Consumer Credit Law and Practice
– A Guide

Consumer Credit Law and Practice
– A Guide

Third Edition

Dennis Rosenthal
Partner, Berwin Leighton Paisner LLP

Tottel
publishing

Tottel Publishing Ltd, Maxwelton House, 41–43 Boltro Road, Haywards Heath, West Sussex, RH16 1BJ

A CIP Catalogue record for this book is available from the British Library.

ISBN   978 1 84766 250 7

Typeset by Phoenix, Chatham, Kent
Printed and bound in Great Britain by Athenaeum, Gateshead, Tyne and Wear

Foreword

Nearly six years have elapsed since the appearance of the second edition of this work, in which my foreword noted the immense complexity of the legal regime governing consumer credit. Little did we think then that we would come to see that regime as one of relative simplicity! The Consumer Credit Act 2006, with its 71 sections and 4 schedules, has introduced a number of major changes. Among other things the Act has modified the framework of the licensing system and introduced the concept of irresponsible lending; removed the limit on the sphere of application of the 1974 Act for consumer-purpose transactions; created new categories of exempt agreement; added several layers to the notice requirements; replaced the concept of extortionate credit bargains with a completely open-ended concept of unfair relationships while providing no criteria whatsoever for determining when a relationship is unfair; and brought consumer credit disputes within the purview of the Financial Ombudsman Service. New statutory instruments have been made and more are in the pipeline. There has been a steady stream of case law, some of it quite difficult to interpret and apply. Finally, a new EC consumer credit directive, based on maximum harmonisation, is about to be finalised and will almost certainly necessitate some changes to our existing legislation on consumer credit.

The need for a guide which is sufficiently detailed to give an accurate picture of the legislation but broad enough to enable the reader to see the wood for the trees has therefore become even more pressing. It is a tribute to Dennis Rosenthal's analytical and presentational skills that in this new edition of his excellent book he has once again succeeded in providing us with just such a guide in language which is both clear and accurate. Whether examining the documentation required for advertisements and agreements, the effect of the statutory provisions on multiple agreements, the new statutory provisions governing default or the rules governing ancillary credit businesses, the reader will rapidly find the answers to most questions. There are also very useful chapters on electronic communications and fraud and money laundering offences and defences.

It therefore gives me great pleasure to recommend this third edition most warmly to all those who have to grapple with UK legislation governing credit, hire and ancillary credit business.

Roy Goode
Oxford, 10 April 2008

Preface

This is a pivotal time for the publication of a new edition of this book, as most of the Consumer Credit Act 2006 has now been implemented and the remainder is about to come into force on 1 October 2008. This edition encompasses all these changes, including those which are imminent and developments in the law and practice since the last edition in 2002.

The book is intended as a comprehensive, informative and critical guide for lawyers, businessmen and students to the complex mass of legislation, regulation, case law and practice relating to consumer credit, consumer hire and ancillary credit business. It is hoped that the reader will find it helpful in navigating the sometimes labyrinthine passages of this complex field of law.

I wish to express my gratitude to my secretary, Jan Jackson, for typing the manuscripts, Sarah Thomas of Tottel Publishing for her assistance in the book's production and to my colleague, Sarah Gatehouse, for reviewing Chapter 28 on accounting and tax aspects. Above all, I am indebted to my mentor, Professor Sir Roy Goode, for his encouragement and to my wife for her tolerance in the course of producing yet another edition.

The law is stated as at 12 May 2008. However, the text includes changes to consumer credit law which are to come into force on 1 October 2008 and consideration of the Consumer Protection from Unfair Trading Regulations 2008.

Dennis Rosenthal
12 May 2008

Contents

Table of Statutes

Table of Statutory Instruments

References are to Paragraph Numbers

Table of Cases

References are to Paragraph Numbers

Chapter 1

Consumer credit law in context

The White Paper on the Consumer Credit Market in the 21st Century[1] sets out the government's vision as one to create an efficient, fair and free market where consumers are empowered to make fully informed decisions and lenders are able to compete. The Paper identifies problems in the consumer credit market which the reforms outlined in the Paper are aimed to address. The problems fall under the following heads:

- informational problems pre-purchase;
- undue surprises post-purchase;
- unfair practices;
- illegal money lenders;
- over-indebtedness.

In 2004 new Consumer Credit Regulations were made relating to pre-contract disclosure, formalities for consumer credit and hire agreements, early settlement, advertisements, electronic communications and default. The Consumer Credit Act 2006 received Royal Assent on 30 March 2006 and is in the course of being fully implemented. An important change in 2007 was the introduction of the new definition of 'individual', especially its limitation to a partnership of no more than three persons, not all of whom are bodies corporate. That year also saw the repeal, in respect of agreements made after 6 April 2007, of s 127(3) to (5), which rendered certain non-compliant regulated agreements automatically unenforceable. Significantly, in April 2007 the unfair relationships provisions between creditors and debtors supplanted the extortionate credit bargain provisions and the Financial Ombudsman Service came into force in relation to consumer credit and consumer hire agreements.

At a time when the final set of the government's reforms are to be implemented, the so-called 'credit crunch' has struck the United Kingdom, as well as Europe and the US, from which it emanated, removing the gloss from the government's reforms. The current turbulent times are concentrating the minds of government, regulators, credit grantors and consumers on the continued avail-ability and affordability of credit. The focus of attention has swung from the control of credit grantors and the practice of consumer credit, to the very source of credit, although this is dictated by economic conditions and beyond the scope of the law and this text.

In April 2008 the financial ceiling, currently £25,000, was removed so that all credit and hire agreements with individuals are within the scope of consumer credit legislation, unless they fall within one or other exemption. Agreements with high net worth debtors and hirers, where they opt out of the regime, and agreements wholly or predominantly for the business purposes of the individual, where the amount exceeds £25,000, are new exemptions. October 2008 sees the introduction of new post-contract transparency requirements, including an annual statement under fixed-sum credit agreements, notice of sums in arrears, notice of default sums and notice of post-judgment interest, together with OFT information sheets to accompany arrears and default notices. The introduction of a more sophisticated and effective licensing regime also commences in October.

In an environment characterised by a weakening of the UK economy, growth of over-indebtedness, the 'credit crunch' and likely continuation of the sub-prime credit crisis, the new legislation will be thoroughly tested.

In January 2008 the European Parliament passed a resolution approving the Common Position, (subject to limited amendment), adopted by the Council for a new Directive on credit agreements for consumers. In April the Council approved the amendments proposed by the European Parliament and the Directive will now need to be implemented by the Member States in 2010. It will repeal Council Directive 87/102/EEC. It is a maximum harmonisation Directive in respect of its subject matter which, in broad terms, is limited to consumer credit agreements of between €200 and €75,000, which are not secured by a land mort-gage. It is left open to Member States to legislate in respect of consumer hire agreements and with regard to consumer credit agreements outside the parame-ters of the Directive.

It is trite to state that European law, emanating from Brussels, is making increasing inroads into UK law in general and UK consumer law in particular. In respect of the latter, we have witnessed European Directives affecting data pro-tection, unfair contract terms, distance contracts, electronic signatures and unfair trading regulations, to name but a few areas where European law has had a sig-nificant impact on UK law.

The very extensive body of legislation, in the form of the Consumer Credit Act 1974, as amended, and the Regulations made under it, imposes a significant bur-den on business and makes it difficult for both the financier and the consumer, to be cognisant of the law and its nuances. It is questionable whether the prolifera-tion of official guidance issued by the regulators, notably the Office of Fair Trading and the Financial Services Authority, serve their intended purpose of informing the public. One thing is clear: '*caveat vendor*' has replaced '*caveat emptor*'.

The Consumer Credit Act 2006 specifically requires the Office of Fair Trading to publish advice and information on how the OFT expects ss 140A to 140C of the Consumer Credit Act 1974, which address the subject of unfair relationships, to interact with Part 8 of the Enterprise Act 2002,[2] to prepare guidance on the fitness test for applicants for licences,[3] guidance on how the OFT proposes to impose requirements on licensees[4] and a statement of policy in relation to how it exercises or proposes to exercise its powers to impose civil penalties.[5] It is unclear what weight will be given to these publications by the courts and it is respectfully submitted that they should be subjected to appropriate scrutiny and challenge and construed as no more than the opinion of the regulator. That is not to suggest that the regulator's opinion carries little weight, but it should be evaluated on the basis of constituting an opinion or point of view.

Official guidance is supplemented by so-called Frequently Asked Questions issued by the regulators, including the Office of Fair Trading. One might question why such extensive questions and answers need to be issued at the very time when the regulations come into force, suggesting perhaps that the regulations are not as clear and self-explanatory as they might be.

Good faith and the concept of treating customers fairly has, it appears, virtually displaced the ideal of legal certainty, with the result that it is increasingly difficult for credit grantors to appreciate or predict how their actions and dealings might be construed. In this respect they are not assisted by the unlimited scope of the unfair relationships provisions. Indeed, with the increasing importance of alternative dispute resolution, including by resort to the Financial Ombudsman Service, consumer credit dispute resolution may well find its natural seat in the home of the creditor or the Financial Ombudsman Service. This is likely to underscore the importance of how the creditor and owner conduct themselves in their day-to-day dealings with the consumer. This, in turn, will underline the importance of the ongoing relationship between creditor and debtor and between owner and hirer, rather than the purely legal aspects of such relationship.

If one were to venture an opinion on how the practice of consumer credit will evolve in the next decade, one might suggest that consumer credit is likely to become more of a relationship issue, with the consumer effectively paying to 'enter the door' of the credit grantor, that being the price for the care and attention which the consumer will come to expect of the credit grantor during the course of their relationship. The days of easy credit and of credit being readily available so as to increase the credit grantor's market share, appear to be over.

The Consumer Credit Act 1974, as amended, including by the Consumer Credit Act 2006, is referred to in the text as CCA 1974.

1 Cm 6040 December 2003.
2 CCA 2006, s 22(1) (CCA 1974, s 140D).
3 CCA 2006, s 30 (CCA 1974, s 25).
4 CCA 2006, s 42 (CCA 1974, s 33E).
5 CCA 2006, s 54 (CCA 1974, s 39C(1)).

Chapter 2

Consumer credit and consumer hire

2.1 MEANING OF 'CREDIT'

The Committee on Consumer Credit Law under the chairmanship of Lord Crowther in the period 1968 to 1971 examined the law as it then was. It laid the foundations for the new consumer credit and consumer hire law in the form of the Consumer Credit Act 1974.

The Crowther Committee deserves credit for breaking the mould of the traditional legal analysis, which considered loans, the subject of the Moneylenders Acts 1900 to 1927, as conceptually different to credit sale, conditional sale and hire-purchase. The distinction between these various forms of facility is formal rather than functional: 'to the customer it is a matter of indifference whether he pays for a motorcar by credit sale or purchase-money loan. The law may distinguish between deferment of the price and the grant of a loan but in commercial terms the distinction is meaningless'.[1]

Accordingly, the legal framework of CCA 1974 was based upon the 'recognition that the extension of credit in a sale or hire-purchase transaction is in reality a loan and that the reservation of title under a hire-purchase or conditional sale agreement or finance lease is in reality a chattel mortgage securing a loan'.[2]

Not surprisingly, therefore, the concept of credit is couched in wide and all-embracing terms. In common parlance 'credit' means the right granted by a creditor to a debtor to defer payment of a debt. 'Credit' has been defined as a sum of money or equivalent purchasing power, as at a shop, available for a person's use; the sum of money that a bank makes available to a client in excess of any deposit and the practice of permitting a borrower to receive goods or services before payment.[3] In *Dimond v Lovell*[4] the Court of Appeal approved an earlier judicial definition of credit as a sum which, in the absence of agreement, would be immediately payable. Thus, deferment of a payment which would otherwise be due is of the essence of credit.[5]

The CCA 1974 defines 'credit' as 'including a cash loan and any other form of financial accommodation',[6] which is indicative of the legislature's objective of bringing within the compass of the regulated regime not only loans but every form of agreement involving credit. It sweeps within its framework the lending of money, the honouring of trading cheques, payments to suppliers by use of credit-tokens and deferment of payment of the purchase price.

It must be said that the definition of 'credit' in the CCA 1974 is not as precise and unambiguous as one might have wished. Thus, were it not for the distinction that the Act makes between credit agreements and hire agreements, it is arguable that 'financial accommodation' might have encompassed hire. After all, in the halcyon days when finance leases were a tax efficient alternative to purchasing equipment, they might have been considered a type of financial accommodation. Likewise, pre-payment schemes for school fees or funeral expenses could be promoted on the basis of financially accommodating the payer. However, the expression 'financial accommodation' must be construed in its context, namely, 'a cash loan and any other form of financial accommodation'. In other words, it is of the same genus as a cash loan. Within the context of the Act as a whole it clearly refers to an accommodation in respect of the advance of a sum of money or its equivalent in goods or services.

The limits of 'financial accommodation' must be drawn at arrangements for the pre-payment of goods or services where the goods or services are not allocated or provided until payment has been effected. In other words, no credit is involved where payment by instalments is not referable or attributable to the grant of credit. In *McMillan Williams v Range*[7] the court stated that where payment is made in advance of services to be rendered, that does not involve the notion of giving credit. As it was impossible to say at the time when the contract was made whether Miss Range would be the debtor or the creditor at the time when the calculation (of salary paid in anticipation of earnings due) came to be made the agreement was not a credit agreement.

In *McMillan Williams v Range* the facts were that there was an arrangement between a Ms Range, an assistant solicitor and the solicitor's firm, McMillan Williams whereby her salary was paid in anticipation of her earnings reaching a certain level at a certain date, subject to an agreement to repay any overpayment made to her. When the agreement was terminated the firm claimed repayment from Ms Range of the excess amount paid to her and she contended that the contract was an unenforceable regulated credit agreement. The Appeal Court held that the nature of the agreement had to be determined at the date of the agreement. It was uncertain at the time when the contract was made whether there would be a surplus or shortfall when the calculation came to be made so that the contract did not involve credit.

In *Nejad v City Index Ltd*[8] it was completely uncertain whether arrangements between the parties would give rise to a debt at all. The court held that there was no credit merely because the arrangements postponed any obligation to pay until such time as the future possible indebtedness had crystallised. The case involved placing bets on the movements of various financial indexes. To place bets the customer was required to open either a 'deposit account', paying in a specified amount as a pre-condition of participation or a 'credit account', based on an assessment of his creditworthiness. In respect of a claim on the credit account, it was alleged that the credit account was an unenforceable one as it did not comply with the requirements of the CCA 1974. The court rejected the submission, stating that the contract was not one for the grant of credit but simply a contract pursuant to which, if the relevant stock exchange index was above or below a specified figure on a specified date, or on early closing of the contract in accordance with City Index's terms and conditions, the customer would pay or receive the appropriate amount of money. There may never be any indebtedness by the customer to City Index and, whether there would, would depend on the movement of the relevant index. Until the closing of the relevant contract between the customer and City Index, it could not be said that there was a debt at all. Accordingly it could not be said that the effect of the agreement in providing what was called a 'credit allocation' to Mr Nejad was to grant him any credit in respect of what would be an indebtedness payable at an earlier date.

An important aspect of the definition of 'credit' is that an item entering into the total charge for credit is not to be treated as credit, even though time is allowed for its payment.[9] This often gives rise to conceptual difficulties. In *Watchtower Investments Ltd v Payne*[10] the question was whether the payment by Watchtower of arrears under a prior mortgage, made contemporaneously with the completion of a consumer credit agreement, constituted the financing of an amount of credit or of a charge for the credit. After a detailed analysis of the law, Gibson LJ, delivering the principal judgment of the Court of Appeal, held that refinancing of arrears was not payment of a charge but amounted to the grant of credit. Whilst this decision appears undoubtedly correct, in *McGinn v Grangewood Securities Ltd*[11] the Court of Appeal held that the facts were distinguishable from those in *Watchtower*. Thus, whilst in *Watchtower* it was a purpose of the new loan that part of the credit was used for repaying arrears under an existing loan, in *McGinn* it was a condition of the grant of the new loan that the arrears under an existing loan be discharged. The Court held that the condition rendered the amount of arrears part of the charges for credit and not part of the credit.

It is respectfully submitted that *McGinn* was wrongly decided. The CCA 1974 expressly recognises, as a form of debtor-creditor credit, restricted-use credit to refinance any existing indebtedness of the debtor's, whether to the creditor or another person.[12]

In the subsequent decision of *London North Securities Ltd v Meadows*[13] the court adopted an intermediate approach. Whilst finding that the credit agreement made it a requirement that all prior arrears be cleared off and that the loan amount was increased to cater for this, the court also found on the facts that the borrowers had agreed that, by signing the documents, the arrears should be paid off and that the loan would provide the sums necessary for this purpose. On that basis payment of the arrears became one of the objective purposes of the transaction so that the arrears amount was part of the credit and not part of the total charge for credit. In the writer's view, for the reasons stated above, there was no need to conduct this analysis in order to arrive at this conclusion.

Viewed from the vantage point of CCA 1974 and the regulations made under it, the conceptual divide between the law which pre-dated the CCA 1974 and its successor regime is revolutionary. Indeed, so far was the functional as opposed to the formal approach adopted that, to a large extent, the distinctions between hire-purchase, credit sale, conditional sale and instalment sale agreements have been reduced by their common features being subsumed in the creation of a debtor-creditor-supplier agreement. This three-party or so-called connected loan agreement contrasts with a simple loan agreement between a debtor and a creditor, unconnected with any third-party supplier. The latter is known as a debtor-creditor agreement. The former Moneylenders Acts 1900 to 1927, the bulk of the Hire-Purchase Act 1964 and the entire Hire-Purchase Act 1965 were replaced.

1   Crowther Report Command 4596, para 6.2.38.
2   Crowther Report Command 4596, para 1.3.7.
3   The Collins English Dictionary.
4   *Dimond v Lovell* [2001] GCCR 2303 at 2316, CA.
5   See *Goode: Consumer Credit Law and Practice* (LexisNexis Butterworths), IC [24.7].
6   CCA 1974, s 9(1).
7   [2004] GCCR 5041, CA.
8   [2001] GCCR 2461, CA.
9   CCA 1974, s 9(4); *Wilson v Robertsons (London) Ltd* [2005] GCCR 5301.
10 [2001] EWCA Civ 1159, [2001] 35 LS Gaz R 32, Times, 22 August.
11 [2002] GCCR 4761, CA.
12 CCA 1974, s 13(b).
13 [2005] GCCR 5381, CA.

2.2   MEANING OF 'CONSUMER'

The second conclusion of the Crowther Committee was that the law ought to distinguish between consumer and commercial transactions. The Moneylenders Acts, for example, applied to all loans regardless of whether they were to individuals or to companies. The Committee was of the view that the purpose of the loan was an inadequate test, being too vague and subjective. It preferred the approach of excluding bodies corporate from the protection afforded to consumers and of setting a financial limit above which consumers were not entitled to statutory protection.

The long title to the CCA 1974 describes it as an Act 'to establish for the protection of consumers a new system, administered by the Director General of Fair Trading, of licensing and other control of traders concerned with the provision of credit for the supply of goods on hire or hire-purchase, and their transactions, in place of enactments regulating moneylenders, pawn-brokers and hire-purchase traders and their transactions; and for related matters'. The legislation is for the protection of the 'consumer' which, oddly, the Act does not define.

In reality, the legislation is for the protection of 'individuals', whether or not they are consumers per se (as opposed to businessmen) provided the credit or hire is not wholly or predominantly for the purposes of a business of the debtor or hirer. 'Individual' means a natural person and includes a partnership of two or three persons or other unincorporated body of persons not consisting entirely of bodies corporate.[1]

Originally, the weakness of the regulatory regime was its failure to adopt what it sought to avoid, namely to apply 'the purpose of the loan test' in distinguishing between consumer and commercial credit, at least to the extent that this was practicable. As a result, consumer credit embraced both business loans to partnerships and commercial loans to individuals. Parliament had no difficulty in disinguishing between non-business and business, or between consumer and non-consumer, transactions e.g. the Unfair Contract Terms Act 1977, the Consumer Protection Act 1987, the CCA 1974, s 101 itself and the Advertisements Regulations made under the Act. The European Parliament similarly distinguished between a consumer and a non-consumer in directives implemented as the Unfair Terms in Consumer Contracts Regulations 1999[3] and the Consumer Protection (Distance Selling) Regulations 2000.[4] Generally, 'consumer' is defined as a natural person who is acting for purposes outside his trade, business or profession.

In 1988 the government, in its Deregulation Initiative, proposed the removal of lending and hiring to businesses from the scope of the Act.[5] Some while later, in 1993, the Office of Fair Trading issued a Consultation Document on the Treatment of Business Consumers under the CCA 1974. This was followed by extensive consultations with the industry and trade associations. Then, in 1994, the Director General of Fair Trading issued a Consultation Document entitled 'Consumer Credit Deregulation'[6] recommending that the government's proposal should be implemented save that licensing should continue to cover all lending and hiring to individuals, including sole traders, partnerships and unincorporated bodies. The Department of Trade and Industry conducted its own consultations by publishing a Consultation Document on 'Deregulation of United Kingdom Consumer Credit Legislation' in 1995 and a further consultation entitled 'Deregulation of Lending and Hiring to Unincorporated Businesses' in 1996. Notwithstanding extensive consultation and overwhelming support for the Deregulation Initiative, the House of Commons Deregulation Committee, which had itself sought the views of various organisations and bodies, surprisingly concluded that it did not believe that the Department of Trade and Industry had adequately addressed the concerns of consumer protection raised by significant numbers of respondents. It voted against the proposal for the deregulation of lending and hiring to businesses and thereby killed off the Deregulation Initiative and eight years of lobbying for change.[7] Lending and hire for business purposes (where the credit amount or rentals prospectively exceeds £25,000) was finally excluded from regulation (save in respect of the provisions relating to unfair relationships between creditor and debtor) by the Consumer Credit Act 2006, with effect from 6 April 2008,[8] some twenty years after the proposal was first mooted.

1 CCA 1974, s 189(1).
2 Council Directive 87/102/EEC of 22 December 1986.
3 SI 1999/2083.
4 SI 2000/2334.
5 'Releasing Enterprise' Cm 512, November 1988, p 24.
6 A Review by the Director General of Fair Trading of the Scope and Operation of the Consumer Credit Act 1974 (June 1994).
7 See 'Consumer Credit' (published by the CCTA), vol 52 (May 1997).
8 CCA 1974, s 16B.

2.3 MEANING OF 'DEBTOR'

A 'debtor' is defined as the individual receiving credit under a consumer credit agreement or the person to whom his rights and duties under the agreement have passed by assignment or operation of law, and, in relation to a prospective consumer credit agreement, includes a prospective debtor.[1] The CCA 1974 does not define a 'prospective consumer credit agreement' nor a 'prospective debtor' but these should be construed in the context of ss 57, 58 and 59 which deal with prospective agreements.

The reader is referred to para 6.7 on the question of the assignability of a debtor's rights and duties under the agreement.

1 CCA 1974, s 189(1) and see also s 140C(2).

2.4   MEANING OF 'HIRER'

Not unexpectedly, 'hirer' is defined in analogous terms to 'debtor'. A 'hirer' is an individual to whom goods are bailed or, in Scotland, hired under a consumer hire agreement, or the person to whom his rights and duties under the agreement have passed by assignment or operation of law and, in relation to a prospective consumer hire agreement, includes the prospective hirer.[1] Once again, the expressions 'prospective consumer hire agreement' and 'prospective hirer' are not defined and must be read in the context of the CCA 1974, ss 57, 58 and 59.

1 CCA 1974, s 189(1) and see also s 140C(2).

2.5   MEANING OF 'CREDITOR'

'Creditor' is the corollary of 'debtor' and is defined as the person providing credit under a consumer credit agreement or the person to whom his rights and duties under the agreement have passed by assignment or operation of law and, in relation to a prospective consumer credit agreement, includes the prospective creditor.[1] The same issues arise as under the definition of 'debtor' above. There are no restrictions on the natural or legal persons, or group of persons, which might constitute the creditor except that, in the case of a legal person, it must have the legal capacity and power to lend, i.e. the lending must be *intra vires*. The creditor may be an individual, a registered company, a partnership, a building society, a mutual society, an association, a charity, a local authority, a trade union, a credit union and the like. The only impact which the CCA 1974 has on the foregoing is that it makes provision for certain types of creditors to be able to enter into exempt agreements under s 16. The reader is referred to Chapter 4 for a full discussion of exempt agreements.

The types of bodies that fall within s 16 and are therefore permitted to enter into exempt agreements are the following: an insurance company, a friendly society, an organisation of employers or organisation of workers, a charity, a land improvement company, a housing authority, a body corporate named or specifically referred to in any public general Act, a body corporate named or specifically referred to in an order referred to in s 16(1)(ff), a building society, and an authorised institution or wholly-owned subsidiary of such an institution. The latter are subsidiaries of banks under the Banking Act 1987 and subsidiaries of deposit-takers under the Banking Co-ordination (Second Council Directive) Regulations 1992.[2] Other wholly-owned subsidiaries, including subsidiaries of building societies, are not exempt creditors for the purpose of s 16.

1 CCA 1974, s 189(1) and see also s 140C(2).
2 Regulation 82(1), Sch 10.

2.6   MEANING OF 'OWNER'

This definition is analogous to that of 'creditor'. An owner is a person who bails or, in Scotland, hires out goods under a consumer hire agreement or the person to whom his rights and duties under the agreement have passed by assignment or operation of law. In relation to a prospective consumer hire agreement, 'owner' includes the prospective bailor or person from whom the goods are to be hired.[1] The Act does not define 'prospective consumer hire agreements' nor 'prospective bailor' and these terms must be read in the context of ss 57, 58 and 59 of the CCA 1974. As to the assignability of the owner's rights and duties, the reader is referred to para 6.7.

As in the case of a 'creditor', any natural or legal person can constitute an owner under a hire agreement. However, the owner must of course have the authority and power to enter into a hire agreement.

Certain hire agreements entered into by specified bodies are exempt from the CCA 1974 but the range is much more restricted than that which applies to credit agreements. The Act does not apply to specified regulated consumer hire agreements for metering equipment where the owner is authorised under an enactment to supply electricity, gas or water or is a public telecommunications operator.[2]

1   CCA 1974, s 189(1).
2   CCA 1974, s 16(6).

2.7   MEANING OF 'CONSUMER CREDIT AGREEMENT'

A consumer credit agreement is an agreement between an individual (as defined in para 2.2 above), the debtor, on the one hand, and any other person, the creditor, on the other hand, by which the creditor provides the debtor with credit of any amount.[1]

1   CCA 1974, s 8(1). Originally the credit amount was restricted by CCA 1974, s 8(2) read with the Consumer Credit (Increase of Monetary Limits) (Amendment) Order 1998, SI 1998/996.

2.8   MEANING OF 'HIRE'

Hire is a form of bailment under which the hirer or bailee receives possession of the chattels or goods and the right to use them in return for payment by the hirer of rent to the bailor or owner and undertakings by the hirer to exercise reasonable care of, and to protect, the goods. At the end of the hire the hirer is obliged to return the goods to the bailor.

The Crowther Report drew attention to the need to bring hire agreements within the regulated fold. Consistent with its approach, the Committee maintained that 'a transaction which is in form a lease may achieve much the same result as an outright sale, as when the lease is for the full working life of the equipment at rentals totalling a sum equivalent to what would be charged for a sale on credit'.[1]

It is remarkable that, in contrast to the opprobrium which credit, money lending and usury have attracted over the centuries and the supervision to which they have become subject, hire has, until recently, remained unregulated. Only terms control, which related to monetary control rather than to affording protection to the hirer, applied to hire as well as to hire-purchase and instalment sale agreements. Terms control covered matters such as minimum down-payments and maximum periods of repayment.[2]

Vestiges of the differential treatment of hire agreements remain in CCA 1974, which deals with hire much less rigorously than with credit. Thus, there is no yardstick for hiring charges comparable to the annual percentage rate of charge, no liability imputed on the lessor corresponding to the creditor's liability under s 75, no equivalent to the unfair relationships provisions and no limit on the level of default charges permitted to be levied under a hire agreement.

1 Crowther Report, Command 4596, para 5.2.7.
2 The Orders applying terms control were first introduced in 1939 and culminated in the final Control of Hiring Order 1977 (as amended) and the Hire-Purchase and Credit Sale Agreements (Control) Order 1976 (as amended). They were revoked by the Control of Hiring and Hire-Purchase and Credit Sale Agreements (Revocation) Order 1982, SI 1982/1034.

2.9   MEANING OF 'CONSUMER HIRE AGREEMENT'

A consumer hire agreement is an agreement made by a person with an individual (as defined in para 2.2 above), the hirer, for bailment or, in Scotland, the hiring of goods to the hirer which is capable of subsisting for more than three months.[1]

In *TRM Copy Centres (UK) Ltd v Lanwall Services Ltd*[2] the court rightly rejected the argument that an agreement which did not stipulate payment for the hire of equipment but required payment to be made only if and when the photocopier was used, constituted a hire agreement. The court commented that under a hire agreement the hirer pays for the hire of the goods which come into his possession even if he does not use them at all. As Professor Goode states (and this was cited with approval by the court), it is abundantly clear that the statutory provisions of CCA 1974 are concerned solely with bailment by way of hire, that is bailment under which the person receiving possession of the goods or equipment is to pay for their use during the period of his lawful possession.[3] The decision was upheld by the Court of Appeal.[4]

If the incorporation of payments other than hire rentals results in the hire agreement being a multiple agreement, consideration must be given to whether the agreement is a unitary multiple agreement or an agreement in parts. However, it is submitted that all payments envisaged by the Agreements Regulations as being capable of being incorporated in a regulated hire agreement militate against the agreement being a multiple agreement by virtue of the inclusion of those payments.

Value added tax is payable on rentals so that they are rentals to be construed as inclusive of value added tax.

In contrast to consumer credit, a distinction has always existed, for very limited purposes, between consumer hire and hire for business purposes in relation to the hirer's right to terminate the hire agreement. Thus, the hirer is given an automatic right to terminate a hire agreement which has run for 18 months unless it is one, *inter alia*, for the purpose of the hirer's business or the goods are hired for the hirer's business of sub-hire.[5] This distinction was retained even though it essentially lost its significance since the exemption of consumer hire agreements for business use under s 16B. Its relevance now is limited to agreements for total rentals not exceeding £25,000, which are still regulated consumer hire agreements.[6]

1 CCA 1974, s 15(1).
2 [2007] All ER(D) 287.
3 Consumer Credit Law and Practice IC [23.75].
4 [2008] All ER (D) 235.
5 CCA 1974, s 101.
6 CCA 1974, s 16B(1).

2.10   CREDIT HIRE

A new form of credit and hire agreement, namely so-called 'credit hire', was formulated by the court in *Dimond v Lovell*.[1] The House of Lords, in upholding the decision of the Court of Appeal, held that a car hire agreement under which hire charges are not payable until after conclusion of the hirer's claim against a third party for damage to the hirer's car, is also a consumer credit agreement, as it involves deferment of the hire charges beyond the time they would otherwise be payable. The court's finding is more palatable under the general law of credit than within the scheme of the CCA 1974. Does the decision mean, for example, that a consumer hire agreement may be combined in one agreement with a credit agreement? The CCA 1974, s 18 and the Consumer Credit (Agreements) Regulations 1983 would suggest otherwise. Does it mean that a consumer hire agreement is incapable of being modified by a regulated modifying agreement to postpone the date of the final rental payment as this would give rise to the need for a consumer credit agreement? In any event, why should a 'postponed' final rental be given a different status than an 'advance rental'?[2]

1 [2001] GCCR 2751, HL.
2 See the trenchant criticism of the case by Professor R.M. Goode in *Consumer Credit Law and Practice* at 1C [24.49] to [24.64].

2.11   CAPACITY OF THE PARTIES

Reference has already been made to the need for the creditor or owner to have legal capacity to enter into the relevant agreement. Generally speaking, this will be manifest from the company's constitution, the partnership deed in the case of a partnership, the constitution, trust deed or rules of an association or charity together with the relevant licence granted to such lender or owner under the CCA 1974, whether a standard licence in respect of the individual organisation or a group licence which covers the organisation.

It will be remembered that, for the purposes of the CCA 1974, an individual is a natural person, a partnership of two or three persons or an unincorporated body of persons not consisting entirely of bodies corporate. Under general principles of contract law most individuals will have capacity to enter into consumer credit and consumer hire agreements.

A minor may enter into a consumer credit or consumer hire agreement but it will be unenforceable against him unless the goods which are the subject of the agreement are necessaries supplied to the minor and the contract is beneficial to him. The lender can then recover the amount spent under the equitable principle of subrogation.[1] The CCA 1974 protects minors by making it an offence for a person, with a view to financial gain, to send to a minor any document inviting him to borrow money, to obtain goods on credit or hire, to obtain services on credit or to apply for information or advice on borrowing money or otherwise obtaining credit or hiring goods.[2]

Leasing by local authorities is restricted by the Local Government and Housing Act 1989 and relevant regulations.[3] Finance leases, in contrast with operating leases, entered into by local authorities fall within the scope of credit arrangements and are subject to a monetary limit on expenditure.

Where the debtor or hirer is a partnership or an unincorporated body of persons, one person may sign the regulated agreement on behalf of such debtor or hirer.[4]

1   *Goode: Consumer Credit Law and Practice* (LexisNexis Butterworths), at 1B [11.12] and see *Chitty on Contracts* (29th edn, 2004) at 8-020.
2   CCA 1974, s 50.
3   Local Authorities (Capital Finance) Regulations 1997, SI 1997/319.
4   CCA 1974, s 61(4) and the Consumer Credit (Agreements) Regulations 1983, SI 1983/1553, reg 6(3)(a).

Chapter 3

Types of credit and credit agreements

3.1 CONSUMER CREDIT AGREEMENT

There is no statutory definition of a credit agreement. However, by inference from various other definitions in the CCA 1974,[1] one might define a credit agreement as an agreement between a creditor and a debtor under which the creditor provides the debtor with a cash loan or any other form of financial accommodation.

A consumer credit agreement is an agreement between an individual ('the debtor') and any other person ('the creditor') by which the creditor provides the debtor with credit of any amount.[2] A regulated consumer credit agreement is a consumer credit agreement which is not an exempt agreement.[3] An exempt agreement is a consumer credit agreement which is specified in or under ss 16, 16A or 16B of the Act.[4]

For the purposes of consumer credit legislation 'individual' has a defined meaning and includes, apart from a natural person, a partnership consisting of two or three persons not all of whom are bodies corporate and an unincorporated body of persons which does not consist entirely of bodies corporate and is not a partnership.[5]

1 In particular s 9.
2 CCA 1974, s 8(1). Prior to 6 April 2008 a consumer credit agreement was subject to a financial ceiling which was then £25,000.
3 CCA 1974, s 8(3).
4 CCA 1974, s 189(1). See further Chapter 4 on exempt agreements.
5 CCA 1974, s 189(1).

3.2 RUNNING-ACCOUNT CREDIT AND FIXED-SUM CREDIT

3.2.1 The distinction between running-account credit and fixed-sum credit

Running-account or revolving credit is a facility under a consumer credit agreement whereby the debtor is enabled to receive from time to time (whether in his own person or by another person) from the creditor or a third party, cash, goods and services (or any of them) to an amount or value such that, taking into account payments made by or to the credit of the debtor, the credit limit (if any) is not at any time exceeded.[1] Examples include bank overdrafts and credit card accounts, whether secured, including on land, or unsecured.

Fixed-sum credit is defined as any other facility under a consumer credit agreement whereby the debtor is enabled to receive credit, whether in one amount or by instalments.[2] The definition of fixed-sum credit is rather infelicitous as the Act defines it by reference to, and in contrast with, running-account credit. Not only is this strange from the point of view of fixed-sum credit being the more common form of credit but it means that one cannot adopt the statutory definition of fixed-sum credit without first defining running-account credit. One would have thought that it was sufficiently simple to define fixed-sum credit independently of running-account credit as a sum of money, certain in amount, which the creditor makes available for borrowing by the debtor in one or more tranches.

1 CCA 1974, s 10(1)(a).
2 CCA 1974, s 10(1)(b).

3.2.2   Features of running-account credit

The common features of a running-account credit account or agreement are a credit limit, the ability continually to pay into the account and to replenish the available credit and the fact that the account usually operates indefinitely until termination by one of the parties. 'Credit limit' is defined as, in respect of any period, the maximum debit balance which under the agreement is allowed to stand on the account during the period, disregarding any term of the agreement allowing that maximum to be exceeded merely temporarily.[1]

The notion of a credit limit (it will be observed from para 3.2.1 above) is not essential to a running-account credit agreement. It was of significance when the Consumer Credit Act applied to credit agreements which did not exceed a specified financial limit. This was the position until 6 April 2008 on which date the Consumer Credit Act 2006 removed the financial limit of £25,000 then applying to consumer credit agreements and consumer hire agreements. With the removal of the financial limit, the only relevance of the anti-avoidance provisions of s 10(3) in their reference to an agreement not exceeding the credit limit, is to consumer credit agreements for business use where the creditor provides the debtor with credit not exceeding £25,000. In relation to running-account credit agreements of that kind, the anti-avoidance provisions of s 10(3) provide that a credit agreement will be assumed not to exceed £25,000 if the credit limit does not exceed that amount or, whether or not there is a credit limit (and if there is, notwithstanding that it exceeds the specified amount), if the debtor is not enabled to draw an amount which exceeds the specified amount or, if the agreement provides that if it so exceeds that amount, the rate of the total charge for credit increases or any other condition favouring the creditor or his associate comes into operation or if, at the time the agreement is made, it is probable, having regard to the terms of the agreement and any other relevant considerations, that the debit balance will not at any time exceed £25,000. In all those cases the running-account credit agreement for business use will be presumed to be a regulated-running account credit agreement. It is a rather odd preservation of what is otherwise an otiose s 10(3), especially as running-account credit for business use is hardly the order of the day in the financing of business requirements.

The characteristics of running-account are also recognised at common law. As early as 1816 in *Clayton's Case*[2] the court defined the agreement in question as a banking account 'where all the sums paid in form one blended fund, the parts of which have no longer any distinct existence'. This passage was also cited in *Re Footman Bower & Co Ltd*[3] where the court described a current account as one where the debtor–creditor relationship of the parties is recorded in one entire account into which all liabilities and payments are carried in order of date, as a course of dealing extending over a considerable period and where the true nature of the debtor's liability is a single and undivided debt for the amount of the balance due on the account, without regard to the several items which as a matter of history contribute to the balance. More recently in *Re Charge Card Services Ltd (No 2)*,[4] the court described a running-account agreement by reference to the reciprocal obligations giving rise to credits and debits in a single running account and a single liability to pay the ultimate balance found due on taking the account.

1 CCA 1974, s 10(2).
2 *Devaynes v Noble* (1816) 1 Mer 572.
3 [1961] 2 All ER 161 at 165, Ch D.
4 *Re Charge Card Services Ltd (No 2)* [1986] 3 All ER 289 at 307, Ch D.

3.2.3 Features of fixed-sum credit

The most common form of fixed-sum credit is a single loan advance although fixed-sum credit will also include a progress or draw-down loan under which the borrower is entitled to draw down the credit amount in tranches. Fixed-sum credit extends beyond loan agreements and includes credit sale, hire-purchase and conditional sale agreements. The underlying principle in treating these identically is the classification of the outstanding amount of the loan or the purchase price or hire-purchase price, as the case may be, as credit and as an ascertained or fixed amount of credit.

3.2.4 Relevance of the distinction between a fixed-sum credit agreement and a running-account credit agreement

The relevance of the distinction between fixed-sum credit and running-account credit, in so far as the Act is concerned, is the fact that they are separate and distinct categories of credit for the purposes of the regulatory regime, subject to different requirements as to the form and content of the regulated credit agreement and give rise to different rights and obligations on the part of the parties. The distinction is also relevant to the issue of multiple agreements and whether fixed-sum credit agreements and running-account credit agreements can be combined in one form of agreement, which it is submitted they cannot.[1]

The regulations distinguish between the obligations of a creditor under a fixed-sum credit agreement and a running-account credit agreement. Distinctions are to be found in the periodicity of issuing statements of account, the event upon which a notice of sums in arrears must be issued, the contents of statements and notices and whether specific statutory notices may be incorporated in other notices or statements.[2]

It is interesting to note that the Consumer Credit (Agreements) Regulations 1983 specifically recognise certain types of credit agreement in the statutory heading to the agreement, but not others. The headings provided for are: hire-purchase agreement, conditional sale agreement, fixed-sum loan agreement and credit card agreement. Notable exceptions are fixed-sum credit agreement (which may take the form of financial accommodation rather than a loan which would generally be identified as an advance of money), credit sale agreement and running-account or revolving credit agreement.[3]

1   See CCA 1974, s 18.
2   See paras 6.1 and 6.2.
3   SI 1983/1553, Sch 1, para 1.

3.3   RESTRICTED-USE CREDIT AND UNRESTRICTED-USE CREDIT

This distinction is the invention of the draftsman of CCA 1974. It is born out of the more important distinction drawn by the legislation between a debtor-creditor-supplier agreement and a debtor-creditor agreement. As the description implies, restricted-use credit is credit whose purpose is prescribed or whose use is monitored by the creditor.

A restricted-use credit agreement is a regulated consumer credit agreement to finance a transaction between the debtor and the creditor or between the debtor and a person other than the creditor (e.g. the supplier) or to re-finance any existing indebtedness of the debtor, whether to the creditor or any other person. An unrestricted-use credit agreement is any other agreement.[1]

If the credit is in fact provided in such a way as to leave the debtor free to use it as he chooses, even though such use would contravene the agreement, the agreement is an unrestricted-use credit agreement.[2]

The distinction between restricted-use and unrestricted-use credit was considered in *Office of Fair Trading v Lloyds TSB Bank plc*[3] in relation to four-party structured credit card agreements. As described in this case, a four-party structure is one where there is interposed between the card issuer and the supplier, the merchant acquirer acting as an independent party. It involves an agreement between the merchant acquirer and the supplier, under which the supplier undertakes to honour the card and the merchant acquirer undertakes to pay the supplier, and an agreement between the merchant acquirer and the card issuer, under which the merchant acquirer agrees to pay the supplier and the card issuer undertakes to reimburse the merchant acquirier. There is, however, no direct contractual link between the card issuer and the supplier.[4] It was argued before the Court of Appeal that where the credit is advanced in relation to transactions entered into under a four-party structure, this is unrestricted-use credit because the card issuer has not itself made any arrangements with the supplier. In such cases the arrangements have been made by the merchant acquirer. The court rejected this contention on the grounds that it cannot make any difference who has made the arrangements with the suppliers. From the point of view of the cardholder, the card can only be used to buy goods or services from the suppliers who have agreed to accept cards carrying the mark or logo in question. The fact that the number of places at which these cards can be presented is very extensive cannot disguise the fact that in contrast to cash they can only be used at places where the relevant sign is displayed.

Some confusion has arisen in identifying whether a sum owing by a borrower to a creditor which is refinanced under a subsequent credit agreement constitutes part of the credit or part of the total charge for credit under the subsequent agreement. In *Watchtower Investments Ltd v Payne*[5] it was held that where part of an advance is to be used to discharge an earlier debt owed to another creditor, it is not part of the cost for credit but part of the credit itself. The court found that it was one of the debtor's purposes in applying for the loan to Watchtower Investments to discharge existing arrears owing to a building society. The court held that payment of the arrears did not form part of the charges because it was not of the nature of a charge for credit as distinct from being part of the credit itself.

Neither the Act nor the Consumer Credit (Total Charge for Credit) Regulations 1980 define 'charges' although the latter sets out in reg 4 the items to be included in the total charge for credit; in summary, interest, other charges at any time payable under the transaction and relevant insurance premiums. In *Watchtower Investments* the court stated that a line can and must be drawn between what constitutes charges and what constitutes credit, the former being payment exacted for the provision of services or the grant or use of facilities relating to the subject matter of the credit agreement, whereas the latter constitutes, for example, the purchase of land or goods under the agreement or amounts under some other agreement relating solely to what is to be provided under that other agreement and unrelated to what is being provided under the credit agreement.[6] The court went on to state that it is necessary to consider all the circumstances, including the documents relating to the agreement in order to ascertain objectively the purpose of the borrowing. The purpose of the court's consideration is to arrive at what in reality is the true cost to the debtor of the credit provided. On the facts the court found that the payment of the arrears was a purpose of the debtor and accordingly the sum in question was part of the credit and not part of the charges.

A different conclusion on the facts was reached in *McGinn v Grangewood Securities Ltd.*[7] Here the court held that a sum advanced under a credit agreement which was used to repay the debtor's arrears under an existing agreement constituted part of the total charge for credit and not the credit amount as it was no part of the debtor's purpose that the sum of arrears should be borrowed from *Grangewood Securities* in order to clear her arrears under her existing mortgage. The sole purpose of the loan was to borrow money in order to extend and refurbish her house. The obligation to discharge the arrears was an obligation to incur a charge payable under the transaction and was therefore part of the true cost of the credit and not part of the credit.

With respect, it appears difficult to reconcile the line of thinking of the courts with the definition of a restricted-use credit agreement in s 11(1)(c), namely an agreement to refinance any existing indebtedness of the debtor's whether to the creditor or another person. Arrears under an existing agreement are surely part of the debtor's indebtedness under that agreement and if those arrears are to be refinanced, whether as a condition of the grant of new credit and entering into a new credit agreement or otherwise, appears irrelevant. The distinction is of course important for the purposes of establishing the financial and related particulars in the agreement and its enforceability under s 127(1) of the Act. In order to avoid any unnecessary confusion or risk, a creditor would be well advised to ensure that it is made clear at the outset that the refinancing of any existing indebtedness is part of the purpose of the loan for which the proposed borrower applies.

1 CCA 1974, s 11(1).
2 CCA 1974, s 11(2).
3 [2006] GCCR 5701 at 5719–5720, CA.
4 At 5704–5705.
5 [2001] GCCR 3055, CA.
6 At 3069.
7 [2002] GCCR 4761, CA.

3.4   DEBTOR-CREDITOR CREDIT AND DEBTOR-CREDITOR-SUPPLIER CREDIT

A debtor-creditor agreement and a debtor-creditor-supplier agreement are descriptive of different types of credit agreements under CCA 1974. One might, however, isolate the credit element from the agreement for the credit. On this basis debtor-creditor-supplier (d-c-s) credit or supplier-connected credit is credit extended by the supplier or dealer to his customer (the debtor) to finance a transaction between himself and the debtor or credit extended by the creditor to the debtor pursuant to or in contemplation of arrangements made by the creditor with the supplier. The latter is commonplace in relation to motor vehicles, home improvements, furniture and equipment. The bank or finance company will have entered into arrangements with a dealer or supplier to assist with the financing of purchases. Often the dealer will have entered into arrangements with more than one source of finance.

In contrast, debtor-creditor credit is unrelated to any supply by the creditor or to any arrangements between the creditor and any supplier. It arises where the creditor advances a loan to a debtor or where a supplier simply introduces a customer to one or other creditor with whom it has no particular arrangements. The credit is debtor-creditor or unconnected-supplier credit. The distinction between debtor-creditor-supplier and debtor-creditor credit applies also to running-account credit. An overdraft on a bank account is debtor-creditor credit whereas an account for a Barclaycard, MasterCard or dedicated in-store card is one for debtor-creditor-supplier credit unless it merely involves a cash advance.

Originally a purpose, but not the sole purpose, of categorising credit agreements was to prevent evasion of CCA 1974 by a creditor grouping together disparate credit agreements and aggregating the credit limits or credit amounts under the agreements, thereby exceeding the financial limit and avoiding regulation. Since the abolition of the financial limit, the distinction between debtor-creditor and debtor-creditor-supplier agreements primarily serves the purpose of distinguishing between the different consequences of such agreements. However, it remains relevant to consumer credit agreements for business use where the £25,000 financial limit on regulated agreements continues to apply.[1]

1   CCA 1974, s 16B.

3.4.1   Debtor-creditor agreements

A debtor-creditor or 'd-c' agreement is a regulated consumer credit agreement for any of the following:

(a)   restricted-use credit to finance a transaction between a debtor and a supplier (other than the creditor) not made under pre-existing arrangements or in contemplation of future arrangements between the creditor and the supplier;

(b)   restricted-use credit to re-finance any existing indebtedness of the debtor, whether to the creditor or any other person; or

(c)   unrestricted-use credit which is not to be used to finance a transaction of the type referred to in (a) above.[1]

Examples of debtor-creditor agreements are bank loans, overdraft facilities, mortgage loans unconnected with a house-builder or property developer and cash advances from an Automated Teller Machine ('ATM').

1   CCA 1974, s 13.

3.4.2   Debtor-creditor-supplier agreements

A debtor-creditor-supplier or 'd-c-s' agreement is a supplier-connected loan, being one of the following:

(a)   A restricted-use credit agreement to finance a transaction between the debtor and the creditor, whether forming part of that agreement or not. Examples are hire-purchase and instalment sale agreements, where the supplier is the creditor himself or a third party, and revolving credit agreements provided by a retailer for its customers.

(b)   A restricted-use credit agreement to finance a transaction between the debtor and a person (the supplier) other than the creditor, which is made by the creditor under pre-existing arrangements or in contemplation of future arrangements between himself and the supplier. Typically this relates to loan facilities agreed between a creditor and supplier for use by the supplier's customers.

(c)   An unrestricted-use credit agreement made by the creditor under pre-existing arrangements between himself and a person (the supplier) other than the debtor in the knowledge that the credit is to be used to finance a transaction between the debtor and the supplier. It is immaterial whether or not the debtor uses the credit for its intended purpose.[1]

It is unfortunate that the terms 'supplier' and 'pre-existing arrangements' which are central to various provisions of the Act, for example the meaning of debtor-creditor-supplier agreement and the application of s 75, are not defined with any great precision. The expression 'supplier' is merely defined in parenthesis in ss 11(1)(b) and 12(c).

'Pre-existing arrangements' is defined in s 187 by reference to 'arrangements' but 'arrangements' is not defined. In *Governor and Co of Bank of Scotland v Alfred Truman*,[2] in deciding whether a party to a transaction was a supplier within the meaning of the Act, the court referred to the judgment of Gloster J in *Office of Fair Trading v Lloyds TSB Bank plc*[3] to the effect that 'arrangements' should be understood and construed in their ordinary popular sense and that there was evidence of a deliberate intention on the part of the draftsman to use broad loose language. It followed that a restricted construction would be contrary to the scheme of that part of the Act. This line of approach was given even more credence by the House of Lords in *Office of Fair Trading v Lloyds TSB Bank*[4] where the court stated that the Crowther Committee and Parliament, when enacting the 1974 Act, did not know how the credit card market would develop but that the language of 'arrangements' used in the Act was capable of embracing the modern relationships between card issuers and suppliers under networks like VISA and MasterCard.

It is submitted that where a finance company finances insurance premiums payable by a borrower and the borrower is introduced to the finance company by the insurance broker which sells the insurance to him, the supplier under the agreement is generally the insurance company and not the broker. If there are no pre-existing or contemplated arrangements between the broker and the finance company, the credit agreement is a debtor-creditor agreement and not a debtor-creditor-supplier agreement.

1   CCA 1974, s 12.
2   [2005] GCCR 5491 at para 95.
3   [2004] GCCR 5061.
4   [2007] ECCR 6101.

3.4.3   Relevance of the distinction between debtor-creditor and debtor-creditor-supplier agreements

The principal differences between d-c and d-c-s agreements are the following:

(a)   the creditor in a d-c-s agreement is liable for any misrepresentation or breach of contract by the supplier,[1]

(b)   the creditor in a d-c-s agreement incurs liability in respect of antecedent negotiations conducted by a credit-broker or supplier in relation to the agreement;[2]

(c)   various consequences attach to linked transactions where the principal agreement is a d-c-s agreement, including the fact that if the d-c-s agreement is cancelled this will generally also undo the linked transaction;[3]

(d)   it is an offence to solicit (canvass) a debtor to enter into a d-c agreement off-trade premises by making oral representations to the debtor or any other individual during a visit carried out for such purpose unless it was preceded by the debtor's signed written request made on a previous occasion;[4]

(e)   there are differences in the prescribed contractual provisions and statutory notices as between d-c and d-c-s agreements;[5] and

(f)   d-c and d-c-s agreements are treated differently under various other sections of the Act and regulations made under the CCA 1974.[6]

1   CCA 1974, s 75(1).
2   CCA 1974, s 56(1).
3   CCA 1974, s 19(1) and (2).
4   CCA 1974, s 49(1).
5   See Schedules to the Consumer Credit (Agreements) Regulations 1983, SI 1983/1553.
6   See CCA 1974, ss 16, 23, 51 and 69–74.

3.5   CANCELLABLE AGREEMENTS

A cancellable agreement is the generic description given to any regulated agreement which is cancellable by the debtor, or hirer, within a stipulated period. Regulated credit agreements are cancellable where negotiations preceding the credit agreement, referred to as antecedent negotiations, included oral representations made by the negotiator in the presence of the debtor.[1] These exclude telephone conversations on the grounds that they are not made in the debtor's presence.

Antecedent negotiations are negotiations conducted with the debtor by the creditor or by a credit-broker in relation to a debtor-creditor-supplier agreement or with the supplier under a linked transaction to a debtor-creditor-supplier agreement.[2]

The meaning of 'representation' in the context of oral representations made in the presence of the debtor (or hirer) in CCA 1974, s 67 was considered in *Moorgate Services Ltd*.[3] The Court of Appeal construed the word 'representation', defined in CCA 1974, s 189(1), as including any condition or warranty, and any other statement or undertaking, whether oral or in writing. It went on to state that the statement must be one of fact or opinion or an undertaking as to the future which is capable of inducing the proposed borrower to enter into the agreement. It need not be shown that it in fact induced the borrower to enter into the agreement. There was no need to enquire into the circumstances of the case to establish whether the particular borrower was likely to have been induced by the statement in question. Nor need it have been intended by the negotiator to induce the agreement. It sufficed if the statement was one which by its nature was capable of inducing an agreement.

If the agreement is signed by the debtor on the trade premises of any of the creditor, the negotiator or a party to a linked transaction (but not on the debtor's own premises) the agreement is not cancellable.[4] In addition, as a separate regime applies to agreements secured on land and to agreements for the purchase of land or for a bridging loan in connection with the purchase of land, such agreements are never cancellable.[5]

A regulated agreement may also be cancellable under the Financial Services (Distance Marketing) Regulations 2004. Under those regulations a contract is cancellable if it is a so-called 'distance contract'. Essentially this is a contract entered into exclusively through use of one or means of distance communication, namely without the simultaneous physical presence of the supplier and the consumer or an intermediary of the supplier and the consumer.[6] A regulated agreement may also be cancellable under the Timeshare Act 1992.

A cancellable regulated credit agreement must set out the debtor's rights of cancellation. Where the agreement is not cancellable, the agreement must contain a statement that the debtor has no right to cancel the agreement under the Consumer Credit Act 1974, the Timeshare Act 1992 or the Financial Services (Distance Marketing) Regulations 2004.[7]

1 CCA 1974, s 67.
2 CCA 1974, s 56.
3 [1999] GCCR 1947, CA.
4 CCA 1974, s 67(b).
5 CCA 1974, s 67(a).
6 SI 2004/2095.
7 See the Consumer Credit (Agreements) Regulations 1983 SI 1983/1553.

3.6   CREDIT-TOKEN AGREEMENTS

A credit-token agreement is a regulated agreement for the provision of credit in connection with the use of a credit-token.[1] A credit-token agreement usually takes the form of a running-account credit agreement.

A credit-token is a document or thing, of whatever kind or description, against the production of which a creditor or a third party will supply cash, goods or services on credit or pay a third party for such supply.[2]

It is an offence to give a person a credit-token if he has not asked for it. The request must be in writing and signed unless the credit-token agreement is a small debtor-creditor-supplier agreement.[3]

1 CCA 1974, s 14(2).
2 CCA 1974, s 14(1).
3 CCA 1974, s 51.

3.7   SOME IRRELEVANT DISTINCTIONS

Secured credit agreements do not constitute a separate category of credit agreement. However, the fact and nature of the security must be set out in the agreement. Furthermore, if the agreement is secured on land, the statutory heading must reflect this and the agreement must be completed in accordance with the advance copy procedure under s 58 of the Act. Whether an agreement is at a fixed or variable rate of interest or interest free also does not affect its categorisation.

3.8 SPECIFIC CONSUMER CREDIT AGREEMENTS

3.8.1 Agreement types recognised by the Agreements Regulations

The Agreements Regulations[1] identify the following specific types of credit agreement regulated by the CCA 1974: a hire-purchase agreement, a conditional sale agreement, a fixed-sum loan agreement and a credit card agreement. All other credit agreements are subsumed under the description, simply of a consumer credit agreement. Further descriptions are added where the agreement is combined with a pawn receipt, where the agreement embodies a credit agreement not regulated by the Act or where the agreement is secured on land.

1 Consumer Credit (Agreements) Regulations 1983, SI 1983/1553 (as amended), Sch 1.

3.8.2 Instalment sale and hire-purchase agreements

3.8.2.1 *Definitions*[1]

Instalment sale agreements, under which the buyer pays the price by instalments, comprise two types of agreement, namely conditional sale and credit sale agreements:

Conditional sale: A conditional sale agreement is an agreement for the sale of goods or land under which the purchase price or part of it is payable by instalments and the property in the goods or land remains in the seller until payment of the purchase price or until the buyer has complied with any other condition precedent stipulated by the agreement for the transfer of title.

Credit sale: A credit sale agreement is a sale under which title passes to the buyer immediately though payment of the purchase price is deferred. Although land might also be sold by way of credit sale, it is somewhat surprising that, in contrast to conditional sale, a credit sale agreement is defined in CCA 1974 by reference only to the sale of goods.

Hire-purchase: A hire-purchase agreement is an agreement under which goods are bailed (or, in Scotland, hired) in return for payment by the bailee (or hirer) and title to the goods passes to that person if the terms of the agreement are complied with (e.g. payment of monthly instalments) and one or more of the following occurs:

(i)   the exercise of an option to purchase by that person;

(ii) the doing of any other specified act by any party to the agreement; and

(iii) the happening of any other specified event.

The hirer under a hire-purchase agreement merely has an option to buy and is not contractually committed to buy. Under the regulated consumer credit regime a hire-purchase agreement is classified as a consumer credit rather than a consumer-hire agreement. This follows from CCA 1974's functional analytical approach, a hire-purchase agreement being construed as a type of secured sale agreement. Hence the reference in the requisite financial particulars relating to a hire-purchase agreement of 'the total amount payable' and 'the amount of credit'. However, it is in truth a hybrid agreement displaying certain characteristics of a hire agreement, as evidenced by the statutory definition's reference to 'hire' and 'bailment', and to 'hirer' and 'bailee'.

The distinction between a conditional sale agreement and a hire-purchase agreement is not always clear and, it would seem, depends upon how the agreement is drafted. Thus, if the agreement is drafted on terms such that if all instalments are paid, the hirer is deemed to have exercised the option to purchase and title in the goods passes to the hirer, even though the hirer is given the option to terminate the agreement at an earlier stage, the courts will construe this as a conditional sale agreement.[2] In contrast, in *Close Asset Finance v Care Graphics Machinery Ltd*[3] the court distinguished the facts from those in *Forthright Finance Ltd v Carlisle Finance Ltd* on the grounds that in *Forthright Finance*, instead of there being an option to purchase, there was a clause which deemed the option to have been exercised if the payments were made and the hirer had to indicate that he would not be taking the goods in order to prevent that happening. In *Close Asset Finance*, on the other hand, there was a standard option to purchase clause, albeit for a nominal amount. The fact that the option to purchase could be exercised for a nominal amount did not detract from the contract as a hire-purchase agreement as, in the words of the court, the law does not go into the question of whether consideration in the contract is sufficient; the option to purchase was not a bogus option, it was an absolutely genuine one. The parties were free to structure their agreements as they wished and in this case had chosen to structure the agreement as a hire-purchase agreement. In each of *Forthright Finance* and *Close Asset Finance* the issue was whether a purchaser of the goods in question acquired title by virtue of purchasing in good faith and without notice of any rights of the original seller in respect of the goods, pursuant to the Sale of Goods Act 1979, s 25 ('buyer in possession after sale').

1 See CCA 1974, s 189(1).
2 *Forthright Finance Ltd v Carlyle Finance Ltd* [1997] 4 All ER 90, CA.
3 [2000] CCLR 43.

3.8.2.2   Structural features of the agreements

In the case of smaller value transactions the customer usually contracts for the goods or services directly with the supplier. The latter then supplies them on instalment credit or hire-purchase terms to the customer. The original supplier is also the creditor. The supplier might then discount the agreements with a finance company or bank, thereby replenishing his supply of funds to finance further consumer transactions.

In larger transactions the customer will identify and select the goods or services as well as their supplier. The supplier then arranges for their financing by a finance company, often one with which the supplier has entered into arrangements. The supplier will then invoice the finance company which will acquire the goods and enter into a conditional sale, credit sale or hire-purchase agreement in respect of them with the customer introduced by the supplier.

The customer might purchase goods from the supplier and sell them to a finance company before buying them back on conditional sale, credit sale or hire-purchase terms. The risk involved in this route is that it may be construed as a disguised secured loan transaction. In the case of a company purchaser, this might render it void for want of registration as a charge under the Companies Act 1985, s 395. Where the purchaser is an individual the risk is twofold. First, the transaction might be construed as a disguised bill of sale and void for want of compliance with and registration under the Bills of Sale Acts.[1] Second, if construed as a disguised loan it may be unenforceable on account of failure to comply with the appropriate Agreements Regulations.[2] The problems are overcome by ensuring that the transactions are in fact genuine, that the finance house has bought the goods in good faith and that the entire transaction is properly documented.

The finance company may require the supplier to grant warranties in respect of the goods. These would normally preserve the seller's implied warranties on a sale and include warranties that the goods are new, not the subject of a previous transaction with the same customer, so as to avoid the possibility of fraud, and that the customer has selected and is satisfied with the goods. The supplier might also enter into a re-purchase agreement with the finance company under which it undertakes to buy back the goods at a predetermined price (e.g. their residual value) if the agreement between the customer and the finance company is terminated, whether on expiry of the agreement or by virtue of early settlement or the customer's breach of the agreement.

1 Bills of Sale Acts 1878–1891; *North Central Wagon Finance Co Ltd v Brailsford* [1962] 1 All ER 502.
2 CCA 1974, ss 61(1)(a), 65 and Consumer Credit (Agreements) Regulations 1983, SI 1983/1553 (as amended).

3.8.2.3   *Characteristics of instalment sale and hire-purchase agreements*

Instalment sale agreement. In an instalment sale agreement the buyer is committed to purchasing whilst in a hire-purchase agreement he retains the option to do so. An instalment sale agreement has all the incidents of a sale agreement. These include the buyer's liability for payment of the purchase price and the application of the Sale of Goods Act 1979 to the contract. The latter in turn embraces the following: an implied term on the part of the seller that he has the right to sell the goods; implied terms that the goods are free from any undisclosed charge or encumbrance and that the buyer will enjoy quiet possession of the goods; an implied term that the goods will correspond with their description and if sold by sample, with that sample. Where goods are sold in the course of a business there is also an implied term that the goods are of satisfactory quality and when the buyer discloses any particular purpose for which he is buying the goods, that they are reasonably fit for that purpose.[1]

In *Barber v NWS Bank plc*[2] the seller of a motor vehicle under a conditional sale agreement was not the owner of the vehicle, which was the subject of a prior finance agreement in the name of a third party with monies outstanding to that party. The purchaser under the conditional sale agreement, on discovering this fact, rescinded the agreement on the grounds of total failure of consideration and demanded the return of all instalments paid. The court found in favour of the purchaser on the grounds that an implied condition (now a term) that the seller had a right to sell the goods under the Sale of Goods Act 1979, s 12 had been breached in that the seller did not have title to the car either at the date of the agreement or at any time thereafter prior to the buyer's letter of rescission.

In the event of termination by the seller by reason of the buyer's breach, the buyer is usually liable for payment of the entire outstanding balance of the purchase price less a discount attributable to the seller's receipt of accelerated payment. However, CCA 1974 stipulates differently in certain situations.[3]

In the event of the buyer's wrongful disposal of goods before he has paid the full purchase price, the 'nemo dat' rule will generally prevent title in the goods passing to their new purchaser.[4] This rule provides that where goods are sold by a person who is not their owner and who does not sell them under the express, implied or apparent authority or with the consent of the owner, the buyer acquires no better title to the goods than the seller had. There are several exceptions to this rule, notably dispositions by mercantile agents, dispositions by sellers and buyers of goods under the Factors Act 1889 and dispositions by a seller in possession after sale or by a buyer in possession after a sale of the goods.[5]

1 Sale of Goods Act 1979, ss 12, 13 and 14. Exclusions are governed by the Unfair Contract Terms Act 1977, s 6 and the Unfair Terms in Consumer Contracts Regulations 1999, SI 1999/2083.
2 [1996] 1 All ER 906, CA.
3 See below.
4 Sale of Goods Act 1979, s 21.
5 Sale of Goods Act 1979, ss 24 and 25 and the Factors Act 1889, s 9. See also *National Employers Mutual General Insurance Association v Jones* [1988] 2 All ER 425, HL.

Hire-purchase agreement. At common law the hirer under a hire-purchase agreement is entitled to terminate the agreement at any time but will be liable to pay the owner damages for early termination and to return the goods to the owner. Where the amount or method of calculation of damages is stipulated at the outset in the agreement it must not exceed a genuine pre-estimate of the likely damages which the owner would suffer in such event.[1]

In both a regulated hire-purchase agreement and a regulated conditional sale agreement, save in exceptional circumstances, the hirer or debtor respectively has the right to terminate the agreement at any time before the final payment falls due.[2] Once the hirer or debtor has paid at least one-third of the total amount payable under the agreement the owner or creditor may not take back the goods against his wishes without a court order, the goods being identified as 'protected goods'.[3] Upon termination the debtor or hirer is liable for no more than the return of the goods, payment of any installation charges and of one-half of the total amount payable under the agreement.[4] If the hirer under a hire-purchase agreement or the buyer under a conditional sale agreement commits a repudiatory breach of the agreement and the owner or creditor terminates the agreement (as he is entitled to do) it is debateable whether he will be entitled to recover more than he would have been entitled to had the customer terminated the agreement. It appears that provided the owner or creditor has served the requisite notice under CCA 1974 and the debtor has not terminated the agreement before the due date for payment under the notice has arisen, the debtor is liable for payment of the full outstanding balance under the agreement. The rule against penalties would then not apply.[5] This conclusion would also accord with the literal meaning of s 99 of the CCA 1974.

The terms implied in hire-purchase agreements are contained in the Supply of Goods (Implied Terms) Act 1973 and are similar to those implied in sale agreements. There is a statutory implied term that the creditor will have a right to sell the goods at the time when the property is to pass, an implied term that the goods are free, and will remain free when the property is to pass, from any charge or encumbrance not disclosed or known to the hirer before the agreement is made and an implied term that the hirer's quiet possession of the goods will remain undisturbed by the creditor or any third person, except of course if the hirer breaches the agreement. This Act also imports into the hire-purchase agreement certain implied terms relating to the goods, namely that they are of satisfactory quality, fit for their purpose, correspond with their description and with any sample.[6]

In *Butterworth v Kingsway Motors Ltd*[7] a hire-purchase agreement was entered into by the owner of a motor vehicle with the hirer, who was given the option of purchasing the vehicle. Until the option had been exercised the vehicle was to remain the property of the owner. Before all instalments had been paid, the hirer purported to make various sales but none of the purported sellers had title to the vehicle at the times when the sales were made. However, the hirer subsequently paid all instalments and exercised the option to purchase, as a result of which title in the vehicle passed to her and served to feed the previously defective titles of the subsequent buyers. Thus, there is no total failure of consideration where at the time of entry into a hire-purchase agreement the seller under the agreement did not have title provided that the seller subsequently has title at the time when the hirer exercises the option to purchase. However, if claims are made before the option to purchase is exercised, the seller may be in breach of the statutory warranty of the right to sell the goods.

In contrast to the position in a sale agreement, an innocent third party cannot acquire good title from a hirer under the Factors Act 1889, s 9 or the Sale of Goods Act, s 25. However, in the case of a motor vehicle which is the subject of a sale agreement to a private purchaser who buys in good faith and without notice of the seller's defective title (and is oblivious to the fact that the vehicle is the subject of a hire-purchase or conditional sale agreement), the purchaser acquires good title even from a hirer under a hire-purchase or conditional sale agreement. This applies equally to a private purchaser from a trade seller.[8] However, it does not extend to a private purchaser buying a motor vehicle from a rogue who had obtained it fraudulently by signing a hire purchase agreement with a forged signature. In such circumstances it was in *Shogun Finance Ltd v Hudson*[9] that the rogue was not the 'debtor' within the meaning of s 27 of the Hire Purchase Act 1964. The seller was liable in conversion to the true owner.

1 *Bridge v Campbell Discount Co Ltd* [1962] 1 All ER 385.
2 CCA 1974, s 99.
3 CCA 1974, s 90.
4 CCA 1974, s 100.
5 See *Goode: Consumer Credit Law and Practice* (LexisNexis Butterworths), at 1C [36.203] citing the decision of Woolf J (as he then was) in *Wadham Stringer Finance Ltd v Meany* [1999] CCR 551.
6 The Supply of Goods (Implied Terms) Act 1973, ss 8, 9 and 10. Exclusions are governed by the Unfair Contract Terms Act 1977, s 6 and the Unfair Terms in Consumer Contracts Regulations 1999, SI 1999/2083.
7 [1954] 2 All ER 694.
8 Sections 27 to 29 of the Hire-Purchase Act 1964 and see the application of these sections in *Stevenson v Beverley Bentinck Ltd* [1976] 2 All ER 606 and *Hichens v General Guarantie Corpn Ltd* [2001] EWCA Civ 359, (2001) Times, 13 March.
9 [2003] GCCR 4971, HL.

3.8.3   Fixed-sum loan agreements

3.8.3.1   Definition

A fixed-sum loan agreement is an agreement under which an ascertained sum is advanced by the creditor to the borrower for a specified period, either for a stipulated purpose or for an unspecified purpose, in return for the repayment of such sum together with interest and any other charges. The loan may relate to the supply of goods or services by a third party. When it is part of a tripartite arrangement or agreement it will fall into the category of a connected loan or a debtor-creditor-supplier agreement. In other cases, namely unconnected loans, it is characterised as a debtor-creditor agreement. The most common form of fixed-sum loan is what is colloquially known as a personal loan agreement.

An agreement is for fixed-sum credit notwithstanding that the borrower may draw down the loan amount in tranches, e.g. on presentation of an architect's certificate or at the borrower's discretion, as in the case of a school fee payments plan.

Fixed-sum loan agreements include cheque or voucher agreements under which the debtor purchases a series of cheques or vouchers on credit to be used at identified stores or suppliers and under which he agrees to repay the credit over a period of time.

As credit is defined in CCA 1974 as including any form of financial accommodation, any agreement under which one party is indebted to the other and is granted a period of time in which to make payment, will involve the grant of credit. If the debtor is an individual, the agreement will be a consumer credit agreement and a regulated agreement if it does not qualify as an exempt agreement. It is important to recognise this fact in practice as if the agreement does not comply with the requirements of a regulated agreement it will be unenforceable without an order of the court and potentially wholly unenforceable.[1] The need to comply is often obscured by the mistaken belief that credit agreements entered into on a one-off basis, as opposed to being entered into as part of a lending business, need not comply. However, the latter is to confuse the dispensation in respect of a non-commercial agreement (an agreement not made by the creditor in the course of a business carried on by him)[2] with the application of the consumer credit regime to even a single regulated agreement. As regards the need to be licensed, the Act states that a person is not to be treated as carrying on a particular type of business merely because occasionally he enters into transactions belonging to a business of that type.[3]

1 CCA 1974 and especially ss 61, 65 and 127.
2 CCA 1974, s 74(1)(a).
3 CCA 1974, s 189(2).

3.8.3.2 Common characteristics of a fixed-sum loan agreement

The Agreements Regulations[1] prescribe the statement of different financial and related particulars for fixed-sum credit agreements as compared with running-account credit agreements. They include, in the case of a debtor-creditor-supplier agreement for fixed-sum credit, a list or other description of the goods, services, things or land to be financed by the agreement and the amount of credit to be provided under the agreement. In contrast with a running-account credit agreement, the creditor under a fixed-sum credit agreement must grant the debtor a rebate of charges on early settlement of the agreement (at least equal to the statutory rebate) where the agreement levies credit charges in respect of the period after the settlement date of the agreement.

The utility of running-account credit agreements, and in particular credit-token agreements, has to a large extent resulted in their replacing fixed-sum loan agreements, credit sale, conditional sale and hire-purchase agreements for retail purchases in the small to medium price range. This is predominantly due to the fact that running-account credit agreements can accommodate more than one transaction without requiring a fresh agreement to be entered into on each occasion, a feature which is particularly appealing to the marketing departments of lending institutions.

Most mortgages take the form of fixed-sum credit agreements secured by a mortgage on the debtor's home.

1 CCA 1974, ss 61(1)(a), 65 and Consumer Credit (Agreements) Regulations 1983, SI 1983/1553 (as amended).

3.8.4 Running-account or revolving credit agreements

3.8.4.1 Agreement types

Running-account or revolving credit agreements include agreements for bank overdrafts, budget accounts, option accounts and charge card accounts.

3.8.4.2 Agreement for overdraft facilities

An overdraft is a loan facility in conjunction with a current account, usually but not necessarily a bank current account, which is repayable on demand.

Bank accounts were previously largely operated by means of cheques but are now increasingly accessed by bank cards, debit cards and ATM cards. Differential interest rates are generally applied to the amount overdrawn, or the balance in debit on the account, depending on whether or not the overdraft has been authorised by the bank.

A bank customer has no entitlement to an overdraft and any transaction which would result in his account being overdrawn may, in the absence of authorisation, be lawfully dishonoured by the bank.

Subject to notification to the Office of Fair Trading, consumer credit agreements enabling a debtor to overdraw on a current account are exempt from the provisions relating to the form and formalities applying to regulated agreements.[1] Although not defined in CCA 1974, a 'current account' is defined, in certain regulations under the Act, as an account under which the customer may, by means of cheques or similar orders payable to himself or to any other person or by any other means, obtain or have the use of money held or made available by the person with whom the account is kept and which records alterations in the financial relationship between such person and the customer.[2]

The expression 'current account' was the subject of judicial consideration in the case of *United Dominions Trust Ltd v Kirkwood*,[3] where the court described it as a running-account maintained for the bank's customer which records payments into and withdrawals from the account and which possesses the following features: the customer may from time to time make payments into and effect withdrawals from the account; the bank must undertake to pay cheques drawn on itself in favour of third parties up to the amount standing to the credit of the customer on the account, debiting the account with such payments; and the bank must undertake to collect cheques for the customer and credit the proceeds to the account.

The Office of Fair Trading has made a Determination to exclude agreements for overdrafts on a current account from the provisions of Part V of CCA 1974 (relating to form and formalities) on certain conditions.[4] They are that the creditor shall have informed the OFT in writing of its general intention to enter into such agreements, that the debtor is informed at the time, or before the agreement is concluded, of any applicable credit limit, the annual rate of interest and charges applicable from time to time, the conditions under which these may be amended and of the procedure for terminating the agreement. In addition, the creditor must undertake to inform the debtor in writing within seven days of the interest rate and charges arising where the debtor overdraws on his current account.

The exemption is of inestimable value and benefit to the entire banking industry and constitutes a vast no-man's land of exempt agreements in the consumer credit terrain. Other provisions of the CCA 1974, including those relating to default and enforcement, apply to these agreements.

1   CCA 1974, s 74(1)(b) and (c).
2   Consumer Credit (Advertisements) Regulations 2004, SI 2004/1484, reg 1(2).
3   [1966] 1 All ER 968, CA.
4   Determination dated 21 December 1989.

3.8.4.3   Budget account agreement

A budget account is a running-account credit agreement with a credit limit which is a multiple of the account holder's periodical payment, usually a monthly payment. The credit limit is commonly 24 times the monthly payment. This is the notional period over which any outstanding balance would be expected to be repaid. Monthly instalments and credit limits are variable, primarily at the instance of the account holder though the creditor may decline such request. Interest is charged on the outstanding balance, ordinarily on a daily basis and debited to the account at monthly intervals.

3.8.4.4 Option account agreement

An option account is a running-account credit agreement with a credit limit selected by the account holder and which requires the account holder to make a regular monthly payment, in a minimum sum usually equal to the greater of a fixed amount or a specified percentage of the monthly outstanding balance. The account holder also has the option of repaying the account balance in full.

3.8.4.5 Characteristics of budget and option account agreements

Budget and option accounts share various common features. These include monthly instalments, which are variable; interest charged on the outstanding balance, usually on a daily basis and debited monthly; the account holder is usually given a limited interest-free period if he repays the full outstanding balance by the due payment date, except in the case of cash withdrawals when interest runs from the date of withdrawal; the interest rate is usually variable; each account is normally operated by means of a credit card.

Budget and option accounts are invariably debtor-creditor-supplier agreements. They may take the form of a store card, in which event they can only be utilised within specified retail outlets with whom the credit card provider has entered into an arrangement for their acceptance. Alternatively, they may take the form of generic cards, utilisable at any outlet accepting such card. If the card issuer is also a member of the Visa or MasterCard organisation and the cards are issued with the Visa or MasterCard symbol, the card can be used wherever that symbol is displayed. The generic card will also usually be a debtor-creditor-supplier agreement by virtue of the creditor having entered into arrangements, directly or indirectly, with the supplier for the acceptance of the card. In so far as the credit card can be used to obtain cash advances, the credit agreement is also a debtor-creditor agreement.

3.8.4.6 Charge card agreement

A charge card agreement is an agreement for the provision of credit under a running-account credit-token agreement, namely a revolving credit agreement operated by means of a credit card, under which the entire outstanding balance is payable in full at regular intervals, usually monthly against receipt of a monthly statement. It is a credit agreement but in so far as it is a debtor-creditor-supplier agreement, it is an exempt agreement and therefore not a regulated agreement.[1] The exemption does not apply to a charge card which is a debtor-creditor agreement, for example a charge card agreement under which cash advances can be obtained with the result that such agreement will need to take the form of a regulated agreement.

1 Consumer Credit (Exempt Agreements) Order 1989, SI 1989/869, art 3(1)(a)(ii).

3.8.4.7   Credit-token agreement

A credit-token agreement (colloquially known as a credit card agreement) is a regulated agreement for the provision of credit in connection with a credit-token.[1] It is the generic description given to such agreements which are invariably in running-account credit form.

A credit-token is a card, cheque, voucher, coupon, stamp, form, booklet or other document or thing given to an individual by a person carrying on a consumer credit business who undertakes that, on the production of it to him (whether or not some other action is also required), he will supply any of cash, goods and services on credit or, on production of it to a third party (whether or not any other action is required), where the third party supplies any of the foregoing, he will reimburse such party in return for payment to him by the debtor.[2]

In *Elliott v Director General of Fair Trading*[3] the defendant, T Elliott & Sons Ltd, had sent to selected members of the public an envelope containing certain materials. One insert contained a statement: 'Your Elliott credit card account valid for immediate use. With your card in your hand, walk into any Elliott shop: give us your signature, show us simple identification, such as a cheque card and walk out of the shop with your purchase and all the credit you need. Please remember to sign your card as soon as you receive it. It is perfectly secure; it cannot be used by anyone until we have their signature in the shop'. A further item was a mock credit card which contained provision for a signature and statements, in summary, as follows: 'This credit card is valid for immediate use; the sole requirement is your signature and means of identification; credit is immediately available if you have a bank account; sign the card as soon as you receive it; it is perfectly secure because it can only be used when a signature has been accepted at an Elliott shop'.

A prosecution was instituted by the Director General of Fair Trading on the grounds that the documents, including the mock card, had been sent to individuals in contravention of CCA 1974, s 51(1) which renders it an offence to give a person a credit-token if he has not asked for it and the request, by virtue of s 51(2), must be in a document signed by the person making it.

The issue turned on the meaning of the word 'undertakes' in the definition of a credit-token as, notwithstanding what the documentation stated, the production of the card did not entitle the customer to the supply of goods on credit but only enabled him to apply for a credit card and despite the wording in the card, the card was not valid for immediate use, even if the customer had a bank account. The court gave short shrift to the defence holding that 'undertakes' does not involve the necessity for any contractual agreement or possibility of contractual agreement. The court stated that one looks at the card and asks whether, on the face or on the back of that card, the defendant company is undertaking that on the production of the card, cash, goods and services (or any of them) will be supplied on credit, to which the court found the answer was 'yes'. The fact that none of the statements was true did not absolve the card from being what it purported to be, namely a credit-token card.

It follows that, if production of some document, whether or not some additional action is required, will result in the supply of, cash, goods or services on credit, the document will constitute a credit-token.

However, 'production' of the document is a requirement, so that notifying the customer by a document, e.g. a customer letter, of his entitlement to the credit, will not constitute a credit-token if there is no requirement that the document needs to be produced in order to obtain the credit. A credit agreement which is pre-signed by the creditor and is sent to a customer guaranteeing him credit on his signing and returning the agreement, or presenting the credit agreement to another, is not a credit-token as it is not within the *genus* or class of documents identified as a credit-token and, moreover, is itself the credit agreement under or in respect of which any relevant credit-token agreement would be operated. If this were not the case, every document comprising a credit agreement, even if not signed by the creditor in advance, would constitute a credit-token if it had not previously been requested by the borrower in writing.

The second limb of the definition of a credit-token refers to a document constituting a credit-token where, on its production to a third party, the third party supplies any cash, goods and services, the person carrying on a consumer credit business will pay the third party for them in return for payment to him by the individual. This second limb of the definition does not specifically require the person carrying on the consumer credit business to grant credit to the individual although, in practice, by virtue of the intervention of the person carrying on a consumer credit business, credit will invariably be granted to the individual.

1 CCA 1974, s 189(1).
2 CCA 1974, s 14(1).
3 [1980] 1 WLR 977.

3.8.4.8 *Common characteristics of running-account credit agreements*[1]

Running-account or revolving credit agreements are inchoate or in suspense until such time as an amount of credit has been drawn down. However, acceptance of a credit-token may take place prior to and independently of utilisation of the credit facility. The debtor accepts a credit-token when it is signed or a receipt for it is signed or it is first used, either by the debtor himself or by a person who, pursuant to the agreement, is authorised by him to use it.[2]

The debtor's liability for misuse of the credit-token is limited by the CCA 1974 (and regulations under it) currently to the sum of £50, save where the person misusing the card acted as the debtor's agent or otherwise used the card or, it is submitted, obtained the card details and any personal identification number, with the debtor's consent.[3] It is submitted that reference to when the card is first used is to be interpreted as meaning when the card is first used to obtain credit and not when it is used for some other purpose, such as a customer identification form or for credit scoring or credit assessment purposes when applying for credit.

A debtor is not liable for any use made of the card after he duly reported its loss or theft to the creditor or that it was for any other reason liable to misuse.[4]

Nor is the debtor liable for any misuse by another person of a credit card in connection with a distance contract.[5]

A credit-token agreement must contain the statutory form relating to the loss or misuse of credit-tokens[6] and specified particulars of the name, address and telephone number of the person to whom notice of any loss, theft or liability to misuse of the credit-token, must be given.[7] Indeed, in the absence of the latter, the debtor will not incur any liability whatsoever following the loss or theft of the card.[8]

A debtor under a running-account credit agreement is entitled to receive regular statements, showing the state of his account, at periodical intervals and, where there has been a movement in his account, at the end of the period during which there has been such movement (e.g. a credit or debit to the account). Where the statement includes a demand for payment it must be furnished within one month of the end of the period to which it relates. In other cases the period for the furnishing of statements varies from six to twelve months.[9]

A notice of variation of a regulated agreement must set out particulars and be served on the debtor not less than seven days before the variation takes effect. Special provision is made where the variation is of the rate of interest payable under the agreement and the interest is charged by reference to the daily outstanding balance. In that case notice of the variation may be given by publication in three national daily newspapers and by displaying the notice at the creditor's premises.[10]

1 See the illuminating discussion in *Goode: Consumer Credit Law and Practice* (LexisNexis Butterworths), IC [25.22] and following.
2 CCA 1974, s 66(2).
3 CCA 1974, ss 83 and 84 and SI 1998/997.
4 *Ibid.*, s 84(3).
5 *Ibid.*, s 84(3A), (3B) and (3C).
6 Consumer Credit (Agreements) Regulations 1983, SI 1983/1553, Sch 2, Pt I, Form 15.
7 Consumer Credit (Credit-Token Agreements) Regulations 1983, SI 1983/1555.
8 CCA 1974, s 84(4).
9 CCA 1974, s 78 and Consumer Credit (Running-Account Credit Information) Regulations 1983, SI 1983/1570.
10 Consumer Credit (Notice of Variation of Agreements) Regulations 1977, SI 1977/328 (as amended).

3.9   LOANS SECURED BY LAND MORTGAGES

3.9.1   Relevance of the Act

As already noted, as a result of the extensive exemption granted by CCA 1974, s 16 and the regulation of regulated mortgage contracts under the Financial Services and Markets Act 2000, the Act does not regulate most consumer credit agreements for the purchase of land, the provision of dwellings or business premises on land or the financing of the alteration, enlarging, repair or improvements of dwellings or business premises on land. Creditors enjoying exempt status under s 16 include all local authorities and bodies specified in an Order made under the Act, namely insurance companies, friendly societies, organisations of employers or workers, charities, land improvement companies, bodies corporate specifically referred to in public general Acts, building societies, banks and wholly-owned subsidiaries of banks (but not subsidiaries of building societies).[1]

As a result of the legislature having thus effectively neutralised so much of the core and raison d'etre of the regime intended for the consumer's protection, the Act now only has relevance to those agreements secured by land mortgages which are not exempt agreements. Exempt agreements are of the kind referred to in s 16 of the Act.[2]

1 See para 4.3.1.
2 *Ibid.*

3.9.2 Characteristics of loans secured by land mortgages

Loans of this kind will generally take the form of a loan agreement signed under hand and a separate and distinct mortgage deed executed by the mortgagor. In the case of a prospective regulated agreement, before sending to the debtor the unexecuted agreement for his signature, the creditor must give the debtor an advance copy of the agreement containing a notice indicating the debtor's right to withdraw from the prospective agreement, accompanied by a copy of the proposed mortgage deed and any other document referred to in the unexecuted agreement. This procedure does not apply to a restricted-use credit agreement to finance the purchase of the mortgaged land or an agreement for a bridging loan in connection with the purchase of the mortgaged land or other land for the reason that these transactions usually need to be concluded speedily.[1]

Where the advance copy procedure applies the agreement for execution by the borrower must be posted to him not less than seven days after the advance copy was given to him. The borrower is then given a further seven days after the day on which the unexecuted agreement is sent for his signature, to consider whether or not he wishes to proceed with the agreement. This interval is known as 'the consideration period' during which the creditor must refrain from approaching the debtor, whether in person, by telephone or letter or in any other way except in response to a specific request made by the borrower after the beginning of the consideration period.[2] It also means that, except in response to such a request, the creditor may not send a surveyor or insurance broker to the debtor. Should the consideration period be broken by the creditor's communication the creditor will have to recommence the procedure with new advance copy documents.

1 CCA 1974, s 58.
2 CCA 1974, s 61(2).

3.9.3 Mortgage types

There are essentially two types of mortgage, a repayment mortgage and an interest-only mortgage. Under a repayment mortgage, monthly instalments comprise both interest and capital, the capital portion representing a repayment of part of the original advance. Under an interest-only mortgage, the monthly instalments are of interest only and the capital, namely the original advance, is repaid in one lump sum ordinarily at the end of the mortgage term. Borrowers under interest-only mortgages are usually advised to enter into an endowment policy or some other investment in order to ensure that they will have available funds to repay the mortgage advance when the mortgage term expires.

There are various sub-sets of mortgage, within the foregoing broad categories. Originally these acquired their nomenclature in a marketing context but with the passing of time the descriptions have acquired a distinct meaning.

Most mortgages are variable rate mortgages, meaning that the interest rate is variable in accordance with the terms of the mortgage. A discounted rate mortgage is a mortgage under which for an initial period of a stated number of years, usually a period not exceeding two years, interest is charged at a stated discount to the lender's standard variable mortgage interest rate. A fixed-rate mortgage is one under which for a stated initial period of time interest is charged at a fixed rate. A capped rate mortgage is one under which the lender's interest rate is capped, again during an initial period, so that although the interest rate is variable it cannot rise above this level. A flexible mortgage is one which permits the borrower to make repayments in excess of the monthly instalments, to take so-called payment holidays during which no monthly instalments need to be paid although interest continues to accrue on the outstanding balance, and sometimes to draw down capital which has been repaid. A cashback mortgage is one under which the borrower receives a lump sum in cash on taking out the mortgage, which is not repayable to the mortgagee, and which the borrower might utilise for any purpose including as part payment of the deposit on the mortgaged property. A home equity release mortgage or lifetime mortgage is a mortgage enabling the borrower to realise the equity acquired in his home and to invest it in a pension or other investment vehicle, particularly in order to provide for ongoing income to the mortgagor on retirement. The capital of the mortgage, and sometimes part or all of the interest accrued under the mortgage, is repayable on the mortgagor's death or at earlier specified events, such as the mortgagor disposing of the mortgaged property or entering sheltered accommodation.

Chapter 4

Regulated agreements and exempt agreements

4.1 MEANING OF A 'REGULATED AGREEMENT'

A regulated agreement is a consumer credit agreement, or consumer hire agreement, other than an exempt agreement, and 'regulated' and 'unregulated' are to be construed accordingly.[1] The table below should assist to identify the classification of the agreement.

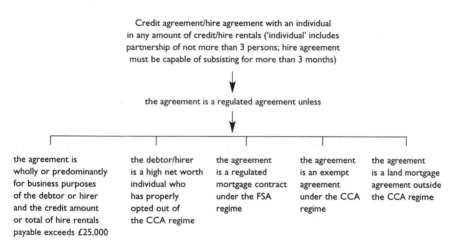

Credit agreement/hire agreement with an individual in any amount of credit/hire rentals ('individual' includes partnership of not more than 3 persons; hire agreement must be capable of subsisting for more than 3 months)

↓

the agreement is a regulated agreement unless

↓

| the agreement is wholly or predominantly for business purposes of the debtor or hirer and the credit amount or total of hire rentals payable exceeds £25,000 | the debtor/hirer is a high net worth individual who has properly opted out of the CCA regime | the agreement is a regulated mortgage contract under the FSA regime | the agreement is an exempt agreement under the CCA regime | the agreement is a land mortgage agreement outside the CCA regime |

---

1 Section 189(1). For a discussion of 'consumer credit agreement' and 'consumer hire agreement', see Chapter 2.

4.2 MEANING OF AN 'EXEMPT AGREEMENT'

CCA 1974 contains provision for the exemption of certain agreements from the scope of the Act. These are known as exempt agreements and are to be distinguished from regulated agreements.

An exempt agreement is an agreement specified in or under ss 16, 16A or 16B of CCA 1974. In order to be able to understand the classification of exempt agreements one should consider the provisions of the Act first and then the regulations made under the relevant section.

There are various types of exempt agreement and the criteria of an exempt agreement may depend upon one or more of the following: the type of creditor, the type of agreement and the type of debtor or hirer.

4.3   TYPES OF EXEMPT AGREEMENT

4.3.1   Credit agreements secured by a land mortgage

Historically, the most important type of exempt agreement has been a credit agreement secured by a land mortgage where the creditor and the credit agreement meet certain criteria set out in CCA 1974, as further qualified by the Consumer Credit (Exempt Agreements) Order 1989.[1]

Certain creditors enjoy total exemption and others only qualified exemption. The former include local authorities in respect of most secured debtor-creditor and debtor-creditor-supplier agreements and housing authorities in respect of an agreement secured by a land mortgage of a dwelling.[2] Qualified exemption applies to building societies, authorised institutions (namely banks) and their wholly-owned subsidiaries and such of the following bodies as have been specifically designated by an Order: insurance companies, friendly societies and charities.

Exempt status is limited to the following types of credit agreement:

(a)   a debtor-creditor-supplier agreement financing the purchase of land or the provision of dwellings on land and secured by a land mortgage on that land;

(b)   a debtor-creditor agreement secured by a land mortgage financing the purchase of land or the provision of dwellings or business premises on land or, where the creditor is a creditor under an agreement for either such purpose, an agreement to finance alterations, repairs or improvements of a dwelling or business premises on any land;

(c)   a debtor-creditor-supplier agreement financing a linked transaction in relation to (a) or (b) above.

There are further limitations in respect of exempt agreements secured by a land mortgage where the creditor is a body specified in the Schedule to the Consumer Credit (Exempt Agreements) Order 1989 or a deposit-taker authorised under the Financial Services and Markets Act 2000.[3]

Notwithstanding the exempt status of these agreements, they are subject to the unfair relationships provisions of CCA 1974.[4]

1   SI 1989/869 (as amended).
2   Section 16(1) and (6A).
3   *Ibid.*, Art 2.
4   Section 16(7A) and see ss 140A to 140D.

4.3.2   Regulated mortgage contracts

Pursuant to the Financial Services and Markets Act 2000 and the Financial Services and Markets Act 2000 (Regulated Activities) Order 2001[1] certain mortgage contracts, known as 'regulated mortgage contracts', were carved out of CCA 1974 (under the ultimate authority of the Department of Trade and Industry) and brought within the scope of the Financial Services and Markets Act 2000 (under the ultimate authority of the Treasury).

A regulated mortgage contract is one which meets the following conditions:

(a)   it is a contract under which the lender provides credit to an individual or to trustees ('the borrower');

(b)   the contract provides for the borrower's obligation to repay to be secured by a first legal mortgage on land (other than timeshare accommodation) in the United Kingdom; and

(c)   at least 40% of that land is used, or is intended to be used as, or in connection with, a dwelling by the borrower or (in the case of credit provided to trustees) by an individual who is a beneficiary of the trust or by a related person.[2]

Regulated mortgage contracts include a lifetime or equity release mortgage. This is a mortgage under which:

(a)   entry into the mortgage is restricted to older customers above a specified age;

(b)   the mortgagee may or may not specify a mortgage term but will not seek full repayment of the loan (nor outstanding interest) until the occurrence of one or more of the following: the death of the customer; the customer leaving the mortgaged land to live elsewhere and having no reasonable prospect of returning (for example by moving into residential care); the customer acquiring another dwelling for use as his main residence; the customer selling the mortgaged land; or the mortgagee exercising its legal right to take possession of the mortgaged land under the terms of the contract; and

(c)   while the customer continues to occupy the mortgaged land as his main residence, prescribed restrictions apply to the repayments which he may be required to make.[3]

In practice the above means that a first legal mortgage on residential property and a further advance by a mortgagee under such mortgage fall under the jurisdiction of the Financial Services Authority and not the Office of Fair Trading under CCA 1974. However, equitable mortgages and second or later legal mortgages on residential property entered into with consumers continue to be governed by the provisions of CCA 1974.

Regulated home purchase plans also fall under the purview of the Financial Services and Markets Act 2000. Although not entirely clear from s 16(6C) of

CCA 1974, this exemption from CCA 1974 applies both to regulated home reversion plans and regulated home purchase plans, as defined in the Financial Services and Markets Act 2000 (Regulated Activities) (Amendment) (No. 2) Order 2006.[4]

Notwithstanding the exempt status of these agreements, they remain subject to the unfair relationships provisions of CCA 1974.[5]

1 SI 2001/544 (as amended).
2 *Ibid.*, art 61.
3 FSA Handbook: Glossary Definition of 'lifetime mortgage'.
4 SI 2006/2383.
5 Section 16(7A) and see ss 140A to 140D.

4.3.3   Extension of land mortgage exemption

An agreement is outside the provisions of CCA 1974 if it is for credit exceeding £25,000 and it is either:[1]

(a)   a consumer credit agreement and any sums due under it are secured by a land mortgage on land outside the United Kingdom; or

(b)   a consumer credit agreement and any sums due under it are secured by a land mortgage on land in the United Kingdom where the condition below is satisfied.

The condition is that at the time the agreement is entered into less than 40% of the land is used, or is intended to be used, as or in connection with a dwelling:

(i)   by the debtor or a person connected with the debtor; or

(ii)   in the case of credit provided to trustees, by an individual who is the beneficiary of the trust or a person connected with such an individual.

For the above purposes the area of any land which comprises a building or other structure containing two or more storeys is to be taken to be the aggregate of the floor areas of each of those storeys. A person is 'connected with' the debtor or an individual who is the beneficiary of a trust if he is:

(i)   that person's spouse or civil partner;

(ii)   a person (whether or not of the opposite sex) whose relationship with that person has the characteristics of the relationship between husband and wife; or

(iii)   that person's parent, brother, sister, child, grandparent or grandchild.

The provision is intended, in part, as a temporary measure to exclude most buy-to-let mortgages, pending the exclusion of the latter from CCA 1974 by a Legislative Reform Order.

1 The Consumer Credit Act 2006 (Commencement No. 4 and Transitional Provisions) Order 2008, SI 2008/831, art 2(1) read with Sch 1.

4.3.4 Exemption relating to high net worth debtors and hirers

A unique exemption introduced by CCA 2006, and which came into force on 6 April 2008, is that relating to high net worth debtors and hirers. The underlying rationale was to permit private banking services a degree of flexibility to offer a wider range of services to those who want them.[1] Originally the justification for this exemption was stated to be that these debtors or hirers have the resources to seek their own legal and financial advice about credit transactions and, secondly, if the exemption were not made available, they might seek to enter into agreements in less regulated jurisdictions.[2] Stated another way, this exemption allows private banking services a degree of flexibility to offer a wide range of services to those who want them.[3]

There is a corollary to this, namely that in view of the removal of the financial limit, credit grantors needed to be placated in relation to the rights of debtors under hire-purchase and conditional sale agreements, particularly the debtor's right to voluntarily terminate the agreement early and pay only one half of the total price of the goods, pursuant to ss 99 and 100 of CCA 1974 and the protection afforded to the debtor in relation to the retaking of protected goods once the debtor has paid at least one third of the total price of the goods, pursuant to s 90 of CCA 1974. The exemption relating to high net worth individuals and the resultant exemption of hire-purchase and conditional sale agreements from the above provisions of CCA 1974 is a welcome development for creditors, particularly those financing the purchase of highly priced vehicles by wealthy individuals.

Originally the criteria proposed for high net worth individuals mirrored those under the Financial Services and Markets Act 2000 (Financial Promotions) Order 2005,[4] but, after some negotiation in the course of the consultation process, the criteria arrived at, as set out in the Consumer Credit (Exempt Agreements) Order 2007,[5] are as follows:

(a) that the individual received during the previous financial year (the year ending 31 March) net income (i.e. total income reduced by the amount of income tax and national insurance contributions) totalling not less than £150,000; or

(b) that the individual had throughout that year net assets (excluding the value of the individual's primary residence or loan secured on it and excluding any rights under a qualifying contract of insurance, pensions and the like) totalling not less than £500,000.

The requirements for exemption are that:[6]

(a) the debtor or hirer is a natural person;

(b) the agreement includes a declaration made by the individual in the form set out in Schedule 1 to the Order;

(c) a statement of high net worth in the form set out in Schedule 2 to the Order has been made in relation to the individual;

(d) the above statement was made during the period of one year ending with the day on which the agreement is made; and

(e)   before the agreement was made a copy of that statement was provided to the debtor or hirer and (if the statement was not made by the creditor or owner), to the creditor or owner.

The statement of high net worth must be made by a qualified accountant or, where the creditor or owner is an authorised deposit-taker, by the creditor or owner, employee or agent of the creditor or owner or an associate of the creditor or owner.[7]

The declaration by the high net worth debtor or hirer must be set out in the consumer credit agreement or consumer hire agreement no less prominently than other information, readily distinguishable from the background medium and signed by the debtor or hirer, 'unless the agreement is so signed'.

The wording of the requirement for signature is unfortunately imprecise. It is therefore advisable that either the declaration should be signed in addition to the agreement being signed, or the signature to the agreement should make it clear that the signature also relates to the declaration. The statutory declaration is worded in the singular number, with the result that if the agreement is entered into by two or more debtors or hirers each of whom is a high net worth individual (and this presupposition must apply as otherwise the individual(s) would need to enter into a regulated agreement), each should sign a separate statutory declaration.

When advice is given to a high net worth individual as regards the consequences of making the declaration, a solicitor might be well advised to take note of the decision in *Royal Bank of Scotland plc v Etridge (No. 2)*,[8] lest an individual allege that he was unduly influenced by his co-debtor or co-hirer into signing the declaration.

If the provisions relating to high net worth individuals are not complied with, the credit agreement or hire agreement is improperly executed and enforceable only on an order of the court.[9]

Notwithstanding their exempt status, the agreements are circumscribed in an important respect, namely by the unfair relationships provisions that apply to agreements between creditors and debtors, pursuant to ss 140A to 140D of CCA 1974.[10]

1   Explanatory Memorandum to the Order issued by the Department of Trade and Industry on 31 March 2007.
2   DTI's Consultation on the draft Order URN 06/1679, August 2006.
3   Explanatory Memorandum to the Regulations DTI, 31 March 2007.
4   SI 2005/1529, art 50.
5   Consumer Credit (Exempt Agreements) Order 2007, SI 2007/1168, Sch 2.
6   *Ibid.*, art 2 read with Sch 1.
7   *Ibid.*, art 2 read with Sch 2.
8   [2001] GCCR 3105, HL.
9   CCA 1974, s 65; and see CCA 1974, s 127.
10 CCA 1974, s 16A(8).

4.3.5   The business exemption

As the CCA 2006 removed the financial limit for consumer credit agreements and consumer hire agreements, so that consumer credit agreements and consumer hire agreements in any amount are regulated agreements, it was decided that agreements that are wholly or predominantly for business purposes should be exempt from regulation, as business lending was outside the intended focus of the Act.[1]

With effect from 6 April 2008, the CCA 1974 no longer regulated a consumer credit agreement by which the creditor provides the debtor with credit exceeding £25,000 or a consumer hire agreement that requires the hirer to make payments exceeding £25,000, if the agreement is entered into by the debtor or hirer wholly or predominantly for the purposes of a business carried on, or intended to be carried on, by him.[2]

If the agreement includes a declaration made in statutory form set out in Schedule 3 to the Consumer Credit (Exempt Agreements) Order 2007 and it, or the agreement incorporating it, has been signed by the debtor or hirer, the agreement is presumed to have been entered into wholly or predominantly for such purposes.[3] It follows that, whilst the declaration is voluntary, it is useful in that it creates a rebuttable presumption that the agreement is for business purposes.

The presumption does not apply, notwithstanding that the debtor or hirer may have signed the declaration, if the creditor or owner, or any person acting on his behalf, knew or had reasonable cause to suspect that the agreement was not entered into for such purposes.[4] Thus, for example, in a car finance transaction, if the customer signs such a declaration but informs the creditor or owner that the vehicle is predominantly for private use and the declaration is to obtain tax benefits, the agreement will not be an exempt agreement. In consequence, the agreement will have been an improperly executed regulated agreement enforceable against the debtor or hirer only on an order of the court.[5] In exercising its discretion in deciding whether to grant an enforcement order, a court will consider the prejudice caused to any person by the contravention in question and the degree of culpability for it.[6]

Where a declaration is signed for the purposes of exempting the agreement, it must:[7]

(a)   comply with the prescribed form;

(b)   be set out in the consumer credit agreement or consumer hire agreement no less prominently than other information in the agreement and be readily distinguishable from the background medium; and

(c)   be signed by the debtor or hirer or where the debtor or hirer is a partnership or an unincorporated body of persons, on its behalf, 'unless the agreement is so signed'. As with the declaration for high net worth individuals, the regulations are imprecise in their stipulation of the signature requirement. It would appear to suffice if it was clear that the signature to the agreement also related to the declaration.

Generally speaking, 'business' has a wide meaning. It must be construed independently of s 189(2) which states that a person is not to be treated as carrying on a particular type of business merely because occasionally he enters into transactions belonging to a business of that type. Each agreement must be considered on its merits, rather than as one of a series of transactions or as a transaction in the course of a business. As the test is whether the agreement itself is entered into wholly or predominantly for the purposes of a business, it does not suffice that it is entered into in the course of a business or partly for business[8] and partly for investment purposes e.g. buy-to-let mortgages.

If the provisions relating to the business exemption are not complied with, the credit agreement or hire agreement is improperly executed and enforceable only on an order of the court.[9]

Notwithstanding their exempt status, the agreements remain subject to the unfair relationships provisions that apply as between creditors and debtors, pursuant to ss 140A to 140D of CCA 1974.[10]

1 Explanatory Memorandum to Order issued by the Department of Trade and Industry on 31 March 2007.
2 CCA 1974, s 16B(1).
3 CCA 1974, s 16B(2).
4 CCA 1974, s 16B(3).
5 CCA 1974, s 65.
6 CCA 1974, s 127(1).
7 Consumer Credit (Exempt Agreements) Order 2007, SI 2007/1168, Art 6 and Sch 3.
8 Contrast this with *Stevenson v Beverley Bentinck Ltd* [1976] 2 All ER 606, CA.
9 CCA 1974, s 65; and see CCA 1974, s 127.
10 CCA 1974, s 16B(6).

4.3.6   Connected loan agreements involving a limited number of repayments

The CCA 1974 does not regulate certain consumer credit agreements where the number of payments to be made by the debtor does not exceed the number specified by the relevant Order.[1] The specific agreements falling within this exempt category are considered below.

4.3.6.1   Purchase finance agreements

The most important agreements in this class are:[2]

(a)   a debtor-creditor-supplier fixed-sum credit agreement where the credit is repayable by four or fewer instalments in a period not exceeding twelve months beginning with the date of the agreement; or

(b)   a debtor-creditor-supplier running-account credit agreement which provides for the making of payments by the debtor in relation to specified periods and that the credit amount referable to a given period is payable by one payment, e.g. a charge card facility such as American Express and Diner's Card or a monthly account with a supplier, where the account has to be settled by one payment.

The above agreements may not relate to the financing of the purchase of land, may not be conditional sale agreements or hire purchase agreements, and may not be secured by a pledge (other than a pledge of documents of title or of bearer bonds).

4.3.6.2   Property finance agreements

The CCA 1974 does not regulate a debtor-creditor-supplier agreement financing the purchase of land under which the number of payments to be made by the debtor does not exceed four.[3]

4.3.6.3   Premium finance agreements

The CCA 1974 does not regulate:[4]

(a)   a debtor-creditor-supplier agreement for fixed-sum credit to finance an insurance premium relating to land or to anything on the land. The creditor must be a creditor under an exempt agreement secured by a land mortgage on that land, the amount of credit must be repayable within the period to which the premium relates and not exceeding twelve months, the number of payments may not exceed twelve and the only constituent of the total charge for credit must be interest at a rate not exceeding that under the credit agreement secured by the land mortgage; or

(b)   a debtor-creditor-supplier agreement for fixed-sum credit to finance a premium under a contract of life insurance which provides for payment on the death of the debtor of a sum not exceeding the amount of credit and total charge for credit. The creditor must be a creditor under an exempt agreement secured by a land mortgage, the only constituent of the total charge for credit must be interest at a rate not exceeding that under the credit agreement secured by the land mortgage and the number of payments to be made by the debtor may not exceed twelve.

4.3.6.4   General overview

An advance payment, deposit or down payment is not included in the maximum number of instalments and may therefore be required to be paid in addition to the instalments.

The courts adopt a strict approach to the interpretation of the period of the agreement and the due date for final payment, in considering whether this falls within the twelve-month period.

Various decisions have been made relating to the type of agreement identified above. In the leading case of *Dimond v Lovell* [5] the House of Lords held that a hire agreement under which the hire charge was not payable until some future event, occurring after the conclusion of the period of hire, was also a credit agreement. As it contained provision for payment with no limit on the duration of the 'credit', save that it was payable on conclusion of the claim for damages, the agreement was potentially repayable outside the twelve-month period. It was conceded by Counsel (without argument) that the agreement was not an exempt agreement.

If the terms of the agreement are such that no payment is capable of being made outside the period of twelve months beginning with the date of the agreement, it will be an enforceable exempt agreement. *Seddon v Tekin* [6] dealt with three actions where similar or identical issues arose. The claimants had entered into broadly similar hire agreements under a 'credit repair facility' for a substitute vehicle under which charges were payable at the commencement of the hire and otherwise on demand, unless a credit hire agreement had been concluded. Credit hire agreements were concluded for a period of 51 weeks in two of the cases and 26 weeks in the other case. In concluding that they were exempt agreements the County Court found that the hypothetical reasonable person would consider that the payment fell due in full at the end of the stated period and that therefore the agreements were valid exempt agreements. This was one of a series of similar cases decided by no less than six other circuit judges.

Similar types of agreement were considered by the Court of Appeal. In *Clark v Ardington Electrical Services* [7] the court held that a credit agreement which stipulated a liability to pay at the end of the credit period, namely after 26 or 51 weeks beginning with the date of the agreement, referred to the legal obligation to make payment at that time and accordingly the agreement was an exempt agreement.

In contrast with the above, the Court of Appeal in *Ketley v Gilbert* [8] found that an agreement where payment was to be made on the expiry of twelve months starting with the date of the agreement, permitted payment to be made outside the statutory period for an exempt agreement. As it did not comply with the requirements stated above, the agreement was unenforceable for want of compliance with the requirements of a regulated credit agreement.

The commencement of the period of twelve months is the date of the agreement. So it was held in *Zoan v Rouamba* [9] where the court stated that where the period within which an act is to be done is expressed to be a period beginning with a specified day, it has been held with equal consistency over the past 40 years or so that the legislature (or the relevant rule-making body, as the case may be) has shown a clear intention that the specified day must be included in the period. As the agreement had to be construed as providing for a period of deferment of payment one day longer than that prescribed, it was not an exempt agreement and therefore unenforceable.

1 CCA 1974, s 16(5)(a) and the Consumer Credit (Exempt Agreements) Order 1989, SI 1989/869 (as amended).
2 *Ibid.*, arts 3(1)(a) and (2).
3 *Ibid.*, art 3(1)(b).
4 *Ibid.*, art 3(1)(c) and (d).
5 *Dimond v Lovell* [2001] GCCR 2751, HL.
6 *Seddon v Tekin, Dowsett v Clifford, Beasly v PPP/Columbus Healthcare* [2001] GCCR 2865 (Oxford County Court).
7 *Clark v Ardington Electrical Services* [2002] GCCR 4691.
8 *Ketley v Gilbert* [2001] GCCR 2951 CA; *King v Daltray*; *Thew v Cole* [2003] All ER (D) 280.
9 *Zoan v Rouamba* [2001] GCCR 2581 CA at 2589.

4.3.7 Low cost credit exemption

CCA 1974 does not regulate certain debtor-creditor agreements (and note the important exclusion of debtor-creditor-supplier agreements) where the credit charge is interest which does not exceed a specified low limit. They are debtor-creditor agreements:[1]

(a) where the creditor is a credit union and the rate of the total charge for credit does not exceed 26.9%. Admittedly, this is not a low rate of charge, but this exemption had its origins in a low level of charge; or

(b) of a type offered to a particular class or particular classes of individuals and not offered to the public generally and under the terms of which the only charge in the total charge for credit is interest which cannot at any time exceed 1% and the highest of the base rates of banks listed in the Order, being the latest rates in operation 28 days before any such time; or

(c) of a type offered to a particular class or particular classes of individuals and not offered to the public generally, under which there can be no increase after the relevant date in the rate or amount of any item in the total charge for credit and in respect of which the rate of the total charge for credit does not exceed the sum of 1% and the highest of the base rates published by banks listed in the Order.

Paragraphs (b) and (c) above do not apply to an agreement under which the total amount to be repaid by the debtor to discharge his indebtedness in respect of the amount of credit may vary according to a formula specified in the agreement and which has effect by reference to movements in the level of any index or to any other factor.[2] Whilst the purpose of the provision is clear, the wording is far from clear.

The *Concise Oxford Dictionary* defines 'class' as 'a group of persons or things having some characteristic in common'. This would probably be too wide a definition for present purposes and the further qualifying expression 'not offered to the public generally' appears to restrict the parameters of 'class' to a group which cannot be described as public generally even if they share some characteristic in common. Employees, members of a club or association, shareholders of a company and other 'ringfenced' classes of persons who share some common characteristics and cannot properly be described as 'the public generally' would fall into this classification.

The expression 'being the latest rates in operation on the date 28 days before any such time' is also unclear. It is submitted that it refers to the highest bank base rate in force 28 days before the date of the agreement and subsequent to that date, the highest bank rate in force 28 days before any variation in the relevant bank base rate. A corresponding variation in the rate of interest under the credit agreement may therefore not come into operation earlier than 28 days after the increase in the relevant base rate.

1 CCA 1974, s 16(5)(b) and the Consumer Credit (Exempt Agreements) Order 1989, SI 1989/869, art 4(1).
2 *Ibid.*, art 4(2) (as amended).

4.3.8 Overseas trade finance

Consumer credit agreements made in connection with trade and goods or services with or between the UK and a foreign country or between two or more foreign countries, where credit is provided in the course of a business carried on by the debtor, are exempt agreements.[1]

Whilst this provision preceded the Consumer Credit Act 2006, which exempts all credit agreements entered into with a debtor or hirer wholly or predominantly for the purposes of a business, these provisions extend beyond this insofar as they do not require the credit agreement to be entered into wholly or predominantly for the purposes of the debtor's business.

1 CCA 1974, s 16(5)(c) and the Consumer Credit (Exempt Agreements) Order 1989, SI 1989/869, art 5.

4.3.9 Exempt consumer hire agreements

A very limited exemption applies to certain consumer hire agreements, namely consumer hire agreements where the owner is a body corporate authorised to supply gas, electricity or water and the subject of the agreement is metering equipment used in connection with that supply.[1]

1 CCA 1974, s 16(6) and the Consumer Credit (Exempt Agreements) Order 1989, SI 1989/869, art 6.

4.4 AGREEMENTS EXCLUDED FROM PART V OF CCA 1974

Certain consumer hire agreements, whilst otherwise regulated by the CCA 1974, are excluded from the provisions of Part V of the Act, namely provisions applying to entry into credit or hire agreements, including formalities applying to regulated agreements. These agreements are identified below.

4.4.1 Small credit agreements

Small agreements, more properly described as small sum agreements, are regulated consumer credit agreements for credit not exceeding £50 (a sum variable by Order).[1] The agreement may be unsecured or secured by a guarantee or indemnity. If it is secured by a pledge, pawn or other security, it is no longer considered a small agreement. The small sum exemption does not apply to hire-purchase or conditional sale agreements. Examples of exempt small agreements are small sum credit sale, cheque trading or credit card agreements.

Part V of CCA 1974 (except ss 55 and 56) which relates to entry into credit or hire agreements, including the form and content of the agreement, does not apply to a small debtor-creditor-supplier agreement for restricted-use credit.[2] However, the exception of s 55, read with the Consumer Credit (Disclosure of Information) Regulations 2004,[3] means that a small debtor-creditor-supplier agreement for restricted-use credit must be preceded by a full Pre-contract Information document under these Regulations.

The legislation contains an anti-avoidance provision which applies in relation to a series of small credit agreements.[4]

1 CCA 1974, s 17 and see the exemptions under ss 51, 74(2), 78(7) and 85(3).
2 *Ibid.*, s 74(2).
3 SI 2004/1481.
4 CCA 1974, s 17(3).

4.4.2   Non-commercial agreements[1]

These are consumer credit agreements or consumer hire agreements not made by the creditor or owner in the course of a business carried on by him.[2] Part V of CCA 1974, which relates to entry into credit or hire agreements, including the form and content of the agreement, does not apply to non-commercial agreements.[3]

1 CCA 1974, ss 74(1)(a) and 189(1).
2 See further at para 21.1.4.
3 *Ibid.*, s 74(1)(c).

4.4.3   Agreements for overdraft facilities[1]

Subject to notification to the Office of Fair Trading, debtor-creditor agreements for overdrafts on current accounts are exempt from the provisions relating to the form of and formalities applying to regulated agreements. They are considered in more detail at para 3.8.4.2. Part V of CCA 1974, which relates to entry into credit or hire agreements, including the form and content of the agreement, does not apply to debtor-creditor agreements for overdraft facilities.[2]

1 CCA 1974, s 74(1)(b).
2 *Ibid.*, s 74(1)(b).

4.4.4   Agreements to finance payments connected with death

Part V of CCA 1974, dealing with agreement requirements, does not apply to the financing of certain specified payments arising on or connected with the death of a person. These relate to payments of tax and court fees. The relevant provisions[1] must be read together with the Determination of the Office of Fair Trading in connection with the same. The indulgence relates to loans for such purposes advanced by the Bank of England or by banks to debtors acting in the course of their trade or profession, e.g. solicitors and accountants administering deceased estates.

In view of the exemption of credit agreements which are wholly or predominantly for business purposes carried on by the debtor, the exclusion of these agreements from Part V of the Act now seems redundant as the agreements are wholly exempt.[2]

1 CCA 1974, s 74(1)(c) read with the Consumer Credit (Payments Arising on Death) Regulations 1983, SI 1983/1554.
2 CCA 1974, s 16B.

4.4.5   Exemption at the discretion of the Office of Fair Trading[1]

The Office of Fair Trading is authorised to vary or waive any of the requirements as to the form and content of regulated agreements where it appears impractical for the applicant to comply with the requirements. The OFT must be satisfied that the exercise of its power will not prejudice the interests of debtors or hirers.

The OFT has granted applications to Housing Associations in relation to social housing agreements for rent and agreements for purchase.

1   CCA 1974, s 60(3) and (4).

4.5   PARTLY REGULATED AGREEMENT

There is no definition of a partly regulated agreement in the CCA 1974. However, the Agreements Regulations[1] recognise such type of agreement, which they describe as a document which embodies an agreement of which at least one part is a credit agreement not regulated by the CCA 1974.

1   Consumer Credit (Agreements) Regulations 1983, SI 1983/1553, Sch 1, para 1.

Chapter 5

Hire agreements

5.1 MEANING OF A HIRE AGREEMENT

A hire agreement is a contract of bailment without any element of sale. The hirer receives both possession and use of the goods hired in return for rental paid to the lessor or owner. He is obliged to return the goods at the end of the agreed term.[1] However simple that definition may appear, it gave rise to substantial dispute in *Dimond v Lovell*.[2] The court was there concerned with whether the agreement was an exempt hire agreement or a regulated credit agreement and, if the latter, as it did not contain the prescribed terms, it was unenforceable. The Court of Appeal held that the fact that the respondent's obligation to pay for the car hire was to be deferred until her damages claim had been concluded meant that the agreement allowed her credit and should therefore have taken the form of a regulated credit agreement. As it did not, the agreement was not properly executed and was unenforceable. The court held that the agreement would also have been a regulated consumer hire agreement if it had been capable of lasting for more than three months. The argument that a contract for the bailment of goods to a hirer could not be both a consumer credit agreement and a consumer hire agreement was rejected by the court. Surprisingly, these issues were not argued on appeal to the House of Lords.

Dimond v Lovell has been followed by a long line of cases in which the lower courts have sought to distinguish the cases before them, on the facts, from those in the House of Lords decision or to raise the unargued issues. A definitive decision on the unargued points is still awaited.

1 9(1) *Halsbury's Laws* (4th edn), para 52.
2 [1999] 3 All ER 1, CA; affd [2000] 2 All ER 897, HL.

5.2 TYPES OF CONSUMER HIRE AGREEMENTS

In contrast to the position in relation to credit agreements where there are various types of consumer credit agreements, there is in fact only one form of consumer hire agreement. The CCA 1974 defines a consumer hire agreement as an agreement made by a person with an individual (which includes a partnership or two or three persons or an unincorporated body of persons not consisting entirely of bodies corporate) for the bailment or hiring of goods, which is capable of subsisting for more than three months.[1] A hire-purchase agreement is classified as a credit and not a hire agreement.[2]

In *TRM Copy Centres (UK) v Lanwell Services*[3] the court rejected the argument that a so-called Location Agreement which stipulated payment for photocopying services, but not a regular rental payment, constituted a regulated hire agreement. The decision was upheld on appeal.[4] Thomas LJ stated that s 15 of CCA 1974 was concerned solely with bailment by way of hire, that a hire agreement could involve reward or recompense other than payment of money but that payment of commission by the owner of photocopying machines to the retailer based on use of the machine was not tantamount to bailment by way of hire by the retailer.

The requirement that the hire agreement must be capable of subsisting for more than three months relates to the period of hire and not the time for payment of hire charges.[5]

A regulated hire agreement is a consumer hire agreement which is not an exempt agreement. Exempt hire agreements are notably those entered into wholly or predominantly for the hirer's business purposes and which require the hirer to make payments exceeding £25,000.[6] Hire agreements for the hire of metering equipment for gas, electricity or water supplies or of equipment owned by specified telecommunication operators are also exempt agreements.[7]

A non-commercial hire agreement is one which is not made by the owner in the course of a business carried on by him. It is a regulated agreement but exempt from CCA 1974's provisions relating to formalities applying to the entry of agreements.[8]

There are two instances of confused drafting in relation to hire agreements. The first relates to small agreements, being those which do not require the hirer to make payments exceeding £50.[9] As with small credit agreements, these were meant to be excluded from certain provisions of CCA 1974 but their minor status appears to have resulted in their being overlooked. Likewise, it was intended that there should be cancellation provisions corresponding to those which apply to regulated credit agreements. By virtue of a drafting error, hire agreements are only cancellable if they were preceded by antecedent negotiations conducted by the owner or the owner's authorised agent.[10]

1 CCA 1974, s 15.
2 *Ibid.*
3 [2007] All ER(D) 287.
4 *TRM Copy Centres (UK) Limited v Lanwall Services Limited* [2008] EWCA Civ 382, CA.
5 *Clark v Ardington Electrical Services* [2003] GCCR 4691, CA.
6 CCA 1974, s 16B(1)(b).
7 CCA 1974, s 16(6) and Consumer Credit (Exempt Agreements) Order 1989, SI 1989/869.
8 CCA 1974, ss 74(1)(a) and 189(1).
9 CCA 1974, s 17(1)(b).
10 CCA 1974, s 56 and see *Branwhite v Worcester Works Finance Ltd* [1969] 1 AC 552, [1968] 3 All ER 104, HL.

5.3 SOME CHARACTERISTICS OF A REGULATED HIRE AGREEMENT

The Supply of Goods and Services Act 1982 imports certain implied terms into hire agreements.[1] These include an implied condition on the part of the lessor that he has a right to transfer possession of the goods by way of hire, and in an agreement for hire, that he will have such right at the time of hire.

There is an implied warranty that the hirer will enjoy quiet possession of the goods for the period of hire except so far as possession may be disturbed by the owner or other person entitled to the benefit of any charge or encumbrance disclosed or known to the hirer before the contract is made.

In the case of a contract for the hire of goods by description, there is an implied condition that the goods will correspond with their description and in a contract for the hire of goods by reference to a sample as well as a description, that the bulk of the goods will correspond with the sample as well as their description. If goods are hired in the course of a business there is also an implied condition that they are of satisfactory quality. Finally, there is an implied term that the goods are in conformity with any particular purpose required and disclosed by the hirer.

A unique aspect of a regulated hire agreement is the right conferred upon the hirer to terminate the agreement 18 months after entering into the agreement, unless the agreement was for a shorter period.[2] The rationale for this is that the hirer should not be bound by a lengthy agreement. However, as a result of industry pressure, this benefit does not apply to rental agreements requiring the hirer to make rental payments in any year exceeding £1,500 (a sum which is variable by Order).[3] This right of termination also does not apply to the common type of lease (e.g. of equipment or motor vehicles) where the goods are hired to the hirer for the purpose of a business carried on by him, or where the hirer holds himself out as requiring the goods for such purpose, and the goods are selected by the hirer and acquired by the owner for the purposes of the agreement, at the hirer's request, from a person other than the owner's associate.[4]

The standard regulated hire agreement, falling within such parameters, will usually contain declarations or acknowledgements by the hirer to the foregoing effect.

A hirer is also not entitled to terminate a lease after 18 months where he requires the goods or holds himself out as requiring them for the purpose of sub-hire or of hiring them to other persons in the course of a business carried on by him.[5]

The Office of Fair Trading is empowered to exempt agreements from the foregoing termination provisions, upon application of an owner intending to enter into hire agreements, if it appears that it would be in the interests of hirers to do so.[6] Whilst applications have been granted, they are relatively rare. Applicants generally have to prove that without the certainty of a long-term hire agreement they could not offer agreements to hirers for the goods in question on terms likely to be acceptable to hirers. They also have to show why the offer of hire agreements by independent leasing companies alone is unsatisfactory, e.g. the need of the supplier company to maintain and service the goods as part of the hire arrangement or by reason of economies of scale underlying the operation.

A new section, introduced by CCA 2006, makes provision for exemption from s 101 of CCA 1974, if it appears to the OFT that it would be in the interests of hirers to exempt consumer hire agreements falling within a specified description. The OFT is then empowered to exempt such agreements by general notice.[7] It remains to be seen to which agreements this power is applied.

At first sight it is difficult to reconcile the continuance of s 101 with the exclusion of hire agreements for the hirer's business purposes, by virtue of s 16B(1)(b) of the Act. However, its continued application can be found in the following limited circumstances:

(a)   where the hire agreement for business purposes does not require rental payments exceeding £25,000; and

(b)   where the hire agreement, albeit for business purposes, is not wholly or predominantly for business purposes.

As already mentioned, hire agreements are cancellable in more limited circumstances than those in which credit agreements are cancellable owing to the more restricted definition of 'negotiator' in respect of hire agreements than credit agreements. Thus, a regulated hire agreement may be cancelled by the hirer if the antecedent negotiations included oral representations made in the presence of the hirer by an individual acting as or on behalf of the negotiator and 'negotiator' is restricted, in the case of hire agreements, to the owner.[8] By a drafting error a leasing transaction concluded through a dealer was omitted from the scope of the cancellability provisions of CCA 1974, s 67. This section refers to oral representations made in the presence of the hirer (or debtor) by an individual acting as or on behalf of the negotiator. 'Negotiator' is defined in CCA 1974, s 56 but, owing to an oversight, the definition omits from the meaning of 'negotiator' a credit broker involved in antecedent negotiations with the hirer prior to the hirer entering into the hire agreement. The supplier who conducts antecedent negotiations in relation to a hire agreement is likewise not included within the meaning of a 'negotiator'.

As a result of the foregoing lacuna in the law, various attempts have been made to hold a dealer liable as agent of the owner. However, following *Branwhite v Worcester Works Finance Ltd*,[9] the courts have held that a dealer through whom business is introduced to a finance house is not in general to be treated as the agent of a finance house, including in respect of representations made by the dealer relating to the goods or the transaction. *Branwhite* related to hire-purchase transactions but the reasoning applies with equal force to leasing and rental agreements entered into with a leasing company on the introduction of a dealer. So the Court of Appeal held in *JD Williams & Co v McCauley Parsons & Jones*[10] and *Woodchester Equipment (Leasing) Ltd v British Association of Canned and Preserved Foods Importers and Distributors Ltd.*[11] In both cases the lessor was held not bound by fraudulent misrepresentations made by the supplier.

The position is otherwise where the finance company holds itself out as the dealer or where, on the facts, the dealer is the agent of the lessor, as when the dealer is authorised to sign for the lessor or authorised to commit the lessor to the terms of the agreement.[12]

A leasing company may also incur liability as the deemed agent of the supplier. Thus, in *Purnell Secretarial Services v Lease Management Services*,[13] Purnell agreed to lease a photocopier from a leasing company which traded under the name of the supplier. Purnell thought it was dealing with the supplier and the court held that the leasing company was estopped from denying such capacity and its apparent authority to make representations on behalf of the supplier.

A regulated hire agreement may be secured, including on land, in which latter event the withdrawal and consideration provisions applying to credit agreements, discussed earlier, would apply.

Consumer hire agreements are subject to 'soft-touch regulation' under CCA 1974 when compared with consumer credit agreements. Thus:

(a)   there is no means of comparing rental charges under consumer hire agreements equivalent to the APR in respect of credit agreements;

(b)   there are no provisions applicable to consumer hire agreements corresponding to the unfair relationships provisions which apply to consumer credit agreements;

(c)   there is no limit on default charges payable under consumer hire agreements in contrast to the position under regulated consumer credit agreements; and

(d)   there is no requirement to issue a regular statement, indeed not even an annual statement, to the hirer.

1 Supply of Goods and Services Act 1982, ss 7, 8, 9 and 10.
2 CCA 1974, s 101(1)–(3).
3 CCA 1974, s 101(7)(a).
4 CCA 1974, s 101(7)(b) and see the meaning of 'associate' in s 184.
5 CCA 1974, s 101(7)(c).
6 CCA 1974, s 101(8).
7 SCCA 1974, s 101(8A).
8 CCA 1974, ss 67 and 56 and see para 3.3.4.
9 [1969] 1 AC 552, [1968] 3 All ER 104, HL.
10 [1999] GCCR 1375, CA.
11 [1999] GCCR 1923, CA.
12 [1994] CCLR 87.
13 [1999] GCCR 1841, CA.

5.4   SPECIFIC CONSUMER HIRE AGREEMENTS

It should be mentioned at the outset that the various consumer hire agreements described in this section are legally identical but functionally different. It should also be pointed out that there is no legal distinction between the expressions 'lease' and 'hire' and that in this text the term 'hire' is used in preference to 'bailment'.

Various types of lease have received statutory recgonition for tax purposes in the Capital Allowances Act 2001. They include 'long funding lease', 'funding lease' and 'finance lease'.[1] For purposes of a consumer hire agreement we are principally concerned with the types of lease identified below.

5.4.1   Finance lease

A finance lease is essentially a financial operation under which goods (usually comprising medium to high cost equipment) are leased under a lease whose minimum or primary term equates to the major part of the equipment's useful life and the rentals are structured to secure payment to the lessor, over the minimum period of the lease, of a sum equal to the capital cost of the leased equipment plus the desired return on capital. The latter will take into account corporation tax, any first year allowances, writing-down allowances and available grants. A finance lease is one that transfers substantially all the risks and rewards of ownership of an asset to the lessee.[1] For capital allowances purposes it has been defined as any arrangements which provide for plant or machinery to be leased or otherwise made available by a person ('the lessor') to another person ('the lessee') and which under generally applied accounting practices fall or would fall to be treated in the accounts of the lessor, or a person connected with him, as a finance lease or a loan or are comprised in arrangements to be so treated.[2] A presumption arises in tax and accounting practice that a lease is a finance lease when the present value of the minimum lease payments, including any initial payment, amounts to substantially all (normally at least 90%) of the fair value of the leased asset.[3]

Under a finance lease the lessee chooses the equipment and then negotiates the purchase terms with the supplier. The lessor provides the finance to meet the purchase price and either purchases the equipment from the supplier and leases it on to the lessee or arranges to acquire it from the ultimate lessee by way of sale by the latter to the lessor and the lease-back of the equipment to the lessee. The payment terms are scheduled to meet the specific cashflow requirements of the lessee in terms of amounts and payment frequency. Indeed, the different rentals and frequency intervals can create quite a kaleidoscopic range of rental patterns. Frequently a balloon (or substantial residual rental) payment is provided for at the end of the primary or minimum rental period. Invariably the hirer is then permitted to continue the agreement into a secondary period, commonly at a nominal or peppercorn rent, usually payable annually. Once the lessor has recovered his desired capital and return on the equipment in the primary period he tends to cease to be concerned with the condition, whereabouts or fate of the leased equipment, although he remains its owner.

A finance lease will usually permit the lessor to increase the rentals if there is a change in tax structure, corporation tax, writing down allowances or other variable factors. This flows from the fact that by such a lease the lessor is aiming to recover a pre-determined return on his capital.

A finance lease will often be structured so as to leave a residual value in the equipment at the end of the primary period. The balloon rental would ordinarily equate to the residual value. The lessee might be given the right, either under the lease or in a side letter agency agreement, to sell the leased equipment at the end of the lease to an independent buyer in an arms length transaction and to retain up to 90% of the net proceeds of sale.

More recent embellishments of finance leases are the provision of services, maintenance and the upgrading of the leased equipment at regular intervals. In a regulated finance lease these additional benefits are provided either free of charge, in other words the rentals would include the additional benefits, or against periodical cash payments as consideration for them, paid to the lessor as agent for their provider.

As compared to an operating lease, where the rentals are generally charged on a straight-line basis over the lease term, a finance lease is recorded in the balance sheet of the lessee as an asset and as an obligation to pay future rentals in an amount equal to the present value of future rentals. Rentals are apportioned between the finance charge and a reduction of the outstanding obligation for future amounts payable. The total finance charge is allocated to accounting periods during the lease term to produce a constant periodic rate of charge and the leased equipment is depreciated over the shorter of the lease term and its useful life. Corresponding entries will be made in the lessor's accounts.

1 Statement of Standard Accounting Practice No 21 (SSAP 21 para 15); International Accounting Standards Committee's Standard on Accounting for Leases (IAS 17); International Financial Reporting Standards (IFRS 17); Capital Allowances Act 2001, ss 70G, 70J and 70N and 219.
2 Capital Allowances Act 2001, s 219(1).
3 See 1 above.

5.4.2 Operating lease

In the case of an operating lease the lessor lets the goods on hire to the hirer for a period related to the hirer's requirements and unrelated to the useful or working life of the goods or the lessor's need to recover his capital outlay and profits. An operating lease may be for as short a period as one day or for a minimum period of several years. The lessor will usually rely on the residual value of the goods to recover the balance of his investment and to earn any additional profit. The residual value is the value of the goods at the expiry of the lease term and is represented by the rental value of the goods under any extended or new lease or the net proceeds of the sale of the goods. In short-term leases the lessor will often assume responsibility for the maintenance, repair and insurance of the goods, whilst in longer-term leases the obligation will generally be passed on to the hirer. Goods commonly hired under operating leases include motor vehicles, television sets, vending machines and small office equipment.

Under an operating lease the lessor may agree to provide a miscellanea of additional benefits such as ingredients for machines, paper for photocopiers, detergents for dishwashers, a chauffeur for a motor vehicle or an operator for a crane.

Operating leases are used where it is desired that the lease equipment should not appear as assets in the lessee's balance sheet or where rules prevent leasing unless some of the risks or rewards of ownership are assumed by the lessor or where writing down allowances available to lessors who enter into finance leases are restricted by the Capital Allowances Act 2001 or the lessor is taxable on the excess of accountancy rental earnings over the normal rent.[1]

It is common for the lessor and supplier to enter into an agreement for the resale of the equipment on expiry of the lease so as to capitalise on any residual value in the equipment. This is especially so in the case of specialist equipment or equipment manufactured to the specific requirements of the hirer as the supplier will be more acquainted with the marketplace and hence better able to dispose of the equipment.

1 See SSAP 21.

5.4.3 Contract hire

This is the name given by the leasing industry to short-term operating leases, especially of motor vehicles and in particular the leasing by finance companies of fleets of motor vehicles. Contract hire agreements are for fixed hire periods, usually of 24 or 36 months, at the end of which the vehicle is returned to the owner and a new lease entered into in respect of a new vehicle. The owner will usually assume the obligation of insuring, maintaining and repairing the vehicle, the cost of which will be borne by the hirer. Lessors of fleets of vehicles will generally undertake to provide a replacement vehicle if for any reason the hired vehicle becomes unusable and to cover ancillary benefits such as AA and RAC membership fees, motor vehicle licence fees and recovery and breakdown service charges. A common feature of motor vehicle contract hire agreements is the imposition of an obligation on the hirer to pay excess mileage charges at the end of the hire period if the vehicle has exceeded the stated anticipated mileage. This is to compensate the lessor for the additional depreciation of the vehicle.

5.4.4   Master lease

A master agreement, as its name implies, is the document which sets out all the terms of the agreement save for the terms relating to the specific transaction which will fall under the general umbrella and be governed by that master agreement. The particular terms relating to the specific transaction will be set out in a schedule to the master agreement. The master agreement will therefore be an inchoate agreement, signed by the parties at the outset of their relationship and the schedule to the agreement will be the specific agreement, signed by the parties each time a transaction is entered into. The schedule will import the terms of the master agreement into the schedule and hence into each individual transaction. The benefit of a master agreement is that it establishes a relationship between the parties and enables the parties to enter into more than one transaction by completing more than one schedule. Master leases are commonly used in leasing transactions where the lessee intends entering into more than one lease with the lessor, e.g. in relation to fleet vehicles.

As a regulated hire agreement must contain all the terms of the agreement other than implied terms, care must be taken in relation to a master lease agreement where the leases will be regulated leases, to ensure that each schedule does in fact contain all the terms of the agreement. This is achieved by each schedule being drafted as a separate regulated hire agreement and embodying the master lease agreement by specifically making reference to it in the schedule.[1]

1 CCA 1974, ss 61(1)(b) and 189(4).

5.4.5   Business finance lease

The Finance & Leasing Association's Business Finance Code of Practice applies to business finance agreements entered into by members of the FLA where the member enters into, or manages, an agreement for the provision to a customer of office equipment, the customer has been introduced by the supplier of that equipment and the value of the equipment supplied does not exceed £50,000. The Code contains key commitments to customers including specific obligations relating to copiers and multi-functional devices. It contains a checklist for business finance customers and a list of specific disclosures which should be made to public sector, including NHS, customers before a business finance agreement is made.[1]

1 Finance & Leasing Association: Business Finance Code of Practice 2006.

5.4.6 Software lease

'Software' is not a term of art. It can be used to refer to diverse items such as the programming part of data processing, the range of services necessary to support the hardware, such as the information loaded into the machine and the directions given to the machine, or it can be taken to refer to support and consultancy services.

Computer programs are not normally sold but licensed to the user, though the hard copy itself may be sold to the customer on a chip, tape, or disk. In this way the use of the program and the number of terminals on which it can be employed are controlled, variations are limited and the copyright protected. Although somewhat of a legal fiction, it is increasingly commonplace for software to be leased. As regards capital allowances, the position is governed by s 71(1) and (2) of the Capital Allowances Act 2001 which provides that if a person carrying on a qualifying activity incurs capital expenditure in acquiring, for the purpose of that activity, the right to use or otherwise deal with computer software, it is to be treated as plant. This means that expenditure on software can qualify for plant and machinery allowances. The Inland Revenue had issued a guidance note on their interpretation of the previous law.[1] The term 'computer software' is not defined for capital allowance purposes but the Revenue consider that the term covers both programs and data, such as books stored in digital form.

Simply calling a software agreement a lease does not necessarily convert it into a lease, as against a licence. A software lessor's ultimate concern is to protect his investment. For this he needs to be satisfied that he can grant to, or procure for, the lessee the necessary rights to enable the lessee to use the software and the lessor must be able to recover its value if the lease is terminated prematurely. The lessor must be in the position of either the ultimate licensor or sub-licensor of the software, with the right to assign the benefit of the licence to a purchaser from him. Interposing the lessor between the software owner, copyright holder or licensor and the lessee has the advantage of giving the lessor control over the hired equipment and software. It results in the lessor incurring express and implied obligations and liability to the lessee or licensee when otherwise the obligations and liability would be those of the software owner directly. In practice commercial considerations play a dominant role and often the software is merely listed as an item of leased equipment together with the hardware, in a lease of the whole. Where, however, the lessor does not possess the right to use or otherwise deal with the computer software, he is not in a position to bundle it in this way and the lessee will need to license the software directly from the software provider.

1 Revenue Interpretation 56(R156).

5.4.7   Lease upgrade

It is common practice for suppliers and lessors of equipment to encourage lessees to upgrade the equipment subject to the lease, particularly in the case of office furniture and equipment. Often the lessee will be offered an inducement by way of reduced rentals or a higher 'part-exchange' value for existing equipment to take on the new equipment.

Any agreement involving an upgrade of existing equipment must, in the case of a regulated hire agreement, comply with the requirements of a modifying agreement, in accordance with the CCA 1974 and the Agreements Regulations under the Act. An upgrade may involve in part a refinancing agreement and in part a new rental agreement. A modifying agreement is not a cancellable agreement unless it is entered into within the cancellation period applicable to the original agreement.

5.5   STRUCTURE OF AN EQUIPMENT LEASE

An 'equipment lease' is not a term of art and may take the form of a finance lease or an operating lease. It has certain characteristic features. The lessee will select the goods from the supplier, satisfy himself that they are suitable for his purpose and either lease them directly from the supplier or from a lessor introduced by the supplier. Often the lessor's identity is immaterial to the lessee who will be mainly concerned with the financial terms of the lease. Indeed, it has become increasingly common for lessees to sign standard form lease agreements with unnamed lessors, leaving it to the supplier to find a lessor with whom he has arranged for the supply of leasing facilities to his customers. It is submitted that until the lessor's identity is disclosed to the lessee in the agreement, one of the essentials of a lease is missing, with the result that it is not a binding agreement and the lessee would be entitled to withdraw from it before it has been accepted.

Frequently a customer, after being invoiced by the supplier, decides that it would be beneficial to lease the equipment. Two approaches might then be adopted. The preferable one is for the original invoice to be cancelled so that the supplier can invoice the proposed lessor directly and enter into the equipment lease with the lessee. The alternative is for the proposed lessee to forward the invoice to his proposed lessor, who will settle it directly with the supplier, and then enter into a lease agreement with the lessee. The original purchase by the lessee will then be deemed to have been effected by the customer as agent for an undisclosed principal, the lessor.

Where the proposed lessee has been in possession of (and possibly used) the equipment for some period, he might enter into a sale and lease-back from the proposed lessor. The courts will scrutinise such transactions to ensure that the transfer of ownership was genuinely intended as a sale and is not tantamount to a disguised loan secured by a mortgage.

To crystallise the relationship between supplier and lessor, the lessor will usually require the supplier to provide him with various warranties and representations. These include warranties relating to the supplier's business, including compliance with the law and the holding of a valid credit-broker's licence; warranties relating to the goods, including that their ownership will pass to the lessor, in respect of their quality and their condition and that they were selected by and meet the requirements of the lessee; a warranty that the lease was accurately and fully completed before signature and appropriate copies handed to the lessee after execution; and in respect of the lessee, a warranty that he requested the goods for business purposes and that the supplier did not give any warranties or make any representations to the lessee other than those contained in the agreement.[1] Frequently the supplier will enter into a re-purchase agreement with the lessor undertaking to re-purchase the equipment in the amount of its residual value on expiry of the lease agreement.

1 *Stoneleigh Finance v Phillips* [1965] 2 QB 537, CA.

Chapter 6

Multiple agreements, modifying agreements; novation, variation and assignment of agreements

6.1 MULTIPLE AGREEMENTS

Undoubtedly one of the most complex provisions of CCA 1974 is s 18 which creates the concept of a multiple agreement. The underlying rationale of the section was to prevent several credit agreements or hire agreements being combined so as to exceed the financial limit which then applied to such agreements and thereby to bypass the provisions which would apply to them if they were separate agreements. In other words, it was an anti-avoidance measure.

At first blush, the removal of the financial limit which applied to consumer credit agreements and consumer hire agreements removes the need for this provision. However, on reflection the section serves to preserve the information provisions which apply under the rigid regulatory regime. Infringement of the section is now less likely to be driven by the desire to avoid the consequences of a regulated agreement than to be attributable to non-compliance for reasons of presentation or business efficacy. As the rationale of the provision is now solely to ensure that different categories of agreement are treated appropriately, it is hoped that the courts will give due recognition to the altered situation when exercising their discretionary enforcement powers under s 127(1).

Section 18 refers to categories of an agreement and to parts of an agreement. 'Category of agreement' is not defined and the only indication as to its meaning is the subsequent qualification by reference to categories of agreement mentioned in CCA 1974 and categories of agreement not so mentioned. In truth, however, this adds little clarity. The drafting is rendered even more complex by a subsection[1] which refers to 'two or more categories of agreement so mentioned', which might be construed as meaning categories of agreement mentioned in the Act or, more likely, all categories previously referred to, namely those mentioned in the Act and those not mentioned in the Act.

A possible meaning of 'category of agreement mentioned in the Act' is each and every type of agreement identified in the CCA 1974, and especially in Part II of CCA 1974, read with the Consumer Credit (Agreements) Regulations 1983.[2] This would, therefore, include the following: a consumer credit agreement, a consumer hire agreement, a consumer credit agreement for running-account credit, a consumer credit agreement for fixed-sum credit or a fixed-sum loan agreement, a credit card agreement, a restricted-use credit agreement, an unrestricted-use credit agreement, a debtor-creditor-supplier agreement, a debtor-creditor agreement, a small agreement, a cancellable (and by contrast a non-cancellable) agreement. In addition CCA 1974 mentions, and defines in s 189, the following more general types of agreement: conditional sale agreement, credit-sale agreement and hire-purchase agreement. Other types of agreement created by the Act are a modifying agreement, a multiple agreement (itself a creature of s 18), a regulated agreement and an unregulated agreement. Types of agreement recently given statutory recognition are an agreement to aggregate and a home credit loan agreement.[3] It would appear that, provided some distinction can be drawn between one type of agreement and another, the agreements will fall into different categories of agreement.

Once having established that an agreement involves more than one category of agreement, one turns to s 18 to consider how that section applies to the agreement. In *National Home Loans Corpn plc v Hannah*,[4] a County Court decision, the court stated that whatever else s 18 was about, it seems clear that in referring to categories it refers to disparate ones and that any other interpretation could be used to produce absurdities.

In *National Westminster Bank plc v Story and Pallister*,[5] the Court of Appeal, after opining that the main purpose of s 18 was to prevent frustration of the CCA 1974's protection to borrowers by the artificial combination of two or more agreements in one and without being required to comment on the meaning of 'category', stated that it was inclined, influenced in part by the positioning of the provision in Part II of the CCA 1974, to construe the word 'category' in the more narrow sense. That is, it applies to different categories within Part II of the CCA 1974 rather than as between every type of agreement for which the Act, in its various parts, provides its own legal regime. On that approach, the court added, restricted-use and unrestricted-use agreements were separate categories of agreement.

An analysis of s 18 does not end with the differentiation of categories of agreement as the section distinguishes between an agreement which falls within two or more categories of agreement and an agreement in parts, each part of which falls within another category of agreement. If an agreement falls within more than one category and those categories are not disparate categories so that they can be combined within one agreement, the agreement can be drafted as a single multiple unitary agreement, i.e. as a single agreement with the same provisions applying to each category of agreement comprised in that agreement. If, on the other hand, the agreement is in parts or the agreement is one within two or more categories which cannot be combined within one unitary agreement, e.g. a conditional sale agreement in respect of a motor vehicle together with a personal loan agreement for fixed sum credit to finance a caravan, each must be drafted as a separate agreement.

In *National Westminster Bank plc v Story and Pallister* the court referred with approval to the Office of Fair Trading's discussion paper on multiple agreements and the suggestion that an agreement is not an agreement in parts if the categories are so interwoven that they cannot be separated without affecting the nature of the agreement as a whole. The court was inclined to the view that the word 'part' includes, but is not restricted to, a facility that is different as to some of its terms from another facility granted under the same agreement or one that can stand on its own as a separate contract or bargain. However, the court was prepared to give 'part' a wider meaning so as to include a facility provided under an agreement by which it could be operated independently of another facility under the same agreement. In other words, it would be enough for an agreement to be in parts for its terms to differ as between the different parts or for a part to be capable of operating as a free-standing agreement, even if it does not in fact do so under the terms of the agreement. In relation to the agreement before it the court came to the conclusion that the written agreement needed to be construed as a whole, without distinguishing the purpose or terms of one loan from those of another.

Where an agreement is in parts, s 18(2) treats each part as a separate agreement in the relevant category in question, so that each part must comply with the requirements of CCA 1974 and, of course, the regulations under the Act. The particulars common to each part need not be set out more than once. Where the agreements are of a completely different type, such as a credit and hire agreement, they cannot be combined as parts within one agreement and must of necessity be set out in separate agreements.

The Agreements Regulations[6] contain some interesting glosses on the subject of multiple agreements, including in relation to the heading to the agreement and the statements of protection and remedies available under CCA 1974. They also make provision for a form of agreement which embodies an agreement of which at least one part is a credit agreement not regulated by the Act.

In one respect the Agreements Regulations expressly countenance and accommodate a multiple agreement. This is where a document embodies a debtor-creditor-supplier agreement or a debtor-creditor agreement and also contains the option of a debtor-creditor-supplier agreement to finance a premium under a contract for payment protection insurance (i.e. covering one or more of accident, sickness, unemployment or death) or a contract of shortfall insurance or a contract relating to the guarantee of goods.[7]

1 CCA 1974, s 18(1)(a).
2 SI 1983/1553 (as amended).
3 SI 2007/1167.
4 [1999] GCCR 2071 at 2078.
5 [2000] GCCR 2381, CA.
6 SI 1983/1553 (as amended) and especially Schs 1 and 2.
7 SI 1983/1553 (as amended), reg 2(8).

6.2 MULTIPLE AGREEMENTS IN PRACTICE

Having regard to the complications and complexities to which a multiple agreement gives rise, one is justified in asking why creditors and owners do not take measures to avoid them. The answer, of course, lies in the practical necessity of combining categories of agreement in a single unitary agreement or parts of an agreement in a single document. The draftsman sometimes has the choice of drafting an agreement which comprises more than one category, as an agreement in parts, setting out the distinctive particulars applying to each part, or as a single unitary agreement, without distinguishing the 'parts'. By way of example of the latter, a credit agreement combining restricted-use and unrestricted-use credit might be drafted in this manner.

Where different provisions apply to different credit amounts or different credit uses, the agreement must, of necessity, take the form of an agreement in parts. The general type of revolving credit agreement, operated by means of a credit card, will give rise to an agreement in parts if different interest rates (and APRs) apply to one or more of cash advances, balance transfers and transactions (purchases of goods and services). This is not always recognised, especially as regards a statement of the credit limit. Reliance appears to be placed upon an implied term that the credit limit is reduced in relation to certain facilities to the extent that the credit has been utilised in relation to other facilities. Payments and outstanding balances in respect of such agreements should be appropriately apportioned. Where a payment is insufficient to discharge the total sum due in respect of all the parts, the borrower has the right of appropriation conferred by CCA 1974, s 81.

Loan agreements commonly incorporate provisions financing premiums under payment protection insurance so as to protect the borrower against certain events arising during the course of the agreement which would affect his ability to make repayments under the loan agreement. The Agreements Regulations[1] specifically permit a debtor-creditor agreement, or a debtor-creditor-supplier agreement to finance a transaction between the debtor and the creditor, to be combined in a single agreement with the option of a debtor-creditor-supplier loan for the financing of a premium under a payment protection insurance contract or a premium under a contract which relates to a guarantee of goods. The insurance contract is one which provides for a sum payable in the event of one or more of accident, sickness, unemployment or death of the borrower before the credit has been repaid and where the sum payable does not exceed the outstanding balance.[2] It should be noted, in passing, that where such insurance is compulsory in that the creditor requires it as a condition of the making of the agreement, the insurance premium does not constitute credit but forms part of the total charge for credit and will therefore not impact on the characterisation of the agreement, nor convert it into a multiple agreement.[3] Where the creditor or owner wishes to make provision for payment protection insurance, but is unable to combine it in the foregoing manner, the payment protection insurance premiums might be financed under a separate credit agreement or take the form of regular cash premiums, usually monthly cash premiums. Provisions relating to the latter can be incorporated in the principal credit agreement and are best dealt with by partitioning those provisions off from the main agreement.

In the case of mortages, including all-monies mortgages, one needs to take care to check that further advances, other than the original, are treated appropriately. Thus, it may be that the original agreement secured by the land mortgage is a regulated agreement and that a subsequent further advance is a separate regulated agreement in its own right. Some regulated agreements secured by a land mortgage permit the borrower to draw down loan amounts from time to time. If the agreement constitutes a single bargain on uniform terms it can take the form of a unitary agreement which may or may not be a multiple agreement. If what is offered is a single facility on a single set of terms, the fact that the facility may be used for different purposes attracting different categories, e.g. unrestricted-use and restricted-use credit for debtor-creditor credit and debtor-creditor-supplier credit, does not change the unitary character of the agreement. The position would be otherwise where the agreement contains separate sets of terms for the different categories of agreement.

It is sometimes necessary to have regard to commercial considerations in order to decide whether an agreement has been artificially constructed so as to avoid the consequences of the law or whether in fact it truly reflects the transaction of the parties. One example where this might arise is in the area of conditional sale and hire-purchase agreements. The Act confers certain rights on the hirer or buyer under such agreements, namely protection in relation to the goods once one-third or more of the total price of the goods has been paid and the limitation of the liability of the buyer or under such agreements should he terminate the agreement.[4] Certain items, such as motor car insurance, do not lend themselves to being sold on hire-purchase or conditional sale terms and the question then arises as to whether they can be combined with the motor vehicle sold on hire-purchase or conditional sale terms.

This was the subject of *Mutual Finance v Davidson (No 2)*[5] where the hire-purchase agreement was drafted outside the then Hire-Purchase Acts of 1938 and 1954 and the hire-purchase agreement showed a single cash price relating to the motor vehicle and the motor vehicle insurance premium. Similar considerations to the CCA 1974 applied. The Court of Appeal held that the insurance premium was a legitimate component of the price and constituted part of the added value of the car. In other words, the buyer had agreed to purchase an insured vehicle under the hire-purchase agreement. The insurance premium was held to be a genuine part of the hire-purchase price of the vehicle which was worth more to the hirer by virtue of the insurance and there was nothing unnatural in the price increase. Another example mentioned by the court was a 'cif' sale of goods contract where the price is often expressed as a single sum although it covers the three elements of cost, insurance and freight. On the basis of such reasoning, a lump sum cash price for a three-year warranty and repair contract for the vehicle could likewise be included in the hire-purchase price of the vehicle. In contrast, a three-year warranty and repair contract payable by instalments would not be capable of being so combined.

Another example where market practice would countenance a combination of elements is a full repairing hire agreement under which the owner undertakes to effect repairs during the period of the agreement. The owner's undertaking to repair is an obligation assumed by it under the agreement. It would not be correct to isolate the hire element from the covenant to repair and appropriate payments to each, unless the agreement itself does so.

An unpleasant surprise may await the draftsman of an agreement which the parties, or at least the party proposing it, construed as an agreement of one kind but is subsequently found to be a combination of agreements of different kinds. Such was the case in *Dimond v Lovell*.[6] The court found the agreement to be a 'credit hire agreement' as it combined both a hire agreement and a credit agreement in circumstances where the lessor allowed the hirer credit on the hire charges until such time as a claim for damages had been concluded in relation to a vehicle involved in a road traffic accident. The Court of Appeal held that the hire agreement was also a consumer credit agreement since it provided for deferment of payment of the hire charges for a period extending beyond the end of the hire. As the agreement was not properly executed as a regulated consumer credit agreement, it was an improperly executed agreement under s 61(1) of CCA 1974 and accordingly unenforceable. The decision was upheld by the House of Lords where Lord Hoffmann stated:[7]

> 'Finally on this issue I should mention that it was submitted to the Court of Appeal that a contract for the bailment of goods to a hirer (such as the bailment of the car to Mrs Dimond) could not be a consumer credit agreement. It was either a consumer hire agreement if it satisfied the requirements of s 15(1) of the Act or it was altogether unregulated. The argument, based upon a passage by Professor Goode (Consumer Credit Legislation 1999 Vol 1, para 456.5, pp 215–215), was rejected by the Court of Appeal … and not pursued before your Lordships.'

Interestingly this comment appears in the learned Lord's speech after he indicated that he experienced difficulty with the analysis of a multiple agreement in parts, saying:

> 'The difficulty I have with this argument is that it seems to sever the provisions that create the debt (hiring the car) from the provisions that allow credit for payment of the debt. Whatever a multiple agreement may be, one cannot divide up a contract in that way. The creation of the debt and the terms in which it is payable must form parts of the same agreement.'

With respect, this is how CCA 1974 might have dealt with multiple agreements, but does not. The court having found that the agreement involved both hire and credit, CCA 1974 does create a bifurcation between the two. Had the court found (which it did not) that only a hiring was involved, with a postponement of the event for payment of the hire rental, the above dictum would have correctly reflected the situation.

As the categories of credit and hire are disparate categories, one way of drafting this agreement within the original framework, was by way of two agreements, a hire agreement and a credit agreement, each complying with the requirements applying to that agreement. An alternative approach would be to extend the period of hire until such time as the claim for damages had been concluded but provide that the hirer may pay such hire charges and end the hire agreement at any earlier time, thereby avoiding the deferment of payment and any notion of credit arising.

1 SI 1983/1553 (as amended).
2 SI 1983/1553 (as amended), reg 2(8).
3 Consumer Credit (Total Charge for Credit) Regulations 1980, S1 1980/51 (as amended), reg 4(1)(c).
4 CCA 1974, ss 99 and 100.
5 [1963] 1 WLR 134, [1963] 1 All ER 133, [1999] GCCR 163, CA.
6 [2001] GCCR 2303.
7 [2001] GCCR 2751 at 2761.

6.3   MODIFYING AGREEMENTS

Another strange creature of statute is the modifying agreement, created by CCA 1974, s 82. This is an agreement which varies or supplements an earlier agreement, not necessarily a regulated agreement. The modifying agreement is treated as revoking the earlier agreement and containing provisions reproducing the combined effect of the two agreements. If, therefore, the new modified agreement fails for any reason, as it has revoked the earlier agreement, both agreements fail. Likewise, if the earlier agreement was supported by a guarantee, as the modifying agreement revokes the earlier agreement, the guarantee is likewise ended. Obligations outstanding in relation to the earlier agreement are treated as outstanding instead in relation to the modifying agreement.[1]

If the earlier agreement is a regulated agreement but the modifying agreement is not then, unless the modifying agreement is for running-account credit, the modifying agreement is treated as a regulated agreement.[2] Originally this provision was mainly of relevance to the situation where the modifying agreement exceeded the financial limit, latterly £25,000, which then applied to a regulated agreement. Since the abolition of the financial limit, the likely relevance of this provision is where the modifying agreement is an exempt agreement.

Regulated mortgage contracts and regulated home purchase plans, (which are subject to the Financial Services and Markets Act 2000), and earlier exempt agreements under s 16(6C), are excepted from the provisions relating to modifying agreements.[3] The proviso relating to a modifying agreement for running-account credit is of no real significance as it does not add to what the CCA 1974 otherwise provides in s 82(4) read with s 10(2). Moreover, it would not be possible for a modifying agreement which is a running-account credit agreement, to vary a fixed-sum credit agreement.

A modifying agreement is not a cancellable agreement unless it is entered into within the cooling-off period of an earlier cancellable agreement.[4] It follows that even if the modifying agreement is entered into in circumstances where ordinarily a regulated agreement would be cancellable, the modifying agreement is not cancellable. A modifying agreement which is a regulated mortgage contract or a regulated home purchase plan is not a cancellable agreement even if it is entered into within the cooling-off period of an earlier cancellable agreement.[5]

A modifying agreement which varies or supplements an agreement which is secured on land, must itself comply with the advance copy procedure of CCA 1974, s 58.

Where it is possible to enter into a fresh regulated agreement, modifying agreements are best avoided as they involve the unique consequence of revoking the original agreement, which could have unexpected and unwanted consequences from the point of view of the creditor or owner. In practice, confusion might also be caused by the presumption that obligations outstanding in relation to the earlier agreement are treated as outstanding in relation to the modifying agreement. The various consequences of entering into a modifying agreement which are set out in s 82(2) are qualified by the words 'for the purposes of the Act' so that, it would appear, the order of priority of mortgages, i.e. a regulated loan secured by a mortgage, would not be affected by the subsequent modification of that agreement. Hence, in circumstances where a regulated agreement was secured by a first mortgage on land and the borrower entered into subsequent mortgages with other mortgagees, the variation of the terms of the original regulated agreement by the modifying agreement would not affect the priority of the original mortgage, which will retain its status as a first charge on the property.

However, it appears that the situation is different in relation to guarantees and indemnities so that a guarantee or indemnity given in respect of a regulated agreement which is subsequently varied by a modifying agreement will be extinguished by the modifying agreement, which will have revoked the earlier agreement, unless the guarantee or indemnity was expressed to extend to the regulated agreement as modified by any subsequent agreement.

Additional complications might arise where a regulated agreement is varied by successive modifying agreements.

The notion of the revocation of the original agreement and its substitution, as it were, by the modifying agreement might serve indirectly to extend the time before which goods under a hire-purchase or conditional sale agreement become protected goods under CCA 1974, s 90 and increase the liability of the hirer or debtor respectively under such an agreement for payment of at least one-half of the total price under s 100. This would not be the case, however, if the goods had become protected goods or the hirer had already paid half of the total price before the modifying agreement was entered into. A further consequence is the extension of the limitation period in respect of any claims which might be brought against a creditor under a credit agreement or a hirer under a hire agreement where the agreement has been modified by a modifying agreement. Finally, a modifying agreement might have the unintended result of the modified agreement being a multiple agreement and, indeed, a multiple agreement in parts.

1   CCA 1974, s 82(2).
2   CCA 1974, s 82(3).
3   CCA 1974, ss 82(2A), (3)(b) and (5A) inserted by the Financial Services and Markets Act 2000 (Consequential Amendments) Order 2005 SI 2005/2967 and the Financial Services and Markets Act 2000 (Consequential Amendments) Order 2008 SI 2008/733.
4   CCA 1974, s 82(5) and (6).
5   CCA 1974, s 82(5A).

6.4   MODIFYING AGREEMENTS IN PRACTICE

Although it is suggested above that modifying agreements should be avoided, there are circumstances where their utilisation is practical, and sometimes unavoidable. Modifying agreements might be used for rescheduling payments, extending the term of an agreement, replacing or upgrading equipment, providing for a further advance and inserting additional agreement provisions. The Agreements Regulations themselves envisage circumstances in which modifying agreements might be used.[1] Thus, they provide for a modifying agreement of a credit agreement where:[2]

(a)   goods, services, land or other things, specified in the earlier agreement, are varied or supplemented or where the cash price of the same is varied;

(b)   the advance payment to be made under the earlier agreement is modified;

(c)   the charge included in the total charge for credit or the credit amount in the case of a fixed-sum credit agreement is varied or supplemented;

(d)   the credit limit under an earlier agreement for running-account credit is varied;

(e) the repayment provisions of an earlier agreement are varied;

(f) any provision for security provided by the debtor in relation to an earlier agreement is varied or additional security is provided; and

(g) any charges on default are varied.

The Regulations envisage the following circumstances where a modifying agreement might vary a hire agreement:[3]

(a) where goods to be hired under an earlier agreement are varied or supplemented;

(b) where any provision of an earlier agreement relating to an advance, hire or other payment is varied;

(c) where any of the provisions of the earlier agreement relating to hire or repayments are varied or supplemented;

(d) where the hire period is varied;

(e) where security provided by the hirer under the earlier agreement is varied; and

(f) where the default charges are varied.

A further advance in relation to a mortgage may give rise to a modifying agreement. For example, a further advance under an existing credit agreement which varies that agreement because it is not within the original facility and requires to be agreed between the debtor and creditor may give rise to a modifying agreement within CCA 1974, s 82(2).

Whilst the Financial Services and Markets Act 2000 (Consequential Amendments) Order 2005[4] appears to provide the necessary exemption of regulated mortgage contracts and regulated home purchase plans from s 82 of CCA 1974, it only exempts such agreements from the provisions applying to modifying agreements under s 82(2) and not variations under s 82(1). Thus the variation of a regulated agreement under a power of variation under that agreement could potentially have given rise to regulation under both CCA 1974 and the Financial Services and Markets Act 2000. The problem is expected to be restored by the passing of amending legislation under a Legislative Reform Order.

The removal of the financial limit on consumer credit agreements has no effect where an agreement varies or supplements an agreement made before 6 April 2008 for the provision of credit exceeding £25,000 and either does not itself provide for further credit to be advanced or is itself an exempt agreement under CCA 1974.[5]

Temporary overdraft arrangements under running-account credit agreements do not give rise to a modifying agreement.[6]

1 SI 1983/1553 (as amended), reg 7.
2 *Ibid.*, Sch 8, Part I.
3 *Ibid.*, Sch 8, Part II.
4 SI 2005/2967.
5 SI 2008/831, art 4.

6 CCA 1974, s 82(4) in respect of regulated agreements and s 74(1)(b) in respect of debtor-creditor agreements on a current account.

6.5 NOVATION

A contract is novated where another party is substituted for one of the original parties to the agreement, so that all rights and duties of one party to the agreement are assumed by another. In other words, novation takes place where two contracting parties agree that a third, who also agrees, shall stand in the relation of either of them to the other. There is a new contract and it is therefore essential that the consent of all parties is obtained. It is with the necessity for consent that the most important difference lies between novation and assignment.[1]

For purposes of the consumer credit regime, it is important to recognise that a modifying agreement cannot be used to effect the novation of an agreement. For example, the transfer of equity in a property securing a regulated loan agreement, say from two spouses to only one of them, unless effected by means of the release of one of the parties, involves a change of parties to the agreement and cannot be dealt with by way of a modifying agreement. Likewise, if parties to an agreement agree to the substitution of new goods for the original goods under the agreement, not by way of remedy of any defect in the original goods or their replacement under an insurance policy as a result of any insurable risk having arisen, this must be dealt with by way of a new agreement. It cannot be effected by means of a modifying agreement as the subject matter of the original agreement will no longer be in existence.[2] However, the corollary is equally relevant. If the Agreements Regulations envisage the relevance and application of a modifying agreement in particular circumstances, then prima facie the modification is not tantamount to a novation.[3]

1 See *Chitty on Contracts: General Principles of Contract* (29th edn, Sweet & Maxwell, 2004) at 19.085.
2 See the discussion in *Goode: Consumer Credit Law and Practice* (LexisNexis Butterworths), at para 1C [35.12].
3 See SI 1983/1553, reg 7.

6.6 VARIATION

It is always possible at common law to vary agreements. Not unexpectedly, the possibility of varying a regulated agreement is also recognised by the CCA 1974. It provides that where, under a power contained in a regulated agreement, the creditor or owner varies the agreement, the variation shall not take effect before notice of it is given to the debtor or hirer in the prescribed manner.[1] It should be recognised that the variation envisaged by this provision is a unilateral variation, one which does not require the agreement of the parties, and which it is possible to effect unilaterally.

The mode of variation is governed by regulations made under the CCA 1974.[2] These require notice of the variation of any regulated agreement to set out particulars of the variation and to be served on the debtor or hirer not less than seven days before the variation takes effect. However, there is provision for an exceptional mode of notice where the variation is of the rate of interest payable under the agreement and the amount of the payments of interest charged under the agreement is determined, both before and after the variation takes effect, by reference to the amount of the balance outstanding established as at daily intervals. Basically this would apply to running-account credit agreements. Where those conditions exist, not less than seven days' prior notice of variation may be given by publication in at least three national daily newspapers or, if it is not reasonably practicable so to publish, in the London Gazette or other appropriate gazette. In each such case, if reasonably practicable so to do, the notice of variation must also be prominently displayed at premises where the agreement to which the variation relates, is maintained.[3]

In the case of a regulated credit agreement where the rate or amount of any item included in the total charge for credit may be varied, the agreement must state the circumstances in which the variation may occur and the time at which it may occur.[4] The Regulations do not restrict the creditor's power to vary and the requirements are satisfied by a statement that the rate is subject to variation by the creditor from time to time.[5]

The Unfair Terms in Consumer Contracts Regulations 1999[6] have considerably circumscribed the unilateral right of a creditor under a credit agreement and an owner under a hire agreement, to vary the agreement. *Prima facie* a term which has the object or effect of enabling the seller or supplier (including a creditor or owner) to alter the terms of the contract unilaterally without a valid reason which is specified in the contract, will be regarded as unfair.[7] An exception is made in relation to a contract for financial services where the supplier reserves the right to alter the rate of interest or the amount of other charges payable by the consumer, without notice, where there is a valid reason, provided that the supplier is required to inform the consumer at the earliest opportunity and the latter is free to dissolve the contract immediately.[8] The further exception is where the seller or supplier reserves the right to alter unilaterally the conditions of a contract of indeterminate duration, provided that he is required to inform the consumer with reasonable notice and the consumer is free to dissolve the contract.[9]

It is common for agreements to contain widely expressed variation clauses permitting the creditor or owner to vary the agreement in a host of specified, or indeed unspecified, circumstances. It will sometimes be open to question whether or not such power, or the exercise of such power, extends beyond the creditor's or owner's rights under the agreement. As noted above, the unilateral power of variation is subject to various legal limitations. It will often equally be open to question whether the purported variation in fact amounts to a new agreement or a modifying agreement. This will be the case where the subsequent variation is dependent upon the agreement of both parties and involves a consideration passing from the promisee to the promisor.

Frequently in the case of credit card accounts, the creditor will issue an entire new set of terms and conditions. Leaving aside the question as to whether the terms are capable of variation, as already noted, this requires the creditor to set out the particulars of the variation. This would normally take the form of a notice setting out the variations accompanied by a set of the new terms. Whilst the relevant regulations require only seven days' advance notice[10] if the creditor is a subscriber to The Banking Code, it will need to give at least 30 days' prior notice of the variations.[11] Subscribers to the Code include banks, building societies and members of the UK Payments Association (APACS).

No variation of an agreement is involved in circumstances where the event is referrable to an ascertainable yardstick which operates independently of the agreement. An example is an agreement with interest at 2% above the Bank of England Base Rate from time to time in force. No notice of variation in respect of the altered interest rate need be given under CCA 1974 though it may still be required under one or other Code of Practice or governing set of Guidelines which applies to the loan. The altered interest rate will in any event be notified to the borrower (albeit retrospectively) in statements issued by the creditor relating to the agreement.

Variation of an agreement is to be distinguished from the grant of a concession or indulgence by the creditor or owner to the other party to the agreement. This amounts to the unilateral withholding by one party of its entitlement to enforce the agreement or any of its rights under the agreement, without entering into a contract with or receiving consideration from the other party for so doing. A concession or indulgence is granted in circumstances where it would alleviate hardship which the other party to the contract would suffer if the contract were enforced. The party granting the concession or indulgence would reserve the right to strictly enforce the terms of the agreement at any future time. In order to avoid any suggestion that the concession amounts to a contractual variation of the agreement, it should be recorded in writing, usually in the form of a letter setting out its terms.

1 CCA 1974, s 82(1).
2 Consumer Credit (Notice of Variation of Agreements) Regulations 1977, SI 1977/328. See especially reg 2.
3 Consumer Credit (Notice of Variation of Agreements) Regulations 1977, SI 1977/328, reg 3.
4 Consumer Credit (Agreements) Regulations 1983, SI 1983/1553, Sch 1, para 18.
5 *Lombard Tricity Finance Ltd v Paton* [1989] 1 All ER 918, CA.
6 SI 1999/2083.
7 SI 1999/2083, reg 5(5) read with para 1(i) of Sch 2.
8 SI 1999/2083, Sch 2, para 2(b).
9 SI 1999/2083, Sch 2, para 2(b).
10 SI 1977/328, reg 2.
11 The Banking Code (March 2005 edn) para 6.4.

6.7 ASSIGNMENT

The assignability of a regulated agreement is the subject of debate. CCA 1974 defines 'creditor' as the person providing credit under a consumer credit agreement or the person to whom his rights and duties under the agreement have passed by assignment or operation of law.[1] 'Owner' is similarly defined. The inclusion of the phrase 'and duties' in the definition has caused some controversy. Professor Goode has described it as a drafting error since, as a matter of contract law, an assignment transfers rights but does not relieve the assignor of his duties to the contracting party. The draftsman of the Act recognises this criticism and maintains that, notwithstanding any assignment, the original creditor should continue to be treated as such until such time, if any, as his duties pass by operation of law to a person who also possesses the rights. Professor Guest, on the other hand, suggests that the meaning of 'creditor' depends upon the policy underlying the particular provision of the Act. In his view, the creditor's or owner's statutory duties to the debtor or hirer respectively will pass by assignment provided that the debtor or hirer receives notice of the assignment.[2] It is submitted that Parliament may have intended to extend the meaning of 'creditor' to include persons to whom the creditor's statutory duties have passed, if only to prevent the assignee evading duties imposed upon the creditor under the Act and in order to facilitate assignments. Clearly, if the agreement does not permit assignment this would override any interpretation to the contrary which might be suggested by the Act.

The Consumer Credit Act 2006 underlines the unique application of the Act to assignments of consumer credit agreements and consumer hire agreements. The following should be noted in this regard:

(a)   'Consumer credit business' and 'consumer hire business' is defined by reference, inter alia, to any business carried on by a person so far as it comprises or relates to his being a creditor under regulated consumer credit agreements or an owner under regulated consumer hire agreements.[3] 'Creditor' or 'owner' have the meanings referred to above and include their respective assignees.

(b)   With regard to unfair relationships 'creditor' and 'debtor' include their respective assignees.[4]

(c)   By virtue of paragraph (a) above, an assignee must also be licensed.[5]

(d)   Obligations of the creditor, unless carried out by the creditor as assignor must be carried out by the assignee. This applies, for example, to the duty to issue statements[6] and statutory notices of sums in arrears, default sums and default notices.[7]

1 CCA 1974, s 189(1).
2 *Goode: Consumer Credit Law and Practice* (LexisNexis Butterworths), para I[61]; *Bennion: Consumer Credit Control* (Sweet & Maxwell), para 1-920; Guest, *Encyclopaedia of Consumer Credit Law*, para 2-190.
3 CCA 1974, s 189(1).
4 CCA 1974, s 140C(2).
5 See also CAA 1974, s 21(1).
6 See CCA 1974, s 77A and s 78.
7 CCA 1974, ss 86B to 87.

Chapter 7

The regulated agreement

7.1   FORM AND CONTENT

7.1.1   Background

It is quite easy to lose sight of the wood for the trees when first considering the contents of a regulated agreement, forgetting that the regulated aspects are merely the overlay to the underlying consumer transaction. This is understandable, having regard to the very detailed and prescriptive approach of the legislature to the content and form of the face or front of a regulated agreement.

The legislative approach, especially to the form of pre-contract information, may in fact be misconceived. The White Paper entitled 'The Consumer Credit Market in the 21st Century' states:[1]

> 'Although the existing legislative provisions require credit agreements to be documented in a prescribed format, there remains confusion among consumers about the information they receive from lenders, due to a lack of clarity. Research indicates that 39% of borrowers only read the main information on the front page of a credit agreement before signing, and are therefore unaware of clauses that may be to their detriment.'

The appropriate response to the above, it is suggested, would have been to furnish the entire agreement to the customer in good time before the agreement is signed and give the customer the opportunity to familiarise himself with all its terms. The legislature could still have required the terms to be clear and transparent and that statutory notices and forms be given due prominence. In fact the response was a halfway measure, namely to expand the information on the front page of the agreement and essentially require this information to be supplied to the consumer before the agreement is made. As the White Paper continues to state:

> 'One of the reasons consumers do not read their credit agreements in detail is due to the way in which the information is presented, and the terminology used. The Government intends to revise the format of agreements to make them clearer and more transparent. This will include a requirement to state key financial particulars in addition to [the following] key information … This is in response to our finding that 81% of borrowers said that they would welcome more information on their rights.

In addition, the key financial information will be required to be presented together as a whole and with appropriate prominence ....'[2]

7.1.2   The elements of a contract

Before turning to the form and content of a regulated agreement, it is worthwhile setting out the elements of a valid contract. They are the following: first, there must be two or more separate and definite parties to the contract; second, those parties must be in agreement, i.e. there must be consensus on specific matters (often referred to in the older authorities as 'consensus ad idem'); third, those parties must intend to create legal relations in the sense that the promises by each side must be enforceable contractual promises; fourth, the promise by each party must be supported by consideration or by some other factor which the law considers sufficient.[3]

In the sphere of consumer credit and hire, the subject matter of the agreement must be identifiable and evident from the contractual terms. Thus, whilst the Consumer Credit (Agreements) Regulations 1983 require statutory headings and information to be contained in the agreement, it does not necessarily follow that complying with such requirements will result in the setting out of all of the essential terms of the contract. A hire-purchase agreement must incorporate the hirer's option to purchase or to terminate the agreement, a conditional sale agreement implies retention of title until full payment of the purchase price, a credit agreement infers the passing of title at the outset and a hire agreement imports the notion of the hire of goods. If, notwithstanding the heading and contents of the agreement, it does not contain the essential provisions relating to an agreement of that type, no agreement may in fact have come into existence or the agreement may be void, at common law.

7.1.3   Form and content of a regulated agreement

The form and contents of a regulated agreement are prescribed by CCA 1974, the Agreements Regulations and the Copy Document Regulations.[4] In fact the requirements relating to the form and content of documents embodying regulated agreements are not set out in the Act itself but in regulations made under s 60. Section 61 sets out the minimum requirements in order for a regulated agreement to be 'properly executed'. If the agreement is improperly executed it is enforceable against the debtor or hirer on order of the court only.[5] In arriving at a decision as to whether to grant an enforcement order the court will have regard to its discretionary powers under s 127(1) and (2).

The minimum requirements of a regulated agreement are set out in s 61(1). A regulated agreement is not properly executed unless:

(a)   a document in the prescribed form, itself containing all the prescribed terms and conforming to regulations under s 60(1), is signed in the prescribed manner both by the debtor or hirer and by or on behalf of the creditor or owner;

(b)   the document embodies all the terms of the agreement, other than implied terms; and

(c)   the document is, when presented or sent to the debtor or hirer for signature, in a state that all its terms are readily legible.

Additionally, where the agreement is a prospective regulated agreement which is to be secured on land, the agreement is not properly executed unless the requirements of s 58(1) are adhered to. It is necessary for the debtor or hirer to be given an advance copy of the unexecuted agreement which contains a notice in the prescribed form indicating the right of the debtor or hirer to withdraw from the prospective agreement.

If the agreement is a cancellable agreement, it is not properly executed if it does not contain a notice in the prescribed form indicating the right of the debtor or hirer to cancel the agreement, how and when that right is exercisable and the name and address of the person to whom notice of cancellation may be given.[6]

We turn next to consider the elements of s 61(1):

(a)   *A document in the prescribed form*: The Agreements Regulations set out the form and content of regulated consumer credit agreements, consumer hire agreements and modifying agreements. The Copy Document Regulations set out general requirements as to the form and content of copy documents. In essence, every copy of an executed agreement, security instrument or other document referred to in CCA 1974 which is delivered or sent to a debtor, hirer or a surety, must be a true copy. This does not mean that it must be an identical or exact copy.

(b)   *Prescribed terms*: Schedule 6 of the Agreements Regulations sets out the prescribed terms. These were originally the minimum terms which a regulated consumer credit, consumer hire or modifying agreement had to contain if the agreement was not to be regarded as improperly executed, for the purposes of s 61(1)(a). Agreements entered into before 6 April 2007 were automatically unenforceable if they failed to contain the prescribed terms. This result was considered not to be incompatible with the European Convention on Human Rights as set out in Schedule 1 to the Human Rights Act 1998.[7] However, the relevant ss 127(3) to (5) have now been repealed in respect of agreements entered into after 6 April 2007,[8] with the result that the prescribed terms of Schedule 6 to the Agreements Regulations have been placed on the same plane as all other information required by s 61(1)(a), as no specific reference to prescribed terms is contained in s 127(1) or (2). This apparently unintended result serves to emasculate Schedule 6 to the Agreements Regulations and is obfuscated by the continuing erroneous reference to s 123(3) in Regulation 6(1) of the Agreements Regulations and in the heading to Schedule 6 to those Regulations.

The current position contrasts strikingly with the legal position prevailing in *Dimond v Lovell*.[9] In that case the hire agreement was for a maximum period of 28 days and, if truly a hire agreement, outside the purview of the

CCA 1974 as it was incapable of subsisting for more than three months. However, as payment of the hire charges was deferred until such time as a claim for damages had been concluded, which time was beyond the conclusion of the hire agreement, the Court of Appeal held that the provision for payment constituted a deferment of that payment, that the letting of the car on hire was the provision of services, that the services had been supplied on credit and that, as the agreement did not contain the prescribed terms of a credit agreement, it was unenforceable. The argument that the deferment did not amount to credit within the meaning of the Act was not put before the House of Lords which therefore restricted itself to the wording of the agreement. In view of references to 'credit facility' and the like, the Court concluded that the agreement was a credit agreement and not a hire agreement. The omission of the prescribed terms of Sch 6 to the Agreements Regulations meant the agreement was unenforceable by virtue of s 127(3).

Following the repeal of s 127(3), in the absence of any special significance attaching to implied terms, a court would need to consider the factors set out in s 127(1) and in s 140A (relating to unfair relationships in cases where the agreement in question is a credit agreement), in deciding whether to grant an enforcement order. It is submitted that the hirer in *Dimond v Lovell* was not prejudiced to any significant extent by the contravention in question and the prevailing practice did not involve any appreciable degree of culpability – the two tests of s 127(1). Nor does it appear that the agreement gave rise to unfair relationships between creditor and debtor, so that it is suggested that the court's finding would be different under the revised law.

A recent example where the court exercised its discretion under s 127(1) and (2) is *Hurstanger Ltd v Wilson*. The court awarded compensation to the debtor rather than rescission, having regard to all the circumstances of the case.[10]

Once a judge has exercised his discretion, the Court of Appeal will not interfere with such discretion unless it can be shown that the trial judge failed to exercise it on the right principles.[11]

The fact that an agreement is not enforceable without an order of the court, does not mean that it does not create liabilities. Thus, in *R v Modupe* the Court of Appeal upheld the appellant's conviction on various charges of false accounting, evasion of liability by deception and theft under the Theft Act 1978, notwithstanding the fact that the agreement was an improperly executed regulated agreement, enforceable against the appellant only on an order of the court. The court opined that the fact that the agreement was not enforceable without an order of the court did not mean that it did not give rise to an existing liability.[12]

(c)   *Signed in the prescribed manner by the debtor or hirer and by or on behalf of the creditor or owner*: The debtor or hirer must himself or herself sign the agreement; it cannot be signed by an agent or attorney on behalf of the debtor or hirer. However, where the debtor or hirer is a partnership or an unincorporated body of persons the agreement may be signed by a person by or on behalf of the debtor or hirer.[13] The Agreements Regulations set out statutory signature boxes which the debtor or hirer must sign. There is no equivalent signature box for the creditor or owner. Significantly, the agreement must be signed by both parties to the agreement, a requirement which is not observed in the case of many running-account credit agreements, where for marketing reasons the creditor's signature is dispensed with, with the result that such agreements are not properly executed.

Where an agreement is intended to be concluded by the use of an electronic communication (within the meaning of the Electronic Communications Act 2000), the signature box may contain 'information about the process or means of providing, communicating or verifying the signature to be made by the debtor or hirer'.[14]

(d) *The document embodies all the terms of the agreement other than implied terms*: A document embodies a provision if it is set out either in the document itself or in another document referred to in it.[15]

(e) *The document is, when presented or sent to the debtor or hirer for signature, in a state that all its terms are readily legible*: There is no further amplification of this requirement in CCA 1974. However, the Agreements Regulations and the Copy Document Regulations require the relevant documents to be easily legible and of a colour which is readily distinguishable from the background medium upon which the information is displayed.[16] The Regulations also require the lettering of the terms to be of equal prominence, except for headings, trade names and names of parties to the agreement.[17]

There are no prescribed print or font sizes and it appears that 'readily legible' in the Act and 'easily legible' in the Regulations have the same meaning, especially as they are used interchangeably.

1 DTI, Con 6040, dated December 2003, para 2.18.
2 *Ibid.*, paras 2.25 and 2.27.
3 9(1) Halsbury's *Laws* (4th edn, LexisNexis Butterworths), para 603.
4 Agreements: CCA 1974, ss 60 and 61 and the Consumer Credit (Agreements) Regulations 1983, SI 1983/1533 (as amended); Copy Agreements: CCA 1974, ss 58 and 64 and the Consumer Credit (Cancellation Notices and Copies of Documents) Regulations 1983, SI 1983/1557 (as amended).
5 CCA 1974, s 65(1).
6 CCA 1974, s 64(1) and (5).
7 See *Wilson v First County Trust Ltd (No 2)* [2003] GCCR 4931, HL.
8 SI 2007/123 (C.6).
9 [1999] 3 All ER 1, [1999] GCCR 2303, CA; affd [2000] 2 All ER 897, HL.
10 [2007] All ER (D) 66, CA.
11 *Nissan Finance UK Ltd v Lockhart* [1999] GCCR 1649, CA.
12 [1999] GCCR 1595, CA.
13 CCA 1974, s 61(4).
14 Agreements Regulations, reg 6(5).
15 CCA 1974, s 189(4).
16 Agreements Regulations, reg 6(2); Copy Document Regulations, reg 2(1).
17 *Ibid.*

7.2   MAKING THE AGREEMENT

7.2.1   **Pre-contract information**

Before a regulated agreement is signed by the customer he must be given pre-contract information. This obligation on the creditor or owner depends on the circumstances, as set out below.

(a)   If the agreement is one to which s 58 of CCA 1974 applies (i.e. an agreement where the customer is given an opportunity to withdraw from a prospective land mortgage), the customer must be given an advance copy of the agreement and the information in (b) below, if applicable.[1]

(b)   If the agreement is a distance contract, the creditor or owner must give the customer the pre-contract information specified by the Financial Services (Distance Marketing) Regulations 2004 in good time prior to the customer being bound by the distance contract.[2]

(c)   In all other cases the creditor or owner must give the customer Pre-Contract Information as specified in, and in a document which accords with the requirements of, the Consumer Credit (Disclosure of Information) Regulations 2004.[3] The information essentially mirrors that contained on the face of the credit or hire agreement to which it relates (i.e. the statutory financial information and statements of protection and remedies). The information must be easily legible, of a colour which is readily distinguishable from the background medium and of equal prominence, save for headings. The document must be separate from the document embodying the relevant agreement, on paper or another durable medium and of a nature that enables the customer to remove it from the place where it is disclosed to him.

One might justifiably question the value of a document which essentially mirrors the financial terms, statements of protection and remedies set out in the agreement, but without the agreement terms. It would appear to be a more sensible approach to require the agreement form itself to be furnished to the customer and to permit him to remove it, and of course read it, before requesting him to sign. The Unfair Terms in Consumer Contracts Regulations 1999 in any event fundamentally assume that this approach is adopted.[4]

1   SI 1983/1557, as amended.
2   SI 2004/2095 and especially regs 7(1), 8(1) and Sch 1.
3   SI 2004/1481.
4   SI 1999/2083 reg 5(5), Sch 2, para 1(i) although this relates to non-core terms of the agreement.

7.2.2   **Making the agreement**

Every regulated agreement must be signed by both parties and where two or more customers enter into the agreement, by each customer. It may be signed by one person on behalf of a partnership or an unincorporated body of persons as debtor or hirer under the agreement.[1] The agreement date must be inserted but the customer's signature need not be dated except in the case of a cancellable agreement.[2]

The customer, and each person where more than one person enters into the agreement as the customer, must be given a copy of the agreement.

In most cases the customer will receive two copies of the agreement, the first being a copy of the unexecuted agreement which the customer receives immediately upon signing the agreement and the second copy, of the executed agreement, signed also by the creditor or owner, which the customer receives within seven days of the latter signing the agreement.[3] Where the creditor or owner is the first to sign the agreement it becomes an executed agreement upon the customer's signature, in which case the customer then receives only one copy of the agreement, namely that signed by both parties.[4] Likewise, if the unexecuted agreement is not presented personally to the debtor or hirer for his signature but the debtor or hirer helps himself to it, such as with a take-one agreement made available from a display rack at a store, there is no requirement to furnish the customer with a copy of the unexecuted agreement. In that event it suffices for the customer to be furnished with a copy of the executed agreement.[5] In practice most take-one leaflets embodying agreements will also contain a copy of the agreement for the customer to keep.

In the case of a cancellable agreement, a notice in the prescribed form indicating the right of the debtor or hirer to cancel the agreement must be set out in every copy of the agreement.[6] Save where the agreement becomes an executed agreement upon the owner's or creditor's signature, a copy of the executed agreement, containing a notice of cancellation rights, must also be posted to the debtor or hirer within seven days following the making of the agreement.[7]

The second copy of a credit-token agreement may be posted to the debtor before the credit-token is given or sent together with the credit-token, even if this is after the foregoing seven-day period.[8] Save in the case of the first credit-token, on the issue of any subsequent credit-token the debtor must be given a copy of the executed agreement.[9] This will usually set out in or with the card carrier.

The cancellation notice gives the debtor five days from the day after receipt of the copy agreement to notify the creditor or owner of his wish to cancel the same.[10] The confluence of the consumer credit regime and the distance marketing regime means that when the regulated agreement is a distance contract, the lengthier period for cancellation of the agreement specified by either regime, applies to the regulated agreement. The Distance Marketing Regulations provide a cancellation period of 14 days beginning with the day after the conclusion of the contract. In the case of a distance contract relating to life insurance or a personal pension the cancellation period is 30 days.[11] There is no right of cancellation in relation to a consumer credit agreement secured by a land mortgage or a restricted-use credit agreement to finance the purchase of land or an existing building or a bridging loan in that connection.[12]

A distance contract is essentially a contract relating to financial services (services of a banking, credit, insurance, personal pension investment or payment nature) concluded between a supplier and a consumer without the simultaneous physical presence of the supplier and the consumer.[13] Financial services include most types of consumer hire agreements.

The relevant cancellation period must, in the case of all cancellable regulated agreements, be inserted in the statutory notice of cancellation rights.[14]

Exemptions from the need to supply notice of cancellation rights apply to certain mail order purchases.[15]

Agreements secured on land follow a reverse sequence to that which applies to cancellable agreements. These transactions are initiated by an advance copy of the agreement, setting out the customer's right of withdrawal from the proposed agreement.[16] This is followed, not less than seven days after the advance copy was given to the debtor or hirer, with the posting of a copy of the signature copy of the agreement. The creditor or owner is not permitted to contact the customer during the period commencing with the giving of the advance copy and ending at the expiry of seven days after the day on which the unexecuted agreement is sent to the customer for his signature, or on its return by the customer after signature by him, whichever occurs first. This period is called the consideration period. It is intended to enable the customer to consider the merits and demerits of entering into the proposed agreement without being bothered by the creditor or owner, or any representative or professional appointee of the creditor or owner, such as a solicitor or surveyor. No communication may take place with the customer during the consideration period, whether in person, by telephone, letter or in any other way except in response to a specific request made by the customer after the beginning of the consideration period.[17] A failure to observe these requirements will render the resulting agreement improperly executed and unenforceable without an order of the court.[18]

The cancellation of or withdrawal from a regulated agreement, will also effect the cancellation of, or withdrawal from, a linked transaction, unless the agreement provides otherwise[19] or the linked transaction is exempt from the consequences of cancellation.[20]

It will have been observed that the agreements regime requires the supply of the original agreement and of appropriate copies. It is respectfully submitted that there is no compliance with the requirements of the CCA 1974 if what is supplied by way of an original agreement is a truncated version of that agreement, which in turn refers to a copy of the agreement enclosed with it. The Act requires an original signature copy of the agreement, as well as any prescribed copy, to be supplied to the customer. Reliance cannot be placed upon s 189(4) which stipulates that a document embodies a provision if the provision is set out either in the document itself or in another document referred to in it. 'Provision' does not extend to a 'copy of the agreement'. One of the aims of the Act is to provide the customer with appropriate and comprehensive information before the agreement is entered into.

Where an agreement is signed by more than one debtor or hirer, each must be provided with all relevant copies of the agreement and of any document referred to in the agreement, such as a mortgage deed or life assurance policy.[21]

---

1   CCA 1974, s 61(4) and the Consumer Credit (Agreements) Regulations 1983, reg 6(3)(a).
2   Consumer Credit (Agreements) Regulations 1983, regs 6(3)(a) and (c).
3   CCA 1974, ss 62 and 63 read with s 185(1)(a).
4   CCA 1974, s 63(1) and (2).
5   CCA 1974, s 63(1) and (2).
6   CCA 1974, s 64(1)(a).
7   CCA 1974, s 64(1)(b).
8   CCA 1974, s 63(4).
9   CCA 1974, s 85.
10 CCA 1974, s 68(1).

11 The Financial Services (Distance Marketing) Regulations 2004, SI 2004/2095, reg 10.

12 *Ibid.*, reg 11.

13 *Ibid.*, reg 2(1).

14 See the Forms in the Schedule to the Consumer Credit (Cancellation Notices and Copies of Documents) Regulations 1983, SI 1983/1557.

15 Consumer Credit (Notice of Cancellation Rights) (Exemptions) Regulations 1983, SI 1983/1558.

16 CCA 1974, s 58.

17 CCA 1974, s 61(2) and (3).

18 CCA 1974, s 61 read with s 65.

19 Consumer Credit (Linked Transactions) (Exemptions) Regulations 1983, SI 1983/1560.

20 See in this connection *Goshawk Dedicated (No 2) Ltd v Governor and Company of Bank of Scotland* [2005] GCCR 5431 and *Governor and Company of the Bank of Scotland v Euclidian (No. 1) Ltd* [2007] All ER (D) 330.

21 CCA 1974, s 185(1).

7.3 AGREEMENT TERMS

7.3.1 General

CCA 1974 lays down essential requirements for a regulated agreement and requires regulations to ensure that the debtor or hirer is made aware of:

(a) the rights and duties conferred or imposed on him by the agreement;

(b) the amount and rate of the total charge for credit (in the case of a consumer credit agreement);

(c) the protection and remedies available to him under the Act; and

(d) any other matters which, in the opinion of the Secretary of State, it is desirable for him to know about in connection with the agreement.

The Act states that regulations may in particular:

(a) require specified information to be included in the prescribed manner in documents, and other specified material to be excluded;

(b) contain requirements to ensure that specified information is clearly brought to the attention of the debtor or hirer, and that one part of a document is not given insufficient or excessive prominence compared with another.[1]

1 CCA 1974, s 60(1) and (2).

7.3.2 Regulated consumer credit agreement

7.3.2.1 *Prescribed terms*

As already noted in para 7.1.3, prescribed terms no longer occupy the higher pedestal which they did prior to 6 April 2007, when the absence of a prescribed term automatically rendered the agreement unenforceable. The prescribed terms, set out in Schedule 6 to the Agreements Regulations, are now of no more importance than the other elements of a regulated agreement set out in s 61(1), namely, that the document is in the prescribed form, conforms to regulations made under s 60(1), is signed in the prescribed manner by the debtor (or hirer) and by or on behalf of the creditor (or owner), embodies all the terms of the agreement other than implied terms and is, when presented or sent to the debtor (or hirer) for signature, in such a state that all its terms are readily legible. In addition, if the agreement is one to which s 58(1) applies, the provisions of that section must have been complied with, the unexecuted agreement must have been sent to the debtor (or hirer) not less than seven days after a copy of it was given to him under s 58(1); during the consideration period the creditor (or owner) must have refrained from approaching the debtor (or hirer) except in response to a specific request made by the debtor (or hirer) after the beginning of the consideration period and no notice of withdrawal by the debtor (or hirer) must have been received by the creditor (or owner) before the sending of the unexecuted agreement.

The prescribed terms are the following: the amount of credit or, in the case of a running-account credit agreement, the credit limit or the manner in which it will be determined or a statement that there is no credit limit; the rate of interest; the repayments, which may be described by reference to a combination of any of the number, amount, frequency and timing of payments, dates of repayments, and the manner in which any of the foregoing may be determined; and any power of the creditor to vary what is payable.[1]

The case of *Dimond v Lovell*[2] affirmed the unenforceability of an agreement which did not contain one of the prescribed terms. This decision was based on s 127(3), which has now been repealed and it offers no guidance on how the court might have construed the absence of a financial, as opposed to a prescribed, term. The same observation may be made in respect of *Watchtower Investments Ltd v Payne*,[3] *McGinn v Grangewood Securities Ltd*[4] and *London North Securities Ltd v Meadows*[5] each of which dealt with the categorisation of, and differentiation between, credit and charges and whether the agreement in question contained the necessary prescribed terms. It is submitted that where, as now, the court is required to exercise its discretion under s 127(1), in circumstances such as those prevailing in the above cases it will endeavour to uphold the agreement. Indeed, why otherwise should the legislature have found fit to repeal s 127(3)?

1   Agreements Regulations SI 1983/1553 (as amended) Sch 6.
2   [2001] GCCR 2751.
3   [2001] GCCR 3055.
4   [2002] GCCR 4761.
5   [2005] GCCR 5381.

7.3.2.2   Information to be contained in a regulated consumer credit agreement

A regulated consumer credit agreement must contain the information set out in Schedule 1 to the Agreements Regulations, namely the following information and in the following order:[1]

(a)   the nature of the agreement, namely one of the statutory headings;

(b)   the parties to the agreement, namely the names and addresses of the parties;

(c)   specified financial and related particulars under the respective headings: 'Key Financial Information', 'Other Financial Information' and 'Key Information';

(d)   under the heading 'Key Information', the relevant statements of protection and remedies set out in Schedule 2 to the Regulations;

(e)   the customer signature box and, where applicable, the separate box required where the agreement is one to which s 58(1) of CCA 1974 applies, or if the agreement is a cancellable agreement or is an agreement under which any person takes any article in pawn and under which the pawn-receipt is not separate from the document embodying the agreement, a separate box immediately above, below or adjacent to the signature box containing the appropriate statutory statement. It should be noted that where the agreement is a cancellable agreement, the notice of cancellation rights needs to be set out above the signature box by virtue of it being part of the 'Key Information' i.e. the 'Key Information' ends before the signature box;

(f)   where the agreement embodies a debtor-creditor-supplier agreement which finances a premium under a contract of insurance under which a sum is payable in the event of the death of the debtor or the debtor suffering an accident, sickness or unemployment before the credit under the agreement becomes payable, or finances a premium under a contract of shortfall insurance or a contract of insurance relating to the guarantee of goods, the agreement must contain a statutory form of consent immediately below the customer signature box and which requires completion and signature by the customer.

The above financial information, statements of protection and remedies, signature and separate boxes, must be set out in the order prescribed by the Agreements Regulations, shown together as a whole and not preceded by any information, apart from trade names, logos or the reference number of the agreement. The foregoing may not be interspersed with any other information or wording, apart from sub-totals of total amounts and cross-references to the terms of the agreement.

1   SI 1983/1553, as amended, reg 2(4) read with Sch 1.

7.3.2.3   *Aspects of the Financial and Related Particulars*

(a)   *Order of the information*: The general view, which is supported by BERR (formerly the Department of Trade and Industry)[1] is that where the Regulations prescribe the ordering of particular information, the order is that which applies to the blocks of information i.e. 'Key Financial Information', 'Other Financial Information' and 'Key Information' rather than to the individual items of information within each block.

(b)   *Total charge for credit etc.*: Where the total charge for credit or rate of interest cannot be exactly ascertained, the creditor may insert information based on assumptions it may reasonably make in all the circumstances.[2] A statement of the assumptions should be included in the terms of the agreement and the terms on the face of the agreement should cross-refer to the assumptions.

In the case of a *running*-account credit agreement, the total charge for credit must be calculated on the following assumptions:[3]

(i)   where there will be a credit limit but that limit is not known at the date of making the agreement, the credit amount is assumed to be £1,500 or where it will be less than £1,500, an amount equal to that limit;

(ii) credit is provided for a year beginning with the relevant date (normally the date of the agreement);[4]

(iii) credit is provided in full on the relevant date;

(iv) where the rate of interest will change at a time provided in the agreement within a period of three years beginning with the date of the making of the agreement, the rate should be taken to be the highest rate obtaining under the agreement in that period;

(v)   where the agreement provides credit to finance the purchase of goods, services, land or other things and also provides one or more of cash loans, credit to refinance existing indebtedness and credit for any other purpose, and the rates of interest and charges differ, the rate of interest and charges shall be those applying to the provision of credit for the purchase of goods etc.;

(vi) the credit is assumed to be repaid in 12 equal instalments at monthly intervals, beginning one month after the relevant date.

The result of the above is that the credit agreement will show one APR even though it may also include provision for balance transfers and cash advances, each at different rates of interest and different charges.

(c) *Amount of repayments*: The amount of each repayment must be stated in the manner required by the Agreements Regulations. Paragraph 13 of Schedule 1 is more restrictive than paragraph 5 of Schedule 6 in only permitting it to be stated in 'the manner in which the amount will be determined' if it cannot be stated in any of the alternative ways specified in paragraph 13. Failure to comply will give rise to a court having to exercise its discretion in respect of the enforceability of the agreement under s 127(1).[5]

(d) *Allocation of payments*: Where different interest rates or different charges or both are at any time payable in respect of credit under the agreement provided for different purposes or different parts of the agreement, the agreement must state the order or proportions in which any amount paid by the debtor, which is insufficient to discharge the total indebtedness, will be applied or appropriated towards the discharge of the sums due.[6] Examples are 'Any payments will be allocated first to pay off arrears, if any, then costs and charges accrued due, if any, and then to reduce the balance outstanding' or 'Payments are allocated first towards interest, second towards other charges and fees, next to balance transfers, followed by purchases, followed by cash advances'.

(e) *Charges*: The agreement must list any charges payable under the agreement upon failure by the debtor or a relative of his to do or refrain from doing anything which he is required to do or refrain from doing. It must also contain a statement indicating any term of the agreement which provides for charges not required to be shown as above or not included in the total charge for credit. This is understood to refer to a general charges provision rather than to a specific charge e.g. a clause requiring the debtor to pay all costs, charges and expenses relating to the enforcement of the credit agreement.[7] 'Charges' clearly does not mean the payment payable on termination of the agreement.

(f) *Cancellation rights*: In the case of a cancellable agreement, the agreement must set out the statutory form relating to the debtor's rights to cancel the agreement. Where the agreement is not a cancellable agreement, whether under CCA 1974, the Timeshare Act 1992 or the Financial Services (Distance Marketing) Regulations 2004, the agreement must contain a statement that the debtor has no right to cancel the agreement under those provisions.[8]

(g) *Amount payable on early settlement*: An agreement for fixed-sum credit for a term of more than one month must set out examples based on the amount of credit to be provided under the agreement, or the nominal amount of either £1,000 or £100, showing the amount that would be payable if the debtor exercises his right under s 94 of the Act to discharge his indebtedness on the date when a quarter, half and three quarters of the term respectively has elapsed, or on the first repayment date after each of those dates. The amounts need to be described as only illustrative and as not taking account of any variation which might occur under the agreement.[9]

(h) *Statutory warnings*:[10] A notice alerting the debtor to the fact that missing payments could have severe consequences and make obtaining credit more difficult, must be inserted in the agreement.

A notice alerting the debtor to the fact that his home may be repossessed if he does not keep up repayments on a mortgage or other debt secured on it, must be inserted in an agreement which is secured on land.

---

1 Guidance Notes issued October 2004.
2 Agreement Regulations, SI 1983/1553, as amended, reg 2(2).
3 *Ibid.*, Sch 7, para 1.
4 *Ibid.*, reg 1(2).
5 See *Hurstanger Ltd v Wilson* [2007] EWCA Civ 299, CA, which was decided before the repeal of s 127(3).
6 *Ibid.*, Sch 1, para 14A.
7 *Ibid.*, Sch 1, para 22.
8 *Ibid.*, Sch 1, para 23.
9 *Ibid.*, Sch 1, para 24.
10 *Ibid.*, Sch 2, Forms 2 and 3.

7.3.3   Regulated consumer hire agreement

7.3.3.1   *Prescribed terms*

As with regulated consumer credit agreements, the Agreements Regulations set out in Schedule 6 the prescribed terms for a regulated hire agreement. These are surprisingly restricted in scope. They are limited to a statement of the term stating how the hirer is to discharge his obligations under the agreement to pay the hire payments. This may be expressed by reference to the combination of the number, amount, frequency and timing or dates of payments or the manner in which any of the foregoing may be determined and any power of the owner to vary what is payable.

7.3.3.2   *Information to be contained in a regulated consumer hire agreement*

A regulated consumer hire agreement must contain the information set out in Schedule 3 to the Agreements Regulations, namely the following information and in the following order:[1]

(a)   the nature of the agreement, namely the statutory heading;

(b)   parties to the agreement, namely the names and addresses of the parties;

(c)   specified financial and related particulars under the respective headings 'Key Financial Information' and 'Key Information';

(d)   under the heading 'Key Information', the relevant statements of protection and remedies set out in Schedule 4 to the Regulations;

(e)   the customer signature box and, where applicable, the separate box containing the appropriate statutory statement required where the agreement is one to which s 58(1) of the Act applies or is a cancellable agreement. Although the Regulations state that the separate box must be immediately above, below or adjacent to the signature box, where the hire agreement is a cancellable agreement it follows from the content of 'Key Information' that it must be set out above the customer signature box.

The financial information, statements of protection and remedies, signature and separate box, if any, must be set out in the order stated in the Agreements Regulations, shown together as a whole and not preceded by any information apart from trade names, logos or the reference number of the agreement. The foregoing may not be interspersed with any other information or wording, apart from sub-totals of total amounts and cross-references to the terms of the agreement.

7.3.3.3   *Aspects of the Financial and Related Particulars*

(a)   *Estimated information*: Where any information relating to the hire payments or other payments (as specified in Schedule 3) cannot be exactly ascertained, estimated information based on such assumptions as the owner may reasonably make in all the circumstances of the case, and an indication of the assumptions made, may be included in the agreement.[2] This would usually take the form of a cross-reference after the relevant information to the assumptions stated in the terms of the agreement.

(b) *Other payments*: One of the listed 'Other payments' is 'any payment payable on termination of the agreement (other than a payment on default to be shown under paragraph 10' of Schedule 3, namely the paragraph relating to the charges). It appears that this refers to the amount payable on termination of the agreement albeit that a similar provision does not exist in relation to credit agreements. In view of the uncertainty, it is advisable to include it by this description under 'Key Financial Information'.

(c) *Cancellation rights*: In contrast to the position in relation to cancellable credit agreements, the Agreements Regulations require the incorporation of a statement that the agreement is non-cancellable only where the agreement is not a cancellable agreement under CCA 1974 and not where it is not cancellable under the Financial Services (Distance Marketing) Regulations 2004.[3] The result is that the statement can be misleading and therefore should, it is submitted, be qualified where the latter regulations result in the agreement being a cancellable agreement.

(d) *Statutory warnings*: A notice alerting the hirer to the fact that missing payments could have severe consequences and may make obtaining credit more difficult, must be inserted in the agreement.

A notice alerting the hirer to the fact that his home may be repossessed if he does not keep up the payments on a hire agreement secured by a mortgage or other security on his home, must be inserted in an agreement which is secured on property.

It is unfortunate that there is inconsistency in the wording of these statutory notices as compared to those applying to a credit agreement.

1 SI 1983/1553, as amended, reg 3(4) read with Sch 3.
2 *Ibid.*, reg 3(2).
3 *Ibid.*, Sch 3, para 11.

7.3.4 Modifying agreements

7.3.4.1 Prescribed terms

A modifying agreement revokes the earlier agreement and contains provisions reproducing the combined effect of the two agreements.[1] Thus, whilst there is not a specific schedule to the Agreement Regulations setting out the prescribed terms of a modifying agreement, in fact the provisions of Schedule 6 apply to the modifying agreement depending upon whether it is an agreement modifying a credit agreement or a hire agreement.

7.3.4.2 Information to be contained in an agreement modifying a credit agreement

An agreement modifying an earlier credit agreement must contain the information set out in Part I of Schedule 8 to the Agreements Regulations, namely the following information and in the following order:[2]

(a)   the nature of the agreement, namely one of the statutory headings;

(b)   the parties to the agreement, namely the names and addresses of the parties;

(c)   specified financial and related particulars under the respective headings: 'Key Financial Information', 'Other Financial Information' and 'Key Information';

(d)   under the heading 'Key Information', the relevant statements of protection and remedies set out in Schedule 2 to the Regulations;

(e)   the customer signature box and, where applicable, the separate box referred to in para 7.3.2.2(e) above.

There is provision for estimated information where certain information cannot be exactly ascertained.[3]

The financial information, statements of protection and remedies, signature and separate boxes, must be set out, in the order stated in the Agreements Regulations, shown together as a whole and not preceded by any information, apart from trade names, logos or the reference number of the agreement. The foregoing may not be interspersed with any other information or wording, apart from sub-totals of total amounts and cross-references to the terms of the agreement.

7.3.4.3   *Information to be contained in an agreement modifying a hire agreement*

An agreement modifying an earlier hire agreement must contain the information set out in Part II of Schedule 8 to the Agreements Regulations, namely the following information and in the following order:[4]

(a)   the nature of the agreement, namely the statutory heading;

(b)   the parties to the agreement, namely the names and addresses of the parties;

(c)   specified financial and related particulars under the respective headings: 'Key Financial Information' and 'Key Information';

(d)   under the heading 'Key Information', the relevant statements of protection and remedies set out in Schedule 4 to the Regulations;

(e)   the customer signature box and, where applicable, the separate box referred to in para 7.3.3.2(e) above.

There is provision for estimated information where certain information cannot be exactly ascertained.[5]

The financial information, statements of protection and remedies, signature and separate boxes, must be set out, in the order stated in the Agreements Regulations, shown together as a whole and not preceded by any information, apart from trade names, logos or the reference number of the agreement. The foregoing may not be interspersed with any other information or wording, apart from sub-totals of total amounts and cross-references to the terms of the agreement.

1   CCA 1974, s 82(2).
2   Regulation 7(4).

3 Regulation 7(3).
4 Regulation 7(11).
5 Regulation 7(10).

7.4   COPIES OF THE AGREEMENT

We have already discussed the requirement for the furnishing of copies of the agreement.[1] This paragraph deals with the contents of the copy of the agreement.

Every copy of an agreement must be a true copy of the original agreement.[2] Although the relevant regulation refers to a copy of an executed agreement, the principle applies equally to a copy of the unexecuted agreement i.e. the first copy or advance copy of the agreement, as the case may be. The copy agreements are governed by the Consumer Credit (Cancellation Notices and Copies of Documents) Regulations 1983 (the 'Copy Document Regulations').[3] The separate forms of notice of cancellation rights are set out in the Schedule to the Regulations.

Certain information may be omitted from a copy, notably any signature box.[4]

Where the agreement falls under s 58(1) of CCA 1974, the advance copy of the agreement must have a specified heading and contain a box indicating the right of the debtor or hirer to withdraw from the prospective agreement, in accordance with the statutory form. Where the agreement is a cancellable agreement, the agreement must include the debtor's or hirer's right to cancel, in statutory form.[5]

Where a notice indicating the right of the debtor or hirer to cancel does not appear prominently on the first page of the copy of the agreement, the copy of the agreement must show on its first page a box containing the statutory statement: 'This is a copy of your agreement for you to keep. It includes a notice about your cancellation rights which you should read'.[6] This requirement creates an anomaly, as the Agreements Regulations do not permit any information other than that which they prescribe, and this statement is not included or envisaged in the information, so that it constitutes a prohibited interspersal. However, it is submitted that the Copy Document Regulations supersede the Agreements Regulations in this respect, as otherwise this requirement would be incapable of fulfilment.

A regulated agreement must embody all the terms of the agreement, other than implied terms.[7] A document embodies a provision if the provision is set out either in the document itself or in another document referred to in it.[8] The Regulations, however, dispense with the need to supply certain copies of documents, notably a document obtained by the debtor or hirer from a person other than the creditor or owner and supplied by the debtor or hirer to the creditor or owner or a document kept or to be kept by the debtor or hirer under the terms, or in consequence, of the agreement.[9]

Where more than one debtor or hirer enters into the agreement, the creditor or owner, as the case may be, must supply copies of the agreement to each of them.[10]

1 At para 7.2.3.
2 SI 1983/1557, as amended, reg 3(1).
3 SI 1983/1557, as amended.
4 *Ibid.*, reg 3(2)(b).

5 *Ibid.*, reg 5.
6 *Ibid.*, reg 5 and Schedule Part V.
7 CCA 1974, s 61(1)(b)
8 *Ibid.*, s 189(4).
9 Regulation 11.
10 CCA 1974, s 185.

Chapter 8

Contract terms

8.1 OVERVIEW

Consumer credit and consumer hire agreements are governed by an array of statutes, regulations and codes of practice. Indeed, the regulatory framework is becoming ever more complex, intricate and all-embracing. The principal relevant statutory enactments are the following:

Consumer Credit Act 1974, as amended, notably by the Consumer Credit Act 2006, and the Regulations made under the Act

Unfair Terms in Consumer Contracts Regulations 1999

Financial Services (Distance Marketing) Regulations 2004

Consumer Protection (Distance Selling) Regulations 2000

Data Protection Act 1998

Electronic Communications Act 2000

Consumer Credit Act 1974 (Electronic Communications) Order 2004

Supply of Goods and Services Act 1982

Supply of Goods (Implied Terms) Act 1973

Unfair Contract Terms Act 1997

Consumer Transactions (Restrictions on Statements) Order 1976

Financial Services and Markets Act 2000.

Financial Services and Markets Act 2000 (Regulated Activities) Order 2001.

The following codes may also impact on the consumer agreement:

The Banking Code

The Codes of Practice of the Finance & Leasing Association

The Code of Practice of the Consumer Credit Trade Association.

In general terms, the above requires that the agreement terms are expressed clearly and in plain intelligible language, that the agreement contains the information prescribed by the relevant Acts and Regulations, laid out in the prescribed order and that the agreement does not contain unfair contract terms. It is a far cry from the notion of freedom of contract and indeed epitomises the converse of the concept of 'caveat emptor'.

8.2   THE SHAPE OF A REGULATED AGREEMENT

Various provisions in the statutory enactments serve to give a regulated agreement a particular shape.

Every regulated agreement requires a prescribed heading and the information relating to the financial and related particulars which must be set out together and as a whole, without interspersals. In general terms a regulated consumer credit agreement must set out, in the following sequence, 'Key Financial Information', 'Other Financial Information' and 'Key Information' followed by the customer's signature box. In general terms a consumer hire agreement must set out, in the following order, 'Key Financial Information' and 'Key Information', followed by the customer's signature box. The contents of each information section is prescribed.[1] The agreement must contain statutory forms of statement and in certain cases these must be adjacent to the financial and related particulars and in others, adjacent to the customer's signature box. Certain statutory forms or notices must be enclosed in a box. Whilst there are no requirements governing the size of the lettering, the agreement must be easily legible and of a colour which is readily distinguishable from the background medium. Subject to limited exceptions the lettering of the terms must be of equal prominence.[2] Prominence as such is not defined and is in some respects a subjective issue. Information regarding the customer's personal data, and how it may be used, should preferably be set out below, but near the customer's signature box, so that it can be shown that the customer consented to the same; alternatively, it may be set out in the agreement itself and the customer's attention drawn to it by a reference close to the signature box.

The Unfair Terms in Consumer Contracts Regulations provide that a contractual term which has not been individually negotiated (ie a term in a standard form contract) is to be regarded as unfair if, contrary to the requirement of good faith, it causes a significant imbalance in the parties' rights and obligations arising under the contract, to the detriment of the consumer.[3] A consumer is defined as any natural person who, in contracts governed by those Regulations, is acting for purposes which are outside his trade, business or profession.

It will readily be appreciated that the draftsman of a consumer agreement must deal with the agreement with a fresh, even handed approach, bearing in mind the rights and obligations of both parties, and the balance between them. The unfairness of a contractual term is assessed as at the date when the contract was concluded, by reference to all circumstances at the time and to all the other terms of the contract or of another contract on which it is dependent.[4]

The Regulations require the written terms of a contract to be expressed in plain, intelligible language. If there is doubt about the meaning of a written term, the interpretation which is most favourable to the consumer will prevail. An unfair term is not binding on the consumer although the contract may continue to bind the parties if it is capable of continuing in existence without the unfair term.[5]

1 Consumer Credit (Agreements) Regulations 1983, SI 1983/1553, as amended.
2 *Ibid.*
3 Unfair Terms in Consumer Contracts Regulations 1999, reg 5(1).
4 Unfair Terms in Consumer Contracts Regulations 1999, reg 6(1).
5 Unfair Terms in Consumer Contracts Regulations 1999, regs 7 and 8.

8.3 SPECIFIC CONTRACT TERMS

In this section we review some of the more common contract terms found in consumer agreements.

8.3.1 Time of performance

It is usual for an agreement to state that time of payment is of the essence. The contract may also stipulate that prompt performance of other obligations is essential.

In general, in the absence of a statement making time of the essence in the performance of an obligation, prompt performance is not essential. Thus, although the party in breach may incur liability for damages or for interest on late payment, his late performance will not constitute a repudiation of the agreement.

The agreement apart, certain statutes expressly provide that performance need only be made within a reasonable time.[1] However, at common law, time of delivery may prima facie be of the essence as in the case of a commercial sale or in the sale of perishable goods or assets which fluctuate in value.

Where time is not expressed to be of the essence it may be made of the essence by service of an appropriate notice on the defaulting party.

In the case of a loan repayable on demand, the creditor need only allow the debtor a reasonable time to obtain the money from some convenient place but is not required to give the debtor time to negotiate a replacement loan.[2]

1 For example, the Sale of Goods Act 1979, s 29(3).
2 *Halsbury's Laws* vol 9(1) (4th edn, LexisNexis Butterworths), para 931.

8.3.2 Breach entitling the innocent party to terminate

A breach of contract always entitles the innocent party to maintain an action for damages but to terminate the contract only if the defaulting party has repudiated the contract or otherwise committed a fundamental breach of the contract. To constitute a repudiation the hirer's or debtor's default must be a breach of condition or go to the root of the contract. The agreement may provide that a particular breach is a fundamental breach which entitles the creditor or owner to terminate it, or it may be so persistent a breach as to constitute a repudiatory breach. It might be noted in this connection that a creditor appears to have almost complete discretion to stipulate the events that attract a right to terminate a hire-purchase agreement.[1]

It may be a question of degree whether or not the conduct of the debtor or hirer amounts to a repudiation. Thus, non-payment of six months' instalments has been held to amount to a repudiation whereas failure to make payment of two instalments was held not to amount to a repudiation.[2] As stated above, if time was expressed to be, or made, of the essence or if an act or omission is expressed to amount to a repudiation of the contract, the courts are likely to treat it as such.[3]

Where the debtor or hirer has neither repudiated the agreement nor committed a fundamental breach of it but the creditor or owner terminates it in the exercise of an express power to do so, the owner's damages are limited to loss suffered through breach up to the date of termination. Any greater compensatory measure will be an unenforceable penalty.[4]

Agreements sometimes provide for their automatic termination on the happening of certain events of default, such as the debtor's or the hirer's bankruptcy. Unfortunately, regulated agreements cannot be terminated automatically, as they require the prior service of a default notice. The benefit of an automatic termination provision is that it can be used to crystallise the creditor's claim on insolvency and can afford protection to the owner of goods which are the subject of a consumer hire agreement, a conditional sale or a hire-purchase agreement, especially from a landlord's right of distress under the Law of Distress Amendment Act 1908.

The application of the law of distress is rendered complex by the abstruse wording of s 4A of the Law of Distress Amendment Act 1908. The landlord's common law right to distrain on goods, whether or not belonging to the tenant, applies to goods held by the tenant under a hire-purchase or conditional sale agreement, unless the agreement has been terminated or during the period between the service of a default notice under CCA 1974 and the date on which the notice expires. Although s 4A of the Law of Distress Amendment Act also refers to consumer hire agreements, these were excluded from the commencement order bringing s 4A into force so that the owner of goods comprised in a leasing or hire agreement, whether within or outside the CCA 1974, remains entitled to invoke the Law of Distress Amendment Act 1908 by serving the requisite declaration on the landlord.[5]

---

1 *Goode: Consumer Credit Law and Practice* (LexisNexis Butterworth), para 1B [11.125].
2 *Yeoman Credit Ltd v Waragowski* [1961] 3 All ER 145, CA, see further *Financings Ltd v Baldock* [1963] 1 All ER 443; *Anglo-Auto Finance Co Ltd v James* [1963] 3 All ER 566, CA.
3 *Lombard North Central plc v Butterworth* [1987] 1 All ER 267, CA.
4 *Chitty on Contracts: General Principles of Contract* (28th edn, 1999) at para 1834; *Financings Ltd v Baldock* [1963] 2 QB 104, CA; *Re Apex Supply Co* [1942] Ch 108.
5 *Goode: Consumer Credit Law and Practice* (LexisNexis Butterworth), para 1C [52.9].

8.3.3 Implied terms

Various statutes import implied terms into contracts.[1] Thus, in the case of a contract of sale, the Sale of Goods Act 1979, ss 12, 13, 14 and 15 import various implied terms, previously called conditions, into the contract of sale. These relate to implied terms as to title, correspondence of the goods with their description, implied terms about the quality or fitness for any particular purpose of goods and that they are of satisfactory quality and, in a contract for sale by a sample, that the bulk will correspond with the sample in quality and will be free from any defect which would not be apparent on reasonable examination of the sample.

The Supply of Goods and Services Act 1982 introduces various implied terms into contracts for the transfer of property in goods and where ownership of goods will pass from the supplier to the customer but which are not sale agreements. It also introduces implied terms into contracts for the hire of goods and into certain contracts for the supply of services. The Act does not apply to a contract for the sale of goods (as to which see above), nor to a hire-purchase agreement (as to which see below).

The implied terms which apply to a transfer of property in goods are contained in s 2 (implied terms as to title), s 3 (implied terms as to the correspondence of the goods with their description), s 4 (implied terms as to the goods' quality or fitness for any particular purpose), s 5 (in the case of the transfer of goods by reference to a sample, the implied condition that the bulk will correspond with a sample in quality, that the transferee will have a reasonable opportunity of comparing the bulk with the sample and that the goods will be free from any defect not apparent on a reasonable examination of the sample).

The Supply of Goods and Services Act 1982 also introduces implied terms in relation to contracts of hire. Thus, in a contract for the hire of goods, there is an implied condition that the bailor (or owner) has a right to transfer possession of the goods by way of hire, that the bailee (or hirer) will enjoy quiet possession of the goods for the period of the hire (s 7), that where the bailor agrees to hire the goods by description, that the goods will correspond with their description, that if he agrees to hire the goods by reference to a sample as well as a description, that the bulk of the goods correspond with the sample and the description (s 6), where the owner hires out the goods in the course of a business, that the goods supplied under the contract are of satisfactory quality (s 9), where the owner hires the goods by reference to a sample that the bulk will correspond with the sample in quality, that the hirer will have a reasonable opportunity of comparing the bulk with the sample and that the goods will be free from any defect which would not be apparent on a reasonable inspection of the sample.

Part IA extends the application of the Supply of Goods and Services Act 1982 to the supply of goods with respect to Scotland.

As its title suggests, the Supply of Goods and Services Act 1982 also applies to the supply of services and it imports implied terms into such a contract. These are to the effect that there is an implied term that the supplier will carry out the service with reasonable care and skill (s 13), that the supplier will carry out the service within a reasonable time (s 14) and that the party contracting with the supplier will pay a reasonable charge (s 15).

Implied terms in relation to hire-purchase agreements are set out in the Supply of Goods (Implied Terms) Act 1973. This sets out implied terms as to title (s 8), an implied term that the goods will correspond with their description (s 9), that where the creditor hires out goods under a hire-purchase agreement in the course of a business, the goods supplied under the agreement are of satisfactory quality (s 10) and an implied term that where goods under a hire-purchase agreement are hired by reference to a sample, that the bulk will correspond with the sample in quality, the person to whom the goods are hired will have a reasonable opportunity of comparing the bulk with the sample and that the goods will be free from any defect which would not be apparent on a reasonable examination of the sample.

Whereas originally the Sale of Goods Act and Supply of Goods and Services Act imported what are now called 'terms' as 'conditions', it is now left for the courts to determine whether, in all the circumstances, the particular breach was a condition entitling the buyer to rescind a contract. Whether or not it is a condition is assisted by further provisions in each of the Acts. Thus, the Sale of Goods Act states that where in the case of contract of sale the buyer would have the right to reject goods by reason of the breach on the part of the seller on the terms implied by ss 13, 14 or 15, but the breach is so slight that it would be unreasonable for him to reject them, then if the buyer does not deal as consumer, the breach is not to be treated as a breach of condition but may be treated as a breach of warranty.[2] Likewise, in the Supply of Goods and Services Act, where in the case of conflict over the transfer of goods, the transferee would have the right to treat the contract as repudiated by reason of a breach on the part of the transferor the term implied by ss 3, 4 or 5(2)(a) or (c) but the breach is so slight that it would be unreasonable for him to do so, then if the transferee does not deal as consumer, the breach is not to be treated as a breach of condition but may be treated as a breach of warranty.[3] These sections apply unless a contrary intention appears in or is to be implied from the contract.

A term can also be implied into a contract via other routes, namely terms implied by custom or trade usage and terms implied by the courts. An example of the latter is the implied term that, where interest rates in an agreement are expressed to be variable, the rates would not be set dishonestly, for an improper purpose, capriciously or arbitrarily.[4] The reader is reminded that a regulated agreement is not required to set out implied terms even though they are contained in and form part of the agreement.[5]

Unless the particular implied terms cannot be excluded, by virtue of any of the provisions referred to below, implied terms can be overridden, superseded or indeed amplified by express terms set out in the agreement or varied by custom or trade usage.

1   (i) Unfair Contract Terms Act 1977, ss 6, 7(3A) and 20 and the provisions there referred to relating to contracts of sale and hire-purchase, namely the Sale of Goods Act 1979, ss 12, 13, 14 and 15 (re sale) and the Supply of Goods (Implied Terms) Act 1973, ss 8, 9, 10 and 11 (re hire-purchase); (ii) The Unfair Contract Terms Act 1977, ss 7 and 21 and the Supply of Goods and Services Act 1982, ss 2 and 7 (re contract for transfer of goods and contract for hire respectively).
2   Sale of Goods Act 1979, s 15A.
3   Supply of Goods and Services Act 1982, s 5A.
4   *Paragon Finance plc v Nash and Staunton* [2002] 1 WLR 685, [2001] 2 All ER (Comm) 1025, CA.
5   CCA 1974, s 61(1)(b).

8.3.4　Unfair contract terms

8.3.4.1　Impact of the Unfair Contract Terms Act 1977

Before entering into credit and hire agreements creditors and owners might in practice seek an acknowledgement from debtors or hirers to the effect that the goods were selected and examined by them before they entered into the agreement and that they were satisfied with the goods. In a non-consumer agreement, being an agreement entered into in the course of a business, the creditor or owner will often seek to exclude any term, condition or warranty, whether express or implied, relating to the goods save for those which cannot be excluded in any circumstances, namely the undertakings, terms, conditions and warranties implied by statute relating to title, the right to transfer property, the absence of any change or encumbrances on the goods and the entitlement to enjoy quiet possession of the goods.

Where the customer is dealing as a consumer, liability for breach of obligations relating to the seller's implied undertakings as to conformity of goods with description or sample, to their quality or fitness for a particular purpose and the corresponding things in relation to a hire-purchase agreement, cannot be excluded or restricted by reference to any contract term. As against a person dealing otherwise as a consumer (i.e. who makes the contract in the course of a business or holds himself out as doing so) the above can be excluded or restricted by reference to a contract term but only in so far as the term satisfies the requirement of reasonableness.[1] Corresponding provisions apply to other contracts, e.g. a hire contract, where possession or ownership of goods passes. In those contracts too, liability in respect of the right to transfer ownership of goods, or give possession or the assurance of quiet possession cannot be excluded or restricted by reference to any contract term except in so far as the term satisfies the requirement of reasonableness.[2]

The Unfair Contract Terms Act sets out the parameters of the reasonableness test. The requirement is that the term must have been a fair and reasonable one, having regard to the circumstances which were, or ought reasonably to have been, known to or in contemplation of the parties when the contract was made.[3] In determining the reasonableness or otherwise of a term, regard needs to be had to the guidelines set out in Sch 2. In summary form they are the following:

(a)　the strength of the bargaining positions of the parties;

(b)　whether the customer received an inducement to agree to the term or had an opportunity of entering into a similar contract with other persons without having to accept a similar term;

(c)　whether the customer knew or ought reasonably to have known of the existence and extent of the term;

(d)　where the term excludes or restricts any relevant liability if some condition is not complied with, whether it was reasonable to expect that compliance with that condition would be practicable; and

(e)　whether the goods were manufactured, processed or adapted to the special order of the customer.

The Unfair Contract Terms Act limits exclusion of liability for negligence. Thus, a person cannot by reference to any contract term, whether in a consumer contract or a non-consumer contract, or to a notice given to persons generally or to particular persons, exclude or restrict his liability for death or personal injury resulting from negligence.[4] In the case of other loss or damage, a person cannot so exclude or restrict his liability for negligence except in so far as the term or notice satisfies the requirement of reasonableness.[5] The reasonableness is judged by the factors referred to above.

A statement limiting or indeed setting out the consumer's rights in respect of defective goods, goods which are not fit for their purpose or which fail to correspond with their description or the consumer's rights generally in connection with a consumer transaction, must be followed in close proximity by a statement that the same does not affect the consumer's statutory rights and that he always remains entitled to assert the same.[6]

The Unfair Contract Terms Act 1977 limits the extent to which standard terms of business can exclude liability for breach of contract where the other party deals as consumer.[7] It also restricts the ambit of indemnities sought from consumers, whilst ensuring that guarantees of consumer goods do not contain unacceptable exclusions or restrictions.[8]

In non-consumer transactions (transactions entered into in the course of a business) certain exclusions are permitted to the extent that it would be fair and reasonable to incorporate them.[9]

1 Unfair Contract Terms Act 1977, s 6(2) and (3).
2 Unfair Contract Terms Act 1977, s 7.
3 Unfair Contract Terms Act 1977, s 11 read with Sch 2.
4 Unfair Contract Terms Act 1977, s 2(1).
5 Unfair Contract Terms Act 1977, s 2(2).
6 Consumer Transactions (Restrictions on Statements) Order 1976, SI 1976/1813 (as amended). See art 3(d).
7 Unfair Contract Terms Act 1977, s 3 and see *Lease Management Services v Purnell Secretarial Services Ltd (Canon (South West) Ltd,* third party) [1994] CCLR 127, (1994) Times, 1 April; *Sovereign Finance Ltd v Silver Crest Furniture Ltd* [1999] ECCR 2187.
8 Unfair Contract Terms Act 1977, ss 4 and 5.
9 Unfair Contract Terms Act 1977, ss 2, 6 and 11 and Sch 2; see also *Photoprint v Forward Trust Group* (1993) 12 Tr LR 146.

8.3.4.2 Impact of the Unfair Terms in Consumer Contracts Regulations 1999

The EC Directive on Unfair Terms in Consumer Contracts (93/13/EEC) resulted, in the first instance, in the enactment of the Unfair Terms in Consumer Contracts Regulations 1994.[1] These were replaced by the Unfair Terms in Consumer Contracts Regulations 1999.[2] Whilst largely to the same effect as the earlier regulations, the new regulations reflect more closely the wording of the Directive. They also introduce for the first time the right of a qualifying body named in Schedule 1 to apply for an injunction to prevent the use of unfair contract terms and empower such bodies to apply for an injunction to prevent their continued use. These rights are exercisable under Part 8 of the Enterprise Act 2002.

The regulations apply in relation to unfair terms in contracts concluded between a seller or a supplier on the one hand and a consumer on the other. A consumer is defined as any natural person who, in contracts covered by the regulations, is acting for purposes which are outside his trade, business or profession. A seller or supplier means any natural or legal person who, in contracts covered by the regulations, is acting for purposes relating to his trade, business or profession, whether publicly owned or privately owned. Although the regulations use the expression 'seller or supplier' they are not restricted to contracts of sale or supply and indeed extend to financial contracts, including security contracts such as mortgages.

At the heart of the regulations is the proscription of unfair terms. A contractual term which has not been individually negotiated is regarded as unfair if, contrary to the requirement of good faith, it causes a significant imbalance in the parties' rights and obligations, arising under the contract, to the detriment of the consumer.[3] In the direct line of attack under the regulations, are standard form contracts about whose terms the consumer has, by definition, little say.

The Regulations provide that a term shall always be regarded as not having been individually negotiated which has been drafted in advance and where as a result the consumer has not been able to influence the substance of the term.[4] Schedule 2 to the Regulations contains an indicative and non-exhaustive list of the terms which may be regarded as unfair.

The unfairness of a contractual term is assessed, taking into account the nature of the goods or services for which the contract was concluded and by referring, at the time of the conclusion of the contract, to all the circumstances attending the conclusion of the contract and to all the other terms of the contract or of another contract on which it is dependent.[5] In so far as it is in plain intelligible language, the assessment of fairness will not relate to the definition of the main subject matter of the contract (the 'core provisions') or the adequacy of the price or remuneration.[6]

The Regulations impose on the draftsman of standard form contracts an onerous obligation to ensure that contracts are evenly balanced as between the rights and obligations of the parties. The requirement of good faith in the Regulations is generally alien to English law. The concept of good faith in English law was originally restricted to contracts of insurance, partnership and employment, all of which involve fiduciary relations. However, it has made inroads into English law largely by its incorporation in various European Community Directives. English statutory law has also imported the civil law notion of good faith via the Uniform Law of International Sales Act 1967 and the Commercial Agents (Council Directive) Regulations 1993.[7]

The Unfair Terms in Consumer Contracts Regulations require written terms of contract to be expressed in plain intelligible language. If there is doubt about the meaning of a written term, the interpretation which is most favourable to the consumer shall prevail.[8] This requirement is analogous to the contra proferentem rule which requires a contract, in the case of ambiguity, to be considered against its proposer. This requirement applies even to core terms which define the nature of the agreement.

An unfair term is not binding on the consumer but the contract continues to bind the parties if it is capable of continuing in existence without the unfair term.

The Office of Fair Trading is obliged to consider any complaint made to it that any contract term drawn up for general use is unfair, unless the complaint is frivolous or vexatious or a qualifying body has agreed to consider the complaint.

Qualifying bodies are empowered to enforce provisions of the regulations. They include the Information Commissioner, the Consumers' Association and the Directors General of the various utility companies. They may apply for an injunction preventing the further use of an unfair term drawn up for general use in contracts with consumers.

Schedule 2 to the Unfair Terms in Consumer Contracts Regulations 1999 sets out an indicative and non-exhaustive list of terms which are considered to be unfair. Some of these are considered in the context of various contractual provisions discussed in the remaining paragraphs of this chapter.

1 SI 1994/3159.
2 SI 1999/2083.
3 Unfair Terms in Consumer Contracts Regulations 1999, reg 5(1).
4 Unfair Terms in Consumer Contracts Regulations 1999, reg 5(2).
5 Unfair Terms in Consumer Contracts Regulations 1999, reg 6(1).
6 Unfair Terms in Consumer Contracts Regulations 1999, reg 6(2).
7 See further the discussion at para 8.3.4.3.
8 Unfair Terms in Consumer Contracts Regulations 1999, reg 7.

8.3.4.3   'Unfairness' and 'good faith'

In *Director General of Fair Trading v First National Bank plc*[1] the court dwelt at some length with the concepts of unfairness and good faith in the earlier Unfair Terms in Consumer Contracts Regulations 1994, but which the corresponding 1999 Regulations largely replicate. Lord Bingham stated:[2]

> 'The requirement of good faith in this context is one of fair and open dealing. Openness requires that the terms should be expressed fully, clearly and legibly, containing no concealed pitfalls or traps. Appropriate prominence should be given to terms which might operate disadvantageously to the customer. Fair dealing requires that a supplier should not, whether deliberately or unconciously, take advantage of the consumer's necessity, indigence, lack of experience, unfamiliarity with the subject matter of the contract, weak bargaining position or any other factor listed in or analogous to those listed in Schedule 2 of the regulations. Good faith in this context is not an artificial or technical concept; nor since Lord Mansfield was its champion, is it a concept wholly unfamiliar to British lawyers. It looks to good standards of commercial morality and practice.'

Surprisingly, the 1999 Regulations, unlike their predecessor, the 1994 Regulations, do not spell out how to assess the presence or absence of good faith. However, the factors set out in the Unfair Terms in Consumer Contracts Regulations 1994, Schedule 2, appear to be relevant to any assessment. They are:

(a)   the strength of the bargaining position of the parties;

(b)   whether the consumer had an inducement to agree to the term;

(c)   whether the goods or services were supplied to the special order of the consumer; and

(d)   the extent to which the seller or supplier has dealt fairly and equitably with the consumer.

To these may be added:[3]

(e) whether the customer knew or ought reasonably to have know of the existence and extent of the term (having regard, amongst other things, to any custom of the trade and any previous course of dealing between the parties);

(f) where the term excludes or restricts any relevant liability if some condition is not complied with, whether (assuming the exemption is permitted in law) it was reasonable at the time of the contract to expect that compliance with that condition would be practicable.[4]

The above regulations apart, and subject to the potential extension of the consideration of unfairness discussed below, the concept of good faith is not one which has until now applied to English contract law generally. But, to quote Professor McKendrick, there are signs that the traditional English hostility towards a requirement of good faith might be abating.[5]

The reader is also referred to the Office of Fair Trading and Abbey National PLC and others[6] relating to the Unfair Contract Terms Regulations and bank charges.

1 [2001] GCCR 3075, HL.
2 At 3086. See also the Opinion of Lord Steyn at 3092.
3 These additional tests are taken from Schedule 2 to the Unfair Contract Terms Act 1977.
4 The reader is referred to the discussion of criteria of fairness and good faith in *Chitty on Contracts*, vol 1 General Principles (29th edn, 2004) at 1-024 and 15-048 following.
5 *Contract law* (6th edn, 2005), p 265 and the cases cited.
6 [2008] EWHC 875 (comm).

8.3.4.4   Unfair relationships and contract terms

The unfair relationships provisions of s 140A of the Act impact directly on consumer credit agreements. Section 140A(1)(a) provides that a court may make an order under s 140B if it determines that the relationship between the creditor and the debtor arising out of the agreement, or the agreement taken with any related agreement, is unfair to the debtor because, inter alia, any of the terms of the agreement or of any related agreement.

Whilst the Unfair Terms in Consumer Contracts Regulations 1999 do not apply to core terms of the contract,[1] the above section of the Act applies to all terms of the contract, including core terms. Thus, unfairness and absence of good faith are criteria against which the consumer credit agreement (although not a hire agreement) might be tested under this section.

1 Regulation 4(2).

8.4   INSURANCE

An agreement relating to the sale or hire of goods will often contain provision for their insurance, usually at the expense of the customer. Invariably insurance premiums are exempt charges for the purposes of calculating the total charge for credit and must be included under 'other payments' in regulated hire agreements. Brief particulars of the insurance cover should be supplied at the time of the agreement, either by incorporation in the agreement terms or by an accompanying leaflet. This will usually be followed by the issue of a certificate of insurance. The agreement might require the customer to procure the noting of the creditor's or owner's interest in the policy by endorsement on the policy or by having the creditor named as loss payee. Whilst most insurers are agreeable to endorsing the policy, they will not bind themselves to making payment to anyone other than the insured who pays the premiums. It is therefore prudent to provide that the customer will hold any policy proceeds received by him in trust for the creditor or owner.

Trading companies are often in a position to arrange block insurance policies to protect their goods and thereby benefit from reduced insurance premiums and the knowledge that their goods have been properly insured.

8.5   DEFAULT

8.5.1   Interest on Default

Under a regulated consumer credit agreement the creditor may not require the debtor to pay default interest, namely interest on sums which in breach of the agreement are unpaid by him, at a rate exceeding the interest rate applying to the agreement. Where the total charge for credit applying to the credit agreement does not include interest, the default interest rate may not exceed the total charge for credit applying to the agreement, excluding any charge attributable to any linked transactions.[1]

It follows that default interest cannot be charged in interest-free transactions. In variable rate transactions the maximum default interest rate will vary with the interest rate applying on the date of the default.

No restrictions apply to default interest in regulated hire agreements. Clearly such interest could not be circumscribed by reference to the total charge for credit (as this does not apply to hire agreements) although it might have been restricted by regulation to bank base rate or some other objective rate.

Where the debtor is entitled to a rebate of charges on early settlement, the rebate is calculated as at the date when the debtor discharges the full indebtedness under his agreement. The creditor is therefore entitled to the full unrebated amount due, together with default interest on the unrebated figure.[2] This is not to suggest that the creditor is entitled to claim principal, unaccrued and unrebated interest and default charges on the aggregate sum, as this would be struck down as a penalty.

In the absence of a default interest clause, no interest would be chargeable on a judgment debt relating to a regulated agreement.[3]

The entitlement of a creditor to charge default interest at the contract rate after, as well as before, any judgment was the subject of a challenge by the Director General of Fair Trading under the Unfair Terms in Consumer Contracts Regulations 1994 in *Director General of Fair Trading v First National Bank plc*.[4] The court stated that it was trite law that once judgment is obtained under the loan agreement for a principal sum and judgment is entered, the contract merges in the judgment and the principal becomes owing under the judgment. However, the parties to a contract may agree that a covenant to pay interest will not merge in any judgment and that interest will be charged on the principal sum even after judgment had been obtained. The court held that such a provision was not a core term as it did not define the main subject matter of the contract nor relate to the adequacy of price or remuneration.

The issue was whether the relevant term was unfair. The Court of Appeal cited *Interfoto Picture Library Ltd v Stiletto Visuals Programmes Ltd*[5] where Bingham LJ stated that:

> 'in many civil law systems and perhaps in most legal systems outside the common law world, the law of obligations recognises and enforces an overriding principle that in making and carrying out contracts parties should act in good faith. This does not simply mean that they should not deceive each other, a principle which any legal system must recognise; its effect is perhaps most aptly conveyed by such metaphorical colloquialisms as "playing fair", "coming clean" or "putting ones cards face upwards on the table". It is a principle of fair and open dealing.'

Approving the statement in Anson's *Law of Contract* the court stated that the 'good faith' element seeks to promote fair and open dealing and to prevent unfair surprise and the absence of real choice. In the court's view a term to which the consumer's attention was not specifically drawn but which may operate in a way in which the consumer might reasonably not expect and which is to his disadvantage may offend the requirement of good faith. Terms must be reasonably transparent and should not operate to defeat the reasonable expectations of the consumer. The consumer, in choosing whether to enter into a contract, should be put in the position where he can make an informed choice.

Turning to the second element in the regulation of unfairness of a contractual term, namely a significant imbalance in the parties' rights and obligations under the contract, the court opined that this would appear to overlap with the absence of a good faith. A term which gives a significant advantage to the seller or supplier without a countervailing benefit to the consumer (such as a price reduction) failed to satisfy the test of fairness. Finally, the element of detriment to the consumer must be present for the term to be unfair.

The Court of Appeal found that the relevant term was unfair within the meaning of the Regulations to the extent that it enabled the bank to obtain judgment against the debtor under a regulated agreement and an instalment order under the County Courts Act 1984, s 21 without the court having to consider whether to make a time order under CCA 1974, s 129, and if it was to make such a time order, whether it should also make an order under CCA 1974, s 136 to reduce the contractual interest rate. Finding in favour of the Director General, the court stated that with its strong bargaining position as against the relatively weak position of the consumer, the bank had not adequately considered the consumer's interests. It found that the relevant term did create unfair surprise and so did not satisfy the test of good faith. It caused a significant imbalance in the rights and obligations of the parties by allowing the bank to obtain interest on a judgment in circumstances where it would not obtain interest under the 1984 Act and the

County Courts (Interest on Judgement Debts) Order 1991 and did not confer any compensatory benefit on the borrower.

The House of Lords, in a unanimous judgment, reversed the judgment of the Court of Appeal.[6] After considering the requirement of good faith and fair dealing it drew attention to the fact that CCA 1974 did not prohibit terms providing for post-judgment interest, even though it required claims to be brought in the county court which could not at the time award statutory interest. The Act itself provided relief by way of time orders (s 129) and the provisions of s 136. The weakness in the regime lay in the procedures: neither the procedure for giving notice of default to the borrower nor the county court forms drew attention to these sections. The Unfair Terms in Consumer Contracts Regulations were directed to the unfairness of a contract term and not the unfair use which a supplier may make of a term. On balance, the court did not consider that a term providing for default interest at the contract rate, rather than at the judgment rate, caused a significant imbalance in the parties' rights and obligations under the contract to the detriment of the consumer in a manner or to an extent which was contrary to the requirement of good faith.

1   CCA 1974, s 93.
2   *Forward Trust v Whymark* [1989] 3 All ER 915, CA.
3   County Court (Interest on Judgment Debts) Order 1991, SI 1991/1184.
4   [1999] GCCR 2601, CA.
5   [1988] 1 All ER 348 at 352. See Appendix to OFT Unfair Contract Terms Bulletin, Case Reports Issue No 9, where the terms of the undertaking are set out.
6   *Director General of Fair Trading v First National Bank plc* [2002] 1 All ER 97, HL.

8.5.2   Default charges

Standard default charges or a tariff of default charges is now commonplace in relation to financial products. They were the subject of the OFT's statement on 'Calculating fair default charges in credit card contracts'. The OFT stated that in its view a fair default charge should:[1]

(a)   be calculated on the basis of a reasonable pre-estimate of the net limited additional administrative costs which occur as a result of the specific breaches of contract and can be identified with reasonable precision;

(b)   reflect a fair attribution of those costs between defaulting consumers;

(c)   be based on a genuine estimate of the numbers of expected instances of default in the relevant period; and

(d)   treat costs other than those net limited additional administrative costs as a general overhead of the credit card business and disregard them for purposes of calculating a default fee.

The OFT effectively required credit card companies to limit their default charges to £12 per default, stating that, as a practical measure, to help encourage a swift change in market practice, it was setting a simple mandatory threshhold for intervention by the OFT on default charges.[2]

1 April 2006 at para 3.27.
2 At para 5.3.

8.6 VARIATION CLAUSES

A clause commonly found in financing agreements, whether of credit or hire, is the ability of the creditor or owner to vary the charges or interest rates and in consequence, the regular payment amounts. Indeed, the Consumer Credit (Agreements) Regulations 1983 recognise the ability of the creditor in the case of consumer credit agreements and the owner in the case of consumer hire agreements, to vary the charges and the hire charge. They require a statement in the financial and related particulars of the relevant agreement to indicate the circumstances in which any variation may occur and, where that information is ascertainable at the time the document is presented or sent to the customer for signature, the time any such variation may occur.

The Consumer Credit (Notice of Variation of Agreements) Regulations 1977 provide the manner in which notice of a variation of a regulated agreement must be given, namely the notice must set out the particulars of the variation and be served on the debtor or hirer not less than seven days before the variation takes effect. An alternative procedure is available, namely notice by publication in various national newspapers, where the amount of payment of interest charged under the agreement is calculated by reference to the daily outstanding balance and the variation relates only to the rate of interest. This usually applies to running-account credit agreements.

Regard must be had to the Unfair Terms in Consumer Contracts Regulations 1999 in relation to such provisions. They stipulate that a term is to be regarded as unfair if it enables the seller or supplier to alter the terms of the contract unilaterally without a valid reason which is specified in the contract.[1] This is qualified by a further paragraph to the effect that the foregoing provisions are without hindrance to the term under which a supplier of financial services reserves the right to alter the rate of interest payable by the consumer or due to the latter, or the amount of other charges for financial services without notice, where there is a valid reason, provided that the supplier is required to inform the other contracting party at the earliest opportunity and the latter is free to dissolve the contract immediately. It is also without hindrance to a term under which a seller or supplier reserves the right to alter unilaterally the condition of a contract of indeterminate duration, provided that he is required to inform the consumer with reasonable notice and that the consumer is free to dissolve the contract.[2]

In *Paragon Finance plc v Staunton and Nash*[3] the Court of Appeal stated that there was an implied term that a rate of interest described as being variable would not be set dishonestly, for an improper purpose, capriciously or arbitrarily.

The power to vary the rate of charge must be distinguished from provisions whereby consumers are locked into contract terms which may themselves constitute unfair contract terms. The Office of Fair Trading has issued guidance on interest variation terms.[4] This sets out, as examples of unfair interest variation terms, unrestricted interest variation terms in mortgage and savings products where consumers are locked in by a requirement to pay an early payment charge on a mortgage or suffer a loss of interest or a charge where consumers give insufficient notice of withdrawal of money from a savings account.

1 Unfair Terms in Consumer Contracts Regulations 1999, Sch 2, para 1(j).
2 Unfair Terms in Consumer Contracts Regulations 1999, Sch 2, para 2(b).
3 [2001] EWCA Cir 1466, [2001] 2 All ER (Comm) 1025, CA.
4 Unfair Contract Terms Guidance: Interest Variation Terms (February 2000).

8.7   SET OFF

It was common practice to exclude the customer's right of counterclaim and set off in relation to payments due by the customer to the creditor or owner in regulated agreements. This right has now been curtailed in relation to consumer contracts by the Unfair Terms in Consumer Contracts Regulations 1999. They deem a term to be unfair which has the object or effect of inappropriately excluding or limiting the legal rights of the consumer vis-à-vis seller or supplier in the event of total or partial non-performance or inadequate performance by the seller or supplier of any of the contractual obligations, including the option of offsetting a debt owed to the seller or supplier against any claim which the consumer may have against him.[1] It is also an unfair term to exclude or hinder the consumer's right to take legal action or exercise any other legal remedy.[2] A consumer contract may, however, legitimately provide for set off by the creditor of any sum standing to the borrower's credit in a savings account with the creditor against any undisputed sum owing by the borrower to the creditor. In other words, offsetting is permissible to the extent that the customer is not in dispute with the other party to the contract.

1 Unfair Terms in Consumer Contracts Regulations 1999, Sch 2, para 1(b).
2 Unfair Terms in Consumer Contracts Regulations 1999, Sch 2, para 1(q).

8.8   CONSOLIDATION

A provision, commonly known as a consolidation clause, entitles the creditor or owner under an agreement with his customer to terminate all other agreements with that customer in the event of his breach. It gives rise to practical problems in relation to regulated agreements. First, a consolidation clause which appears first in one agreement cannot be imported as a term into an earlier agreement except by way of variation or modification of the earlier agreement. Second, in a regulated agreement a default notice is required before a party is entitled to exercise his rights arising from the default, so that a default notice would have to be served in respect of each agreement, giving the customer an opportunity to remedy the breach, before a consolidation clause could effectively be invoked. Third, CCA 1974 itself contains provisions regulating the appropriation of payments by the customer.[1] Finally, the right of consolidation is open to the same objections as the right of set off, as discussed at para 8.7, by virtue of the Unfair Terms in Consumer Contracts Regulations 1999.

1 CCA 1974, s 81.

8.9 'ENTIRE AGREEMENT' CLAUSE

It was common practice to insert an 'entire agreement clause' in consumer agreements, stating that the agreement contained all the terms agreed between the parties relating to its subject matter. The inclusion of such a clause in consumer contracts has been challenged by the Office of Fair Trading as constituting an unfair contract term particularly as it limits the seller's or supplier's obligation to respect commitments undertaken by his agents.[1] The Office of Fair Trading is especially concerned with the attempted exclusion of representations which may have been made by the dealer or the dealer's representatives to the conclusion of a contract.

However, there is a good reason for consumer credit and consumer hire agreements to state that the agreement contains all its terms for not only does it put the consumer on notice that this is the basis upon which the contract is entered into, but it accords with the rationale of the Consumer Credit Act which states that a regulated agreement is not properly executed unless the document embodies all the terms of the agreement, other than implied terms.[2] If the agreement had to be read with any additional written or oral terms or representations, it would by definition not have been properly executed. Moreover, the Unfair Terms in Consumer Contracts Regulations stipulate that they do not apply to contractual terms which reflect mandatory statutory or regulatory provisions.[3]

It is suggested that the correct approach is to assume that the regulated agreement does contain all its terms, that a clause in the agreement to such effect is not prima facie an unfair term but that it would be advisable to draw the customer's attention to the provision on the face of the agreement. If representations were made in connection with entry into the agreement it would be more appropriate to challenge the agreement on the grounds that it did not contain all its terms.

1 Unfair Terms in Consumer Contracts Regulations 1999, Sch 2, para 1(n).
2 CCA 1974, s 61(1)(b).
3 Unfair Terms in Consumer Contracts Regulations 1999, reg 4(2)(a).

8.10 ASSIGNABILITY

Regulated agreements will generally prohibit the customer assigning the agreement or his rights or duties under the agreement. On the other hand, the creditor or owner will usually assert his right to assign the benefit of the agreement and the right to transfer his obligations under the agreement. By concluding an agreement on these terms, the customer is deemed to have given his consent to the assignment.

The right of assignment is subject to the Unfair Terms in Consumer Contracts Regulations as a term is regarded as unfair which has the effect or object of giving the seller or supplier the possibility of transferring his rights and obligations under the contract, where this may serve to reduce the guarantees for the consumer, without the latter's agreement.[1] In other words, in the absence of the customer's consent to a transfer assignment, the customer's rights under the agreement must at least be ensured. For example, if a leading clearing bank were to have the right to assign variable rate agreements to a sub-prime lender which might exercise its right to vary the interest rate under the agreement to an almost extortionate rate, the customer would be unduly prejudiced. For this reason, the right of assignment or transfer needs to be qualified, possibly by a direct reference to the wording of the regulation, eg provided that the assignment does not reduce the guarantees for the consumer, without the latter's agreement. In passing, it might also be noted that the relevant paragraph of the regulations makes reference to the right of the seller or supplier to transfer not only his rights, but also his obligations under the contract.

1 Unfair Terms in Consumer Contracts Regulations 1999, Sch 2, para 1(p).

Chapter 9

Rights of the debtor and hirer during the lifetime of the agreement

This Chapter outlines the rights of a debtor or hirer to documents and information during the course of an agreement. Chapter 10, by contrast, addresses the obligations of a creditor or owner to keep the customer informed of the state of his agreement by the issue of notices and statements of account.

9.1 ENTITLEMENT TO COPIES OF THE AGREEMENT AND TO DOCUMENTS

A debtor or hirer under a regulated agreement is entitled to receive at least one copy of the agreement. In the ordinary case, where the debtor or hirer signs first and the creditor or owner second, two copies of the agreement must be supplied to the customer. One copy, of the unexecuted agreement, is supplied with the original agreement which the customer is to sign and a second copy, of the executed agreement, signed by both parties, must be given to the debtor or hirer within seven days following the making of the agreement.[1] 'Give' means deliver or send by an appropriate method. 'Appropriate method' means post or transmission in the form of an electronic communication in accordance with s 176A(1).[2]

As a general rule the copy agreement must also be accompanied by a copy of any document referred to in the agreement.[3] There are exceptions to this rule and the following need not be supplied: a document obtained by the customer from a third party and supplied to the creditor or owner (e.g. an insurance policy); a copy of a mail order catalogue where the agreement complies with the description specified in the Schedule to the Consumer Credit (Notice of Cancellation Rights) (Exemption) Regulations 1983; a document, not being a security, which relates to title to property or to the rights or duties of the debtor or hirer in respect of such property (e.g. a title deed or a lease); a document to be kept by the customer under the terms of, or in consequence of, the agreement (e.g. premium receipts, life policy, vehicle registration documents). The latter could not be used as a device to overcome a statutory requirement, e.g. a subsequent fresh regulated agreement which refers to the earlier agreement, requires the earlier agreement to be copied, notwithstanding a term in the earlier agreement to the effect that the customer must retain it. Other copies of documents that need not be supplied are the following:

(a)   a copy of an entry in a register contained by or on behalf of a government department or other body charged with a public administrative or statutory function and open to public inspection (e.g. birth, marriage and death certificates, charge certificates and an extract from the Land Register);

(b)   an enactment (subject to a limited exception); a document, other than an enactment, published by or on behalf of a government department or other body charged with a public administrative or statutory function; in the case of a modifying agreement, a document embodying the terms of the earlier agreement (subject to various exceptions);

(c)   in the case of an unexecuted agreement, where the agreement is to be or is secured on land, any document referred to in the agreement where the debtor or hirer has earlier been supplied with a copy of that document in an identical form by virtue of any requirement of the CCA 1974. This dispensation only applies where the document was supplied pursuant to a requirement of the CCA 1974 and therefore excludes a situation, for example, where the document was supplied under an earlier agreement. Thus, where an advance copy of an agreement secured on land is supplied with a mortgage, a mortgage deed in an identical form need not be copied again with the signature copy of the agreement. However, if the customer enters into a subsequent loan agreement secured by the original all-monies mortgage, the mortgage deed must again be copied with the second loan agreement.[4]

Where the creditor or owner signs first and the debtor or hirer signs second, so that an executed agreement comes into being upon the customer's signature, there is an obligation to supply only one copy of the agreement, namely a copy of the executed agreement and not also of the unexecuted agreement. Professor Goode extends this to the situation where both parties sign on the same occasion, notwithstanding that the customer signs first and the creditor or owner signs second, giving a wider interpretation to the words 'on the *occasion* of his [the customer] signing it [the document] became an executed agreement'.[5] A copy of the unexecuted agreement is also not required where the agreement is neither presented personally nor sent to the customer for signature. An example of such a case is where the customer takes a leaflet form containing a regulated agreement, usually a credit-token agreement, from a leaflet dispenser in a store, colloquially known as a 'take-one'.[6] Where a second copy is not required, in the case of a cancellable agreement, the creditor or owner must send a separate notice of cancellation rights to the customer within seven days of the making of the agreement.[7] The notice must be sent either by post or by transmission in the form of an electronic communication in accordance with s 176A(1).[8]

In the case of a credit-token agreement, the second copy may be sent by post or by electronic communication even after the seven-day period has expired if it is sent together with the credit-token.[9] The notice of cancellation rights may likewise be sent by post or electronic communication before or with the credit-token.[10]

1 CCA 1974, s 62.
2 Section 64(1) read with s 189(1).
3 CCA 1974, s 62.
4 Consumer Credit (Cancellation Notices and Copies of Documents) Regulations 1983, SI 1983/1557, reg 11.
5 CCA 1974, s 63(2)(b) and *Goode: Consumer Credit Law and Practice*, para IC [30.62].
6 CCA 1974, s 63(1) and (2).
7 CCA 1974, s 64(1).
8 Section 64(1) read with s 189(1).
9 CCA 1974, s 63(4).
10 CCA 1974, s 64(2).

9.2 RIGHT TO CANCEL THE AGREEMENT

In the case of a cancellable agreement, the original and each copy of the agreement must include a notice of the customer's cancellation rights and, where a second copy of the agreement is not required, a separate notice of cancellation rights must still be provided.[1] In each case, the second copy of the agreement or the notice must be sent to the customer by post or by transmission in the form of an elecronic communication (i.e. by email).[2] The latter applies if:

(a) the person to whom it is transmitted agrees that it may be delivered to him by being transmitted to a particular electronic address in an electronic form;

(b) it is transmitted to that address in that form, and the form in which the document is transmitted is such that any information in the document is capable of being stored for future reference for an appropriate period in a way which allows the information to be reproduced without charge.[3]

If the customer wishes to cancel the agreement he may do so by completing and forwarding the statutory cancellation form within the so-called 'cooling-off' period ending five days after receipt of the second copy of the agreement or of the notice, as appropriate.[4] A notice in any other form indicating the customer's intention to cancel the agreement will also operate as a cancellation notice.

A notice of cancellation sent by post is deemed to be served at the time of posting and if sent by email at the time of transmission and otherwise on the working day immediately following the day of transmission.[5]

Cancellation will have the effect of cancelling the agreement and any linked transaction and of withdrawing any offer by the customer to enter into a linked transaction.[6] Effectively the transaction is undone, void ab initio, and each party must reimburse the other for any sums paid under or in contemplation of the transaction and return any goods given in part-exchange or make a payment in lieu of the same.[7]

If, under the cancelled agreement, the customer is in possession of any goods, he has a lien on those goods until any payment due to him by the trader has been made.

In the case of a debtor-creditor-supplier agreement for restricted-use credit which is used to finance the doing of work or the supply of goods to meet an emergency or for the supply of goods which, before the cancellation became effective, had become incorporated or affixed to any land or things not comprised in the agreement, the customer is liable for payment of only the cash price of the goods. So, for example, where a trader installs kitchen equipment with the customer's consent (provided the equipment constitutes goods within the meaning of the Sale of Goods Act 1979, s 61(1)), the customer will only be liable for payment of the cash price and not for any credit charge, if he cancels the agreement within the prescribed time. It is therefore prudent for traders to wait for the cancellation or cooling-off period to expire before supplying goods or services under a cancellable agreement.[8]

The cancellation period is extended where the agreement is a distance contract under the Financial Services (Distance Marketing) Regulations 2004.[9] The cancellation period is 14 calendar days beginning with the day after the distance contract is concluded.[10] A contract is concluded when the offeror is made aware of the offeree's acceptance. In the case of a distance contract relating to life insurance or a personal pension, the cancellation period is 30 calendar days in place of 14 calendar days.[11]

Cancellation rights analogous to those under the Act are contained in the Consumer Protection (Cancellation of Contracts Concluded Away from Business Premises) Regulations 1987, dealing with cold-call or doorstep selling of goods and services, and in the Timeshare Act 1992. They contain similar provisions to those under the CCA 1974 and expressly provide that they do not apply where the Act applies to the agreement in question.

1   CCA 1974, s 64.
2   CCA 1974, ss 63(3), 64(1)(b), 189(1) and 176A(1).
3   Section 176A(1).
4   CCA 1974, s 68.
5   Section 69(7)(b).
6   Subject to the Consumer Credit (Linked Transactions) (Exemptions) Regulations 1983, SI 1983/1560. See also *Goshawk Dedicated (No 2) Ltd v Governor and Company of Bank of Scotland* [2005] GCCR 5431.
7   CCA 1974, s 69(1) and (4); *Colesworthy v Collman Services* [1993] CCLR 4.
8   CCA 1974, s 69(2).
9   SI 2004/2095.
10   *Ibid.*, reg 10(1) and (2).
11   *Ibid.*, reg 10(5).

9.3   WITHDRAWAL RIGHTS

Withdrawal rights are cancellation rights in reverse, namely a customer's right to withdraw from an agreement before entering into it. They are provided in respect of agreements secured on land. The customer is given a so-called 'consideration period' in which to decide whether or not he wishes to proceed with the agreement. The consideration period begins with the furnishing of the advance copy of the agreement and ends at the expiry of seven days after the day on which the unexecuted agreement is sent to him for signature, or on its return by the customer after signature by him, if earlier.[1]

1   CCA 1974, s 58.

9.4 ENTITLEMENT TO INFORMATION

The debtor, hirer and surety are each entitled, on written request and payment of a nominal fee, to copies of the executed agreement and of each document referred to in the agreement and to a signed statement by the creditor setting out prescribed financial information regarding the state of repayment of the agreement. The creditor or owner must comply with any such request within the prescribed period of 12 working days. If a creditor or owner defaults, he is not entitled to enforce the agreement whilst the default continues.[1]

Subject to the court's power to grant relief under CCA 1974, s 172, a statement by a creditor or owner of information to a debtor or hirer under ss 77(1), 78(1) or 79(1), to a debtor for a figure for early settlement under s 97(1) or of information to sureties under ss 107(1), 108(1) or 109(1) is binding on the creditor or owner.

1 See CCA 1974 sections below, read with Consumer Credit (Prescribed Periods for Giving Information) Regulations 1983, SI 1983/1569:
77(1) – Duty to give information to debtor under fixed-sum credit agreement.
78(1) – Duty to give information to debtor under running-account credit agreement.
79(1) – Duty to give information to hirer under consumer hire agreement.
103(1) – Duty to give information to debtor or hirer a regulation termination statement or serve counter-notice.
107(1) – Duty to give information to surety under fixed-sum agreement.
108(1) – Duty to give information to surety under running-account credit agreement.
109(1) – Duty to give information to surety under consumer hire agreement.
110(1) – Duty to give debtor or hirer copy of any security instrument executed in relation to agreement after making of agreement.

9.5 EARLY SETTLEMENT

A debtor under a regulated credit agreement is entitled to complete repayments ahead of time whenever he wishes to do so. This is achieved by the debtor establishing from the creditor the amount required to settle the account and forwarding payment to him. The debtor is not required to give the creditor any advance period of notice. The notice may also incorporate other information such as the exercise of the option to purchase goods under a hire-purchase agreement or deal with any other matter arising on, or in relation to termination of the agreement e.g. cancellation of an insurance policy.[1]

On the debtor's request, the creditor must furnish a settlement statement within seven working days, setting out prescribed information.[2]

To counter-balance the effect of the rebate which the creditor is obliged to give the debtor, and particularly to compensate the creditor for initial setting-up costs, the creditor is entitled notionally to postpone the settlement date for purposes of the rebate calculation to the date of expiry on 28 days following the day on which the creditor received a request in writing for a statement from the debtor. The right to postpone only arises if the debtor's request was in writing.[3] The settlement date may be further postponed for purposes of calculating the rebate.[4]

A debtor or hirer ('the customer') may serve on the creditor or owner ('the trader') a termination notice stating that the customer has discharged his indebtedness to the trader and that the agreement has ended, and requiring the trader to provide, within the prescribed period of 12 working days, a notice confirming that those statements are correct or a counter-notice setting out the particulars in request of which the termination notice is alleged to be wrong. The counter-notice will be binding on the trader even if erroneous, unless a court is prepared to grant relief.[5]

1 CCA 1974, s 94.
2 See para 9.6.4. below.
3 Consumer Credit (Settlement Information) Regulations 1983, SI 1983/1564, reg 3.
4 See para 9.6.2 below.
5 CCA 1974 s 172 and see *Lomard North Central plc v Stobart* [1990] CCLR 53, CA.

9.6   REBATE ON EARLY SETTLEMENT

9.6.1   Entitlement to a rebate

Upon early settlement of a credit agreement, the debtor has a statutory entitlement to a rebate on the amount of charges attributable to the period after the settlement date. The rebate applies to a fixed-sum, (but not running-account), credit agreement, which is discharged wholly or becomes payable in full (including as a result of any default) before the time fixed by the agreement where the agreement includes charges payable in respect of the period after the settlement date. It applies irrespective of whether the agreement is settled in full voluntarily by the debtor, the credit under the agreement is refinanced or the outstanding balance is repaid following a breach of the agreement. Where the debtor settles the agreement voluntarily, he must give written notice of early settlement, but no period is prescribed and the notice may accompany the payment.[1]

There is no entitlement to a rebate when the debtor terminates a hire-purchase agreement or conditional sale agreement under s 99 of CCA 1974 as in that case the debtor's liability is limited by s 100 of the Act.[2]

1 CCA 1974, s 95 and Consumer Credit (Early Settlement) Regulations 2004, SI 2004/1483.
2 *Ibid.*, reg 2(3).

9.6.2   Calculation of the rebate

The rebate is calculated on the charges element only, and not the credit amount, and specifically on the charges which would have arisen after the settlement date under the agreement but for its early settlement.

For the purposes of calculating the rebate, the settlement date may be postponed by one month or 30 days where the credit is repayable over a period of more than one year from the agreement date.[1]

The rebate is calculated in accordance with the formula set out in Consumer Credit (Early Settlement) Regulations.[2] The statutory rebate is the minimum rebate the creditor is required to grant the debtor, the creditor being free to offer the debtor a greater rebate.

In *Forward Trust v Whymark*[3] the court held that a creditor was entitled to claim the unrebated payment due by the debtor, as the debtor's entitlement to a rebate arises only upon actual discharge of the indebtedness and not when the demand for payment is made.

1 Consumer Credit (Early Settlement) Regulations 2004, SI 2004/1483, reg 6.
2 *Ibid.*, reg 4.
3 [1989] 3 All ER 915, CA.

9.6.3 Exclusions from the rebate calculation

Certain items may be excluded from the rebate calculation. They include taxes, duties etc., sums paid under linked transactions before the settlement date and sums payable under linked transactions for insurance contracts, for guarantees of goods or for the operation of current or deposit accounts and any fee or commission payable under a credit brokerage contract. In other words, all the foregoing charges are not subject to a rebate in the event of early settlement.[1]

1 Consumer Credit (Early Settlement) Regulations 2004, SI 2001/1483, reg 3.

9.6.4 Statement of rebate

The settlement statement provided by the creditor to the debtor must set out, inter alia, details of the agreement, parties to the agreement, the amount of payment required to be made before taking into account any rebate, the amount of any rebate on early settlement or a statement that the debtor is not entitled to a rebate, the rebated settlement amount, the settlement date and the statement explaining how the rebate has been calculated.[1]

1 CCA 1974, s 97 and the Consumer Credit (Settlement Information) Regulations 1983, SI 1983/1564, reg 2 and Schedule. See also *Home Insulation v Wadsley* [1988] CCLR 25.

9.6.5 Hire agreements

Although, as already noted, in certain instances a hirer may terminate a hire agreement once it has run for 18 months, there is otherwise no statutory entitlement to early termination or to a rebate on the termination sum payable in the event of early settlement. However, at common law and under the rules of equity, there are limitations. Thus, whilst it is open to the parties to stipulate in the contract a sum to be paid as liquidated damages in the event of a breach, the sum so fixed as at the date of the contract must be a reasonable pre-estimate of the loss or damages likely to result from the breach. It may not constitute a penalty, such as a sum which is intended to deter the hirer from terminating the agreement or to give the owner an additional windfall in the event of breach.[1]

1 See, for example, *Bridge v Campbell Discount Co Ltd* [1962] 1 All ER 385.

9.7 PROTECTED GOODS

Once a debtor under a regulated hire-purchase or a regulated conditional sale agreement has paid the creditor one-third or more of the total cost of the goods and ownership of the goods remains in the creditor, the creditor may not recover possession of the goods from the debtor without an order of the court.[1] The goods falling within this section are referred to as 'protected goods'. Where the agreement also provides for an amount to be paid in respect of the installation of goods, reference to one-third of the total price is construed as a reference to the aggregate of the installation charge plus one-third of the remainder of the total price of the goods.[2]

There is an important provision to the effect that once goods have become protected goods and are comprised, whether alone or with other goods, in a later agreement or a modifying agreement, they remain protected goods and also 'infect' the remaining goods under the new or modifying agreement so that all the goods become protected goods.[3] This is important in relation to add-on agreements.

'Payment' includes tender,[4] and payment pursuant to a judgment. However, both payment and tender mean payment and tender of the full amount which is due so that if the debtor merely offers to pay sufficient to make up one-third of the total purchase price of the goods at a time when a greater amount is owing, e.g. a larger instalment or the full outstanding balance, the creditor is entitled to reject such payment or tender, with the result that the goods do not become protected goods and can be recovered without an order of the court.[5]

If the creditor or owner breaches the foregoing provisions by recovering protected goods without obtaining a court order, the regulated agreement, if not previously terminated, terminates automatically and the debtor is released from all liability under the agreement and is entitled to recover from the creditor all sums paid under the agreement.[6] Sums payable under the agreement include sums paid by way of deposit or part-exchange allowance.[7]

It has been suggested that goods are not protected goods even though one-third or more of the total price may have been paid, unless the debtor is in breach of the agreement.[8] This cannot be the case as it would be absurd to suggest that a debtor who had paid more than one-third and was not in breach is in a worse position than a debtor who had defaulted under his agreement. The reference in CCA 1974, s 90 to the debtor being in breach is simply a statement of the circumstances in which a creditor would normally be impelled to recover possession of his goods as, in the absence of default by the debtor, the creditor would have no reason to do so. Section 90 also appears in that part of the Act which deals with default and termination and the heading to s 90 and the following sections is 'Further Restriction of Remedies for Default'.

In appropriate citcumstances a court may grant equitable relief against forfeiture of insalments upon a customer's breach of an agreement when the sum forfeited was out of all proportion to the damage suffered and when it would be unconscionable for the creditor or owner to retain the money. In exercising its discretion a court will take into account the following factors:

(a) whether or not the debtor or hirer is in default under the agreement;

(b) whether significant prejudice would be caused to the creditor or owner by the grant of the relief; and

(c) whether the refusal of relief would give the creditor or owner a subsantial windfall profit or cause the debtor or hirer a disproportionate loss.[9]

1 CCA 1974, s 90(1).
2 CCA 1974, s 90(2).
3 CCA 1974, s 90(3) and (4).
4 CCA 1974, s 189(1).
5 See Treitel, *The Law of Contract* (10th edn, 1999), p 698 and *Dixon v Clarke* (1848) 5 CB 365; *Read's Trustee in Bankruptcy v Smith* [1951] Ch 439, [1951] 1 All ER 406.
6 CCA 1974, s 91.
7 *Branwhite v Worcester Works Finance Ltd* [1969] 1 AC 552, [1999] GCCR 397, HL.
8 *Chitty on Contracts* vol 2 (29th edn, Sweet & Maxwell, 2004) at 38–308.
9 *Ibid.*, 38–308 and see *Barton, Thompson & Co Ltd v Stapling Machines Co* [1966] 2 All ER 222 and *Transag Haulage Ltd v Leyland DAF Finance plc and Lease Plan UK Ltd* [1999] GCCR 1819.

9.8 APPROPRIATION OF PAYMENTS

At common law a debtor or hirer who has several agreements with a creditor or owner may appropriate payments made by him in such order and manner as he deems fit. The CCA 1974 preserves such right.[1] If the debtor or hirer does not appropriate his payments to different agreements, there are statutory restrictions on the rights of appropriation by the creditor or owner in the case of a hire-purchase or conditional sale agreement, consumer hire agreement or agreement in respect of which any security is provided. In these instances the payments must be appropriated towards satisfation of the sums due under the various agreements in the proportions which those sums bear to one another.[2]

1 CCA 1974, s 81(1).
2 CCA 1974, s 81(2).

9.9 TIME ORDERS

A debtor or hirer is given various opportunities to apply to a court for a time order. A time order may provide for payment by the debtor, hirer or any surety of any sum owed under a regulated agreement or a security, by such instalments and at such times as the court considers reasonable, having regard to the means of the debtor, hirer or surety. It may also provide for remedy by the debtor or hirer of any breach of a regulated agreement (other than for non-payment) within such period as the court may specify.[1]

A time order may be applied for, either in response to an application or action by a creditor or owner for an enforcement order or an order to recover possession of goods or land, or at the instance of the debtor or hirer, including after his receipt of an arrears notice.[2]

1 CCA 1974, s 129(2).
2 Section 129(1).

9.10   CONTRACTING OUT

In the context of a customer's rights, a term is void if it is inconsistent with a provision for the protection of the debtor or hirer, his relative or any surety. This will extend also to a waiver by a debtor or hirer of any protection afforded to him by the regulatory regime.[1]

1 CCA 1974, s 173.

Chapter 10

Post-contract information

10.1 BACKGROUND

Whilst CCA 1974 originally made provision for the furnishing of statements in relation to running-account credit agreements, government was of the view that there was a lack of ongoing information provided to debtors under a consumer credit agreement. As the perspective was one from the angle of the escalation of debt, it is perhaps not surprising that more emphasis was placed upon a lack of consumer information to debtors rather than to hirers under regulated agreements although it applies equally to debtors and hirers. To quote from the White Paper:[1]

> 'A contributory fact identified in relation to the escalation of debt, has been the lack of ongoing information that many borrowers receive concerning their credit agreement. This is a particular concern to consumers who fall into arrears, as they are often unaware of the consequences of charges on their account, default costs for missed payments, compound interest on the amount owed or underpayment on the accumulation of their debt. At present, although the CCA contains some duties on the lender to provide information, these are generally only triggered by a request from the consumer. There is no obligation on the lender to provide regular statements or, crucially, to inform consumers when payments have been missed.'

In consequence, CCA 2006 introduced various new post contract information requirements, as follows:

(a)   annual statements to be provided in relation to fixed-sum credit agreements but not in respect of hire agreements;

(b)   additional provisions to be contained in statements relating to running-account credit agreements;

(c)   notice of sums in arrears under fixed-sum credit agreements and hire agreements;

(d)   notice of default sums;

(e)   notice of interest payable on judgment debts; and

(f)   information sheets on arrears and defaults, prepared by the Office of Fair Trading, to accompany notices of arrears and notices of default respectively.

1 White Paper: Fair, Clear and Competitive: The Consumer Credit Market in the 21st Century (Cm 6040 December 2003).

10.2   ANNUAL STATEMENTS OF ACCOUNT UNDER FIXED-SUM CREDIT AGREEMENTS

This is a new requirement introduced by s 6 of CCA 2006 (s 77A of CCA 1974). The statutory requirement is that the creditor under a regulated agreement for fixed-sum credit must, within the period of one year beginning with the day after the day on which the agreement is made, give the debtor a statement of account and thereafter a statement of account at intervals of not more than one year. A creditor who fails to comply with this obligation is not entitled to enforce the agreement during the period of non-compliance, and the debtor has no liability to pay any sum of interest or any default sum during the period of non-compliance.

The Consumer Credit (Information Requirements and Duration of Licences and Charges) Regulations 2007[1] stipulate that the first statement must relate to a period beginning with the date of the making of the agreement and ending on a date not more than 30 days before the date the statement is given. Any subsequent statement must relate to a period beginning on the day immediately after the end of the period to which the preceding statement related and end on a date not more than 30 days before the date the subsequent statement is given.[2] The regulations therefore create the potential awkward effect of annual statements having to relate to successive periods of one year less a day (i.e. a one-day receding annual period).

As 'give' is defined in the Act to mean 'deliver or send by an appropriate method'[3] ('appropriate method' means post or transmission in the form of an electronic communication[4]) it is only necessary for the statement to be posted, and not received, by the relevant date.

As regards fixed-sum credit agreements entered into before the coming into force of the requirement for annual statements, the period of one year in respect of such agreements commences on the date CCA 2006, s 6 comes into force, namely 1 October 2008.[5]

The prescribed contents of the statement are set out in Parts 1 and 2 of Schedule 1 to the Regulations[6] and include the period to which the statement relates, details of the creditor, information specific to the agreement and specified statutory forms of wording under the following headings:

(a)   'Settling your credit Agreement early'

(b)   'Dispute resolution'

(c)   'Paying less than the agreed sum'

and where the statement relates to a hire-purchase or conditional sale agreement, a statutory form of wording under the heading shown as: 'Termination: Your rights'.[7]

Where the fixed-sum credit agreement relates to a home credit loan agreement, it must include certain additional information and statutory statement.[8]

The duty to provide annual statements applies equally to agreements entered into before the relevant regulations came into force, i.e. before 1 October 2008, and in that the case the first statement must be provided within one year beginning with that date. Provision is made for certain information to be omitted from the statement relating to agreements entered into before such date.[9]

Statements must be in plain, intelligible language and certain specified forms of wording are required to appear together as a whole and not interspersed with any other information or wording. The wording must be easily legible and of a colour which is readily distinguishable from the background medium upon which it is displayed.[10] There are prescribed rules regarding prominence of the information and wording.[11]

1 SI 2007/1167, as amended.
2 *Ibid.*, reg 11.
3 Section 189(1).
4 CCA 2006, Sch 3, para 2(2).
5 *Ibid.*
6 Reg 4, Sch 1, Parts 1 and 2.
7 *Ibid.*, Part 3.
8 *Ibid.*, reg 12.
9 *Ibid.*, regs 46 to 50 and CCA 2006, Sch 3, para 2.
10 *Ibid.*, regs 36 to 38.
11 *Ibid.*, reg 40.

10.3 STATEMENTS OF ACCOUNT UNDER RUNNING-ACCOUNT CREDIT AGREEMENTS

At the outset CCA 1974 obligated creditors under running-account credit agreements to furnish regular statements of account.[1] The contents of statements under running-account credit agreements is prescribed by the Consumer Credit (Running-Account Credit Information) Regulations 1983 and the schedule to those regulations.[2] These requirements have been supplemented by those under the Consumer Credit (Information Requirements and Duration of Licences and Charges) Regulations 2007.[3]

The statement of account must also contain the prescribed form of wording relating to the order or proportions in which any amount paid by the debtor which is insufficient to discharge the total debt then due, will be applied by the creditor towards the discharge of the sums due in respect of amounts of credit provided for different purposes or different parts of the agreement. This corresponds to a similar requirement in the Agreements Regulations.

There is additional statutory wording which must be included in statements under running-account credit agreements as prescribed by the above regulations.[4]

Depending upon the circumstances, the specified statutory forms of wording relate to the following:[5]

(a)   'Minimum payments'

(b)   'You have failed to make a minimum payment'

(c)   'Dispute resolution'.

Statutory periods are laid down for the sending of statements of account. Where the statement includes a demand for payment, the statement must be sent within one month from the end of the period to which the statement relates. Where the statement does not include a demand for payment and there is a nil balance throughout the period to which the statement relates or at the end of the period to which the statement relates, a 12-monthly statement must be sent. Where it does not include a demand for payment and there is a debit or credit balance on the account at the end of the period, the statement must be sent within six months of the end of the period to which the statement relates.[6] Whilst failure to comply is not an offence, repeated non-compliance by a creditor is conduct which may be taken into account by the Office of Fair Trading in relation to the fitness of the creditor to continue to be licensed under the Act.[7] Periodic statements are not binding on the creditor[8] although estoppel may apply.[9]

The rules regarding the form and formalities set out in the final paragraph under 10.2 above apply equally to statements under running-account credit agreements.

1   CCA 1974, s 78(4).
2   Consumer Credit (Running-Account Credit Information) Regulations 1983, SI 1983/1570, reg 2.
3   SI 2007/1167, regs 13 to 18 read with Sch 2.
4   SI 2007/1167, regs 13 to 18.
5   *Ibid.*, Sch 2.
6   Consumer Credit (Running-Account Credit Information) Regulations 1983, SI 1983/1570, reg 3.
7   CCA 1974, ss 25(2) and 170(2).
8   CCA 1974, ss 170 and 172.
9   See *United Overseas Bank v Jiwani* [1977] 1 All ER 733.

10.4   NOTICE OF SUMS IN ARREARS

Notice of sums in arrears is an innovation introduced by CCA 2006.[1] It applies to fixed-sum credit agreements, running-account credit agreements and hire agreements. Fixed-sum credit agreements include hire-purchase agreements and conditional sale agreements.

Under fixed-sum credit agreements or hire agreements the creditor or owner respectively must, within 14 days when two contractual payments are in arrears, and thereafter at six monthly intervals whilst the account is in arrears, send the debtor or hirer respectively a notice of arrears. Where the payment is due at weekly or shorter intervals, the trigger is four rather than two contractual payments in arrears. The obligation to issue the arrears notice only applies if the shortfall is no less than the sum of the last two payments which the debtor or hirer is required to have made. The obligation ceases once the debtor or hirer is no longer in arrears or a judgment is given in relation to the agreement requiring a payment to be made by the debtor or hirer.[2]

In the case of running-account credit agreements, the creditor is obliged to issue an arrears notice within 14 days when two contractual payments have been missed and the last two payments have not been made. The obligation continues even after the grant of a judgment, whilst there is still a sum to be paid under the judgment.

If the creditor or owner fails to issue an arrears notice when required, he is not entitled to enforce the agreement during the period of non-compliance and the debtor or hirer does not incur any liability to pay any sum of interest or default sum during the period of non-compliance.[3]

As regards agreements entered into before the statutory requirement for notices of arrears, the start date for determining any arrears is the coming into force of CCA 2006, s 9. In other words the relevant arrears are those arising after 1 October 2008, the relevant date for the commencement of CCA 2006, s 9.[4]

The contents of the notice of sums in arrears are prescribed by the Consumer Credit (Information Requirements and Duration of Licences and Charges) Regulations 2007.[5] The notice must contain the information set out in the Regulations, which includes the following:

(a) a form of wording to the effect that the notice is given in compliance with the 1974 Act because the debtor or hirer is behind with his payments under the agreement;

(b) a form of wording encouraging the debtor or hirer to discuss the state of his account with the creditor or owner;

(c) the information specified in the relevant Regulations read with Schedule 3;

(d) in the case of an arrears notice under a fixed-sum credit agreement or hire agreement, the amount of the shortfall under the agreement which gave rise to the duty to give the notice. This information appears to apply only to the first arrears notice. On receipt of a request for further information about the shortfall, the creditor or owner must give the debtor or hirer in relation to each of the sums comprising the shortfall, notice of the amount of the sums, the date on which they became due and the amounts paid by the debtor or hirer;[6]

(e) in arrears notices under fixed-sum credit and hire agreements, other than the first arrears notice, additional prescribed information must be set out.[7]

The information to be included in notice of sums in arrears under running-account credit agreements is set out in the relevant Regulations.[8] The notice of arrears relating to a running-account credit agreement but inexplicably not that relating to a fixed-sum credit agreement or a hire agreement, may be incorporated in a statement or other notice which the creditor gives the debtor in relation to the agreement by virtue of any other provision of CCA 1974.[9] In such a case the notice need not contain so much of the information as is required to be included in the other notice or under CCA 1974 under which the notice is given.[10]

Arrears notices must be accompanied by the current information sheet on arrears prepared by the Office of Fair Trading[11] and must include a statutory notice drawing the customer's attention to its inclusion.[12]

As regards agreements entered into before the relevant sections come into force, the obligation to give the first notice does not arise under a fixed-sum credit agreement or hire agreement until at least two payments have fallen due after the section has come into force and the arrears are at least in the sum of the last two (or four, as the case may be) payments that the debtor or hirer has been required to make.[13]

In the case of running-account credit agreements, the obligation in relation to pre-existing agreements does not arise until at least two payments have fallen due after the section has come into force and the last two payments have not been made.[14]

1 Sections 9 to 12, inserting ss 86B, 86C and 86D of CCA 1974 with effect from 1 October 2008, by virtue of SI 2007/1167.
2 CCA 1974, s 86B(4).
3 CCA 1974, s 86D.
4 CCA 2006, Sch 3, paras 6(2) and 7(2).
5 Consumer Credit (Information Requirements and Duration of Licences and Charges) Regulations, SI 2007/1167, regs 19 to 24 read with Sch 3.
6 CCA 1974, s 86B(2)(a) read with reg 19(2)(a) and Sch 3, Part 2 of the above Regulations.
7 CCA 1974, s 86B(2)(b) read with reg 19(3) and Sch 3, Part 3 of the above Regulations.
8 Regulation 24 read with Sch 3 of the above Regulations.
9 CCA 1974, s 86C(4).
10 Regulation 25 of the above Regulations.
11 CCA 1974, s 86B(6) and 86C(3), regs 19(1)(e) and 24(1)(e) and Sch 3, Part 5 of the above Regulations.
12 Regulations 19(1)(e) and 24(1)(e) and Sch 3, Part 5 of the above Regulations.
13 CCA 2006, Sch 3, para 6(1) and (2).
14 CCA 2006, Sch 3, para 7.

10.5 DEFAULT NOTICES

Service of a default notice on the debtor or hirer is necessary before the creditor or owner may, by a reason of breach by the debtor or hirer of regulated agreement, terminate the agreement, demand earlier payment of any sum, recover possession of any goods or land or treat any right conferred on the debtor or hirer by the agreement as terminated, restricted or deferred, or enforce any security.[1]

This does not prevent a creditor from treating the debtor's right to draw upon any credit as restricted or deferred and taking such steps as may be necessary to make the restriction or deferment effective.[2]

The default notice must be in paper form and comply with the relevant regulations.[3] The notice must specify the nature of the alleged breach, if the breach is capable of remedy, what action is required to remedy it and the date before which that action is to be taken; if the breach is not capable of remedy, the sum, if any, required to be paid as compensation for the breach and the date before which it is to be paid.[4] A date specified for the date of remedy must be not less than 14 days after the date of service of the default notice.[5]

The default notice might also set out what action the creditor or owner will take if the debtor or hirer respectively fails to remedy the breach within the pre-scribed period within the prescribed time.[6]

The form and contents of a default notice are set out in the Consumer Credit (Enforcement, Default and Termination Notices) Regulations 1983, as amended.[7] These Regulations were materially amended by the Consumer Credit (Information Requirements and Duration of Licences and Charges) Regulations 2007.[8] Notably, the latter prescribe a statutory notice of the cus-tomer's right under a hire-purchase or conditional sale agreement to end the agreement at any time before the final payment falls due and a warning that this right may be lost if the customer does not act before the date shown. They also require a statement in statutory form where the creditor or owner is entitled to charge post-judgment interest in connection with a judgment sum. The default notice must be accompanied by the current Office of Fair Trading information sheet on default and must include a statutory notice drawing the customer's attention to its inclusion.[9]

The 1983 Regulations and the 2007 Regulations require the lettering in default notices to be easily legible, of a colour which is readily distinguishable from the background medium and prescribe the prominence of wording in the notice.

1 CCA 1974, s 87(1).
2 *Ibid.*, s 87(2).
3 Consumer Credit (Enforcement, Default and Termination Notices) Regulations 1983 SI 1983/1561 and see the Schedules to the Regulations. 'Paper form' is prescribed by reg 2(4A).
4 *Ibid.*, s 88(1).
5 *Ibid.*, s 88(2).
6 *Ibid.*, s 85(5).
7 SI 1983/1561.
8 CCA 1974, s 88(4A) and the Consumer Credit (Information Requirements and Duration of Licences and Charges) Regulations 2007, SI 2007/1167.
9 *Ibid.*, reg 33(3)(c).

10.6 NOTICE OF DEFAULT SUMS

CCA 2006 introduces the new concept of a notice of default sums. A default sum is a sum (other than a sum of interest) which is payable by a debtor or hirer under a regulated agreement in connection with a breach of the agreement by him, but does not include a sum which, as a consequence of the breach of an agreement, is payable earlier than it would otherwise have been.[1] In short, it is a fee or charge payable in respect of the customer's default under the agreement.

The creditor or owner must give the customer notice of the default sum within 35 days of the default sum becoming payable.[2] The content of the notice is set out in the Consumer Credit (Information Requirements and Duration of Licences and Charges) Regulations 2007.[3] The notice must include a copy of the current default information sheet prepared by the Office of Fair Trading.[4]

Significantly, interest on default sums may only be charged at a simple rate even if, as is usually the case, interest on the principal debt is calculated at a com-pound rate of interest.[5] There is no liability to pay interest on the default sum in the period of 29 days following the day on which the debtor or hirer is given notice of the default sum.[6]

The restriction of interest to simple interest also applies to agreements entered into before the section came into force, but only as regards default sums payable after the commencement of CCA 2006, s 13, namely 1 October 2008.[7]

The notice of default sum may be incorporated in a statement or other notice which the creditor or owner gives the debtor or hirer in relation to the agreement by virtue of another provision of CCA 1974.[8] In such a case there is no need to duplicate the information which is required to be included in the other notice by virtue of a provision of CCA 1974.[9]

If the creditor or owner fails to give the notice, he is not entitled to enforce the agreement until the notice of default sum has been given.[10]

In recent times the Office of Fair Trading has taken a strident approach to default charges, commencing with its statement on 'Calculating fair default charges in credit card contracts' in April 2006.[11] The OFT's view is that, in essence, default charge provisions are open to challenge on grounds of unfairness if they have the object of raising more in revenue than is reasonably expected to be necessary to recover certain limited administrative costs incurred by the credit card issuer. It maintained that credit card default fees had been set at a significantly higher level than was fair for the purposes of the Unfair Terms in Consumer Contracts Regulations 1999. In the view of the OFT, a default charge should:

(a)   be calculated on the basis of a reasonable pre-estimate of the net limited additional administrative costs which occur as a result of the specific breaches of contract and can be identified with a reasonable precision;

(b)   reflect a fair attribution of those costs between defaulting consumers;

(c)   be based on a genuine estimate of the total number of expected instances of default in the relevant period; and

(d)   treat costs other than those net of limited administrative additional costs as a general overhead of the credit card business and disregard them for purposes of calculating a default fee.[12]

To help encourage a swift change in market practice, the OFT set a simple monetary threshold for intervention by the OFT on default charges, at £12. The OFT opined that the basic principles enunciated by it in its statement applied also to other analogous default charges in consumer contracts, for example agreements for bank overdrafts, mortgages and store card agreements.

The OFT's statement created a sea-change in the treatment of default charges on the part of creditors, from card issuers in relation to credit card agreements to banks in respect of charges for overdraft facilities and a backlash on the part of credit institutions in their approach to levying charges for services which were previously free or at a low rate of charge, e.g. charges for balance transfers, annual fees for credit cards and the like. It remains to be seen where the pendulum ultimately settles on the clock-face of credit and banking charges.

1   CCA 1974, s 187A.
2   SI 2007/1167, reg 28.

3 SI 2007/1167, regs 29 to 32.
4 CCA 1974, s 88(4A).
5 *Ibid.*, ss 586F(2) and 86E(4).
6 CCA 2006, Sch 3, paras 9(1) and (2).
7 *Ibid.*, s 86E(4).
8 *Ibid.*, s 86E(3).
9 SI 2007/1167, reg 32.
10 CCA 1974, s 86E(5).
11 OFT 842.
12 *Ibid.*, para 3.27.

10.7 NOTICE OF INTEREST ON JUDGMENT DEBTS

CCA 2006 introduced the new requirement that creditors and owners give notice to judgment debtors of interest payable on the judgment amount, following the grant of judgment. This may be interest at the contract rate or interest at the judgment rate. The notice must be given after the obtaining of judgment and subsequently at intervals of not more than six months. No liability to pay post-judgment interest accrues before the day on which the first required notice is given or subsequently in respect of the period in which any required notice has not been given.[1]

The above only applies to judgments made after the commencement of the relevant section, namely CCA 2006, s 17.[2]

The notice may be incorporated in a statement or other notice which the creditor or owner gives to the debtor or hirer in relation to the agreement by virtue of any other provision of the Act.[3]

The requirement to give notice does not apply in relation to post-judgment interest which is required to be paid by virtue of s 74 of the County Courts Act 1984, s 4 of the Administration of Justice (Scotland) Act 1972 or Art. 127 of the Judgments Enforcement (Northern Ireland) Order 1981.[4]

The content of notices of intention to recover post-judgment interest is set out in the Consumer Credit (Information Requirements and Duration of Licences and Charges) Regulations 2007.[5]

1 CCA 1974, s 130A(1) to (3).
2 CCA 2006, Sch 3, para 13.
3 CCA 1974, s 130A(5).
4 CCA 1974, s 130A(7).
5 SI 2007/1167, reg 34 read with Sch 5.

10.8 PROVISIONS APPLICABLE TO VARIOUS NOTICES

10.8.1 'Agreement to aggregate'

This is a new concept, introduced by the Consumer Credit (Information Requirements and Duration of Licences and Charges) Regulations 2007.[1] An agreement to aggregate is defined as an agreement, whether arising by conduct or otherwise, made between the creditor and the debtor:

(a) concerning two or more agreements for fixed-sum credit between the creditor and the debtor where at least one such agreement is a regulated credit agreement; and

(b) which permits or requires the debtor to aggregate all individual payments under the agreements mentioned in paragraph (a) above and pay them at the same time.

It will be noted that the concept does not apply to agreements for running-account credit, nor to hire agreements. Various concessions are made in respect of agreements to aggregate, including in relation to the content of statements[2] and notices of sums in arrears.[3]

1 SI 2007/1167, reg 2.
2 *Ibid.*, regs 7 to 9.
3 *Ibid.*, regs 19(2)(d) to 23.

10.8.2   Formalities

Many of the rules are common to notices and statements. Enforcement, default and termination notices must be in paper form[1] but all other notices and statements may be sent by an 'appropriate method', meaning by post (and hence in a paper form) or by electronic communication, where the recipient agrees to the latter.[2] Notices must set out the prescribed information together as a whole, not interspersed with any other information or wording. They must be easily legible and of a colour which is readily distinguishable from the background medium. Information and wording must be equally prominent except for certain specified wording which may be more prominent than other wording.[3]

1 *Ibid.*, reg 39 and the Consumer Credit (Enforcement, Default and Termination Notices) Regulations 1983, SI 1983/1561, reg 2(4A).
2 CCA 1974, ss 189(1) and 176A.
3 *Ibid.*, regs 36 to 40.

10.8.3   Charges for notices etc.

No charge may be levied for statements or notices.[1] This prohibition does not extend to default notices. Whilst not expressly stipulated in legislation, the charges for the latter must be reasonable and may not exceed the cost incurred by the creditor or owner in producing and administering the same.

1 CCA 1974, s 77A(3) re statements under fixed-sum credit agreements; there is no equivalent provision for statements under running-account credit agreements;
  s 86B(7) and 86C(5) re notice of sums in arrears;
  s 86E(6) re notice of default sums;
  s 130A(4) re notice of judgment interest.

10.8.4   Errors and omissions

Where a notice or statement contains an error or omission which does not affect the substance of the information or forms of wording which it is required to contain, it does not on that ground alone constitute a breach of the relevant regulations.[1] It follows that a breach which does affect the substance, presumably invariably only a material breach, would have the effect of that notice or statement being regarded as not having been given.

In contrast s 172 of CCA 1974 makes certain statements binding on a creditor or owner, namely statements given in response to a debtor, hirer or surety exercising his entitlement under the Act to request information in relation to the state of his agreement. Whilst s 172(2) states that the notice is binding on the trader, s 172(3) provides that where the statement or notice is shown to be incorrect, the court may direct such relief, if any, to be given to the creditor or owner as appears to it to be just.[2]

1 SI 2007/1167, reg 41.
2 But estoppel may apply: *United Overseas Bank v Jiwani* [1977] 1 All ER 733.

10.8.5   Dispensing notice

Where an agreement is entered into with two or more debtors, any (but not all) of the debtors may sign a dispensing notice, dispensing with the creditor's need to send a statement to him. The dispensing notice ceases to be operational if it is revoked or any of the debtors dies.[1] A dispensing notice which is operative in relation to an agreement, is also operative in relation to any modifying agreement.[2]

1 CCA 1974, s 185(2), 2(A) and (2C).
2 CCA 1974, s 185(2D).

10.9   PROVISIONS APPLICABLE TO SPECIFIC AGREEMENT TYPES

10.9.1   Store card agreements

Specific provision relating to store cards was introduced as a result of the Store Cards Market Investigation conducted by the Competition Commission following a referral to it by the Office of Fair Trading under the Enterprise Act 2002 in March 2004.

Store card statements must contain certain prescribed information.[1] In summary form, the information is: the current APR on purchases; an estimate of the amount of interest payable for the next month if the customer only makes the minimum payment; the minimum payment warning; the amount of each insurance charge accompanied by a description of the charge on the basis of its calculation; a list of any charges payable in the event of late payment or default; an explanation and the basis of the calculation of the interest amount; the relevant annual rates of interest; the payment options including payment by direct debit; how any insurance cover relating to the store card account can be reviewed.

Where the APR is 25% or more the store card provider must also prominently display an APR warning on the face of each monthly statement.

1 Store Cards Market Investigation Order, 27 July 2006, Sch 2.

10.9.2   Home credit loan agreements

Specific requirements apply to information relating to home credit loan agreements. This was introduced by the Consumer Credit (Information Requirements and Duration of Licences and Charges) Regulations 2007[1] as a result of recommendations made by the Competition Commission following its enquiry into the Home Credit Market pursuant to a referral to it by the Office of Fair Trading under the Enterprise Act 2002, in December 2004.

A home credit loan agreement is a debtor-creditor agreement which satisfies either or both of the following conditions:

(a)   the agreement provides that all or most of the sums payable by the debtor are to be collected by or on behalf of the creditor at the debtor's home or the home of a natural person who makes payments to the creditor on the debtor's behalf or, to be so collected if the debtor so wishes;

(b)   at the time the agreement is entered into, the debtor could reasonably expect, from representations made by or on behalf of the creditor at or before that time, that all or most of the sums payable will be collected as set out above, or so collected if the debtor so wished.[2]

In addition to the above, pursuant to the Competition Commission's Home Credit Market Investigation Order 2007,[3] there is a duty on a creditor under a home credit loan agreement, within 7 days after receiving a request to that effect, to give the debtor a statement complying with the Order. The Order also contains provisions relating to early settlement rebates which need to be calculated on the assumption that early settlement will take place not later than 13 days, rather than 28 days, under an ordinary credit agreement. A creditor is required to supply product information to a debtor on request and positive, delinquent and default data at least monthly to credit reference agencies on all accounts it has entered into.

The provisions applying to home credit accounts are attributable to the desire to open up the market to greater competition. The message is intended to be relayed both to consumers and to other suppliers. Indeed, the Order requires lenders to publish information on the price of loans on a website, making it easier for customers in particular to shop around and compare offers.

1   SI 2007/1167.
2   SI 2007/1167, reg 2.
3   Home Credit Market Investigation Order 2007 dated 13 September 2007.

10.9.3   General observation

Notwithstanding the imposition of further requirements on store card and home credit providers, their markets have been left relatively intact although customers are now being urged by regulatory requirements to consider utilising cheaper credit facilities.

Chapter 11

Linked transactions

11.1 MEANING OF A 'LINKED TRANSACTION'

Inevitably it was necessary to deal with transactions which are related to or ancillary to the principal credit or hire agreement. The need for this is especially present where the principal agreement is a cancellable agreement and where it is in fact cancelled. The question then arises as to the impact that it has on related transactions.

A linked transaction is defined as a transaction entered into by the debtor or hirer, or his relative, with another person, in relation to an actual or prospective regulated agreement ('the principal agreement') of which it does not form part, if it falls within one or other of the following alternative heads. First, if the transaction is entered into in compliance with a term of the principal agreement. Second, if the principal agreement is a debtor-creditor-supplier agreement and the transaction is financed, or to be financed, by the principal agreement. Third, if the transaction was suggested to the debtor or hirer or his relative by one of a specified number of persons (essentially the creditor or owner) and the debtor or hirer enters into the agreement for one of a specified range of purposes. The purposes are inducing the creditor or owner to enter into the principal agreement, any other purpose related to the principal agreement or where the principal agreement is a restricted-use credit agreement, a purpose related to a transaction financed, or to be financed, by the principal agreement.[1]

A notable exception from linked transactions is any agreement for the provision of security but it appears that s 113(8) of the CCA 1974 brings security for linked transactions back into the 'linked transaction syndrome'.[2]

The principal agreement is the regulated credit or hire agreement. In practice a linked transaction might take the form of one or other of a life assurance contract, an insurance contract, a contract relating to the guarantee or warranty of goods, a maintenance and service agreement or a contract for the purchase of goods or the supply of services ancillary to the principal contract such as supplemental health insurance, a regular savings plan, an agreement for a current account and the like.

1 CCA 1974, s 19(1) and (2).
2 CCA 1974, s 19(1). See also ss 105 to 124 and especially s 113(8).

11.2   LEGAL ASPECTS OF A LINKED TRANSACTION

A linked transaction entered into before the making of the principal agreement has no effect until such time as that agreement is made.[1] Thus, although on the face of it the agreement constituting the linked transaction might appear to be valid and binding, it is in fact inchoate and in suspense until the main agreement to which it relates is made. It follows that the linked transaction is unenforceable by either party until such time. When the principal agreement comes into force, it will also trigger the coming into force of the linked transaction and, apparently, may not do so with retrospective effect to the date when the linked transaction was entered into.

It would appear to follow, a fortiori from the foregoing, that the withdrawal of a party from a prospective regulated agreement will also constitute a withdrawal from any linked transaction. Although this would appear to be an obvious inference, it is expressly provided for.[2] Notice of withdrawal may be oral or in writing.

In the case of a cancellable agreement, notice by the debtor or hirer of cancellation of the agreement will also serve as cancellation of any linked transaction.[3] The result is that the hirer or debtor is entitled retrospectively to the extinction of his liability and to repayment of all sums paid. However, in certain circumstances the debtor will remain liable for payment of the cash price. This will be so where the agreement is a debtor-creditor-supplier agreement for restricted-use credit financing the doing of work or supply of goods to meet an emergency or the supply of goods which, before service of the notice of cancellation, had by the act of the debtor or his relative, become incorporated in any land or thing not comprised in the agreement or any linked transaction. In those circumstances any cancellation by the debtor will cancel any agreement or linked transaction in so far as it relates to credit or the payment of any charge for credit, leaving the debtor liable for payment of the cash price of the goods or services.

The effect of the debtor's exercise of the right to cancel the credit agreement is that the agreement and any linked transaction, including the contract of supply, are treated as though they had never been entered into and any money paid by the debtor under or in contemplation of the agreement or the linked transaction is recoverable by him and he is released from all liability for future payments. Except in the situation mentioned, the supplier under a linked transaction would not be entitled to the return of his goods as there is no common law restitutionary principle to fall back on.[4]

In other circumstances where the debtor or hirer cancels the credit agreement, hire agreement or linked transaction after he has obtained possession of the goods, he is required to return the goods and in the meanwhile to take reasonable care of them.[5]

Where a debtor discharges his liability under a regulated consumer credit agreement, he and his relative will at the same time be discharged from any liability which has not yet accrued due under a linked transaction.[6] This flows from the fact that a linked transaction rides on the back of the principal agreement.

Any charges payable under a linked transaction which is entered into in compliance with a term of the principal agreement (but not charges under other linked transactions), are included in the total charge for credit under the principal agreement.[7]

The 'linked agreement' provisions of CCA 1974 can have absurd results. Fortunately these were avoided in the case of *Citibank International plc v Schleider*,[8] which is nevertheless illustrative of the potential absurdities arising from the sections of the Act. In that case it was argued that a relatively minor agreement, a regulated interest credit agreement, had been improperly executed, with the result that the main mortgage transaction, which was a linked transaction in relation to it, was unenforceable, the main mortgage being ancillary to the regulated agreement which CCA 1974 deems to be the principal agreement. The court rejected the argument on the grounds that the credit agreement was not a restricted-use credit agreement and therefore not a debtor-creditor-supplier agreement within s 12, with the result that the main mortgage loan was not a linked transaction within s 19(1)(b).

1 CCA 1974, s 19(3).
2 CCA 1974, s 57(1).
3 CCA 1974, s 69.
4 CCA 1974, s 69(2).
5 CCA 1974, s 72.
6 CCA 1974, s 96.
7 Consumer Credit (Total Charge for Credit) Regulations 1980, SI 1980/51, regs 4(1)(b) and 1(2).
8 [2001] GCCR 2281.

11.3   EXEMPT LINKED TRANSACTIONS

The following linked transactions are excluded from most of the above provisions applying to linked transactions (but not from inclusion in the total charge for credit):

(a)   contracts of insurance;

(b)   other contracts in so far as they contain a guarantee of goods;

(c)   transactions comprising or effected under:

(i)   any agreement for the operation of any account (including any savings account) for the deposit of money; or

(ii)   any agreement for the operation of a current account.[1]

As noted above, a contract of insurance is excluded from the meaning of 'linked transactions' for certain purposes, but these purposes do not include the calculation of the total charge for credit. Indeed, a premium under a contract of insurance payable under the transaction (which includes a linked transaction under CCA 1974, s 19(1)(a)) is now expressly included in the total charge for credit where the making or maintenance of the contract of insurance is required by the creditor as a condition of the making of the agreement and for the sole purpose of ensuring complete or partial repayment of the credit and of the charges included in the total charge for credit in the event of the debtor's death, invalidity, illness or unemployment.

Specified linked transactions are excluded from:

(a) the operation of s 19(3) of the Act, which provides that a linked transaction entered into before the making of the regulated consumer credit agreement or regulated hire agreement to which it relates has no effect until such time, if any, as that agreement is made;

(b) s 69(1)(ii) which provides that a notice of cancellation served by the debtor or hirer under a cancellable agreement shall operate to cancel any linked transaction and to withdraw any offer by the debtor or hirer or his relative, to enter into a linked transaction; and

(c) the operation of s 96(1) which provides that where the indebtedness of the debtor under a regulated consumer credit agreement is discharged before the time fixed by the agreement, he and any relative of his, shall be discharged from any liability under a linked transaction other than a debt which has already become payable.

In *Goshawk Dedicated (No 2) Ltd v Governor and Company of Bank of Scotland*[2] it was held that cancellation of the credit agreement did not result in cancellation of the insurance policy, by virtue of the Consumer Credit (Linked Transactions) (Exemptions) Regulations 1983, which had the effect of excluding the policy from constituting a linked transaction. The relevant 'Note' to the cancellation notice in the regulated credit agreement was therefore applicable and the bank was correct in appending it to the notice of the customer's cancellation rights. This case was followed in *Governor and Company of the Bank of Scotland v Euclidian (No 1) Ltd*.[3] However, with respect, it is not clear that the cases were correctly decided, not least because the parties to a regulated consumer credit or regulated consumer hire agreement are at liberty to contract otherwise, namely to agree that cancellation of the credit or hire agreement will affect the linked transaction, so that the 'Note' would make no sense if it indicated the contrary.[4]

1 Consumer Credit (Linked Transactions) (Exemptions) Regulations 1983, SI 1983/1560.
2 [2005] GCCR 5431.
3 [2007] GCCR 6051.
4 See the writer's comments on the case at note 3 above.

11.4   UNFAIR RELATIONSHIPS AND LINKED TRANSACTIONS

The unfair relationships provisions are extensive and discussed in detail in Chapter 23. For present purposes it should be pointed out that linked transactions are subject to the provisions of ss 140A and 140B of CCA 1974, which set out the meaning and consequences of unfair relationships arising between creditors and debtors. References in those sections to an agreement related to a credit agreement, and which are likewise subject to those provisions, are deemed to refer also to a linked transaction in relation to the credit agreement or a linked transaction in relation to a credit agreement consolidated by a subsequent credit agreement.[1]

The unfair relationships provisions apply to a credit agreement of any amount and to both regulated credit agreements and exempt agreements.[2] There is a corresponding provision relating to linked transactions, so that a transaction is a linked transaction even if the credit agreement to which it relates is not a regulated consumer credit agreement.[3]

1 Section 140C(4)(b).
2 Section 140C(1).
3 Section 140C(5).

Chapter 12

Credit-brokers

12.1 MEANING OF 'CREDIT BROKERAGE'

The business of credit brokerage has several facets. First and most commonly, it is the effecting of introductions of individuals desiring to obtain credit or goods on hire to persons carrying on a consumer credit or a consumer hire business. Second, subject to the exception below, it comprises the introduction of individuals desiring to obtain credit to finance a dwelling to be occupied by them or their relatives to persons carrying on a business in the course of which they provide credit secured on land. Third, credit brokerage is the introduction of individuals desiring to obtain credit or to obtain goods on hire, to other credit-brokers. Finally, it generally also includes the introduction of individuals to persons carrying on business in relation to exempt agreements.[1]

The principal exception to credit brokerage results from the fact that generally first legal mortgages for residential purposes now fall under the Financial Services and Markets Act 2000 ('FSMA'). As such mortgages are exempt from the CCA regime, so is credit brokerage involving them.

Thus it is not credit brokerage for a person to effect the introduction of an individual desiring to obtain credit, if the introduction is made to:

(a) an authorised person within the meaning of FSMA who has permission to enter into a relevant agreement as lender or home purchase provider; or

(b) a qualifying broker, namely an authorised or exempt person under FSMA.[2]

Accordingly, mortgage arranging and mortgage advising falling within the purview of the Financial Services and Markets Act 2000 are exempt from the provisions of the consumer credit regime.

Credit brokers generally include motor car dealers, retailers and home improvement suppliers. Solicitors and accountants are licensed credit brokers by virtue of the group licences applying to them. Insurance brokers who introduce their customers to sources of credit or hire facilities need to be licensed, as do employers who introduce their staff to providers of credit.

A prime credit-broker, to coin a phrase, is an institution which acts variously as both lender and credit-broker. It will scour the market for the most suitable loan for the potential borrower and also offer its own loan product, if that happens to be the most appropriate. It is the equivalent role to that of an independent financial adviser, in the financial services arena, which also offers its own products range.

The Internet has expanded the range of credit-brokers. Individuals introduced to sources of credit or hire, or to credit-brokers, via the Internet, are enjoying the services of a credit-broker. The credit-broker needs to be licensed as such.

A notable exception to credit brokerage is an introducer canvassing debtor-creditor-supplier agreements or consumer hire agreements off trade premises, not in the capacity of an employee.[3]

1   CCA 1974, s 145(2) to (4).
2   CCA 1974, s 146(5A) and 5(D).
3   CCA 1974, s 146(5).

12.2   MEANING OF 'EFFECTING OF INTRODUCTIONS'

To effect introductions of prospective debtors to prospective creditors is to bring them into contact with each other, whether personally, by correspondence, by telephone, via the Internet or in any other manner. Although the relevant section only refers in terms to one-way introductions, namely introductions of individuals desiring to obtain credit to those in business to provide it,[1] it appears that credit brokerage includes introductions moving the other way, namely introductions of prospective creditors or owners to prospective debtors or hirers respectively.[2]

An intermediary does not act as a credit-broker merely by advertising credit facilities as a result of which an individual makes contact with the provider of credit or hire. Nor does an intermediary effect introductions to credit grantors by making the latter's application forms available in display boxes or helping the prospective debtor to complete the form.[3] In the case of an estate agent it has been held that merely sending particulars of a property to a potential purchaser does not amount to introducing the purchaser to the vendor.[4] However, on the credit scene, sending details of a loan offer in the name of the lender to a potential borrower would, it is submitted, amount to an introduction to the lender. Whether a particular action amounts to the effecting of an introduction is largely a question of fact to be determined on the merits of each case. If the criteria were to be too widely cast, then every bank, hotel or restaurant in the country advertising the services of Access or American Express or any other credit card company and providing leaflets relating to the services they provide would need a licence. This could not be what parliament intended.[5]

A person is engaged in credit brokerage not only when he directly effects an introduction but also when the introduction is effected by his agent.[6] It is therefore not possible to overcome a refusal by the Office of Fair Trading to issue a credit brokerage licence, by appointing an agent to act as credit-broker on behalf of oneself.

No credit brokerage business is involved by a trader simply accepting payment by credit card or trading check. However, if a retailer conducts his own in-house credit card scheme in conjunction with a third party as the credit provider, the retailer will be carrying on a credit brokerage business. If a trader actively recruits customers to a credit card scheme he will also need to be licensed as a credit-broker.

It is not credit brokerage business to recommend a source of credit where no commission or other arrangement exists between the party recommending the source of credit and the credit provider. The same applies to consumer hire. The activity of introducing only corporate customers to a source of credit or hire is also not credit brokerage.

The role of the credit-broker may be pivotal to the categorisation of the credit agreement. Thus, if the credit-broker is the supplier under the credit agreement and the creditor has entered into, or proposes entering into, arrangements or an agreement with the supplier, the credit agreement entered into between the creditor and the debtor will be a debtor-creditor-supplier agreement, with all the consequences flowing from that categorisation.[7]

A credit-broker's introduction may take the form of an automatic referral by the credit-broker of all enquirers for credit to a credit provider, without any active intervention on the part of the credit-broker. Indeed, the introduction may be effected by an automated system. Whether the potential debtor should not in fact be given an opportunity to reflect upon the identity and reputation of the proposed lender and his credit terms, is another issue.

1 CCA 1974, s 145(2).
2 Compare *Goode: Consumer Credit Law and Practice* (LexisNexis Butterworths), para IC [48.34]; Bennion, *Consumer Credit Act Manual* (3rd edn, Sweet & Maxwell), p 153; and Guest, *Encyclopaedia of Consumer Credit Law* (Sweet & Maxwell), 2–146.
3 *Brookes v Retail Credit Cards Ltd* (1985) 150 JP 131, [1986] CCLR 5.
4 *Christie Owen & Davis plc v King* 1998 SCLR 786.
5 See note 1 above.
6 *Hicks v Walker* (1984) 148 JP 636, [1999] GCCR 721.
7 CCA 1974, ss 12(b) and (c).

12.3 CONDUCT OF CREDIT BROKERAGE BUSINESS

The business of credit brokerage falls into the category of an ancillary credit business. A licence is required in order to be able to conduct the business of credit brokerage.[1] 'Business' has been defined in general terms as including every trade, occupation or profession and so as to apply to single transactions as well as long-term ventures.[2]

Although the Act defines 'business' as including a profession or trade, it also provides that a person is not to be treated as carrying on a particular type of business merely because occasionally he enters into transactions belonging to a business of that type. In addition, no credit brokerage is involved where the individual is introduced to the provider of non-commercial agreements as, by definition, the provider is not engaged in a consumer credit business, a business involving exempt agreements, a consumer hire business or a business involving exempt hire agreements.[3]

Particular circumstances may support the notion of a business, whether of credit brokerage or otherwise, even in the case of just one introduction or transaction.

In *R v Marshall*[4] the court had to consider whether a double-glazing salesman, who offered financial arrangements to customers in the form of credit facilities, at a time when he was unlicensed, was carrying on an unlicensed credit brokerage business in breach of CCA 1974, ss 39(1) and 145. The Court of Appeal quashed the conviction of the court of first instance. The trial court had been too restrictive in its direction to the jury when it stated that if all that the defendant did was occasionally make introductions, not as part of his way of selling his goods or services, but only because he was assisting customers who wanted that help, he did not break the law. The court cited with approval a passage in *Consumer Credit Legislation* (now *Consumer Credit Law and Practice*) that 'regularity of activity is necessary before that activity can be regarded as a business activity so as to attract the licensing provisions. Thus, a person making occasional bridging loans for his clients or customers would not on that account alone be carrying on a consumer credit business'.[5]

It is submitted that the test as to whether a person is carrying on a business is more sophisticated than a question of regularity of activity. For example, a person may set up in business with the declared intention of conducting a certain type of business, although he merely enters into one transaction of that type, after which, say, the business folds. Thus the declared purpose of a business, including where a person advertises or announces himself as carrying on a business, is relevant to the determination of whether that person is in fact carrying on such business. This was also the view of the Court of Appeal in *Conroy v Kenny*.[6]

1   CCA 1974, s 21.
2   *Cornelius v Phillips* [1918] AC 199.
3   See CCA 1974, ss 189(1) and 145(1), (2) and (3).
4   *R Marshall* [1999] GCCR 1345, CA.
5   See Goode, *Consumer Credit Law and Practice*, para 1C [48.12].
6   [1999] 1 WLR 1340, CA.

12.4   LICENSING OF CREDIT-BROKERS

A credit-broker must be licensed in order to be able to carry on a credit brokerage business.[1] Engaging in unlicensed credit brokerage business constitutes an offence.[2] The licence must cover all business names of the licensee and a licensee commits an offence if he carries on a business in a business name not specified in the licence.[3]

The provisions relating to an application for a licence and the qualifications for a licence apply also to a licence to conduct the business of credit brokerage.

The following practices are considered unfair in relation to credit brokerage services:[4]

(a)   failing to return fees in excess of £5 when a consumer does not take up a loan or enter into an agreement within six months of an introduction to a lender, for whatever reason, contrary to CCA 1974, s 155;

(b)   inducing consumers to enter into agreements for mortgage arrangements where the licensee ought to have known the outcome of the loan application was uncertain. This can only refer to where the broker irresponsibly involves the customer in incurring unnecessary delay and expense (e.g. in relation to valuation and surveyor's fees); and

(c) purporting, notwithstanding the provisions of CCA 1974, ss 155 and 173(1), to set terms as to when fees paid as commission will become refundable, in stating that such fees are non-returnable, or that the consumer would only be entitled to a refund of a portion of the original fee.

Credit providers and leasing companies commonly enter into agreements with credit-brokers under which the broker is appointed the exclusive or non-exclusive broker, or possibly the agent of the company, with appropriate commission arrangements. The agreements will regulate the conduct of credit-brokers. Most credit and hire companies will be members of the Consumer Credit Trade Association or the Finance & Leasing Association. The codes of these Associations require their members to ensure that credit-brokers and others with whom they have commercial dealings affecting consumers carry on their activities lawfully and with integrity. They are required to vet credit-brokers with whom they deal, to monitor their activities and to decline to accept further business from them when their conduct falls below the requisite standard of integrity and competence. More specifically, the codes require them to take reasonable steps to ensure that credit-brokers do not impose undue pressure on consumers to enter into agreements and do not permit customers to sign blank application forms.

Credit and hire companies generally supply credit-brokers with procedural guides or instructions governing how agreements are to be completed, how a customer is to be identified, the criteria for the grant of credit and guidance on intercepting fraudulent applications. The appointment as credit-broker by a creditor or leasing company is viewed as an asset by the credit-broker. This serves as some assurance to the consumer that the credit-broker will maintain certain minimum standards in his dealings with the consumer.

1 CCA 1974, s 21.
2 CCA 1974, s 39(1).
3 CCA 1974, ss 39(2), and 24.
4 Office of Fair Trading – Consumer Credit Licences: Guidance for holders and applicants (published 2003).

12.5 CREDIT-BROKERS WITH REFERENCE TO UNFAIR RELATIONSHIPS

The conduct of credit-brokers is relevant in determining whether the relationship between the creditor and debtor is unfair because of anything done, or not done, by the credit-broker acting on behalf of the creditor, either before or after the making of the agreement or any related agreement.[1]

In deciding whether to make a determination, the court must have regard to all matters it thinks relevant. A creditor transacting on an ongoing basis with a specific credit-broker should therefore procure undertakings from the credit-broker to conduct himself lawfully, fairly, in accordance with OFT guidance and relevant codes of practice. Moreover, as any claim would lie against the creditor, without an automatic right of recourse against the credit-broker, the creditor should obtain an appropriate indemnity from the credit-broker including in respect of any acts, omissions and representations made by the credit-broker on his behalf.

1 CCA 1974, s 140A.

12.6   CREDIT-BROKER AS AGENT

12.6.1   The position at common law

At common law, in the absence of an agreement establishing the credit-broker as agent of the finance company, the credit-broker acting in his capacity as the dealer or supplier of the goods or equipment, is not the agent of the finance company. This was the decision in the leading case of *Branwhite v Worcester Works Finance*.[1]

The House of Lords approved the following statement of Pearson LJ in *Mercantile Credit Co Ltd v Hamblin*:[2]

> 'There is no rule of law that in a hire-purchase transaction the dealer never is, or always is, acting as agent for the finance company or as agent for the customer. In a typical hire-purchase transaction the dealer is a party in his own right, selling his car to the finance company, and he is acting primarily on his own behalf and not as a general agent for either of the other two parties. There is no need to attribute to him an agency in order to account for his participation in the transaction. Nevertheless the dealer is to some extent an intermediary between the customer and the finance company, and he may well have in a particular case some ad hoc agencies to do particular things on behalf of one or the other or it may be both of those two parties. For instance, if the car is delivered by the dealer to the customer after the hire-purchase agreement has been concluded, the dealer must be making delivery as agent of the finance company.'

The Court in *Branwhite* held that the mere possession by the dealer of the finance company's forms was not enough to constitute an agency and that neither filling in the forms on behalf of the intending purchaser, nor receiving a deposit from him, amounted to acting as agent for the finance company. It is also clear from the cases that the dealer's mere receipt of commission from the finance company does not make him an agent of the finance company.

It follows that the finance company is also not fixed with any knowledge that the dealer (which is not its agent) may have of defective title in the goods.[3]

Branwhite's case was applied to a leasing agreement in *Woodchester Equipment (Leasing) Ltd v British Association of Canned and Preserved Foods Importers and Distributors Ltd*[4] where Millet LJ stated:

> 'There is no rule of law that in a hire-purchase transaction that the supplier is the agent of the finance company for the purpose of procuring the customer to offer to acquire goods on hire-purchase. There is equally no rule of law that the supplier is not the agent of the finance company for that purpose. The question is a question of fact in every case. This was settled by the decision of the House of Lords in *Branwhite v Worcester Works Finance Ltd* ([1969] 1 AC 552).

That case also decided that the facts that the finance company has provided the supplier with a stock of its forms to enable him to provide one to a prospective customer, and that it has also provided the supplier with the information necessary to enable him to calculate and inform the customer of the amounts of the initial payment and subsequent periodic payments which the finance company will require, neither constitute the supplier [and] the agent of the finance company as a matter of law, nor amount to evidence that he is such an agent in fact. These facts are entirely consistent with all parties acting as principals in their own interests.

In my judgment the same applies to a leasing agreement; see the decision of this court in *J D Williams & Co v McCauley* ([1994] CCLR 78). In such a case, the supplier wishes to sell goods and the customer wishes to hire them. These conflicting objectives can both be accommodated only by the interposition of a third party, such as a finance company, which buys the goods from a supplier and in turn lets them on hire to the customer. Such a transaction involves three parties and two contracts, one of sale and the other of hire. These contracts are capable of being concluded by the parties without the interposition of any agency, so that a finding of agency requires, in my judgment, to be supported by clear evidence.'

1 *Branwhite v Worcester Works Finance Ltd* [1969] 1 AC 552, [1999] GCCR 397, HL; see also *Mynshul Asset Finance v Clarke (t/a Peacock Hotel)* referred to in [1992] CLY 487; *Moorgate Mercantile Leasing v Isobel Gell and Ugolini Dispensers (UK) Ltd* [1988] CCLR 1. Compare *Woodchester Leasing Equipment Ltd v R M Clayton and D M Clayton (t/a Sudbury Sports)*, decision of the Sudbury County Court (October 1993) where the Court found the suppliers to be the agent of the plaintiff leasing company, resulting in a cancellable lease under CCA 1974, s 67. It drew the rather forced inference from the fact that the agreement was highly advantageous to the supplier and the leasing company. See also Chapter 13 on 'Agency'.
2 [1965] 2 QB 242, CA at 269.
3 *Car and Universal Finance Co Ltd v Caldwell* [1964] 1 All ER 290, CA.
4 [1999] GCCR 1923 CA at 1932.

12.6.2   Agency under the Act and the regulations

In the common 'three-party' hire-purchase or instalment sale agreement the dealer is a credit-broker who sells the goods which are the subject of the proposed credit agreement to the creditor. The creditor then delivers those goods on credit terms to the debtor. That agreement, being a hire-purchase or instalment sale agreement, is a debtor-creditor-supplier agreement and any negotiations conducted by the dealer in relation to those goods or to the transaction financed or to be financed by the credit agreement are deemed to be conducted by the dealer in his capacity as agent of the creditor as well as in his actual capacity.[1] This means that the creditor is bound by any statements or representations made by the dealer in relation to the goods or the transaction. This might include an associated or linked agreement.[2]

Included in these negotiations, known as 'antecedent negotiations', are statements made when the credit-broker first enters into communications with the debtor or hirer, namely advertisements, discussions and correspondence.[3] 'Antecedent negotiations' are any negotiations with a debtor conducted by a credit-broker in relation to goods sold or proposed to be sold by the credit-broker to the creditor before forming the subject matter of a debtor-creditor-supplier agreement under s 12(a) of CCA 1974.[4]

In *Forthright Finance Ltd v Ingate*[5] Mrs Ingate, the debtor, had agreed to buy a motor car under a three-party conditional sale agreement with the third party, Carlyle Finance. The car dealers, who set up the agreement, also agreed to take the debtor's existing car, which was the subject of a conditional sale agreement with Forthright Finance under which a sum of money was still owing, by way of part exchange. The car dealers also undertook to pay the balance owing under that agreement but before doing so, went into liquidation.

The Court of Appeal found, on the facts, that there were not two independent transactions, one relating to the discharge of the sum owing in respect of the part exchanged vehicle and the other relating to the financing of the new vehicle, but that the two transactions were linked aspects of one transaction. In the court's judgment, s 56(1)(b) meant that there must be goods sold or proposed to be sold by the credit-broker to the creditor which will form the subject matter of a debtor-creditor-supplier agreement. If that condition is fulfilled, one next enquires whether there were negotiations in relation to those goods. If there were, then all that was said by the creditor-broker in those negotiations is deemed to have been said on behalf of the creditor. On the other hand, what is said in any other negotiations which do not relate to those goods, is not deemed to be said on behalf of the creditor.

The court held that the negotiations, including those in respect of the part exchange, all related to the goods to be sold because they were all part of one transaction. In the circumstances, the finance company of the second vehicle, Carlyle Finance Ltd, was vicariously liable for representations by the dealer as a negotiator within s 56. As stated by Henry J:

> 'Using the old familiar language of "hirer, dealer and finance company" the clear statutory effect of s 56 of the Consumer Credit Act of 1974 is to make the dealer, in addition to his liability in his "actual capacity", the finance company's agent in situations where he would not be at common law because he would not have had the authority express or implied so to act. The machinery for doing this is to be found in s 56(2) of the Act, making him the finance company's agent in negotiations with [the hirer] ....'

In contrast to *Forthright Finance Ltd v Ingate* is the case of *Black Horse Ltd v Langford*[6] where the court held that the phrase 'sold or proposed to be sold' in CCA 1974, s 56(1)(b) only applies to the credit-broker which actually sold or proposed to sell the goods to the creditor and not to any intermediate credit-broker. In this case the credit-broker which made the representations, Castleford Trade Car Centre, introduced the transaction to another credit-broker, North Riding Finance, which in turn introduced the defendant, Langford, to the finance company, Black Horse, the supplier on hire-purchase of the motor vehicle to Langford. It was held that the original credit-broker's promise to discharge the outstanding balance under an existing hire-purchase agreement of Langford was not deemed to have been made by him as agent of the claimant, Black Horse, under s 56 as that credit-broker did not sell the vehicle to Black Horse. The decision appears to be correct but will be of little comfort to any person relying on the original dealer's representation as binding the ultimate creditor or supplier.

An error in the drafting of s 56 has given rise to the anomalous position that it does not extend to negotiators of hire agreements, so that s 56 does not bind the owner under a hire agreement[7] to antecedent negotiations entered into by the negotiator, unless the negotiator was in fact the owner's agent. This result is dramatically different from that in relation to a negotiator in respect of a credit agreement where the creditor is bound by the antecedent negotiations of the negotiator. Section 56 does not exclude situations where, as a matter of fact, one party negotiated as agent of another, including a dealer as agent of the hiring company. Thus, in *Woodchester Leasing Equipment Ltd v Clayton*[8] the Court was satisfied that the defendant had been induced to enter into the leasing agreement by the representations made to him by the supplier and concluded that in all the circumstances of the case it defied belief that the plaintiff leasing company did not know of the kind of inducements which the supplier would hold out, approve of their use and encourage the supplier to make them. Accordingly, it found that the supplier was acting as agent for the leasing company.

A credit-broker is deemed to be the agent of the creditor or hiring company for various other purposes, such as receiving various notices, including a notice of withdrawal from a prospective agreement, a notice of cancellation in respect of a cancellable agreement and a notice rescinding the agreement. These deemed agency provisions may not be excluded by agreement as they are intended for the protection of the debtor or hirer.[9]

An intention made known to a credit-broker by a consumer may be imputed to the creditor or leasing company. For example, if a customer makes known to a credit-broker the purpose for which he proposes purchasing goods or hiring goods under a hire-purchase agreement, there is an implied condition that the goods supplied under the agreement are reasonably fit for that purpose. The credit-broker's knowledge is imputed to the creditor. The presumption can be dislodged if it can be shown that the hirer or buyer has not relied upon, and that it would be unreasonable for him to rely upon, the skill or judgement of the creditor or credit-broker.[10]

It is submitted that, in the absence of agreement to the contrary between the credit-broker and the finance company, the limited agency of the credit-broker will not result in the finance company being liable for the credit-broker's wrongful or tortious acts or omissions, including any under the Trade Descriptions Act 1968 or the Consumer Protection Act 1987.

1 CCA 1974, s 56(2).
2 *UDT v Whitfield* [1987] CCLR 60. Cf *Northgran Finance Ltd v Ashley* [1963] 1 QB 476.
3 CCA 1974, s 56(4).
4 CCA 1974, s 56(1)(b).
5 [1999] GCCR 2213 at 2220, CA. Compare this decision to *Powell v Lloyds Bowmaker Ltd* [1999] GCCR 3523 (Sheriff's Court).
6 [2007] EWHC 907 (QB) [2007] ALL ER (D) 214 [2007] GCCR 6001.
7 *Moorgate Mercantile Leasing v Isobell Gell and Ugolini Dispensers (UK) Ltd* [1988] CCLR 1; *Lloyds Bowmaker Leasing Ltd v John R MacDonald* [1999] GCCR 3443 (Sheriff's Court).
8 Reported in Consumer Credit Trade Association Journal, January 1994, vol 48 no 5, p 2; for *UDT v Whitfield* see note 2, above.
9 CCA 1974, s 173.
10 Sale of Goods Act 1979, s 14(3); [1999] GCCR 721 Supply of Goods (Implied Terms) Act 1973, s 10(3); and see *R&B Customs Brokers Co Ltd v United Dominions Trust Ltd* [1999] GCCR 1195, CA.

12.7   CONSEQUENCES OF UNLICENSED CREDIT BROKERAGE

It is an offence to conduct business as a credit-broker if not licensed to do so. In addition, agreements introduced by an unlicensed credit-broker are only enforceable against the debtor or hirer on an order of the Office of Fair Trading pursuant to an application made to him. Amongst the factors which the OFT will take into account in arriving at its decision are how far debtors and hirers were prejudiced by the credit-broker's conduct and the degree of culpability of the applicant in facilitating the carrying on by the credit-broker of his unlicensed business.[1]

The creditor or owner is only concerned to ensure that his immediate introducer is licensed. However, any credit-broker in a chain of credit-brokers must be licensed. It does not avail a person who has been refused a credit brokerage licence to by-pass the restrictions upon him by introducing applicants for credit through a licensed credit-broker. Indeed, he and all those involved in any such scheme might be convicted as accomplices to contravening the CCA 1974's provisions governing credit brokerage.[2]

1   CCA 1974, s 149.
2   *Hicks v Walker* [1984] Crim LR 495, [1999] GCCR 721.

12.8   CREDIT-BROKERAGE FEES

Credit-brokers are entitled to charge customers a credit brokerage fee. Often, however, they will be remunerated exclusively by the creditor or leasing company. This is especially so in the case of interest-free credit where, by definition, no charge is levied on the consumer. Where the consumer is required to pay a charge for credit, the credit company and the credit-broker may share the charges between them.

Where a credit-broker levies a charge on the customer for his services, the credit brokerage fee forms part of the total charge for credit and the annual percentage rate of charge ('APR'), and must be shown in any agreement and, where required, in any advertisement. Originally the credit brokerage fee was exempted from the total charge for credit and it was only included in the calculation some nine years after the Total Charge for Credit Regulations were first enacted. A remaining anomaly is that credit brokerage fees charged in respect of hire agreements are reflected in neither the hire charge nor the hire agreement.

If a consumer does not enter into a regulated agreement or an agreement for a house mortgage under the CCA regime within six months of the introduction, the credit-broker must reimburse the consumer with the amount of any credit brokerage fee in excess of £5 levied on the consumer. This also applies to cancelled regulated agreements.[1]

The right to recover brokerage fees does not apply where the fee or commission relates to the effecting of an introduction of an individual desiring to obtain credit if the introduction is made to an authorised person, within the meaning of the Financial Services and Markets Act 2000, who has permission under that Act to enter into a relevant agreement as a lender or home purchase provider, or to a qualifying broker with a view to that individual obtaining credit under a relevant agreement. By relevant agreement is meant an agreement which is secured by a land mortgage or is or forms part of a regulated home purchase plan and entry into which by a lender or home purchase provider is a regulated activity for the purposes of the 2000 Act. A qualifying broker is a person who may effect introductions of that kind without contravening the general prohibition within the meaning of s 19 of that Act.[2]

There is no upper limit on the amount which a credit-broker can charge but in practice credit brokerage fees are restricted by virtue of their impact on the APR and ultimately by the unfair relationships provisions of ss 140A and 140D. These factors are relevant only to credit and not hire agreements.

The provisions relating to recovery of credit brokerage fees also apply to any other fee or commission for the services charged by a credit-broker to an individual. In the case of an individual desiring to obtain credit under a consumer credit agreement, any sum payable or paid by him to a credit-broker, otherwise than as a fee or commission for the credit-broker's services, is treated as such a fee or commission for the purposes of the right to recover brokerage fees, if it enters into, or would enter into, the total charge for credit.[3]

1 CCA 1974, s 155. The sum is variable by Order.
2 CCA 1974, ss 155(2A), 146(5A) and (5D).
3 CCA 1974, s 155(4).

12.9 CREDIT-BROKERS AND FIDUCIARY RELATIONSHIPS

Where a credit-broker introduces a non-status or sub-prime borrower to a lender in respect of a secured loan, he must observe the Non-Status Lending Guidelines for Lenders and Brokers issued by the Office of Fair Trading.[1] They require him to disclose the existence and nature of any commission or other payment payable by the lender and the implications of the same with regard to the borrower, so as to clear any potential conflict of interest on the part of the broker. In practice it means that the broker must obtain the borrower's informed consent to the commission payment.

Where a credit-broker receives payment of a fee from his customer, whether a debtor or hirer, it places the credit-broker in a fiduciary situation with regard to his customer. As a fiduciary he is required to act loyally for the customer and not to put himself in a position where he has a conflict of interest. If he is also to be paid a commission or fee by the lender, he can only discharge his fiduciary duty to his customer by obtaining his informed consent with the full knowledge of all the material circumstances and of the nature and the extent of his interest, including disclosure of the fact that he is to receive a commission from the lender and the amount of the commission. The consent should be accompanied by a warning to the effect that payment of the commission to the broker might mean that he is not in a position to give unbiased advice. This was the principle of the decision in *Hurstanger Ltd v Wilson*.[2]

A fiduciary relationship might also arise in circumstances where the customer relies upon the broker to advise him. Merely recommending a particular finance company is not, it is submitted, tantamount to advice and does not create a fiduciary relationship between the finance company and the customer.

The remedy for breach of the fiduciary duty is in equity. The court has a discretion as to whether or not to grant rescission of the contract resulting from the credit-broker's introduction or to grant compensation to the broker's client for the broker's breach of fiduciary duty. In the circumstances of *Hurstanger* the court considered that the defendants were adequately compensated by awarding them the sum of £240, equal to the commission which the credit-broker received from the lender, plus interest. It held that to rescind the transaction altogether would be unfair and disproportionate.

1 Revised November 1997 OFT 192.
2 [2007] All ER (D) 66, [2007] GCCR 5951, CA.

12.10   ADVERTISING BY CREDIT-BROKERS

Chapter 9 on the advertising of credit and hire facilities also applies to advertising by credit-brokers.

It is worthwhile noting specifically that the exclusion from the Consumer Credit (Advertisements) Regulations 2004 of advertisements to provide credit or hire for the purposes of another person's business does not include a business carried on by the advertiser or by any person acting as a credit-broker in relation to the credit or hire facility to which the advertisement relates. Accordingly, any such advertisements are governed by these regulations.[1]

1 SI 2004/1484, reg 10(1) and (2).

12.11   OTHER REGULATED ACTIVITIES OF CREDIT-BROKERS

Credit-brokers often act as independent financial advisers or intermediaries in relation to activities regulated under the Financial Services and Markets Act 2000 (Regulated Activities) Order 2001.[1] These activities include accepting deposits, issuing electronic money, effecting and carrying out contracts of insurance, dealing in investments as principal, dealing in investments as agent, arranging deals in investments, managing investments, assisting in the administration and performance of a contract of insurance, safeguarding and administering investments and advising on investments. Investments include deposits, electronic money, contracts of insurance, regulated mortgage contracts, regulated home reversion plans and regulated home purchase plans.

A contract is a regulated mortgage contract if, at the time it is entered into, the following conditions are met:

1.   the contract is one under which a person ('the lender') provides credit to an individual or to trustees ('the borrower');

2.   the contract provides for the obligation of the borrower to repay to be secured by a first legal mortgage on land (other than timeshare accommodation) in the United Kingdom; and

3. at least 40% of that land is used, or is intended to be used, as or in connection with a dwelling by the borrower or (in the case of credit provided to trustees) by an individual who is a beneficiary of the trust, or by a related person.[2]

A person conducting any of the above activities must be authorised by the Financial Services Authority under the Financial Services and Markets Act 2000 or, for more limited purposes, be an appointed representative or agent of an authorised person. The appointed representative or agent must have a contract with an authorised person permitting him to carry on business of a prescribed description. The principal must accept responsibility in writing for the activities of the appointed representative and the principal is responsible, to the same extent as if he had expressly permitted it, for anything done or omitted by the appointed representative or agent in carrying on the business for which he has accepted responsibility.[3]

An introducer appointed representative is an appointed representative appointed by a firm whose scope of appointment is limited to effecting introductions and distributing non real-time financial promotions. An introducer appointed representative must enter into an agreement with his principal, similar to an appointed representative, and broadly similar rules apply to him. However, whilst an appointed representative must register as an approved person with the Financial Services Authority, an introducer appointed representative is not required to do so.

1 SI2001/544, as amended.
2 *Ibid.*, art 61(3).
3 Financial Services and Markets Act 2000 (Appointed Representative) Regulations 2001, SI 2001/1217, as amended.

Chapter 13

Agency

13.1   AGENCY AT COMMON LAW

The relationship of principal and agent may be constituted by agreement between principal and agent, whether express or implied, or from the conduct or situation of the parties. The relationship may also be constituted retrospectively, by subsequent ratification by the principal of acts done on his behalf. A person may also be estopped from denying that another person acted as his agent. Finally, a person may be liable under the doctrine of apparent authority in respect of another who is not his agent at all.[1]

An agent is in a fiduciary relationship with his principal, regardless of whether the agency contract expresses or recognises the same. Thus:

> 'Agency need not be contractual; and although there is much overlap with common law duties the notion of fiduciary obligation stems from equity and is independent of contract. It is submitted that the law's control over the agent's exercise of his powers of intervention is not to be derived from contract terms alone. As was said in a subsequent case: "The essence of a fiduciary obligation is that it creates obligations of a different character from those deriving from the contract itself." '[2]

Even where the relationship is contractual, the law imposes overriding obligations, remedies and relief:

> 'A too casual failure to recognise the requirements of a fiduciary position, and sometimes a short-sighted assumption that all relevant duties are prescribed in a contract, can be and has been responsible for serious misbehaviour in the financial markets and elsewhere, as is shown by many litigated cases in the last quarter-century.'[3]

The fiduciary relationship between a principal and an agent was the subject of *Hurstanger Ltd v Wilson*[4] where the court held that a credit-broker who receives a payment from the debtor for acting as his agent and also has an arrangement with the creditor to receive commission (whether or not he in fact receives such commission) is under a fiduciary duty to make full disclosure to the debtor and to obtain his informed consent to receiving such payment from the creditor. In the absence of such disclosure and consent, the agent will have received a secret commission in breach of his fiduciary duty.[5]

1 *Bowstead & Reynolds on Agency* (Sweet & Maxwell, 2006) para 2-001.
2 loc. cit at 6-034.
3 loc. cit at 6-034.
4 [2007] All ER (D) 66, CA.
5 See the discussion at para 12.9.

13.2   CONTRACTS (RIGHTS OF THIRD PARTIES) ACT 1999

Before turning to the statutory provisions creating an agency relationship under the CCA 1974, it should be mentioned that a contract might, directly or indirectly, confer upon a person who is not a party to the contract, namely a third party, the right to enforce a term of the contract. It will do so if the contract expressly provides such right or if the term purports to confer a benefit on a third party unless, in the latter case, it appears on a proper construction of the contract, that the parties to the contract did not intend the term to be enforceable by the third party. The third party must be expressly identified in the contract by name, as a member of a class or as answering a particular description or the agreement must purport to confer a benefit on him. The third party need not be in existence when the contract is made.

In a leasing or hire-purchase contract, if rights are conferred upon identifiable third parties in the event of a breach of the contract, for example upon the provider of maintenance of a motor vehicle, they would be enforceable by that provider.

13.3   RELATIONSHIP BETWEEN THE FINANCE COMPANY AND THE DEALER OR RETAILER

In the leading case of *Branwhite v Worcester Works Finance Ltd*,[1] the House of Lords stated that a dealer may, in some circumstances, be held out by a finance company as its agent. However, the court approved the following statement in *Mercantile Credit Co Ltd v Hamblin*:[2]

> 'There is no rule of law that in a hire-purchase transaction the dealer never is, or always is, acting as agent for the finance company or as agent for the customer. In a typical hire-purchase transaction the dealer is a party in his own right, selling his car to the finance company, and he is acting primarily on his own behalf and not as general agent for either of the other two parties. There is no need to attribute to him an agency in order to account for his participation in the transaction. Nevertheless, the dealer is to some extent an intermediary between the customer and the finance company, and he may well have in a particular case some ad hoc agencies to do particular things on behalf of one or the other or it may be both of those two parties. For instance, if the car is delivered by the dealer to the customer after the hire-purchase agreement has been concluded, the dealer must be making delivery as agent of the finance company.'

This decision has since been applied to leasing agreements in *JD Williams & Co v McCauley*[3] and *Woodchester Equipment (Leasing) Ltd v British Association of Canned and Preserved Foods Importers and Distributors Ltd.*[4] In the latter the court stated that the authority of *Branwhite* establishes beyond peradventure that unless some very exceptional factual material is present, a relationship of principal and agent does not arise between a finance company entering into a hire-purchase agreement and the dealer or retailer. This principle, the court held in *Woodchester*, extended equally to leasing agreements. It is immaterial that a finance company has supplied the dealer with a stock of its forms to enable it to provide one to the dealer's prospective customer and that it has supplied the supplier with information necessary to enable him to calculate and inform the customer of the financial details; these do not constitute the supplier and the agent of the finance company as a matter of law, nor amount to evidence that he is such an agent in fact. The court held that these facts are entirely consistent with all parties acting as principal in their own interest. The interposition of the supplier or dealer between the finance company and the customer is necessitated simply by the fact that the finance company sells the goods to the supplier who in turn lets them on hire or hire-purchase to the customer. Such a transaction necessarily involves three parties and two contracts, one of sale and the other of lease or hire-purchase. These contracts are capable of being concluded by the parties without the interposition of any agency. A finding of agency requires to be supported by clear factual evidence and is not to be assumed from the relationship between the parties.

If, on the other hand, the finance company in fact appoints the supplier or dealer as its agent, an agency relationship will exist as an express provision of the contract between them.

1 [1968] 3 All ER 104, [1999] GCCR 39 7, HL.
2 [1964] 3 All ER 592 at 600.
3 [1999] GCCR 1375, CA.
4 [1999] GCCR 1923 at 1926 and 1932, CA.

13.4 AGENCY UNDER THE CONSUMER CREDIT ACT

13.4.1 Antecedent negotiations

The CCA 1974, s 56, importantly provides that certain negotiations by a credit-broker or by the supplier are deemed to be conducted by such person in the capacity of agent of the creditor as well as in his actual capacity. The negotiations are so-called antecedent negotiations, namely negotiations with a debtor or hirer conducted by a credit-broker in relation to goods sold or proposed to be sold by the credit-broker to the credit or, before forming the subject matter of a debtor-creditor-supplier agreement in the form of a restricted-use agreement to finance a transaction between the debtor and the creditor. Likewise, negotiations are deemed to be conducted by the supplier as agent for the creditor where the negotiations relate to a transaction financed or to be financed by a debtor-creditor-supplier agreement to finance a transaction between the debtor and a supplier, other than the creditor.[1] An agreement is void if, and to the extent that, it purports to provide that a person acting as, or on behalf of a negotiator, is to be treated as the agent of the debtor or hirer or to relieve a person from liability for acts or omissions of any person acting as, or on behalf of, a negotiator.[2]

The limitation of the scope of the s 56 agency provision is evidenced by *Black Horse Ltd v Langford*.[3] The court held that the phrase 'goods sold or proposed to be sold', in s 56(1)(b) applies only to the credit-broker who actually sells or proposes to sell the goods to the creditor and not to any other credit-broker in the chain of credit-brokers leading to the conclusion of the transaction. Ironically, it highlights the advantage to finance companies of dealing with intermediary credit-brokers, rather than directly with the supplier credit-broker.

The provisions of s 56, though not for any logical reason, do not apply the relationship of agency to a dealer involved in antecedent negotiations in relation to the making of a regulated hire agreement (as opposed to a regulated credit agreement).

The agency relationship, where it exists, extends to the entire spectrum of negotiations which precede entering into the agreement, including negotiations by the dealer relating to the part-exchange of a vehicle prior to the creditor entering into a conditional sale agreement.[4]

Antecedent negotiations commence when the negotiator and the debtor or hirer first enter into communication, including communication by advertisement and, although the CCA 1974 describes them as 'antecedent negotiations' they may even include negotiations following the making of the agreement.[5]

1 CCA 1974, ss 56(1)(b) and (c) and 56(2).
2 CCA 1974, s 56(3).
3 [2007] All ER (D) 214.
4 *Forthright Finance Ltd v Ingate (Carlyle Finance Ltd, third party)* [1999] GCCR 2213, CA.
5 CCA 1974, s 56(4).

13.4.2   Agent relating to disclosure of business use

The Consumer Credit Act does not regulate a consumer credit agreement by which the creditor provides the debtor with credit exceeding £25,000 or a consumer hire agreement that requires the hirer to make payments exceeding £25,000 if the agreement is entered into by the debtor or hirer, wholly or predominantly for the purposes of a business carried on, or intended to be carried on, by him. This presumption does not apply if, when the agreement is entered into, the creditor or owner or any person who acted on his behalf in connection with entering into the agreement, knows or has reasonable cause to suspect, that the agreement is not entered into wholly or predominantly for the purposes of a business carried on, or intended to be carried on, by the debtor or hirer.[1]

It follows that if a person who acts as an agent for the creditor or owner is informed by the debtor or hirer that he is entering into the agreement wholly or predominantly for the purpose of business, the agreement will be an unregulated agreement. There is no need to prove that the information was actually passed to the creditor or owner.

The words 'acted on his behalf in connection with the entering into the agreement' are not entirely clear but it would be safe to assume that they encompass an ordinary dealer even though, following *Branwhite v Worcester Works Finance Ltd*, such a dealer is not construed as the agent of the creditor or owner.

1 CCA 1974, s 16B(1) and (3).

13.4.3   Relevance to establishing unfair relationships between creditor and debtor

The signifcance of any act or omission by an agent of a creditor emerges from the unfair relationships provisions of the Consumer Credit Act. Thus, in considering whether the relationship between the creditor and the debtor arising out of the agreement is unfair to the debtor, one of the grounds is anything done, or not done, on behalf of the creditor either before or after the making of the agreement or any related agreement.[1] The court is bound to take into account all matters it thinks relevant. Accordingly, the conduct of any person acting as agent of the creditor will be a relevant issue for consideration.

1 CCA 1974, s 140A.

13.4.4   Agent for receiving notices

The Act deems certain persons to be the agent of the creditor or owner for specified purposes. Each of the following is deemed to be the agent of the creditor or owner for the purpose of receiving a notice of withdrawal from a prospective regulated agreement, a cancellation notice in respect of a cancellable agreement or a notice rescinding the agreement:

(a)   a credit-broker or supplier who is the negotiator in antecedent negotiations; and

(b)   any person who, in the course of a business carried on by him, acts on behalf of the debtor or hirer in any negotiations for the agreement.[1]

The hirer under a regulated consumer hire agreement is entitled to terminate the agreement by giving notice to any person entitled or authorised to receive the rental payments.[2] Likewise, a debtor under a hire-purchase or conditional sale agreement may terminate the agreement by giving notice to any person entitled or authorised to receive the sums payable under the agreement.[3]

A credit-broker or supplier who is the negotiator in antecedent negotiations is also deemed to be the agent of the creditor in respect of any repayments of credit or of interest and for the re-delivery of any goods under a cancelled agreement.[4]

Where a person is deemed to receive a notice or payment as agent of the creditor or owner under a regulated agreement, he is deemed to be under a contractual duty to the creditor or owner to transmit the notice or remit the payment to him forthwith.[5]

1 CCA 1974, ss 57(3), 68(6) and 102(1).
2 CCA 1974, s 101(1).
3 CCA 1974, s 99(1).
4 CCA 1974, ss 71(4) and 72(6).
5 CCA 1974, s 175.

13.4.5   Debtor's agent

So far as the debtor is concerned, the debtor under a regulated consumer credit agreement is not liable to the creditor for any loss arising from any use made of the credit facility by another person not acting, or to be treated as acting, as the debtor's agent.[1] However, except in relation to a distance contract within the meaning of the Consumer Protection (Distance Selling) Regulations 2000,[2] the debtor under a credit-token agreement can be made liable for £50 of the creditor's loss.[3]

1 CCA 1974, s 83.
2 SI 2000/2334.
3 CCA 1974, s 84.

13.4.6   Contracting out

Finally, it should be mentioned that the various agency provisions cannot be excluded or negated by contract as this would offend CCA 1974, s 173. Subject to limited exceptions, this section provides that a term in a regulated agreement or linked transaction or in any other agreement relating to an actual or prospective regulated agreement or linked transaction is void if and to the extent that it is inconsistent with a provision for the protection of the debtor or hirer, his relative or any surety.[1]

1 CCA 1974, s 173.

Chapter 14

The supplier and related supplies

14.1 THE SUPPLIER UNDER THE CONSUMER CREDIT ACT 1974

In relation to the supply of goods or services on credit, as we have already noted, there are two types of debtor-creditor-supplier (d-c-s) agreements, namely two-party and three-party d-c-s agreements. In a two-party d-c-s agreement the supplier is also the provider of the credit. This is the case in credit sale, conditional sale and hire-purchase agreements.

In a three-party d-c-s agreement the credit facility and the title to the goods pass from different sources. Thus, where a retailer supplies goods which are financed by a separate finance company, the retailer passes the title and the finance company provides the credit.

The CCA 1974 identifies the supplier obliquely, by reference to the third person to a credit transaction, namely as the party to the transaction with the debtor, other than the creditor, in the case of a three-party d-c-s agreement and as the creditor himself in the case of a two-party d-c-s agreement.

A useful distinction between the two kinds of supplier is provided by the Consumer Protection Act 1987. This refers to the supplier in the two-party d-c-s agreement as the ostensible supplier and the supplier in the three-party d-c-s agreement as the effective supplier. Section 46 of the Consumer Protection Act 1987 provides that in the case of a hire-purchase agreement, conditional sale agreement or credit sale agreement or an agreement for the hiring of goods, the effective supplier and not the ostensible supplier will be treated as supplying goods to the customer for the purposes of that Act.

CCA 1974, s 75 renders the creditor liable for any misrepresentation or breach of contract by the supplier. The creditor is entitled to a statutory indemnity by the supplier for any loss suffered by the creditor in satisfying such liability, including costs reasonably incurred by him in defending proceedings instituted by the debtor.[1] It is submitted that a creditor facing potential claims under CCA 1974, s 75 may apply to the court under the Contracts (Rights of Third Parties) Act 1999 or the Third Parties (Rights against Insurers) Act 1930, as appropriate, for the purpose of establishing rights transferred to or vested in the creditor.[2]

The Advertisements Regulations use the expression 'dealer' synonymously with 'supplier'. 'Dealer' is defined in the Regulations as, in relation to a hire-purchase, credit sale or conditional sale agreement under which he is not the creditor, a person who sells or proposes to sell goods, land or other things to the creditor before they form the subject matter of any such agreement and, in relation to any other agreement, means a supplier or his agent.[3] In commercial parlance, 'dealer' is used in preference to 'supplier'.

1   CCA 1974, s 75. See further para 16.4.4.
2   See *Re OT Computers* [2004] 1 All ER (Comm) 320, [2003] GCCR 4951.
3   Consumer Credit (Advertisements) Regulations 2004, SI 2004/1484, reg 1(2).

14.2   DEALER AGREEMENTS

Creditors and providers of hire facilities will often enter into agreements with dealers to govern their relationship, including the terms of supply, commission arrangements, credit criteria, compliance with laws and regulations, buy-back arrangements and agency appointment for the sale of goods on expiry of the agreement.

It is common practice to require the dealer to give warranties and indemnities, either in a master agreement or in respect of each credit or hire agreement entered into in respect of goods supplied by the dealer. Thus, the dealer might be required to warrant that any initial payment or deposit had been received by him, that the agreement was correctly completed before it was signed by the customer, that the requisite statutory copies were supplied to the customer, that the goods were the dealer's unencumbered property and that, upon acceptance of the supply by the dealer, ownership of the goods would pass to the creditor or lessor, as the case may be.

Dealer agreements may contain restrictive covenants seeking to prevent the dealer from transacting with other finance companies during the term of the dealer's agreement with the finance company.

In view of the value attached to customer lists, dealer agreements might contain provisions seeking to protect the confidentiality of, and rights of ownership to, customer names and addresses.

A typical dealer agreement will contain terms governing the substantive relationship between the creditor or owner and the dealer and provisions relating to:

(i)   submission of agreements;

(ii)   credit referencing and credit criteria;

(iii)   making of agreements;

(iv)   reimbursement by creditor or owner of cash price of goods and payment of commission to dealer;

(iv)   marketing and advertising;

(v)   operation of a negative stop list;

(vi)   debt collection procedures;

(vii)   restrictions on the use of customer information;

(viii) confidentiality provisions;

(ix) compliance with the law, relevant codes of practice and OFT Guidance;

(x) customer complaints procedure;

(xi) dispute resolution procedure;

(xii) rights of assignment;

(xiii) provisions applying on termination;

(xiv) governing law and jurisdiction.

14.3 EXTENDED WARRANTIES

In addition to statutory warranties and guarantees, which may not be excluded or restricted in the case of consumer agreements, suppliers might offer customers additional protection by way of extended warranties to cover goods supplied by them. Typically this cover extends the warranty or guarantee applying to the goods for a period after the manufacturer's guarantee has expired.

Following a reference by the Office of Fair Trading in July 2002 under the Fair Trading Act 1973, the Competition Commission investigated the market for extended warranties on electrical goods. In consequence of the Competition Commission's Report, an Order was made in January 2005, which came into force on 6 April 2005,[1] and essentially relates to a product designed to be connected to an electricity supply or powered by batteries for domestic purposes. The Order requires a person who offers to supply a consumer with an extended warranty, either directly or on behalf of a third party, to display the price of the extended warranty, provide specified information and produce a written quotation in store, in newspaper advertisements and other media, catalogues and websites. Written quotations must be available for acceptance for 30 days. The consumer has 45 days to cancel the extended warranty if it is to apply for more than one year.

Arranging, advising on and selling extended warranties is a regulated activity and will require the principal offering the same to be authorised under the Financial Services and Markets Act 2000. However, the agent offering the same will usually be exempt from the requirement to be authorised as an agent, as the sale by an agent of a 'connected insurance product' is not a regulated activity.[2] The exemption only applies to the sale of a contract of insurance which is complementary to non-motor goods.

Other insurance which 'piggy backs' on credit or hire agreements is mechanical breakdown insurance which might be sold 'as an optional extra' in respect of agreements involving motor vehicles and fraud protection cover which might be offered free of charge as an incentive to applicants for credit cards. The provider of such insurances, and the intermediary, will generally need to be authorised under the Financial Services and Markets Act 2000.

1 The Supply of Extended Warranties on Domestic Electrical Goods Order 2005, SI 2005/37. Note that the cancellation and termination rights under Art 8 do not apply to a distance contract.
2 Financial Services and Markets Act 2000 (Regulated Activities) Order 2001, SI 2001/544, as amended, art 72B.

14.4   INSURANCE AND THE REGULATED AGREEMENT

Insurance companies offer insurance in connection with credit or hire transactions in respect of associated insurable risks. These include third party motor vehicle insurance, comprehensive insurance cover and Guaranteed Asset Protection (GAP) insurance in the case of motor vehicles, insurance of goods, usually in the form of comprehensive insurance cover and property insurance in respect of mortgaged land. In addition, life assurance may be taken up on the life of the borrower in the context of an endowment mortgage or as collateral security for a loan. Arranging, advising on and selling insurance products is a regulated activity under the Financial Services and Markets Act 2000 and will require authorisation by the FSA.

Contracts of insurance are excluded from the normal rule that linked transactions entered into before the regulated agreement have no effect until that agreement is made. It follows that cancellation of a regulated agreement will not (at least, in the writer's view, in the absence of a contractual term to the contrary), terminate a contract of insurance.[1]

The attractiveness of insurance is enhanced by the fact that insurance premiums are excluded from the total charge for credit in regulated credit agreements, subject to one exception. The exception is a premium under a contract of insurance payable under the transaction by the debtor or a relative of his, where the making or maintenance of the contract of insurance is required by the creditor (i) as a condition of the making of the agreement and (ii) for the sole purpose of ensuring complete or partial repayment of the credit, and complete or partial repayment to the creditor of such of those charges included in the total charge for credit as are payable to him under the transaction, in the event of the death, invalidity, illness or unemployment of the debtor.[2] The expression 'transaction' is defined in the Regulations. The term 'invalidity' is an infelicitous substitution for the 'incapacity' of the debtor.

1   CCA 1974, s 19 and Consumer Credit (Linked Transactions) (Exemptions) Regulations 1983, SI 1983/1560.
2   Regulation 4 of the Consumer Credit (Total Charge for Credit) Regulations 1980, SI 1980/51 (as amended).

14.5   PAYMENT PROTECTION INSURANCE ('PPI')

Payment protection insurance encompasses various categories of cover intended to protect the customer against liability to make repayments under credit or hire agreements when unable to do so. It may include insuring the customer against his inability to pay if he is made redundant, suffers an accident, falls ill, ceases to be employed or dies.

PPI has undergone radical reform in the way in which it is permitted to be sold to consumers. Originally it was commonly sold to borrowers and hirers by way of a negative option, whereby the customer was asked to make an election only if he did not wish to take out such insurance, as opposed to positively electing for PPI. This incurred the wrath of the consumer lobby, which persuaded the then

Director General of Fair Trading to declare that he would regard the continuing sale of payment protection insurance by negative option as calling into doubt the licensee's licence under CCA 1974.[1]

Life assurance and general insurance were transferred from the authority of the then Department of Trade and Industry to the Treasury in December 2001 and January 2005 respectively, when they came under the regulatory powers of the Financial Services Authority. Accordingly, arranging, advising on and selling insurance products, such as PPI, are regulated activities and require authorisation by the FSA. Regulation of PPI falls under the ICOBS section of the FSA Handbook. The Rules govern all aspects of the insurance, including identifying client needs, advising, product information, customer's rights of cancellation, claims handling and complaints.

Payment protection insurance may be dealt with in various different ways. First, it may be financed and constitute the main or only subject matter of the agreement. In this case it invariably needs to be documented as a regulated debtor-creditor-supplier agreement. Second, it may be ancillary to the main subject matter of a regulated agreement. In that case, it is included in the total charge for credit where the conditions referred to in para 14.4 apply. Otherwise it is excluded from the charge for credit and APR, so where it is optional or not for the sole purpose referred to above, it does not augment the charge for credit. Finally, payment protection insurance may be paid for by regular, usually monthly, cash premiums, in which event it is not financed. It will then take the form of a regular periodical policy, in respect of which failure to pay the premium will result in the policy lapsing.

In February 2004 the OFT made a reference to the Competition Commission under the Enterprise Act 2002 for an investigation into the supply of PPI. The findings of the Commission are now awaited.

1 Press Release of 28 October 1992.

14.6 CARD PROTECTION COVER

The credit industry has spawned a secondary industry which is involved in all aspects of the protection of credit cards. In return for a premium or membership fee the card protection companies or card notification organisations will provide a range of services such as the confidential registration of all the member's cards; an emergency helpline to notify card issuers of the loss or theft of cards to stop their further use; payment of a sum, by way of protection against fraudulent use of cards; an emergency cash loan; arrangements for the replacement of cards; lost key registration; valuable property and document protection; lost luggage recovery etc.

Taking advantage of opportunities created by cards being lost or stolen, these agencies also offer to replace lost keys, pay hotel bills, replace airline tickets and provide emergency car hire.

In *Card Protection Plan Ltd v Comrs of Customs and Excise*[1] the House of Lords held that arrangements of this kind constitute insurance business as the dominant purpose is one of insurance. Accordingly, the transaction is to be regarded for VAT purposes as comprising a principal exempt insurance supply, with the other supplies in the transaction being ancillary, so that they are to be treated as exempt for VAT purposes.[2]

1 [2001] 2 All ER 143, HL.
2 Value Added Tax Act 1983, ss 2(1) and 2(2); s 17(1); Sch 6, Group 2 – Insurance.

14.7   PROVIDERS OF MAINTENANCE SERVICES

Borrowers and hirers are usually required to maintain goods in proper working condition, fair wear and tear excepted and, in the case of the hire of motor vehicles, to have them serviced regularly.

Where, under the agreement, the owner makes arrangements for the maintenance of the vehicles, routine servicing costs will often be included in the rentals. Where they are not, the owner will collect the maintenance payments by way of monthly cash sums, other than financed monthly payments, to avoid problems in relation to the categorisation of the agreement.

A separate maintenance contract in conjunction with the hire or credit agreement will usually be a linked transaction with the result that cancellation of the regulated agreement will also result in cancellation of the maintenance contract.

14.8   SUPPLIERS UNDER DISTANCE CONTRACTS

The Consumer Protection (Distance Selling) Regulations 2000[1] introduced a new era in consumer protection. The regulations define a 'distance contract' as any contract concerning goods or services concluded between a supplier and a consumer under an organised distance sales or service provision scheme run by the supplier who, for the purpose of the contract, makes exclusive use of one or more means of distance communication up to and including the moment at which the contract is concluded.[2]

'Means of distance communication' is defined as any means which, without the simultaneous physical presence of the supplier and the consumer, may be used for the conclusion of a contract between those parties. It includes addressed or unaddressed printed matter, letter, press advertising with order form, catalogue, telephone, videophone, electronic mail, facsimile and teleshopping.[3] The Regulations specify the information which the supplier must give to the consumer prior to the conclusion of the contract. That information includes the consumer's right of cancellation within seven working days beginning with the day after that on which he receives the goods or the contract is concluded, in the case of a contract for the supply of services.

Cancellation of an agreement for the supply of goods and services automatically cancels a related credit agreement.[4] The consumer repays any portion of the credit before the expiry of one month following the cancellation of the credit agreement or, in the case of a credit agreement repayable by instalments, before the date on which the first instalment is due, no interest is payable on the amount repaid.[5] A further permutation of the Regulations is that they require the supplier to perform the contract within a maximum period of 30 days after the day the consumer sent his order to the supplier. If the supplier fails to perform within this time, he is obligated to reimburse the consumer with any sum paid by him or on his behalf, including by a creditor.[6]

The Regulations are not restricted to regulated credit agreements but apply to an agreement between a creditor and a consumer for the provision of credit in any amount. Although not expressly stated, the regulations also appear to apply to the provision of goods on hire, hire-purchase or sold under a credit sale or conditional sale agreement, as these are contracts concerning goods, rather than contracts relating (exclusively) to financial services, which are exempted from the Regulations.[7]

1 Consumer Protection (Distance Selling) Regulations 2000, SI 2000/2334.
2 Consumer Protection (Distance Selling) Regulations 2000, reg 3(1).
3 Consumer Protection (Distance Selling) Regulations 2000, Sch 1.
4 Consumer Protection (Distance Selling) Regulations 2000, reg 15.
5 Consumer Protection (Distance Selling) Regulations 2000, reg 16.
6 Consumer Protection (Distance Selling) Regulations 2000, reg 19.
7 Consumer Protection (Distance Selling) Regulations 2000, reg 5(1)(c) read with Sch 2.

14.9 CONTRACTS MADE IN THE CONSUMER'S HOME OR PLACE OF WORK

Following the receipt of complaints regarding the earlier Consumer Protection (Cancellation of Contracts Concluded away from Business Premises) Regulations 1987[1] (to protect consumers in respect of contracts concluded away from business premises), Citizens Advice Bureau lodged a super-complaint with the OFT in 2002. This led to an OFT market study of doorstep selling. In September 2006 the government published its response to the public consultation, in the form of draft Cancellation of Contracts made in a Consumer's Home or Place of Work etc. Regulations 2008.[2] The Regulations extend the cooling-off period and cancellation rights applying to contracts made during unsolicited visits by traders, to contracts made during solicited visits, require a notice of customer cancellation rights to be displayed in the contractual document, set the cooling-off period at seven days (starting on receipt of the notice of cancellation rights) and provide for automatic cancellation of a related credit agreement where a cancellation notice is served on a trader.

1 SI 1987/2117, which implement Directive 85/577/EEC, a minimum harmonisation Directive.
2 These regulations are still in draft form at the time of writing. They will in due course repeal and replace SI 1987/2117.

14.10 TIMESHARE AGREEMENTS

Timeshare agreements are regulated by the Timeshare Act 1992 and Orders made under that Act.[1]

The Timeshare Act 1992 imposes on the offeror of the timeshare agreement, classified by the Act as the operator, obligations to provide pre-contractual information about the proposed accommodation which must also be referred to in any advertisement for timeshare rights. The Timeshare Act lays down obligatory terms for the timeshare agreement, an obligation to provide a translation of the agreement in the language of the EEA state in which the accommodation is situated, and requires a notice of the right to cancel to be set out in the agreement.

The Timeshare Act makes separate provision for a timeshare credit agreement, which is an agreement under which credit is granted to fully or partly cover the price payable for the timeshare. The Timeshare Act imposes mandatory provisions for cancellation of a timeshare credit agreement[2] and these prevail over those laid down in CCA 1974.[3] When a timeshare agreement is cancelled, any related timeshare credit agreement is also cancelled.[4] The debtor may, however, cancel the credit agreement without cancelling the timeshare agreement. When the credit agreement is cancelled, it remains enforceable by the creditor in so far as it relates to payment of credit and payment of interest. However, if the debtor repays the whole or a part of the credit before expiry of one month following the giving of notice of cancellation or the automatic cancellation of the timeshare agreement or, in the case of credit repayable by instalments, before the due date of the first instalment, no interest is payable on the amount repaid.[5]

The Timeshare Act 1992 was amended by the Timeshare Act 1992 (Amendment) Regulations 2003.[6] The Timeshare Act 1992 is extended to apply also where the timeshare accommodation is situated in another EEA state but the parties to the timeshare agreement are subject to the jurisdiction of the UK courts. Notice of the right to cancel a timeshare agreement must now be set out in the agreement itself.

Where a timeshare agreement is financed by a regulated debtor-creditor-supplier agreement, the creditor under the agreement assumes obligations pursuant to CCA 1974, ss 56 and 75, notwithstanding that the property which is the subject of the timeshare agreement is situated outside the jurisdiction of the United Kingdom. So it was held in *Jarrett v Barclays Bank plc*; *Jones v First National Bank plc*; *Peacock v First National Bank plc*.[7] Morrit LJ stated that the claims against the defendants, as lenders, on grounds of misrepresentation and breach of contract, did not have as their object the tenancies of immovable property (i.e. the timeshare accommodation). Rather, the foundation of the claims under CCA 1974, ss 56 and 75 was the debtor-creditor-supplier agreement, to which the personal statutory rights conferred on the debtor by CCA 1974 were attached. It followed that the debtors under the various credit agreements were able to institute proceedings against their respective creditors for misrepresentation or breach of contract by the sellers of the timeshares.

It is submitted that a regulated agreement may not import the law of the jurisdiction where the timeshare properties are situated if the effect would be to exclude rights conferred on the debtor by CCA 1974. This would conflict with the anti-avoidance provisions of CCA 1974, s 173 and constitute an unfair term under the Unfair Terms in Consumer Contracts Regulations 1999.[8]

1   Timeshare (Cancellation Notices) Order 1992, SI 1992/1942 and Timeshare (Repayment of Credit on Cancellation) Order 1992, S1 1992/1943.
2   Timeshare Act 1992, s 3.
3   Timeshare Act 1992, ss 1(5), (6), (6A) and 6.
4   Timeshare Act 1992, s 6A.

5 Timeshare Act 1992, s 7.
6 SI 2003/1922.
7 [1999] QB 1, [1999] GCCR 2151, CA.
8 SI 1999/2083, reg 5(5) read with Sch 2, para 1(q).

Chapter 15

Ancillary credit business

15.1 MEANING OF ANCILLARY CREDIT BUSINESS

An ancillary credit business is a business which comprises or relates to credit brokerage, debt-adjusting, debt-counselling, debt-collecting, debt administration, the provision of credit information services, or the operation of a credit reference agency.[1]

'Business' includes a profession or trade, but a person is not to be treated as carrying on a particular type of business merely because occasionally he enters into transactions belonging to a business of that type.[2] We consider the question of 'carrying on business' at para 21.1.4.

The business of credit brokerage was discussed in Chapter 12 and we shall now consider the other ancillary credit businesses.

1 CCA 1974, s 145(1).
2 CCA 1974, s 189(1) and (2).

15.2 DEBT-ADJUSTING, DEBT-COUNSELLING AND DEBT-COLLECTING

Although each of the above is classified as a separate ancillary credit business, they will be considered together. From a practical point of view they are usually carried on together by the same persons and CCA 1974 contains provisions common to each activity.

On a practical plane, credit-brokers are often also licensed to carry on the businesses of debt-adjusting, debt-counselling and debt-collecting. Less frequently, they will also be licensed to carry on the business of a credit reference agency. The more restricted types of businesses, namely those involving the carrying on of the businesses of debt-adjusting and debt-counselling, are to be found in the form of the Citizens' Advice Bureaux, Age Concern, the Institute of Business Counsellors and various advice centres.

Each of the ancillary credit businesses is defined by reference to debts due under consumer credit or consumer hire agreements. Debt-adjusting is negotiating with the creditor or owner, on behalf of the debtor or hirer, terms for the discharge of a debt, or taking over, in return for payments by the debtor or hirer, his obligation to discharge a debt or any similar activity concerned with the liquidation of a debt.[1] It is not debt-adjusting if the debt in question is due under an agreement secured by a land mortgage or the agreement is, or forms part of, a regulated home purchase plan ('relevant agreement') where entering into the agreement constituted a regulated activity under the Financial Services and Markets Act 2000 ('FSMA').[2]

Debt-counselling is the giving of advice to debtors or hirers about the liquidation of debts.[3] It is not debt-counselling for a person to give advice to a debtor about the liquidation of debts if the debt in question is due under a relevant agreement, as identified above, and giving that advice is a regulated activity under FSMA.[4]

Debt-collecting is the taking of steps to procure payment of debts due under consumer credit or consumer hire agreements.[5] The debts which are the subject of debt-adjusting, debt-counselling and debt-collecting can arise under consumer credit or hire agreements, whether regulated or exempt agreements. There is no exemption corresponding to the exemptions above for FSMA regulated activities.

It is not debt-adjusting, debt-counselling or debt-collecting for a person to do anything in relation to an agreement if that person is any of the following:

(a)   the creditor or owner under the agreement;

(b)   the supplier in relation to the agreement;

(c)   a credit-broker who has acquired the business of the person who was the supplier in relation to the agreement; or

(d)   not, by virtue of CCA 1974, s 146(5), treated as a credit-broker and the agreement was made as a result of an introduction which, by virtue of that section, is to be disregarded.

It should be remembered that creditor/owner includes the person to whom the creditor's/owner's respective rights and duties under the agreement have passed by assignment or operation of law.[6]

In order to facilitate the conduct of their principal business, practising barristers or advocates, and solicitors engaging in contentious business, are not regarded as carrying on any ancillary credit business.[7]

1   CCA 1974, s 145(5).
2   CCA 1974, s 146(5B) and (5D).
3   CCA 1974, s 145(6).
4   CCA 1974, s 146(5C) and (5D).
5   CCA 1974, s 145(7).
6   CCA 1974, s 189(1).
7   CCA 1974, s 146(1).

15.3   DEBT ADMINISTRATION; PROVIDING CREDIT INFORMATION SERVICES

Debt administration is the taking of steps to perform duties, or to exercise or enforce rights, under a consumer credit agreement or a consumer hire agreement, on behalf of the creditor or owner, so far as the taking of such steps is not debt-collecting.[1] As noted above, the creditor or owner includes an assignee of the creditor or owner.

It is not debt administration for a person to take steps to perform duties, or to exercise or enforce rights, under an agreement on behalf of the creditor or owner if that person is any of the following:

(a) the creditor or owner under the agreement;

(b) the supplier in relation to the agreement;

(c) a credit-broker who has acquired the business of the person who was the supplier in relation to the agreement; or

(d) not, by virtue of CCA 1974, s 146(5) treated as a credit-broker and the agreement was made as a result of an introduction which, by virtue of that section, is to be disregarded.[2]

A person provides credit information services if he takes any of the following steps, or gives advice to an individual in relation to the taking of any of the following steps, namely steps with a view to:

(a) ascertaining whether a credit information agency (other than that person himself if he is one) holds information relevant to the financial status of an individual;

(b) ascertaining the contents of such information held by such an agency;

(c) securing the correction of, the omission of anything from, or the making of any other kind of modification of, such information so held; or

(d) securing that such an agency which holds such information stops holding it or does not provide it to another person.[3]

A credit information agency means any of the following:

(a) a person who carries on a consumer credit business or a consumer hire business;

(b) a person who carries on a business so far as it comprises or relates to credit brokerage, debt-adjusting, debt-counselling, debt-collecting, debt administration or the operation of a credit reference agency;

(c) a person who carries on a business which would be a consumer credit business except that it comprises or relates to consumer credit agreements being, otherwise than by virtue of s 16(5)(a), exempt agreements; or

(d) a person who carries on a business which would be a consumer hire business except that it comprises or relates to consumer hire agreements being, otherwise than by virtue of s 16(6) exempt agreements.[4]

1 CCA 1974, s 145(7A).
2 CCA 1974, s 146(7).
3 CCA 1974, s 145(7B) and (7C).
4 CCA 1974, s 145(7D).

15.4   RESTRICTIONS ON DEBT COLLECTING

A debt-collector is required to use reasonable restraint in the debt-collection methods employed by him. Thus, he may not unreasonably harass the debtor with demands for payment so that, in respect of the frequency or the manner of making any demand, or of any threat or publicity accompanying it, he causes the debtor or his family distress or humiliation. He may also not make false representations about possible criminal proceedings.[1]

A debt-collector may not send letters which convey a threat unless it is used to reinforce a demand which he has proper and reasonable grounds for making.[2] A breach of the foregoing constitutes an offence and, more seriously, the debt-collector stands to lose his licence.[3]

The Office of Fair Trading publishes Debt Collection Guidance from time to time.[4] The Guidance makes it clear that the misdemeanours of a debt collector will be visited upon a licence holder who employs that debt collector, by calling into question that licence holder's fitness. The aim of the OFT is to ensure that creditors and owners do not ignore the unfair practices of debt collectors, whether in-house or external, acting on their behalf. The debt collection guidance sets out what the OFT regard as unfair business practices under the heads 'Communication', 'False Representation of authority and/or legal position', 'Physical/psychological harassment', 'Deceptive and/or unfair methods', 'Charging for Debt Collection', 'Debt Collection Visits' and 'Statute barred debts'.

The OFT identifies unfair practices in relation to communications as including use of official looking documents intended or likely to mislead debtors as to their status e.g. documents made to resemble court claims; leaving out or presenting information in such a way that it creates a false or misleading impression or exploits debtor's lack of knowledge; unnecessary and unhelpful use of legal and technical language e.g. use of Latin phrases, and contacting debtors at unreasonable times.

The OFT prohibits persons contacting debtors by misrepresenting the authority and/or the correct legal position e.g. claiming to work on instructions from the courts, claiming to be bailiffs or, in Scotland, sheriff officers or messenger-at-arms; falsely implying or stating that action can or will be taken when it legally cannot e.g. referring to bankruptcy or sequestration proceedings when the balance is too low to qualify for such proceedings or claiming a right of entry when no court order to this effect has been granted; misrepresenting status or backing, such as using a logo which falsely implies government backing; taking or threatening to take court action in the wrong jurisdiction e.g. against a Scottish debtor in an English court unless legally justified.

Under the head of physical/psychological harassment, the OFT lists as examples of unfair practices, contacting debtors at unreasonable times and at unreasonable intervals; pressurising debtors to sell property, to raise funds by further borrowing or to extend their borrowing; using more than one debt collection business at the same time; not informing the debtor when their case has been passed on to a different debt collector; pressurising debtors to pay in full, in unreasonably large instalments or to increase payments when they are unable to do so; acting in a way likely to publicly embarrass the debtor.

Under the heading of deceptive and/or unfair methods, the OFT identifies the following: sending demands for payment or disclosing details to an individual, when it is uncertain that the individual is the debtor in question; refusing to deal with appointed or authorised third parties such as Citizens' Advice Bureaux, independent advice centres or money advisers; operating a policy, without reason, of refusing to negotiate with debt management companies; and not ceasing collection activity whilst investigating a reasonable queried or disputed debt.

In relation to charging for debt collection, the OFT guidance prescribes that charges should not be levied unfairly, such as claiming collection costs from the debtor in the absence of express contractual or other legal provision; not giving an indication in credit agreements of the amount of any charges payable on default; and applying unreasonable charges and charges which are disproportionate to the main debt. In the case of a regulated agreement there is of course the requirement under the Consumer Credit (Agreements) Regulations 1983, that the credit agreement must include an indication of any charges payable on default, failing which the agreement is not properly executed and is only enforceable against the debtor on an order of the court.[5]

On the subject of debt collection visits, the OFT prohibits those visiting debtors from acting in an unclear or threatening manner e.g. not making the purpose of any proposed visit clear; visiting a debtor when it is known that he is vulnerable; entering a property uninvited; visiting or threatening to visit debtors without prior agreement when the debt is deadlocked or disputed or not giving adequate notice of the time and date of a visit.

As regards a debt which is statute barred, the OFT regards it unfair to pursue the debt if the debtor has heard nothing from the creditor during the relevant limitation period. On the other hand, if a creditor has been in regular contact with the debtor before the debt is statute barred, then the OFT does not consider it unfair to continue to recover the debt provided that the creditor does not furnish the debtor with any false or misleading information.

The Office of Fair Trading has issued 'Complaint Evidence Checklist for Advisers' which it expects licensees to complete in order to enable the OFT to check whether there has been compliance with the OFT's Debt Collection Guidance.

The Office of Fair Trading has published Debt Management Guidance to regulate advice on the restructuring and rescheduling of debts, contacting debtors for such purposes and setting out minimum standards to be met by Debt Management Companies (DMCs) if they are to be judged fit to hold a consumer credit licence.[6]

1 Administration of Justice Act 1970, s 40.
2 Malicious Communications Act 1988, s 1.
3 For an example see *Credit Default Register and Holmes v Secretary of State for Trade and Industry* [1993] CCLR 59; [1993] CL 84.
4 See the Guidance issued in July 2003 (updated December 2006) OFT 664.
5 CCA 1974, ss 61(1)(a), 65 and Consumer Credit (Agreements) Regulations 1983, Sch 1.
6 December 2001.

15.5 CREDIT REFERENCE AGENCIES

A credit reference agency is a person carrying on a business comprising the furnishing of persons with information relevant to the financial standing of individuals and being information collected by the agency for that purpose.¹ There are three limbs to the activity of credit referencing: collecting information, furnishing information to others and that the information must relate to the financial standing of individuals i.e. their creditworthiness.

It follows that if the information is only gathered for the collector's own use, e.g. a bank or leasing company, the activity does not constitute the operation of a credit reference agency business. However, if a company in a group of companies furnishes its associate companies with information regarding the credit status of individuals, it will be conducting a credit reference agency business. If an organisation only serves the purpose of controlling personal data, e.g. by setting up and operating a data system, without both collecting information on the financial standing of others and imparting that information to other persons, it is not conducting the business of a credit reference agency.

Whilst there are numerous operations which conduct ancillary credit businesses and a vast number which carry on credit brokerage businesses, there are only two major credit reference agencies in the United Kingdom, Experian Ltd and Equifax plc.

As noted at para 2.6.9, an applicant for credit or hire facilities is entitled to obtain the name and address of any credit reference agency used by the creditor or leasing company. The request must be made within 28 days of the ending of the negotiations. The credit reference agency must, within the prescribed period of 7 working days, and on payment of the prescribed fee, furnish the customer with a copy of the file relating to him and a statement of his rights in relation to the file. The file (in relation to an individual) means all the information about him kept by the credit reference agency, regardless of how the information is stored and 'copy of the file' is respect of information not in plain English, means a transcript reduced into plain English.²

If an individual who has been given information by a credit reference agency under the Data Protection Act 1998, s 7 or CCA 1974, s 158, considers that an entry in his file is incorrect, and if not corrected is likely to prejudice him, he may give notice to the agency requiring it either to remove the entry from the file or to amend it. The credit reference agency is required to act on that instruction within 28 days. If a dispute cannot be satisfactorily resolved the consumer can invoke the assistance of the Office of Fair Trading.³

Within the prescribed period, a credit reference agency must furnish the corrected particulars to all persons to whom, in the preceding six months, it furnished information relating to the financial standing of the consumer.⁴ Credit reference agencies may, with the approval of the Office of Fair Trading, refuse to disclose information to consumers who carry on a business where disclosure would adversely affect the service provided by them to customers.⁵

Information held by credit reference agencies in relation to an individual includes information about the individual on the electoral roll (in order to check the address), and judgments supplied by Registry Trust Ltd, an independent organisation established by the Lord Chancellor's Department for keeping the Register of County Court Judgments or CCJs entered for sums of money in the county courts in England and Wales. The agencies also hold records of Scottish judgments, called decrees, for a period of six years. These records are usually kept on file for six years. Credit reference agencies hold details of bankruptcies and information on property repossessions, each for six years, as well as details of credit accounts of individuals and specifically information relating to late payments.

Credit reference agencies also provide a payment profile service, providing details of the financial commitments and payment performance of an individual, which is a valuable aid to underwriting. They will supply a copy of the mortgage possession register, confirming details of properties which have been surrendered to, or repossessed by, mortgage lenders, and hold records on non-registered businesses, such as sole traders and partnerships. They might also offer underwriting services and credit account services, such as the production of statements for customers, and control and audit reports for credit companies.

In 1992 the then Data Protection Registrar (now the Information Commissioner) instituted proceedings against the main credit reference agencies with a view to preventing them from furnishing information about persons living at the same address as the data subject about whom a credit reference was sought, on the grounds that such information was irrelevant. As a result of those hearings before the Data Protection Tribunal, an Enforcement Notice was issued under the terms of which lenders are restricted to searching credit reference agencies for information only about an applicant for credit and other people with the same surname, or with a different name if it is reasonable to believe that such person is the data subject or has been living as a member of the same family as the data subject in a single household.[6]

Needless to say, credit reference agencies must comply with the Data Protection Principles set out in the Data Protection Act 1998, Sch 1. These principles include the following requirements: that personal data should be processed fairly and lawfully; shall be obtained only for one or more specified and lawful purposes; must be adequate, relevant and not excessive in relation to the purposes for which they are processed; need to be accurate and kept up to date; may not be kept for longer than is necessary; and must be processed in accordance with the rights of data subjects. Appropriate technical and organisational measures must be taken against unauthorised or unlawful processing of personal data and against accidental loss or destruction of, or damage to, personal data. Personal data may not be transferred to a country outside the European Economic Area unless that country ensures an adequate level of protection of the rights and freedoms of the subjects in relation to the processing of personal data.

In general, credit reference agencies retain records for six years for the use of credit grantors. Records of bankruptcies are held for six years after the date of bankrkuptcy, records of County Court Judgments are held for six years after the date of the judgment, and account records are held for six years from the date of the last entry on that record.

Data controllers must ensure that the necessary security measures are in place to safeguard personal data. If a controller uses the services of a data processor, the security arrangements must be recorded in a written agreement between the parties.[7]

1 CCA 1974, s 145(8).
2 CCA 1974, s 158.
3 CCA 1974, ss 158 and 159 and the Consumer Credit (Credit Reference Agency) Regulations 1977, SI 1977/329.

4 Consumer Credit (Conduct of Business) (Credit References) Regulations 1977, SI 1977/330 as amended by the Consumer Credit (Conduct of Business) (Credit References) (Amendment) Regulations 2000, SI 2000/291.
5 CCA 1974, s 160.
6 See *Goode: Consumer Credit Law and Practice* (LexisNexis Butterworths), at para VIII, D [23.1].
7 Data Protection Act 1998, Sch 1, Pt 1, reg 7; Pt II, para 12(a).

15.6   UNFAIR RELATIONSHIPS AND ANCILLARY CREDIT BUSINESS

The manner in which ancillary credit business, of whatever kind, is carried on, may have an impact upon a credit agreement by virtue of the unfair relationships provisions of CCA 1974.[1] Section 140A expressly states that the relationship between the creditor and the debtor arising out of the agreement may be unfair to the debtor because of the way in which the creditor has exercised or enforced any of his rights under the agreement or any related agreement or because of any other thing done, or not done, by or on behalf of, the creditor, either before or after making the agreement or any related agreement. Thus, in addition to the OFT's powers in relation to licensing, the courts may in the event of misconduct on behalf of a provider of ancillary credit business services, make an order in any of the terms set out in s 140B. It therefore behoves a creditor to ensure that it, and any party carrying on ancillary credit business on its behalf, does so in a lawful and unimpeachable manner.

1 CCA 1974, s 140A following.

15.7   LICENSING OF PERSONS CARRYING ON AN ANCILLARY CREDIT BUSINESS

A person may not carry on an ancillary credit business unless licensed in respect of that category under CCA 1974. Any misconduct on the part of a licensee in respect of ancillary credit business may jeopardise the licence, in whole or in part.[1]

1 See generally Chapter 21 post.

Chapter 16

Credit cards and other payment cards

16.1 STRUCTURE OF CREDIT CARD TRANSACTIONS

Credit card transactions fall into one of two structures. The first is a three-party structure which involves (i) an agreement between the card issuer and the cardholder to extend credit by paying for goods or services purchased by the cardholder from suppliers who have agreed to honour the card and, where applicable, advancing cash and/or agreeing to discharge the amount owing under other cards of the cardholder by way of balance transfers; (ii) an agreement between the card issuer and the supplier under which the supplier agrees to accept the card in payment and the card issuer agrees to pay the supplier; (iii) an agreement between the cardholder and the supplier for the purchase of goods or services and any other benefits (such as cash advances and balance transfers).

The second type of structure is a so-called four-party structure which has developed out of the use made by card issuers of merchant acquirers to recruit new suppliers willing to accept the issuer's card. In this situation there is interposed between the card issuer and the supplier the merchant acquirer acting as an independent party. The merchant acquirer and supplier enter into an agreement under which the supplier undertakes to honour the card and the merchant acquirer undertakes to pay the supplier. The merchant acquirer and the card issuer enter into an agreement under which the merchant acquirer agrees to pay the supplier and the card issuer undertakes to reimburse the merchant acquirer. There is no direct contractual link between the card issuer and the supplier.

A further development of the four-party structure is the interposition of large international credit card operating networks, such as VISA and MasterCard, which involve the addition of a clearing house system. Under the rules of the VISA and MasterCard networks, the card issuer enters into an agreement with its customer to extend credit in connection with the purchase of goods or services (and/or the advance of cash and provision of balance transfers) from any supplier who has agreed to honour the network card. The merchant acquirers recruit suppliers to the network, rather than to an individual card issuer, and the supplier undertakes to honour the network card regardless of the identity of the issuer. The card issuer undertakes to reimburse the merchant acquirer even though unaware of his identity or existence.[1]

As a matter of practice, VISA and MasterCard will not permit card issuers to join their operating networks unless they are authorised by the Financial Services Authority under the Financial Services and Markets Act 2000 with authority to collect deposits (i.e. banks) or the card issuer is ultimately owned by such an institution or a similar authorised financial institution abroad.

1 See *Office of Fair Trading v Lloyds TSB Bank plc* [2006] GCCR 5701, CA at 5704-5; *Re Charge Card Services Ltd* [1983] 3 All ER 289 at 301, [2000] GCCR 1231; *Customs and Excise Commissioners v Diners Club Ltd* [1999] GCCR 1213, CA.

16.2 LEGAL CHARACTERISATION OF PAYMENT BY CREDIT CARD

In contrast to payment by cheque, which operates as a conditional payment, a payment by credit card is an absolute, unconditional payment of the relevant amount on the date the payment is effected.[1] It is unaffected by any subsequent failure of the card issuer or merchant acquirer to effect payment to the supplier. If the supplier fails to recover payment from the card issuer or merchant acquirer, he has no right of recovery against the cardholder.

There is no possibility of making a post-dated payment by credit card, as there is in the case of payment by cheque. From the point of view of the supplier this underlines the need to check, prior to accepting payment by credit card, that the cardholder's account does in fact have the necessary funds in place to enable the credit card payment to be effected. If the cardholder exceeds his credit limit and the card issuer subsequently refuses to meet the liability, the supplier will have accepted the risk of loss of recovery of payment. From the point of view of the cardholder who wishes to order goods on day one but to postpone payment until receipt of delivery of the goods, he is unable to achieve this where payment is made by credit card but he is protected against any breach of contract, including non-receipt of the goods or misrepresentation by the supplier, by virtue of the card issuer's (creditor's) joint and several liability with the supplier under s 75 of the Act. Section 75 protection also applies to the use made of a credit card abroad.[2]

Section 75 liability only attaches to a debtor-creditor-supplier agreement (falling within s 12(b) or (c) of the Act). It does not extend to a cash withdrawal (or to goods or services paid by cash withdrawn) by means of a credit card, which is an unrestricted-use debtor-creditor agreement under s 13(c). Section 75 also does not apply to a balance transfer, which is a restricted-use debtor-creditor agreement under s 13(b), to refinance any existing indebtedness of the debtor's. A balance transfer does not extinguish the liability of the original creditor under a debtor-creditor-supplier agreement preceding the balance transfer, albeit that the original indebtedness is refinanced.

Additional cardholders receive their cards, and make their payments, in the capacity as agent of the debtor under the credit card agreement. The additional cardholder is not himself a debtor under the agreement and is not, for example, entitled to any rights as debtor, including rights under s 75 of the Act, rights to receive notices, statements etc. In contrast, each joint debtor is equally entitled to the rights of a debtor under the agreement.

A credit card cheque is a cheque drawn under a credit card agreement (where the agreement so provides) and can be used where transactions by card are not accepted. Payment by such cheque is subject to the Bills of Exchange Act 1882 and is not tantamount to payment by credit card.

1 *Re Charge Card Services Ltd* [1999] GCCR 95, [2000] GCCR 1231, CA.
2 *Office of Fair Trading v Lloyds TSB Bank plc.* loc. cit. at 5738-9.

16.3 LIABILITY FOR THEFT, LOSS OR MISUSE OF A CREDIT CARD

The debtor under a regulated consumer agreement is not liable to the creditor for loss arising from use of the credit facility by another person not acting, or to be treated as acting, as the debtor's agent.[1] However, this provision does not prevent the debtor under a credit-token agreement from being made liable to the extent of £50 (or the credit limit if lower) for loss to the creditor arising from use of the credit-token by other persons prior to the creditor being given notice that the credit-token has been lost or stolen or is for any other reason liable to misuse. On the other hand, where the credit token is acquired by another person with the debtor's consent, the debtor's liability for loss to the creditor, arising out of use made of the credit-token, is unlimited.[2]

Where a payment card is used in connection with a 'distance contract', the cardholder is not even liable for the first £50 of loss but is entitled to be re-credited, or to have all sums returned by the card issuer, in the event of fraudulent use of his payment card by another person not acting, or to be treated as acting, as his agent.[3] This applies to all distance contracts, namely any contracts concerning goods, services or financial services concluded between a supplier and a consumer under an organised distance sale or service provision scheme run by the supplier who, for the purpose of the contract, makes exclusive use of one or more means of distance communication, up to and including the moment at which the contract is concluded.[4] Means of distance communication includes printed matter, letter, press advertising with order forms, telephone, electronic mail and teleshopping. It does appear, however, that the Distance Selling Regulations and the Distance Marketing Regulations, especially as regards amendment of CCA 1974, have been poorly drafted so as to result in some striking ambiguity.

If the debtor alleges that any use made of the credit-token has not been authorised by him, the onus of proof falls on the creditor to prove either that the use was so authorised or that the use occurred before the creditor had been given notice of the loss, theft or misuse.[5]

The Agreements Regulations prescribe a statutory form of statement, which must be set out in the agreement, relating to the theft, loss or misuse of the credit-token. Particulars of the name, address and telephone number of the person to whom theft, loss or misuse of a credit-token is to be notified, must be set out prominently and so as to be easily legible.[6] Where the agreement requires confirmation of loss in writing, it shall be treated as taking effect if not confirmed in writing within 7 days.[7]

The Banking Code overlaps and to some extent conflicts with the CCA 1974, and governs liability in respect of cards generally. The common denominator in relation to all cards and Personal Identification Numbers (PINs) is that the liability of the cardholder or borrower is limited to £50 unless the cardholder acted fraudulently or without reasonable care. If the card is misused with the cardholder's permission he may be liable for all losses. The Code generally places the burden of proof on the card issuer.

In furtherance of ensuring the security of cards, the Banking Code contains provisions for the protection of the PIN and how this should be notified to the customer, and obligates cardholders to notify card issuers as soon as possible of the loss, theft, or possible misuse of a card or disclosure of a PIN.

1 Consumer Credit Act 1974, s 83.
2 *Ibid.*, s 84.
3 Consumer Protection (Distance Selling) Regulations 2000, SI 2000/2334, reg 21(2) and the Financial Services (Distance Marketing) Regulations 2004, SI 2004/2095, reg 14(1).
4 Consumer Protection (Distance Selling) Regulations 2000, reg 3(1) and reg 2(1).
5 Consumer Credit Act 1974, s 171(4).
6 Consumer Credit (Agreements) Regulations 1983, Sch 2, Part I; Consumer Credit (Credit-Token Agreements) Regulations 1983, SI 1983/1555.
7 CCA 1974, s 84(5).

16.4 ASPECTS OF THE REGULATORY REGIME

16.4.1 Unsolicited credit-tokens

It is an offence to give a person a credit-token if he has not requested it in a document signed by him. Usually the customer's signature is contained in the credit-token agreement itself. The prohibition does not extend to the provision of a credit-token to a person for use under a credit-token agreement already made, or to a renewal or replacement of a credit-token or in relation to the issue of a credit-token under a small debtor-creditor-supplier agreement.[1]

An apparently innocent 'customer privilege letter' enabling the customer to obtain credit on the presentation of the letter to a store will almost certainly contravene the prohibition. A document may constitute a credit-token even though the creditor's undertaking to supply cash, goods or services has no contractual force. It will also be a credit-token notwithstanding that the customer's entitlement to credit is still subject to credit vetting and approval. Furthermore, it will be a credit-token even if the undertaking to grant credit is in fact false. If, on the other hand, without prior solicitation, the customer is furnished with a document to assist in identifying him to a credit grantor as a privileged customer or as a customer entitled to be granted credit, for example by reference to an account number or other means of identification, the provision or furnishing of such information, as it is not itself a document or other tangible item, will not constitute an offence.[2]

1 Consumer Credit Act 1974, s 51.
2 *Elliott v Director General of Fair Trading* [1980] 1 WLR 977.

16.4.2   The Banking Code

The Banking Code is a voluntary code which sets standards of good banking practice for financial institutions in their dealings with personal customers in the United Kingdom. Its subscribers include banks, building societies, credit card companies and National Savings & Investments institutions. The Code is produced jointly by the Association for Payment Clearing Services, the British Bankers' Association and the Building Societies Association.

The Code makes special provision for cards and PINs and specifically credit cards. Subscribers to the Code are required to furnish prospective customers with information in the form of a Summary Box setting out the main features of the credit card, before the customer commits to a credit card agreement. Among the other obligations imposed on credit card issuers are the following: a duty to tell the customer how the card works and to supply the customer with terms and conditions; an obligation to assess the customer's ability to repay when assessing the credit limit; an obligation to issue monthly statements unless the account has a nil balance and has not been used; an obligation that the minimum repayment amount covers more than that month's interest; a duty to notify a customer when an introductory promotional interest rate is about to come to an end; the customer's right to decline receiving credit card cheques. The Summary Box for credit cards was introduced in 2003 and extended to credit card cheques in 2006.

16.4.3   The APR

The Consumer Credit (Agreements) (Amendment) Regulations 2004[1] and the Consumer Credit (Advertisements) Regulations 2004[2] introduced new assumptions for the purpose of calculating the percentage rate of charge (APR) in running-account agreements in place of the previous assumptions. The assumptions are that:

(i)   in any case where there will be a credit limit, but that limit is not known at the date of the making of the agreement, the amount of the credit to be provided shall be taken to be £1,500 or, in a case where the credit limit will be less than £1,500, an amount equal to that limit;

(ii)   the credit is provided for a period of one year beginning with the relevant date;

(iii)   the credit is provided in full on the relevant date;

(iv)   where the rate of interest will change at a time provided in the agreement, within a period of three years beginning with the date of the making of the agreement, the rate shall be taken to be the highest rate at any time obtaining under the agreement in that period;

(v)   where the agreement provides credit to finance the purchase of goods, services, land or other things and also provides one or more of cash loans, credit to refinance existing indebtedness of the debtor's, whether to the creditor or another person and credit for any other purpose, and either or both different rates of interest and different charges are payable in relation to the credit for all or some of those purposes, the rate of interest and charges payable in relation to the whole of the credit are those applicable to the provision of credit for the purchase of goods etc.; and

(vi) the credit is repaid in 12 equal instalments, at monthly intervals beginning one month after the relevant date.

The requirement that the APR in relation to cash advances and balance transfers is the same as that applicable to purchases, has led to considerable confusion and indeed is partly responsible for the Super Complaint by Which? referred to in para 18.7.2 below.

The APR is the mathematical representation of the total charge for credit and is calculated in accordance with the Consumer Credit (Total Charge for Credit) Regulations 1980.[3] Strangely, these regulations do not provide for any leeway in the statement of the APR, in contrast with the provisions in Schedule 7 to the Consumer Credit (Agreements) Regulations 1983[4] and Schedule 1 to the Consumer Credit (Advertisements) Regulations 2004,[5] as follows:

(a) the APR may be shown at the rate which exceeds the APR by not more than one or a rate which falls short of the APR by not more than 0.1 or in a case to which paragraphs (b) or (c) below apply, the rate determined in accordance with the relevant paragraph;

(b) in an agreement under which all repayments but one are equal and one repayment does not differ from any repayment by more whole pence than there are repayments, there may be included in the document a rate found under reg 7 of the Total Charge for Credit Regulations as if that one repayment were equal to the other repayments to be made under the agreement;

(c) in the case of an agreement under which three or more repayments are to be made at equal intervals and the interval between the relevant date and the first repayment is greater than the interval between the repayments, there may be included a rate found under reg 7 of the Total Charge for Credit Regulations as if the interval between the relevant date and the first repayment were shortened so as to be equal to the interval between the repayments.

1 SI 2004/1482, Sch 4, para 15 and see Consumer Credit (Agreements) Regulations 1983, SI 1983/1553, as amended, Sch 7.
2 SI 2004/1484, Sch 1, para 1.
3 SI 1980/51.
4 SI 1983/1553.
5 SI 2004/1484.

16.4.4   The creditor's liability under s 75

Section 75 of the Act provides that if the debtor under a debtor-creditor-supplier agreement falling within s 12(b) of (c) has, in relation to a transaction financed by the agreement, any claim against the supplier in respect of a misrepresentation or breach of contract, he has a like claim against the creditor who, with the supplier, is accordingly jointly and severally liable to the debtor. The section does not apply to a claim under a non-commercial agreement or so far as the claim relates to any single item to which the supplier has attached a cash price not exceeding £100 or more than £30,000. The creditor is entitled to a statutory indemnity by the supplier for loss suffered by the creditor in satisfying any such claim, including costs incurred by him in defending proceedings instituted by the debtor.[1]

In relation to credit card transactions, the long-standing issue as to whether the creditor is liable under s 75 for purchases made by a borrower under a credit card transaction entered into outside the United Kingdom, was finally answered in the affirmative by the House of Lords in *Office of Fair Trading v Lloyds TSB Bank plc.*[2] Lord Hoffmann stated that there was nothing in the language of s 75(1) to exclude foreign transactions. In so far as it was alleged that the section had the effect of legislating extra-territorially, he stated that extra-territorial effect means seeking to regulate the conduct or affect the liabilities of people over whom the United Kingdom has no jurisdiction. In this case the Office of Fair Trading accepted that s 75(1) applied only to agreements with a creditor carrying on business in the United Kingdom. The effect of the section was equivalent to the statutory implication of a term in the contract between a United Kingdom creditor and the debtor by which the former accepts joint and several liability with the supplier. If the supplier is foreign, the Act does not purport to regulate his conduct or impose liabilities upon him. It is only the United Kingdom creditor who is affected. As regards the argument that s 75(1) was dependent upon the enforceability of the statutory indemnity of the creditor by the supplier under s 75(2), Lord Hoffmann stated that if this was Parliament's intention, it would have said so and that it was not obvious why there should be such a link.

In his Opinion, Lord Mance emphasised the need for consumer protection, which was the fundamental purpose of the Consumer Credit Act 1974. He referred to the Crowther Committee Report, which led to the enactment of the Act, and its observation that the law's task was to maintain a fair balance between the creditor and the debtor and that in considering which of two innocent parties should bear the greater loss, it was much easier for the business creditor to do so than the individual debtor. In distinguishing between so-called 'connected' and 'unconnected' loans, the Committee had felt that the connected lender should incur a primary liability for supplier's misrepresentation or breach along the lines reflected in s 75(1). Commenting on the expression 'arrangements' in the definition of a debtor-creditor-supplier agreement, Lord Mance stated that the language of 'arrangements' used in the Act is well capable of embracing the modern relationships between card issuers and suppliers under networks like VISA and MasterCard. Finally, the statutory indemnity in s 75(2), did no more than reflect a well-recognised restitutionary right at English common law.

The obvious problem of a creditor (and corresponding benefit to a debtor) with s 75, is that it imposes virtual unlimited liability on a creditor for use made by the debtor of the credit card, whether in the United Kingdom or abroad. It arises even if only the deposit, or part of the price of a transaction, is paid for by means of the credit card.

Charge card transactions and debit card transactions, including electronic transfers of funds at point of sale, and cash withdrawals, do not attract the provisions or protection of s 75 as they are not debtor-creditor-supplier agreements. For the avoidance of doubt the Act expressly excludes arrangements for the electronic transfer of funds from a current account at a bank from the scope of arrangements between a creditor and a supplier.[3] A second or additional cardholder who is authorised by the debtor to make purchases (by means of a separate card) under a debtor-creditor-supplier agreement cannot invoke the provisions of s 75 as such a person is not the 'debtor' under the agreement.[4]

1 Section 75(1), (2) and (3).
2 [2007] All ER (D) 466, [2007] GCCR 6101, HL.
3 CCA 1974, s 187(3A).
4 See further para 16.4.5 below.

16.4.5   Additional cardholders

The terms of a credit-token agreement commonly permit cards to be used by authorised users or additional cardholders. However, these persons are not the debtor under the credit agreement. It follows that in a contract of supply entered into by an authorised user or additional cardholder, they would not enjoy the protection afforded by s 75, as the section only extends to a transaction financed by a debtor-creditor-supplier agreement where the debtor, and not any other person, has a claim against the supplier. Unless the authorised person acted as the debtor's agent, the debtor would not have any claim against the supplier arising from the transaction. In any event 'debtor' in s 189(1) is the individual receiving credit under a consumer credit agreement or the person to whom his rights and duties under the agreement have passed by assignment or operation of law.

The OFT in its Guidance Note on s 75, states that untested by court action is the liability of a credit card company when a purchase has been made by an additional cardholder.[1] However, in February 2001 the OFT issued a note on s 75 under the heading 'Transactions by Authorised Second Users'[2] which refers to its views in an earlier report of the Office on Connected Lender Liability (March 1994) and which views it reiterates. In that report the OFT stated:

> 'Most card-issuers allow a second card to be issued on a single account, usually to the spouse of the account holder. The holder of the second card thus becomes an authorised user of the account. The Office's view in such cases is that the second card-user is acting as the agent of the principal cardholder and that any claims under s 75 in relation to purchases made by the second user should be made by the principal cardholder. It is a well-established principle of agency law that a person who is entitled to pledge the credit of another acts as that other's agent.
>
> Card-issuers are evidently keen, for commercial reasons, to promote the use of second cards. Moreover, they can recover from the principal cardholder any debts arising from transactions entered into by an authorised second card-user. In these circumstances card-issuers cannot reasonably argue that they should have no s 75 liability in respect of authorised users. The evidence available to

the Office suggests that, in practice, card-issuers may offer to settle some s 75 claims on an *ex gratia* basis. In contested cases, however, it appears that card-issuers have sometimes relied upon the second user's not being the debtor, as defined in the Act, and sought to ignore the agency connection between him and the principal cardholder. Some county court judges, moreover, appear to have accepted this. It is the Office's view that card-issuers should act on the basis of the agency connection that undoubtedly exists, and meet claims arising from transactions of authorised second users.'

It is submitted that the Office's reasoning is flawed. The entitlement of an additional cardholder or authorised person to utilise the principal cardholder's credit under the account is the extension of a facility and not the creation of an agency relationship. The additional cardholder is not the debtor and is not authorised to make any representations, or to be at the receiving end of representations or the beneficiary of any rights in respect of breaches of contract, as the 'debtor' or agent of the debtor.

The corollary of the foregoing is that the debtor's claim under s 75 only lies against the creditor under the debtor-creditor-supplier agreement. However, 'creditor' is defined in s 189 as including the person to whom the creditor's right and duties under the agreement have passed by assignment or operation of law and it is submitted that the debtor would have an equal claim against the creditor's assignee. In any event the creditor could not avoid liability by assignment as this would constitute an unfair contract term under the Unfair Terms in Consumer Contracts Regulations 1999.[3]

1 Consumer Credit Act 1974: Section 75 – Equal Liability (June 2000).
2 Consumer Credit Act 1974: Section 75 – Transactions by Authorised Second Users (February 2001).
3 See especially the Unfair Terms in Consumer Contracts Regulations 1999, Sch 2, para 1(p).

16.5 SPECIFIC TYPES OF CREDIT CARD

Credit cards are distinguished by their purpose or the method by which the outstanding balance on a credit card account is discharged.

16.5.1 Store card

A store card is a payment card, usually in the form of a credit card, issued with respect to the purchase of the goods, services or facilities of one retailer or retailers who are members of a single group of interconnected bodies corporate or retailers who belong to a store card network who trade under a common name. In each case the card has associated retail benefits, such as special discounts, special cardholder retail offers and the like.

Following the Store Cards Market Investigation conducted by the Competition Commission, the latter made an Order entitled the 'Store Cards Market Investigation Order', which came into force on 1 May 2007.[1]

The Order imposes obligations in respect of the following:

(a) Information on statements including:

> (i) a statement of the current APR applicable to purchases;
>
> (ii) an estimate of interest payable in the following month if the card-holder only makes a minimum payment;
>
> (iii) a warning outlining the consequences of only making minimum payments;
>
> (iv) the basis of insurance charges;
>
> (v) late payment or default of charges;
>
> (vi) the basic assumptions used in calculating the estimate of interest payable in the following month;
>
> (vii) contact details for amending or cancelling insurance sold with the store card and a brief summary of insurance cover.

(b) The APR warning, to the effect that the rate of interest on the account may be higher than on other sources of credit and that it may be costly to leave balances owing on the account after the interest-free period.

(c) Provision and display of the facility to pay outstanding balances by direct debit.

(d) The requirement that insurances which are generally offered in conjunction with credit cards, such as payment protection insurance, price protection and purchase protection, be sold as separate insurances.

Store cards take the form of either Option Account cards or, less frequently, Budget Account cards.

1 Store Cards Market Investigation Order – Date of Report – 7 March 2006. Date of Order – 27 July 2006. Note that the Order applies to all store cards, whether in the form of payment or credit cards.

16.5.2 Option account card

An option account card is sometimes mistakenly called a charge card. It is a credit card issued in respect of an option account, where the borrower selects the credit limit which is to apply to his account. The borrower must then make a monthly payment in a minimum sum, usually between £5 and £10, or between 2% to 5% of the outstanding balance, whichever is the greater. The borrower may also at any time discharge the outstanding balance in full.

16.5.3 Budget account card

Budget accounts have largely been overtaken by option accounts. A budget account card is a credit card issued in connection with a budget account, under which the borrower agrees to pay a fixed monthly amount, selected by him, and the credit limit is set as a multiple of the fixed monthly payment. The credit limit is usually 24 times the monthly payment, based on the deceptive assumption that the fully utilised credit limit would be discharged within two years.

16.5.4   Affinity card

This is a card where the issuer undertakes to pay a specified percentage of the transaction costs to a charity, either of the customer's or the creditor's choice.

16.5.5   Charge card

A charge card is descriptive of two quite distinct types of credit card. In the strict sense it is the description of a card that requires the customer under the terms of his account to settle the outstanding balance in full by one payment within a pre-scribed period following the date of his monthly statement, resulting in a limited period of interest-free credit. The agreement for such an account is an exempt agreement, not regulated by the CCA 1974.[1]

As a charge card agreement is not a regulated credit card agreement the provisions of the CCA 1974 relating to unsolicited credit-tokens do not apply to it. However, the Code of Banking Practice prohibits subscribers issuing cards, which includes charge cards, to customers except pursuant to a request or where the card is supplied in replacement of an earlier card.

A charge card is also the description applied to a 't and e' (travel and entertainment) card. Typical examples are American Express and Diners Club Cards.

1   Consumer Credit (Exempt Agreements) Order 1989, SI 1989/869, art 3(1)(a)(ii).

16.5.6   Co-branded or loyalty card

This is a card, usually a credit card, whose utilisation earns the cardholder points which can then be used to secure discounts on purchases or services from a related or sponsoring company. It is in fact no more than a marketing tool used to win or preserve market share in a saturated market.

16.6   OTHER PAYMENT CARDS

16.6.1   Prepaid cards

Prepaid or pre-payment cards fall within the scope of the Financial Services and Markets Act 2000 and specifically the Financial Services and Markets Act 2000 (Regulated Activities) Order 2001.[1]

In summary, prepaid cards constitute 'electronic money' and the issuing of electronic money is a regulated activity under the above Order. 'Electronic money' is defined as monetary value as represented by a claim on the issuer which is stored on an electronic device, issued on receipt of funds and accepted as a means of payment by persons other than the issuer.[2] In order to carry on such an activity by way of a business, the issuer must either be an authorised person or an exempt person under the Financial Services and Markets Act 2000.

Significantly, a sum is not a deposit for the purposes of the Order if it is immediately exchanged for electronic money.[3]

Provision is made in the Order for the exemption of small issuers of electronic money. Essentially the exemption applies to an electronic device on which the monetary value stored is subject to a maximum amount of not more than €150 and where the total liabilities of the issuer do not exceed the stipulated ceiling, or where the electronic money is accepted as a means of payment only by subsidiaries of the issuer or other members of the issuer's group, or where the electronic money is accepted as a means of payment in the course of business by not more than 100 persons within the same premises or local area (such as a shopping centre, airport, university campus) or which have a close financial or business relationship with the issuer, such as a common marketing or distribution scheme.[4]

A prepaid card is also known as an electronic purse and is becoming increasingly more commonplace. It includes cards such as the Oyster card, prepaid telephone cards and travel cards, prepaid MasterCard and VISA cards and prepaid gift cards. It is interesting to note that as recently as March 2005, in referring to the electronic purse, the Banking Code comments that the electronic purse is not yet a product in common use.

At the request of HM Treasury the Banking Code sets out limited provisions relating to the electronic purse, in order to comply with EU requirements. It states that the electronic purse should be treated as cash in a wallet and that if the card is lost or stolen, any credit amount on that card will be lost. However, in the absence of fraud or lack of care, liability for misuse of monies in the electronic purse is limited to £50.[5]

It is submitted that prepaid cards are not credit tokens within the meaning of s 14 of CCA 1974 as no credit is involved and the card issuer does not undertake payment to a third party in return for payment by the cardholder.[6] On the contrary, the third party undertakes to pay no more than the cardholder has *already* paid into the card.

1 SI 2001/544, as amended, art 93.
2 *Ibid.*, art 3(1).
3 *Ibid.*, art 9A.
4 *Ibid.*, art 9C.
5 The Banking Code 2005, para 12.
6 Consumer Credit Act 1974, s 14(1). See also *Goode: Consumer Credit Law and Practice* (LexisNexis Butterworths), paras 1C [25.69] to [25.80].

16.6.2   Debit card

The trend in relation to card usage is markedly in favour of debit cards over credit cards. This evolution could not have taken place but for the increasing number of consumers who hold current accounts, the consequence of a development from weekly to monthly wage payments. The lower cost of an overdraft on a current account than a credit card account also accounts for the increasing popularity of non-credit cards.

A debit card is used in conjunction with a current account to obtain cash at an 'ATM', or to effect payment and obtain cash by electronic funds transfer at point of sale ('EFTPOS'). It dispenses with the need for cheques and can be used for amounts in excess of those guaranteed by cheque guarantee cards.

The account holder's bank account is debited and funds transferred in about the time that it takes to clear a cheque, approximately three working days. The card has no pre-set transaction limit. The only limit is the amount available to the customer under his current account. A major advantage to the supplier is the speed with which he receives payment, albeit in return for a commission payable by him, usually at a lower rate than under a credit card transaction.

There is controversy as to whether or not a debit card is a credit-token for the purposes of CCA 1974. According to Professor Guest such a card is a credit-token under CCA 1974, s 14(1)(b), as a deemed provision of credit will arise under s 14(3). The regulated agreement for the provision of such credit will be a debtor-creditor-supplier agreement. On the other hand, Professor Goode maintains that an agreement for the issue of a debit card is not a credit agreement but merely an agreement providing for a convenient payment mechanism and that in all probability a debit card is not a credit-token.[1] These arguments also extend to cash cards (or ATM cards).[2] Whatever the position may be, banks have endeavoured to structure their debit card agreements as exempt agreements under the Consumer Credit (Exempt Agreements) Order 1989, art 3(1)(a)(ii).

The most common debit card schemes in place in the United Kingdom are those operated by Switch Card Services, backed by numerous banks and building societies, the Connect Scheme operated by the VISA network and the Delta debit card.

1 Guest, *Consumer Credit Law* (Sweet & Maxwell), 2–015; *Goode: Consumer Credit Law and Practice* (LexisNexis Butterworths), para 1C [24.84].
2 Guest, *Consumer Credit Law* (Sweet & Maxwell), 2–015; *Goode: Consumer Credit Law and Practice* (LexisNexis Butterworths), paras 1C [25.69] to [25.80].

16.6.3   Cheque guarantee card

This is a card issued by a bank or a building society for use in connection with a cheque. It is not a credit card. If used in conjunction with the drawing of a cheque, the bank or building society guarantees payment of individual cheques in the amount shown on the card, usually £50, but often up to £250. The obligation undertaken by the guarantor to the supplier, through the agency of the customer when he uses the cheque guarantee card, is not to dishonour the cheque on presentation for want of funds in the customer's bank account, up to the amount guaranteed.

16.6.4   Eurocheque card

This is a cheque guarantee card which can be used with a Eurocheque to pay for goods or services or used to withdraw cash from ATMs or cash machines in the UK and other countries.

Chapter 17

Security

17.1 TYPES OF SECURITY

The CCA 1974 envisages a range of security in relation to actual or prospective consumer credit agreements, consumer hire agreements and linked transactions. Such security includes a mortgage, charge, pledge, bond, debenture, indemnity, guarantee, bill, note or other right provided by the debtor or hirer, or at his request, express or implied, to secure the carrying out of the obligations of the debtor or hirer under the agreement.[1]

1 CCA 1974, s 189(1).

17.2 FORM AND CONTENT OF SECURITY DOCUMENTS

Any security provided in relation to a regulated agreement by the debtor, hirer or a third party must be in writing. Whilst guarantees and indemnities are further regulated, there are no specific regulations covering other forms of security.[1]

A regulated agreement must embody any security provided by the debtor or hirer. This means that the agreement must set out all the provisions of the security or expressly refer to the security document.[2] Significantly, this requirement only applies to security provided by the debtor or hirer, and not that provided by a third person, whether or not at the request of the debtor or hirer. It will therefore also not encompass a guarantee or indemnity which, by definition, will not be provided by the debtor or hirer.

Where the agreement is secured on land, the words 'secured on' followed by the address of the land must appear at the end of the statutory heading to the regulated agreement.[3] The agreement must also contain the statutory form of statement: 'YOUR HOME MAY BE REPOSSESSED etc.'.[4]

The CCA 1974's provisions relating to the form of security document are additional to those provided for elsewhere. We will now deal with specific types of security.

1 CCA 1974, s 105 and Consumer Credit (Guarantees and Indemnities) Regulations 1983, SI 1983/1556.
2 CCA 1974, s 105(9); Consumer Credit (Agreements Regulations) 1983, as amended, Sch 1, para 20 and Sch 3, para 9.
3 *Ibid.*, Sch 1, para 1; Sch 3, para 1.
4 *Ibid.*, Sch 2, para 3; Sch 4, para 3.

17.2.1 Guarantee and indemnity

Section 4 of the Statute of Frauds (1677) requires a guarantee to be in writing and signed by the party to be charged or by some other person lawfully authorised by him. The section only applies to guarantees and not to indemnities which constitute primary obligations. However, in the case of guarantees or indemnities securing obligations under regulated or linked transactions, the Consumer Credit (Guarantees and Indemnities) Regulations[1] prescribe the form and formalities that apply to them. These include the following requirements:

(i)   a prescribed heading;
(ii)   prescribed minimum information;
(iii)   a statement of the surety's rights in statutory form;
(iv)   a statutory form of signature box.

As with regulated agreements, there are requirements relating to the prominence of certain lettering and the legibility of the document.

A guarantee or indemnity must be signed by or on behalf of the surety. The document must embody all the terms of the security other than implied terms, and when presented to the surety for his signature it must be accompanied by a copy of the document, together with a copy of any other document referred to in it (e.g. the agreement secured by it). Where the security is provided before the regulated agreement is made, a copy of the subsequently executed agreement, together with a copy of any other document referred to in it, must be given to the surety within seven days of the regulated agreement being made. Otherwise a copy of the executed agreement and of any document referred to in it must be given to the surety when the security is provided. Failure to comply with these requirements will ordinarily result in the security being unenforceable against the surety save on an order of the court.[2]

A weakness of the regulations is that they do not make specific provision for continuing guarantees.

The foregoing requirements are in addition to the common law requirement that a guarantee or indemnity must either be given for consideration or executed as a deed in accordance with the Law of Property (Miscellaneous Provisions) Act 1989.

The Banking Code requires its subscribers to encourage prospective guarantors to take independent legal advice and to set out such recommendation in the guarantee forms.

1 CCA 1974, s 105 and Consumer Credit (Guarantees and Indemnities) Regulations 1983, SI 1983/1556.
2 CCA 1974, s 105(5) and (7).

17.2.2 The mortgage

A mortgage, in the case of goods, is a transfer of ownership to the creditor by way of security, upon the express or implied condition that the asset will be reconveyed to the debtor when the sum secured has been paid. Where the debtor wishes to remain in possession of the mortgaged goods or chattels, he must register a bill of sale under the Bills of Sale Acts 1878 to 1891. Bills of sale are most commonly used in the financing of motor vehicles. This is in order to avoid the consequences of the one-third ('protected goods') and one-half ('total liability on termination') rules which apply to hire-purchase and conditional sale agreements under CCA 1974, ss 90 and 100 respectively.

The Bills of Sale Acts specify the chattels capable of being charged, the form of bill of sale together with its attestation and affidavit and the mode and place of its registration. Registration serves as notice to the world of the chattel mortgage, which is essential in view of the fact that the mortgagor remains in possession of the mortgaged chattel.

Mortgages or charges of property, whether goods or land, by a company are registrable under the Companies Act 1985, s 395.

The more common type of mortgage used to secure a regulated agreement is a land mortgage. There are two types of land mortgages, a mortgage by demise for a term of years absolute (i.e. a lease) or the more usual form of charge by way of legal mortgage.

The mortgage deed might itself provide for the method of payment or, alternatively, the agreement secured by it will provide for the method of payment. The two main methods are the 'repayment mortgage' and the 'endowment', or so-called 'interest only' mortgage. The former requires repayment of the loan during the term by regular, usually monthly, payments of capital and interest. The latter provides for the payment of the loan by regular, usually monthly, instalments of interest only and repayment of the capital sum of the loan by one lump sum at the end of the term. In the case of an endowment mortgage the capital sum is repaid out of the proceeds of a life assurance policy on the life of the mortgagor or a third party which is assigned to the mortgagee at the time of the execution of the mortgage. Within this broad framework, there are various variations on the theme, either in relation to the mode of payment or the form of security.

There are various payment combinations which are offered as distinctive mortgage products. These include the fixed-rate mortgage, the low start or discounted mortgage, the capped mortgage, the collateral mortgage and the cash-back mortgage. Most of these terms simply refer to the beneficial mortgage terms granted in the early years of the mortgage, usually the first two to five years. The objective is to assist financially the mortgagor at a time when ordinarily his earnings would be low. The beneficial terms are, however, invariably linked to some 'lock-in' provision requiring the mortgagor to compensate the mortgagee for its subsidy by payment of a redemption penalty if the mortgagor redeems the security during the beneficial period. The particular term and payment amount may be open to challenge under the Unfair Terms in Consumer Contracts Regulations 1999.[1]

A flexible mortgage is one which, during the mortgage term, entitles the mortgagor to make payments, as and when he pleases, in excess of the instalment payment, to take payment holidays (without the non-payment of the monthly instalment constituting a breach of the mortgage), to obtain a re-advance of repaid principal and so on. An offset mortgage is a mortgage which entitles the mortgagor to set off interest accrued on his savings account against the accrued interest charged on his mortgage, thereby saving the income tax otherwise payable on the interest accrued on the savings account.

Mortgages can be combined with repayment vehicles such as a unit trust, ISA (Individual Savings Account) and a pension policy. Each of these involves payment by the mortgagor into an additional investment or pension scheme, the ultimate proceeds of which can be utilised in reduction or discharge of the loan secured on the mortgaged property.

In its endeavours to set minimum standards for mortgages the Treasury, in October 1999, established so-called CAT (Charges, Access and Terms) standards for mortgages, later to be extended to ISAs and other financial products. They are voluntary standards aimed at preventing confusing marketing and hidden charges. There are minimum standards for qualifying mortgage products in three key areas: fair charges, easy access and terms which are fair, clear, not misleading and easy to understand.

1 See also the OFT's Guidance Note on 'Fairness and Unfairness in Interest Variation Terms' (February 2000).

17.2.3   Regulated mortgage contract ('RMC')

The Financial Services and Markets Act 2000 ('FSMA') sets out a complex web of mortgage regulation under the supervision of the Financial Services Authority ('FSA'). It regulates the so-called 'regulated mortgage contract' as defined in the Financial Services and Markets Act 2000 (Regulated Activities) Order 2001, art 61(3)(a).[1] A regulated mortgage contract is a contract which, at the time it is entered into, meets the following conditions:

(a)   the lender provides credit to an individual or to trustees; and
(b)   the obligation of the borrower to repay is secured by a first legal mortgage on land (other than timeshare accommodation) in the United Kingdom, at least 40% of which is used, or is intended to be used as, or in connection with, a dwelling by the borrower or (in the case of credit provided to trustees) by an individual who is a beneficiary of a trust, or by a related person.

In contrast with a regulated agreement under CCA 1974, an 'individual' borrower does not include a partnership or other unincorporated body of persons not consisting entirely of bodies corporate. A regulated mortgage contract is restricted to credit secured by a first legal mortgage and this excludes any later mortgage and also equitable mortgages.

Regulated mortgage contracts include the following types of mortgage:

(a)   *Regulated Lifetime Mortgage Contract*. This is a so-called 'lifetime mortgage' or 'equity release mortgage'. These are usually entered into by retired persons, to provide a lump sum or regular advances to assist with their financial requirements. There are no monthly repayments under the mortgage and the interest accrues, usually at a fixed rate, throughout the mortgage term. The capital and accrued interest is only repayable on the mortgagor's death or the earlier vacation of the property or if the mortgagor enters into residential care. The mortgage is then repaid solely out of the proceeds of sale of the property. If there is a shortfall, repayment of the unpaid balance is waived by the mortgagee.

(b) *Regulated Home Purchase Plan.* This involves a home purchase provider buying a qualifying interest or undivided share in land in the UK which is held on trust for the home purchase provider. The home purchaser is obliged to buy the interest over the course, or at the end of, a specified period. The home purchaser is entitled to occupy at least 40% of the land.

(c) *Regulated Home Reversion Plan.* This is an arrangement under which the plan provider (the investor) buys all or part of a qualifying interest in land from the reversion seller. The reversion seller is entitled to occupy at least 40% of the land. The arrangement ends on the happening of a specified qualifying termination event.

The FSA has responsibility for the regulation of promotional literature and advertising for 'qualifying credit', namely all lending and mortgage advice by firms authorised by the FSA for mortgage purposes, regardless of whether the lending is secured by a first or second mortgage. If a lender only lends against second mortgages and is therefore not authorised by the FSA, its advertising is subject to the regime under CCA 1974.

Advice in relation to mortgages, both in respect of first and second mortgages, and the regulation of intermediaries and mortgage brokers, falls under the supervision of the FSA.

The FSA requires delivery of disclosure documents, both before and after completion of the mortgage. Pre-sale disclosure is justified on the grounds that it enhances informed decision-making and affords an appropriate degree of consumer protection. It takes place both before the mortgage application is made and at the mortgage offer stage. Further disclosure must be made at the start of the mortgage in order to provide a consumer with a definitive reference document to enable him to verify that everything has been set up correctly. Finally there is periodical disclosure during the lifetime of the mortgage, for example by way of annual statements.

Most residential first mortgages are regulated mortgage contracts. Some first mortgages, namely those not qualifying as regulated mortgage contracts and all second mortgages, fall into one of the following three categories: (i) unregulated agreements, governed by neither the FSMA 2000 nor CCA 1974, (ii) exempt agreements under CCA 1974, or (iii) regulated agreements under CCA 1974.

1 SI 2000/544, as amended.

17.2.4 Exempt mortgages

A consumer credit agreement is an exempt agreement if the creditor under the agreement is one of the exempt institutions referred to in CCA 1974, s 16, read with the Consumer Credit (Exempt Agreements) Order 1989, and the agreement is for one of the purposes mentioned in s 16, read with the provisions of the Exempt Agreements Order.

The main categories of exempt credit agreements secured by a second mortgage (and which will therefore fall under neither the FSMA 2000 or CCA 1974 regimes) are where the creditor is an exempt institution (referred to above) and the agreement is:

(a)   a debtor-creditor-supplier agreement, secured by a second mortgage, financing a transaction which is a linked transaction in relation to the purchase of land;

(b)   a debtor-creditor agreement, secured by a second mortgage, financing (i) the purchase of land or (ii) the provisions of dwellings or business premises on land or (iii) the alteration, enlarging, repair or improvement of a dwelling or business premises on any land, or (iv) refinancing any existing indebtedness of the debtor under any agreement by which the debtor was provided with credit for any of the foregoing purposes. (Head (b)(iii) will only be exempt if the creditor is also the creditor under the first mortgage.)

A mortgage is also exempt from CCA 1974 if it secures an agreement for credit exceeding £25,000 which is either:[1]

(a)   a consumer credit agreement if any sums due under it are secured by a land mortgage on land outside the United Kingdom; or

(b)   a consumer credit agreement if any sums due under it are secured by a land mortgage on land in the United Kingdom where the condition below is satisfied.

The condition is that at the time the agreement is entered into less than 40% of the land is used, or is intended to be used, as or in connection with a dwelling:

(i)   by the debtor or a person connected with the debtor; or

(ii)   in the case of credit provided to trustees, by an individual who is the beneficiary of the trust or a person connected with such an individual.

For the above purposes the area of any land which comprises a building or other structure containing two or more storeys is to be taken to be the aggregate of the floor areas of each of those storeys. A person is 'connected with' the debtor or an individual who is the beneficiary of a trust if he is:

(i)   that person's spouse or civil partner;

(ii)   a person (whether or not of the opposite sex) whose relationship with that person has the characteristics of the relationship between husband and wife; or

(iii) that person's parent, brother, sister, child, grandparent or grandchild.

Where the second mortgage is not exempt, it will be regulated by CCA 1974 and regulations made under that Act, regardless of whether the monies are advanced for business or private use purposes.

Lenders under first legal mortgages, firms which carry on their mortgage administration and mortgage intermediaries in respect of such mortgages, namely those introducing and advising on them, must be authorised by the FSA and meet its financial resource requirements.

1 The Consumer Credit Act 2006 (Commencement No. 4 and Transitional Provisions) Order 2008, SI 2008/831, art 2(1) read with Sch 1.

17.2.5 The charge

A charge does not depend on delivery of possession or transfer of ownership of the property charged, but comprises an agreement between the creditor and the debtor by which a particular asset is appropriated to the satisfaction of the debt so that the creditor is entitled to look to the asset and its proceeds to discharge the indebtedness in priority to the claims of unsecured creditors.

In the case of a receivable, a charge will take the form either of an assignment or negotiation, namely delivery of the bill of exchange, negotiable certificate of deposit or other instrument, together with an endorsement. In order to vest a receivable in the assignee at law and to enable the assignee to sue solely in his own name, the assignment must be in writing, under the hand of the assignor, absolute and not by way of charge, relate to the whole of the debt and be notified to the debtor in writing.[1]

Apart from the foregoing, the only formalities relating to a mortgage or charge of land or an interest in land, including an equitable charge, are those stipulated by the Law of Property (Miscellaneous Provisions) Act 1989, which requires such document to be by way of deed and executed as a deed in accordance with its provisions.

1 Law of Property Act 1925, s 136.

17.2.6 Bills of sale

Bills of sale are governed by the Bills of Sale Act 1878 and Bills of Sales Act (1878) Amendment Act 1882. This rather dated legislation is still utilised by creditor grantors especially in the motor finance industry, in order to avoid the provisions of ss 99 and 100 of CCA 1974 applying. In contrast to the position under a regulated hire-purchase or conditional sale agreement, if a personal loan agreement is secured by a bill of sale the borrower is not entitled to terminate the agreement and to pay only one half of the total sum payable.

Bills of sale must take the form set out in the Schedule to the Bills of Sale Act (1878) Amendment Act 1882. This creates practical difficulties where the loan agreement is a regulated agreement for the reason that the statutory form of the bill of sale only allows for repayment of the principal sum, together with interest and no other charges, by equal payments. Failure to comply with the requisite form renders the bill of sale void.

The bill of sale must be attested by a solicitor and the attestation of the execution of the bill of sale, together with an affidavit relating to its execution, must be filed at the Queens Bench Division of the High Court of Justice.

17.2.7 Contractual set-off

Contractual set-off is not a true security, though it fulfils a security function. It gives no right over the creditor's asset (i.e. the debt), but merely an entitlement to set off one personal obligation against another.[1]

Contractual set-off is wider than equitable set-off. Contractual set-off is an arrangement for the mutual setting-off of personal obligations between parties. However, in the case of the debtor's insolvency, the Insolvency Act 1986 does not permit the creditor to obtain for himself a better position by virtue of the set-off arrangements than those to which he is entitled under the Insolvency Act.[2]

1 Goode, *Commercial Law* (2nd edn, LexisNexis Butterworths, 1995), p 657.
2 Goode, *Commercial Law* (2nd edn, LexisNexis Butterworths, 1995). See also *British Eagle International Airlines Ltd v Compagnie Nationale Air France* [1975] 1 WLR 758, HL.

17.2.8 Charge over a credit balance

In *Re Charge Card Services Ltd*[1] Millet J (as he then was) held that it was conceptually impossible for a debtor (e.g. a bank with whom monies are deposited by its customer) to become its own creditor. It follows that a depositor of monies in a savings account cannot effectively charge such monies, or the credit balance, in favour of the bank. Legal opinion remained divided on the issue.[2] However, in *Re Bank of Credit and Commerce International SA (No 8)*[3] Lord Hoffmann, delivering the decision of the House of Lords, held that a bank could take a charge over its customer's deposit.

1 [1987] Ch 150.
2 See Goode, *Commercial Law* (3rd edn, 2004), pp 611–612.
3 [1998] AC 214 (see the criticism of this case in Goode, 'Commercial Law in the Next Millennium', *The Hamlyn Lectures* (49th Series, Sweet & Maxwell)).

17.2.9 'Flawed asset' and negative pledge clauses

A 'flawed asset' is the description given to an agreement between a depositor of monies and the depositee in terms of which the depositor agrees not to withdraw the monies except on fulfilment of certain conditions. This does not amount to a security interest but merely qualifies the bank's repayment obligation.

In a negative pledge, the obligor merely undertakes in favour of the obligee not to grant any other security over the asset without the obligee's consent. A mortgagor's undertaking not to enter into any other mortgage without the first mortgagee's consent is an example of a negative pledge. Breach of such negative pledge merely gives rise to a personal liability and is therefore not a security interest.[1]

1 Goode, *Commercial Law* (3rd edn, 2004), p 613.

17.2.10 Pledge

A pledge is the actual or constructive delivery of possession of an asset to the creditor by way of security. Ownership remains with the pledgor but the pledgee enjoys a limited legal interest in the asset which encompasses the right to use the asset at his own risk so long as this will not impair it, to sell his interest as pledgee or assign it by way of gift, to deliver the asset to another for safe-keeping, to sub-pledge the asset on the same conditions as he holds it and to sell the asset in the event of default in payment by the pledgor.

As equity considers as done that which ought to be done, an agreement for the pledge of specified property together with the passing of consideration, will result in the creation of a security interest.

17.2.11   Assignment

Security may be created by assignment. Thus, a life policy or other insurance policy may be assigned by way of security. This is done in one of two ways. First, it may be effected by written assignment together with notice of assignment to the insurer.[1] Alternatively, it may be achieved by endorsement of the policy under the Policies of Assurance Act 1867 or by assignment in the form prescribed in the schedule to that Act.

1   Law of Property Act 1925, s 136.

17.2.12   Contractual lien

A possessory lien may be created at common law or by contract. The essential distinction between a contractual lien and a pledge is that in pledge possession is given for the purpose of security, whereas in the case of lien possession is given for some independent purpose. The terms of the contract limit the holder of the lien to a right to withhold possession of the asset as security for payment and do not confer rights of sale.

17.2.13   Pawn

A pawn is any article subject to a pledge. The earlier Pawnbrokers Acts 1872–1960 were repealed by CCA 1974, of which ss 114 to 122 deal with pledges and pawns.

When a person takes an article by way of pawn under a regulated agreement, he must give a pawn receipt in the prescribed form. Where the pawn-receipt forms part of a document embodying a regulated consumer credit agreement or modifying agreement, its form is governed by the Agreements Regulations. If the pawn-receipt is separate from such document, its form is governed by the Consumer Credit (Pawn-Receipts) Regulations 1983.[1]

A pawn is redeemable within a period of not less than six months from the time it is taken and until the expiry of such longer period as the parties may stipulate or the expiry of the agreement secured by the pledge if earlier. Even then, it remains redeemable until it is realised by the pawnee. Special provision is made for a statutory declaration or, in certain circumstances, a written statement to replace a pawn-receipt where the latter has been lost or stolen.

In *Wilson v Robertsons (London) Ltd*[2] Wilson appealed against a decision of the county court and claimed that the credit agreements were invalid owing to the inclusion of the document fee in the amount of credit and further, that as some of the agreements had been backdated this resulted in a failure to provide the statutory redeemable period of six months. The appeal succeeded on both grounds. The court referred to s 116 of CCA 1974 which provides for a minimum redemption period of six months and to s 173 of the Act which stipulates that it is not possible to contract out of the statutory protections accorded by the Act. Reliance was placed on the House of Lords decision in *Wilson v Secretary of State for Trade and Industry/First County Trust Ltd (No 2)*.[3] There the House of Lords opined that CCA 1974 was, like the Moneylenders Act 1927 before it, designed to tackle a significant social problem. The activities of some money lenders had given the money lending business a bad reputation. Something had to be done to protect the borrower, who frequently, indeed normally, would be in a weak bargaining position. Protection of borrowers was the social policy behind the legislation. Part of that policy was to be achieved by setting stringent rules which had to be complied with by the lender if his money lending agreement was to be enforceable.

When a pawn has become realisable by the pawnee, the latter may sell it after giving the pawnor not less than 14 working days' notice of his intention. Within 20 working days of the sale, the pawnee must give the pawnor the prescribed information in writing as to the sale, its proceeds and expenses.

1 SI 1983/1566.
2 [2005] GCCR 5301 esp at 5305.
3 [2003] GCCR 4931, HL.

17.2.14   Negotiable instruments

In order to prevent the circumvention of the CCA 1974's provisions the law does not permit a creditor to take a negotiable instrument other than a bank note or cheque, in discharge of any sum payable under a regulated agreement or by any surety in relation to the agreement. Likewise a creditor or owner may not take a negotiable instrument as security for the discharge of any such sum payable to him. A contravention of this provision will result in the agreement or security being enforceable only on an order of the court.[1]

1 CCA 1974, ss 123 and 124.

17.3   RIGHTS OF SURETY DURING THE LIFETIME OF THE SECURITY

A surety is entitled to require the creditor or owner to furnish him, within 12 working days, with a copy of the executed agreement, or any document referred to in it, a copy of the security instrument and a statement signed by, or on behalf of, the creditor or owner showing, inter alia, the amount outstanding to him under the secured agreement.[1]

Where a creditor or owner defaults with any of these foregoing obligations, the security is unenforceable whilst the default continues and if it continues for one month he commits an offence.

A creditor or owner is also obliged to furnish the surety with a copy of any default notice, enforcement notice or notice of termination in non-default cases served on the debtor or hirer. If he fails, the security is enforceable against the surety only on an order of the court.

1 CCA 1974, ss 107 to 111 and Consumer Credit (Cancellation Notices and Copies of Documents) Regulations 1983, SI 1983/1557, as amended, reg 10.

17.4 PRECAUTIONS TO BE TAKEN BY A CREDITOR OR OWNER IN TAKING SECURITY

The long line of cases since *Barclays Bank plc v O'Brien*[1] highlights the precautions to be taken by a creditor or owner, in taking security, when it is put on enquiry as to the circumstances in which that person agrees to stand surety, especially where there is an emotional relationship or a relationship of trust between the surety and the debtor. The court stated that a creditor was put on enquiry when a wife offered to stand surety for her husband's debts by the combination of two factors. These are the fact that the transaction on its face is not to the financial advantage of the wife and, secondly, that there is a substantial risk in such a transaction that, in procuring the wife to act as surety, the husband had committed a legal or equitable wrong that entitled the wife to set aside the transaction. To avoid being fixed with constructive notice, the court opined that a creditor should take steps to bring home to the wife the risks she was running by standing surety and to advise her to take independent advice. A creditor would satisfy those requirements if it insisted that the wife attend a private meeting, in the absence of the husband, with a representative of the creditor at which she was told of the extent of her liability as surety, warned of the risks she was running and urged to take independent legal advice.

The foregoing case, involving persons having a special relationship to each other and one standing as surety for the other, giving rise to constructive notice on the part of the bank lender, contrasts with the situation where the wife enters into a joint borrowing with her husband. If a wife is induced by the undue influence of her husband to charge the matrimonial home as security for a loan made to her husband and herself jointly, the lender would not be affected by the undue influence if the husband was not the lender's agent, the lender had no actual knowledge of any undue influence and there was no indication that the transaction was anything other than a normal loan to a husband and wife for their joint benefit.[2]

The leading decision on a creditor's duty in relation to a proposed charge by a wife of her interest in favour of the bank as security for the indebtedness of her husband or his business, is that of *Royal Bank of Scotland plc v Etridge (No 2)*.[3] This involved consolidated appeals in eight cases, each arising out of a transaction in which a wife charged the interest in her home in favour of a bank, one of which was the Royal Bank of Scotland, under the undue influence of her husband. The House of Lords ruled that where it was proposed that a wife should charge her interest in her home in favour of a bank as security for the indebtedness of her husband or his business, specific clear and simple procedures should be operated in the future, as minimum requirements, to protect the wife and reduce to an acceptable level the risk that she had been misled or coerced by her husband so that the lender might make the advance in reasonable confidence that, if necessary, the security would be enforceable.

The decision is the climax to the long line of decisions commencing with *Barclays Bank plc v O'Brien* in 1993. In summary:

(a)   The bank is put on inquiry whenever a wife offers to stand surety for her husband's debts and vice versa and likewise in the case of unmarried couples where the bank is aware of the relationship. On the other hand, where the money is advanced to the parties jointly, the bank is not put on inquiry unless it is aware that the loan is not being made for joint purposes. However, cases where the wife stands surety for the debts of a company, even when she is a shareholder in the company, are not to be equated with joint loans. The bank is put on inquiry in such cases even when the wife is a director or company secretary.

(b)   In *O'Brien* it was stated that a bank could reasonably be expected to take steps to bring home to the wife the risks she was running and to advise her to take independent advice. The House of Lords held that that was applicable to past transactions. For the future the bank was to *insist* that the wife attend a private meeting with its representative at which she was told of the extent of her liability and of the risk she was running and she would be urged to take independent advice. Exceptionally, to be safe, the bank had to insist on the wife being separately advised.

(c)   As regards the content of the legal advice, it was not for the solicitor to veto the transaction by declining to confirm to the bank that he had explained the documents and the attendant risks to the wife. If he considered the transaction not in her best interests, he should give her reasoned advice to that effect. However, if it was clear that the wife was being grievously wronged, the solicitor should decline to act further. The solicitor's advice should cover at least the following matters:

(i)   the solicitor must explain the nature of the documents and the practical consequences they would have for her if she signed them;

(ii)   the solicitor must point out the seriousness of the risks involved. He should discuss her financial means including her understanding of the value of the property concerned and whether she or her husband had assets from which repayment could be made if the business failed;

(iii) the solicitor must make it clear that the wife has a choice and that the decision is hers alone;

(iv)   the solicitor must check whether the wife wishes to proceed and whether she is content for him to write to the bank confirming the various matters or whether, for instance, she would prefer him to negotiate on the terms with the bank.

(d)   The solicitor might also act for the husband or the bank provided that he was satisfied that it was in the wife's best interest and that it would not give rise to any conflict of duty or interest.

(e)   If the solicitor failed to act properly, the wife had a remedy in damages for negligence against him. The mere fact that the bank asked the solicitor, for its own purposes, to advise the wife did not make him the bank's agent in giving that advice. In the ordinary case deficient advice was a matter between the wife and the solicitor. The bank was entitled to proceed on the assumption that the solicitor had done his job by advising the wife properly.

(f) As regards obtaining the solicitor's confirmation, the bank should:

    (i) check directly with her the name of the solicitors who wished to act for her and communicate directly with her for that purpose;

    (ii) as the bank was likely to have a better picture of the husband's financial affairs it should provide the solicitor with the financial information he needs for that purpose. The bank would first need to obtain the consent of its customer to the disclosure of that confidential information and if it is not forthcoming, the transaction will not be able to proceed;

    (iii) if the bank believed that the wife had been misled, it must notify the wife's solicitors of the facts giving rise to the belief or suspicion; and

    (iv) the bank should in every case obtain from the wife's solicitor written confirmation to the effect that he had fully explained to her the nature of the documents and the practical implications they would have for her. She should be told that the purpose of the requirement was that thereafter she should not be able to dispute that she was legally bound by the documents once she had signed them.

1 *Barclays Bank plc v O'Brien* [1994] 1 AC 180, HL.
2 *CIBC Mortgages plc v Pitt* [1994] 1 AC 200, HL.
3 [2001] UKHL 44, [2001] 4 All ER 449.

17.5 UNFAIR RELATIONSHIPS AND SECURITY

The provisions of ss 140A to 140C of CCA 1974, relating to unfair relationships between creditors and debors, which are discussed in detail in Chapter 23, also apply to security taken for a credit agreement.[1] Thus, references in those sections to an agreement related to a credit agreement include references to a security provided in relation to the credit agreement or to security taken for an agreement which is subsequently consolidated by a further credit agreement or to a linked transaction in relation to either such agreement. As the provisions relating to unfair relationships apply to a credit agreement in any amount, and whether or not an exempt agreement, the unfair relationships provisions likewise apply to security taken for any such agreement.[2]

1 CCA 1974, s 140C(4)(c).
2 CCA 1974, s 140C(6).

17.6 GENERAL OBSERVATIONS

The regulatory regime applying to security is somewhat ambivalent. So far as documentation is concerned it veers from being highly regulated in the case of guarantees and pawns to being relatively relaxed in relation to mortgages and assignments.

A surety is inextricably involved from the outset in the making of the agreement and in any subsequent proceedings which may be brought for its enforcement. In the case of an agreement secured on land, where the debtor is not the mortgagor, he will be furnished with advance copies of the credit agreement and the mortgage. Similarly, where a guarantee is provided in advance of a regulated agreement being entered into, the guarantor is involved with the transaction before it is made. In other situations, the surety only becomes involved at the time when the agreement is entered into by the debtor or hirer.

Care needs to be taken in relation to an all-monies mortgage or charge or a continuing guarantee to ensure that it does not unwittingly catch within its grasp agreements between creditor and debtor, or between owner and hirer, which were not intended to be secured by it.

Where security is provided by a third party and is a condition of the making of the agreement, the provision of the security is not a term of the agreement and does not require to be embodied in the regulated agreement.

The provisions of CCA 1974 may not be evaded by the use of any security.[1]

1 CCA 1974, s 113.

Chapter 18

The total charge for credit and APR

18.1   RELEVANCE OF THE TOTAL CHARGE FOR CREDIT

The Crowther Committee considered that it was of primary importance for borrowers to be able to compare different costs of credit so as to be able to make an informed choice. The result was a set of rules governing the constituents of charges and formulae for their calculation. With effect from April 2000 the various formulae were replaced by a single equation.[1]

The total charge for credit must be stated in agreements and relevant advertisements. The relevant regulations provide permissible tolerances in the disclosure of the APR. Thus, the APR may be stated at a rate which exceeds the APR by not more than one or falls short of the APR by not more than 0.1.[2]

The amount of credit and the total charge for credit are mutually exclusive so that an item entering into the total charge for credit may not be treated as credit even though time is allowed for its payment.[3] This was also the core of the decision in *Wilson v First County Trust Ltd (No 1)*[4] where the court held that the inclusion of a document fee as part of the loan amount had the effect that the credit amount was misstated.

Charges which must, by law, be excluded from the total charge for credit might properly be included in the amount of credit if they are financed.

Possibly with the exception of the calculation and statement of the APR in respect of credit cards, the APR is recognised as an objective yardstick of the cost of credit. Indeed, provided that the APR is applied in a uniform manner there is no need for the public to be aware of how it is composed. In Consultation Paper CP 98 issued by the FSA in June 2001 on the subject of future control of residential mortgages, it stated that the APR is a long-established tool for enabling consumer comparison of the total costs of alternative forms of credit and that in response to an earlier consultation paper, most respondents supported the use of the APR and continuity of the approach in the consumer credit regime. The reasons given included the view that the APR is the best measure available, that it enjoys some consumer recognition, and that it allows comparison between secured and unsecured credit although it worked best as a comparator between like products.

1 Consumer Credit (Total Charge for Credit Regulations) 1980, SI 1980/51, reg 7.
2 Consumer Credit (Agreements) Regulations 1983, SI 1983/1553, as amended, Sch 7, para 1; Consumer Credit (Advertisements) Regulations 2004, SI 2004/1484, Sch 1, para 2.

3 CCA 1974, s 9(4).
4 [2001] QB 407, [2001] GCCR 2901, CA and see [2003] GCCR 4931, HL.

18.2   CALCULATION OF THE APR

The total charge for credit is expressed as an annual percentage rate of charge ('APR') in accordance with the equation set out in the Consumer Credit (Total Charge for Credit) Regulations 1980, reg 7.[1] This replaces the formulae which were previously contained in the Regulations and was inserted by the Consumer Credit (Total Charge for Credit, Agreements and Advertisements) (Amendment) Regulations 1999.[2] The Order implements the amendment made in Directive 90/88 to the Consumer Credit Directive 87/102, namely the introduction of a single method of calculating the APR in Member States of the EU. As the method of calculation is an equation, applicable in all cases, it can only be established with the use of a calculator.

The APR must be rounded to one decimal place. If the figure at the second decimal place is 5 or more, the figure at the first decimal place is increased by one.[3]

1 Consumer Credit (Total Charge for Credit Regulations) 1980, SI 1980/51, as amended.
2 SI 1999/3177.
3 Consumer Credit (Total Charge for Credit Regulations) 1980, SI 1980/51, as amended, regs 6 and 6A.

18.3   STATEMENT OF THE APR

The Advertisements Regulations[1] specify how and when the APR and the typical APR must be stated in an advertisement. The typical APR is an APR at or below which the advertiser reasonably expects, on the date on which the advertisement is published, that credit will be provided under at least 66% of the agreements which will be entered into as a result of the advertisement. In the case of an advertisement in respect of the business of a credit brokerage, 'advertiser' means the person carrying on the business of credit brokerage.[2]

Schedule 1 to the Advertisements Regulations and Schedule 7 to the Agreements Regulations[3] contain assumptions which must be applied in the calculation and disclosure of the total charge for credit and APR in running-account credit agreements.

Both the Advertisements Regulations and the Agreements Regulations contain provisions relating to permissible tolerances in the disclosure of the APR, to the effect that there is compliance with the requirements to show the APR if the APR is stated at a rate which exceeds the APR by not more than one or a rate which falls short of the APR by not more than 0.1 or a rate determined as set out in the next paragraph.

Where all repayments but one are equal and that one repayment does not differ from the others by more whole pence than there are repayments of credit, the APR may be calculated as if that one repayment were equal to the other repayments. Where three or more repayments are to be made at equal intervals and the interval between the relevant date (i.e. the date of the agreement) and the first repayment is greater than that between the repayments, the APR may be calculated as if the interval between the relevant date and the first repayment were shortened so as to be equal to the intervals between the repayments.[4]

1 SI 2004/1484, reg 8.
2 *Ibid.*, reg 1(2).
3 SI 1983/1553, as amended.
4 SI 1983/1553, Sch 7; SI 2004/1484, Sch 2.

18.4   CHARGES INCLUDED IN THE TOTAL CHARGE FOR CREDIT

The total charge for credit comprises three elements of charge.[1] They are, first, the total of the interest on the credit which may be provided under the agreement. Secondly, it includes other charges at any time payable under the transaction by or on behalf of a debtor or relative of his whether to the creditor or any other person, e.g. legal fees, documentation charge, credit brokerage charges. Thirdly, the total charge for credit includes any premium under a contract of insurance, payable under the transaction by the debtor or a relative of his, where the making or maintenance of the contract of insurance is required by the creditor:

(a)   as a condition of making the agreement; and

(b)   for the sole purpose of ensuring complete or partial repayment of the credit, and complete or partial payment to the creditor of those charges included in the total charge for credit as are payable under the transaction in the event of the death, invalidity, illness or unemployment of the debtor. The various charges are included notwithstanding that the whole or part of the charge may be repayable at any time or that the consideration may include matters not within the transaction or subsisting at a time not within the duration of the agreement.

'Transaction' in respect of which charges are included, is widely defined and includes a linked transaction entered into in compliance with a credit agreement, any contract for the provision of security relating to the agreement, a credit brokerage contract relating to the agreement and any other contract to which the debtor or his relative is a party and which the creditor requires to be made or maintained as a condition of the making of the agreement.[2]

There is some confusion in CCA 1974 as to whether an option to purchase fee in a hire-purchase agreement is part of the total charge for credit. Notwithstanding the wording of s 9(3) read with the definition of 'total price' in s 189(1), it is submitted that it is part of the total charge for credit and not the credit amount.[3]

1 Consumer Credit (Total Charge for Credit Regulations) 1980, SI 1980/51, as amended, reg 4.
2 Consumer Credit (Total Charge for Credit Regulations) 1980, SI 1980/51, as amended, reg 1(2).
3 See also Consumer Credit (Total Charge for Credit) Regulations, SI 1980/51, reg 4; *Goode: Consumer Credit Law and Practice* (LexisNexis Butterworths), IC [29.149] and *Humberclyde Finance Ltd v Thompson* [1999] ECCR 2141 CA.

18.5   CHARGES EXCLUDED FROM THE TOTAL CHARGE FOR CREDIT

Certain charges are excluded from the total charge for credit with the result that even though they are payable under the agreement, they are not included in the APR.[1] The main exclusions are the following:

(a)   Default charges: this includes payments such as default interest in the event of late payment, charges relating to correspondence and administration fees incurred in the event of a debtor's default and costs relating to litigation.

Under a separate provision, default interest may not exceed the interest rate applying to an agreement or, in the absence of such interest rate, the rate of the total charge for credit applying to the agreement, excluding any charges arising under a linked transaction.[2] It follows that no default charges can be charged under an interest free credit agreement.

In practice the range of default-type charges has expanded considerably over the years and includes charges for stopping a cheque, charges for bounced and unpaid cheques, for special presentation of cheques and for returned unpaid cheques or dishonoured standing orders and direct debits, and for correspondence relating to the unauthorised use of an overdraft. There are administration charges, likewise not included in the total charge for credit, which might be debited to an account, if a payment is not made in accordance with the Conditions of Use, on requesting a duplicate statement or voucher, on the replacement of a lost or damaged card, on returning a dividend warrant; charges relating to arrears letters, default letters and arrears administration charges.

(b)   Charges relating to debtor-creditor-supplier agreements which would also be payable if the transaction was for cash, e.g. delivery or installation charge.

(c)   A charge relating to services or benefits incidental to the agreement and which the debtor voluntarily undertook to pay before entering into the credit agreement.

(d)   Charges for arrangements for the care, maintenance or protection of land or goods without which the land or goods could not be reasonably enjoyed or used. These would include car maintenance charges. Also excluded from the charge for credit are maintenance and service charges if they are substantially the same as those available under comparable arrangements from a person who is not the creditor or supplier or credit broker who introduced the debtor and the creditor. Where arrangements are made with the person chosen by the debtor and are subject to the creditor's consent, that consent may not be unreasonably withheld.

(e)   Charges for money transmission services, e.g. charges for cheques, for banker's drafts, for payments by telegraphic transfer, by CHAPS or by SWIFT.

(f) Any charge for a guarantee, other than a guarantee which is required by the creditor as a condition of making the agreement and the purpose of which is to ensure the complete or partial repayment of the credit, and complete or partial payment of such of the charges included in the total charge for credit as are payable, in the event of the death, invalidity, illness or unemployment of the debtor.

(g) Charges for the transfer of funds and charges for keeping an account intended to receive payment towards repayment of the credit and the payment of interest and other charges, except where the debtor does not have reasonable freedom of choice in the matter and where such charges are abnormally high.

(h) A premium under a contract of insurance other than a contract of insurance as referred to in para 18.4.

1 Consumer Credit (Total Charge for Credit Regulations) 1980, SI 1980/51 (as amended), reg 5.
2 CCA 1974, s 93.

18.6 GENERAL ASSUMPTIONS FOR CALCULATION OF THE TOTAL CHARGE FOR CREDIT

Apart from the assumptions relating to the calculation of the APR which apply to running-account credit agreements, referred to in para 18.3 above, the following are the principal assumptions which apply to the calculation of the total charge for credit:[1]

(1) In the case of a land-related agreement which provides for the possibility of the variation of the rate of interest following the occurrence of an event which is certain to occur and where the date or earliest date of its occurrence can be ascertained when the agreement is made, the assumption that such variation will take place on such date.

(2) Except in land-related agreements (as to which see para (1) above) where the transaction provides for a variation of the rate or amount of any item included in the total charge for credit following the happening of an event, the assumption that such event will not occur, unless it is certain that such event will occur and where the date or earliest date of its occurrence can be ascertained when the agreement is made.

(3) Each provision of credit and each repayment of credit and of the charge for credit shall be assumed to be made at the earliest time provided under the agreement.

(4) Where the amounts of repayments or the intervals between them are not stated in the agreement and a constant rate of charge is specified in respect of equal periods, then the charge is calculated on the debit balance at the start of the period and the amount of any repayment of credit or of the charge for credit is assumed to be the minimum amount payable by the debtor.

(5) Where the amount of the credit cannot be ascertained when the agreement is made, in the case of a running-account credit agreement when there is a credit limit it shall be assumed to be the credit limit and in any other case it shall be assumed to be £100.

(6) Where the period for which credit is provided cannot be ascertained when the agreement is made, the period shall be assumed to be one year.

(7) Where, in the case of a land-related agreement falling within para (1) above, the amount of the variation cannot be ascertained when the agreement is made. It shall be assumed that the rate or level will be the standard variable rate of interest which would be applied by the lender on the date the agreement is made.

(8) Where the period for which the credit cannot be ascertained when the agreement is made and the rate or amount of any item of charge will alter within one year of the agreement date, the date or amount shall be taken to be the highest rate or amount pertaining during that year.

(9) Where the earliest date for provision of credit cannot be ascertained, it shall be assumed to be the date of the making of the agreement.

(10) If a charge is payable at an unknown date, it shall be assumed to be payable when the agreement is made or if the debtor cannot reasonably be expected to make payment on that date, on the earliest date when he can reasonably be expected to make payment.

Complications arise in deciding which assumptions prevail over others although the Regulations provide some assistance, as in the case of Pt IV of the Regulations where it is provided that reg 13 shall be applied first. Of concern, too, is the fact that it appears that several of the assumptions, notably those contained in regs 2(1)(d) and 16, conflict with Council Directive 87/102 EEC (as amended), especially art 1a, para 6, of the latter.

1 Consumer Credit (Total Charge for Credit Regulations) 1980, SI 1980/51, as amended, regs 2, 12, 13, 14, 15, 15A, 16, 17 and 18.

18.7 CREDIT CARD INTEREST CALCULATIONS

18.7.1 Introductory interest rates

In 2001 the Office of Fair Trading issued advice on the calculation of APRs in relation to running-account credit when the agreement, or a part (e.g. balance transfer) commences with a low rate of interest for a specified period, e.g. six months, and then moves on to the standard rate. It took the view, that, first, the period for which credit is provided must be determined in accordance with regs 1(3)(b) and 13 of the Total Charge for Credit Regulations; secondly, the APR must be calculated taking into account both the introductory interest rate and the standard interest rate subsequently applying, so as to create a so-called 'blended

APR'; thirdly, the OFT considered it desirable that the interest rate in advertising is presented as an annual rate, as this would be more readily understood by consumers. A statement of any other rate might be misleading.[1]

An argument to the contrary would require the period of the agreement to be determined by reference to the assumption in reg 14 of the Total Charge for Credit Regulations, namely that the period of credit is not ascertainable at the outset, so that it is deemed to be for one year and the APR should be calculated by reference to that period.

1 OFT advice issued to the Association for Payment Clearing Services ('APACS') (October 2001) for transmission to its Members.

18.7.2   Credit card comparisons

In April 2007 Which? launched a super-complaint about the way credit card companies calculated interest charges.[1] It maintained that the top 20 credit card providers used 12 different methods to apply interest charges to their customer's accounts. The super-complaint argued that APRs cannot be trusted or used in like-for-like comparisons. The complaint claimed that summary boxes and terms and conditions on their own seldom provided sufficient information on issuers' interest calculation methods that APRs were not comparable as between cards. In its response in June 2007[2] the OFT stated that it would initiate a negotiated approach to finding a way for consumers to make well informed decisions about the best card product for their needs, without restricting the commercial freedom of card issuers. It considered that the outcome of the super-complaint should be undertaken with the banking industry and consumer bodies in a voluntary initiative to increase transparency surrounding the cost of credit arising from the use of credit cards. In February 2008 the OFT published its report.[3] The OFT:

(a)   found that approximately 70% of consumers who had taken out a credit card in the last three years did not shop around at all;

(b)   found that consumers had problems comparing financial products in general and credit cards in particular;

(c)   recommended that to make selecting the right card much easier:

   (i)   the FSA should introduce a price comparison website for credit cards as part of its 'moneymadeclear' website (the report reveals that the FSA had already agreed to run the credit card comparison on its website);

   (ii)   summary boxes should present information regarding the credit cards in a consistent way and preferably in tabular form;

   (iii)   terminology should be standardised wherever possible and should be used by all credit card issuers; and

   (iv)   an ongoing consumer education strategy should be established, to which the OFT would contribute, to emphasise the benefits of shopping around for credit cards and to assist in finding the best card for the particular consumer.

The report recognised that 39% of the population did not have access to the internet. The OFT recommended a one-page information sheet which it would design with the credit card industry, FSA and other interested parties to meet the requirements of lower literacy consumers.

With increasing uniformity of product presentation and readier access to comparative information, not only will the consumer be better served, but he will be expected to act more responsibly in making his credit card selection. The greater availability of comparative information will mean that the credit grantor's offering will be placed under closer security by the consumer. However, this should serve to alleviate the obligation of responsible lending as the consumer is assisted by the information in arriving at a decision on the most apporopriate credit card for his purposes in all the circumstances.

1 Under s 11 of the Enterprise Act 2002.
2 OFT 935.
3 OFT 987.

Chapter 19

Advertising and promoting credit and hire facilities

19.1 OVERVIEW

Advertising is the showcase or introduction to a credit or hire agreement. Unlike the position under the Financial Services and Markets Act 2000, which also provides for a regime for the control of advice in relation to investments which fall under that Act, advice relating to hire or credit agreements is not regulated by the CCA 1974.

An 'advertisement' is defined as including every form of advertising, whether in a publication, by television or radio, by display of notices, signs, labels, showcards or goods, by distribution of samples, circulars, catalogues, price lists or other material, by exhibition of pictures, models or films or in any other way and references to the publishing of advertisements is construed accordingly. 'Advertiser' means any person indicated by the advertisement as willing to enter into the transactions to which the advertisement relates.[1]

As will be observed, an advertisement is defined by reference to form rather than to substance. It does mean that any representation can be construed as an advertisement.

An advertisement is regulated by CCA 1974 if it is published for the purposes of a business carried on by the advertiser indicating that he is willing to provide credit or to enter into hire agreements.[2]

Advertisements which relate to exempt agreements (other than exempt agreements secured on land) are exempt from the provisions of CCA 1974.[3] They are:

(a) advertisements relating to specified debtor-creditor-supplier agreements under which the number of payments to be made by the debtor does not exceed a specified number, (excluding agreements financing the purchase of land);

(b) advertisements relating to consumer credit agreements which are exempt agreements by virtue of the rate of the total charge for credit charged under such agreements;

(c) advertisements relating to consumer credit agreements which are exempt agreements by virtue of their having a connection with a country outside the United Kingdom; and

(d) advertisements for consumer hire agreements which are exempt agreements because they are made by specified public bodies.

An advertisement relating to an investment activity (such as a regulated mortgage contract or payment protection insurance), within the meaning of s 21 of the Financial Services and Markets Act 2000, is outside the Consumer Credit regime.[4]

Advertisements relating to the business of credit brokerage, debt adjusting, debt counselling or transactions concerned with the liquidation of debts, or advertisements to provide credit information services are regulated by the CCA 1974 and the Consumer Credit (Advertisements) Regulations 2004 (the 'Advertisements Regulations').[5]

The advertising regime relating to consumer credit and consumer hire agreements is now an amalgam of the Consumer Credit Act 1974, the Advertisements Regulations and the Consumer Protection from Unfair Trading Regulations 2008 ('the Unfair Trading Regulations'). Credit advertisements are governed by CCA 1974 and the Advertisements Regulations 2004. Hire advertisements are governed by CCA 1974 and the Unfair Trading Regulations. The latter implemented Directive 2005/29/EC of the European Parliament and Council concerning unfair business-to-consumer commercial practices. As the Directive also relates to consumer hire advertising, most of the provisions relating to the advertising of consumer hire have been artificially (and it is submitted, unnecessarily) removed from CCA 1974 and are to be found in the Unfair Trading Regulations.

Further dissection of CCA 1974 is to be found in the substitution of various of the Unfair Trading Regulations for the regulations relating to hire advertisements in the Advertisements Regulations, disembodying the purposive format of the former for the sake of the comprehensiveness of the latter. Moreover, it results in the detailed provisions of the Advertisements Regulations realting to hire advertisements being removed and not replaced. Most surprising of all, the Unfair Trading Regulations repeal the core provision of CCA 1974, s 46, which rendered it a criminal offence for an advertisement of facilities to which the Act applied to convey information which was false or misleading in a material respect.

1 CCA 1974, s 189.
2 CCA 1974, s 43(1).
3 Consumer Credit (Exempt Advertisements) Order 1985, SI 1985/621.
4 CCA 1974, ss 43(3A), 151(2A) and SI 2004/1484, reg 10.
5 CCA 1974, s 151.

19.2 THE CONSUMER CREDIT (ADVERTISEMENTS) REGULATIONS 2004[1]

19.2.1 Advertisements exempt from the Regulations

The Regulations do not apply to any advertisement which, whether expressly or by implication, indicates clearly that a person is willing to provide credit for the purposes of another person's business and does not indicate (whether expressly or impliedly), that a person is willing to do either of those things other than for the purposes of such a business.[2] The reference to 'business' does not include a business carried on by the advertiser or any person acting as a credit-broker in relation to the credit to which the advertisement relates.

The Regulations do not apply to any advertisement which is a communication of an invitation or inducement to engage in investment activity within the meaning of s 21 of the Financial Services and Markets Act 2000, other than an exempt generic communication.[3]

The Regulations do not apply to an advertisement which is a communication of an invitation or inducement to enter into a regulated mortgage contract within the meaning of art 61 of the Financial Services and Markets Act 2000 (Regulated Activities) Order 2001.[4]

1 SI 2004/1484, as amended.
2 *Ibid.*, reg 10(1) and (2).
3 *Ibid.*, reg 10(3).
4 *Ibid.*, reg 10(5).

19.2.2 Application of the Advertisements Regulations

The pricipal regulations governing credit advertisements for consumer credit are the Consumer Credit (Advertisements) Regulations 2004[1] ('the Advertisements Regulations'). Prior to the coming into force of the Consumer Protection from Unfair Trading Regulations 2008, the Advertisements Regulations also applied to hire advertisements.

The Advertisements Regulations apply to any person who causes an advertisement to be published.[2] Every credit advertisement must use plain and intelligible language, be easily legible, or in the case of any information given orally, clearly audible, and specify the name of the advertiser.[3] This might be the advertiser's name in its consumer credit licence.

Certain credit advertisements must specify the typical APR. The typical APR means the APR at or below which the advertiser reasonably expects, at the date on which the advertisement is published, that credit will be provided under at least 66% of the agreements which will be entered into as a result of the advertisement. In the case of an advertisement by a credit-broker, the advertiser means the person carrying on the business of credit-brokerage.[4]

A credit advertisement must specify the typical APR if the advertisement:

(a)   specifies any other rate of charge;

(b)   includes information relating to any of the following: frequency, number and amount of repayments of credit, other payments and charges, or the total amount payable by the debtor;

(c)   indicates in any way, including by means of the name given to the business or an address used by a business for the purposes of electronic communication, that:

    (i)   credit is available to persons who might otherwise consider their access restricted, or

    (ii)   any of the terms on which credit is available is more favourable (either in relation to limited period or generally) than corresponding terms applied in any other case or by any other creditors, or

(d)   includes any incentive to apply for credit or to enter into an agreement
      under which credit is provided.[5]

The Office of Fair Trading takes a wide view of the meaning of 'incentive'.[6] It
considers an incentive to include not only a gift or special offer but also a statement such as 'nothing to pay for a year', 'buy now, pay next June', 'no deposit
on orders before 1 May'. In the writer's view, if the credit agreement is one
whereby the debtor can settle the credit amount free of interest and other charges
within 12 months, after which the agreement is interest-bearing, advertising the
credit as interest-free for 12 months does not amount to an incentive, especially
if the advertisement describes the entire product, namely the interest-free period
and the interest-bearing period. Advertising the former is no more than advertising a quality or characteristic of the credit agreement. It is no more an incentive
than a statement of the customer's option to purchase under a hire-purchase
agreement.

  Where the typical APR must be stated, it must be given greater prominence
than any other rate of charge, any of the information to be contained in a credit
advertisement specified in Schedule 2 to the Advertisements Regulations, any of
the information specified above which triggers the requirement to state the typical APR and, where the advertisement is in printed or electronic form which
includes any of the items listed in Schedule 2, at least one and a half times the
size of the characters in which those items appear.[7]

  The APR must be denoted as '…% APR' and, if variable, accompanied by the
word 'variable'. The typical APR must be accompanied by the word 'typical'.

  A credit advertisement may not indicate the range of APRs other than by
specifying, with equal prominence, both:

(a)   the APR which the advertiser reasonably expects at the date on which the
      advertisement is published would be the lowest APR at which credit would
      be provided under not less than 10% of the agreements which will be
      entered into as a result of that advertisement; and

(b)   the APR which the advertiser reasonably expects at that date would be the
      highest APR at which credit will be provided under any other agreement
      which will be entered into as a result of that advertisement.[8]

The inclusion of certain information in the credit advertisement triggers the
need for other information. Thus, a statement of any amount relating to the
frequency, number and amount of repayments of credit, other payments and
charges or the total amount payable by the debtor, triggers the requirement to
state:

(a)   all other information listed in Schedule 2 to the Advertisements Regula-
      tions; and

(b)   a personal address at which the advertiser may be contacted, except in the
      case of advertisements published by means of television or radio broadcast,
      advertisements on the premises of a dealer not intended to be taken away or
      advertisements which include the name and address of the dealer or credit-

broker.[9] All such information must be given equal prominence and shown together as a whole.

1 SI 2004/1484 as amended.
2 *Ibid.*, reg 2.
3 *Ibid.*, reg 3.
4 SI 2007/827, reg 2(2).
5 SI 2004/1484, reg 8(1).
6 Credit Advertising (September 2005) OFT 016.
7 SI 2004/1484, reg 8(5).
8 *Ibid.*, reg 8(2).
9 *Ibid.*, reg 4.

19.2.3 Restrictions on certain expressions

Use of the following expressions in credit advertisements is restricted:

(a) the word 'overdraft' or any similar expression except an agreement enabling the debtor to overdraw on a current account;

(b) the expression 'interest free' or any similar expression indicating that a customer is liable to pay no greater amount in respect of a transaction financed by credit than he would be liable to pay as a cash purchaser;

(c) the expression 'no deposit' or any similar expression except where no advance payments are to be made;

(d) the expression 'loan guaranteed' or 'pre-approved' or any similar expression, except where the agreement is free of any conditions regarding the credit status of the debtor; or

(e) the expression 'gift', 'present' or any similar expression, except where the debtor is not required to return the credit or items that are the subject of the claim;

(f) the expression 'weekly equivalent' or any expression to the like effect or any other periodical equivalent, unless weekly payments or other periodical payments are provided for under the agreement.[1]

1 SI 2004/1484, reg 9.

19.2.4 Advertisements which include security

Where the credit advertisement is for a facility for which security is or may be required, the advertisement must state that fact.[1]

Regulation 7 sets out the statutory warning notices which the advertisement must contain where the security comprises a mortgage or charge on the debtors' home. In the case of an advertisement which is published by means of television or radio broadcast in the course of programming, the primary purpose of which is not advertising or is published by exhibition of a film (other than by television broadcast), or contains only the name of the advertiser, the statutory security warnings may be omitted.[2]

1 SI 2004/1484, reg 7(1).
2 *Ibid.*, reg 7(8).

19.2.5   Miscellaneous

The Advertisements Regulations contain specific provisions relating to credit advertisements in dealers' publications covering a calendar or seasonal period and advertisements in dealers' publications relating to credit under a debtor-creditor-supplier agreement.[1]

1 SI 2004/1484, regs 5 and 6.

19.2.6   'Together as a whole' and 'prominence'

The Advertisements Regulations require certain information to be shown 'together as a whole' and also prescribe the degree of prominence of different types of information.[1]

Regulation 4(2) requires Schedule 2 information to be of equal prominence and to be shown together as a whole. The OFT takes the view that all items of information in question must be shown together in one place so that they are capable of being (and are likely to be) read as a whole and that this will generally mean on the same page and in the same part of the page.[2] The OFT also states that if an individual item is repeated elsewhere in the advertisement, such that it is no longer 'together as a whole' with the other information required to be set out with it, it must be accompanied by a repetition of all the other items. In the case of advertising on the Internet, the OFT is of the view that the requirement that information be shown 'together as a whole' is not satisfied if the information is presented on separate pages of a website or if it is necessary to 'click' between items on a website. The consumer should be able to see all the information together on one screen, or by scrolling down a single page.

Whilst in most instances it would be feasible in practice to meet the OFT's requirements, it is open to question whether it is necessary to adopt the stringent approach the OFT suggests. In the first place, the Regulations do not (as the OFT accepts) prohibit interspersals in the information. Secondly, provided that a reader would ordinarily read the information together as a whole, information contained in more than one page should satisfy the requirements. It might also be mentioned that the requirements of the Advertisements Regulations relate to an advertisement for credit (and in their original unamended form, also for hire). Whilst Schedule 2 information includes the cash price, an advertisement for the sale of the car might show the cash price in large print, separately from an advertisement relating to the credit available for its purchase, the latter complying with the Schedule 2 requirements. The reader is also referred to para 22.5 on online advertising.

The typical APR must be stated in an advertisement with greater prominence than other specified information.[3] Likewise statutory warnings relating to security must be given greater prominence than certain other specified information.[4] In the OFT's view prominence must be assessed in the context of the advertisement as a whole which should generally be considered from the perspective of the reader or listener. This appears correct, as prominence is a subjective issue.

1 The Consumer Credit (Advertisements) Regulations 2004, SI 2004/1484, Regs 4(2), 7(6) and (7), 8(2) and 5.
2 Consumer Credit (Advertisements) Regulations 2004. Frequently Asked Questions (September 2005) OFT 746.
3 Regulation 8(5) and see para 19.2.2 above.
4 Regulations 7(6) and (7).

19.3 CONSUMER PROTECTION FROM UNFAIR TRADING REGULATIONS 2008[1]

19.3.1 Concepts embodied in the Regulations

The Regulations apply to commercial practices, namely any act, omission, course of conduct, representation or commercial communication, including advertising and marketing, by a trader, directly connected with the promotion, sale or supply of a product to or from consumers.[2] 'Product' means any goods or services and includes immovable property, rights and obligations.[3]

The standard of conduct required is one which evidences professional diligence, meaning the standard of special skill and care which a trader may reasonably be expected to exercise towards consumers, which is commensurate with honest market practice or the general principle of good faith, in each case in the trader's field of activity.[4]

Reference in the Regulations to the concept of 'materially distorting the economic behaviour' means, in relation to an average consumer, appreciably to impair the average consumer's ability to make an informed decision, causing him to take a transactional decision he would not have taken otherwise.[5]

'Average consumer' is defined by reference to the material characteristics of such an average consumer, including his being reasonably well informed, reasonably observant and circumspect. Due regard must be had to the members of a vulnerable group of consumers.[6]

1 SI 2008/1277.
2 Regulation 2(1).
3 Regulation 2(1).
4 Regulation 2(1).
5 Regulation 2(1).
6 Regulation 2(2) to (6).

19.3.2   Unfair commercial practices: general

A commercial practice is unfair in relation to goods (including immovable property) or services if:

(a)   it contravenes the requirements of professional diligence; and

(b)   materially distorts or is likely to materially distort the economic balance of the average consumer with regard to the goods or services.[1]

1 Regulation 3(2).

19.3.3   Unfair commercial practices: specific

(1)   Misleading action

A commercial practice is unfair if:

(a)   it is a misleading action.[1] This includes:

    (i)   if it contains false information in relation to matters listed in reg 5(4) or in any way deceives or is likely to deceive the average consumer in relation to the matters listed; and

    (ii)   causes or is likely to cause the average consumer to take a transactional decision he would not have taken otherwise;[2]

(b)   it concerns any marketing of goods or services, including comparative marketing, which creates confusion with any goods, services, trade marks, trade names etc. of a competitor; or

(c)   it concerns any failure by a trader to comply with a commitment in a code of conduct if the trader indicates that he is bound by that code and it causes or is likely to cause the average consumer to take a transactional decision he would not have taken otherwise.[3]

1 Regulation 3(4)(a).
2 Regulation 5(2).
3 Regulation 5(3).

(2)   Misleading omission

A commercial practice is unfair if it is a misleading omission.[1] It is a misleading omission if, in its factual context, taking into account the matters specified in reg 6(2), the commercial practice:

(i)   omits material information;

(ii)   hides material information;

(iii)   provides material information in a manner which is unclear, unintelligible, ambiguous or untimely; or

(iv)   fails to identify its commercial intent, unless this is apparent from the context.[2]

(3) Aggressive commercial practices

A commercial practice is unfair if it is an aggressive commercial practice,[3] that is, in its factual context, taking into account all of its features and circumstances:

(a)   it significantly impairs or is likely significantly to impair the average consumer's freedom of choice or conduct in relation to the goods or services though the use of harassment, coercion or undue influence; and

(b)   it thereby causes or is likely to cause him to take a transactional decision he would not have taken otherwise.[4]

Factors to be taken into account are listed in reg 7(2).

1 Regulation 3(4)(b).
2 Regulation 6(1).
3 Regulation 3(4)(c).
4 Regulation 7(1).

(4) Specific unfair commercial practices

Schedule 1 to the Regulations lists 31 practices which in all circumstances are considered unfair.

(5) Offences and defences

Various offences and defences are set out in Part 3 of the Regulations. The defences include the commission of an offence due to the default of another person, the so-called due diligence defence and the innocent publication of an advertisement.

19.4 OFFENCES RELATING TO CREDIT ADVERTISING

Contravention of the advertising provisions of the CCA 1974 and the Advertisements Regulations constitutes an offence. The offence is committed by the publisher of the advertisement, any person who in the course of business carried on by him devised the advertisement and any person who procured publication of the advertisement.[1] As it gives rise to criminal liability, wherever possible the provisions will be construed in favour of the alleged offender. This contrasts with the approach of the Advertising Standards Authority ('ASA') in its application of the British Codes of Advertising and Sales Promotion. The ASA will often uphold objections to advertisements on the grounds that they are misleading in circumstances where the courts might have refused to convict. However, the ASA's role is quite different to that of the courts. It acts as an arbiter of what is legal, decent, honest and truthful, rather than as a judge of the advertiser's intent.

The Office of Fair Trading might itself intervene in advertising campaigns and require the advertiser, when the OFT considers it to be in breach of CCA 1974, to cease publishing an advertisement. The OFT will generally act in this regard pursuant to its enforcement powers under Part 8 of the Enterprise Act 2002.

The CCA 1974 contains a unique specific prohibition. If an advertisement indicates that the advertiser is willing to provide credit under a restricted-use credit agreement relating to goods or services to be supplied by any person, the advertiser commits an offence if at the time the advertisement is published, that person is not holding himself out as prepared to sell the goods or provide the services for cash.[2] The provision is intended to outlaw any offer of credit in relation to goods or services which cannot also be bought for cash. Though infrequently applied in the courts, it is of considerable practical significance.

We turn next to briefly consider some cases involving breaches of the advertising regulations.

In *Jenkins v Lombard North Central plc*[3] it was successfully argued on the finance company's behalf that an advertisement stating the cash price of a vehicle in a sticker attached to the vehicle was not a credit advertisement at all as it did not indicate the advertiser's willingness to provide credit. The court referred to *Maurice Binks (Turf Accountants) Ltd v Huss*[4] where it was stated that a suggestion derived from the knowledge of the advertiser's business which was obtained not from the advertisement itself did not amount to an indication. As the House of Lords refused leave to appeal, it can be assumed that it concurred in the view that surrounding circumstances should not be taken into account in determining the construction of the expression 'indicating a willingness to provide credit'.

Contrasting circumstances are to be found in *R v Kettering Magistrates Court, ex p MRB Insurance Brokers Ltd*.[5] This turned on whether a wrongly stated APR in a regulated agreement constituted a misleading indication as to price, in contravention of s 20 of the Consumer Protection Act 1987. The court found that the statement of an APR as 28.3% when in fact it was an APR of approximately 64% was a misleading price indication.

In *Metsoja v H Norman Pitt & Co Ltd*[6] it was held that an advertisement for 0% APR where the purchaser was in fact given a less favourable part-exchange allowance than was available to a cash purchaser, constituted a misleading advertisement. The court also found that the advertisement contravened reg 7(c) of the then Consumer Credit (Advertisements) Regulations 1989. This regulation prohibited the use of the expression 'interest free' (or any expression to the like effect) indicating that a customer is liable to pay no greater amount in respect of a transaction financed by credit than he would be liable to pay as a cash purchaser, except where the total amount payable does not exceed the cash price. Regulation 7(c) is replicated as reg 9(b) in the Consumer Credit (Advertisements) Regulations 2004.

Where 'interest free' credit is advertised but a purchaser for cash, unlike a credit purchaser, may, with the aid of a dividend card, receive back cash in due course, the court in *Holman v Co-operative Wholesale Society Ltd*[7] held that this contravened reg 7(c) above.

In *Roller Group Ltd and Roller Finance Ltd v Sumner*[8] an advertisement was found to be misleading where the price quoted for a new car was stated exclusive of the cost of delivery, road fund tax and number plates. A contravention of CCA 1974, s 46 (since repealed) did not require the false or misleading information to relate to the terms of credit.

In *Currys Ltd v Jessop*[9] an advertisement containing the phrase 'nothing to pay for three months' was held to be misleading in circumstances where payments only commenced after three months but interest in fact began to accrue immediately from the date of purchase. In contrast, in *Dudley Metropolitan Borough v Colorvision plc*[10] the court found that the expression 'Your purchase absolutely free. If we cannot meet our competitors' price ask for details' would be interpreted by the average citizen as not meaning that he could expect a free item but rather a price reduction if a rival offered better terms.

1 CCA 1974, s 47.
2 CCA 1974, s 45.
3 [1999] GCCR 623.
4 [1971] 1 All ER 104.
5 [2000] GCCR 2701.
6 [1999] GCCR 1339.
7 [2001] GCCR 2777.
8 [1995] CCLR 1.
9 [1999] GCCR 3407.
10 [1999] GCCR 2135.

19.5 OTHER STATUTORY CONTROLS

There are various statutory controls which apply to the entire range of advertisements, whether or not relating to credit, regulated or unregulated. The main relevant statutes are the Trade Descriptions Act 1968, the Misrepresentation Act 1967, the Unfair Contract Terms Act 1977 and the Property Misdescriptions Act 1991. Principal applicable statutory instruments are the Consumer Transactions (Restrictions on Statements) Order 1976 and the Property Misdescriptions (Specified Matters) Order 1992.

19.6 NON-STATUTORY CONTROLS

The Advertising Standards Authority ('ASA') is the independent body set up by the advertising industry to monitor the rules laid down in the advertising codes. It has the support of the advertising industry and operates through the Committee of Advertising Practice ('CAP'). The ASA regulates the content of advertisements, sales promotions and direct marketing in the UK. The British Code of Advertising, Sales Promotion and Direct Marketing is the rule book for non-broadcast advertisements, sales promotions and direct marketing communications. There are separate codes for radio and TV advertising and for all other types of advertisements.

The main principles of the advertising codes are that advertisements should not mislead, cause harm or offend. All marketing communications should be legal, decent, honest and truthful and should be prepared with a sense of responsibility to consumers and to society. Specifically in relation to CCA 1974, the codes provide that the OFT will continue to regulate consumer loans under that Act and that the FSA is responsible for the regulation of first charge mortgage lending and selling, as well as certain secured loans and the activities of insurance intermediaries. However, the ASA retains responsibility for financial marketing communications that cover non-technical elements of communications, such as statements which cause serious or widespread offence, social responsibility and the truthfulness of claims that do not relate to specific characteristics of financial products.

The BCAP Radio Advertising Standards Code ('the Radio Code') applies to all advertisements and services licensed by Ofcom. Product placement and sponsorship continue to be governed by Ofcom's Code, operated through the Radio Advertising Clearance Centre. The Radio Code contains specific provisions relating to financial products and services and requires advertisements to present information in terms that do not mislead, whether by exaggeration, misuse or otherwise. Advertisements must comply with the laws and regulations applying to them.

The BCAP Television Advertising Standards Code ('TV Code') sets out the rules that govern advertisements, on any television channel licensed by Ofcom. They mirror the principles of the above codes.

The ASA and CAP do not adopt a legalistic approach towards sanctions but endeavour to ensure that non-compliant marketing communications are amended, withdrawn or stopped as early as possible. The ASA publishes rulings, which itself might adversely affect an advertiser. The ASA and CAP also maintain a rapport with the OFT and other bodies with responsibility for administering laws relating to advertising and if necessary those bodies might be urged to take further action.

The Banking Code 2008 requires its subscribers, namely banks, building societies and banking service providers, to ensure that all advertising and promotional material is clear, fair, reasonable and not misleading.

19.7   ENFORCEMENT OF ADVERTISING CONTROLS

The advertising regime under CCA 1974 and the Unfair Trading Regulations is enforced by the OFT and Local Weights and Measures Authorities. Contravention of the Unfair Trading Regulations can be enforced under the Enterprise Act 2002 as a Community Infringement. Under Part 8 of the Act the OFT can issue an enforcement order and take proceedings against the offending party.

Chapter 20

The credit market and credit marketing

20.1 ENTITLEMENT TO CREDIT

Some of the greatest dilemmas faced by the socio-economic foundations of society are to be found in the credit arena, namely how to match the expectations of individuals' entitlement to credit on the one hand with the willingness of credit grantors to advance credit at affordable rates on the other hand; to meet the expectations of individuals in a consumer society given to spending without resulting in over-indebtedness and holding creditors accountable for the same. These contradictions mirror those on the international plane where we have in the past witnessed sovereign states borrow beyond their means only subsequently to appeal for their indebtedness to be written off.

The problems are exacerbated by the fact that credit has become an essential constituent of everyday life. Most individuals have a need to borrow at one time or another, whether in order to pursue their studies, a business or profession, to purchase a dwelling, motor vehicle, assist with expenses associated with a holiday, wedding and general living expenses. Indeed, credit supplies the means to enable individuals to achieve their multifarious goals. Given that the grant of credit is generally not an act of charity but a function of business, it needs to be profitable. Consumer credit law is concerned with the governance of the wants and desires of the parties at opposite ends of the spectrum.

The situation is well described in the following extract from the Quinquennial Review of the Insolvency Service 2000:[1]

> 'Credit is an essential element of everyday life. Business involves taking risks and all who invest recognise that businesses may fail for a variety of reasons, from bad luck to incompetence and fraud. Over the last century the level of personal indebtedness has been rising; and more people have entered business on their own account or using a limited company. Most people are in debt one way or another whether by having a mortgage, paying for essential services in arrears, using credit cards or taking out specific loans; and most businesses are funded at least in part by bank overdrafts and loans, hire, hire purchase and supplier credit.'

This theme, but with the ultimate consequence of over-indebtedness, was the subject of the Over-indebtedness Summit Conference held in London in October 2000 when the Minister for Consumer Affairs stated:[2]

'The availability of credit is a key, possibly essential, requirement for consumers in today's society. For most it brings a means of easier access to services and goods, and provides consumers with greater flexibility in making best use of their income. I do not want to clamp down on the innovation which has enabled many consumers safely to realise their dreams. But for some consumers it can, often through a change of circumstance but also on occasions through over-commitment, result in over-indebtedness ... The average debt for a consumer with repayment problems has increased by a quarter since 1997, and now stands at £21,000. The overall level of unsecured debt has risen 70% in just five years ... I want us to gain a greater understanding of the causes and effects of over-indebtedness and by means of a constructive dialogue, look at how we can encourage, through practical solutions, more responsible lending and borrowing.'

These sentiments were also echoed by the Council of the European Union which, on 26 November 2001, passed a resolution on consumer credit and indebtedness. The resolution notes that over-indebtedness affects a significant and growing number of European consumers in all the Member States. It advocates that consideration be given at Community level to implementing measures to develop cross-border credit with measures to prevent over-indebtedness throughout the credit cycle. It further recommends the harmonisation of preventive measures, cooperation on the study and prevention of over-indebtedness and finding ways of monitoring over-indebtedness within the internal market.[3]

In the UK, it was noted in the White Paper on Consumer Credit Market in the 21st Century, while the majority of consumers do not experience any difficulties with borrowing, 20% of households who have credit, experience difficulties, while 7% have levels of credit use associated with over-indebtedness.[4] The longer-term trend would appear to suggest that debt is becoming a problem for an increasing number of households with the debt to disposable income ratio across the household sector continuing to rise, driven by the growth in secured lending. On the other hand, the household debt to total assets ratio, which includes both financial and housing wealth in total assets, has remained little changed since 2002 and the data for 2006 shows that the ratio is just under 17%. Household wealth, including both housing and financial assets, was £7.5 trillion in 2006, with household secured and unsecured debt equal to approximately 17% of this figure.[5]

Whilst there is no generally accepted definition of over-indebtedness, it has been defined in terms of a household having 25% of its annual income spent on repaying consumer debt or 50% on repaying consumer credit and mortgages or having at least four credit commitments.[6]

1 Published by the Department of Trade and Industry.
2 Speech of Dr Kim Howells given on 30 October 2000.
3 Official Journal of the European Communities (2001/c 364/01).
4 CM 6040 December 2003, p 5.
5 Household Debt Monitoring Paper HI 2007: BERR Consumer and Competition Policy Directorate (December 2007 URN 07/401A), pp 5 and 17.
6 White Paper on The Consumer Credit Market in the 21st Century (CM 6040 December 2003 para 5.5).

20.2 LENDING INSTITUTIONS

The usual institutions that grant loans to individuals are banks, building societies and finance companies. The latter include specialist dedicated finance companies as well as the credit arms of insurance companies and other institutions which finance their respective products and services, such as insurance company subsidiaries which finance insurance premiums.

Most mainstream lenders belong to one or other association, such as the British Bankers Association, the Building Societies Association, the Finance & Leasing Association and the Consumer Credit Trade Association.

The availability of credit to those less able to afford it is being facilitated by the expansion of credit unions. A credit union is a financial cooperative owned and controlled by its individual members. Credit union members are encouraged to save their money by purchasing shares in the credit union out of which funds loans are made to members. Credit unions are a worldwide phenomenon found in approximately 100 countries, comprising some 46,000 credit unions serving over 170 million members. As at September 2006, there were 557 registered credit unions in the United Kingdom, with a combined membership exceeding half a million individuals.[1] They operate under the provisions of the Credit Unions Act 1979, as amended by the Financial Services and Markets Act 2000, and are regulated and supervised by the Financial Services Authority.

Lending by credit unions is governed by the FSA Handbook. Lending powers are determined by whether the credit union is a so-called Version 1 credit union or a Version 2 credit union. A Version 1 credit union is one whose permission includes a requirement that it must not lend more than £15,000 or such lesser amount as may be specified, in excess of a member's shareholding. Member's shareholding means any shares held by a member in the credit union. A Version 2 credit union is any other credit union. A Version 1 credit union must, notwithstanding the above, not lend more than £7,500 in excess of the borrowing member's shareholding unless it has a capital to total assets ratio of at least 5%. A Version 1 credit union must not lend for a period of more than 5 years unsecured and 10 years secured. A Version 2 credit union may lend up to £15,000 in excess of the borrowing member's shareholding or 1.5% of total shares in the credit union in excess of the borrowing member's shareholding, whichever is the greater. A Version 2 credit union must not lend for a period of more than 10 years unsecured and 25 years secured. A credit union with permission to enter into a regulated mortgage contract must not enter into such a contract for a term of more than 25 years.[2]

A debtor-creditor agreement, where the creditor is a credit union and the rate of the total charge for credit does not exceed 26.9%, is an exempt agreement.[3] Rather incongruously, advertisements for such loans are not exempt from the Consumer Credit (Advertisements) Regulations 2004.

Special arrangements for providing financial support to students is contained in the Teaching and Higher Education Act 1998.[4] The scheme operates on the borderline between public and private law and student loans are statutory rather than contractual in character. The loans are made by the Student Loans Company acting as agent of the Secretary of State and, being statutory rather than contractual, CCA 1974 does not apply to them.

Certain housing associations, in partnership with banks or building societies, provide low cost credit to tenants. There are also schemes to provide loans to those who cannot get loans elsewhere.

1 See FSA Financial Returns Data on Credit Unions.
2 FSA Handbook CRED 10.3 Lending Limits.
3 Consumer Credit (Exempt Agreements) Order 1989, SI 1989/8694, art 4(1)(a).
4 See also Education (Student Loans) (Repayment) Regulations 2000, SI 2000/944, as amended.

20.3   ELIGIBILITY FOR CREDIT

Whilst there are no statutory preconditions to the grant of credit, practical considerations dictate that credit is not granted recklessly and regardless of the ability of the borrower to repay. However, this is not a sufficient guarantee of prudent lending practice, for which purpose one needs to turn to various codes of practice and to the general principles underlining the CCA 1974.

The Banking Code[1] requires its subscribers to assess the applicant borrower's ability to repay before lending any money. Factors to be taken into account include the applicant's income and financial commitments, how he has handled his finances in the past, information obtained from credit reference agencies, from other lenders, and from the applicant's employer and landlord, information supplied by the applicant, credit assessment techniques, such as credit scoring, and any security provided.

The Code of Practice of the Finance & Leasing Association requires its subscribers, as responsible lenders, to ensure that all lending is subject to sound and proper credit assessment and lists the criteria for this purpose.[2] The Code of Practice of the Consumer Credit Trade Association likewise stipulates that before granting credit, hire or lease facilities, members must evaluate the customer's ability to repay.[3]

The Office of Fair Trading is authorised to, and will take into account, imprudent and reckless lending policies in determining whether a lender is a fit person to engage in activities covered by a Standard Licence under CCA 1974 under its powers under s 25(2).

1 The Banking Code (March 2008), para 13.1.
2 FLA Lending Code 2006 para 1C.1 and s 5.
3 CCTA Code of Practice (2008), paras 4.2.1 to 4.2.3.

20.4   RESPONSIBLE LENDING

The issue of unfair relationships is the subject of a later chapter. In the present context it is appropriate to refer to the Guidelines for Lenders and Borrowers on Non-Status Lending published by the Office of Fair Trading.[1] These Guidelines apply to all lenders and brokers involved in mortgages or other secured loans to non-status borrowers. Non-status or sub-prime borrowers are individuals with impaired credit ratings or who might find it difficult to obtain finance on normal

terms and conditions from high street bankers, building societies and other traditional lending institutions. Such borrowers are variously described as non-status,
non-conforming or sub-prime borrowers. The Guidelines highlight the following
general principles which are to be applied by lenders:

(a)   there should be transparency in all dealings with potential and actual bor-
      rowers, with full and early disclosure and explanation of all contract terms
      and conditions and all fees and charges payable;

(b)   there should be no high-pressure selling and adequate time should be
      allowed for the borrower to reflect on the terms and conditions of the loan
      and to obtain independent advice before signing;

(c)   advertising and other promotional material should not mislead, and there
      should be no cold-calling or canvassing off-trade premises without the bor-
      rower's prior consent;

(d)   brokers should disclose at the outset their status with regard to the borrower
      and the lender, and the extent of the service offered to the borrower,
      together with any brokerage fee or commission payable by the borrower or
      the lender;

(e)   lenders should take all reasonable steps to ensure that brokers and other
      intermediaries regularly marketing their products do not engage in unfair
      business practices, or act unlawfully, and that they serve the best interests of
      the borrower;

(f)   contract terms and conditions should be fair, and should be written in plain
      English to ensure as far as possible that borrowers understand the nature of
      the loan agreement and their rights and responsibilities under it;

(g)   there should be responsible lending, with all underwriting decisions subject
      to the proper assessment of the borrower's ability to repay and taking full
      account of all relevant circumstances; and

(h)   any ancillary charges (for example, on default or early settlement) should
      be brought to the attention of the borrower before the agreement is entered
      into and should reflect as closely as possible the costs reasonably incurred
      by the lender and not already recovered at the time when the charges are
      made.

The Guidelines also contain directions relating to advertising and marketing,
transparency in the relationship between lender and borrower and between broker and borrower, and set parameters to selling methods. In short, they advocate
responsible lending. The Guidelines were referred to and applied in *Hurstanger
Ltd v Wilson.*[2]

   The corollary to the Guidelines is the fact that no creditor is compelled to lend
and, indeed, no individual has an inherent right to receive credit. In the realm of
finance, there is no equivalent to the old adage, give credit where credit is due.

   The reader is also referred to the chapter on the licensing regime at para 21.2
and Chapter 23 on Unfair Relationships.

1   November 1997 OFT 192.
2   [2007] GCCR 5951, CA.

20.5   CREDIT SCORING

One of the yardsticks used by lenders to determine a borrower's capacity to borrow is credit scoring. This evaluates information provided by the borrower and other information obtained by the creditor and allocates points for each item of relevant information. Creditors operate different types of credit scoring systems, very often of their own creation, and dependent upon the experience they have gained in their sector of business over a period of time.

The Guide to Credit Scoring Practice (1993)[1] agreed between different organisations, lays down principles applying to the implementation and operation of the Guide and principles of decision making. Credit grantors may not discriminate on the grounds of sex, race, religion or colour and are obliged to have regard to all relevant legislation including the following: CCA 1974, Sex Discrimination Act 1975, Race Relations Act 1976, Fair Trading Act 1973, Employment Protection Consolidation Act 1978 and the Data Protection Act 1998, each with its amendments and regulations made under it.

The Credit Scoring Guide expressly permits credit grantors to take factors other than the credit score into account when making a decision. These factors may include verification of identity, validation of application details, applicant's income and existing commitments, credit reference agency information, credit grantor's own prior experiences relevant to that application and any security offered. Significantly, the Guide permits credit grantors to refuse credit if they reasonably believe that servicing the account would place the safety of their property, agents or employees at risk.

There are other types of credit scoring techniques such as artificial intelligence or behavioural scoring. These are statistically derived assessments of the future credit risk of an existing customer based on the characteristics relating to his conduct of an existing account. Another technique takes the form of computer programs which incorporate a body of useful human knowledge in such a way that they can provide support in decision making.

Credit grantors will usually procure credit references from one of the principal credit reference agencies operating in the United Kingdom. The most important types of information held by such credit reference agencies are electoral roll information, public information about past debts and account information.

Various codes of practice, including that of the Finance & Leasing Association, require the creditor to notify the applicant in advance whether it will be using a credit scoring system and if the credit application is declined, to give the applicant an opportunity to have that decision reviewed.

The Data Protection Act 1998 lays down limits on automated credit processing. It confers the right on an individual at any time, by notice in writing to a data controller, to require the data controller to ensure that no decision taken by or on the data controller's behalf, which significantly affects the individual, is based solely on the processing by automatic means of personal data in respect of the individual's creditworthiness. Moreover, even where no such notice has been served, but the credit decision has been made on that basis, the data controller must, as soon as reasonably practicable, notify the individual that the decision was taken on that basis. The individual is then entitled, within 21 days of receiving such notice, to require the data controller to reconsider that decision or to take a new decision on a different basis, and if the data controller fails to take such action, the individual is entitled to compensation for damage or distress suffered as a result.[2]

1 Drawn up by the following organisations in the credit industry: British Bankers Association, Building Societies Association, Consumer Credit Association (UK), Consumer Credit Trade Association, Council of Mortgage Lenders, Credit Card Research Group, Finance and Leasing Association, Institute of Credit Management, Mail Order Traders Association and Retail Credit Group; together with storecard developers and credit reference agencies. The Guide is currently under review.
2 Data Protection Act 1998, ss 12 and 13.

20.6 ENTITLEMENT TO INFORMATION ON CREDIT STATUS

Debtors and hirers are entitled to require their creditors and owners respectively to notify them of any credit reference agency to which the creditor, owner or negotiator during antecedent negotiations, applied for information about their financial standing.[1] A credit reference agency must, within seven working days, respond to the enquirer's request by giving the consumer a copy of the file relating to him together with a statement in the prescribed form of the consumer's rights to require any incorrect information to be corrected.[2] Reference to 'file' means all the information kept by the credit reference agency, regardless of how the information is stored and 'copy of the file', in respect of information not in plain English (for example, in computer language) means a transcript reduced into plain English. Similar rights to those under CCA 1974 are conferred on an individual in respect of information held by a data controller, under the Data Protection Act 1998.[3]

An individual given information under either the Data Protection Act or CCA 1974 who considers that an entry in his file is incorrect, and that if not corrected it is likely to cause him prejudice, may give notice to the credit reference agency requiring it either to remove the entry from the file or to amend it. Within 28 days after receiving such notice, the credit reference agency must by notice inform the objector that it has removed the entry from the file, amended it or taken no action. The objector is given further rights dependent upon what action the agency takes.[4] The credit reference agency must also, within ten days after giving notice of having removed or corrected a file, notify the relevant particulars to every person to whom it has, in the six months preceding the individual's request, furnished information relevant to the financial status of the individual concerned.[5]

If a creditor or owner is not willing to enter into a regulated agreement, he must inform the credit-broker, or the applicant borrower or hirer directly, of such fact and of any agency from whom, during the negotiations relating to the proposed agreement, he applied for information about the financial standing of the applicant. The credit-broker must, on request, furnish a debtor or hirer with the details of any credit reference agency consulted by him.[6]

1　CCA 1974, s 157.
2　CCA 1974, ss 158 and 159.
3　Data Protection Act 1998, s 7.
4　CAA 1974, s 159.
5　Consumer Credit (Conduct of Business) (Credit References) Regulations 1977, SI 1977/330, as amended by the Consumer Credit (Conduct of Business) (Credit References) (Amendment) Regulations 2000, SI 2000/291.
6　Consumer Credit (Conduct of Business) (Credit References) Regulations 1977, SI 1977/330, as amended by the Consumer Credit (Conduct of Business) (Credit References) (Amendment) Regulations 2000, SI 2000/291.

20.7　QUOTATIONS AND PRE-CONTRACT INFORMATION

20.7.1　Quotations

The CCA 1974 envisaged that credit grantors and providers of hire facilities might provide customers with written quotations on request before entering into agreements. The Act makes provision for regulations governing the form and content of any document by which a person, who carries on a consumer credit business or consumer hire business, or a business in the course of which he provides credit to individuals secured on land, gives prospective customers information about the terms on which he is prepared to do business.[1]

The original regulations were the Consumer Credit (Quotations) Regulations 1989. Although businesses expended considerable sums in ensuring that they were in a position to provide quotations, potential borrowers and hirers rarely requested quotations with the result that this entire section of the Act effectively became a dead letter. The regulations were abolished with effect from March 1997.[2]

The Quotations Regulations were resurrected a year later, but solely in respect of land mortgages and in a very limited respect.[3] They prescribe the insertion of the wealth or risk warnings of credit advertisements also in quotations. Where a person who carries on a consumer credit business, a consumer hire business or business in the course of which he provides credit to individuals secured on land, provides a quotation to a prospective customer in connection with a prospective credit agreement or a prospective agreement for the hire of goods which would or might be secured on the customer's home, he must include in the quotation a statement that such security would or might be required, and the wealth or risk warning. In the case of a credit agreement: it reads: 'Your home is at risk if you do not keep up repayments on a mortgage or other loan secured on it'. In the case of a hire agreement it reads: 'Your home is at risk if you do not keep up payments on a hire agreement secured by a mortgage or other security on your home'. Similar provision is made for quotations provided by credit-brokers.

There was a perceived need to provide a different warning statement in relation to lifetime or equity release mortgages. These are credit agreements secured by a mortgage on the debtor's home under which no instalments of credit and no payment of interest are due or capable of becoming due while the debtor continues to occupy the mortgaged land as his main residence. The regulations also apply to a mortgage loan which may require interest payments but which does not require full or partial repayment of the secured sum while the debtor continues to occupy the mortgaged land as his main residence and which the creditor cannot repossess or sell during that period. In these cases the warning statement is the following: 'Check that this mortgage will meet your needs if you want to move or sell your home or if you want your family to inherit it. If you are in doubt, seek independent advice'.[4]

There is no obligation to provide a quotation although, where a quotation is provided, it is mandatory for the quotation to contain the various warning statements.

1 CCA 1974, s 52.
2 Consumer Credit (Quotations) (Revocation) Regulations 1997, SI 1997/211.
3 Consumer Credit (Content of Quotations) and Consumer Credit (Advertisements) (Amendment) Regulations 1999, SI 1999/2725.
4 Consumer Credit (Advertisements and Content of Quotations) (Amendment) Regulations 2000, SI 2000/1797.

20.7.2 Pre-contract information

The recent innovation of Pre-Contract Information has generally displaced quotations which, in any event, have largely been a dead-letter. Pre-Contract Information is required to be supplied in relation to all regulated consumer credit and consumer hire agreements not secured on land, either by reason of the Consumer Credit (Disclosure of Information) Regulations 2004[1] or the Financial Services (Distance Marketing) Regulations 2004 in relation to distance contracts.[2]

1 SI 2004/1481.
2 SI 2004/2095.

20.8 CONDUCTING BUSINESS OFF TRADE PREMISES

20.8.1 Canvassing

It is an offence to canvass debtor-creditor agreements (as opposed to d-c-s agreements) off trade premises. Canvassing involves soliciting the entry by the customer into a regulated agreement by making oral representations during a visit by the canvasser carried out for the purpose of making such representations.[1]

It is not canvassing if the visit takes place in response to a written signed request made by or on behalf of the person making it and the request was made on a previous occasion. There is also no canvassing if the place at which the oral representations are made are the premises where business is carried on by the creditor or owner, the supplier, the canvasser or the person whose employee or agent the canvasser is, or the consumer. The inclusion of the consumer's premises is significant as it is excluded from business premises for determining whether an agreement is cancellable.

Two interesting practical problems arise. First, it is necessary to establish whether the visit was in fact carried out for the purpose of making such oral representations or for some other purpose in the course of which the opportunity arose to canvass a debtor-creditor agreement. Second, what is meant by a 'previous occasion', in relation to the request for the visit? It is submitted that sufficient time and purpose must distinguish the two visits and that ideally, though not necessarily, the visits should be made on separate days.

1 CCA 1974, ss 48 and 49.

20.8.2   Proposals for contracts made in a consumer's home or place of work

Draft regulations, currently the subject of consultation, relate to the proposals set out below. Contracts between a consumer and a trader made:

(a)   during a visit by the trader to the consumer's home or place of work or to the home of another individual;

(b)   during an excursion organised by the trader away from his business premises; or

(c)   after an offer made by the consumer during such visit or excursion

are cancellable within a period of seven days from the date of receipt by the consumer of a notice of the right to cancel from the trader. If the draft regulations, namely the Cancellation of Contracts made in a Consumer's Home or Place of Work etc. are adopted, they will apply regardless of whether or not the trader's visit was solicited by the consumer except that they will not apply to a contract made during a solicited visit where the contract is secured on land.

20.9   CIRCULARS TO MINORS

Persons under 18 years of age do not have contractual capacity.[1] The capacity of a person to enter into a consumer hire or consumer credit agreement is governed by the ordinary rules of contract. A minor may enter into such an agreement but it will be unenforceable against him unless it relates to necessaries and the contract is beneficial to the minor. However, if the contract is ratified by the minor on attaining majority, it becomes an enforceable contract. Prior to that time the court has the power to order restitution by the minor of property acquired by him under the contract.[2]

It is an offence, for financial gain, to send to a minor any document inviting him to borrow money, to obtain goods on credit or hire, to obtain services on credit or to apply for information or advice on borrowing money or otherwise obtaining credit or hiring goods.[3] Rather strangely, it is not an offence to invite a minor orally to apply for credit. Nor do the Advertisements Regulations prescribe a statement that no credit is available to minors, except by inference where advertisements might fall into the hands of minors.

Codes of practice generally advocate that special care is taken in relation to applications for credit from young people (those aged between 18 and 21).

In practice finance companies insert in their promotional literature a statement to the effect that the credit or hire facility is not available to persons under 18 years of age. This alone would not suffice if traders in fact solicit business from minors or do not take sufficient care to avoid doing so. Credit advertisements and insertions in such magazines or periodicals read predominantly by minors would create a presumption that they were addressed to minors, or also to minors. Where a document is received by a minor at a school or educational establishment for minors, there is an assumption that it was sent to the minor.

By way of defence the person charged may prove that he did not know or had no reasonable cause to suspect that the recipient was a minor. Thus, in the case of *Alliance and Leicester Building Society v Babbs*[4] the Society sent circulars for loans to 750,000 account holders without seeking to distinguish between recipients above and below the age of 18. The circular did, however, state that loans were not available to applicants under the age of 18 years of age and the Society's computer program was also written so as to prevent loans being granted to persons under age. The court acquitted the Society on the grounds that the document, read as a whole, was not an invitation to persons under 18 years and that it was not the Society's intention to obtain financial gain from minors. The only logical inference to be drawn from the evidence was that when the brochures were sent out, indiscriminately though that may have been, it was not the Society's intention to obtain financial gain from any person who at the time of receipt of such brochure was a minor.

1 Family Law Reform Act 1969, s 1.
2 *Goode: Consumer Credit Law and Practice* (LexisNexis Butterworths), para IB[11.12].
3 CCA 1974, s 50.
4 [1999] GCCR 1657.

20.10 UNSOLICITED CREDIT-TOKENS

It is an offence to give a person a credit-token if it has not been preceded by a signed request.[1] This does not apply to small debtor-creditor-supplier agreements, to the issue of a credit-token under a credit-token agreement which has already been made or to the renewal or replacement of a credit-token previously issued under the agreement.

The definition of a credit-token is very wide, so that it is of no avail to a defendant to maintain that the production of a credit-token would not itself procure cash goods or services on credit if, for example, the presenter of the credit-token also has to complete an application form and to meet credit criteria.

It is worthwhile setting out the definition of a 'credit token'. It is as a card, cheque, voucher, coupon, stamp, form, booklet or other document or thing given to an individual by a person carrying on a consumer credit business who undertakes:

(a)   that on the production of it (whether or not some other action is also required) he will supply cash, goods and services (or any of them) on credit; or

(b)   that where, on the production of it to a third party (whether or not any other action is also required), the third party supplies cash, goods and services (or any of them) he will pay the third party for them (whether or not deducting any discount or commission), in return for payment to him by the individual.[2]

Thus, in *Elliott v Director General of Fair Trading*[3] the trader was convicted notwithstanding that the card was merely designed to entice customers to enter the shop and customers still had to meet various criteria before they became entitled to credit. The card was a credit-token even though it was not capable of contractually binding its issuer.

1   CCA 1974, s 51.
2   CCA 1974, s 14.
3   [1980] 1 WLR 977, [1999] GCCR 537.

20.11   OFFICIAL GUIDANCE

The OFT generally supervises business practices and standards and when it becomes aware of undesirable business practices issues guidelines to the industry at large. We shall briefly consider principal guidance issued by the OFT in the context of consumer credit.

Inertia selling or selling by way of negative option involves an offer to sell a product or facility, the acceptance of which takes the form of the customer refraining from stating that he does not wish to take up the same. The contractual provisions are drafted in the manner that the customer agrees to take up or is deemed to have taken up a certain product or facility, unless he indicates otherwise by, say, ticking a box. The practice was particularly prevalent in relation to payment protection or credit insurance and was condemned by the then Director General of Fair Trading, Sir Bryan Carsberg, in October 1992 in the following terms:

> 'It is an essential principle of fair trading that customers should have a free and informed choice as to whether they wish to buy insurance or not. I regard it as unacceptable if this freedom of choice is systematically diminished by requiring customers positively to opt out to avoid being charged for this insurance. I hope that those who sell credit insurance in this way will now move to end this practice. If they do not do so their licences may be at risk.'

In February 1997 the then Director General of Fair Trading, John Bridgeman, warned lenders and brokers involved in loans to customers with poor credit ratings, that they risked losing their credit licences if they misled borrowers or persuaded them to take loans beyond their ability to pay. This was followed by the issue of guidelines for lenders and brokers in the so-called non-status lending market in July 1997, and revised guidelines in November 1997, which still prevail. The 'Non-Status Lending: Guidelines for lenders and borrowers' apply to secured lending to borrowers with impaired or low credit ratings who would find it difficult generally to obtain finance from traditional sources on normal terms and conditions.[1] The Guidelines also implore lenders and brokers to consider extending them to their business activity generally. The Guidelines lay down the following broad principles:

(a) there should be transparency in all dealings with potential and actual borrowers, with full and early disclosure and explanation of all contract terms and conditions, fees and charges;

(b) there should be no high-pressure selling, and adequate time should be allowed for the borrower to reflect on the terms and conditions of the loan and to obtain independent advice before signing;

(c) advertising and other promotional material should not mislead, and there should be no cold-calling or canvassing off trade premises without the borrower's prior consent;

(d) the broker should disclose at the outset his status with regard to the borrower and the lender and the extent of the service offered, together with any brokerage fee or commission payable by the borrower or the lender;

(e) lenders should take all reasonable steps to ensure that brokers and other intermediaries regularly marketing their products do not engage in unfair business practices or act unlawfully and that they serve the best interests of the borrower;

(f) contract terms and conditions should be fair and written in plain English;

(g) there should be responsible lending, with underwriting decisions subject to a proper assessment of the borrower's ability to repay and taking full account of all relevant circumstances;

(h) any ancillary charges (for example, on default or early settlement) should be brought to the attention of the borrower before the agreement is entered into and should reflect as closely as possible costs reasonably incurred by the lender not already recovered at the time when the charges are made.

The Office of Fair Trading issues Guidance Notes, some pursuant to statutory obligation under the Consumer Credit Act 1974. They include Guidance on advertising at a rate expressed as an 'APR from ___%',[2] Guidance on Discounted APRs and PPI relating to advertisements which offer discounted APRs linked to payment protection insurance.[3] Guidance on s 75 under the title 'Consumer Credit Act 1974 Section 75 – Equal Liability',[4] 'Transactions by Authorised Second Users',[5] Guidance on regulations under CCA 1974 made in 2004, including the Early Settlement Regulations, the Agreements Regulations, the Advertisements Regulations and Guidance on aspects of the Consumer Credit Act 2006, including Unfair Relationships and Consumer Credit Licensing.

1 Non-status Lending: Guidelines for lenders and brokers (Revised November 1997) OFT 192.
2 Credit Advertising – 'from APRs' (February 2000).
3 Discounted APRs and PPI (February 2000).
4 Consumer Credit Act 1974, s 75 – Equal Liability.
5 Section 75 of CCA: Transactions by Authorised Second Users (February 2001).

20.12   CODES OF PRACTICE

The government's stated expectation is that all creditors should be covered by, and comply with, principles-based codes of practice.[1] However, with so much legislation, primary and subordinate and official guidance in place, this appears to be an ideal rather than a necessary aim. Nonetheless, many creditors and lessors do belong to trade associations which require their members to comply with their codes of practice.

Codes of practice of relevant trade associations lay down principles and guidelines for the marketing of credit and hire services. They include the Codes of Practice of the Finance & Leasing Association, the Consumer Credit Trade Association and the Consumer Credit Association of the United Kingdom.

The Finance and Leasing Association ('FLA') has an extensive code governing all consumer credit, hire or lease agreements and separate codes for business transactions and for business with Local Authorities and the National Health Service. Each code contains key commitments. The Business Code of Practice deals extensively with lease transactions where the FLA member enters into or manages any agreement for the provision to a customer of office equipment or vending machines, where the member has been introduced by the supplier of that equipment, either directly or through a broker or other intermediary, and where the value of the equipment supplied to the customer does not exceed £50,000. There are additional provisions relating to the hiring of photocopiers. The Code contains detailed provisions relating to the content of a hire agreement and contains a checklist for all lessees which must be supplied to customers with their lease agreement documentation.

In general, all codes advocate the use of plain English in communications with customers and the disclosure of relevant information to customers, with due notice being given to customers of any variations to contract terms. Members of the relevant associations are urged to act responsibly and prudently in marketing, both in relation to advertising and the granting of facilities. Members are urged to satisfy themselves as to the customers' ability to repay and to encourage customers in financial difficulties to inform them of their difficulties at the earliest opportunity. The various codes lay down minimum standards for credit brokers and the monitoring of the same. The codes contain provision for the protection of confidential customer information. They also set out procedures for airing customer complaints. Certain of the codes require that debt collection procedures conform to the highest ethical standards. In relation to guarantors, some require credit grantors to advise individuals proposing to give guarantees of their potential liability and the advisability of seeking independent legal advice before entering into the guarantees.

The Banking Code 2008 is a voluntary code adopted by banks and building societies in their relations with personal customers in the United Kingdom and sets minimum standards of good banking practice. The Business Banking Code 2008, does the same in respect of the relationship between subscribing banks and small businesses (with a turnover not in excess of £1 million p.a.). The Codes are revised every three years.

The Banking Code for personal customers was first published in 1992 and is reviewed every three years. Except for institutions involved solely in corporate banking and money market activities, most banks and building societies subscribe to the Banking Code. Among its provisions the Banking Code 2008 contains new provisions on treating customers fairly and lending responsibly (s 2), requires its subscribers to provide customers with important information about unsecured loans in a summary box in pre-sale material (s 3) and to proactively contact customers who may be heading towards financial difficulty (s 4).

The Code of Practice for Traders on Price Indications is the subject of an Approval Order made by the Secretary of State.[2] Section 20 of the Consumer Protection Act 1987 makes it a criminal offence for a person in the course of his business to give consumers a misleading price indication about goods, services, accommodation or facilities. The Code deals, amongst other matters, with price comparisons and recommended retail prices.

1 White Paper on the Consumer Credit Market in the 21st Century (CM 6040 December 2003 para 3.42).
2 Consumer Protection (Code of Practice for Traders on Price Indications) Approval Order 2005, SI 2005/2705.

20.13 DISTANCE SELLING AND DISTANCE MARKETING

20.13.1 Distance selling

The Consumer Protection (Distance Selling) Regulations 2000[1] apply to contracts relating to goods or services between a supplier and a consumer under an organised distance sales or service provision scheme whereby the supplier makes exclusive use of one or more means of distance communication. These include printed matter, letter, press advertising with order form, catalogue, telephone, radio, videophone, videotext, electronic mail, facsimile and 'teleshopping'. The regulations do not apply to contracts relating to the supply of financial services, including investment services, insurance and banking services.

Before entering into a distance contract, the consumer must be provided with prescribed information relating to the proposed contract including the identity of the supplier, the main characteristics of the goods or services, their price, delivery costs and arrangements for payment, delivery or performance. The consumer is also given a 'cooling off period' – the right to cancel the contract within a prescribed period – and must be notified of his cancellation rights. The cancellation period in the case of contracts for the supply of goods begins with the day on which the contract is concluded and ends on expiry of seven working days commencing the day following that on which the consumer receives the goods. Where the supplier has not given notice of cancellation rights at the outset but does so within three months of the consumer receiving the goods, the cancellation period ends seven working days beginning with the day after that on which the consumer receives the information. Where cancellation rights are not notified, the consumer may cancel the contract during the period of three months and seven working days following the day after which he received the goods. The cancellation period in the case of contracts for the supply of services is calculated similarly, with the substitution of the day on which the contract is concluded for the day of delivery of the goods.

If a consumer cancels a contract, he must be reimbursed with any sums paid by him or on his behalf, including by a creditor, and is entitled to the return of any security provided in relation to the contract. Any related credit agreement is similarly cancelled. A related credit agreement is one under which fixed-sum credit, which fully or partly covers the price under a cancelled contract, is granted by the supplier or by another person, under an arrangement between that person and the supplier. 'Fixed-sum credit' has the meaning it bears under the CCA 1974. The type of credit agreement envisaged by a 'related credit agreement' is equivalent to a debtor-creditor-supplier agreement in the regulated scenario.

Following cancellation of a related credit agreement, if the consumer repays the whole or a portion of the credit before the expiry of one month following the cancellation of the credit agreement or, in the case of credit repayable by instalments, before the date on which the first instalment is due, no interest is payable on the amount repaid. Where any security has been provided under a related credit agreement, the duty imposed on the consumer to repay credit and any interest is suspended until any property lodged by way of security is returned to him. The regulations require the consumer to take care of the goods, the subject of a cancelled contract, until their return to the supplier. However, the consumer can tender their return at his own premises but may then be required to pay the supplier's costs of recovering the goods.

In the absence of agreement to the contrary, a supplier of goods or services must perform the contract within 30 days. Where a supplier is unable to perform the contract with the period for performance, the obligations of a creditor under a related credit agreement apply as if the consumer had given a valid notice of cancellation.

A consumer may cancel a payment where fraudulent use has been made of a payment card in relation to a distance contract. The card issuer must then credit him with all sums debited in connection with such contract. 'Payment card' includes a credit card, charge card, debit card and store card.

The Distance Selling Regulations are prolix and not without difficulty. It is submitted that the regulations also apply to hire-purchase and credit-sale agreements.

1 SI 2000/2334.

20.13.2   Distance marketing

Whilst the Distance Selling Regulations apply to non-financial goods or services, the Financial Services (Distance Marketing) Regulations 2004[1] apply to distance contracts in respect of financial services.

Financial services means any service of a banking, credit, insurance, personal pension, investment or payment nature.

A distance contract is a contract concerning one or more financial services concluded between a supplier and a consumer under an organised distance sales or service-provision scheme run by the supplier or by an intermediary who, for the purposes of that contract, makes exclusive use of one or more means of distance communication up to and including the time at which the contract is concluded. 'Distance communication' is any means which, without the simultaneous physical presence of the supplier and the consumer, may be used for the marketing of the service between those parties.

The Regulations prescribe, inter alia, pre-contract information which must be provided by the supplier to the consumer in good time prior to the latter being bound by the contract. They also prescribe a cancellation period of 14 days, beginning with the day after the day on which the consumer receives the contract. In the case of life assurance or a personal pension, the cancellation period is 30 days.

The Regulations largely mirror the Distance Selling Regulations, including with regard to fraudulent use which may be made of a payment card in connection with a distance contract.

1 SI 2004/2095.

20.14   PLAIN ENGLISH

The Plain English Campaign was founded in 1979 as a non-profit making and independent institution for the promotion of documents in plain English. Documents achieving such standards are awarded the so-called Crystal Mark. To date it has been awarded for documents produced, inter alia, by finance and leasing organisations, banks, building societies and insurance companies.

The campaign for plain intelligible language received indirect statutory recognition by the Unfair Terms in Consumer Contracts Regulations 1994, subsequently replaced by the Unfair Terms in Consumer Contracts Regulations 1999.[1] The latter provides that a seller or supplier must ensure that any written term of a contract is expressed in plain, intelligible language. If there is doubt about the meaning of a written term, the interpretation which is most favourable to the consumer shall prevail. Provision is also made for the grant of injunctions against any person using or recommending use of an unfair term. The reader is referred to the earlier discussion on unfair contract terms.[2]

HM Treasury has set so-called 'CAT Standards' for mortgages and credit card agreements. 'CAT' is an acronym for fair Charges, easy Access and decent Terms but the essential features of such compliant products are much more detailed. They are voluntary standards which constitute a benchmark against which standard terms of mortgages and credit card products can be measured and are intended as a form of reassurance to customers. CAT standards do not convey a government assurance in respect of the terms to which they apply.

1 SI 1994/3159; SI 1999/2083.
2 See para 8.3.4.

20.15   OTHER STATUTORY CONTROLS

Various other statutes govern the marketing of credit and hire facilities, directly or indirectly, notably the Consumer Protection from Unfair Trading Regulations 2008, the Trade Descriptions Act 1968, the Prices Acts 1974 and 1975 and the

Consumer Protection Act 1987. They are wide-ranging and include controls on unfair commercial practices and aggressive commercial practices.[1]

1 See further Chapter 19.

20.16   THE COMMON LAW

From time to time the courts impose breaks on 'the unruly marketing horse'. In a recent case the finance company had 'personalised' its standard agreement forms by utilising a trading style similar to that of a well-known equipment supplier and, with its consent, creating the impression that the customer was dealing with the supplier and not the finance company. The court found that the finance company had adopted a deliberately misleading trading practice, without intending to defraud the customer, and granted the customer relief on the basis of estoppel.[1]

1 *Lease Management Services v Purnell Secretarial Services (Canon (South West)) Ltd* [1994] CCLR 127.

Chapter 21

The licensing regime

21.1 'CARRYING ON A BUSINESS' AND THE REQUIREMENT FOR A LICENCE

21.1.1 Requirement for a licence

Subject to various limited exceptions, a licence known as a 'standard licence', is required to carry on a consumer credit business, a consumer hire business or an ancillary credit business.[1] A business is only authorised to carry on the activities for which it is licensed and only in the name or names appearing in the licence. Contravention of these requirements give rise to the commission of criminal offences.[2]

Part III CCA 1974, comprising more than forty sections, covers the licensing of a consumer credit business, a consumer hire business. and an ancillary credit business. By an oversight the Consumer Credit Act 2006 did not amend the heading 'Licensing of Credit and Hire Business' to Part III of the Act to accommodate the inclusion of references to an ancillary business.[3]

In practice it is usually advisable for an applicant for a licence to apply for the licence in all categories other than the category of a credit reference agency, unless in fact it is also to conduct business as a credit reference agency. A licence is not required where the business relates exclusively to exempt agreements.

Credit brokerage is the effecting of introductions of individuals to other credit-brokers or to persons conducting consumer credit business or consumer hire business. Conduct which falls short of effecting such introductions does not require a licence. Thus, an intermediary who merely advertises credit facilities, makes applications for credit available in display boxes and assists prospective debtors to complete the forms, does not require to be licensed. A licence is required where the intermediary passes the names of prospective borrowers to a credit grantor or the provider of hiring services, provides financial advice in connection with loans and communicates directly with credit grantors or providers of hiring services.[4]

A regulated agreement made by a person acting in the course of a consumer credit business or a consumer hire business when the creditor or owner is unlicensed, is enforceable against the debtor or hirer only on an order made on an application by the creditor or owner to the Office of Fair Trading.[5] A regulated agreement made by a creditor or owner where the debtor or hirer was introduced by an unlicensed credit-broker is enforceable only on an application by the credit-broker, creditor or owner to the OFT.[6] The trader or his successor in title may apply to the OFT for an order that an agreement for the services of a person carrying on an ancillary credit business made when unlicensed is to be treated as if made when licensed.[7] Where there is a chain of credit-brokers, provided that the credit-broker who is the immediate introducing party of the agreement to the creditor or provider of hiring services is licensed, the agreement is enforceable. In all cases where a party which is required to be licensed conducts business without a licence it commits an offence and anyone knowingly assisting or participating in such an arrangement is guilty of conspiring to commit such offence.[8]

A person who only enters into non-commercial agreements does not need to be licensed as, by definition, the agreements are not made in the course of a business carried on by him.[9]

1 CCA 1974, s 21.
2 CCA 1974, ss 39(1), 24 and 39(2).
3 CCA 1974, s 21 as amended by CCA 2006, s 33(1).
4 CCA 1974, s 145(2) and see Chapter 12.
5 CCA 1974, s 40(1) and (2).
6 CCA 1974, s 149(1) and (2).
7 CCA 1974, s 148(1) and (2).
8 CCA 1974, s 39(1).
9 This follows from the definition of a non-commercial agreement in s 189(1) and from s 21.

21.1.2   Consumer credit business and consumer hire business

A consumer credit business is any business carried on by a person so far as it comprises or relates to:

(a)   the provision of credit by him; or

(b)   otherwise his being a creditor under regulated consumer credit agreements.[1]

A consumer hire business is any business carried on by a person so far as it comprises or relates to:

(a)   the bailment or (in Scotland) the hiring of goods by him; or

(b)   otherwise his being an owner under regulated consumer hire agreements.[2]

1 CCA 1974, s 189(1).
2 *Ibid.*

21.1.3   Ancillary credit business

Sections 147 to 155 address specific matters relating to the licensing of ancilliary credit businesses. An ancilliary credit business is any business so far as it comprises or relates to:

(a)   credit brokerage;

(b)   debt-adjusting;

(c)   debt-counselling;

(d)   debt-collecting;

(e)   debt administration;

(f)   the provision of credit information services; or

(g)   the operation of a credit reference agency.[1]

1   CCA 1973, s 145(1).

21.1.4   'Carrying on a business'

CCA 1974 does not provide any helpful definition of what is meant by 'carrying on a business'. The phrase is utilised in connection with the definition of a consumer credit business, a consumer hire business and a non-commercial agreement, each as defined in s 189. 'Business' is defined in the same section as including a profession or trade. Section 189(2) states that a person is not to be treated as carrying on a particular type of business merely because occasionally he enters into transactions belonging to a business of that type. According to Professor Goode, a person is not considered to enter into a transaction 'in the course of' a business unless he does so with some degree of regularity as an integral part of his business.[1] On the other hand it appears that a single transaction with a view to setting that person up in business might be construed as a transaction in the course of a business. Although not a decision on the same provision, in *GE Capital Bank Ltd v Rushton*[2] the court decided that a person is to be regarded as carrying on a trade or business even though, at the time when he purchased vehicles from a company, he had not taken any formal steps to set himself up as a motor dealer and at that stage had not even decided where to store them while they were awaiting disposal. However, as he had clearly decided to purchase them as a business venture with a view to selling them at a profit, purchasing the vehicles was no less a step in carrying on a business of purchasing motor vehicles for the purpose of offering or exposing them for sale than it would have been if he had already prepared a showroom or forecourt to receive them, thus rendering the purchaser a trade purchaser within the meaning of s 29(2) of the Hire-Purchase Act 1964. It is a question of fact in all the circumstances whether a person is carrying on a business.

In *Hare v Schurek*,[3] the Court of Appeal held that a motor trader, licensed under the Act as a credit-broker but not in the category of consumer credit and who had entered into a one-off loan agreement granting credit to his customer, did not need to be licensed to grant credit. Mann LJ, delivering the principal judgment of the court, dwelt upon the issue as to whether an occasional agreement amounted to a non-commercial agreement, defined in the Act as a consumer credit agreement or a consumer hire agreement not made by the creditor or owner in the course of a business carried on by him. However, the issue was more correctly identified by Lloyd J as one addressed by CCA 1974, s 189(2) to the effect that a person is not to be treated as carrying on a particular type of business merely because occasionally he enters into transactions belonging to a business of that type.

In *R v Marshall*[4] the appellant, a, double-glazing salesman, had offered financial arrangements to customers in the form of credit agreements when he was not licensed to do so. Evidence was led of six such transactions during a period of 16 months. It was submitted that these transactions fell within the meaning of CCA 1974, s 189(2), having been entered into merely occasionally and therefore not requiring a licence. On appeal against his conviction for carrying on an unlicensed credit brokerage business, the court of appeal held that the trial judge had misdirected the jury by stating that if the appellant had made at least two transactions it proved that they were a part of the client's business when in fact it was for the jury to decide what was meant by the word 'occasionally' in s 189(2). The court also rightly pointed out that there was no justification for distinguishing between transactions initiated by the seller and those initiated by the customer.

In *Conroy v Kenny*[5] the Court of Appeal, in considering the business of money lending, stated that to determine whether a person carried on a business as an unlicensed moneylender the first question was whether, at the date on which the particular loan was made, the business of that person was one of money lending. If so, the test was satisfied. If not, the judge should go on to consider whether that person advertised or announced himself or held himself out in any way as carrying on that business. It was not necessary to prove that a number of loans had been made over a period of time in order to establish that a money lending business was being carried on at the relevant date.

1 *Goode: Consumer Credit Law and Practice* (LexisNexis Butterworths), IC [23.141] and see the cases cited there.
2 [2005] GCCR 5541, CA.
3 [1999] GCCR 1669, CA.
4 [1999] GCCR 1345, CA.
5 [1999] 1 WLR 1340, CA.

21.2   CONSUMER CREDIT LICENCE

21.2.1   Application for a licence

A licence may take the form of either a standard licence or a group licence.[1] From 6 April 2008 most standard licences are issued on an indefinite basis, subject to an initial charge and periodic (five-yearly) maintenance charges. Group licences must be renewed every five years.

A standard licence is issued by the Office of Fair Trading to a person named in the licence on an application made by him and covers the activities described in the licence. A group licence is a licence issued by the OFT, on application or on the OFT's own motion, which during the period that the OFT thinks fit, covers such persons and activities as are described in the licence. Group licences are issued to organisations in respect of their members or participants and have been issued to cover, inter alia, all solicitors holding practising certificates in England,

Wales, Scotland and Northern Ireland, chartered accountants holding practising certificates in those jurisdictions, members of the Association of Certified Accountants, Citizens' Advice Bureaux, Advice Centres and Higher Education Institutions. As with standard licences, group licences only apply to the businesses referred to in them. The OFT has published guidance for standard licences and group licence-holders and applicants.[2]

The terms of a standard licence will specify whether, as will usually be the case, it is issued for an indefinite period or only for a limited period (of five years) and in the latter event, that period. A group licence has effect for a limited period only unless the OFT thinks that there is good reason why it should have effect indefinitely.[3] Charges for standard licences and group licences are payable before the end of each payment period.[4] The licensee may, for good reason, apply to extend the period for payment.[5] If the charge is not paid by the due date, or any extended date, the standard licence terminates.[6]

An application for a standard licence must state, in relation to each type of business covered by the application, whether the applicant is applying for the licence to cover the business with no limitation or to cover the business in so far as it falls within one or more description of business, as described in the application. This is a new requirement introduced by the Consumer Credit Act 2006.[7]

The types of business which may be covered by a licence are:

(a)   a consumer credit business;

(b)   a consumer hire business;

(c)   a business so far as it comprises or relates to credit brokerage;

(d)   a business so far as it comprises or relates to debt-adjusting;

(e)   a business so far as it comprises or relates to debt-counselling;

(f)   a business so far as it comprises or relates to debt-collecting;

(g)   a business so far as it comprises or relates to debt administration;

(h)   a business so far as it comprises or relates to the provision of credit information services;

(i)   a business so far as it comprises or relates to the operation of a credit reference agency.

Applications for standard licences and group licences are made to the OFT. An application for a standard licence currently takes a minimum of twenty-five working days. The applicant for a standard licence must show that he is a fit person to carry on the type of business as specified above.[8]

When granting a licence, the OFT must consider any circumstances appearing to it to be relevant. They include:

(a)   the applicant's skills, knowledge and experience in relation to the specified business;

(b)   the above in relation to other persons intended to participate in the licensed business;

(c)   practices and procedures the applicant proposes to implement in connection with the business;

(d)   evidence tending to show that the applicant or any of the applicant's employees, agents or associates or any controller or associate of the applicant, if a body corporate, has:

    (i)   committed any offence involving fraud, dishonesty or violence, has contravened any provision under CCA 1974 or Part 16 of the Financial Services and Markets Act 2000 relating to the consumer credit jurisdiction or any other enactment regulating the provision of credit to individuals or other transactions with individuals;

    (ii)   contravened any provision in force in any EEA State corresponding to any referred to above;

    (iii)   practised discrimination in connection with the carrying on of any business; or

    (iv)   engaged in business practices which are deceitful, oppressive or otherwise unfair or improper, whether unlawful or not.[9]

A licence only authorises the licensed person to trade in the name or names for which the licence is granted.[10] If the trader wishes to add any name or there is a change in any of the information supplied by him when applying for the licence, he must formally apply to vary the licence. A company, individual or partnership need only apply for one standard licence in respect of all outlets, all business activities covered by the CCA 1974 and all business names under which it operates.

A licence is not transferable or assignable and is generally not transmissible on death.[11]

1 CCA 1974, s 22.
2 'Do you need a credit licence? An introduction to consumer credit licences', OFT 147-08 (March 2008); 'Group Licensing Regime', OFT 990 (April 2008).
3 CCA 1974, s 22(1A) to (D), read with SI 2004/1167.
4 CCA 1974, s 28A.
5 CCA 1974, s 28B, read with SI 2004/1167.
6 Section 28C(4).
7 CCA 1974, s 24A.
8 CCA 1874, s 25.
9 CCA 1974, s 25(2A).
10 CCA 1974, s 24.
11 CCA 1974, s 22(2).

21.2.2   The fitness test

An applicant for a licence and a licensee must satisfy the Office of Fair Trading that:

(a)   he is a fit person to be involved in the relevant activities; and

(b)   the name under which he is licensed is not misleading or undesirable.

The OFT applies a risk-based approach to licensing and requires to be satisfied regarding the applicant's credit competence, integrity and compliance with the law.[1]

The fitness requirement continues for the duration of the licence and the OFT will keep the licensee's fitness under review (SI 2008/1277 which came into force on 26 May 2008).

The OFT is under a statutory duty to prepare and publish guidance on how it determines whether persons are fit to carry on the type of business applied for or the business as described in the licence, if different. The guidance is subject to revision from time to time.[2]

The following practices, according to subject matter, are considered unlawful, unfair or improper.[3]

(a) Actions prohibited under the Consumer Protection from Unfair Trading Regulations 2008

The Consumer Protection from Unfair Trading Regulations (in force from 2008) prohibit unfair commercial practices that distort consumers' decisions. They contain:

- a general duty on businesses dealing with consumers not to trade unfairly;

- prohibitions against misleading actions and omissions, and aggressive commercial practices;

- in Schedule 1 of the Regulations, 31 specific practices that are always considered to be unfair.

(b) Credit brokerage services and fees

- Failing to return fees in excess of £5 when a consumer does not take up a loan or enter into an agreement within six months of an introduction to a lender, for whatever reasons, contrary to s 155 of the Consumer Credit Act 1974.

- Inducing consumers to enter into agreements for mortgage arrangements where the licensee knew or ought to have known that the outcome of the loan application was uncertain.

- Setting terms covering when fees paid as commission become refundable which state that such fees are non-returnable and/or that the consumer would only be entitled to a refund of a proportion of the original fee, contrary to ss 155 and 173(1) of the Consumer Credit Act 1974.

(c) Consumer credit advertising

- Using false or misleading statements in order to induce consumers to enter into a contract, by way of misleading information relating to finance contrary to Regulation 5(2) of the Consumer Protection from Unfair Trading

Regulations 2008 or Regulations 3 or 4 of the Business Protection from Misleading Marketing Regulations 2008.

- Advertising in a way that contravenes paragraphs 5, 6 or 7 of Schedule I of the Consumer Protection from Unfair Trading Regulations 2008.

- Hiding important details about credit deals in the small print.

- Failing to include information required under the Consumer Credit (Advertisements) Regulations 2004 (such as the Typical APR and other required financial information).

(d)   Consumer credit agreements

- Requiring consumers to enter into credit agreements in a manner not meeting the requirements of proper execution as prescribed by s 61(1)(a) to (c) of the Consumer Credit Act 1974.

- Requiring consumers to sign credit agreements that are not easily legible and are difficult to understand.

- Failing to comply with the information provision requirements of the Consumer Credit Act 1974.

- Failing to include key information required under the Consumer Credit (Agreements) (Amendment) Regulations 2004.

- Using terms that are unfair contrary to the Unfair Terms in Consumer Contracts Regulations 1999.

(e)   Consumer goods and services

- Inducing consumers to enter into contracts for the purchase of goods by making false statements about the descrioption and availability of goods, contrary to the Sale of Goods Act 1968 and/or the Consumer Protection from Unfair Trading Regulations 2008.

- Inducing consumers to enter into contracts for the provision of services by knowingly, recklessly or negligently making false statements as to the nature of those services, contrary to the Consumer Protection from Unfair Trading Regulations 2008.

- Failing to carry out work as agreed or with reasonable care and skill.

- Failing to perform contractual obligations to consumers, and failing, when in breach of contract, to give a refund, to pay damages, or to provide the goods or services as agreed.

- Failing to give consumers any or any adequate redress when in breach of any other legal duty owed to them.

- Selling of unroadworthy vehicles, contrary to s 75(5) of the Road Traffic Act 1988.

(f)   Responsibilities under the Company Directors Disqualification Act 1986

Directly or indirectly taking part in the management of a company without leave of the court, contrary to s 1(1) of the Company Directors Disqualification Act 1986.

(g)   Business advertisements

Causing an advertisement to be published that did not make it clear that the goods were being sold in the course of a business, contrary to the Business Advertisements (Disclosure) Order 1977 and para 22 of Schedule 1 of the Consumer Protection from Unfair Trading Regulations 2008.

(h)   Handling money in the course of business administration

- Inappropriate or improper dealing with money held in trust for clients.

- Misappropriating business funds without having regard to the interests of creditors.

(i)   Companies Act 1985

- Failing to ensure that accounts are prepared and delivered for filing to the Registrar of Companies in accordance with ss 227, 241 and 242 of the Companies Act 1985.

- Failing to ensure that annual returns are delivered for filing with the Registrar of Companies in accordance with ss 363 and 365 of the Companies Act 1985.

- Failure to ensure that the accounting records of a company are sufficient to comply with s 221 of the Companies Act 1985.

(j)   Credit repair

- Encouraging consumers to lie to the courts so as to set county court judgments aside, in order to improve credit ratings and thus to obtain loans.

- Publishing advertisements promising to remove negative information from credit reference files even if they are accurate and timely.

- Failing to refund fees paid upfront, where services are not subsequently provided.

- Providing worthless 'money back' guarantees as follow-up literature to consumers in order to induce consumers to continue to proceed with credit repair services.

(k)   Non-status lending

- Inducing consumers to borrow on excessive or oppressive terms against the security of their homes without regard to their ability to repay the loan.

- Offers of inappropriate loans that fail to take into account the consumer's ability to repay, sometimes with catastrophic results.

- Marketing or targeting loans explicitly at consumers in debt.

- Failing (as a broker) to act in the best interests of the borrower; a preoccupation with the value of the security rather than the borrower's credit-worthiness ('equity lending').

- Imposing substantial brokerage or other advance fees separately, while failing to explain that such fees could be charged and deducted from the loan. (Note that charges do not form part of the credit amount by virtue of CCA 1974, s 9(4)).

- Imposing very high interest rates, and increasing interest rates when a loan is in arrears, sometimes in breach of s 93 of the Consumer Credit Act 1974.

- Illegally canvassing agreements in consumers' homes, when not licensed to do so.

- Providing misleading documentation that fails to give, or misrepresents, key information, including misquoting interest rates and APRs.

- Improperly tying-in insurance products that the consumer is unaware of/misled about.

- Falsifying information as to a borrower's income or other aspects of their financial status in order to secure the loan.

- Misrepresenting the form, nature, purpose or long-term implications of loan agreements.

- Using unacceptably high-pressure selling techniques or engaging in any other aggressive commercial practices contrary to reg 7 of the Consumer Protection from Unfair Trading Regulations 2008.

(l)   Irresponsible lending

Lending irresponsibly contrary to the provisions of s 25(2B) of the Consumer Credit Act 1974, by failing to take reasonable care in making loans or advancing lines of credit, including making only limited or no enquiries about consumers' income before offering loans, and failing to take full account of the interests of consumers in doing so.

1 Consumer Credit Licensing: General Guidance for licensees and applicants on fitness and requirements: OFT January 2008 (OFT 969).
2 CCA 1974, s 25A and the above Guidance.
3 Annex to the above Guidance.

21.3   OFFENCES BY THE LICENSEE

It is an offence to engage in any activity for which a licence is required, when unlicensed or unlicensed in respect of that activity.[1]

A licensee under a standard licence who carries on business under a name not specified in the licence commits an offence.[2] In practice, difficulties arise in relation to companies in the course of formation or in the course of changing their names which wish to apply for a standard licence in the company's proposed new name. The company may only apply to the OFT for the change of name of the licensee once the Certificate of Incorporation, or the Certificate of Incorporation on Change of Name, as the case may be, has been issued by the Registrar of Companies. An application to vary a licence should therefore be made to the OFT simultaneously with the relevant application to the Registrar of Companies in order to expedite the issue of the licence, or the varied licence, as appropriate.

Changes in the officers of the licensee, of the controller of the licensee, or of the members of a partnership must be notified to the OFT within 21 working days. Changes in the officers of a company which is a controller of a licensee must be notified to the licensee within 14 working days. Failure to so notify constitutes an offence.[3]

1 CCA 1974, s 39(1).
2 CCA 1974, s 39(2).
3 CCA 1974, s 36.

21.4 VARIATION OF LICENCES

21.4.1 Variation by request

On an application by the licensee, the OFT may by notice to the licensee vary the licence by removing a limitation, adding a description of business or removing a description of business.[1]

21.4.2 Compulsory variation

Where at a time during the currency of a licence the OFT is of the opinion that if a licence had expired, it would not have been minded to grant a renewal of the licence, it may by notice to the licensee add a description of business or, more likely, remove a description of business, vary the licence so that it covers the carrying on of that type of business only in so far as it falls within one or more description of business, or so that it no longer covers the carrying on of a type of business at all or in any other way. In the case of a group licence, it may vary the terms of the licence.[2]

The procedure in relation to compulsory variation is that the OFT issues the licensee with a notice of the proposed variation and invites the licensee to submit representations to the OFT in accordance with s 34 of the Act.[3]

1 CCA 1974, s 30.
2 CCA 1974, s 31(1).
3 CCA 1974, s 31(2).

21.5   SUSPENSION AND REVOCATION OF LICENCES

Where at any time during the currency of a licence the OFT is of the opinion that if the licence had expired it would have been minded not to renew it and therefore it should be revoked or suspended, it must, in the case of a standard licence, inform the licensee that it is minded to revoke the licence or suspend it until a specified date or indefinitely, stating its reasons and in the case of a group licence issue a general notice to the same effect. The OFT must invite the licensee to submit representations in accordance with s 34 of the Act.[1]

A licensee may apply to the OFT to end the suspension of a licence.[2]

1   CCA 1974, s 32.
2   CCA 1974, s 33.

21.6   POWER TO IMPOSE REQUIREMENTS

Important new provisions were inserted in CCA 1974 by CCA 2006 relating to the powers of the Office of Fair Trading to regulate the conduct of licensees.

Where the OFT is dissatisfied with any matter in connection with a business being carried on by a licensee or an associate or former associate of a licensee, or a proposal to carry on such business, or with any conduct of any of the above it may, by notice to the licensee, require him to do or not to do or to cease doing anything specified in the notice.[1] The OFT is given similar powers to impose requirements on supervisory bodies in relation to group licences.[2]

A person may not be required, under s 33A or 33B, to compensate or otherwise to make amends to another person.[3] This does not, however, preclude any person making a claim against a licensee for any matter addressed by the OFT under ss 33A and 33B.

Before making a determination to impose a requirement on a person under s 33A or 33B or to refuse an application in relation to a requirement, the OFT must give a notice to every relevant person informing him, with reasons, of its intention to make the determination and inviting him to submit representations.[4]

The OFT is statutorily bound to prepare and publish guidance in relation to how it exercises or proposes to exercise its powers under ss 33A to 33C and must issue revised guidance from time to time.[5]

The procedure for addressing a licensee's representations are dealt with in s 34 of the Act. A new s 34A, inserted by CCA 2006, empowers the OFT, as part of its determination, to authorise the licensee to carry on for a stated period, specified activities or activities of specified descriptions which, because of that determination, the licensee will no longer be licensed to carry on. This is a useful provision which addresses a hiatus which existed under the original Act. As part of its determination, the OFT may, inter alia, provide for persons other than the licensee to carry on activities under the authorisation, specify requirements which must be complied with, prevent a named person from being an employee and ensuring that access to premises is given to officers of the OFT to enable them to inspect documents or to observe the carrying on of activities.[6]

1 CCA 1974, s 33A.
2 CCA 1974, s 33B.
3 Section 33C(3).
4 Section 33D.
5 Section 33E and see Consumer Credit Licensing: General Guidance for licensees and applicants on fitness and requirements. OFT January 2008 (OFT 969).
6 Section 34A(5).

21.7 OBLIGATION TO PROVIDE INFORMATION

A licensee must, within 21 working days after a change takes place in any particulars entered in the Consumer Credit of Public Register, notify the OFT of such change, using the official OFT form.[1]

Where the OFT issues a general notice requiring information or documents, whether prior to or subsequent to the issue of a standard or group licence, the licensee must furnish the further information and documents required by that notice.[2]

The OFT may, by notice to the licensee under a standard licence or the original applicant for a group licence, require him to provide such information, or to produce such documents, as may be specified in the notice. The OFT may also require such information or production of documents from any other person if it has reason to suspect that such person has committed a relevant act or omission.[3]

The OFT may, by notice to a licensee, secure access to premises to observe the carrying on of a business or to inspect documents or obtain information. It may also exercise such right in relation to a person who it has reason to suspect has committed a relevant act or omission.[4]

1 CCA 1974, s 36.
2 CCA 1974, s 36A.
3 CCA 1974, s 36B.
4 CCA 1974, s 36C.

21.8 OFT'S POWER TO IMPOSE CIVIL PENALTIES

If the Office of Fair Trading is satisfied that a person has failed to comply with a requirement imposed on him in relation to his licence or to notify changes or provide information, it may impose a penalty of up to £50,000 in respect of each failure.[1] The person concerned must be given an opportunity to submit representations.[2]

The OFT is statutorily bound to issue a statement of policy on civil penalties, as revised from time to time.[3]

1 CCA 1974, s 39A.
2 CCA 1974, s 39B.
3 CCA 1974, s 39C and see Consumer Credit Licensing: Statement of policy on civil penalties. OFT January 2008 (OFT 971).

21.9   APPEALS PROCEDURE

A licensee or applicant for a licence who is aggrieved with a decision of the OFT has a right of appeal to the Consumer Credit Appeals Tribunal.[1] This is a new body created under CCA 2006 and which is part of the Tribunals Service, an agency of the Ministry of Justice. It replaces appeals to the Secretary of State for Trade and Industry. The Tribunal will fall under the aegis of the First Tier Tribunal under the Tribunals, Courts and Enforcement Act 2007. A party to an appeal to the Tribunal may, with leave, appeal on a point of law to the Court of Appeal or, in Scotland, to the Court of Session and, with leave from that court, to the House of Lords. The Rules governing licensing appeals are the Consumer Credit Appeals Tribunal Rules 2008.[2]

It was held in *Credit Default Register Ltd v Secretary of State for Trade and Industry*[3] that, provided relevant evidence had been adduced and the right tests had been applied, the decision of the Secretary of State should not be set aside on appeal to the court. The appellant had originally appealed to the Secretary of State under the CCA 1974 against the revocation of a debt-collecting licence. The evidence was that it had abused and breached the Insolvency Rules 1986 by making wholesale mailings of statutory demands for payments, using the threat of bankruptcy proceedings with no intention of carrying it out but in order to intimidate debtors and had, in various other ways, been guilty of improper behaviour in debt-collecting practices. The Secretary of State had acted upon and accepted the report commissioned by it, finding that the appellant had over a long period of time engaged in business practices appearing to be deceitful or oppressive or otherwise improper within the meaning of CCA 1974, s 25(2)(d).

1   CCA 1974, ss 40A and 41A.
2   SI 2008/668.
3   [1999] GCCR 1663.

21.10   CONSUMER CREDIT PUBLIC REGISTER[1]

A register of applications for, and holders of, consumer credit licences is held at the Consumer Credit Licensing Bureau of the Office of Fair Trading, Fleetbank House, 2–6 Salisbury Square, London EC47 8JX (020-7211-8608; email: enquiries@oft.gov.uk). The register covers all licences, past and present, and holds the names of everyone who has a licence or who has applied for a licence. The register is open to the public. The OFT will provide basic information on licence holders free of charge, including the commencement date of a licence, types of activities covered, authorised trading names and the main business address of the licence holder. This information can be provided over the telephone.

Other information which is available relates to requirements imposed on licensees by the OFT, licences which have been surrendered or otherwise expired, licences and applications which the OFT is formally considering revoking or refusing, licences which have been revoked and applications which have been refused by the OFT, including a summary of the reasons for such action and the outcome of any appeal and licences which have ended due to bankruptcy or the death of the licensee. The Public Register also contains information relating to orders in respect of credit agreements made by unlicensed traders, exemptions of licensees from parts of CCA 1974 and details of group licences.

The Licensing Bureau will provide copies of documents relating to a licence holder and certify them as authentic if required, against payment of a small fee.

Licence holders and applicants for licences are listed by both personal and business names on a computerised index.

1 CCA 1974, s 35.

21.11   LICENSING STATISTICS[1]

New standard licences

	Apr 05/ Mar 06	Apr 06 / Mar 07	Cumulative totals 1976 to 2007
Applications received	14,912	16,513	600,294
Licences issued	14,138	13,944	574,331

Existing licences: action instigated by licensees

	Apr 05 / Mar 06	Apr 06 / Mar 07
Renewal of licences:		
Applications received	8,999	9,087
Renewal licences issued	9,365	7,833
Licences allowed to lapse	36,418	19,324
Variations of the terms of licences:		
Applications received	3,953	4,007
Variations granted	3,649	3,491
Changes in particulars about licensees:		
Notifications received	11,878	10,484
Voluntary surrender of licences:		
Notices of surrender received	1,316	978

Complaints

The Consumer Credit Fitness Investigation and Enforcement Teams at the OFT received a total of 2,582 enquiries and complaints about licensed traders between April 2006 and March 2007.

Notices issued

Between April 2006 and March 2007 the OFT served 94 notices on applicants and licensees about their fitness to be granted, or to retain, a licence, made up as follows:

'Minded to revoke' an existing licence	28
'Minded to refuse' an application for a licence	58
'Minded to refuse renewal' of an existing licence	6
'Minded to refuse the application to vary' an existing licence	0
'Minded to grant the application, but in terms different from those applied for'	2

Licensing decisions and appeals

	2005/6	2006/7
Notices served on applicants and licensees regarding fitness:		
number served	155	94
not determined in earlier years	40	31
Total	195	125
Cases concluded as follows:		
favourable determination	50	23
adverse determination	75	54
application withdrawn	20	6
licence surrendered	9	10
application made of no effect	0	0
licence expired	4	2
licence of no effect	2	0
'Minded to' notice withdrawn	3	2
other outcomes	0	0
still under consideration at end of period	32	28
Total	195	125
Appeals to the Secretary of State:		
lodged	16	6
brought forward from earlier years	15	13
Total	31	19

Unlicensed trading

In the Financial Year 2006-7, the OFT granted five validation orders.

1 Extracted from Annex B to the Office of Fair Trading Report and Resource Accounts relating to the financial year 2006–2007, issued pursuant to the Enterprise Act 2002.

21.12 EVALUATION OF THE LICENSING SYSTEM

There is no doubt that the Consumer Credit Act 2006 has drastically improved and strengthened the licensing system which was introduced by the original Consumer Credit Act 1974. The weakness of the licensing system was highlighted in the White Paper 'Fair, Clear and Competitive: The Consumer Credit Market in the 21st Century' issued by the then Secretary of State for Trade and Industry in December 2003. This stated that the licensing system did not take into account inter alia a trader's ability to conduct its credit business in a fit manner by ensuring that staff were properly trained or that adequate systems had been put in place and that the problem was compounded by limitations on the OFT's powers to investigate ongoing activities of the licensee. If a trader behaved in a way, which although undesirable, did not breach a specific provision of the Act, the OFT was powerless to gain the information it needed to consider properly whether the licence should be revoked. A further weakness was the lack of flexibility in the imposition of intermediate measures to promote compliance. The OFT could only refuse, vary, suspend or revoke a licence, each of which might put the licensee out of business and was therefore only used in the most serious of cases. The only alternative to such draconian action was to take no action at all, beyond informal warnings, which meant in practice that the OFT did not have appropriate sanctions for a range of infractions.[1]

It appears that all the objectives of the White Paper in relation to licensing have been achieved and were incorporated in the Consumer Credit Act 2006. It remains to be seen how the OFT's powers are exercised in practice but it would not be surprising to find that the OFT models itself closely on the way the Financial Services Authority administers and enforces the Financial Services and Markets Act regime.

1 Paragraphs 3.5 to 3.7.

Chapter 22

Electronic communications

22.1 COMPLETING THE REGULATED AGREEMENT ONLINE

Whilst the Consumer Credit Act 1974, in its original form, preceded the advent of common electronic communications, amendments to the Act and the Regulations under the Act have brought it up to date with the electronic age. Thus, a regulated agreement might be in an electronic form and signed by an electronic signature.

Section 61(1)(c) of CCA 1974 requires the terms of the agreement to be readily legible. The Consumer Credit (Agreements) Regulations 1983 refer to the agreement being easily legible and, where applicable, of a colour which is readily distinguishable from the background medium upon which the information is displayed.[1] A similar requirement applies to the copy of the agreement.[2]

The agreement copies, whether of the unsecured agreement, or the agreement secured on land, must be sent by an appropriate method.[3] The expression 'appropriate method' means post or transmission in the form of an electronic communication if:[4]

(a) the person to whom it is transmitted agrees that it may be delivered to him by being transmitted to a particular electronic address in a particular electronic form,

(b) it is transmitted to that address in that form, and

(c) the form in which the document is transmitted is such that any information in the document which is addressed to the person to whom the document is transmitted is capable of being stored for future reference for an appropriate period in a way which allows the information to be reproduced without change.

Where a document is transmitted electronically, as above, unless the contrary is proved, it is treated (save in respect of the notice of cancellation, as to which see below) as having been delivered on the working day immediately following the day on which it is transmitted.[5]

Where an agreement is cancellable, a notice in the prescribed form indicating the right of the debtor or hirer to cancel the agreement and how and when that right is exercisable, must be included in every copy of the agreement and sent by an appropriate method, as described above, to the debtor within seven days following the making of an agreement.[6] Whether or not the notice of a cancellation is actually received by the creditor or owner, it is deemed to have been served on the creditor or owner in the case of a notice transmitted by electronic communication, at the time of the transmission. This equates to the time when a notice of cancellation sent by post is deemed to have been served, namely at the time of the posting.[7]

The signature of a regulated agreement may be effected by electronic signature, as impliedly recognised by reg 6(5) of the Agreements Regulations which provide that, where an agreement is intended to be concluded by the use of an electronic communication, there might be included in the signature box information about the process or means of providing, communicating or verifying the signature to be made by the debtor or hirer.[8]

1 SI 1983/1553, reg 6(2)(a).
2 SI 1983/1557, reg 2(1).
3 Sections 63(2) and (3); s 61(2(b).
4 Section 189(1) and s 176A(1).
5 Section 176A(2) and s 189(1).
6 Section 64(1)(b) and see also s 64(2).
7 Section 69(7).
8 SI 1983/1553, reg 6(5).

22.2 POST-CONTRACT INFORMATION

Statements, notice of sums in arrears, notice of default sums, notice of interest payable on judgment debts and notice of termination may all be given electronically if:

(a) the person to whom it is transmitted agrees that it may be delivered to him by being transmitted to a particular electronic address in a particular electronic form,

(b) it is transmitted to that address in that form, and

(c) the form in which the document is transmitted is such that any information in the document which is addressed to the person to whom the document is transmitted is capable of being stored for future reference for an appropriate period in a way which allows the information to be reproduced without change.[1]

By way of exception to the general position that a document may be sent in electronic form is any enforcement, default or termination notice, which must always be given to the debtor or hirer in paper form.[2]

1 Section 189(1): definitions of 'give', 'serve', 'appropriate method' and s 176A.
2 SI 1983/1561, reg 2(4A).

22.3   ELECTRONIC SIGNATURE

An electronic signature is associated with an electronic document. It is used to give the recipient of the document confirmation that the communication comes from the person who it purports to come from. It is also essential to ensure that the electronic signature has not been tampered with.

The procedure known as encryption is used to create a digital signature by the holder of a private key issued specifically for the individual. Encryption is a way of encoding information and turning (or locking) normal readable text into something which is unreadable (a coded series of numbers and/or letters) which can be unlocked by the holder of the relevant key (decoding device) which will then transfer it back into normal readable form.[1]

Electronic signatures give rise to various problems, not least the difficulty in proving that the individual named as the borrower or hirer has actually signed the agreement. The Electronic Communications Act 2000 describes how an electronic signature may be admitted in evidence and taken as a valid means of establishing the authenticity of documents. Section 7 provides that in any legal proceedings an electronic signature incorporated into, or logically associated with, a particular electronic communication or particular electronic data and the certification by any person of such signature, is admissible in evidence in relation to any question as to the authenticity of the communication or data or as to the integrity of the communication or data. The section sets out the meaning of an electronic signature and how the signature is to be certified.

The Act also contains provision for a register of approved providers of cryptography support services.

1   See generally Amanda C. Brook and Rafi Azim-Khan, *E-Business: The practical guide to the laws* (2nd edn, Spiramus Press, 2008).

22.4   ONLINE SERVICES

Various websites provide online services, including credit brokerage and comparisons of charges and other features of credit products. These sites are subject to the usual contract law provisions including in relation to data protection and privacy policy, advertising and marketing, offer and acceptance, distance contracts, rights of cancellation, payment by card, protection against fraudulent use of a payment card and electronic communications.

22.5   ONLINE ADVERTISING

The Advertisements Regulations require certain information to be shown 'together as a whole'.[1] The OFT interprets this to mean that the consumer should be able to see all of the information together on one screen or by scrolling down a single page; it does not suffice for the information to be shown on separate pages of a website.[2] Whilst this will generally be true, so that a banner advertisement, for example, which cannot contain all the prescribed information, will bc linked in its permissible content, it is possible to envisage advertisements which commence on one page and necessarily continue on a click-through page, e.g. information on page 1, continued with an electronic coupon on page 2 and without any impermissible interspersal in the text. Such an advertisement might well, in its context, show the required information 'together as a whole'.

1 The Consumer Credit (Advertisements) Regulations 2004, SI 2004/1484, reg 4(2).
2 Consumer Credit (Amendments) Regulations 2004: Frequently asked questions. OFT 746 (September 2005) paras 10.14 and 10.15.

Chapter 23

Unfair relationships

23.1   THE LAW

Sections 19 to 22 of the Consumer Credit Act 2006 introduced the new concept
and test of unfair relationships in respect of credit agreements with individuals
(including small partnerships) relating to credit in any amount (ss 140A to 140D
Consumer Credit 1974). The provisions mark a radical departure from the corresponding provisions on extortionate credit bargains which they replace and
which were generally considered to be ineffective, principally because of the
heavy burden of proof on the debtor. In order to establish that an agreement
amounted to an extortionate credit bargain the debtor had to prove that the transaction required him to make payments which were grossly exorbitant or that the
transaction otherwise grossly contravened ordinary principles of fair dealing.

The unfair relationships provisions empower a court to make an order in connection with a credit agreement if it determines that the relationship between the
creditor and the debtor arising out of the agreement (or the agreement taken with
any related agreement) is unfair to the debtor because of one or more of the following:

(a)   any of the terms of the agreement or of any related agreement;

(b)   the way in which the creditor has exercised or enforced any of his rights
       under the agreement or any related agreement;

(c)   any other thing done (or not done) by, or on behalf of, the creditor either
       before or after the making of the agreement or any related agreement.[1]

In deciding whether to make a determination a court must have regard to all matters it thinks relevant (including matters relating to the creditor and matters relating to the debtor). A court must, except to the extent that it is not appropriate to
do so, treat anything done (or not done) by, or on behalf of, or in relation to, an
associate or a former associate of the creditor as if done (or not done) by, or on
behalf of, or in relation to, the creditor. A court may make a determination in relation to a relationship notwithstanding that it may have ended.[2]

A court which finds that a credit agreement gives rise to unfair relationships
has extensive powers. They include requiring the creditor, or any associate or

former associate of the creditor, to repay in whole or in part any sum paid by the debtor or by a surety under or in relation to the agreement or to do or to refrain from doing anything in connection with the agreement or any related agreement. A court may reduce or discharge any sum payable by the debtor or a surety in respect of the agreement or any related agreement, set aside any duty imposed on the debtor or a surety and alter the terms of the agreement or any related agreement.[3]

For the purposes of these provisions, 'creditor' and 'debtor' include persons to whom their respective rights and duties under the agreement have passed by assignment or operation of law. Where two or more persons are the creditor or the debtor, the provisions apply to any one or more of those persons.[4]

A 'related agreement' is a credit agreement which is consolidated by a subsequent credit agreement, or a linked transaction in relation to the credit agreement or a security provided in relation to either such agreement.[5]

The unfair relationships provisions came into force on 6 April 2007.[6] The provisions are retrospective to an agreement whenever made, except for an agreement completed before 6 April 2007,[7] that is one under which no sum is payable or will still become payable.[8] The provisions reflect a swing of the pendulum in favour of the debtor to the detriment of the creditor. As will have been noted, 'unfair relationships' is very widely defined, the courts are given extensive powers in relation to agreements which are found to contravene the sections and a debtor or surety need merely allege that the relationship between the creditor and the debtor arising out of the agreement is unfair to the debtor, for the onus of proof to shift to the creditor to prove the contrary.[9]

1 Section 140A(1).
2 Section 140A(2), (3) and (4).
3 Section 140B.
4 Section 140C(2).
5 Section 140C(4).
6 SI 2007/123, art 3(2) read with Sch 2.
7 CCA 2006, s 69 read with Sch 3, para 14(2).
8 CCA 2006, s 69 read with Sch 3, para 1.
9 CCA 2006, s 140B(9).

23.2   A NOTE ON INTERPRETATION

A few observations might be made on the interpretation of the 'unfair relationships' provisions of s 140A(1).

The provisions relate to the relationship between the creditor and the debtor, something more enduring and permanent than the underlying cause of unfairness or even than any imbalance, in the rights and obligations arising under the contract, to the detriment of the consumer.[1] The status of unfair relationships is a deduction which a court is required to make on the basis of the existence of one or more of the factors set out in s 140A(1) but is not to be equated with those factors as otherwise the provisions would have omitted all mention of unfair relationships and merely referred to unfairness as between the creditor and the debtor.

Interestingly, the expression 'related agreement' is not defined, although 'an agreement related to a credit agreement' is described in s 140C(4). Definitions of 'associate' and 'linked transaction' can be found in s 189(1).

1 Compare the Unfair Terms in Consumer Contracts Regulations 1999, SI 1999/2083, reg 5(1).

23.3 CRITIQUE OF THE LAW

Some lawyers maintain that the provisions are so vaguely drafted that they are unlikely to comply with Article 1, Protocol 1, of the European Convention on Human Rights, which was incorporated into UK law by the Human Rights Act 1998 and that they violate the constitutional principle of legal certainty. An Opinion to this effect[1] was considered by the Joint Committee on Human Rights of the UK Parliament. It concluded that EU case law expressly acknowledges that some laws are required by their subject matter to be flexible, that there is suitable guidance available as to the meaning of 'unfair' in the case law and that, while citizens must be able to foresee the consequences of their conduct, if needs be with appropriate advice, creditors can and should be able to obtain sufficient advice about the meaning of 'unfairnes' by seeking the meaning of that term in other closely analogous contexts. Whilst specific guidance as to the meaning of 'unfair' in relation to the 'unfair relationships' provisions might be desirable, the Committee considered that the absence of such guidance in the Act did not render the unfair relationship provisions incompatible with Article 1, Protocol 1, of the European Convention on Human Rights.[2]

Let us briefly consider the three separate limbs to s 140A(1), set out in para 23.1 above.

The first test or limb of unfair relationships is whether the relationship arising out of the agreement is unfair to the debtor because of any of the terms of the agreement or of any related agreement. As the relationship is linked to the terms of the agreement, the courts are required to determine the fairness of the contractual relationship between creditor and debtor by reference to the agreement or any regulated agreement. This can be done by referring to other relevant legislation, such as the Unfair Contract Terms Act 1977, the Unfair Terms in Consumer Contracts Regulations 1999 and relevant case law.

In addition to the Common Law and its prohibition against penalties, courts might also resort to the law of equity. In the context of mortgages (admittedly a creature of equity) equity will give relief if the contractual terms are unfair, oppressive or unconscionable. For example, in *Multiservice Bookbinding Ltd v Marden*,[3] the court stated that the classic example of an unconscionable bargain is where advantage is taken of a young, inexperienced or ignorant person to introduce a term which no sensible, well advised person would have accepted.

In *Director General of Fair Trading v First National Bank plc*[4] the House of Lords had to consider the provision in the then Unfair Terms in Consumer Contracts Regulations 1994 that a contractual term which has not been individually negotiated is unfair if, contrary to the requirement of good faith, it causes a significant imbalance in the parties' rights and obligations to the detriment of the consumer. It opined that good faith in this context was not an artificial or technical concept, nor a concept unfamiliar to British lawyers. The law looked to good standards of commercial morality and practice.

The government's eleventh hour amendment to the Bill, by the introduction of s 25(2B) of CCA 1974 requiring licensees to lend responsibly, will provide further legislative support for this limb.

The unfair relationships provisions also apply to the terms of any related agreement.[5] A credit agreement may therefore give rise to unfair relationships because of any of the terms of the underlying agreement financed by the credit agreement. The connection between a supply agreement and a financing agreement is well recognised in hire-purchase, conditional sale, credit sale and connected loan or debtor-creditor-supplier agreements. Whilst the new provision marks a considerable shift in emphasis, as it encompasses all personal loan agreements, and of necessity puts financiers on their guard in relation to the terms of supply agreements financed by them, it is already in the reasonable expectation of creditors that their potential liability extends to the terms of transactions financed by their credit agreements. However, it should be noted in this regard that the unfair relationships provisions effectively impose on creditors liability equivalent to that under s 75 of CCA 1974 in circumstances where the statutory indemnity under that section may not be available to them.

The second test or limb of 'unfair relationships' is whether the relationship is unfair to the debtor because of the way in which the creditor has exercised or enforced any of his rights under the agreement or any related agreement. This means that the fairness of an agreement can be tested not merely by what is stated in the agreement on the date it is entered into, but also on how the agreement is operated and enforced in practice. This would include any variation of the agreement, its terms and debt collection procedures. For example, where an interest rate under a credit agreement starts at a fair and competitive rate but is varied frequently and to rates unconnected to generally prevailing interest rates, the agreement will be open to challenge under this section.

The House of Lords in *Wilson v First County Trust Ltd*[6] stated that inherent in Article 1 of the First Protocol of the European Convention on Human rights is the need to hold a fair balance between the public interest and the protection of the fundamental rights of creditors. The fairness of a system of law governing the contractual or proprietary rights of private persons is a matter of public concern and Parliament is charged with the primary responsibility for deciding whether the means chosen to deal with a social problem are both necessary and appropriate. The court added that the more severe the sanction, the more important it is that the law should be unambiguous.

Given that s 140B of CCA 1974 confers on the court a wide range of remedies, it appears likely that this limb will be considered to be not unduly wide or uncertain in its ambit, as the court will order a remedy which fits the particular circumstances. Moreover the section is restricted to the manner in which the creditor, and not any person under the related agreement, has exercised or enforced his rights.

The third test or limb of 'unfair relationships' is whether the relationship arising out of the agreement is unfair to the debtor because of any other thing done or not done by or on behalf of the creditor (or by any associate or former associate of the creditor) either before or after the making of the agreement or any related agreement. The act or omission in question need not be limited, or necessarily linked, to the credit agreement. Indeed, the inference must be that this test or limb extends to circumstances beyond the first two limbs.

It is submitted that this limb is so widely couched as to impose obligations upon creditors which are incapable of certainty or circumscription. Indeed, that is the very object of the provision. In the words of Lord Sainsbury in Grand Committee considering the Bill:[7]

> 'I believe it would assist noble Lords if I briefly explain the Government's position in relation to the test and the need to define unfair relationships.
>   The new test is general so that it can catch all unfair relationships. It does not exist in a vacuum - Parliament and Ministers have already specified in other legislation those terms and practices that are unfair when considered alone. The new test is broader and is directed at looking at the substance of the relationship between the debtor and the creditor. This consideration will depend on the circumstances of the particular case. The court can consider anything that is relevant in deciding that there is an unfair relationship. Therefore, we do not want to give undue emphasis to some things by spelling them out, as this could mean that in practice the range of issues that the court considers is limited. It is not possible to define an unfair relationship as being certain things, or combinations of specific types of conduct, without limiting it in some way. That would serve to reduce the effeciveness of the test and the ability of the court to tackle unfair relationships – whatever form they take'.

It is respectfully submitted that the breadth and vagueness of this provision and the fact that it gives no indication of the type of conduct which is relevant (even though s 140A(2) obliges the court only to have regard to matters it thinks relevant), or the time preceding or following the contract within which the act or omission must have occurred, results in imposing obligations on creditors which are uncertain and unquantifiable. Arguably, the third limb creates a fiduciary relationship between creditor and debtor, something which is beyond the scope of a credit agreement.

It is submitted that the third limb produces an unfair balance between the public interest and the protection of the fundamental rights of creditors and conflicts with the provisions of Article 1, Protocol 1, of the European Convention on Human Rights. It appears to fail the tests in *Wilson v First County Trust Ltd.*[8]

One might usefully contrast the third limb with the more specific test in the Unfair Commercial Practices Directive. Under the Directive a commercial practice is unfair if it is contrary to the requirements of professional diligence and it materially distorts or is likely to materially distort the economic behaviour with regard to the product, of the average consumer whom it reaches or to whom it is addressed or the average member of the group when a commercial practice is directed to a particular group of consumers.[9]

There are exceptional factors which ought to influence a court in adopting a restrictive approach to the interpretation of s 140A(1). The first is the fact that the provisions apply retrospectively to a credit agreement whenever made (CCA 2006, Sch 3, para 14)) as well as to an agreement or relationship which has ended (s 140A(4) of CCA 1974). The second is the fact that the 'unfair relationships' provisions can be invoked merely on application or assertion of the same by the debtor or surety. Thirdly, Parliament had the opportunity to set parameters to the law in the interest of fairness and certainty for both debtor and creditor when it is a principle of legal policy that law should be certain and predictable.[10]

1 By Michael Beloff QC and Andrew Hunter in their Opinion. See Hansard vol 674 No 47 p 1040.
2 Joint Committee on Human Rights First Report dated 24 October 2005.
3 [1978] 2 All ER 489.
4 [2001] GCCR 3075.
5 Section 140A(1).
6 [2003] GCCR 4931.
7 Hansard vol 675 No 56 GC 159.
8 See note 6 above.
9 Directive 2005/29/EC of 11 May 2005 concerning unfair business-to-consumer commercial practices, Art 5, para 2(b).
10 Bennion, *Statutory Interpretation* (4th edn, LexisNexis Butterworths), s 266 and *Halsbury's Laws of England* (LexisNexis Butterworths), vol 44(1) para 1434.

23.4 OFT GUIDANCE

The Office of Fair Trading is required to publish guidance indicating how it expects ss 140A to 140C of the Act to interact with Part 8 of the Enterprise Act 2002.[1] The Enterprise Act 2002 empowers the Office of Fair Trading and other enforcement bodies to enforce certain consumer credit legislation.

Pursuant to the above obligation, the Office of Fair Trading has issued draft Guidance on Unfair Relationships,[2] which is subject to amendment from time to time. Commenting on the third limb of unfair relationships (at para 23.1(c) above) the OFT Guidance states that this would include, for example, pre-contract business practices (such as advertising) and post-contract actions not based on a right (such as demanding sums of money the consumer has not agreed to pay). Relevant omissions might include failure to provide key information in a clear and timely manner (or at all), or to disclose material facts. It will also encompass acts or omissions which are non-commercial.

In order for the OFT to take action under the Enterprise Act 2002, the infringement must also harm the collective interests of consumers in the United Kingdom. Whilst the unfair relationships provisions apply to an individual relationship between a lender and a borrower, as the lender may enter into such relationships with more than one consumer it may, by virtue of acts or omissions, give rise to unfairness which has an adverse effect on a number of consumers.

The OFT identifies two broad headings of unfair practices, namely contract terms and business practices. Under contract terms it will take into account the Unfair Terms in Consumer Contracts Regulations 1999 and, where appropriate, the Unfair Contract Terms Act 1977. The former provides that a contractual term, if not individually negotiated, is unfair if contrary to the requirement of good faith it causes a significant imbalance in the parties' rights and obligations under the contract, to the detriment of the consumer. The OFT Guidance states that a number of court decisions and the OFT's own published regulatory guidance emphasise that the requirement of good faith embodies a general principle of fair and open dealing, with suppliers being expected, in drafting contracts, to respect consumers' legitimate interests. However, a term may be unfair under the Regulations without necessarily giving rise to an unfair relationship as, for example, where the term may be insufficiently central to the relationship between the parties so as to make the relationship as a whole unfair to the borrower. Equally, a term may not be unfair for the purposes of the Regulations but may still result in an unfair relationship. Thus, the Regulations preclude an assessment of fairness in relation to so-called 'core terms' but such terms may nevertheless give rise to a finding of an unfair relationship. Likewise, whilst the Regulations do not apply to terms which have been individually negotiated between the parties, the particular provisions may give rise to unfair relationships. The same considerations apply to the interest rate or APR under a credit agreement, which would normally be core terms.

Turning to business practices, the OFT Guidance distinguishes between practices which give rise to an unfair relationship and are in breach of the law and practices which are not necessarily in breach of the law. The former include breaches of the Unfair Commercial Practices Directive, as implemented into UK law in the form of the Consumer Protection from Unfair Trading Regulations 2007. The latter include irresponsible lending or business practices which contravene general guidance issued by the OFT e.g. in relation to non-status lending, debt collection and debt management.

The OFT would also consider issues of fairness in other contexts, such as whether there has been a breach of the rules or principles of the Financial Services Authority, for example in relation to linked insurance products such as payment protection insurance sold with a loan and generally whether there has been compliance with the FSA's principles relating to Treating Customers Fairly. The OFT would also take account of compliance with industry codes of practice, especially in relation to fairness and responsible lending, and with findings by the Financial Ombudsman Service.

Apart from the Office of Fair Trading, the other enforcers in relation to Part 8 of the Enterprise Act 2002 are general enforcers such as Local Authority Trading Standards Services, designated enforcers such as the Financial Services Authority and Community Enforcers, namely a designated entity in another EEA state.

1 CCA 1974, s 140D.
2 OFT 854 dated December 2006, revised April 2008.

23.5   TREATING CUSTOMERS FAIRLY ('TCF')

In the context of unfair relationships it is relevant to point out that the Financial Services Authority has spearheaded a drive identifying the criteria to be applied in ascertaining whether customers are treated fairly. In this regard the FSA published, in July 2006, a document entitled 'Treating Customers Fairly – towards fair outcomes for consumers' in which it identified six Outcomes which have become known as principles characterising 'Treating Customers Fairly'. They are the following:

1.   Consumers can be confident that they are dealing with firms where the fair treatment of customers is central to the corporate culture.

2. Products and services marketed and sold in the retail market are designed to meet the needs of identified consumer groups and are targeted accordingly.

3. Consumers are provided with clear information and are kept appropriately informed, during and after the point of sale.

4. Where consumers receive advice, the advice is suitable and takes account of their circumstances.

5. Consumers are provided with products that perform as firms have led them to expect, and associated service is of an acceptable standard and as they have been led to expect.

6. Consumers do not face unreasonable post-sale barriers imposed by firms to change product, switch provider, submit a claim or make a complaint.

Subsequent to the above, the FSA produced further documents on the theme of treating customers fairly, namely 'Responsibilities of Providers and Distributors for the Fair Treatment of Customers'; 'Treating Cusomers Fairly – Culture'; 'Treating Customers Fairly – Guide to Management Information' and 'Treating Customers Fairly (TCF) in Product Design'.[1]

In November 2007 the FSA published 'Treating Customers Fairly: measuring outcomes'[2] in which it reported that overall there was limited evidence that firms' work on TCF was translating into improved outcomes. The FSA stated that it was committed to working with firms and others to improve its ability to measure and evaluate the extent to which firms were delivering the TCF Outcomes.

1 July 2007.
2 November 2007.

Chapter 24

Enforcement and dispute resolution

24.1 ENFORCEMENT

As a general rule a creditor or owner is not entitled to enforce a term of a regulated agreement without giving the debtor or hirer the prescribed notice, namely not less than seven days' written[1] notice in paper form.[2]

Enforcement of an agreement means demanding earlier payment of any sum or recovering possession of any goods or land or treating any right conferred on the debtor or hirer by the agreement as terminated, restricted or deferred.

By way of exception, there is no need to give such prior written notice of enforcement when the agreement is not for a specified duration, as in the case of a running-account credit agreement.[3] A creditor may treat a debtor's right to draw on any credit as restricted or deferred and take steps to enforce such restriction or deferment without giving the debtor prior notice of any kind.[4] Thus, in a running-account credit card agreement the creditor is entitled to put a stop on the further use of the account or the further use of a credit-token without prior notice to the debtor.

Owing to the creditor's general obligation of treating customers fairly, it is always advisable to give a reasonable period of notice, which may be a longer period of notice than that prescribed by legislation.

1 CCA 1974, s 76 and Consumer Credit (Enforcement, Default and Termination Notices) Regulations 1983, SI 1983/1561 (as amended).
2 *Ibid.*, reg 2(4A).
3 CCA 1974, s 76(2).
4 CCA 1974, s 87(2).

24.2 DEFAULT

A creditor or owner may not proceed against a debtor or hirer, where the debtor or hirer is in default under the agreement, without first serving a notice of default in the prescribed form.[1] The notice must be in paper form, give the debtor or hirer at least 14 days to remedy any breach capable of remedy and be accompanied by the current OFT default information sheet.[2] Such notice is required before the creditor or owner is entitled to terminate the agreement, to demand earlier payment of any sum, to recover possession of any goods or land, to treat any right conferred on the debtor or hirer by the agreement as terminated, restricted or deferred or to enforce any security. Where a creditor or owner seeks to recover goods under a regulated hire-purchase, conditional sale or hire agreement, he must prove that the hirer's or buyer's possession would be adverse to his rights. This necessitates a demand for delivery of the goods in the default article.[3]

As in the case of enforcement proceedings, a notice is not required for the creditor to treat a debtor's right to draw upon any credit as restricted or deferred and to take such steps as may be necessary to make the restriction or deferment effective.

When a default notice overstated the amount due it has been held to be ineffective.[4]

In the case of a material or repudiatory breach (or one which is of the essence) of an unregulated agreement entitling the creditor to terminate the agreement, the creditor can recover, as damages (and the agreement will usually so stipulate), the unpaid balance of the total price, less the value of any repossessed goods and a discount in respect of the creditor's receipt of accelerated payment.[5] Any agreement may, by its terms, provide that a particular breach is of the essence.[6]

A creditor or owner may not harass his debtor or send letters which causes the debtor anxiety or stress.[7]

1 CCA 1974, s 87 and see the regulations referred to at para 24.1.
2 *Ibid.*, ss 88(2), 88(4A) and reg 2(4A). See also Chapter 10 above.
3 CCA 1974, s 134(1).
4 *Woodchester Lease Management Services Ltd v Swain & Co* [1998] All ER (D) 339, [1999] ECCR 2255, CA.
5 *Yeoman Credit Ltd v Waragowski* [1961] 3 All ER 145; see further *Financings Ltd v Baldock* [1963] 1 All ER 443.
6 *Lombard North Central plc v Butterworth* [1987] 1 All ER 267, CA.
7 Administration of Justice Act 1970, s 40 and Malicious Communications Act 1988.

24.3   TERMINATION OF AGREEMENT IN NON-DEFAULT CASES

A creditor or owner who wishes to terminate a regulated agreement which contains a contractual right of termination and where the customer is not in default, must give the debtor or hirer written notice of termination in the prescribed form.[1] This applies when the agreement is for a specified period and that period has not ended when the notice is given.[2]

The above requirements do not prevent the creditor from treating the debtor's right to draw on any credit as restricted or deferred and taking steps to enforce the same.[3]

1 CCA 1974, s 98(1) and see the regulations referred to at para 24.1.
2 CCA 1974, s 98(2)(a) and (b).
3 CCA 1974, s 98(4).

24.4   NOTICE ON SURETIES

Where a default or termination notice is served on a debtor or hirer, a copy of the notice, in paper form, must also be served by the creditor or owner on any surety.[1]

Failure to serve such notice will result in the security being enforceable against the surety on an order of the court only.

1 CCA 1974, s 111.

24.5   RECOVERY OF POSSESSION OF GOODS OR LAND

A creditor or owner is not entitled to enter into any premises to take possession of goods which are the subject of a regulated hire-purchase agreement, a regulated conditional sale agreement or a regulated consumer hire agreement except on an order of the court.[1]

A creditor is not entitled to recover possession of land from a debtor under a regulated conditional sale agreement relating to land except on an order of the court.

An entry in contravention of the foregoing is actionable as a breach of statutory duty giving rise to a claim in damages.[2]

Where goods have been lawfully repossessed following the termination of an agreement and the hirer or debtor pays the arrears the court may, as a matter of equity, grant relief.[3]

1 CCA 1974, s 92(1).
2 CCA 1974, s 92(2).
3 *Goker v NWS Bank plc* [1990] CCLR 34.

24.6   RETAKING PROTECTED GOODS

Where the debtor is in breach of a regulated hire-purchase or a regulated conditional sale agreement relating to goods and has paid to the creditor one-third or more of the total price of the goods, and the property in the goods remains in the creditor, the creditor is not entitled to recover possession of the goods from the debtor except on an order of the court. If the creditor does recover the goods without a court order, the regulated agreement is deemed to be terminated and the debtor released from all liability under the agreement. In addition the debtor is entitled to recover from the creditor all sums paid by him under the agreement.[1] If, however, the hirer consents to recovery at the time when repossession is sought, the creditor may take the goods without an order of the court. It will be necessary for the creditor to show that the hirer's consent was informed and voluntary.[2]

In *Transag Haulage Ltd v Leyland DAF Finance plc and Lease Plan UK Ltd*,[3] the facts were that the owner terminated the agreements, as it was entitled to do, upon the appointment of an administrative receiver to the hirer under hire-purchase agreements; the administrative receiver wished to carry on the business as a going concern and sought relief in order to retain the fleet of 12 vehicles under the hire-purchase agreements to enable it to fulfil contracts for the transportation of goods. The court (in the Chancery Division) held that although it had no jurisdiction to grant relief from forfeiture of merely contractual rights, it had equitable jurisdiction to grant relief from forfeiture of proprietary rights, namely the hirer's contingent right to purchase the vehicles under the hire-purchase agreements and would grant such relief where the hirer had been guilty of no default in payment, no financial loss would be caused to the creditor and to refuse relief would result in a substantial windfall profit for the creditor and a disproportionate loss for the hirer. There appears to be no reason why such equitable relief should not be similarly available in the case of regulated agreements.

The notion of relief from forfeiture was extended by the House of Lords to apply also to monies held in an escrow account, pending resolution of claims to it, in *On Demand Information plc (in administrative receivership) v Michael Gerson (Finance Credit) plc*.[4] A court had previously acceded to an application for an interim order for the sale of the equipment pursuant to RSC Order 29, r 4. In reversing the decision of the Court of Appeal and allowing the appeal, Millet LJ stated that, given the purpose of the rule, it was clear that the conversion of the property into money effected by the sale of the equipment was not intended to prejudice the parties' rights. The whole purpose of the sale was to preserve the value of their rights and particularly the rights of the ultimate successful party.

If a claimant believes it is entitled to relief from forfeiture, it should act expeditiously and where necessary, as in the above case, obtain an order of the court for the sale of the goods and payment of the proceeds into an escrow account pending resolution of the conflicting claims to the monies.

1   CCA 1974, ss 90 and 91.
2   CCA 1974, s 173(3) and see *Chartered Trust plc v Pitcher* [1988] RTR 72, [1987] LS Gaz 1147.
3   [1999] GCCR 1819.
4   [2002] All ER (D) 116 (April), [2003] GCCR 4651, HL.

24.7   CONSEQUENCES OF FAILURE TO COMPLY WITH THE NOTICE PROVISIONS

Where a creditor or owner takes action without complying with the requisite notice provisions, including failing to give the debtor or hirer the prescribed period of time for remedying any remediable breach, the debtor or hirer may be entitled to one or more of the following: to recover damages; to recover possession of goods or land removed from him; to a prohibitory injunction to restrain the creditor or owner from taking action or a mandatory injunction to restore the position to what it was before the creditor or owner took action.

It is always open to a creditor or owner to remedy any failure to serve an enforcement or default notice by subsequently serving the same. This may, however, require him to recommence legal proceedings where they have already been instituted.

24.8   WHERE FORMAL NOTICE IS NOT REQUIRED

Where the creditor or owner is entitled to rescind the agreement on the grounds, for example, of the debtor's or hirer's misrepresentation (whether fraudulent, negligent or innocent) he is not obliged to serve a default notice before rescinding the agreement. A default notice is also not required where the creditor or owner wishes to sue for accrued arrears (although an arrears notice will be required) or for damages, unless he also proceeds against the surety.

Creditors and owners will generally operate debt collection procedures. Letters issued prior to formal default or enforcement notices which are not, and do not purport to be, a notice of arrears, notice of default sums, notice of default or an enforcement notice are permissible and do not need not comply with any formalities.

24.9 LAND MORTGAGES

A land mortgage securing a regulated agreement is enforceable on an order of the court only.[1]

1 CCA 1974, s 126.

24.10 JUDICIAL CONTROL

Court proceedings in relation to regulated agreements must be brought in the County Court. Any action instituted in a High Court will be transferred to the County Court.[1]

1 CCA 1974, s 141; *Sovereign Leasing plc v Ali*; *Sovereign Leasing plc v Martindale* [1992] CCLR 1.

24.11 ENFORCEMENT ORDERS IN CASE OF INFRINGEMENT

The court's discretion in cases of infringement of the CCA 1974's provisions is governed by s 127. This provides that in the case of an application for an enforcement order relating to improperly executed agreements, improperly executed security instruments, failure to serve a copy of a notice on a surety or the taking of negotiable instruments in contravention of s 122 (which prohibits a creditor or owner taking a negotiable instrument, other than a bank note or cheque in discharge of any sum payable under a regulated agreement) the court must dismiss the application if it considers it just to do so. In deciding whether it is just to do so the court must have regard, inter alia, to the prejudice caused to any person by the contravention in question and the degree of culpability for it.[1]

In making an enforcement order the court may reduce or discharge any sum payable by the debtor or hirer or any surety, to compensate him for any prejudice suffered.[2] Thus, in *National Guardian Mortgage Corporation v Wilkes*[3] where the creditor failed to serve an advance copy of the secured loan agreement, the court held that as the borrower might have borrowed at a lower rate were she to have had the benefit of the consideration period, the borrower should be awarded credit equivalent to 40% of the interest claimed.

1 CCA 1974, s 127(1).
2 CCA 1974, s 127(2).
3 [1993] CCLR 1.

24.12 TIME ORDERS

A debtor or hirer may apply for a time order after he has received a notice of sums in arrears.[1] Application for a time order may only be made if he has given notice of his intention to apply for a time order to the creditor or owner and a period of at least 14 days has elapsed after the day on which such notice was given.[2] The notice must set out details of the proposal by the debtor or hirer.[3]

Where a creditor or owner applies to the court for an enforcement order or an order to enforce any security or to recover possession of any goods or land to which a regulated agreement relates or on an application by a debtor or hirer following service of a default, enforcement or termination notice, the court may, in its discretion, make a time order.

A time order relates either to payments or to the remedying of a breach. A time order relating to payments may be made by the court, in its discretion, under which the debtor, hirer or surety is ordered to make payment of the sum owed under a regulated agreement or a security, by such instalments and at such times, as the court deems reasonable. A time order in relation to the remedying of a breach is an order on the debtor or hirer to remedy a breach, other than non-payment of money, within such period as the court may specify.

In making time orders courts might reduce both the rate of interest and the amount of monthly instalments. A court is unlikely to make a time order where there has been a history of default, where the instalments which the debtor can afford will not meet the accruing interest and where there is no realistic prospect of the debtor's financial position improving. In considering making a time order the court must have regard to both the creditor's and the debtor's position.[4]

A concomitant of the court's power to make time orders is the court's power to vary agreements and securities under CCA 1974, s 136. This enables a court, in an order made by it, to include such provision as it considers just for amending any agreement or security in consequence of a term of the order. The issue of time orders and the court's power to vary under s 136, was considered in the context of default interest at the contract interest rate (rather than the judgment rate) in the case of *Director General of Fair Trading v First National Bank plc*.[5]

In *Southern and District Finance plc v Barnes*; *J & J Securities v Ewart and Equity Home Loans Ltd v Lewis*[6] the Court of Appeal laid down three principles relating to time orders. First, a time order relates to a sum owed under a regulated agreement or a security and means any sum which the lender is entitled to recover by action, in other words, a sum which is due and payable. If the full loan has not been called in, the only sum owed is the outstanding arrears. Second, the power to vary agreements in s 136 can only be exercised in consequence of the term of a time order and where the making of the variation is just. Third, where application is made for a time order or a possession order of property mortgaged as security for a regulated agreement, the court must first consider whether it is just to make a time order by taking into account all the circumstances and the position of the creditor as well as the debtor. The Court of Appeal upheld the judgment of the court of first instance which had rescheduled the instalments due under the agreement over a fresh period of 15 years and reduced the rate of interest to nil. In so doing, the court exercised its power under s 136 to amend the agreement in consequence of a term of a time order under s 129.

A time order may provide for the rescheduling of future instalments which have not yet fallen due, grant time for the payment of arrears or vary the rate of interest.[7]

1 CCA 1974, s 129(1)(ba).
2 CCA 1974, s 129A(1).
3 CCA 1974, s 129A(2).
4 *First National Bank plc v Syed* [1991] 2 All ER 250, [1999] GCCR 1533, CA.
5 [2000] GCCR 2601, CA.
6 [1999] GCCR 1935, CA.
7 *Cedar Holdings Ltd v Thompson* [1993] CCLR 7. See the contrary decision in *Ashbroom Facilities v Bodley* [1992] CCLR 31 which was not followed.

24.13   FINANCIAL RELIEF FOR A HIRER

Where the owner under a regulated consumer hire agreement recovers posses-sion of goods, the subject of the agreement, otherwise than by action, the hirer may apply to the court for relief. Relief includes the repayment of the whole or part of any sum paid by the hirer to the owner in respect of the goods and termi-nation of the obligation to continue to make rental payments.[1]

1 CCA 1974, s 132.

24.14   CLAIMS FOR DELIVERY OF GOODS UNDER A HIRE-PURCHASE OR CONDITIONAL SALE AGREEMENT

Where a claimant claims the delivery of goods let under a hire purchase agree-ment or sold under a conditional sale agreement, it must set out specified partic-ulars in a prescribed order, including whether notice under s 76(1) or s 98(1) of the CCA 1974 has been served and the date that it was served.[1]

Where, in relation to a regulated hire-purchase or conditional sale agreement, it appears to the court just to do so, the court may make a 'return order', namely an order for return to the creditor of goods to which the agreement relates or a 'transfer order' for the transfer to the debtor of the creditor's title to the goods.[2]

None of the foregoing provisions derogates from the provisions of the Torts (Interference with Goods) Act 1977 and indeed s 3(8) of that Act specifically states that it is without prejudice to the remedies afforded by the CCA 1974, s 133.

1 See Civil Procedure Rules and Practice Directions, para 6.4.4, Practice Directives supplementary Pt 16 and Civil Procedure Rules (CPR), Order 6 at cc 6.6 to 6.6.3. The pleading requirements in hire-purchase claims have not changed.
2 CCA 1974, s 133.

24.15   DISTRESS FOR RENT BY LANDLORD OF DEBTOR OR HIRER

At common law the landlord is entitled to distrain on any goods on the leased premises, whether or not they are owned by the tenant. Some relief was granted to sub-tenants and parties connected with the tenant by the Law of Distress Amendment Act 1908 which allows such persons to give notice to a landlord identifying property as their own. The protection afforded by the Law of Distress Amendment Act 1908 does not extend to goods which are in the possession of the tenant with the consent of the true owner where the tenant has become their reputed owner.

The owner of goods comprised in a leasing agreement, whether within or outside the CCA 1974, should therefore serve a declaration on the landlord of the premises notifying the landlord that the tenant has no right of property or beneficial interest in the goods.

The landlord's common law right to distrain on goods extends also to goods under a hire-purchase or conditional sale agreement unless it has been terminated or is an agreement within the CCA 1974 in respect of which a default or termination notice is in force. It is therefore advisable for unregulated agreements to contain an automatic termination provision to prevent the landlord's distress rights coming into operation.

24.16   ADDITIONAL POWERS OF THE COURT

(a)   On an application of the creditor or owner under a regulated agreement the court may make a protection order, namely an order protecting the property of the creditor or owner, or property subject to any security, pending the determination of any proceedings.[1]

(b)   The CCA 1974 empowers a court to impose conditions in any order or to suspend the operation of any term of the order, if it considers it just to do so. The court may also include such provision as it considers just for amending any agreement or security in consequence of a term of the order.[2]

(c)   Under the Torts (Interference with Goods) Act 1977, in addition to remedies available to a creditor or owner under CCA 1974, an action will also lie against a bailee in conversion for any loss or destruction of goods which he has allowed whilst the goods were in his care.

(d)   The remedies and measures discussed in this chapter are in addition to those available to the parties at common law for breach of contract or misrepresentation, whether fraudulent, negligent or innocent.

(e)   An order of the court in relation to a regulated agreement cannot include interest on the judgment debt. However, there is no bar to a creditor suing for both the principal amount and any default interest due under the regulated agreement[3] provided that this would not amount to seeking to enforce an unfair contract term.[4]

1   CCA 1974, s 131.
2   CCA 1974, ss 135 and 136 and see *Cedar Holdings Ltd v Jenkins* [1988] CCLR 34.
3   County Court (Interest on Judgment Debts) Order 1991, SI 1991/1184 and see *Forward Trust Ltd v Whymark* [1990] 2 QB 670, [1999] GCCR 1363, CA.
4   See para 24.12 and *Director General of Fair Trading v First National Bank plc* [2000] GCCR 2601, CA.

24.17 CONSEQUENCES OF DEATH OF THE DEBTOR OR HIRER

If the regulated agreement is fully secured, the creditor or owner under a regulated agreement is not entitled, by reason of the death of the debtor or hirer, to terminate the agreement, demand earlier payment of any sum, recover possession of any goods or land, treat any right conferred on the debtor or hirer as terminated, restricted or deferred or enforce any security.[1] If the agreement was only partly secured or unsecured, the creditor or owner may do any of the foregoing on an order of the court only.[2]

1 CCA 1974, s 86. Note that this section employs the expressions 'fully secured', 'partly secured' or 'unsecured'. It is submitted that 'fully secured' means security to the full value of the outstanding indebtedness under the agreement.
2 CCA 1974, s 86.

24.18 CLAIMS FOR POSSESSION OF MORTGAGED PROPERTY

Possession claims are governed by the Civil Procedure Rules (CPR) including Practice Directive PD 16.[1] The Defence Form raises the question as to whether, in the case of a regulated agreement, the defendant wants the court to consider whether the terms of the original agreement are fair. The borrower is also reminded of the right to apply for a time order in the form 'do you intend to apply to the court for an order changing the terms of your loan agreement?'.

1 Generally on claims, defences and contentious (litigation) procedures see *Goode: Consumer Credit Law and Practice* (LexisNexis Butterworths), vol 5 Division XII.

24.19 SURETIES

Where an agreement has been secured by a surety, whether a guarantor or indemnifier, a copy of any enforcement notice, termination notice or default notice must also be served in paper form on the surety, containing the prescribed heading, stating that it is the surety's copy of such notice. Failure to comply will result in the security being enforceable against the surety on an order of the court only.[1]

1 CCA 1974, s 111 and Consumer Credit (Cancellation Notices and Copies of Documents) Regulations 1983, SI 1983/1557, reg 10.

24.20 FINANCIAL OMBUDSMAN SERVICE

The complaint handling jurisdiction of the Financial Ombudsman Service (FOS) was extended on 6 April 2007 to consumer credit complaints.[1] The procedures are set out in the FSA Handbook, Sourcebook Dispute Resolution: Complaints (DISP). DISP 3 governs 'Complaint handling procedures of the Financial Ombudsman Service'.

Before the ombudsman can consider a complaint he must be satisfied that the licensee under CCA 1974 had the requisite eight weeks from receipt of the complaint, to consider the complaint. Where a licensee fails to send a final response to the complainant by the end of eight weeks, the ombudsman will consider the complaint. The ombudsman will attempt to resolve the complaint at the earliest possible stage and by whatever means appears appropriate, including by mediation or investigation.[2]

1 CCA 1974, s 226A following.
2 FSA Handbook, DISP 3.2.

Chapter 25

Fraud, money laundering, offences and defences

25.1 FRAUD: THE EXTENT OF THE PROBLEM

It is trite to state that fraud is a cancerous virus which pervades all sectors of the credit industry: payment and credit cards, retail credit, mortgage finance and motor, asset and general finance. The fraudster might operate alone or as a member of an organised group, nationally or internationally.[1]

Fraud, though not exclusively credit fraud, costs the UK economy a minimum of £13.9 billion annually.[2] In respect of card fraud, as a result of the success of 'Chip and PIN', face-to-face fraud has continued to drop since its introduction. Card fraud loss in the UK in 2006 amounted to £428 million of which 'card-not-present' fraud accounted for approximately half of the losses. 'Card-not-present' fraud arises when the cardholder does not present the card when making the purchase e.g. card use over the telephone or via the Internet. In 2006 cheque fraud in the UK totalled £30.6 million.[3]

1 For a survey and analysis of part of the problem see 'The Prevention of Cheque and Credit Card Fraud' by Michael Levi, Paul Bissell and Tony Richardson, Paper No 26 issued by the Home Office Crime Prevention Unit (June 1991).
2 Report commissioned by the Association of Chief Police Officers Economic Crime Portfolio Group ('ACPO'), February 2007.
3 Figures published by APACS in Fraud: The Facts 2007.

25.2 FRAUD: THE LAW

The legislation governing fraud was dramatically simplified by the Fraud Act 2006 which received Royal Assent on 8 November 2006 and came fully into force on 15 January 2007. It has changed the face of anti-fraud legislation in the United Kingdom largely by simplifying the definition of fraud and closing loopholes which existed previously.

The Fraud Act 2006 sets out various fraud offences, as follows:

(a) Fraud by false representation. In essence this involves dishonestly making a false representation and intending, by making the representation, to make a gain for oneself or to cause a loss to another. The representation may be express or implied and made in any form to any system or device designed to receive, convey or respond to communications.[1]

(b) Fraud by failing to disclose information. This essentially takes place where a person dishonestly fails to disclose to another person information which he is under a legal duty to disclose and intends, by so doing, to make a gain for himself or to cause loss to another.[2]

(c) Fraud by abuse of position. This is essentially caused where a person who occupies a position in which he is expected to safeguard, or not to act against, the financial interests of another person, dishonestly abuses that position and intends, by so doing, to make a gain for himself or to cause loss to another.[3]

(d) Participating in a fraudulent business carried on by a sole trader etc. A person commits this offence if he is knowingly a party to the carrying on of a business which is outside s 458 of the Companies Act 1985 (offence of fraudulent trading) and with the intent to defraud creditors of any person or for any other fraudulent purpose.[4]

(e) Obtaining services dishonestly. Essentially this offence is committed if a person obtains services for himself or another by a dishonest act in that he has no intention of making payment for them in full or at all.[5]

Some offences appertaining to fraud remain governed by legislation which preceded the Fraud Act 2006 and has not been repealed. The offences include:

(a) dishonestly retaining a wrongful credit;[6]

(b) unauthorised access to computer material with intent to commit or facilitate the commission of offences;[7]

(c) conspiracy to defraud or conspiracy to commit an offence;[8]

(d) false accounting;[9]

(e) forgery.[10]

---

1 Section 2.
2 Section 3.
3 Section 4.
4 Section 9.
5 Section 11.
6 Theft Act 1968, s 24A.
7 Computer Misuse Act 1990, ss 1 to 3A as amended by the Police and Justice Act 2006.
8 Criminal Justice Act 1987, s 12; Criminal Law Act 1977, s 1.
9 Theft Act 1968, s 17.
10 Forgery and Counterfeiting Act 1981.

25.3 FRAUD PREVENTION

Various organisations, systems and procedures have been established and techniques introduced in order to prevent, or at least limit, fraud.

In order to combat fraud it is essential to nip it in the bud by early detection. This is especially so where the fraudulent activity is being undertaken by conspirators, whether local, national or international. Combating fraud effectively presupposes the following:

(a) the sharing and exchange of information;

(b) rapid reaction and response;

(c) cooperation and action on the part of the police and the enforcement authorities;

(d) an effective and up to date civil and criminal law; and

(e) the fraudsters being brought to justice.

The law on fraud must be clear, firm, uncompromising and effective, and perceived as such, so that fraud prevention and control is not viewed by the criminal fraternity as the achilles heal of the criminal system.

25.3.1 Organisations which combat fraud

CIFAS is a system for preventing fraud. Established in 1991, it facilitates the exchange of information by its members, particularly the sharing of allegedly fraudulent applications for credit or services. Members can also exchange information about accounts which are suspected of being used fraudulently or insurance claims which are suspected of being made fraudulently. When a CIFAS member identifies a fraud, a warning is placed against the address linked to the application or account, thereby alerting other CIFAS members when they check against that address. In 2007 CIFAS identified 185,000 alleged frauds and saved industry just under £1 billion of loss through fraud.

The principal credit reference agencies provide software packages which enable their subscribers to identify suspect fraud.

The Association for Payment Clearing Services ('APACS') was established in 1985 to manage the payment clearing systems and oversee money transmission in the United Kingdom. It founded a Plastic Fraud Prevention Forum to fight the battle against plastic card fraud. It identifies as the main types of fraud: counterfeit cards, fraudulent possession of card details, fraud on lost or stolen cards, mail non-receipt fraud, application fraud, ATM fraud and cross-border fraud. The Fraud Intelligence Bureau, established by APACS, shares information between banks and the police on all types of card fraud.

Mortgage fraud grew rapidly in the late 1980s and was often the product of collusion between borrowers, solicitors and valuers. As a result, the Building Societies Association hosts a panel of building societies and other institutions which share their experience and discuss how to identify and tackle fraud. Fraud was also a motivating factor in the establishment of the Council of Mortgage Lenders, which has a fraud prevention committee.

HPI Limited and Car Data Check are registering and information service businesses which enable creditors with security interests in vehicles, arising under hire-purchase, conditional sale or loan agreements, to register their interests on a register. Potential purchasers of vehicles can check whether the vehicles they propose purchasing have security interests registered against them.

HPI Limited also holds a so-called 'condition alert register' relating to vehicles which have been the subject of a major damage insurance claim and where the insurer has declined to have the vehicle repaired as the vehicle has been written off. It serves as an alert to potential purchasers in relation to the condition of the vehicle. Other registers held relate to stolen vehicles, vehicles that are at risk from fraud or theft, vehicles which have undergone registration plate changes since April 1990 and a register recording dates of first registration.

The Dedicated Cheque and Plastic Crime Unit ('DCPCU') is a special police unit that focuses on cheque and plastic card fraud and is sponsored by the banking industry through APACS.

25.3.2   Procedures to combat fraud

Procedures for combating fraud are limitless. They extend from applying prudent checks on the identification of customers, ensuring that goods proposed to be leased exist and are not already the subject of an existing lease agreement, implementing floor limits in stores so that credit approvals are required for purchases above a pre-set limit, to personal delivery of credit cards to customers at their bank branches and safeguards in relation to PINs.

25.3.3   Fraud prevention techniques

At the basic level, the most effective measure to prevent credit fraud is for credit grantors to share information on persons who have made fraudulent applications for credit or have otherwise evidenced fraudulent misuse of credit. Such an information base is clearly enhanced by the comprehensiveness and exhaustiveness of the data base.

Chip and PIN technology is at the forefront of the fight against plastic card fraud. As at January 2007 the UK banks and card companies had issued 138 million Chip and PIN cards, representing 97% of the UK's 142 million payment cards.[1] A chip card is a plastic card containing a microchip which has highly secure memory and processing capabilities and can be recognised by the gold-coloured contact plate on the front of the card. Chip cards are also known as integrated circuit cards ('ICCs') or smart cards and are designed to international specifications set by the international card schemes Europay Mastercard and Visa. A PIN is a personal identification number ('PIN') which enables customers to withdraw cash and use other services at a cash machine or at the point of sale.

Another method of tackling fraud is by way of knowledge-based systems, namely checking for unusual purchasing patterns in order to detect the fraudulent use of cards.

Personal identification methods such as iris scanning and fingerprint recognition have been promoted from time to time but it appears that such technology is not sufficiently reliable or cost effective to meet the current requirements of the

UK card industry. However, as the government appears intent on introducing identification cards with biometric identification features, the introduction of such features into credit cards appears likely in the medium to long term.

Most internet fraud involves using card details which have been obtained fraudulently in order to make card-not-present transactions. Various methods and devices exist to prevent or detect fraud, notably the automated address and card security code checking system which allows merchants to verify the billing address of card holders and to cross check coded digits on cards. In order to protect data against being intercepted by hackers certified organisations encrypt data.[2]

1 *Fraud: The Facts 2007*, published by APACS.
2 See further Chapter 22.

25.4 MONEY LAUNDERING

The Money Laundering Regulations 2007[1] implement Directive 2005/60/EC of the European Parliament and of the Council of 26 October 2005 on the prevention of the use of the financial system for the purpose of money laundering and terrorist financing. The Regulations apply, inter alia, to so-called 'relevant persons', which include credit institutions and financial institutions.[2] They are required to apply customer due diligence measures where the relevant person establishes a business relationship, carries out an occasional transaction, suspects money laundering or terrorist financing or doubts the veracity or adequacy of documents, data or information previously obtained for the purposes of identification or verification.[3] The relevant person must apply, on a risk-sensitive basis, enhanced customer due diligence measures and enhanced ongoing monitoring where the customer was not physically present for identification purposes or the customer is a politically exposed person.[4] Customer due diligence measures involve identifying the customer and verifying the customer's identity on the basis of documents, data or information obtained from a reliable and independent source and obtaining information on the purpose and intended nature of the business relationship.[5]

The Regulations prescribe record-keeping, procedures and training; supervision and registration; and enforcement. The Office of Fair Trading is the supervisory authority to ensure compliance by licensees in respect of consumer credit business and has issued guidance on their operation.[6] The Financial Services Authority is the supervisory body of authorised persons except in so far as they may be licensed to conduct consumer credit business.

The general thrust of the Regulations is to require relevant businesses to:

(a) set up checks, controls and procedures in order to prevent money laundering or terrorist financing;

(b) train staff in the procedures;

(c) appoint a nominated officer to receive and consider internal disclosures and to make suspicious activity reports ('SARs') to the Serious Organised Crime Agency ('SOCA');

(d)   institute procedures to identify customers, verify the customers' identity and obtain information of the purpose or nature of the business relationship ('customer due diligence');

(e)   have in place ongoing monitoring of the business relationship; and

(f)   maintain records of the customers' identity and business relationships for five years.

The Regulations adopt a risk-based approach and place the ultimate responsibility of compliance with senior management. Breach of certain of the Regulations constitutes a criminal offence.

Failure to comply with the Regulations places the relevant person at the risk of letting criminal offences under the Regulations and also criminal offences under the Proceeds of Crime Act 2002.

1   SI 2007/2157.
2   Regulation 3.
3   Regulation 7.
4   Regulation 14.
5   Regulation 5.
6   Money Laundering Regulations 2007, November 2007, OFT 954.

25.5   OFFENCES, PENALTIES AND DEFENCES

25.5.1   Overview

The criminal law is the forum of last resort in relation to the enforcement of consumer credit law so that the sparsity of prosecutions under CCA 1974 should not be viewed as evidence of the ineffectiveness of criminal sanctions. The authority of the Office of Fair Trading under the Act, the Fair Trading Act 1973 and the Enterprise Act 2002 have to some extent relegated the criminal law to a subsidiary position in relation to the enforcement of consumer credit law. This position is likely to continue as a result of the new powers of the OFT to impose civil penalties.[1]

1   See para 25.5.3 below.

25.5.2   Offences

There are thirty-five offences under CCA 1974 and these, together with their mode of prosecution and the sentences they carry, are summarised in Sch 1 to the Act.

It is submitted that there is a basic flaw in consumer credit law in so far as certain fundamental breaches of CCA 1974 and the regulations give rise simultaneously to both criminal and civil sanctions, the civil sanctions sometimes resulting in the unenforceability of the agreement. As a higher degree of proof is required in criminal cases, it may result in an acquittal in circumstances where a civil court, deciding the same issue, might find that there had been a breach of the relevant regulations. The decision of the court in *National Westminster Bank v Devon County Council and Devon County Council v Abbey National plc*,[1] which was a successful appeal from a criminal conviction, is an illustration. This case had far-reaching consequences, not least of which was the amendment of the Consumer Credit (Total Charge for Credit) Regulations 1980.

The creation of criminal offences for infringements of CCA 1974 has from time to time aroused views of disbelief on the part of the judiciary, disbelief that reputable institutions which acted in good faith should find themselves prosecuted for breaches of abstruse and difficult regulations.[2] The reputation of an institution is not, however, a relevant factor, and reference to it distorts the issue in question.

1 [1999] GCCR 1685, see also Chapter 18.
2 See the above decision at p 1692.

25.5.3 Civil penalties

The Consumer Credit Act 2006 introduced, for the first time, civil penalties into consumer credit law. The Office of Fair Trading is empowered to impose civil penalties where it is satisfied that a person has failed or is failing to comply with a requirement imposed on him by virtue of ss 33A, 33B or 36A of CCA 1974, which set out the power of the OFT to impose requirements on licensees, the power of the OFT to impose requirements on supervisory bodies and the duty to notify changes etc., respectively. The penalty amount may not exceed £50,000 but, as it relates to each offence committed, the total sum may exceed that amount. Section 39B sets out the procedure relating to the imposition of penalties. The OFT is obligated to prepare and publish a statement of policy in relation to the exercise of its power to impose penalties.[1]

1 CCA 1974, s 49C and see Consumer Credit Licensing, Statement of Policy on Civil Penalties, January 2008, OFT 971.

25.5.4 Defences and the approach of the courts

It is not intended to deal with defences generally but to highlight a specific defence under the Act and to outline the approach of the courts.

It is a defence for a person charged with an offence under CCA 1974 to prove both:

(a) that the act or omission was due to a mistake or to reliance on information supplied, or to an act or omission by another person, or to an accident or some other cause beyond the person's control; and

(b) that the person took all reasonable precautions and exercised all due diligence to avoid such an act or omission by the person or any other person under his control.[1]

The defence was pleaded in the case of *Coventry City Council v Lazarus*.[2] The respondents traded in partnership as a garage and advertised credit for used motor vehicles without complying with the Consumer Credit (Advertisements) Regulations 1989. Failure to comply was not in issue, but the respondents argued that they had relied upon advice given by the Retail Motor Industry's Federation and had received a visit from the Area Manager who had offered advice concerning the advertisements. According to the evidence, the respondents relied on the information but the court found that they had not exercised all due diligence to avoid the publication of the offending advertisements.

An interesting analogous case is *Tesco Supermarkets Ltd v Nattrass*.[3] This involved a prosecution under the Trade Descriptions Act 1968 which provides a defence for the person charged to prove that the commission of the offence was due to a mistake or to reliance on information supplied to the person or to the act or default of another person and that the accused took all reasonable precautions and exercised all due diligence to avoid the commission of the offence. The court stated that the defence was plainly intended to make a just and reasonable distinction between an employer who is wholly blameless and ought to be acquitted and an employer who was in some way at fault. Although on the facts, a chain of command was set up through regional and district supervisors, the acts and omissions of shop managers was found not to constitute those of the company itself which was therefore acquitted.

Where a person deliberately flouts the law, the courts will usually impose a custodial sentence. In *R v Curr*[4] an unlicensed trader advanced moneys to customers by way of loan and acted in deliberate defiance of the law. In addition to imposing a fine, the court considered a sentence of imprisonment justified because of the appellant's attitude to the law. Similarly, in *R v Priestly*[5] which involved offences under the Trade Descriptions Act 1968 and unlicensed trading under CCA 1974, where the trader had engaged in activities in a manner which, with his experience, he knew was contrary to the law and did so quite brazenly, the court considered it appropriate to impose a prison sentence.

A misstated APR in a credit agreement was held to be a misleading indication as to price in breach of the Consumer Protection Act 1987, s 21 in the case of *R v Kettering Magistrates Court, ex p MRB Insurance Brokers Ltd*.[6] The court stated that CCA 1974, s 170(1), which provides that a breach of any requirement under the Act will incur no civil or criminal sanction except to the extent expressly provided by or under the Act, is merely intended to clarify (by disapplying) the common law rules relating to breaches of an act of parliament. It does not prevent a person being charged under legislation other than the Act itself and did not preclude a prosecution under the Consumer Protection Act 1987.

1 CCA 1974, s 168(1).
2 [1999] GCCR 1909.
3 [1971] 1 QB 133.
4 [1999] GCCR 533, CA.
5 [1999] GCCR 641, CA.
6 [2001] GCCR 2701.

Chapter 26

Data protection

26.1 DATA PROTECTION ACT 1998

The Data Protection Act 1998 ('DPA 1998') has relevance to the consumer credit regime in two respects: it imposes obligations on credit grantors and providers of hire facilities and, second, it confers rights on consumers. Its application is confined to personal data, being data which relate to a living individual and who can be identified from those data or from those data and other information which is in the possession, or likely to come into the possession, of the data controller.

A 'data controller' is a person who, either alone or jointly or in common with others, determines the purposes for which and the manner in which any personal data are processed.

'Data' is information which is processed by equipment operating automatically in response to instructions given for that purpose or which is recorded with the intention that it should be so processed, or which is recorded as part of a relevant filing system (i.e. structured by reference to individuals or criteria relating to individuals so that information about a particular individual is readily available) or which forms part of an accessible record or which is recorded information held by a public authority.

'Processing' is widely defined and includes obtaining, recording or holding information or data or carrying out any operation on the information or data, including organisation, retrieval, disclosure, adjustment or erasure of data.[1]

1 These definitions are a précis of those in DPA 1998, s 1(1).

26.2 DATA PROTECTION PRINCIPLES

The DPA 1998 lays down eight data protection principles.[1] They are as follows:

(1) personal data shall be processed fairly and lawfully and, in particular, shall not be processed unless:

  (a) at least one of the conditions in Sch 2 is met, and

  (b) in the case of sensitive personal data, at least one of the conditions in Sch 3 is also met;

(2)   personal data shall be obtained only for one or more specified and lawful purposes, and shall not be further processed in any manner incompatible with that purpose or those purposes;

(3)   personal data shall be adequate, relevant and not excessive in relation to the purpose or purposes for which they are processed;

(4)   personal data shall be accurate and, where necessary, kept up to date;

(5)   personal data processed for any purpose or purposes shall not be kept for longer than is necessary for that purpose or those purposes;

(6)   personal data shall be processed in accordance with the rights of data subjects under the DPA 1998;

(7)   appropriate technical and organisational measures shall be taken against unauthorised or unlawful processing of personal data and against accidental loss or destruction of, or damage to, personal data; and

(8)   personal data shall not be transferred to a country or territory outside the European Economic Area unless that country or territory ensures an adequate level of protection for the rights and freedoms of data subjects in relation to the processing of personal data.

Of the conditions set out in Sch 2, the most common is that the data subject has given his consent to the processing. The most common condition to apply in the case of those set out in Sch 3 is that the data subject has given his explicit consent to the processing of sensitive personal data.

1 DPA 1998, Sch 1, Pt I.

26.3   PROCESSING OF PERSONAL DATA

Personal data must be processed fairly and lawfully and only if the conditions referred to below are met ('the first data protection principle').[1]

    Personal data may only be processed if the conditions of Schedule 2 to DPA 1998 are met. Sensitive personal data may only be processsed if, in addition, at least one of the conditions in Schedule 3 to the Act is met.[2]

    'Sensitive personal data' comprises personal data consisting of information as to the racial or ethnic origin of the data subject, his political opinions, his religious beliefs, whether he is a member of a trade union, his physical or mental condition, his sexual life, the commission or alleged commission by him of an offence or information of any proceedings for any offence or any sentence.[3]

    Personal data processed for purposes of the prevention or detection of crime, the apprehension or prosecution of offenders, or the assessment or collection of any tax or duty are exempt from the first data protection principle (except to the extent to which compliance is required with Schs 2 and 3) and from provisions granting the data subject access rights to personal data, where this is likely to prejudice any of the above purposes.[4]

    The circumstances in which sensitive personal data may be processed, in addition to those specified in Schedule 2, are where the processing:

(a)   is in the substantial public interest;

(b)   is necessary for the purposes of the prevention or detection of any unlawful act; and

(c)   must necessarily be carried out without the explicit consent of the data subject being sought, so as not to prejudice those purposes.[5]

1   DPA 1998, s 4(1) and (2), read with Sch 1, Principle 1
2   DPA 1998, s 4(3).
3   DPA 1998, s 2.
4   DPA 1998, s 29.
5   Data Protection (Processing of Sensitive Personal Data) Order 2000, SI 2000/417. See also SI 2002/2905 and SI 2006/2068.

26.4   DATA SHARING

Data is shared in the credit industry by banks, building societies, finance companies, leasing companies and intermediaries, essentially via credit reference agencies. Sharing data amounts to the disclosure of information or data by transmission, dissemination or otherwise making the same available and accordingly constitutes 'processing' as defined in s 1(1) of DPA 1998. As such, the processing must be attended to fairly and lawfully and must meet at least one of the conditions in Schedule 2 to the Act and, in the case of sensitive personal data, also at least one of the conditions in Schedule 3 to the Act.

   CIFAS, a company limited by guarantee, operates the UK's fraud prevention service primarily for the UK financial services industry. It facilitates the sharing of what can generically be described as fraud data. Another scheme for sharing data is that set up by the Steering Committee on Reciprocity (SCOR), comprising representatives of various trade associations and the principal credit reference agencies. The SCOR Principles of Reciprocity are a set of guidelines governing the sharing of personal credit performance and related data for the prevention of over-indebtedness, fraud and money laundering and to support debt recovery and debt tracing, with the aim of promoting responsible lending.

   There are no obstacles to the sharing of data within the European Economic Area (EEA), subject to compliance with the Member State's data protection laws. As regards sharing data outside the EEA, if data is shared with the USA, the user of the data must commit to the Safe Harbour Principles. Other countries deemed to have adequate data protection safeguards by the European Commission are Argentina, Canada, Guernsey, Isle of Man and Switzerland. Outside the above countries and the US, the US user must commit to comply with standard EU model clauses relating to data protection.

26.5   CONSENT CLAUSES

Before personal data relating to an individual is accessed, whether at the application or agreement stage, the person obtaining that information, usually the creditor or lessor, must provide the following information to the proposed customer: the identity of the data controller and if he has a nominated representative the identity of that representative; the purposes for which the data are intended to be processed; and any further information which is necessary, having regard to the specific circumstances in which the data are to be processed, to enable the data processing to be fair. This includes information as to the source of any personal data.

A typical notification clause in an agreement might read as follows:

'Data Protection: Use of Your Information

In considering whether to enter into this agreement we will search your record at credit reference agencies. They will add to their record about you details of our search and your application and this will be seen by other organisations that make searches. We will also add to your record with the credit reference agencies details of your agreement with us and your payment record under this agreement. These records will be shared with other organisations and may be used by them to consider your further applications for credit and credit related services and to trace debtors, recover debts and for fraud prevention. We may also check your details with fraud prevention agencies and if you provide us with false information or we suspect fraud, this may be recorded. Fraud prevention agencies will also share their records with other organisations to help make decisions. We may also use information about you for marketing our other products to you. If you do not wish to receive such information, you should write to us at any time.

Please telephone us on freephone .... if you want to have details of the credit reference and fraud prevention agencies from whom we obtain and to whom we pass information about you. You have a legal right to these details. You also have a right to receive a copy of the information we hold about you if you apply to us in writing. A fee will be payable.'

26.6   ASSOCIATED RECORDS

For some time the Data Protection Commissioner, now called the Information Commissioner, expressed concern at the credit industry's use of so-called 'third party data' the assumption of a financial connection on the basis of shared surname and current or previous address.

The credit industry duly recognised the need for change, reinforced by the DPA 1998, and the Human Rights Act 1998. A working party was set up in 1999 comprising representatives of various trade associations resulting in agreement on an additional data protection notice to be included in the general data protection notice. It reads as follows:

'Use of Associated Records

Before entering into any agreement with you we may search records at credit reference agencies which may be linked to records relating to your spouse/partner or other persons with whom you are linked financially and other members of your household. For the purposes of this application you may be treated as financially linked and you will be assessed with reference to "associated records".

Where any search or application is completed involving joint parties, you both consent to our recording details at credit reference agencies. As a result, an "association" will be created which will link your financial records and your associate's information may be taken into account when future searches are made by us or another lender unless you file a "disassociation" at the credit reference agencies.'

It will be apparent that consent clauses in application and agreement forms have become almost as lengthy as the forms themselves and will often necessitate an extra page being appended to the form. Where applications are entered into over the internet, the data protection notice must be included on the relevant page of the trader's website and there must be evidence that the customer read and consented to that notice, especially where explicit consent is required to sensitive personal data. Applications over the telephone must likewise be preceded by the consent notice being read to the customer. In these cases the notice can be replicated in the agreement form itself so as to make the customer's consent abundantly clear.

26.7   NOTIFICATION/REGISTRATION

The system of notification under the DPA 1998 replaced the registration scheme under the Data Protection Act 1984 and produces a register of data controllers. No personal data may be processed unless an entry in respect of the data controller is included in the register maintained by the Information Commissioner. When a notification is made by a data controller, in addition to the registrable particulars, the general description of the security measures taken to protect the personal data must be notified.

Apart from general information relating to the data controller, the notification form requires the data controller to include the purposes for which personal data are being or are to be processed, a description of the data subjects about whom data are to be held, a description of the data classes, a list of the recipients of the data, and information as to where the data are to be transferred outside the European Economic Area.

26.8   FREEDOM OF INFORMATION ACT 2000

This Act provides individuals with access to information held by public authorities, as defined in Schedule 1 to the Act. They include government departments, the House of Commons, the House of Lords, local government bodies, bodies falling under the National Health Service, maintained schools and other educational institutions, police forces and specified Advisory Committees, Boards, Councils and Agencies. Various items of information are exempt from the duty to provide information, either absolutely exempt or conditionally exempt.[1]

1   See s 2 and Part 11; see s 2(3) for absolute exemptions.

26.9 RIGHTS OF INDIVIDUALS

26.9.1 Right of subject access

The DPA 1998 and CCA 1974 allow individuals to find out what information is held about them on computer and certain paper records. This is known as the right of subject access.

An individual or partnership is entitled to receive information held by credit reference agencies. Whilst the right is secure, the source of the right is somewhat muddled, as will be seen below.

Under CCA 1974, a creditor, owner or negotiator must, within seven working days after receiving a written request, furnish a debtor or hirer with the name and address of any credit reference agency to which it applied for information about the applicant's financial standing.[1]

The duty of the credit reference agency to supply information is set out in CCA 1974 in relation to requests received from partnerships or any other unincorporated body of persons and in the DPA 1998 in respect of requests received from a living individual. Why this unnecessary bifurcation was resorted to is not clear. Under CCA 1974 a credit agency must, within the period of seven working days after receiving a written request and the prescribed fee, furnish the consumer with a copy of the file relating to it kept by the agency.[2] Under the DPA 1998 the individual is entitled to be given a description of the personal data held, the purposes for which they are held, the recipients to whom they are to be disclosed, and the source of those data. Further, where processing by automatic means of personal data is undertaken, e.g. credit scoring, the data subject is entitled to be informed of the logic involved in taking that decision. The information must be requested in writing and the prescribed fee paid.[3]

An individual who considers an entry in his file to be incorrect, and if not corrected that he is likely to suffer prejudice, may give notice to the agency requiring it to be removed.[4]

Where there is information on the individual's file about people in his family with whom he has no financial connection, he can write to the agency to disassociate himself from them.

1 CCA 1974, s 157(1).
2 CCA 1974, s 15(1) *ibid.*, read with the Consumer Credit (Credit Reference Agency) Regulations 1977, SI 1977/329.
3 Data Protection Act 1998, s 7(1) and (2) read with the Data Protection (Subject Access) (Fees and Miscellaneous Provisions) Regulations 2000, SI 2000/191.
4 CCA 1974, s 159 and the procedure set out there.

26.9.2 Right to prevent processing likely to cause damage or distress

An individual is entitled at any time by notice in writing to a data controller to require the data controller to cease, or not to begin, processing or processing for a specified purpose in a specified manner, any personal data relating to him on the grounds that it is causing or likely to cause substantial damage or distress to him and that the damage or distress is unwarranted.[1] The data controller must then follow the procedure set out in the DPA 1998, s 10.

1 DPA 1998, s 10(1).

26.9.3 Right to prevent processing for direct marketing

An individual is entitled at any time by notice in writing to a data controller to require the data controller to cease, or not to begin, processing data relating to him for the purpose of direct marketing.[1]

1 DPA 1998, s 11.

26.9.4 Right in relation to automatic decision-taking

An individual is entitled at any time, by notice in writing to a data controller, to require the data controller to ensure that no decision taken by or on behalf of the data controller, which significantly affects that individual, is based solely on the processing by automatic means of personal data relating to him, e.g. his performance at work, his creditworthiness, his reliability or his conduct.[1]

1 DPA 1998, s 12.

26.9.5 Right to compensation

An individual who suffers damage or distress by reason of any contravention by the data controller of any requirements of the DPA 1998 is entitled to compensation.[1]

1 DPA 1998, s 13(1).

26.10 REMEDIAL ACTION

An individual may apply to a court to order a data controller to rectify, block, erase or destroy data relating to him, including data containing an expression of opinion based on inaccurate data.[1]

1 DPA 1998, s 14(1).

26.11 TELECOMMUNICATIONS

Concurrently with the requirement to implement Data Protection Directive 95/46/EC Member States had to implement the Telecommunications Data Protection Directive 97/66/EC. It was brought into effect in the United Kingdom as the Telecommunications (Data Protection and Privacy) (Direct Marketing) Regulations 1998.[1] These Regulations:

(a)   prohibit the use of automated calling systems for direct marketing, except where in a particular case, the call subscriber has given his consent;

(b)   prohibit communication by facsimile transmission of direct marketing material except where the call subscriber has previously given his consent; and

(c)   prohibit unsolicited calls for direct marketing purposes either where in a particular case the call subscriber has previously notified the caller that such calls should not be made or where the call subscriber's number is, at his request, included in the record kept by the Director General of Communications of numbers not wishing to receive unsolicited calls (a so-called 'stop list'). Whilst individuals have the right to opt out of unsolicited telephone sales, corporate customers have no such right. Automated calling systems, however, must be built on the prior consent of both corporate and individual subscribers.

1   SI 1998/3170.

26.12   USE OF CUSTOMER LISTS AND DATABASES

The first data protection principle requires personal data to be processed fairly and lawfully.

If customer lists are intended to be used for direct marketing purposes by parties to a contract or by third parties, even if no data is actually disclosed, this must be explained to the customer in advance and his consent obtained. This may be in the form of a positive or negative option e.g. tick this box if you do not wish to receive marketing materials. List rentals and 'host' mailings by a list owner on behalf of a third party require the list owner to notify his sources of information, namely consumers, that he intends to use the data in this way. Third parties include any separate legal entity, even a subsidiary company within the same group.

If an individual has indicated his wish not to receive unsolicited mail, a data user who processes personal information about that individual so as to cause further unsolicited mail to be dispatched, is likely to breach the first data protection principle.

Use of databases, including customer lists, is subject to the Copyright and Rights in Databases Regulations 1997[1] and the rules relating to Database Practice in the British Code of Advertising, Sales Promotion and Direct Marketing.

1   SI 1997/3032.

26.13   CODES OF PRACTICE

Various codes of practice applying to the credit industry contain provisions relating to data protection. They will usually have received the approval of the Information Commissioner.

26.14 OTHER CONFIDENTIALITY SAFEGUARDS

26.14.1 The *Tournier* principle and exceptions

In the leading case of *Tournier v National Provincial and Union Bank of England*[1] the court held that there is a contractual duty of secrecy implied in the relationship of banker and customer. It enunciated four exceptions, namely:

(a) where disclosure is under compulsion by law;

(b) where there is a duty to the public to disclose;

(c) where the interests of the bank require disclosure; and

(d) where the disclosure is made by the express or implied consent of the customer.

1 [1924] 1 KB 461, CA. See also *Christofi v Barclays Bank plc* [1999] 4 All ER 437, *Robertson v Canadian Imperial Bank of Commerce* [1995] 1 All ER 824, *Barclays Bank plc v Taylor* [1989] 3 All ER 563.

26.14.2 The Banking Code

The Banking Code stipulates that a subscriber must treat as private and confidential all financial information relating to private customers. Banks undertake not to reveal the customer's name and address or details about the customer to anyone, including other companies in the banking group, except in the four exceptional cases stated in the paragraph above.

Banks undertake not to use the exception at (c) above as a ground for giving information about accounts to anyone else, including other companies in the banking group, for marketing purposes.

26.14.3 Use of the electoral register

The refusal by an electoral registration officer to allow an elector to have his name removed from an electoral register before it was sold to a commercial concern for marketing purposes was held to constitute both a breach of his right to respect for his private and family life under Art 8 of the European Convention on Human Rights and an invalid interference with his right to vote.[1] The issues raised by the *Robertson Case* were resolved by The Representation of the People (England and Wales) (Amendment) Regulations 2002.[2] These regulations provide for the creation of two versions of the register – a full version and an edited version. The full version is supplied to a limited number of organisations, principally government departments and credit reference agencies. The edited version is available for sale to anyone, although individuals may object to their details being included in the edited version.[3]

1 *R (on the appliction of Robertson) v City of Wakefield Metropolitan Council* [2001] All ER (D) 243.
2 SI 2002/1871.
3 See *Encyclopedia of Data Protection & Privacy* (Sweet & Maxwell), at 1–165.

Chapter 27

Funding and outsourcing

27.1 INTRODUCTION

This is a vast subject and one which falls more properly within the scope of corporate finance. Nevertheless, it is relevant to include brief mention of the methods whereby credit and hire facilities are financed and a note on the outsourcing of services.

Credit grantors and providers of hire facilities do not usually enjoy an entirely free hand in raising funds. Various restrictions in relation to capital adequacy requirements apply to banks, building societies and other credit institutions. Companies are restricted by virtue of the provisions of their constitution, memoranda and articles of association (although greatly reduced by the weakening of the ultra vires doctrine[1]) and associations and institutions by their rules and constitutions. Leasing companies which are banks fall under the supervision of the FSA and leasing transactions are ordinarily treated as loans for the purposes of calculating the institution's risk/asset ratio.

1 Companies Act 1985, s 35A.

27.2 METHODS OF FINANCING

The primary criteria which apply to the selection of sources of funding are their cost, efficiency (including accounting treatment) and tax effectiveness. These, in their various orders of priority, will ultimately dictate the method of funding adopted.

27.2.1 Equity

Equity or share capital is the risk-bearing capital of a company and can take the form of various classes of shares such as ordinary, preference or deferred shares, each with their separate rights. Every company, unless it is a company limited by guarantee (and which is usually utilised for non-profit making associations or charities) requires to have a share capital.

27.2.2   Deposits

Banks, building societies and other authorised deposit-taking institutions will utilise the monies received by way of deposit from customers and their members for lending on to borrowers. The importance of this source of funding was recently highlighted by the funding crisis involving Northern Rock plc which relied almost exclusively on the availability of wholesale funding. When banks ceased to lend to each other Northern Rock's funding resource dried up.

27.2.3   Borrowing

There are many types and sources of loans ranging from simple bank loan facilities, such as sterling dealing lines, to Eurocurrency floating rate loans. The appropriate type of loan facility will be determined by the factors already mentioned, the amount to be raised and the ease with which this can be achieved.

A loan may be a fixed sum loan or an overdraft or other revolving credit facility and may be raised from one or several lenders, in the form of a syndicated loan. In the case of more mature and larger companies, borrowings may be effected by the issue of debenture loan stock, secured on the assets of the borrowing company. Eurobonds, debt securities denominated in a foreign currency, might also be used to raise funds abroad.

The capacity of a company to raise funds is dependent upon its ability to provide security, its gearing ratio (the relationship between its indebtedness and its equity capital) and its ability to meet its repayment obligations. Together these will affect the borrower's credit rating which will, in turn, have a direct bearing on the cost of loan finance; in simple terms, the higher the credit rating of the borrower, the cheaper will be its cost of funding.

27.2.4   Funding of leasing companies

Whilst many of the methods of funding described above apply equally to leasing companies, they also enjoy certain unique methods of raising finance.

Head-lease finance involves interposing the lessee company between a superior lessor and the ultimate lessee. The head-lease takes the form of a master lease corresponding to a wholesale funding line of credit, and sharing all the characteristics of a lease. Its benefit is that the leasing company can be certain of the availability of leasing finance provided that the lease agreement entered into by the leasing company mirrors the provisions of the head lease agreement and that the tax and capital allowance provisions of the lease agreement match the corresponding provisions of the head lease. The ultimate sub-lessee may or may not be made aware of the existence of the head lease agreement at the outset or at all.

At the other end of the spectrum, leasing finance may be raised after leases have already been concluded. This would normally involve the assignment by the lessor, either by way of security or outright assignment, of the underlying lease receivables on their own or together with the transfer of the leased equipment.

Depending upon the commercial considerations, a lessor might enter into a total refinancing package substituting the financier as the lessor in new leasing agreements with the lessee, by way of novation of the original leases.

Accounting for leases and hire-purchase contracts, including sale and lease-back transactions, is subject to the Statement of Standard Accounting Practice.[1]

1 Statement of Standard Accounting Practice SSAP 21 or IAS 17 in the case of public companies.

27.2.5 Stock-in-trade finance

The expression 'stock-in-trade finance' is used as a generic description of on-going funding arrangements available to a dealer who provides his own finance. Examples are unit-stocking finance and block discounting or periodical assignments of agreements.

Unit-stocking finance is the arrangement whereby vehicles are supplied on consignment to dealers with the consignor invariably retaining title to the vehicles. The consignment may take the form of conditional sale under which the dealer only incurs liability for the purchase price of a vehicle when the dealer effects a sale of the vehicle to a customer. Unit-stocking finance is in fact a method of subsidised extended credit.

Block discounting is a form of receivables financing. It takes place after the dealer has entered into the relevant finance or lease agreements. Under a block discounting agreement the dealer might sell the receivables under the agreements (alone or together with title to the underlying goods) to a financier. The dealer may then continue to collect the receivables as disclosed or undisclosed agent for the financier. Commercial considerations will often dictate that no notice of the assignment is given to the customers so that the arrangement constitutes merely an equitable assignment. Where notice of the assignment is given to customers (e.g. where the purchaser of the receivables collects payments directly from customers), the arrangement constitutes a legal assignment. Block discounting might also take the form of a loan by a financier secured by a charge on the finance and leasing agreements.

27.2.6 Refinancing techniques

27.2.6.1 Securitisation

Securitisation is a financing technique whereby the originator of a pool of assets (such as residential or commercial mortgages, credit card or other receivables, personal loans or leases) sells or transfers such assets to a special-purpose vehicle ('SPV') which funds the purchase by issuing debt securities (typically medium-term notes or commercial paper) into the capital markets. The debt securities are typically divided into several different layers or 'tranches' with the junior tranche absorbing any losses first and attracting the highest rate of return as compensation. The transaction is structured so that the income produced by the purchased assets is sufficient for the issuing vehicle to fund the payment obligations arising under the debt securities and to redeem them at maturity.

There are many reasons why an originator may choose securitisation over other financing techniques, including the opportunity to remove assets from its balance sheet for regulatory (in the case of a bank originator) and/or accounting purposes (in some cases without the need for an actual sale of the assets) thereby freeing up capital for further investment, the opportunity to access diverse funding sources and the opportunity to access the cheaper funding often offered by the capital markets. The rules governing structures for originators which are UK banks are set out in the FSA Handbook. Originators in the UK looking to remove assets from their balance sheet for accounting purposes using securitisation will have to do so in accordance with either IFRS or UK GAAP.

Securitisation is usually associated with refinancing of assets which have already been originated, but this is not necessarily the case. A variation of the theme is the creation, in advance of the credit or leasing agreements coming into existence, of a SPV which acts as a borrowing company, whose sole activity is to purchase and fund selected credit and leasing receivables. It is possible to structure the transaction so that the SPV would be off balance sheet to all parties to the transaction.

27.2.6.2   Swaps

The swap market assists traders to solve financial problems arising out of variations in interest rates and currency exchange rates, different taxation regimes, rates of inflation and degrees of creditworthiness.

In its simplest form a swapped contract is an agreement between two parties by which one agrees to pay the other on a specified date amounts calculated by reference to the interest which would have accrued over a given period on the same notional principal sum, assuming different rates of interest to be payable.[1]

1 *Hazell v Hammersmith and Fulham London Borough Council* [1991] 2 WLR 372 at 378–9, HL.

27.2.6.3   Cash settlement systems

Grantors of credit facilities which operate internationally, such as credit card companies, might enter into a multilateral netting agreement in order to avoid duplicated foreign exchange deals and so as to avoid additional fund transfer costs. Each party to the agreement settles its position by a transfer in the local currency to a local netting centre and all local netting centres settle their positions vis-à-vis the international netting centre. In this way the number and amount of cross-border remittances and the volume of foreign exchange transactions required to effect the settlement of outstanding liability is reduced.

27.3   OUTSOURCING

An increasingly common phenomenon is the outsourcing by consumer lending firms of IT and telecommunications, business process or facilities management services.

Outsourcing is defined as:[1]

> 'an arrangement of any form between a firm and a service provider by which that service provider performs a process, a service or an activity which would otherwise be taken by the firm itself.'[2]

The FSA has always expressed concerns that outsourcing creates operational risk. The central theme to the FSA's approach is set out in SYSC 3.2.G. In simple terms it states that a firm cannot contract out of its regulatory obligations. Outsourcing should not be considered a method for reducing a firm's regulatory obligations. It goes on to illustrate the point by stating that, under Principle 3, a firm should take reasonable care to supervise the discharge of outsourced functions by its contractor.

The implementation of the Markets in Financial Instruments Directive[3] ('MiFID') and the Capital Requirements Directive[4] ('CRD') has not altered the FSA's general approach but has introduced additional regulatory provisions derived directly from the EU legislation, with which firms must comply. These additional regulatory provisions cover issues such as the following:

- obligation to avoid undue additional operational risk;

- obligation to have adequate policies and procedures;

- notification to the FSA;

- due diligence;

- service management;

- disclosure, audit and maintenance of records;

- confidential information;

- business continuity and termination;

- written agreement.

Further consideration of this area is outside the scope of this book.[5]

1 Commission Directive No. 2006/73/EC implementing Directive 2004/39/EC of the European Parliament and of the Council as regards organisational requirements and operating conditions for investment firms and defined terms for the purposes of that Directive ('MiFID Implementing Directive').
2 Article 2(6) of the MiFID Implementing Directive.
3 Directive 2004/39/EC of the European Parliament and of the Council on the markets in financial instruments amending Council Directives 85/611/EC and 93/6/EEC and Directive 2000/12/EC of the European Parliament and of the Council and repealing Council Directive 93/22/EEC ('MiFID').
4 Capital Requirements Directive.
5 See 'Outsourcing Contracts – a Practical Guide' by Amanda Lewis, published by City & Financial Publishing, which provides a comprehensive description of the business and legal issues relating to outsourcing, and includes a chapter on all of the FSA guidance relevant to outsourcing.

Chapter 28

Miscellaneous accounting and tax aspects

28.1 ACCOUNTING FOR LEASES AND HIRE-PURCHASE CONTRACTS

The subject is governed by SSAP 21, the Statement of Standard Accounting Practice of the Institute of Chartered Accountants in England and Wales and Financial Reporting Standard 5 ('FRS 5') entitled 'Reporting the Substance of Transaction'. SSAP 21 codifies accepted practice for some aspects of lease accounting and requires assets held under finance leases and the related leasing obligations to be capitalised on a company's balance sheet. Capitalisation of assets held under finance leases results in the company's assets and obligations being readily apparent. Hire-purchase contracts which are of a financing nature are to be accounted for on a similar basis to finance leases.

A lease is a finance lease if it transfers substantially all the risks and rewards incidental to ownership and a lease is classified as an operating lease if it does not.[1]

Whether a lease is classified as one or the other depends on the substance of the transaction rather than the form of the contract. A lease would normally be classified as a finance lease if the lease term is for the major part of the economic life of the asset or if, at the inception of the lease, the present value of the minimum lease payments, including any initial payment, amounts to substantially all (normally 90% or more) of the fair value of the leased asset.[2] Since a lessor and lessee are obliged to apply the test independently, each may treat the asset differently in their accounts.

1 IAS 17 and SSAP 21, para 15. See also paras. 5.4.1 and 5.4.2 above.
2 IAS 17; SSAP 21 para 15.

28.1.1 Accounting by lessee

A finance lease should be recorded in the balance sheet of a lessee as an asset subject to an obligation to pay the rentals. At the inception of the lease the sum to be recorded both as an asset and as a liability should be the present value of the minimum lease payments, derived by discounting them at the interest rate implicit in the lease. In practice the fair value of the asset will often be a sufficiently close approximation to the present value of the minimum lease payments and may then be substituted for it.

The total finance charge under a finance lease should be allocated to accounting periods during the lease term so as to produce a constant periodic rate of charge on the remaining balance. The asset should be depreciated over the shorter of the lease term and the asset's useful life. In the case of a hire-purchase contract which has the characteristics of a finance lease, the asset should be depreciated over its useful life. The rental under an operating lease should be charged on a straight-line basis over the lease term.

28.1.2   Accounting by lessor

The payments due from the lessee under a finance lease should be recorded as a debt in the amount of the net investment in the lease after making provision for any bad and doubtful rentals receivable. The payments should be allocated to accounting periods so as to give a constant periodic rate of return on the lessor's net cash investment and release in each period.

Tax-free grants which are available to the lessor against the purchase price of assets for leasing should be spread over the period of the lease.

In the case of operating leases, the asset should be recorded as a fixed asset and depreciated over its useful life. Rental income should be recognised on a straight-line basis over the period of the lease.

28.1.3   Manufacturer or dealer lessor

A manufacturer or dealer lessor should not recognise a selling profit under an operating lease. The selling profit under a finance lease should be restricted to the excess of the fair value of the asset over the manufacturer's or dealer's cost less any grants receivable by the manufacturer or dealer.

28.2   SALE AND LEASEBACK TRANSACTIONS

28.2.1   Accounting by the seller/lessee

SSAP 21 provides that in a sale and lease-back transaction which results in a finance lease, any apparent profit or loss should be deferred and amortised in the financial statements of the seller/lessee over the shorter of the lease term and the useful life of the asset. A sale and lease-back arrangement where there is also an option for the seller/lessee to repurchase the asset will now be governed by FRS5.[1]

In the case of an operating lease, if the transaction is established at fair value, any profit or loss should be recognised immediately. Separate rules apply where the sale price is below or above fair value.

Finance Act 2004 introduced anti-avoidance legislation to prevent double tax benefits arising in the leaseback of plant or machinery by retention of capital allowances at the same time as obtaining a deduction for the leaseback rentals.[2]

1 See FRS 5, para 4 and Application Note B – Sale and Repurchase Agreements.
2 Capital Allowances Act 2001, ss 228A to 228M.

28.2.2 Accounting by the buyer/lessor

A buyer/lessor should account for a sale and lease-back in the same way as he accounts for other leases.

28.3 LEASING AND TAXATION

HMRC has issued a statement of practice[1] setting out their approach to leases where SSAP 21 has been applied and where it has not.

1 HMRC Statement of Practice 3/91.

28.3.1 Cases where SSAP 21 is applied

Notwithstanding that SSAP 21 requires a proportion of the rentals payable to be treated as capital repayment, the rentals remain, in law, revenue payments for the use of the asset and for tax purposes the whole of the rentals should be allocated to the periods of account for which the asset is leased. Normally the finance charge element of the rentals will be deductible in computing the profits of that period. In determining what proportion of the lessee's capital repayment element should be allowed for tax purposes in a period of account, HMRC will normally be prepared to accept the properly computed commercial depreciation of the asset charged to the profit and loss account.

28.3.2 Cases where SSAP 21 is not applied

As finance lease rentals are revenue payments for the use of the asset over time, in accordance with correct principles of commercial accounting they should be allocated to the periods of account for which the asset is leased under the 'accruals' concept. For tax purposes, the rentals are deductible in computing profits on the same basis as they are allocated to the periods of account under the accruals concept. There is no entitlement to deduct the rentals for tax purposes merely by reference to the due dates of payments.

28.3.3 Exceptions

Where the period of the lease payments is less than the commercial life expectancy of the leased equipment relief is only available over the economic life of the leased equipment.

28.4 CAPITAL ALLOWANCES

Capital allowances are the amount of depreciation allowed by HMRC to be off-set against taxable profits and are governed by the Capital Allowances Act 2001. Allowances can be claimed on the cost of plant or machinery (qualifying expenditure) purchased for use in a qualifying activity (e.g. a trade).[1] Qualifying expenditure in respect of each item is allocated to a pool on which the owner claims the allowances.

Special provisions apply to cars. If a car is not a qualifying car (e.g. not a car for hire) and capital expenditure incurred on it exceeds £12,000, it must be allocated to a single asset pool and annual writing down allowances cannot exceed £3,000.[2] Cars costing less than £12,000 are allocated to the taxpayer's main pool for capital allowances purposes.

A separate class pool is used to capture total expenditure relating to long life assets or assets leased overseas. Long-life assets are plant or machinery with a useful economic life of at least 25 years. They only attract writing down allowances of 6%, calculated annually on a reducing balance.[3] All other assets are allocated to the main pool. The writing down allowances on short-life assets is 25%, calculated annually on a reducing balance.[4]

Certain qualifying expenditure qualifies for first year allowances. This includes expenditure incurred by a small or medium sized enterprise on plant or machinery, excluding expenditure on long life assets (currently at 40% first year allowance)[5] and expenditure on energy-saving plant and machinery (currently 100% first year allowance).

As regards hire-purchase agreements, the plant or machinery is treated as owned by the person who hires and shall or may become the owner of the asset at any time when he is entitled to the benefit of the contract, so far as it relates to the plant and machinery. At the time that the plant and machinery is brought into use by the hirer for the purposes of a qualifying activity, he is treated as having incurred all capital expenditure in respect of the same.[6] However this does not apply to expenditure incurred on plant or machinery which is a fixture.[7]

The lessor, as owner of equipment under the lease, is generally entitled to all allowances in relation to the assets. An exception is made where the plant or machinery is provided by the lessee, the lessee incurs capital expenditure for the purposes of a qualifying activity and the lessee does not own the plant or machinery.[8]

Allowances under the Capital Allowances Act 2001 are only available if the person carries on a qualifying activity, notably a trade, profession or vocation or the special leasing of plant or machinery.[9]

1 'Qualifying Activity' is defined in chapter 2 of Part 2 of the Act.
2 Capital Allowances Act 2001, s 74 and see also ss 75–79.
3 Capital Allowances Act 2001, s 91 for meaning of 'long-life asset' and s 102.
4 Capital Allowances Act 2001, s 83 for meaning of 'short-life asset' and s 56.

5 The rate of 40% applies for expenditure incurred on or after 6 April 2008 for income tax purposes and on or after 1 April 2008 for corporation tax purposes.
6 Capital Allowances Act 2001, s 67.
7 Capital Allowances Act 2001, ss 69 and 173.
8 Capital Allowances Act 2001, s 70.
9 Capital Allowances Act 2001, ss 11 and 15.

28.5 'FUNDING LEASE' AND 'LONG FUNDING LEASE'

Finance Act 2006 introduced the new concepts of a 'funding lease' and a 'long funding lease' into the Capital Allowances Act 2001.[1] The intention of the regime is to treat lease finance and loan finance in the same way and the regime is therefore restricted to leases which are essentially financing transactions.

A 'funding lease' is a lease of plant or machinery which, at its inception, meets one or more of the following tests: a finance lease test, a lease payments test or the useful economic life test, subject to specified exceptions.[2]

A 'long funding lease' is a funding lease which meets the following conditions: it is not a short lease, it is not an excluded lease of so-called background plant or machinery for a building and it is not excluded by the *de minimis* provision for plant or machinery leased with land.[3]

Under the new regime, capital allowances in respect of long funding leases are given to the lessee rather than to the lessor. The lessee may qualify for first year allowances in respect of expenditure on the provision of the leased plant or machinery. Only those sums which, in accordance with generally accepted accounting practice would be treated as finance charges, can be deducted from the lessee's taxable profits. The lessor is disabled from claiming allowances which he would otherwise have been entitled to in respect of the leased plant or machinery and the rental earnings for the relevant period is the amount which, in accordance with generally accepted accounting practice, would be treated as the gross return on the investment.[4]

1 Capital Allowances Act 2001, ss 70A to 70YJ.
2 *Ibid.*, s 70 J.
3 *Ibid.*, s 70 G.
4 See paras 7.121 to 7.140 (and generally) *Tolley's Capital Allowances 2007–8*, 20th ed. by K. Walton and D. Smailes.

28.6 VALUE ADDED TAX[1]

28.6.1 Loans

The making of loans and the granting of credit is exempt from VAT. This includes credit granted in connection with the supply of goods or services provided that a separate charge is made for the credit and disclosed to the customer.[2]

1 Value Added Tax Act 1994, s 31 and Sch 9, Part II, Group 5; Value Added Tax Regulations 1995, SI 1995/2518; HMRC Notice 701/49 VAT: Finances.
2 See HMRC Notice 701/49 para 4.2 and also *Customs & Excise Comrs v Diners Club Ltd* [1989] 2 All ER 385, CA.

28.6.2 Supplies by credit, debit and charge card companies

Charges made by credit or charge card companies to retailers who accept the cards in payment for goods or services they have provided are exempt. This includes interchange fees and charges in the form of a discount on the amount reimbursed to the retailer or other outlet. Charges made by a debit card issuer to the retailer or outlet which accepts the cards are also exempt.

Charges payable by cardholders such as interest, annual membership and the like, are exempt.[1]

The following charges by ATM providers are also exempt supplies: charges for the facility to obtain money, the provision of money, transaction processing or the operation of accounts.[2]

1 HMRC Notice 701/49 para 4.8.
2 *Ibid.*, para 2.9.

28.6.3 Instalment credit finance

The charges for credit supplied under a hire-purchase, conditional sale or credit sale agreement, without involving a finance company, are exempt from VAT if the amount of such charges is separately disclosed to the customer.[1]

If the transaction is financed by a finance company which becomes the owner of the goods, the retailer's supply of goods to the finance company is taxable. The finance company's supply of the goods to the customer is taxable but the separate supply of credit is exempt if the credit charge is disclosed seperately to the customer.

Option fees in a hire-purchase agreement, documentation fees, arrangement fees and similar additional fees in conditional sale and credit sale agreements are exempt from VAT provided that the fees are specified in the agreement and do not exceed a total of £10 and the agreement includes an exempt supply of instalment credit finance.[2]

In *Primback Ltd v Comrs of Customs & Excise*[3] the Court of Appeal held that retailers who sold furniture on interest free credit to customers with the finance company buying the furniture at a lower price than that paid by customers, were not obliged to pay VAT on the full retail price but only on the sums received from the finance company. It was the court's view that to require retailers to pay VAT on the full price paid by the customers rather than on the sum the retailers actually received from the finance company was to require payment of VAT on an exempt supply, in conflict with art 27 of the Sixth Directive of 17 May 1977 on the Harmonisation of Turnover Taxes (77/388/EEC). The House of Lords referred the matter to the European Court for a preliminary ruling. The European Court overruled the Court of Appeal finding that, since an agreement between the claimant retailer and the customer in each case was that the customer would pay the full advertised price, which was known in advance and invoiced as such and did not vary according to the method of payment, that price was the consideration for the goods and the taxable amount.[4]

1 Value Added Tax Act 1994, Sch. 9, Group 5, Item 3.
2 Value Added Tax Act 1994, Sch. 9, Group 5, Item 4.
3 [1996] CCLR 81, CA.
4 [2001] 1 WLR 1693.

28.6.4   Credit brokerage and intermediary services

Charges levied by a credit-broker, mortgage broker or money broker for arrangements for any advance of money or the grant of any credit are exempt from VAT provided that the intermediary takes an active part in arranging a specific supply which is clearly envisaged at the time the services are supplied. The arrangements may include helping the client to complete the application form, checking completed application forms and forwarding the forms to the grantor of the loan or credit. Simply introducing a customer to a credit broker or to the grantor of credit finance will not result in the services being exempt from VAT. For the exemption to apply to the 'bringing together' of customer and creditor, the intermediary must be involved in an active, independent and transparent role and not merely act 'in the shoes' of the creditor.[1]

Supplies which may be connected with financial services but which are not exempt include debt collection and credit control services.

1 HMRC Guidance on VAT and Finance (HMRC 701/49 para 9).

28.6.5   Equipment leasing

Rentals under leasing or hire agreements are subject to VAT whether the agreement is a finance lease or an operating lease. VAT must be charged on each rental due under the lease agreement. The tax point, namely the date which determines when the tax must be paid by the finance company, is usually the earlier of the issue of a VAT invoice or receipt of the rental payment.

Where the lease or hire agreement contains an option to purchase clause, i.e. where it is a hire-purchase or lease purchase agreement, no VAT is payable in respect of the finance charges.[1]

1 Value Added Tax Act 1994, Sch 9, Part II, Group 5, item 3.

28.6.6   Taxable services

The supply of credit management services, when the supplier does not grant the credit, is taxable.[1] The supply of debt collection services is taxable.[2]

1 Value Added Tax Act 1994, Sch 9, Group 5, Item 5; HMRC Notice 701/49 para 4.10.
2 HMRC Notice 701/49 para 5.10.

28.6.7   Bad debt relief

Bad debt relief can be claimed on supplies of goods made by way of hire-purchase or conditional sale where the customer has defaulted. Supplies have two components, a supply of goods and a supply of associated finance. Suppliers are permitted to allocate each payment received from defaulting customers to goods and to finance in the same ratio as the total costs of goods and the total cost of finance to the customer.[1] In the case of repossessed goods, where the disposal of the repossessed goods are subject to VAT, a supplier need not deduct the proceeds of the disposal from the outstanding debt of the customer when claiming bad debt relief.[2]

1   Customs and Excise Business Brief 19/2001 issued 7 December 2001.
2   Regulation 170A of the Value Added Tax Regulations 1995 (1995/2518) and see Revenue & Customs Brief 14/07 issued 13 February 2007.

Chapter 29

The European Community perspective

29.1 THE ROAD TO EUROPEAN COMMUNITY HARMONISATION

29.1.1 The background

Council Directive 87/102/EEC embodied minimum harmonisation of consumer credit law across the European Community and largely reflected the basic elements of consumer credit law in the United Kingdom. The Directive was amended on two occasions, first by the Directive of 22 February 1990 (90/88/EEC) and then by the Directive of 16 February 1998 (98/7/EEC).

In 1995 the Commission presented a report on the operation of the Directive and undertook a consultation with interested parties. It presented a report in 1996 which disclosed substantial differences between the laws of the Member States in consumer credit law.

In June 2001 the European Commission issued a Discussion Paper for the further amendment of Directive 87/102/EEC. It followed the Commission's conclusion in 1995 (some six years earlier!) that the Directive was no longer sufficiently in step with the situation of the consumer credit market. The Commission ordered a series of studies on a range of subjects: mortgage credit in the EEA; methods of calculation of the APR; harmonisation of cost elements of the APR; the role of intermediaries in the grant of consumer credit; and consequences of non-performance of the credit agreement. The Commission was troubled by the fact that there had been only marginal growth in the grant of credit across the European frontier-free market.

In September 2002 the Commission proposed a Directive aimed at full harmonisation of national legislation. This was rejected by the European Parliament in April 2004. The Commission then submitted an amended proposal enunciating the following guidelines:

(1) redefinition of the Directive's scope so as to adapt it to the new market situation and better tracking of the demarcation line between consumer credit and real estate credit;

(2) new arrangements to take account not only of creditors but also credit intermediaries;

(3) an information framework for the credit grantor to enable him to better appreciate the risks involved in the grant of credit;

(4) more comprehensive information for consumers and guarantors;

(5) more equitable sharing of responsibilities between the consumer and 'the professional'; and

(6) improvement in the processing of payment incidents.

The driving force behind the new Directive is to be found in the Recitals to the Directive of 2008. In summary they state the following:

The *de facto* and *de jure* situation resulting from national differences in some cases leads to distortions of competition among creditors in the Community and creates obstacles in the internal market where Member States havve adopted different mandatory provisions more stringent than those provided for in Directive 87/102/EEC. This restricts consumers' ability to make direct use of the gradually increasing availability of cross-border credit. Those distortions and restrictions may in turn have consequences in terms of the demand for goods and services.[1] The development of a more transparent and efficient credit market within the area without internal frontiers is vital in order to promote the development of cross-border activities.[2] Full harmonisation is necessary in order to ensure that all consumers in the Community enjoy a high and equivalent level of protection of their interests and to create a genuine internal market.[3]

In May 2007 the Council of the European Union, by a qualified majority reached, agreement on the Commission's modified proposal for a Directive on credit agreements for consumers to replace the existing Consumer Credit Directive.

The key features of the Council's agreement were the following:

(1) application: the Directive will not apply to specified exempt consumer credit agreements, to consumer credit agreements secured by a land mortgage or to hire agreements;

(2) pre-contractual and contractual information: there was to be standard information in the form of pre-contractual information, to enable borrowers to compare different offers;

(3) right of withdrawal: as a general principle the consumer was to have a period of fourteen calendar days to withdraw from a credit agreement without having to provide a reason;

(4) early repayment: a debtor should be able to discharge fully or partially his obligations under a credit agreement at any time and be entitled to a reduction in the total cost of credit. Where the agreement is at a fixed rate of interest, the creditor should be entitled to prescribed compensation;

(5) APR and 'borrowing rate': the APR and the 'borrowing rate' must be stated in advertising information, pre-contractual information and contractual information. In contractual information for overdrafts, the creditor might state either the borrowing rate and charges, or the APR;

(6)   assignment of rights: a consumer must be informed of any assignment of the agreement except where the original creditor, in agreement with the assignee, continues to service the credit.

The Common Position of the Council was reached in September 2007 and amended, in limited respects, by the European Parliament in January 2008. The amended version was accepted by the Commission on 25 February 2008 and approved by the Council on 7 April 2008. The Directive must be implemented by the Member States by 12 May 2010, two years after its publication in the Official Journal of the European Union.

29.1.2   The Consumer Credit Directive

The following are the principal provisions of the Directive:

(a)   It applies to credit agreements with consumers relating to credit of between €200 and of €75,000, repayable after more than one month. It does not apply to credit agreements secured by a mortgage or to hire agreements.

(b)   Advertising, which indicates an interest rate or the cost of credit, must include prescribed standard information.

(c)   In good time before the consumer is bound by a credit agreement or an agreement for overdraft facilities, the creditor or credit intermediary as appropriate, must supply the consumer with pre-contractual information in the form of the Standard European Consumer Credit Information, as set out in the relevant Annex to the Directive.

(d)   Member States must ensure that credit checks are carried out and determine how the obligation to assess the creditworthiness of the customer is to operate. Creditors and credit intermediaries must supply the consumer with sufficient information and explanations to enable him to assess the suitability of the proposed credit agreement.

(e)   Member States must ensure access to databases to creditors from other Member States in order to facilitate cross-border credit.

(f)   Prescribed formalities apply to credit agreements and the consumer under a fixed-term credit agreement is entitled to request an amortisation table.

(g)   The consumer may end a so-called open-end credit agreement free of charge at any time, subject to a maximum notice period of one month.

(h)   The consumer has a 14-day period in which to withdraw from a credit agreement without having to state a reason. Where Member States have legislation in place in respect of linked agreements that provide that funds cannot be made available before a specified period, they may allow the withdrawal period to be reduced at the consumer's request. (This does not apply to the UK as it does not have such legislation.)

(i)   The consumer is entitled to repay the credit early at any time. The creditor will be entitled to fair and objectively justified compensation for costs directly linked to early repayment of credit up to 1% of the amount of credit repaid early (or 0.5% if the repayment takes place within 12 months of the end of the credit agreement). Member States may allow lenders to claim further compensation upon proof of greater loss. Any compensation may not exceed an amount of interest the consumer would have paid during the period between early repayment and the termination date.

(j)   The Directive contains a mathematical equation for the calculation of the Annual Percentage Rate of Charge (APR).

(k)   Member States must ensure that creditors are supervised by an independent authority.

(l)   The Directive sets minimum standards for credit intermediaries in respect of the disclosure of their powers and fees.

(m) Member States must set up out-of-court dispute resolution procedures.

(n)   The creditor must give the consumer notice of the arrangement of his agreement, unless the creditor continues to service the agreement *vis à vis* the consumer.

The Directive is a maximum harmonisation Directive which means that Member States may not impose lesser or greater requirements than those set out in the Directive in relation to its subject matter. However, Member States remain free to prescribe their own requirements in relation to areas outside the Directive.

1   Recital (4).
2   Recital (6).
3   Recital (9).

29.2   THE DIRECTIVE'S IMPACT ON CCA 1974

Where the Directive directly addresses matters governed by CCA 1974, it sets maximum standards and prescriptions with which UK law must conform and which it may not exceed. This will require amendment of CCA 1974 by some time in 2010.

In areas which will not be governed by the Directive, UK law in general, and CCA 1974 in particular, is likely to continue to regulate. These areas include the following:

(a)   consumer hire agreements;

(b)   consumer credit agreements for business use where the credit amount does not exceed £25,000. (It is to be noted that the Directive defines 'consumer' as a natural person who, in transactions covered by the Directive, is acting for purposes which are outside his trade, business or profession);

(c)   consumer credit agreements where the credit amount exceeds €75,000;

(d) exempt agreements under s 16A where the credit amount exceeds £75,000 (exemption relating to high net worth debtors and hirers) and s 16B (exemption relating to businesses) in relation to agreements under paragraph (b) above;

(e) hire-purchase agreements, although the UK Parliament might decide to bring them within the scope of the legislation implementing the Directive, on account of hire-purchase agreements being treated as credit agreements in CCA 1974;

(f) the hirer's right of early termination under a hire-purchase agreement and the buyer's right of early termination under a conditional sale agreement (s 99 of CCA – so-called 'voluntary termination' or 'VT') as this relates to early termination of the agreement and not early repayment under Art 16 of the Directive). Once again the UK Parliament might choose to bring this within the scope of the implementing legislation;

(g) post-contract information requirements including statements and statutory notices;

(h) regulation of ancillary credit business, except for credit brokerage to the extent that it is governed by the provisions of the Directive governing credit intermediaries;

(i) joint and several liability under s 75 of CCA 1974 (as expressly recognised by Recital (9) of the Directive).

29.3 CREDIT INSTITUTIONS AND THE EUROPEAN PASSPORT

The Second Banking Directive of 89/646/EEC on credit institutions provided for the co-ordination of laws, regulations and administrative provisions relating to the taking up and pursuit of the business of credit institutions. Inter alia, it distinguishes between a 'home Member State' and a 'host Member State'. A home Member State is a Member State in which a credit institution has been authorised in accordance with the Council Directive 77/780/EEC. A host Member State is a Member State in which a credit institution has a branch or in which it provides services.

A home Member State is responsible for the authorisation of credit grantors and a host Member State is obliged to permit the credit institution of a home Member State to operate in its territory. Minimum requirements are laid down for the grant of authorisation of credit institutions in home Member States. The Directive contains a list of activities which are subject to regulation by Member States. These include lending, financial leasing, issuing and administering means of payment, (such as credit cards, travellers' cheques and bankers' drafts), guarantees, money broking and credit reference services.

The Banking Co-ordination (Second Council Directive) Regulations 1992[1] gave effect to the Second Council Directive on the coordination of loans, regulations and administrative provisions relating to the taking up and pursuit of the business of credit institutions (Directive 89/646/EEC). The regulations coined the expression 'UK institution' which means a UK authorised institution or a UK subsidiary. A credit institution is a UK authorised institution if it is incorporated in the United Kingdom, has its principal place of business in the United Kingdom and, in the case of a bank, is authorised by the FSA under Pt IV of the Financial Services and Markets Act 2000 (FSMA 2000) (previously by the Bank of England under the Banking Act or by the Building Societies' Commission under the Building Societies Act).

The regulations established the concept of a 'European authorised institution', which is a European institution or a European subsidiary with equivalent authorisation. As a result of the Directive and the regulations, banks and building societies, and their subsidiaries, are able to enjoy the benefits of holding a so-called 'European passport' which enable them to conduct banking, consumer credit and investment business throughout the European Community.

Before a UK firm can exercise passport rights in another Member State it must give the FSA notice of intention to establish a branch in the host state, the FSA must have given a consent notice to the host state regulator and the latter must have notified the firm of the applicable provisions or two months must have elapsed since the date on which the FSA gave the consent notice. If the FSA refuses consent the authorised person may refer the matter to the Tribunal set up under that Act.[2]

A firm authorised in another Member State ('the home state') which intends to carry on regulated activities (i.e. governed by the FSMA 2000) in the UK ('the host state') must comply with corresponding requirements to those governing UK firms wanting to exercise passport rights in another EEA state.[3]

The Second Council Directive has been replaced by the Banking Directive 2000 (2000/12/EC) and the above Regulations by regulations made under FSMA 2000.[4] Firms in other Member States which wish to operate in the UK are subject to the same approval regime, as spelt out in s 31(1)(b) and Sch 3 of the FSMA 2000.

1 SI 1992/3218.
2 FSMA 2000, ss 31(1)(b) and 37, read with Sch 3, para 19.
3 FSMA 2000, s 31(1)(c) read with Sch 4.
4 Financial Services and Markets Act 2000 (Consequential Amendments and Repeals) Order 2001, SI 2001/3649, which came into force on 1 December 2001.

29.4   LICENSING AND CONSUMER CREDIT EEA FIRMS

The very inelegant description of a 'consumer credit EEA firm' refers to an EEA firm which does not have its head office in the UK, falls within para 5(a), (b), or (c) of Sch 3 to the FSMA 2000 and carries on, or seeks to carry on, consumer credit, consumer hire or ancillary credit business for which a licence would ordinarily be required.[1]

Such a firm does not need a Standard Licence to carry on any activity which the firm is permitted to conduct under para 15 of Sch 3 to the FSMA 2000.

The provisions of the CCA 1974 requiring a person to hold a licence in order to carry on a permitted activity do not apply to a firm which qualifies for authorisation as a result of paras 12 and 13 of Sch 3 to the FSMA, unless the Director

General of Fair Trading has exercised the power conferred on him by FSMA 2000, s 203 in relation to the firm. Under s 203 the Director General of Fair Trading is given power to prohibit the carrying on of consumer credit business by a consumer credit EEA firm if that firm or any of its employees does any of the things specified in CCA 1974, s 25(2)(a) to (d). This relates to the fitness of a person to be a licensee under the Act.

1 See footnote 4 to para 29.3 and especially Art 189A.

29.5 UNFAIR CONTRACT TERMS

The Directive on Unfair Terms in Consumer Contracts 93/13/EEC aimed to approximate the laws, regulations and administrative provisions of the Member States relating to unfair terms in contracts concluded between a seller or supplier and a consumer where the contract has not been individually negotiated. It thus also extends to standard form credit and hire agreements.

A contractual term will be regarded as unfair if, contrary to the requirement of good faith, it causes a significant imbalance in the parties' rights and obligations to the detriment of the consumer. In the assessment of whether a particular term is unfair, the Directive adopts similar tests to the Guidelines to be found in the Unfair Contracts Terms Act 1977.

The Directive also requires agreements to be drafted in plain, intelligible language. In the event of ambiguity, the provision will be interpreted in favour of the consumer.

The Directive was implemented in the United Kingdom by the Unfair Terms in Consumer Contracts Regulations 1994,[1] which came into force in July 1995 and they have since been replaced by the Unfair Terms in Consumer Contracts Regulations 1999,[2] which came into force in October 1999.

1 SI 1994/3159.
2 SI 1999/2083.
3 See the discussion on the Regulations at paras 8.3.4.1, 8.3.4.2 and 8.3.4.3

29.6 INJUNCTIONS DIRECTIVE

The so-called 'Injunctions Directive', Directive 98/27/EC, was made in May 1998 and provided for qualified bodies in Member States to be empowered to institute injunction proceedings for the protection of consumers' interests and to stop any non-compliance with specified Council Directives. They include Directives relating to misleading advertising, contracts negotiated away from business premises, consumer credit, television broadcasting, package travel and holidays, unfair terms in consumer contracts, timeshare contracts and distance contracts.

The Directive was enacted in the United Kingdom originally by way of the Stop Now Orders (EC Directive) Regulations 2001[1] and now in the form of enforcement orders under Part 8 of the Enterprise Act 2002.

1 SI 2001/1422.

29.7 APPLICABLE LAW AND JURISDICTION

29.7.1 Applicable law

The applicable law in respect of a consumer contract is determined by the Contracts (Applicable Law) Act 1990 which implements the Convention on the Law Applicable to Contractual Obligations (the 'Rome Convention') of 1980. The Convention displaces the common law conflict of law rules.

Article 3 of the Convention provides that a contract shall be governed by the law chosen by the parties. Article 4(1) provides that, in the absence of a choice of law, the contract should be governed by the law of the country with which it is most closely connected. Article 4(2) presumes this to be the country where the party who is to effect the performance has at the time of the conclusion of the contract, his habitual residence or, in the case of a body corporate or unincorporate, its central administration or, if entered into within the course of that party's trade of profession, the country in which the principal place of business is situated or the performance is to be effected.

Article 5(2) states that, notwithstanding the provisions of Art 3, a choice of law made by the parties shall not have the result of depriving the consumer of the protection afforded to him by the mandatory rules of the law of the country in which he has his habitual residence:

(i) if in that country the conclusion of the contract was preceded by a specific invitation addressed to him or by advertising, and he had taken in that country all the steps necessary on his part for the conclusion of the contract, or

(ii) if the other party or his agent received the consumer's order in that country.

However, Art 5 does not apply to a contract for the supply of services where the services are to be supplied to the consumer exclusively in a country other than that in which he has his habitual residence.

Where the debtor resides or carries on business in England, he is *prima facie* within the protective provisions of CCA 1974. But such residence is not enough if that is the only point of contact with England. The transaction itself must have some real anchorage in England if CCA 1974 is to apply e.g. the essential steps necessary for the making of the contract were taken in England or the agreement results from advertising, negotiations etc. in England or the credit is to be advanced or repaid in England.[1]

If parties to a consumer credit agreement falling under a jurisdiction other than under English law, choose English law to govern their contract, they do not thereby contract into the provisions of CCA 1974. To quote Goode:

> 'The application of the CCA 1974 depends on the spatial reach which Parliament wanted it to have. If the connections with England are considered by the court such as to attract the CCA 1974 it will apply even if the agreement is otherwise governed by a foreign law. Conversely, if the connections with England are considered insufficient to bring the agreement within the Act it will not apply, despite the choice of English law, for the CCA 1974 operates only

within its own spatial limitations and is unaffected by conflict of law rules, which can neither reduce not expand its scope, except so far as the CCA 1974 itself otherwise provides.'[2]

The leading illustration of the spatial reach of CCA 1974 is *Office of Fair Trading v Lloyds TSB Bank plc*[3] where the House of Lords held that the liability of a creditor under s 75 of the CCA 1974 extends to credit agreements financing a supply transaction abroad.

Whilst the *lex situs* generally governs contracts relating to immovable property, where a credit agreement was entered into in England to finance timeshare purchasers in Portugal and Spain, *Jarrett v Barclays Bank plc*[4] held that a claim that the vendors had been guilty of misrepresentation and breach of contract against the defendants was justiciable under s 75 of CCA 1974 by reason of the defendants' status as debtors under regulated debtor-creditor-supplier agreements.

1 *Goode: Consumer Credit Law and Practice* (LexisNexis Butterworths), IC, [49.86].
2 *Ibid.*, EC, 49.59–49.80.
3 [2007] GCCR 6101, HL.
4 [1999] CGGR 2151, CA.

29.7.2 Jurisdiction

If the defendant is domiciled in a Member State, the Jurisdiction Rules in the Brussels Convention, (incorporated as Schedule 1 into the Civil Jurisdiction and Judgments Act 1982) apply. In all other cases, the jurisdiction rules or the national laws of the particular country will apply. Under the former, if one or more of the parties domiciled in a Member State has agreed that a court of a Member State shall have jurisdiction to settle any dispute, that court will have jurisdiction. Such jurisdiction is exclusive unless the parties have agreed otherwise.

CCA 1974 provides that for the purposes of the Act, any reference to 'the court' means, in relation to England and Wales, the county court, in relation to Scotland the sheriff court and in relation to Northern Ireland the High Court or the county court. In the absence of a contrary indication in CCA 1974, those courts have exclusive jurisdiction in respect of all actions and applications where specific reference is made to 'the court'. The Civil Procedure Rules provide that a claim may be commenced in any of the county courts, subject to the restrictions set out in the relevant Practice Direction.[1]

1 CPR, PD 7, para 7.1.

Chapter 30

Critical reflections on consumer credit legislation

The Consumer Credit Act 1974 was envisaged as a comprehensive, all-embracing piece of legislation which, together with the regulations made under it, would 'establish for the protection of consumers a new system, administered by the Director General of Fair Trading [now the Office of Fair Trading], of licensing and other control of traders concerned with the provision of credit, or the supply of goods on hire or hire-purchase, and their transactions, in place of the present enactments regulating moneylenders, pawnbrokers and hire-purchase traders and their transactions; and for related matters'.[1]

Over time, at least so far as mortgages are concerned, the Act has lost its comprehensive and all-embracing quality. Mortgages were largely removed from the Act by the extension of the exemption under s 16 to most mortgages granted by insurers, building societies and deposit-takers or banks. Subsequently most first legal mortgages and further advances were removed from its provisions and brought under the regime governed by the Financial Services and Markets Act 2000. This development, together with the Financial Services Authority acquiring jurisdiction over all insurance products, notably payment protection insurance, brought the Financial Services Authority into the forefront of consumer credit, resulting in a formal liaison between the Office of Fair Trading and the Financial Services Authority in respect of the control of lenders, as evidenced by the principles relating to Treating Customers Fairly and the convergence of consumer and competition policy. Other consumer protection legislation, notably in the form of the Unfair Terms in Consumer Contracts Regulation 1999 (and in due course in all probability also the Consumer Protection from Unfair Trading Regulations 2008) is producing a merger in policy and approach between the two regulators.

So far as hire is concerned, the provisions of the Consumer Credit Act and the Consumer Credit (Advertisements) Regulations 2004 relating to hire advertisements have been replaced by provisions in the Consumer Protection from Unfair Trading Regulations 2008.

The fragmentation of the Consumer Credit Act 1974 and the regulation of its original subject matter under diverse pieces of legislation has produced a complex multi-piece jigsaw which is far from easy to comprehend and apply, not least by consumers for whose benefit the law is intended.

The Consumer Credit Act 1974 has, of course, been considerably amended over the past 30 years, especially by the Consumer Credit Act 2006. The latter removed the financial limit which previously applied to regulated agreements.

This has largely rendered redundant certain provisions of the Act, particularly s 18 on multiple agreements which was originally envisaged as an anti-avoidance provision to protect consumers against creditors and lessors combining regulated agreements in order to avoid the consequences of the Act. Whilst the provision still serves a limited purpose in relation to agreements which remain subject to a financial limit, currently £25,000, its presence on the statute book in respect of all regulated agreements is a continuing potential threat to the validity of regulated agreements, out of proportion to its usefulness. The concept of 'an agreement to aggregate' in the Consumer Credit (Information Requirements and Duration of Licences and Charges) Regulations 2007 perhaps suggests the way forward for the legislature.

The removal of the financial limit will cause problems and frustration in relation to credit and hire agreements where these could previously have been avoided, in the case of a majority of agreements, by the agreement exceeding the financial limit. By way of example, the inability of a consumer who wishes to expedite the completion of a prospective land mortgage by shortening or waiving the consideration period prescribed by s 61(2) and the inability of an elderly pensioner who wishes to enter into a credit agreement by means of a power of attorney (as the Act makes no provision for the same) now applies to all consumer credit agreements, regardless of the credit amount.

With the growth of consumer indebtedness and the increase in home repossessions, assisting debtors with their problems, especially by rescheduling debt, is not made easier by the absence of provision in the legislation for by-passing regulated modifying agreements.

Taking a broader view of relevant legislation, it is noteworthy how primary legislation is increasingly amended by subordinate legislation. Currently a Legislative Reform Order is being proposed to amend sections of the Consumer Credit Act relating to buy-to-let agreements, statements and modifying agreements.

Amendment or replacement of the Bills of Sale Acts 1878 and 1882, as amended by the Bills of Sale Act 1890, is long overdue. More than a century's practice has passed since they were enacted and there is urgent need for reform of practice and to bring the statutory requirements applying to bills of sale in line with those which apply to regulated agreements. Indeed, a fresh consideration of, and approach to, chattel mortgages generally would be a welcome development.

The unfair relationships provisions of the Consumer Credit Act, the various pre-contract and post-contract information requirements under the Regulations and the plethora of relevant Acts and Regulations, have hugely increased the legislative burden on creditors and lessors. Quite apart from current economic conditions, they will result in the increased cost of credit and hire facilities to consumers. Whether this will lead consumers to look for equivalent facilities in other Member States of the European Community, particularly after the implementation of the new EC Directive on Consumer Credit in 2010, remains to be seen. Ultimately, the test of the success of recent consumer credit legislation is whether it serves to enhance consumer protection and benefits the consumer, commensurate with any increased cost of consumer credit and hire facilities, without reducing consumer choice.[1]

1   Long title to the Act (31 July 1974).

ANNEX

Consumer Credit Act 1974

Arrangement of sections

Schedules

An Act to establish for the protection of consumers a new system, administered by the Director General of Fair Trading, of licensing and other control of traders concerned with the provisions of credit, or the supply of goods on hire or hire-purchase, and their transactions, in place of the present enactments regulating moneylenders, pawnbrokers, and hire-purchase traders and their transactions; and for related matters

[31st July 1974]

PART I DIRECTOR GENERAL OF FAIR TRADING

1   General functions of OFT.

(1)   It is the duty of the Office of Fair Trading ('the OFT')—

    (a)   to administer the licensing system set up by this Act,

    (b)   to exercise the adjudicating functions conferred on it by this Act in relation to the issue, renewal, variation, suspension and revocation of licences, and other matters,

    (ba)   to monitor, as it sees fit, businesses being carried on under licences;

    (c)   generally to superintend the working and enforcement of this Act, and regulations made under it, and

    (d)   where necessary or expedient, itself to take steps to enforce this Act, and regulations so made.

(2)   It is the duty of the OFT, so far as appears to it to be practicable and having regard both to the national interest and the interests of persons carrying on businesses to which this Act applies and their customers, to keep under review and from time to time advise the Secretary of State about—

    (a)   social and commercial developments in the United Kingdom and elsewhere relating to the provision of credit or bailment or (in Scotland) hiring of goods to individuals, and related activities; and

    (b)   the working and enforcement of this Act and orders and regulations made under it.

2   Powers of Secretary of State.

(1)   The Secretary of State may by order—

    (a)   confer on the OFT additional functions concerning the provision of credit or bailment or (in Scotland) hiring of goods to individuals, and related activities, and

    (b)   regulate the carrying out by the OFT of its functions under this Act.

(2)   The Secretary of State may give general directions indicating considerations to which the OFT should have particular regard in carrying out its functions under this Act, and may give specific directions on any matter connected with the carrying out by the OFT of those functions.

(3)   The Secretary of State, on giving any directions under subsection (2), shall arrange for them to be published in such manner as he thinks most suitable for drawing them to the attention of interested persons.

(4)   With the approval of the Secretary of State and the Treasury, the OFT may charge, for any service or facility provided by it under this Act, a fee of an amount specified by general notice (the 'specified fee').

(5)   Provision may be made under subsection (4) for reduced fees, or no fees at all, to be paid for certain services or facilities by persons of a specified description, and references in this Act to the specified fee shall, in such cases, be construed accordingly.

(6)   An order under subsection (1)(a) shall be made by statutory instrument and shall be of no effect unless a draft of the order has been laid before and approved by each House of Parliament.

(7)   References in subsection (2) to the functions of the OFT under this Act do not include the making of a determination to which section 41 (appeals from OFT to the Tribunal) applies.

3

...

4 *Dissemination of information and advice.*

The OFT shall arrange for the dissemination, in such form and manner as it considers appropriate, of such information and advice as it may appear to it expedient to give to the public in the United Kingdom about the operation of this Act, the consumer credit jurisdiction under Part 16 of the Financial Services and Markets Act 2000, the credit facilities available to them, and other matters within the scope of its functions under this Act.

5

...

6

(1) An application to the OFT under this Act is of no effect unless the requirements of this section are satisfied.

(2) The application must be in writing, and in such form, and accompanied by such information and documents, as the OFT may specify or describe in a general notice,

(2A) The application must also be accompanied—

    (a) in the case of an application for a licence or for the renewal of a licence, by the charge payable by virtue of section 6A;

    (b) in any other case, by the specified fee.

(3) Where the OFT receives an application, it may by notice to the applicant at any time before the determination of the application require him to provide such information or documents relevant to the application as may be specified or described in the notice.

(4) The OFT may by notice require the applicant to publish details of his application at a time or times and in a manner specified in the notice.

(5) Subsection (6) applies where a general notice under subsection (2) comes into effect—

    (a) after an application has been made; but

    (b) before its determination.

(6) The applicant shall, within such period as may be specified in the general notice, provide the OFT with any information or document—

    (a) which he has not previously provided in relation to the application by virtue of this section;

    (b) which he would have been required to provide with his application had it been made after the general notice came into effect; and

    (c) which the general notice requires to be provided for the purposes of this subsection.

(7) An applicant shall notify the OFT, giving details, if before his application is determined—

    (a) any information or document provided by him in relation to the application by virtue of this section is, to any extent, superseded or otherwise affected by a change in circumstances; or

    (b) he becomes aware of an error in or omission from any such information or document.

(8) A notification for the purposes of subsection (7) shall be given within the period of 28 days beginning with the day on which (as the case may be)—

    (a)   the information or document is superseded;

    (b)   the change in circumstances occurs; or

    (c)   the applicant becomes aware of the error or omission.

(9) Subsection (7) does not require an applicant to notify the OFT about—

    (a)   anything of which he is required to notify it under section 36; or

    (b)   an error in or omission from any information or document which is a clerical error or omission not affecting the substance of the information or document.

6A Charge on applicants for licences etc.

(1) An applicant for a licence, or for the renewal of a licence, shall pay the OFT a charge towards the costs of carrying out its functions under this Act.

(2) The amount of the charge payable by an applicant shall be determined in accordance with provision made by the OFT by general notice.

(3) The provision that may be made by the OFT under subsection (2) includes—

    (a)   different provision in relation to persons of different descriptions;

    (b)   Provision for no charge at all to be payable by persons of specified descriptions.

(4) The approval of the Secretary of State and the Treasury is required for a general notice under subsection (2)

7 Penalty for false information.

A person commits an offence if, for the purposes of, or in connection with, any requirement imposed or other provision made by or under this Act, he knowingly or recklessly gives information to the OFT, or to an officer of the OFT, which, in a material particular, is false or misleading.

8 Consumer credit agreements.

(1) A consumer credit agreement is an agreement between an individual ('the debtor') and any other person ('the creditor') by which the creditor provides the debtor with credit of any amount.

(2) ...

(3) A consumer credit agreement is a regulated agreement within the meaning of this Act if it is not an agreement (an 'exempt agreement') specified in or under section 16, 16A or 16B.

PART II CREDIT AGREEMENTS, HIRE AGREEMENTS AND LINKED TRANSACTIONS

9 Meaning of credit.

(1) In this Act 'credit' includes a cash loan, and any other form of financial accommodation.

(2)   Where credit is provided otherwise than in sterling it shall be treated for the purposes of this Act as provided in sterling of an equivalent amount.

(3)   Without prejudice to the generality of subsection (1), the person by whom goods are bailed or (in Scotland) hired to an individual under a hire-purchase agreement shall be taken to provide him with fixed-sum credit to finance the transaction of an amount equal to the total price of the goods less the aggregate of the deposit (if any) and the total charge for credit.

(4)   For the purposes of this Act, an item entering into the total charge for credit shall not be treated as credit even though time is allowed for its payment.

10   Running-account credit and fixed-sum credit.

(1)   For the purposes of this Act—

(a)   running-account credit is a facility under a consumer credit agreement whereby the debtor is enabled to receive from time to time (whether in his own person, or by another person) from the creditor or a third party cash, goods and services (or any of them) to an amount or value such that, taking into account payments made by or to the credit of the debtor, the credit limit (if any) is not at any time exceeded; and

(b)   fixed-sum credit is any other facility under a consumer credit agreement whereby the debtor is enabled to receive credit (whether in one amount or by instalments).

(2)   In relation to running-account credit, 'credit limit' means, as respects any period, the maximum debit balance which, under the credit agreement, is allowed to stand on the account during that period, disregarding any term of the agreement allowing that maximum to be exceeded merely temporarily.

(3)   For the purposes of paragraph (a) of section 16B(1), running-account credit shall be taken not to exceed the amount specified in that paragraph ('the specified amount') if—

(a)   the credit limit does not exceed the specified amount; or

(b)   whether or not there is a credit limit, and if there is, notwithstanding that it exceeds the specified amount—

(i)   the debtor is not enabled to draw at any one time an amount which, so far as (having regard to section 9(4)) it represents credit, exceeds the specified amount, or

(ii)   the agreement provides that, if the debit balance rises above a given amount (not exceeding the specified amount), the rate of the total charge for credit increases or any other condition favouring the creditor or his associate comes into operation, or

(iii) at the time the agreement is made it is probable, having regard to the terms of the agreement and any other relevant considerations, that the debit balance will not at any time rise above the specified amount.

11   Restricted-use credit and unrestricted-use credit.

(1)   A restricted-use credit agreement is a regulated consumer credit agreement—

(a)   to finance a transaction between the debtor and the creditor, whether forming part of that agreement or not, or

(b)   to finance a transaction between the debtor and a person (the 'supplier') other than the creditor, or

(c) to refinance any existing indebtedness of the debtor's, whether to the creditor or another person,

and 'restricted-use credit' shall be construed accordingly.

(2) An unrestricted-use credit agreement is a regulated consumer credit agreement not falling within subsection (1), and 'unrestricted-use credit' shall be construed accordingly.

(3) An agreement does not fall within subsection (1) if the credit is in fact provided in such a way as to leave the debtor free to use it as he chooses, even though certain uses would contravene that or any other agreement.

(4) An agreement may fall within subsection (1)(b) although the identity of the supplier is unknown at the time the agreement is made.

12 Debtor-creditor supplier agreements.

A debtor-creditor-supplier agreement is a regulated consumer credit agreement being—

(a) a restricted-use credit agreement which falls within section 11(1)(a), or

(b) a restricted-use credit agreement which falls within section 11(1)(b) and is made by the creditor under pre-existing arrangements, or in contemplation of future arrangements, between himself and the supplier, or

(c) an unrestricted-use credit agreement which is made by the creditor under pre-existing arrangements between himself and a person (the 'supplier') other than the debtor in the knowledge that the credit is to be used to finance a transaction between the debtor and the supplier.

13 Debtor-creditor agreements.

A debtor-creditor agreement is a regulated consumer credit agreement being—

(a) a restricted-use credit agreement which falls within section 11(1)(b) but is not made by the creditor under pre-existing arrangements, or in contemplation of future arrangements, between himself and the supplier, or

(b) a restricted-use credit agreement which falls within section 11(1)(c), or

(c) an unrestricted-use credit agreement which is not made by the creditor under pre-existing arrangements between himself and a person (the 'supplier') other than the debtor in the knowledge that the credit is to be used to finance a transaction between the debtor and the supplier.

14 Credit-token agreements.

(1) A credit-token is a card, check, voucher, coupon, stamp, form, booklet or other document or thing given to an individual by a person carrying on a consumer credit business, who undertakes—

(a) that on the production of it (whether or not some other action is also required) he will supply cash, goods and services (or any of them) on credit, or

(b) that where, on the production of it to a third party (whether or not any other action is also required), the third party supplies cash, goods and services (or any of them), he will pay the third party for them (whether or not deducting any discount or commission), in return for payment to him by the individual.

(2) A credit-token agreement is a regulated agreement for the provision of credit in connection with the use of a credit-token.

(3) Without prejudice to the generality of section 9(1), the person who gives to an individual an undertaking falling within subsection (1)(b) shall be taken to provide him with credit drawn on whenever a third party supplies him with cash, goods or services.

(4) For the purposes of subsection (1), use of an object to operate a machine provided by the person giving the object or a third party shall be treated as the production of the object to him.

15 Consumer hire agreements.

(1) A consumer hire agreement is an agreement made by a person with an individual (the 'hirer') for the bailment or (in Scotland) the hiring of goods to the hirer, being an agreement which—

(a) is not a hire-purchase agreement, and

(b) is capable of subsisting for more than three months,

(c) ...

(2) A consumer hire agreement is a regulated agreement if it is not an exempt agreement.

16 Exempt agreements.

(1) This Act does not regulate a consumer credit agreement where the creditor is a local authority, or a body specified, or of a description specified, in an order made by the Secretary of State, being—

(a) an insurer,

(b) a friendly society,

(c) an organisation of employers or organisation of workers,

(d) a charity,

(e) a land improvement company,

(f) a body corporate named or specifically referred to in any public general Act.

(ff) a body corporate named or specifically referred to in an order made under—

section 156(4), 444(1) or 447(2)(a) of the Housing Act 1985,

section 156(4) of that Act as it has effect by virtue of section 17 of the Housing Act 1996 (the right to acquire),

section 223 or 229 of the Housing (Scotland) Act 1987, or

Article 154(1)(a) or 156AA of the Housing (Northern Ireland) Order 1981 or Article 10(6A) of the Housing (Northern Ireland) Order 1983, or

(g) a building society, or

(h) a deposit-taker.

(2) Subsection (1) applies only where the agreement is—

(a) a debtor-creditor-supplier agreement financing—

(i) the purchase of land, or

(ii) the provision of dwellings on any land, and secured by a land mortgage on that land; or

(b)   a debtor-creditor agreement secured by any land mortgage; or

(c)   a debtor-creditor-supplier agreement financing a transaction which is a linked transaction in relation to—

   (i)   an agreement falling within paragraph (a), or

   (ii)   an agreement falling within paragraph (b) financing—

      (aa)   the purchase of any land, or

      (bb)   the provision of dwellings on any land,

and secured by a land mortgage on the land referred to in paragraph (a) or, as the case may be, the land referred to in sub-paragraph (ii).

(3)   Before he makes, varies or revokes an order under subsection (1), the Secretary of State must undertake the necessary consultation.

(3A) The necessary consultation means consultation with the bodies mentioned in the following table in relation to the provision under which the order is to be made, varied or revoked:

TABLE

Provision of subsection (1)	Consultee
Paragraph (a) or (b)	The Financial Services Authority
Paragraph (d)	Charity Commission
Paragraph (e), (f) or (ff)	Any Minister of the Crown with responsibilities in relation to the body in question
Paragraph (g) or (h)	The Treasury and the Financial Services Authority

(4)   An order under subsection (1) relating to a body may be limited so as to apply only to agreements by that body of a description specified in the order.

(5)   The Secretary of State may by order provide that this Act shall not regulate other consumer credit agreements where—

(a)   the number of payments to be made by the debtor does not exceed the number specified for that purpose in the order, or

(b)   the rate of the total charge for credit does not exceed the rate so specified, or

(c)   an agreement has a connection with a country outside the United Kingdom.

(6)   The Secretary of State may by order provide that this Act shall not regulate consumer hire agreements of a description specified in the order where—

(a)   the owner is a body corporate authorised by or under any enactment to supply electricity, gas or water, and

(b)   the subject of the agreement is a meter or metering equipment,

or where the owner is a provider of a public electronic communications service who is specified in the order.

(6A) This Act does not regulate a consumer credit agreement where the creditor is a housing authority and the agreement is secured by a land mortgage of a dwelling.

(6B) In subsection (6A) 'housing authority' means —

(a)   as regards England and Wales, the Housing Corporation and an authority or body within section 80(1) of the Housing Act 1985 (the landlord condition for secure tenancies), other than a housing association or a housing trust which is a charity;

(b) as regards Scotland, a development corporation established under an order made, or having effect as if made under the New Towns (Scotland) Act 1968, the Scottish Special Housing Association or the Housing Corporation;

(c) as regards Northern Ireland, the Northern Ireland Housing Executive.

(6C) This Act does not regulate a consumer credit agreement if—

(a) it is secured by a land mortgage and entering into the agreement as lender is a regulated activity for the purposes of the Financial Services and Markets Act 2000; or

(b) it is or forms part of a regulated home purchase plan and entering into the agreement as home purchase provider is a regulated activity for the purposes of that Act.

(6D) But section 126, and any other provision so far as it relates to section 126, applies to an agreement which would (but for subsection (6C)(a)) be a regulated agreement.

(6E) Subsection (6C) must be read with—

(a) section 22 of the Financial Services and Markets Act 2000 (regulated activities: power to specify classes of activity and categories of investment);

(b) any order for the time being in force under that section; and

(c) Schedule 2 to that Act.

(7) ...

(7A) Nothing in this section affects the application of sections 140A to 140C.

(8) In the application of this section to Scotland, subsection (3A) shall have effect as if the reference to the Charity Commission were a reference to the Lord Advocate.

(9) In the application of this section to Northern Ireland subsection (3A) shall have effect as if any reference to a Minister of the Crown were a reference to a Northern Ireland department and any reference to the Charity Commission were a reference to the Department of Finance for Northern Ireland.

(10) In this section—

(a) 'deposit-taker' means—

(i) a person who has permission under Part 4 of the Financial Services and Markets Act 2000 to accept deposits,

(ii) an EEA firm of the kind mentioned in paragraph 5(b) of Schedule 3 to that Act which has permission under paragraph 15 of that Schedule (as a result of qualifying for authorisation under paragraph 12 of that Schedule) to accept deposits,

(iii) any wholly owned subsidiary (within the meaning of the Companies Act 1985) of a person mentioned in sub-paragraph (i), or

(iv) any undertaking which, in relation to a person mentioned in sub-paragraph (ii), is a subsidiary undertaking within the meaning of any rule of law in force in the EEA State in question for purposes connected with the implementation of the European Council Seventh Company Law Directive of 13 June 1983 on consolidated accounts (No. 83/349/EEC), and which has no members other than that person;

(b) 'insurer' means—

(i) a person who has permission under Part 4 of the Financial Services and Markets Act 2000 to effect or carry out contracts of insurance, or

    (ii)   an EEA firm of the kind mentioned in paragraph 5(d) of Schedule 3 to that Act, which has permission under paragraph 15 of that Schedule (as a result of qualifying for authorisation under paragraph 12 of that Schedule) to effect or carry out contracts of insurance,

but does not include a friendly society or an organisation of workers or of employers.

(11) Subsection (10) must be read with—

    (a)   section 22 of the Financial Services and Markets Act 2000;

    (b)   any relevant order under that section; and

    (c)   Schedule 2 to that Act.

16A   Exemption relating to high net worth debtors and hirers

(1)   The Secretary of State may by order provide that this Act shall not regulate a consumer credit agreement or a consumer hire agreement where—

    (a)   the debtor or hirer is a natural person;

    (b)   the agreement includes a declaration made by him to the effect that he agrees to forgo the protection and remedies that would be available to him under this Act if the agreement were a regulated agreement;

    (c)   a statement of high net worth has been made in relation to him; and

    (d)   that statement is current in relation to the agreement and a copy of it was provided to the creditor or owner before the agreement was made.

(2)   For the purposes of this section a statement of high net worth is a statement to the effect that, in the opinion of the person making it, the natural person in relation to whom it is made—

    (a)   received during the previous financial year income of a specified description totalling an amount of not less than the specified amount; or

    (b)   had throughout that year net assets of a specified description with a total value of not less than the specified value.

(3)   Such a statement—

    (a)   may not be made by the person in relation to whom it is made;

    (b)   must be made by a person of a specified description; and

    (c)   is current in relation to an agreement if it was made during the period of one year ending with the day on which the agreement is made.

(4)   An order under this section may make provision about—

    (a)   how amounts of income and values of net assets are to be determined for the purposes of subsection (2)(a) and (b);

    (b)   the form, content and signing of—

        (i)   statements of high net worth;

        (ii)   declarations for the purposes of subsection (1)(b).

(5)   Where an agreement has two or more debtors or hirers, for the purposes of paragraph (c) of subsection (1) a separate statement of high net worth must have been made in relation to each of them; and paragraph (d) of that subsection shall have effect accordingly.

(6) In this section—

'previous financial year' means, in relation to a statement of high net worth, the financial year immediately preceding the financial year during which the statement is made;

'specified' means specified in an order under this section.

(7) In subsection (6) 'financial year' means a period of one year ending with 31st March.

(8) Nothing in this section affects the application of sections 140A to 140C.

16B Exemption relating to businesses

(1) This Act does not regulate—

   (a) a consumer credit agreement by which the creditor provides the debtor with credit exceeding £25,000, or

   (b) a consumer hire agreement that requires the hirer to make payments exceeding £25,000,

if the agreement is entered into by the debtor or hirer wholly or predominantly for the purposes of a business carried on, or intended to be carried on, by him.

(2) If an agreement includes a declaration made by the debtor or hirer to the effect that the agreement is entered into by him wholly or predominantly for the purposes of a business carried on, or intended to be carried on, by him, the agreement shall be presumed to have been entered into by him wholly or predominantly for such purposes.

(3) But that presumption does not apply if, when the agreement is entered into—

   (a) the creditor or owner, or

   (b) any person who has acted on his behalf in connection with the entering into of the agreement,

knows, or has reasonable cause to suspect, that the agreement is not entered into by the debtor or hirer wholly or predominantly for the purposes of a business carried on, or intended to be carried on, by him.

(4) The Secretary of State may by order make provision about the form, content and signing of declarations for the purposes of subsection (2).

(5) Where an agreement has two or more creditors or owners, in subsection (3) references to the creditor or owner are references to any one or more of them.

(6) Nothing in this section affects the application of sections 140A to 140C.

17 Small agreements.

(1) A small agreement is—

   (a) A regulated consumer credit agreement for credit not exceeding £50, other than a hire-purchase or conditional sale agreement: or

   (b) a regulated consumer hire agreement which does not require the hirer to make payments exceeding £50,

   being an agreement which is either unsecured or secured by a guarantee or indemnity only (whether or not the guarantee or indemnity is itself secured).

(2)   Section 10(3)(a) applies for the purposes of subsection (1) as it applies for the purposes of 16B(1)(a).

(3)   Where—

(a)   two or more small agreements are made at or about the same time between the same parties, and

(b)   it appears probable that they would instead have been made as a single agreement but for the desire to avoid the operation of provisions of this Act which would have applied to that single agreement but, apart from this subsection, are not applicable to the small agreements,

this Act applies to the small agreements as if they were regulated agreements other than small agreements.

(4)   If, apart from this subsection, subsection (3) does not apply to any agreements but would apply if, for any party or parties to any of the agreements, there were substituted an associate of that party, or associates of each of those parties, as the case may be, then subsection (3) shall apply to the agreements.

18   Multiple agreements.

(1)   This section applies to an agreement (a 'multiple agreement') if its terms are such as—

(a)   to place a part of it within one category of agreement mentioned in this Act, and another part of it within a different category of agreement so mentioned, or within a category of agreement not so mentioned, or

(b)   to place it, or a part of it, within two or more categories of agreement so mentioned.

(2)   Where a part of an agreement falls within subsection (1), that part shall be treated for the purposes of this Act as a separate agreement.

(3)   Where an agreement falls within subsection (1)(b), it shall be treated as an agreement in each of the categories in question, and this Act shall apply to it accordingly.

(4)   Where under subsection (2) a part of a multiple agreement is to be treated as a separate agreement, the multiple agreement shall (with any necessary modifications) be construed accordingly; and any sum payable under the multiple agreement, if not apportioned by the parties, shall for the purposes of proceedings in any court relating to the multiple agreement be apportioned by the court as may be requisite.

(5)   In the case of an agreement for running-account credit, a term of the agreement allowing the credit limit to be exceeded merely temporarily shall not be treated as a separate agreement or as providing fixed-sum credit in respect of the excess.

(6)   This Act does not apply to a multiple agreement so far as the agreement relates to goods if under the agreement payments are to be made in respect of the goods in the form of rent (other than a rentcharge) issuing out of land.

19   Linked transactions.

(1)   A transaction entered into by the debtor or hirer, or a relative of his, with any other person ('the other party'), except one for the provision of security; is a linked transaction in relation to an actual or prospective regulated agreement (the 'principal agreement') of which it does not form part if—

(a)   the transaction is entered into in compliance with a term of the principal agreement; or

(b) the principal agreement is a debtor-creditor-supplier agreement and the transaction is financed, or to be financed, by the principal agreement; or

(c) the other party is a person mentioned in subsection (2), and a person so mentioned initiated the transaction by suggesting it to the debtor or hirer, or his relative, who enters into it—

    (i) to induce the creditor or owner to enter into the principal agreement, or

    (ii) for another purpose related to the principal agreement, or

    (iii) where the principal agreement is a restricted-use credit agreement, for a purpose related to a transaction financed, or to be financed, by the principal agreement.

(2) The persons referred to in subsection (1)(c) are—

(a) the creditor or owner, or his associate;

(b) a person who, in the negotiation of the transaction, is represented by a credit-broker who is also a negotiator in antecedent negotiations for the principal agreement;

(c) a person who, at the time the transaction is initiated, knows that the principal agreement has been made or contemplates that it might be made.

(3) A linked transaction entered into before the making of the principal agreement has no effect until such time (if any) as that agreement is made.

(4) Regulations may exclude linked transactions of the prescribed description from the operation of subsection (3).

20   Total charge for credit.

(1) The Secretary of State shall make regulations containing such provisions as appear to him appropriate for determining the true cost to the debtor of the credit provided or to be provided under an actual or prospective consumer credit agreement (the 'total charge for credit'), and regulations so made shall prescribe—

(a) what items are to be treated as entering into the total charge for credit, and how their amount is to be ascertained;

(b) the method of calculating the rate of the total charge for credit.

(2) Regulations under subsection (1) may provide for the whole or part of the amount payable by the debtor or his relative under any linked transaction to be included in the total charge for credit, whether or not the creditor is a party to the transaction or derives benefit from it.

21   Businesses needing a licence.

(1) Subject to this section, a licence is required to carry on a consumer credit business or a consumer hire business or an ancillary credit business.

(2) A local authority does not need a licence to carry on a business.

(3) A body corporate empowered by a public general Act naming it to carry on a business does not need a licence to do so.

PART III LICENSING OF CREDIT AND HIRE BUSINESSES

Licensing principles

22   *Standard and group licences.*

(1)   A licence may be—

   (a)   a standard licence, that is a licence, issued by the OFT to a person named in the licence on an application made by him, which, whilst the licence is in effect, covers such activities as are described in the licence, or

   (b)   a group licence, that it a licence, issued by the OFT (whether on the application of any person or of its own motion), which, whilst the licence is in effect, covers such persons and activities as are described in the licence.

(1A) The terms of a licence shall specify—

   (a)   whether it has effect indefinitely or only for a limited period; and

   (b)   if it has effect for a limited period, that period.

(1B) For the purposes of subsection (1A)(b) the period specified shall be such period not exceeding the prescribed period as the OFT thinks fit (subject to subsection (1E)).

(1C) A standard licence shall have effect indefinitely unless—

   (a)   the application for its issue requests that it have effect for a limited period only; or

   (b)   the OFT otherwise thinks there is good reason why it should have effect for such a period only.

(1D) A group licence shall have effect for a limited period only unless the OFT thinks there is good reason why it should have effect indefinitely.

(1E) Where a licence which has effect indefinitely is to be varied under section 30 or 31 for the purpose of limiting the licence's duration, the variation shall provide for the licence to expire—

   (a)   in the case of a variation under section 30, at the end of such period from the time of the variation as is set out in the application for the variation; or

   (b)   in the case of a variation under section 31, at the end of such period from the time of the variation as the OFT thinks fit;

but a period mentioned in paragraph(a) or (b) shall not exceed the prescribed period.

(2)   A licence is not assignable or, subject to section 37, transmissible on death or in any other way.

(3)   Except in the case of a partnership or an unincorporated body of persons, a standard licence shall not be issued to more than one person.

(4)   A standard licence issued to a partnership or an unincorporated body of persons shall be issued in the name of the partnership or body.

(5)   The OFT may issue a group licence only if it appears to it that the public interest is better served by doing so than by obliging the persons concerned to apply separately for standard licences.

(5A) A group licence to carry on a business may limit the activities it covers in any way the OFT thinks fit.

(6)   The persons covered by a group licence may be described by general words, whether or not coupled with the exclusion of named persons, or in any other way the OFT thinks fit.

(7)   The fact that a person is covered by a group licence in respect of certain activities does not prevent a standard licence being issued to him in respect of those activities or any of them.

(8)   A group licence issued on the application of any person shall be issued to that person, and general notice shall be given of the issue of any group licence (whether on application or not).

(9)   ...

(10) ...

23   Authorisation of specific activities.

(1)   Subject to the terms of the licence, a licence to carry on a business covers all lawful activities done in the course of that business, whether by the licensee or other persons on his behalf.

(2)   ...

(3)   A licence covers the canvassing off trade premises of debtor-creditor-supplier agreements or regulated consumer hire agreements only if, and to the extent that, the licence specifically so provides; and such provision shall not be included in a group licence.

(4)   The OFT may by general notice specify other activities which, if engaged in by or on behalf of the person carrying on a business, require to be covered by an express term in his licence.

24   Control of name of business.

A standard licence authorises the licensee to carry on a business under the name or names specified in the licence, but not under any other name.

24A   Applications for standard licences

(1)   An application for a standard licence shall, in relation to each type of business which is covered by the application, state whether the applicant is applying—

(a)   for the licence to cover the carrying on of that type of business with no limitation; or

(b)   for the licence to cover the carrying on of that type of business only so far as it falls within one or more descriptions of business.

(2)   An application within subsection (1)(b) in relation to a type of business shall set out the description or descriptions of business in question.

(3)   References in this Part to a type of business are references to a type of business within subsection (4).

(4)   The types of business within this subsection are—

(a)   a consumer credit business;

(b)   a consumer hire business;

(c)   a business so far as it comprises or relates to credit brokerage;

(d)   a business so far as it comprises or relates to debt-adjusting;

(e)   a business so far as it comprises or relates to debt-counselling;

(f)   a business so far as it comprises or relates to debt-collecting;

(g)   a business so far as it comprises or relates to debt administration;

(h)   a business so far as it comprises or relates to the provision of credit information services;

(i)   a business so far as it comprises or relates to the operation of a credit reference agency.

(5)   The OFT—

(a)   shall by general notice specify the descriptions of business which can be set out in an application for the purposes of subsection (2) in relation to a type of business;

(b)   may by general notice provide that applications within subsection (1)(b) cannot be made in relation to one or more of the types of business within subsection (4)(c) to (i).

(6)   he power of the OFT under subsection (5) includes power to make different provision for different cases or classes of case.

25   Licensee to be a fit person.

(1)   If an applicant for a standard licence—

(a)   makes an application within section 24A(1)(a) in relation to a type of business, and

(b)   satisfies the OFT that he is a fit person to carry on that type of business with no limitation,

he shall be entitled to be issued with a standard licence covering the carrying on of that type of business with no limitation.

(1A)…

(1AA)   If such an applicant—

(a)   makes an application within subsection (1)(b) of section 24A in relation to a type of business, and

(b)   satisfies the OFT that he is a fit person to carry on that type of business so far as it falls within the description or descriptions of business set out in his application in accordance with subsection (2) of that section,

he shall be entitled to be issued with a standard licence covering the carrying on of that type of business so far as it falls within the description or descriptions in question.

(1AB)   If such an applicant makes an application within section 24A(1)(a) or (b) in relation to a type of business but fails to satisfy the OFT as mentioned in subsection (1) or (1AA) (as the case may be), he shall nevertheless be entitled to be issued with a standard licence covering the carrying on of that type of business so far as it falls within one or more descriptions of business if—

(a)   he satisfies the OFT that he is a fit person to carry on that type of business so far as it falls within the description or descriptions in question;

(b)   he could have applied for the licence to be limited in that way; and

(c)   the licence would not cover any activity which was not covered by his application.

(1AC) In this section 'description of business' means, in relation to a type of business, a description of business specified in a general notice under section 24A(5)(a).

(1AD) An applicant shall not, by virtue of this section, be issued with a licence unless he satisfies the OFT that the name or names under which he would be licensed is or are not misleading or otherwise undesirable.

(1A)...

(1B) If an application for the grant of a standard licence—

(a) is made by a person with permission under Part 4 of the Financial Services and Markets Act 2000 to accept deposits, and

(b) relates to a listed activity,

the Financial Services Authority may, if it considers that the OFT ought to refuse the application, notify him of that fact.

(1C) In subsection (1B) 'listed activity' means an activity listed in Annex 1 to Directive 2006/48/EC of the European Parliament and of the Council of 14 June 2006 relating to the taking up and pursuit of the business of credit institutions or in Annex I to the markets in financial instruments directive (2004/39/EC) and references to deposits and to their acceptance must be read with—

(a) section 22 of the Financial Services and Markets Act 2000;

(b) any relevant order under that section; and

(c) Schedule 2 to that Act.

(2) In determining whether an applicant for a licence is a fit person for the purposes of this section the OFT shall have regard to any matters appearing to it to be relevant including (amongst other things)—

(a) the applicant's skills, knowledge and experience in relation to consumer credit businesses, consumer hire businesses or ancillary credit businesses;

(b) such skills, knowledge and experience of other persons who the applicant proposes will participate in any business that would be carried on by him under the licence;

(c) practices and procedures that the applicant proposes to implement in connection with any such business;

(d) evidence of the kind mentioned in subsection (2A).

(2A) That evidence is evidence tending to show that the applicant, or any of the applicant's employees, agents or associates (whether past or present) or, where the applicant is a body corporate, any person appearing to the OFT to be a controller of the body corporate or an associate of any such person, has—

(a) committed any offence involving fraud or other dishonesty or violence;

(b) contravened any provision made by or under—

(i) this Act;

(ii) Part 16 of the Financial Services and Markets Act 2000 so far as it relates to the consumer credit jurisdiction under that Part;

(iii) any other enactment regulating the provision of credit to individuals or other transactions with individuals;

(c) contravened any provision in force in an EEA State which corresponds to a provision of the kind mentioned in paragraph (b);

(d) practised discrimination on grounds of sex, colour, race or ethnic or national origins in, or in connection with, the carrying on of any business; or

(e) engaged in business practices appearing to the OFT to be deceitful or oppressive or otherwise unfair or improper (whether unlawful or not).

(2B) For the purposes of subsection (2A)(e), the business practices which the OFT may consider to be deceitful or oppressive or otherwise unfair or improper include practices in the carrying on of a consumer credit business that appear to the OFT to involve irresponsible lending.

(3) In subsection (2A), 'associate', in addition to the persons specified in section 184, includes a business associate.

25A Guidance on fitness test

(1) The OFT shall prepare and publish guidance in relation to how it determines, or how it proposes to determine, whether persons are fit persons as mentioned in section 25.

(2) If the OFT revises the guidance at any time after it has been published, the OFT shall publish it as revised.

(3) The guidance shall be published in such manner as the OFT thinks fit for the purpose of bringing it to the attention of those likely to be affected by it.

(4) In preparing or revising the guidance the OFT shall consult such persons as it thinks fit.

(5) In carrying out its functions under this Part the OFT shall have regard to the guidance as most recently published.

26 Conduct of business.

(1) Regulations may be made as to—

(a) the conduct by a licensee of his business; and

(b) the conduct by a consumer credit EEA firm of its business in the United Kingdom.

(2) The regulations may in particular specify—

(a) the books or other records to be kept by any person to whom the regulations apply;

(b) the information to be furnished by such a person to those persons with whom—

(i) that person does business, or

(ii) that person seeks to do business,

and the way in which that information is to be furnished.

Issue of licences

27 Determination of applications.

(1) Unless the OFT determines to issue a licence in accordance with an application it shall, before determining the application, by notice—

(a) inform the applicant, giving its reasons, that, as the case may be, it is minded to refuse the application, or to grant it in terms different from those applied for, describing them, and

    (b)   invite the applicant to submit to the OFT representations in support of his application in accordance with section 34.

(2)   If the OFT grants the application in terms different from those applied for then, whether or not the applicant appeals, the OFT shall issue the licence in the terms approved by it unless the applicant by notice informs it that he does not desire a licence in those terms.

27A   *Consumer credit EEA firms*

(1)   Where—

    (a)   a consumer credit EEA firm makes an application for a standard licence, and

    (b)   the activities covered by the application are all permitted activities,

the OFT shall refuse the application.

(2)   Subsection (3) applies where—

    (a)   a consumer credit EEA firm makes an application for a standard licence; and

    (b)   some (but not all) of the activities covered by the application are permitted activities.

(3)   In order to be entitled to be issued with a standard licence in accordance with section 25(1) to (1AB) in relation to a type of business, the firm need not satisfy the OFT that it is a fit person to carry on that type of business so far as it would involve any of the permitted activities covered by the application.

(4)   A standard licence held by a consumer credit EEA firm does not at any time authorise the carrying on of an activity which is a permitted activity at that time.

(5)   In this section 'permitted activity' means, in relation to a consumer credit EEA firm, an activity for which the firm has, or could obtain, permission under paragraph 15 of Schedule 3 to the Financial Services and Markets Act 2000.

28   *Exclusion from group licence.*

Where the OFT is minded to issue a group licence (whether on the application of any person or not), and in doing so to exclude any person from the group by name, it shall, before determining the matter—

    (a)   give notice of that fact to the person proposed to be excluded, giving its reasons, and

    (b)   invite that person to submit to the OFT representations against his exclusion in accordance with section 34.

Charges for indefinite licences

28A   *Charges to be paid by licensees etc. before end of payment periods.*

(1)   The licensee under a standard licence which has effect indefinitely shall, before the end of each payment period of his, pay the OFT a charge towards the costs of carrying out its functions under this Act.

(2)   The original applicant for a group licence which has effect indefinitely shall, before the end of each payment period of his, pay the OFT such a charge.

(3)   The amount of the charge payable by a person under subsection (1) or (2) before the end of a payment period shall be determined in accordance with provision which—

   (a)   is made by the OFT by general notice; and

   (b)   is current on such day as may be determined in accordance with provision made by regulations.

(4)   The provision that may be made by the OFT under subsection (3)(a) includes—

   (a)   different provision in relation to persons of different descriptions (including persons whose payment periods end at different times);

   (b)   Provision for no charge at all to be payable by persons of specified descriptions.

(5)   The approval of the Secretary of State and the Treasury is required for a general notice under subsection (3)(a).

(6)   For the purposes of this section a person's payment periods are to be determined in accordance with provision made by regulations.

28B   *Extension of period to pay charge under s. 28A*

(1)   A person who is required under section 28A to pay a charge before the end of a period may apply once to the OFT for that period to be extended.

(2)   The application shall be made before such day as may be determined in accordance with provision made by the OFT by general notice.

(3)   If the OFT is satisfied that there is a good reason—

   (a)   why the applicant has not paid that charge prior to his making of the application, and

   (b)   why he cannot pay that charge before the end of that period,

   it may, if it thinks fit, by notice to him extend that period by such time as it thinks fit having regard to that reason.

(4)   The power of the OFT under this section to extend a period in relation to a charge—

   (a)   includes the power to extend the period in relation to a part of the charge only;

   (b)   may be exercised even though the period has ended.

28C   *Failure to pay charge under 28A*

(1)   This section applies if a person (the 'defaulter') fails to pay a charge—

   (a)   before the end of a period (the 'payment period') as required under section 28A; or

   (b)   where the payment period is extended under section 28B, before the end of the payment period as extended (subject to subsection (2)).

(2)   Where the payment period is extended under section 28B in relation to a part of the charge only, this section applies if the defaulter fails—

   (a)   to pay so much of the charge as is not covered by the extension before the end of the payment period disregarding the extension; or

   (b)   to pay so much of the charge as is covered by the extension before the end of the payment period as extended.

(3)   Subject to subsection (4), if the charge is a charge under section 28A(1), the defaulter's licence terminates.

(4) If the defaulter has applied to the OFT under section 28B for the payment period to be extended and that application has not been determined—

  (a) his licence shall not terminate before the application has been determined and the OFT has notified him of the determination; and

  (b) if the OFT extends the payment period on that application, this section shall have effect accordingly.

(5) If the charge is a charge under section 28A(2), the charge shall be recoverable by the OFT.

Renewal, variation, suspension and revocation of licences

29 *Renewal.*

(1) If the licensee under a standard licence, of limited duration or the original applicant for, or any licensee under, a group licence of limited duration, wishes the OFT to renew the licence, whether on the same terms (except as to expiry) or on varied terms, he must, during the period specified by the OFT by general notice or such longer period as the OFT may allow, make an application to the OFT for its renewal.

(2) The OFT may of its own motion renew any group licence.

(3) The preceding provisions of this Part apply to the renewal of a licence as they apply to the issue of a licence, except that section 28 does not apply to a person who was already excluded in the licence up for renewal.

(3A) In its application to the renewal of standard licences by virtue of subsection (3) of this section, section 27(1) shall have effect as if for paragraph (b) there were substituted—

  '(b) invite the applicant to submit to the OFT in accordance with section 34 representations—

    (i) in support of his application; and

    (ii) about the provision (if any) that should be included under section 34A as part of the determination were the OFT to refuse the application or grant it in terms different from those applied for.'

(4) Until the determination of an application under subsection (1) and, where an appeal lies from the determination, until the end of the appeal period, the licence shall continue to have effect, notwithstanding that apart from this subsection it would expire earlier.

(5) …

(6) General notice shall be given of the renewal of a group licence.

30 *Variation by request.*

(1) If it thinks fit, the OFT may by notice to the licensee under a standard licence—

  (a) in the case of a licence which covers the carrying on of a type of business only so far as it falls within one or more descriptions of business, vary the licence by—

    (i) removing that limitation;

    (ii) adding a description of business to that limitation; or

    (iii) removing a description of business from that limitation;

(b)   in the case of a licence which covers the carrying on of a type of business with no limitation, vary the licence so that it covers the carrying on of that type of business only so far as it falls within one or more descriptions of business;

(c)   vary the licence so that it no longer covers the carrying on of a type of business at all;

(d)   vary the licence so that a type of business the carrying on of which is not covered at all by the licence is covered either—

(i)   with no limitation; or

(ii)   only so far as it falls within one or more descriptions of business; or

(e)   vary the licence in any other way except for the purpose of varying the descriptions of activities covered by the licence.

(1A) The OFT may vary a licence under subsection (1) only in accordance with an application made by the licensee.

(1B) References in this section to a description of business in relation to a type of business—

(a)   are references to a description of business specified in a general notice under section 24A(5)(a); and

(b)   in subsection (1)(a) (apart from sub-paragraph (ii)) include references to a description of business that was, but is no longer, so specified.

(2)   In the case of a group licence issued on the application of any person, the OFT, on an application made by that person, may if it thinks fit by notice to that person vary the terms of the licence in accordance with the application; but the OFT shall not vary a group licence under this subsection by excluding a named person, other than the person making the request, unless that named person consents in writing to his exclusion.

(3)   In the case of a group licence from which (whether by name or description) a person is excluded, the OFT, on an application made by that person, may if it thinks fit, by notice to that person, vary the terms of the licence so as to remove the exclusion.

(4)   Unless the OFT determines to vary a licence in accordance with an application it shall, before determining the application, by notice—

(a)   inform the applicant, giving its reasons, that it is minded to refuse the application, and

(b)   invite the applicant to submit to the OFT representations in support of his application in accordance with section 34.

(5)   General notice shall be given that a variation of a group licence has been made under this section.

31   *Compulsory variation.*

(1)   Where at a time during the currency of a licence the OFT is of the opinion that, if the licence had expired at that time(assuming, in the case of a licence which has effect indefinitely, that it were a licence of limited duration), it would, on an application for its renewal or further renewal on the same terms (except as to expiry), have been minded to grant the application but on different terms, and that therefore it should take steps mentioned in subsection (1A), it shall proceed as follows.

(1A) Those steps are—

(a)   in the case of a standard licence, steps mentioned in section 30(1)(a)(ii) and (iii), (b), (c) and (e);

(b)   in the case of a group licence, the varying of terms of the licence.

(1B) The OFT shall also proceed as follows if, having regard to section 22(1B) to (1E), it is of the opinion—

    (a)   that a licence which has effect indefinitely should have its duration limited; or

    (b)   in the case of a licence of limited duration, that the period during which it has effect should be shortened.

(2)   In the case of a standard licence the OFT shall, by notice—

    (a)   inform the licensee of the variations the OFT is minded to make in the terms of the licence, stating its reasons, and

    (b)   invite him to submit to the OFT in accordance with section 34 representations—

        (i)   as to the proposed variations; and

        (ii) about the provision (if any) that should be included under section 34A as part of the determination were the OFT to vary the licence.

(3)   In the case of a group licence the OFT shall—

    (a)   give general notice of the variations it is minded to make in the terms of the licence, stating its reasons, and

    (b)   in the notice invite any licensee to submit to it representations as to the proposed variations in accordance with section 34.

(4)   In the case of a group licence issued on application the OFT shall also—

    (a)   inform the original applicant of the variations the OFT is minded to make in the terms of the licence, stating its reasons, and

    (b)   invite him to submit to the OFT representations as to the proposed variations in accordance with section 34.

(5)   If the OFT is minded to vary a group licence by excluding any person (other than the original applicant) from the group by name the OFT shall, in addition, take the like steps under section 28 as are required in the case mentioned in that section.

(6)   General notice shall be given that a variation of any group licence has been made under this section.

(7)   A variation under this section shall not take effect before the end of the appeal period.

(8)   Subsection (1) shall have effect in relation to a standard licence as if an application could be made for the renewal or further renewal of the licence on the same terms (except as to expiry) even if such an application could not be made because of provision made in a general notice under section 24A(5).

(9)   Accordingly, in applying subsection (1AA) of section 25 in relation to the licence for the purposes of this section, the OFT shall treat references in that subsection to the description or descriptions of business in relation to a type of business as references to the description or descriptions of business included in the licence in relation to that type of business, notwithstanding that provision under section 24A(5).

32 *Suspension and revocation.*

(1)   Where at a time during the currency of a licence the OFT is of the opinion that if the licence had expired at that time (assuming, in the case of a licence which has effect indefinitely, that it were a licence of limited duration) it would have been minded not to renew it, and that therefore it should be revoked or suspended, it shall proceed as follows.

(2)   In the case of a standard licence the OFT shall, by notice—

    (a)   inform the licensee that, as the case may be, the OFT is minded to revoke the licence, or suspend it until a specified date or indefinitely, stating its reasons, and

    (b)   invite him to submit to the OFT in accordance with section 34 representations—

        (i)   as to the proposed revocation or suspension; and

        (ii)   about the provision (if any) that should be included under section 34A as part of the determination were the OFT to revoke or suspend the licence.

(3)   In the case of a group licence the OFT shall—

    (a)   give general notice that, as the case may be, it is minded to revoke the licence, or suspend it until a specified date or indefinitely, stating its reasons, and

    (b)   in the notice invite any licensee to submit to it representations as to the proposed revocation or suspension in accordance with section 34.

(4)   In the case of a group licence issued on application the OFT shall also—

    (a)   inform the original applicant that, as the case may be, the OFT is minded to revoke the licence, or suspend it until a specified date or indefinitely, stating its reasons, and

    (b)   invite him to submit representations as to the proposed revocation or suspension in accordance with section 34.

(5)   …

(6)   General notice shall be given of the revocation or suspension of a group licence.

(7)   A revocation or suspension under this section shall not take effect before the end of the appeal period.

(8)   Except for the purposes of section 29, a licensee under a suspended licence shall be treated, in respect of the period of suspension, as if the licence had not been issued; and where the suspension is not expressed to end on a specified date it may, if the OFT thinks fit, be ended by notice given by it to the licensee or, in the case of a group licence, by general notice.

(9)   The OFT has no power to revoke or to suspend a standard licence simply because, by virtue of provision made in a general notice under section 24A(5), a person cannot apply for the renewal of such a licence on terms which are the same as the terms of the licence in question.

33   Application to end suspension.

(1)   On an application made by a licensee the OFT may, if it thinks fit, by notice to the licensee end the suspension of a licence, whether the suspension was for a fixed or indefinite period.

(2)   Unless the OFT determines to end the suspension in accordance with the application it shall, before determining the application, by notice—

    (a)   inform the applicant, giving its reasons, that it is minded to refuse the application, and

    (b)   invite the applicant to submit to the OFT representations in support of his application in accordance with section 34.

(3)   General notice shall be given that a suspension of a group licence has been ended under this section.

(4) In the case of a group licence issued on application—

    (a) the references in subsection (1) to a licensee include the original applicant;

    (b) the OFT shall inform the original applicant that a suspension of a group licence has been ended under this section.

Further powers of OFT to regulate conduct of licensees etc

33A Power of OFT to impose requirements on licensees

(1) This section applies where the OFT is dissatisfied with any matter in connection with—

    (a) a business being carried on, or which has been carried on, by a licensee or by an associate or a former associate of a licensee;

    (b) a proposal to carry on a business which has been made by a licensee or by an associate or a former associate of a licensee; or

    (c) any conduct not covered by paragraph (a) or (b) of a licensee or of an associate or a former associate of a licensee.

(2) The OFT may by notice to the licensee require him to do or not to do (or to cease doing) anything specified in the notice for purposes connected with—

    (a) addressing the matter with which the OFT is dissatisfied; or

    (b) securing that matters of the same or a similar kind do not arise.

(3) A requirement imposed under this section on a licensee shall only relate to a business which the licensee is carrying on, or is proposing to carry on, under the licence under which he is a licensee.

(4) Such a requirement may be framed by reference to a named person other than the licensee.

(5) For the purposes of subsection (1) it is immaterial whether the matter with which the OFT is dissatisfied arose before or after the licensee became a licensee.

(6) If—

    (a) a person makes an application for a standard licence, and

    (b) while dealing with that application the OFT forms the opinion that, if such a licence were to be issued to that person, it would be minded to impose on him a requirement under this section,

    the OFT may, before issuing such a licence to that person, do (in whole or in part) anything that it must do under section 33D or 34(1) or (2) in relation to the imposing of the requirement.

(7) In this section 'associate', in addition to the persons specified in section 184, includes a business associate.

33B Power of OFT to impose requirements on supervisory bodies

(1) This section applies where the OFT is dissatisfied with the way in which a responsible person in relation to a group licence—

    (a) is regulating or otherwise supervising, or has regulated or otherwise supervised, persons who are licensees under that licence; or

    (b) is proposing to regulate or otherwise to supervise such persons.

(2)   The OFT may by notice to the responsible person require him to do or not to do (or to cease doing) anything specified in the notice for purposes connected with—

  (a)   addressing the matters giving rise to the OFT's dissatisfaction; or

  (b)   securing that matters of the same or a similar kind do not arise.

(3)   A requirement imposed under this section on a responsible person in relation to a group licence shall only relate to practices and procedures for regulating or otherwise supervising licensees under the licence in connection with their carrying on of businesses under the licence.

(4)   For the purposes of subsection (1) it is immaterial whether the matters giving rise to the OFT's dissatisfaction arose before or after the issue of the group licence in question.

(5)   If—

  (a)   a person makes an application for a group licence, and

  (b)   while dealing with that application the OFT forms the opinion that, if such a licence were to be issued to that person, it would be minded to impose on him a requirement under this section,

  the OFT may, before issuing such a licence to that person, do (in whole or in part) anything that it must do under section 33D or 34(1) or (2) in relation to the imposing of the requirement.

(6)   For the purposes of this Part a person is a responsible person in relation to a group licence if—

  (a)   he is the original applicant for it; and

  (b)   he has a responsibility (whether by virtue of an enactment, an agreement or otherwise) for regulating or otherwise supervising persons who are licensees under the licence.

33C   Supplementary provision relating to requirements

(1)   A notice imposing a requirement under section 33A or 33B may include provision about the time at or by which, or the period during which, the requirement is to be complied with.

(2)   A requirement imposed under section 33A or 33B shall not have effect after the licence by reference to which it is imposed has itself ceased to have effect.

(3)   A person shall not be required under section 33A or 33B to compensate, or otherwise to make amends to, another person.

(4)   The OFT may by notice to the person on whom a requirement has been imposed under section 33A or 33B vary or revoke the requirement (including any provision made under subsection (1) of this section in relation to it) with effect from such date as may be specified in the notice.

(5)   The OFT may exercise its power under subsection (4) in relation to a requirement either on its own motion or on the application of a person falling within subsection (6) or (7) in relation to the requirement.

(6)   A person falls within this subsection in relation to a requirement if he is the person on whom the requirement is imposed.

(7) A person falls within this subsection in relation to a requirement if—

   (a) the requirement is imposed under section 33A;

   (b) he is not the person on whom the requirement is imposed;

   (c) the requirement is framed by reference to him by name; and

   (d) the effect of the requirement is—

   (i) to prevent him being an employee of the person on whom the requirement is imposed;

   (ii) to restrict the activities that he may engage in as an employee of that person; or

   (iii) otherwise to prevent him from doing something, or to restrict his doing something, in connection with a business being carried on by that person.

33D Procedure in relation to requirements

(1) Before making a determination—

   (a) to impose a requirement on a person under section 33A or 33B,

   (b) to refuse an application under section 33C(5) in relation to a requirement imposed under either of those sections, or

   (c) to vary or to revoke a requirement so imposed,

   the OFT shall proceed as follows.

(2) The OFT shall give a notice to every person to whom subsection (3) applies in relation to the determination—

   (a) informing him, with reasons, that it is minded to make the determination; and

   (b) inviting him to submit to it representations as to the determination under section 34.

(3) This subsection applies to a person in relation to the determination if he falls within, or as a consequence of the determination would fall within, section 33C(6) or (7) in relation to the requirement in question.

(4) This section does not require the OFT to give a notice to a person if the determination in question is in the same terms as a proposal made to the OFT by that person (whether as part of an application under this Part or otherwise).

33E Guidance on requirements

33E Guidance on requirements

(1) The OFT shall prepare and publish guidance in relation to how it exercises, or how it proposes to exercise, its powers under sections 33A to 33C.

(2) If the OFT revises the guidance at any time after it has been published, the OFT shall publish it as revised.

(3) The guidance shall be published in such manner as the OFT thinks fit for the purpose of bringing it to the attention of those likely to be affected by it.

(4) In preparing or revising the guidance the OFT shall consult such persons as it thinks fit.

(5) In exercising its powers under sections 33A to 33C the OFT shall have regard to the guidance as most recently published.

Miscellaneous

34   Representations to OFT.

(1) Where this section applies to an invitation by the OFT to any person to submit representations, the OFT shall invite that person, within 21 days after the notice containing the invitation is given to him or published, or such longer period as the OFT may allow—

   (a) to submit his representations in writing to the OFT, and

   (b) to give notice to the OFT, if he thinks fit, that he wishes to make representations orally,

and where notice is given under paragraph (b) the OFT shall arrange for the oral representations to be heard.

(2) In reaching its determination the OFT shall take into account any representations submitted or made under this section.

(3) The OFT shall give notice of its determination to the persons who were required to be invited to submit representations about it or, where the invitation to submit representations was required to be given by general notice, shall give general notice of the determination.

34A   Winding-up of standard licensee's business

(1) If it thinks fit, the OFT may, for the purpose of enabling the licensee's business, or any part of his business, to be transferred or wound up, include as part of a determination to which subsection (2) applies provision authorising the licensee to carry on for a specified period—

   (a) specified activities, or

   (b) activities of specified descriptions,

which, because of that determination, the licensee will no longer be licensed to carry on.

(2) This subsection applies to the following determinations—

   (a) a determination to refuse to renew a standard licence in accordance with the terms of the application for its renewal;

   (b) a determination to vary such a licence under section 31;

   (c) a determination to suspend or revoke such a licence.

(3) Such provision—

   (a) may specify different periods for different activities or activities of different descriptions;

   (b) may provide for persons other than the licensee to carry on activities under the authorisation;

   (c) may specify requirements which must be complied with by a person carrying on activities under the authorisation in relation to those activities;

and, if a requirement specified under paragraph (c) is not complied with, the OFT may by notice to a person carrying on activities under the authorisation terminate the authorisation (in whole or in part) from a specified date.

(4) Without prejudice to the generality of paragraph (c) of subsection (3), a requirement specified under that paragraph may have the effect of—

(a) preventing a named person from being an employee of a person carrying on activities under the authorisation, or restricting the activities he may engage in as an employee of such a person;

(b) preventing a named person from doing something, or restricting his doing something, in connection with activities being carried on by a person under the authorisation;

(c) securing that access to premises is given to officers of the OFT for the purpose of enabling them to inspect documents or to observe the carrying on of activities.

(5) Activities carried on under an authorisation shall be treated for the purposes of sections 39(1), 40, 148 and 149 as if carried on under a standard licence.

35 The register.

(1) The OFT shall establish and maintain a register, in which it shall cause to be kept particulars of—

(a) applications not yet determined for the issue, variation or renewal of licences, or for ending the suspension of a licence;

(b) licences which are in effect, or have at any time been suspended or revoked or terminated by section 28C, with details of any variation of the terms of a licence;

(ba) requirements imposed under section 33A or 33B which are in effect or which have been in effect, with details of any variation of such a requirement;

(c) decisions given by it under this Act, and any appeal from those decisions; and

(d) such other matters (if any) as he thinks fit.

(1A) The OFT shall also cause to be kept in the register any copy of any notice or other document relating to a consumer credit EEA firm which is given to the OFT by the Financial Services Authority for inclusion in the register.

(2) The OFT shall give general notice of the various matters required to be entered in the register, and of any change in them made under subsection (1)(d).

(3) Any person shall be entitled on payment of the specified fee—

(a) to inspect the register during ordinary office hours and take copies of any entry, or

(b) to obtain from the OFT a copy, certified by the OFT to be correct, of any entry in the register.

(4) The OFT may, if it thinks fit, determine that the right conferred by subsection (3)(a) shall be exercisable in relation to a copy of the register instead of, or in addition to, the original.

(5) The OFT shall give general notice of the place or places where, and times when, the register or a copy of it may be inspected.

36 Duty to notify changes.

(1) Within 21 days working days after a change takes place in any particulars entered in the register in respect of a standard licence or the licensee under section 35(1)(d) (not being a change resulting from action taken by the OFT), the licensee shall give the OFT notice of the change; and the OFT shall cause any necessary amendment to be made in the register.

(2)   Within 21 working days after—

    (a)   any change takes place in the officers of—

        (i)   a body corporate, or an unincorporated body of persons, which is the licensee under a standard licence, or

        (ii)   a body corporate which is a controller of a body corporate which is such a licensee, or

    (b)   a body corporate which is such a licensee becomes aware that a person has become or ceased to be a controller of the body corporate, or

    (c)   any change takes place in the members of a partnership which is such a licensee (including a change on the amalgamation of the partnership with another firm, or a change whereby the number of partners is reduced to one),

the licensee shall give the OFT notice of the change.

(3)   Within 14 working days after any change takes place in the officers of a body corporate which is a controller of another body corporate which is a licensee under a standard licence, the controller shall give the licensee notice of the change.

(4)   Within 14 working days after a person becomes or ceases to be a controller of a body corporate which is a licensee under a standard licence, that person shall give the licensee notice of the fact.

(5)   Where a change in a partnership has the result that the business ceases to be carried on under the name, or any of the names, specified in a standard licence the licence shall cease to have effect.

(6)   ...

36A   *Further duties to notify changes etc.*

(1)   Subsections (2) to (4) apply where a general notice under section 6(2) comes into effect.

(2)   A person who is the licensee under a standard licence or who is the original applicant for a group licence shall, in relation to each relevant application which he has made and which was determined before the general notice came into effect, provide the OFT with any information or document—

    (a)   which he would have been required to provide with the application had the application been made after the general notice came into effect; and

    (b)   which the general notice requires to be provided for the purposes of this subsection.

(3)   Any such information or document shall be provided within such period as may be specified in the general notice.

(4)   Subsection (2) does not require a person to provide any information or document—

    (a)   which he provided in relation to the application by virtue of section 6;

    (b)   which he has previously provided in relation to the application by virtue of this section; or

    (c)   which he would have been required to provide in relation to the application by virtue of subsection (5) but for subsection (6).

(5) A person who is the licensee under a standard licence or who is the original applicant for a group licence shall, in relation to each relevant application which he has made, notify the OFT giving details if, after the application is determined, any information or document which he—

    (a) Provided in relation to the application by virtue of section 6, or

    (b) has so provided by virtue of this section,

is, to any extent, superseded or otherwise affected by a change in circumstances.

(6) Subsection (5) does not require a person to notify the OFT about a matter unless it falls within a description of matters specified by the OFT in a general notice.

(7) A description may be specified for the purposes of subsection (6) only if the OFT is satisfied that the matters which would fall within that description are matters which would be relevant to the question of—

    (a) whether, having regard to section 25(2), a person is a fit person to carry on a business under a standard licence; or

    (b) whether the public interest is better served by a group licence remaining in effect than by obliging the licensees under it to apply separately for standard licences.

(8) A person who is the licensee under a standard licence or who is the original applicant for a group licence shall, in relation to each relevant application which he has made, notify the OFT about every error or omission—

    (a) in or from any information or document which he provided by virtue of section 6, or which he has provided by virtue of this section, in relation to the application; and

    (b) of which he becomes aware after the determination of the application.

(9) A notification for the purposes of subsection (5) or (8) shall be given within the period of 28 days beginning with the day on which (as the case may be)—

    (a) the information or document is superseded;

    (b) the change in circumstances occurs; or

    (c) the licensee or the original applicant becomes aware of the error or omission.

(10) This section does not require a person to notify the OFT about—

    (a) anything of which he is required to notify it under section 36; or

    (b) an error in or omission from any information or document which is a clerical error or omission not affecting the substance of the information or document.

(11) In this section 'relevant application' means, in relation to a person who is the licensee under a standard licence or who is the original applicant for a group licence—

    (a) the original application for the licence; or

    (b) an application for its renewal or for its variation.

36B Power of OFT to require information generally

(1) The OFT may by notice to a person require him—

    (a) to provide such information as may be specified or described in the notice; or

    (b) to produce such documents as may be so specified or described.

(2) The notice shall set out the reasons why the OFT requires the information or documents to be provided or produced.

(3) The information or documents shall be provided or produced—

   (a) before the end of such reasonable period as may be specified in the notice; and

   (b) at such place as may be so specified.

(4) A requirement may be imposed under subsection (1) on a person who is—

   (a) the licensee under a standard licence, or

   (b) the original applicant for a group licence,

   only if the provision or production of the information or documents in question is reasonably required for purposes connected with the OFT's functions under this Act.

(5) A requirement may be imposed under subsection (1) on any other person only if—

   (a) an act or omission mentioned in subsection (6) has occurred or the OFT has reason to suspect that such an act or omission has occurred; and

   (b) the provision or production of the information or documents in question is reasonably required for purposes connected with—

      (i)   the taking by the OFT of steps under this Part as a consequence; or

      (ii) its consideration of whether to take such steps as a consequence.

(6) Those acts or omissions are acts or omissions which—

   (a) cast doubt on whether, having regard to section 25(2), a person is a fit person to carry on a business under a standard licence;

   (b) cast doubt on whether the public interest is better served by a group licence remaining in effect, or being issued, than by obliging the persons who are licensees under it, or who would be licensees under it, to apply separately for standard licences;

   (c) give rise, or are likely to give rise, to dissatisfaction for the purposes of section 33A(1) or 33B(1); or

   (d) constitute or give rise to a failure of the kind mentioned in section 39A(1).

36C   Power of OFT to require access to premises

(1) The OFT may by notice to a licensee under a licence require him to secure that access to the premises specified or described in the notice is given to an officer of an enforcement authority in order for the officer—

   (a) to observe the carrying on of a business under the licence by the licensee; or

   (b) to inspect such documents of the licensee relating to such a business as are—

      (i)   specified or described in the notice; and

      (ii) situated on the premises.

(2) The notice shall set out the reasons why the access is required.

(3) The premises which may be specified or described in the notice—

   (a) include premises which are not premises of the licensee if they are premises from which he carries on activities in connection with the business in question; but

   (b) do not include premises which are used only as a dwelling.

(4) The licensee shall secure that the required access is given at such times as the OFT reasonably requires.

(5) The OFT shall give reasonable notice of those times.

(6) Where an officer is given access to any premises by virtue of this section, the licensee shall also secure that persons on the premises give the officer such assistance or information as he may reasonably require in connection with his observation or inspection of documents (as the case may be).

(7) The assistance that may be required under subsection (6) includes (amongst other things) the giving to the officer of an explanation of a document which he is inspecting.

(8) A requirement may be imposed under subsection (1) on a person who is—

    (a) the licensee under a standard licence, or

    (b) the original applicant for a group licence,

only if the observation or inspection in question is reasonably required for purposes connected with the OFT's functions under this Act.

(9) A requirement may be imposed under subsection (1) on any other person only if—

    (a) an act or omission mentioned in section 36B(6) has occurred or the OFT has reason to suspect that such an act or omission has occurred; and

    (b) the observation or inspection in question is reasonably required for purposes connected with—

        (i) the taking by the OFT of steps under this Part as a consequence; or

        (ii) its consideration of whether to take such steps as a consequence.

(10) In this section—

    (a) references to a licensee under a licence include, in relation to a group licence issued on application, references to the original applicant; and

    (b) references to a business being carried on under a licence by a licensee include, in relation to the original applicant for a group licence, activities being carried on by him for the purpose of regulating or otherwise supervising (whether by virtue of an enactment, an agreement or otherwise) licensees under that licence in connection with their carrying on of businesses under that licence.

36D Entry to premises under warrant

(1) A justice of the peace may issue a warrant under this section if satisfied on information on oath given on behalf of the OFT that there are reasonable grounds for believing that the following conditions are satisfied.

(2) Those conditions are—

    (a) that there is on the premises specified in the warrant information or documents in relation to which a requirement could be imposed under section 36B; and

    (b) that if such a requirement were to be imposed in relation to the information or documents—

        (i) it would not be complied with; or

        (ii) the information or documents would be tampered with.

(3) A warrant under this section shall authorise an officer of an enforcement authority—

    (a) to enter the premises specified in the warrant;

    (b) to search the premises and to seize and detain any information or documents appearing to be information or documents specified in the warrant or information or documents of a description so specified;

    (c) to take any other steps which may appear to be reasonably necessary for preserving such information or documents or preventing interference with them; and

    (d) to use such force as may be reasonably necessary.

(4) An officer entering premises by virtue of this section may take such persons and equipment with him as he thinks necessary.

(5) In the application of this section to Scotland—

    (a) the reference to a justice of the peace includes a reference to a sheriff;

    (b) for 'information on oath' there is substituted 'evidence on oath'.

(6) In the application of this section to Northern Ireland the reference to a justice of the peace shall be construed as a reference to a lay magistrate.

36E   Failure to comply with information requirement

(1) If on an application made by the OFT it appears to the court that a person (the 'information defaulter') has failed to do something that he was required to do by virtue of section 36B or 36C, the court may make an order under this section.

(2) An order under this section may require the information defaulter—

    (a) to do the thing that it appears he failed to do within such period as may be specified in the order;

    (b) otherwise to take such steps to remedy the consequences of the failure as may be so specified.

(3) If the information defaulter is a body corporate, a partnership or an unincorporated body of persons which is not a partnership, the order may require any officer who is (wholly or partly) responsible for the failure to meet such costs of the application as are specified in the order.

(4) In this section—

'court' means—

    (a) in England and Wales and Northern Ireland, the High Court or the county court;

    (b) in Scotland, the Court of Session or the sheriff;

'officer' means—

    (a) in relation to a body corporate, a person holding a position of director, manager or secretary of the body or any similar position;

    (b) in relation to a partnership or to an unincorporated body of persons, a member of the partnership or body.

(5) In subsection (4) 'director' means, in relation to a body corporate whose affairs are managed by its members, a member of the body.

36F   Officers of enforcement authorities other than OFT

(1) A relevant officer may only exercise powers by virtue of section 36C or 36D in pursuance of arrangements made with the OFT by or on behalf of the enforcement authority of which he is an officer.

(2) Anything done or omitted to be done by, or in relation to, a relevant officer in the exercise or purported exercise of a power by virtue of section 36C or 36D shall be treated for all purposes as having been done or omitted to be done by, or in relation to, an officer of the OFT.

(3) Subsection (2) does not apply for the purposes of any criminal proceedings brought against the officer, the enforcement authority of which he is an officer or the OFT in respect of anything done or omitted to be done by the officer.

(4) A relevant officer shall not disclose to a person other than the OFT information obtained by his exercise of a power by virtue of section 36C or 36D unless—

(a) he has the approval of the OFT to do so; or

(b) he is under a duty to make the disclosure.

(5) In this section 'relevant officer' means an officer of an enforcement authority other than the OFT.

37 Death, bankruptcy etc. of licensee.

(1) A licence held by one individual terminates if he—

(a) dies, or

(b) is adjudged bankrupt, or

(c) becomes a person who lacks capacity (within the meaning of the Mental Capacity Act 2005) to carry on the activities covered by the licence.

(1A) A licence terminates if the licensee gives the OFT a notice under subsection (1B).

(1B) A notice under this subsection shall—

(a) be in such form as the OFT may by general notice specify;

(b) contain such information as may be so specified;

(c) be accompanied by the licence or give reasons as to why it is not accompanied by the licence; and

(d) be signed by or on behalf of the licensee.

(2) In relation to a licence held by one individual, or a partnership or other unincorporated body of persons, or a body corporate, regulations may specify other events relating to the licensee on the occurrence of which the licence is to terminate.

(3) Regulations may—

(a) Provide for the termination of a licence by subsection (1) or (1A), or under subsection (2), to be deferred for a period not exceeding 12 months, and

(b) authorise the business of the licensee to be carried on under the licence by some other person during the period of deferment, subject to such conditions as may be prescribed.

(4) This section does not apply to group licences.

38 Application of s. 37 to Scotland and Northern Ireland.

(1) In the application of section 37 to Scotland the following shall be substituted for paragraphs (b) and (c) of subsection (1)—

'(b) has his estate sequestrated, or

(c) becomes incapable of managing his own affairs.'

(2) In the application of section 37 to Northern Ireland the following shall be substituted for subsection (1)—

'(1) A licence held by one individual terminates if—

(a) he dies, or

(b) he is adjudged bankrupt or his estate and effects vest in the official assignee under section 349 of the Irish Bankrupt and Insolvent Act 1857, or

(c) a declaration is made under section 15 of the Lunacy Regulation (Ireland) Act 1871 that he is of unsound mind and incapable of managing his person or property, or an order is made under section 68 of that Act in consequence of its being found that he is of unsound mind and incapable of managing his affairs.'.

39   Offences against Part III.

(1) A person who engages in any activities for which a licence is required when he is not a licensee under a licence covering those activities commits an offence.

(2) A licensee under a standard licence who carries on business under a name not specified in the licence commits an offence.

(3) A person who fails to give the OFT or a licensee notice under section 36 within the period required commits an offence.

39A   Power of OFT to impose civil penalties

(1) Where the OFT is satisfied that a person (the 'defaulter') has failed or is failing to comply with a requirement imposed on him by virtue of section 33A, 33B or 36A, it may by notice to him (a 'penalty notice') impose on him a penalty of such amount as it thinks fit.

(2) The penalty notice shall—

(a) specify the amount of the penalty that is being imposed;

(b) set out the OFT's reasons for imposing a penalty and for specifying that amount;

(c) specify how the payment of the penalty may be made to the OFT; and

(d) specify the period within which the penalty is required to be paid.

(3) The amount of the penalty shall not exceed £50,000.

(4) The period specified in the penalty notice for the purposes of subsection (2)(d) shall not end earlier than the end of the period during which an appeal may be brought against the imposition of the penalty under section 41.

(5) If the defaulter does not pay the penalty to the OFT within the period so specified—

(a) the unpaid balance from time to time shall carry interest at the rate for the time being specified in section 17 of the Judgments Act 1838; and

(b) the penalty and any interest payable on it shall be recoverable by the OFT.

39B Further provision relating to civil penalties.

(1) Before determining to impose a penalty on a person under section 39A the OFT shall give a notice to that person—

    (a) informing him that it is minded to impose a penalty on him;

    (b) stating the proposed amount of the penalty;

    (c) setting out its reasons for being minded to impose a penalty on him and for proposing that amount;

    (d) setting out the proposed period for the payment of the penalty; and

    (e) inviting him to submit representations to it about the matters mentioned in the preceding paragraphs in accordance with section 34.

(2) In determining whether and how to exercise its powers under section 39A in relation to a person's failure, the OFT shall have regard to (amongst other things)—

    (a) any penalty or fine that has been imposed on that person by another body in relation to the conduct giving rise to the failure;

    (b) other steps that the OFT has taken or might take under this Part in relation to that conduct.

(3) General notice shall be given of the imposition of a penalty under section 39A on a person who is a responsible person in relation to a group licence.

(4) That notice shall include the matters set out in the notice imposing the penalty in accordance with section 39A(2)(a) and (b).

39C Statement of policy in relation to civil penalties

(1) The OFT shall prepare and publish a statement of policy in relation to how it exercises, or how it proposes to exercise, its powers under section 39A.

(2) If the OFT revises the statement of policy at any time after it has been published, the OFT shall publish it as revised.

(3) No statement of policy shall be published without the approval of the Secretary of State.

(4) The statement of policy shall be published in such manner as the OFT thinks fit for the purpose of bringing it to the attention of those likely to be affected by it.

(5) In preparing or revising the statement of policy the OFT shall consult such persons as it thinks fit.

(6) In determining whether and how to exercise its powers under section 39A in relation to a person's failure, the OFT shall have regard to the statement of policy as most recently published at the time the failure occurred.

(7) The OFT shall not impose a penalty on a person under section 39A in relation to a failure occurring before it has published a statement of policy.

40 Enforcement of agreements made by unlicensed trader.

(1) A regulated agreement is not enforceable against the debtor or hirer by a person acting in the course of a consumer credit business or a consumer hire business (as the case may be)

if that person is not licensed to carry on a consumer credit business or a consumer hire business (as the case may be) of a description which covers the enforcement of the agreement.

(1A) Unless the OFT has made an order under subsection (2) which applies to the agreement, a regulated agreement is not enforceable against the debtor or hirer if—

    (a)   it was made by the creditor or owner in the course of a consumer credit business or a consumer hire business (as the case may be); and

    (b)   at the time the agreement was made he was not licensed to carry on a consumer credit business or a consumer hire business (as the case may be) of a description which covered the making of the agreement.

(2)   Where—

    (a)   during any period a person (the 'trader' has made regulated agreements in the course of a consumer credit business or a consumer hire business (as the case may be), and

    (b)   during that period he was not licensed to carry on a consumer credit business or a consumer hire business (as the case may be) of a description which covered the making of those agreements,

he or his successor in title may apply to the OFT for an order that the agreements are to be treated for the purposes of subsection (1A) as if he had been licensed as required.

(3)   Unless the OFT determines to make an order under subsection (2) in accordance with the application, it shall, before determining the application, by notice—

    (a)   inform the applicant, giving its reasons, that, as the case may be, it is minded to refuse the application, or to grant it in terms different from those applied for, describing them, and

    (b)   invite the applicant to submit to the OFT representations in support of his application in accordance with section 34.

(4)   In determining whether or not to make an order under subsection (2) in respect of any period the OFT shall consider, in addition to any other relevant factors—

    (a)   how far, if at all, debtors or hirers under the regulated agreements in question were prejudiced by the trader's conduct,

    (b)   whether or not the OFT would have been likely to grant a licence covering the making of those agreements during that period on an application by the trader, and

    (c)   the degree of culpability for the failure to be licensed as required.

(5)   If the OFT thinks fit, it may in an order under subsection (2)—

    (a)   limit the order to specified agreements, or agreements of a specified description or made at a specified time;

    (b)   make the order conditional on the doing of specified acts by the applicant.

(6)   This section (apart from subsection (1)) does not apply to a regulated agreement made by a consumer credit EEA firm unless at the time it was made that firm was precluded from entering into it as a result of—

    (a)   a consumer credit prohibition imposed under section 203 of the Financial Services and Markets Act 2000; or

    (b)   a restriction imposed on the firm under section 204 of that Act.

(7)   Subsection (1) does not apply to the enforcement of a regulated agreement by a consumer credit EEA firm unless that firm is precluded from enforcing it as a result of a prohibition or restriction mentioned in subsection (6)(a) or (b).

(8) This section (apart from subsection (1)) does not apply to a regulated agreement made by a person if by virtue of section 21(2) or (3) he was not required to be licensed to make the agreement.

(9) Subsection (1) does not apply to the enforcement of a regulated agreement by a person if by virtue of section 21(2) or (3) he is not required to be licensed to enforce the agreement.

Appeals

40A   *The Consumer Credit Appeals Tribunal*

(1) There shall be a tribunal known as the Consumer Credit Appeals Tribunal ('the Tribunal').

(2) The Tribunal shall have the functions conferred on it by or under this Part.

(3) The Lord Chancellor may by rules make such provision as he thinks fit for regulating the conduct and disposal of appeals before the Tribunal.

(4) Schedule A1 (which makes provision about the Tribunal and proceedings before it) shall have effect.

(5) But that Schedule does not limit the Lord Chancellor's powers under subsection (3).

41   *Appeals to Secretary of State under Part III.*

(1) If, in the case of a determination by the OFT such as is mentioned in column 1 of the table set out at the end of this section, a person mentioned in relation to that determination in column 2 of the table is aggrieved by the determination he may, within the specified period, appeal to the Tribunal.

(1A) The means for making an appeal is by sending the Tribunal a notice of appeal.

(1B) The notice of appeal shall—

    (a)   be in the specified form;

    (b)   set out the grounds of appeal in the specified manner; and

    (c)   include the specified information and documents.

(1C) An appeal to the Tribunal is to be by way of a rehearing of the determination appealed against.

(1D) In this section 'specified' means specified by rules under section 40A(3).

(2)   …

(3)   …

(4)   …

(5)   …

TABLE

Determination	Appellant
Refusal to issue, renew or vary licence in accordance with terms of application.	The applicant.
Exclusion of person from group licence.	The person excluded.
...	...
Compulsory variation, or suspension or revocation, of standard licence.	The licensee.
Compulsory variation, or suspension or revocation, of group licence.	The original applicant or any licensee.
Refusal to end suspension of licence in accordance with terms of application.	The applicant.
Determination— (a) to impose a requirement under section 33A or 33B; (b) to refuse an application under section 33C(5) in relation to a requirement imposed under either of those sections; or (c) to vary or revoke a requirement so imposed.	A person who falls within section 33C(6) or (7) in relation to the requirement unless the OFT was not required to give a notice to him in relation to the determination by virtue of section 33D(4).
Imposition of penalty under section 39A.	The person on whom the penalty is imposed.
Refusal to make order under section 40(2), 148(2) or 149(2) in accordance with terms of application.	The applicant.
Imposition of a prohibition or restriction or the variation of a restriction.	The firm concerned.
Refusal of an application for the revocation of a prohibition or restriction.	The firm concerned.
Imposition of, or refusal to withdraw, consumer credit prohibition under section 203 of the Financial Services and Markets Act 2000.	The consumer credit EEA firm concerned.
Imposition of, or refusal to withdraw, a restriction under section 204 of the Financial Services and Markets Act 2000.	The consumer credit EEA firm concerned.

41A   *Appeals from the Consumer Credit Appeals Tribunal*

(1) A party to an appeal to the Tribunal may with leave appeal—

  (a) in England and Wales and Northern Ireland, to the Court of Appeal, or

  (b) in Scotland, to the Court of Session,

  on a point of law arising from a decision of the Tribunal.

(2) For the purposes of subsection (1) leave to appeal may be given by—

    (a) the Tribunal; or

    (b) the Court of Appeal or the Court of Session.

(3) An application for leave to appeal may be made to the Court of Appeal or the Court of Session only if the Tribunal has refused such leave.

(4) If on an appeal under this section the court considers that the decision of the Tribunal was wrong in law, it may do one or more of the following—

    (a) quash or vary that decision;

    (b) substitute for that decision a decision of its own;

    (c) remit the matter to the Tribunal for rehearing and determination in accordance with the directions (if any) given to it by the court.

(5) An appeal may be brought from a decision of the Court of Appeal under this section only if leave to do so is given by the Court of Appeal or the House of Lords.

(6) Rules under section 40A(3) may make provision for regulating or prescribing any matters incidental to or consequential on an appeal under this section.

(7) In this section 'party' means, in relation to an appeal to the Tribunal, the appellant or the OFT.

42 *Further appeal on point of law.*

(1) . . .

(2) . . .

(3) . . .

PART IV SEEKING BUSINESS

Advertising

43 *Advertisements to which Part IV applies.*

(1) This Part applies to any advertisement, published for the purposes of a business carried on by the advertiser, indicating that he is willing—

    (a) to provide credit, or

    (b) to enter into an agreement for the bailment or (in Scotland) the hiring of goods by him.

(2) An advertisement does not fall within subsection (1) if the advertiser does not carry on—

    (a) a consumer credit business or consumer hire business, or

    (b) a business in the course of which he provides credit to individuals secured on land, or

    (c) a business which comprises or relates to unregulated agreements where—

(i)   the law applicable to the agreement is the law of a country outside the United Kingdom, and

(ii)   if the law applicable to the agreement were the law of a part of the United Kingdom it would be a regulated agreement.

(3)   An advertisement does not fall within subsection (1)(a) if it indicates—

(a)   ...

(b)   that the credit is available only to a body corporate.

(3A) An advertisement does not fall within subsection (1)(a) in so far as it is a communication of an invitation or inducement to engage in investment activity within the meaning of section 21 of the Financial Services and Markets Act 2000, other than an exempt generic communication.

(3B) An 'exempt generic communication' is a communication to which subsection (1) of section 21 of the Financial Services and Markets Act 2000 does not apply, as a result of an order under subsection (5) of that section, because it does not identify a person as providing an investment or as carrying on an activity to which the communication relates.

(4)   An advertisement does not fall within subsection (1)(b) if it indicates that the advertiser is not willing to enter into a consumer hire agreement.

(5)   The Secretary of State may by order provide that this Part shall not apply to other advertisements of a description specified in the order.

44   *Form and content of advertisements.*

(1)   The Secretary of State shall make regulations as to the form and content of advertisements to which this Part applies, and the regulations shall contain such provisions as appear to him appropriate with a view to ensuring that, having regard to its subject-matter and the amount of detail included in it, an advertisement conveys a fair and reasonably comprehensive indication of the nature of the credit or hire facilities offered by the advertiser and of their true cost to persons using them.

(2)   Regulations under subsection (1) may in particular—

(a)   require specified information to be included in the prescribed manner in advertisements, and other specified material to be excluded;

(b)   contain requirements to ensure that specified information is clearly brought to the attention of persons to whom advertisements are directed, and that one part of an advertisement is not given insufficient or excessive prominence compared with another.

45   *Prohibition of advertisement where goods etc not sold for cash.*

If an advertisement to which this Part applies indicates that the advertiser is willing to provide credit under a restricted-use credit agreement relating to goods or services to be supplied by any person, but at the time when the advertisement is published that person is not holding himself out as prepared to sell the goods or provide the services (as the case may be) for cash, the advertiser commits an offence.

46   *False or misleading advertisements.*

...

47   Advertising infringements.

(1)   Where an advertiser commits an offence against regulations made under section 44 or against section 45 or would be taken to commit such an offence but for the defence provided by section 168, a like offence is committed by—

(a)   the publisher of the advertisement, and

(b)   any person who, in the course of a business carried on by him, devised the advertisement, or a part of it relevant to the first-mentioned offence, and

(c)   where the advertiser did not procure the publication of the advertisement, the person who did procure it.

(2)   In proceedings for an offence under subsection (1)(a) it is a defence for the person charged to prove that—

(a)   the advertisement was published in the course of a business carried on by him, and

(b)   he received the advertisement in the course of that business, and did not know and had no reason to suspect that its publication would be an offence under this Part.

Canvassing etc

48   Definition of canvassing off trade premises (regulated agreements).

(1)   An individual (the 'canvasser') canvasses a regulated agreement off trade premises if he solicits the entry (as debtor or hirer) of another individual (the 'consumer') into the agreement by making oral representations to the consumer, or any other individual, during a visit by the canvasser to any place (not excluded by subsection (2)) where the consumer, or that other individual, as the case may be, is, being a visit—

(a)   carried out for the purpose of making such oral representations to individuals who are at that place, but

(b)   not carried out in response to a request made on a previous occasion.

(2)   A place is excluded from subsection (1) if it is a place where a business is carried on (whether on a permanent or temporary basis) by—

(a)   the creditor or owner, or

(b)   a supplier, or

(c)   the canvasser, or the person whose employee or agent the canvasser is, or

(d)   the consumer.

49   Prohibition of canvassing debtor-creditor agreements off trade premises.

(1)   It is an offence to canvass debtor-creditor agreements off trade premises.

(2)   It is also an offence to solicit the entry of an individual (as debtor) into a debtor-creditor agreement during a visit carried out in response to a request made on a previous occasion, where—

(a)   the request was not in writing signed by or on behalf of the person making it, and

    (b)   if no request for the visit had been made, the soliciting would have constituted the canvassing of a debtor-creditor agreement off trade premises.

(3)   Subsections (1) and (2) do not apply to any soliciting for an agreement enabling the debtor to overdraw on a current account of any description kept with the creditor, where—

    (a)   the OFT has determined that current accounts of that description kept with the creditor are excluded from subsections (1) and (2), and

    (b)   the debtor already keeps an account with the creditor (whether a current account or not).

(4)   A determination under subsection (3)(a)—

    (a)   may be made subject to such conditions as the OFT thinks fit, and

    (b)   shall be made only where the OFT is of opinion that it is not against the interests of debtors.

(5)   If soliciting is done in breach of a condition imposed under subsection (4)(a), the determination under subsection (3)(a) does not apply to it.

50   *Circulars to minors.*

(1)   A person commits an offence, who, with a view to financial gain, sends to a minor any document inviting him to—

    (a)   borrow money, or

    (b)   obtain goods on credit or hire, or

    (c)   obtain services on credit, or

    (d)   apply for information or advice on borrowing money or otherwise obtaining credit, or hiring goods.

(2)   In proceedings under subsection (1) in respect of the sending of a document to a minor, it is a defence for the person charged to prove that he did not know, and had no reasonable cause to suspect, that he was a minor.

(3)   Where a document is received by a minor at any school or other educational establishment for minors, a person sending it to him at that establishment knowing or suspecting it to be such an establishment shall be taken to have reasonable cause to suspect that he is a minor.

51   *Prohibition of unsolicited credit-tokens.*

(1)   It is an offence to give a person a credit-token if he has not asked for it.

(2)   To comply with subsection (1) a request must be contained in a document signed by the person making the request, unless the credit-token agreement is a small debtor-creditor-supplier agreement.

(3)   Subsection (1) does not apply to the giving of a credit-token to a person—

    (a)   for use under a credit-token agreement already made, or

    (b)   in renewal or replacement of a credit-token previously accepted by him under a credit-token agreement which continues in force, whether or not varied.

Miscellaneous

52 Quotations.

(1) Regulations may be made—

(a) as to the form and content of any document (a 'quotation') by which a person who carries on a consumer credit business or consumer hire business, or a business in the course of which he provides credit to individuals secured on land, gives prospective customers information about the terms on which he is prepared to do business;

(b) requiring a person carrying on such a business to provide quotations to such persons and in such circumstances as are prescribed.

(2) Regulations under subsection (1)(a) may in particular contain provisions relating to quotations such as are set out in relation to advertisements in section 44.

(3) In this section, 'quotation' does not include—

(a) any document which is a communication of an invitation or inducement to engage in investment activity within the meaning of section 21 of the Financial Services and Markets Act 2000; or

(b) any document (other than one falling within paragraph (a)) provided by an authorised person (within the meaning of that Act) in connection with an agreement which would or might be an exempt agreement as a result of section 16(6C).

53 Duty to display information.

Regulations may require a person who carries on a consumer credit business or consumer hire business, or a business in the course of which he provides credit to individuals secured on land (other than credit provided under an agreement which is an exempt agreement as a result of section 16(6C)(a)), to display in the prescribed manner, at any premises where the business is carried on to which the public have access, prescribed information about the business.

54 Conduct of business regulations.

Without prejudice to the generality of section 26, regulations under that section may include provisions further regulating the seeking of business by a person to whom the regulations apply who carries on a consumer credit business or a consumer hire business.

PART V ENTRY INTO CREDIT OR HIRE AGREEMENTS

Preliminary matters

55 Disclosure of information.

(1) Regulations may require specified information to be disclosed in the prescribed manner to the debtor or hirer before a regulated agreement is made.

(2) A regulated agreement is not properly executed unless regulations under subsection (1) were complied with before the making of the agreement.

56 Antecedent negotiations.

(1) In this Act 'antecedent negotiations' means any negotiations with the debtor or hirer—

(a) conducted by the creditor or owner in relation to the making of any regulated agreement, or

(b) conducted by a credit-broker in relation to goods sold or proposed to be sold by the credit-broker to the creditor before forming the subject-matter of a debtor-creditor-supplier agreement within section 12(a), or

(c) conducted by the supplier in relation to a transaction financed or proposed to be financed by a debtor-creditor-supplier agreement within section 12(b) or (c),

and 'negotiator' means the person by whom negotiations are so conducted with the debtor or hirer.

(2) Negotiations with the debtor in a case falling within subsection (1)(b) or (c) shall be deemed to be conducted by the negotiator in the capacity of agent of the creditor as well as in his actual capacity.

(3) An agreement is void if, and to the extent that, it purports in relation to an actual or prospective regulated agreement—

(a) to provide that a person acting as, or on behalf of, a negotiator is to be treated as the agent of the debtor or hirer, or

(b) to relieve a person from liability for acts or omissions of any person acting as, or on behalf of, a negotiator.

(4) For the purposes of this Act, antecedent negotiations shall be taken to begin when the negotiator and the debtor or hirer first enter into communication (including communication by advertisement), and to include any representations made by the negotiator to the debtor or hirer and any other dealings between them.

57 Withdrawal from prospective agreement.

(1) The withdrawal of a party from a prospective regulated agreement shall operate to apply this Part to the agreement, any linked transaction and any other thing done in anticipation of the making of the agreement as it would apply if the agreement were made and then cancelled under section 69.

(2) The giving to a party of a written or oral notice which, however expressed, indicates the intention of the other party to withdraw from a prospective regulated agreement operates as a withdrawal from it.

(3) Each of the following shall be deemed to be the agent of the creditor or owner for the purpose of receiving a notice under subsection (2)—

(a) a credit-broker or supplier who is the negotiator in antecedent negotiations, and

(b) any person who, in the course of a business carried on by him, acts on behalf of the debtor or hirer in any negotiations for the agreement.

(4) Where the agreement, if made, would not be a cancellable agreement, subsection (1) shall nevertheless apply as if the contrary were the case.

58 Opportunity for withdrawal from prospective land mortgage.

(1) Before sending to the debtor or hirer, for his signature, an unexecuted agreement in a case where the prospective regulated agreement is to be secured on land (the 'mortgaged

land'), the creditor or owner shall give the debtor or hirer a copy of the unexecuted agreement which contains a notice in the prescribed form indicating the right of the debtor or hirer to withdraw from the prospective agreement, and how and when the right is exercisable, together with a copy of any other document referred to in the unexecuted agreement.

(2) Subsection (1) does not apply to—

    (a) a restricted-use credit agreement to finance the purchase of the mortgaged land, or

    (b) an agreement for a bridging loan in connection with the purchase of the mortgaged land or other land.

59 Agreement to enter future agreement void.

(1) An agreement is void if, and to the extent that, it purports to bind a person to enter as debtor or hirer into a prospective regulated agreement.

(2) Regulations may exclude from the operation of subsection (1) agreements such as are described in the regulations.

Making the agreement

60 Form and content of agreements.

(1) The Secretary of State shall make regulations as to the form and content of documents embodying regulated agreements, and the regulations shall contain such provisions as appear to him appropriate with a view to ensuring that the debtor or hirer is made aware of—

    (a) the rights and duties conferred or imposed on him by the agreement,

    (b) the amount and rate of the total charge for credit (in the case of a consumer credit agreement),

    (c) the protection and remedies available to him under this Act, and

    (d) any other matters which, in the opinion of the Secretary of State, it is desirable for him to know about in connection with the agreement.

(2) Regulations under subsection (1) may in particular—

    (a) require specified information to be included in the prescribed manner in documents, and other specified material to be excluded;

    (b) contain requirements to ensure that specified information is clearly brought to the attention of the debtor or hirer, and that one part of a document is not given insufficient or excessive prominence compared with another.

(3) If, on an application made to the OFT by a person carrying on a consumer credit business or a consumer hire business, it appears to the OFT impracticable for the applicant to comply with any requirement of regulations under subsection (1) in a particular case, it may, by notice to the applicant direct that the requirement be waived or varied in relation to such agreements, and subject to such conditions (if any), as it may specify, and this Act and the regulations shall have effect accordingly.

(4) The OFT shall give a notice under subsection (3) only if it is satisfied that to do so would not prejudice the interests of debtors or hirers.

61   Signing of agreement.

(1)   A regulated agreement is not properly executed unless—

   (a)   a document in the prescribed form itself containing all the prescribed terms and conforming to regulations under section 60(1) is signed in the prescribed manner both by the debtor or hirer and by or on behalf of the creditor or owner, and

   (b)   the document embodies all the terms of the agreement, other than implied terms, and

   (c)   the document is, when presented or sent to the debtor or hirer for signature, in such a state that all its terms are readily legible.

(2)   In addition, where the agreement is one to which section 58(1) applies, it is not properly executed unless—

   (a)   the requirements of section 58(1) were complied with, and

   (b)   the unexecuted agreement was sent, for his signature, to the debtor or hirer by an appropriate method not less than seven days after a copy of it was given to him under section 58(1), and

   (c)   during the consideration period, the creditor or owner refrained from approaching the debtor or hirer (whether in person, by telephone or letter, or in any other way) except in response to a specific request made by the debtor or hirer after the beginning of the consideration period, and

   (d)   no notice of withdrawal by the debtor or hirer was received by the creditor or owner before the sending of the unexecuted agreement.

(3)   In subsection (2)(c), 'the consideration period' means the period beginning with the giving of the copy under section 58(1) and ending—

   (a)   at the expiry of seven days after the day on which the unexecuted agreement is sent, for his signature, to the debtor or hirer, or

   (b)   on its return by the debtor or hirer after signature by him, whichever first occurs.

(4)   Where the debtor or hirer is a partnership or an unincorporated body of persons, subsection (1)(a) shall apply with the substitution for 'by the debtor or hirer' of 'by or on behalf of the debtor or hirer'.

62   Duty to supply copy of unexecuted agreement.

(1)   If the unexecuted agreement is presented personally to the debtor or hirer for his signature, but on the occasion when he signs it the document does not become an executed agreement, a copy of it, and of any other document referred to in it, must be there and then delivered to him.

(2)   If the unexecuted agreement is sent to the debtor or hirer for his signature, a copy of it, and of any other document referred to in it, must be sent to him at the same time.

(3)   A regulated agreement is not properly executed if the requirements of this section are not observed.

63   Duty to supply copy of executed agreement.

(1)   If the unexecuted agreement is presented personally to the debtor or hirer for his signature, and on the occasion when he signs it the document becomes an executed agreement, a copy of the executed agreement, and of any other document referred to in it, must be there and then delivered to him.

(2) A copy of the executed agreement, and of any other document referred to in it, must be given to the debtor or hirer within the seven days following the making of the agreement unless—

 (a) subsection (1) applies, or

 (b) the unexecuted agreement was sent to the debtor or hirer for his signature and, on the occasion of his signing it, the document became an executed agreement.

(3) In the case of a cancellable agreement, a copy under subsection (2) must be sent by an appropriate method.

(4) In the case of a credit-token agreement, a copy under subsection (2) need not be given within the seven days following the making of the agreement if it is given before or at the time when the credit-token is given to the debtor.

(5) A regulated agreement is not properly executed if the requirements of this section are not observed.

64   Duty to give notice of cancellation rights.

(1) In the case of a cancellable agreement, a notice in the prescribed form indicating the right of the debtor or hirer to cancel the agreement, how and when that right is exercisable, and the name and address of a person to whom notice of cancellation may be given—

 (a) must be included in every copy given to the debtor or hirer under section 62 or 63, and

 (b) except where section 63(2) applied, must also be sent by an appropriate method to the debtor or hirer within the seven days following the making of the agreement.

(2) In the case of a credit-token agreement, a notice under subsection (1)(b) need not be sent by an appropriate method within the seven days following the making of the agreement if either—

 (a) it is sent by an appropriate method to the debtor or hirer before the credit-token is given to him, or

 (b) it is sent by an appropriate method to him together with the credit-token.

(3) Regulations may provide that except where section 63(2) applied a notice sent under subsection (1)(b) shall be accompanied by a further copy of the executed agreement, and of any other document referred to in it.

(4) Regulations may provide that subsection (1)(b) is not to apply in the case of agreements such as are described in the regulations, being agreements made by a particular person, if—

 (a) on an application by that person to the OFT, the OFT has determined that, having regard to—

  (i)   the manner in which antecedent negotiations for agreements with the applicant of that description are conducted, and

  (ii) the information provided to debtors or hirers before such agreements are made,

 the requirement imposed by subsection (1)(b) can be dispensed with without prejudicing the interests of debtors or hirers; and

 (b) any conditions imposed by the OFT in making the determination are complied with.

(5) A cancellable agreement is not properly executed if the requirements of this section are not observed.

65   Consequences of improper execution.

(1)   An improperly-executed regulated agreement is enforceable against the debtor or hirer on an order of the court only.

(2)   A retaking of goods or land to which a regulated agreement relates is an enforcement of the agreement.

66   Acceptance of credit-tokens.

(1)   The debtor shall not be liable under a credit-token agreement for use made of the credit-token by any person unless the debtor had previously accepted the credit-token, or the use constituted an acceptance of it by him.

(2)   The debtor accepts a credit-token when—

(a)   it is signed, or

(b)   a receipt for it is signed, or

(c)   it is first used,

either by the debtor himself or by a person who, pursuant to the agreement, is authorised by him to use it.

Cancellation of certain agreements within cooling-off period

67   Cancellable agreements.

A regulated agreement may be cancelled by the debtor or hirer in accordance with this Part if the antecedent negotiations included oral representations made when in the presence of the debtor or hirer by an individual acting as, or on behalf of, the negotiator, unless—

(a)   the agreement is secured on land, or is a restricted-use credit agreement to finance the purchase of land or is an agreement for a bridging loan in connection with the purchase of land, or

(b)   the unexecuted agreement is signed by the debtor or hirer at premises at which any of the following is carrying on any business (whether on a permanent or temporary basis)—

(i)   the creditor or owner;

(ii)   any party to a linked transaction (other than the debtor or hirer or a relative of his);

(iii)   the negotiator in any antecedent negotiations.

68   Cooling-off period.

The debtor or hirer may serve notice of cancellation of a cancellable agreement between his signing of the unexecuted agreement and—

(a)   the end of the fifth day following the day on which he received a copy under section 63(2) or a notice under section 64(1)(b), or

(b)   if (by virtue of regulations made under section 64(4)) section 64(1)(b) does not apply, the end of the fourteenth day following the day on which he signed the unexecuted agreement.

69   Notice of cancellation.

(1)   If within the period specified in section 68 the debtor or hirer under a cancellable agreement serves on—

    (a)   the creditor or owner, or

    (b)   the person specified in the notice under section 64(1), or

    (c)   a person who (whether by virtue of subsection (6) or otherwise) is the agent of the creditor or owner,

a notice (a 'notice of cancellation') which, however expressed and whether or not conforming to the notice given under section 64(1), indicates the intention of the debtor or hirer to withdraw from the agreement, the notice shall operate—

    (i)   to cancel the agreement, and any linked transaction, and

    (ii)   to withdraw any offer by the debtor or hirer, or his relative, to enter into a linked transaction.

(2)   In the case of a debtor-creditor-supplier agreement for restricted-use credit financing—

    (a)   the doing of work or supply of goods to meet an emergency, or

    (b)   the supply of goods which, before service of the notice of cancellation, had by the act of the debtor or his relative become incorporated in any land or thing not comprised in the agreement or any linked transaction,

Subsection (1) shall apply with the substitution of the following for paragraph (i)—

    '(i)   to cancel only such provisions of the agreement and any linked transaction as—

        (aa)   relate to the provision of credit, or

        (bb)   require the debtor to pay an item in the total charge for credit, or

        (cc)   subject the debtor to any obligation other than to pay for the doing of the said work, or the supply of the said goods'.

(3)   Except so far as is otherwise provided, references in this Act to the cancellation of an agreement or transaction do not include a case within subsection (2).

(4)   Except as otherwise provided by or under this Act, an agreement or transaction cancelled under subsection (1) shall be treated as if it had never been entered into.

(5)   Regulations may exclude linked transactions of the prescribed description from subsection (1)(i) or (ii).

(6)   Each of the following shall be deemed to be the agent of the creditor or owner for the purpose of receiving a notice of cancellation—

    (a)   a credit-broker or supplier who is the negotiator in antecedent negotiations, and

    (b)   any person who, in the course of a business carried on by him, acts on behalf of the debtor or hirer in any negotiations for the agreement.

(7)   Whether or not it is actually received by him, a notice of cancellation sent to a person shall be deemed to be served on him—

    (a)   in the case of a notice sent by post, at the time of posting, and

    (b)   in the case of a notice transmitted in the form of an electronic communication in accordance with section 176A(1), at the time of the transmission.

70   Cancellation: recovery of money paid by debtor or hirer.

(1)   On the cancellation of a regulated agreement, and of any linked transaction—

(a)   any sum paid by the debtor or hirer, or his relative, under or in contemplation of the agreement or transaction, including any item in the total charge for credit, shall become repayable, and

(b)   any sum, including any item in the total charge for credit, which but for the cancellation is, or would or might become, payable by the debtor or hirer, or his relative, under the agreement or transaction shall cease to be, or shall not become, so payable, and

(c)   in the case of a debtor-creditor-supplier agreement falling within section 12(b), any sum paid on the debtor's behalf by the creditor to the supplier shall become repayable to the creditor.

(2)   If, under the terms of a cancelled agreement or transaction, the debtor or hirer, or his relative, is in possession of any goods, he shall have a lien on them for any sum repayable to him under subsection (1) in respect of that agreement or transaction, or any other linked transaction.

(3)   A sum repayable under subsection (1) is repayable by the person to whom it was originally paid, but in the case of a debtor-creditor-supplier agreement falling within section 12(b) the creditor and the supplier shall be under a joint and several liability to repay sums paid by the debtor, or his relative, under the agreement or under a linked transaction falling within section 19(1)(b) and accordingly, in such a case, the creditor shall be entitled, in accordance with rules of court, to have the supplier made a party to any proceedings brought against the creditor to recover any such sums.

(4)   Subject to any agreement between them, the creditor shall be entitled to be indemnified by the supplier for loss suffered by the creditor in satisfying his liability under subsection (3), including costs reasonably incurred by him in defending proceedings instituted by the debtor.

(5)   Subsection (1) does not apply to any sum which, if not paid by a debtor, would be payable by virtue of section 71, and applies to a sum paid or payable by a debtor for the issue of a credit-token only where the credit-token has been returned to the creditor or surrendered to a supplier.

(6)   If the total charge for credit includes an item in respect of a fee or commission charged by a credit-broker, the amount repayable under subsection (1) in respect of that item shall be the excess over £5 of the fee or commission.

(7)   If the total charge for credit includes any sum payable or paid by the debtor to a credit-broker otherwise than in respect of a fee or commission charged by him, that sum shall for the purposes of subsection (6) be treated as if it were such a fee or commission.

(8)   So far only as is necessary to give effect to section 69(2), this section applies to an agreement or transaction within that subsection as it applies to a cancelled agreement or transaction.

71   Cancellation: repayment of credit.

(1)   Notwithstanding the cancellation of a regulated consumer credit agreement, other than a debtor-creditor-supplier agreement for restricted-use credit, the agreement shall continue in force so far as it relates to repayment of credit and payment of interest.

(2) If, following the cancellation of a regulated consumer credit agreement, the debtor repays the whole or a portion of the credit—

    (a)   before the expiry of one month following service of the notice of cancellation, or

    (b)   in the case of a credit repayable by instalments, before the date on which the first instalment is due,

no interest shall be payable on the amount repaid.

(3) If the whole of a credit repayable by instalments is not repaid on or before the date specified in subsection (2)(b), the debtor shall not be liable to repay any of the credit except on receipt of a request in writing in the prescribed form, signed by or on behalf of the creditor, stating the amounts of the remaining instalments (recalculated by the creditor as nearly as may be in accordance with the agreement and without extending the repayment period), but excluding any sum other than principal and interest.

(4) Repayment of a credit, or payment of interest, under a cancelled agreement shall be treated as duly made if it is made to any person on whom, under section 69, a notice of cancellation could have been served, other than a person referred to in section 69(6)(b).

72   Cancellation: return of goods.

(1) This section applies where any agreement or transaction relating to goods, being—

    (a)   a restricted-use debtor-creditor-supplier agreement, a consumer hire agreement, or a linked transaction to which the debtor or hirer under any regulated agreement is a party, or

    (b)   a linked transaction to which a relative of the debtor or hirer under any regulated agreement is a party,

is cancelled after the debtor or hirer (in a case within paragraph (a)) or the relative (in a case within paragraph (b)) has acquired possession of the goods by virtue of the agreement or transaction.

(2) In this section—

    (a)   'the possessor' means the person who has acquired possession of the goods as mentioned in subsection (1),

    (b)   'the other party' means the person from whom the possessor acquired possession, and

    (c)   'the pre-cancellation period' means the period beginning when the possessor acquired possession and ending with the cancellation.

(3) The possessor shall be treated as having been under a duty throughout the pre-cancellation period—

    (a)   to retain possession of the goods, and

    (b)   to take reasonable care of them.

(4) On the cancellation, the possessor shall be under a duty, subject to any lien, to restore the goods to the other party in accordance with this section, and meanwhile to retain possession of the goods and take reasonable care of them.

(5) The possessor shall not be under any duty to deliver the goods except at his own premises and in pursuance of a request in writing signed by or on behalf of the other party and served on the possessor either before, or at the time when, the goods are collected from those premises.

(6)   If the possessor—

    (a)   delivers the goods (whether at his own premises or elsewhere) to any person on whom, under section 69, a notice of cancellation could have been served (other than a person referred to in section 69(6)(b)), or

    (b)   sends the goods at his own expense to such a person,

he shall be discharged from any duty to retain the goods or deliver them to any person.

(7)   Where the possessor delivers the goods as mentioned in subsection (6)(a), his obligation to take care of the goods shall cease; and if he sends the goods as mentioned in subsection (6)(b), he shall be under a duty to take reasonable care to see that they are received by the other party and not damaged in transit, but in other respects his duty to take care of the goods shall cease.

(8)   Where, at any time during the period of 21 days following the cancellation, the possessor receives such a request as is mentioned in subsection (5), and unreasonably refuses or unreasonably fails to comply with it, his duty to take reasonable care of the goods shall continue until he delivers or sends the goods as mentioned in subsection (6), but if within that period he does not receive such a request his duty to take reasonable care of the goods shall cease at the end of that period.

(9)   The preceding provisions of this section do not apply to—

    (a)   Perishable goods, or

    (b)   goods which by their nature are consumed by use and which, before the cancellation, were so consumed, or

    (c)   goods supplied to meet an emergency, or

    (d)   goods which, before the cancellation, had become incorporated in any land or thing not comprised in the cancelled agreement or a linked transaction.

(10)   Where the address of the possessor is specified in the executed agreement, references in this section to his own premises are to that address and no other.

(11)   Breach of a duty imposed by this section is actionable as a breach of statutory duty.

73   Cancellation: goods given in part-exchange.

(1)   This section applies on the cancellation of a regulated agreement where, in antecedent negotiations, the negotiator agreed to take goods in part-exchange (the 'part-exchange goods') and those goods have been delivered to him.

(2)   Unless, before the end of the period of ten days beginning with the date of cancellation, the part-exchange goods are returned to the debtor or hirer in a condition substantially as good as when they were delivered to the negotiator, the debtor or hirer shall be entitled to recover from the negotiator a sum equal to the part-exchange allowance (as defined in subsection (7)(b)).

(3)   In the case of a debtor-creditor-supplier agreement within section 12(b), the negotiator and the creditor shall be under a joint and several liability to pay to the debtor a sum recoverable under subsection (2).

(4)   Subject to any agreement between them, the creditor shall be entitled to be indemnified by the negotiator for loss suffered by the creditor in satisfying his liability under subsection (3), including costs reasonably incurred by him in defending proceedings instituted by the debtor.

(5) During the period of ten days beginning with the date of cancellation, the debtor or hirer, if he is in possession of goods to which the cancelled agreement relates, shall have a lien on them for—

    (a) delivery of the part-exchange goods, in a condition substantially as good as when they were delivered to the negotiator, or

    (b) a sum equal to the part-exchange allowance;

and if the lien continues to the end of that period it shall thereafter subsist only as a lien for a sum equal to the part-exchange allowance.

(6) Where the debtor or hirer recovers from the negotiator or creditor, or both of them jointly, a sum equal to the part-exchange allowance, then, if the title of the debtor or hirer to the part-exchange goods has not vested in the negotiator, it shall so vest on the recovery of that sum.

(7) For the purposes of this section—

    (a) the negotiator shall be treated as having agreed to take goods in part-exchange if, in pursuance of the antecedent negotiations, he either purchased or agreed to purchase those goods or accepted or agreed to accept them as part of the consideration for the cancelled agreement, and

    (b) the part-exchange allowance shall be the sum agreed as such in the antecedent negotiations or, if no such agreement was arrived at, such sum as it would have been reasonable to allow in respect of the part-exchange goods if no notice of cancellation had been served.

(8) In an action brought against the creditor for a sum recoverable under subsection (2), he shall be entitled, in accordance with rules of court, to have the negotiator made a party to the proceedings.

Exclusion of certain agreements from Part V

74 Exclusion of certain agreements from Part V.

(1) This Part (except section 56) does not apply to—

    (a) a non-commercial agreement, or

    (b) a debtor-creditor agreement enabling the debtor to overdraw on a current account, or

    (c) a debtor-creditor agreement to finance the making of such payments arising on, or connected with, the death of a person as may be prescribed.

(2) This Part (except sections 55 and 56) does not apply to a small debtor-creditor-supplier agreement for restricted-use credit.

(2A) In the case of an agreement to which the Consumer Protection (Cancellation of Contracts Concluded away from Business Premises) Regulations 1987 apply the reference in subsection (2) to a small agreement shall be construed as if in section 17(1)(a) and (b) '£35' were substituted for '£50'.

(3) Subsection (1)(b) or (c) applies only where the OFT so determines, and such a determination—

    (a) may be made subject to such conditions as the OFT thinks fit, and

    (b) shall be made only if the OFT is of opinion that it is not against the interests of debtors.

(3A) Not withstanding anything in subsection (3)(b) above, in relation to a debtor-creditor agreement under which the creditor is the Bank of England or a bank within the meaning of the Bankers' Books Evidence Act 1879, the OFT shall make a determination that subsection (1)(b) above applies unless it considers that it would be against the public interest to do so.

(4)   If any term of an agreement falling within subsection (1)(c) or (2) is expressed in writing, regulations under section 60(1) shall apply to that term (subject to section 60(3)) as if the agreement were a regulated agreement not falling within subsection (1)(c) or (2).

PART VI MATTERS ARISING DURING CURRENCY OF CREDIT OR HIRE AGREEMENTS

75   *Liability of creditor for breaches by supplier.*

(1)   If the debtor under a debtor-creditor-supplier agreement falling within section 12(b) or (c) has, in relation to a transaction financed by the agreement, any claim against the supplier in respect of a misrepresentation or breach of contract, he shall have a like claim against the creditor, who, with the supplier, shall accordingly be jointly and severally liable to the debtor.

(2)   Subject to any agreement between them, the creditor shall be entitled to be indemnified by the supplier for loss suffered by the creditor in satisfying his liability under subsection (1), including costs reasonably incurred by him in defending proceedings instituted by the debtor.

(3)   Subsection (1) does not apply to a claim—

(a)   under a non-commercial agreement, or

(b)   so far as the claim relates to any single item to which the supplier has attached a cash price not exceeding £100 or more than £30,000.

(4)   This section applies notwithstanding that the debtor, in entering into the transaction, exceeded the credit limit or otherwise contravened any term of the agreement.

(5)   In an action brought against the creditor under subsection (1) he shall be entitled, in accordance with rules of court, to have the supplier made a party to the proceedings.

76   *Duty to give notice before taking certain action.*

(1)   The creditor or owner is not entitled to enforce a term of a regulated agreement by—

(a)   demanding earlier payment of any sum, or

(b)   recovering possession of any goods or land, or

(c)   treating any right conferred on the debtor or hirer by the agreement as terminated, restricted or deferred,

except by or after giving the debtor or hirer not less than seven days' notice of his intention to do so.

(2)   Subsection (1) applies only where—

(a)   a period for the duration of the agreement is specified in the agreement, and

(b) that period has not ended when the creditor or owner does an act mentioned in sub-section (1),

but so applies notwithstanding that, under the agreement, any party is entitled to terminate it before the end of the period so specified.

(3) A notice under subsection (1) is ineffective if not in the prescribed form.

(4) Subsection (1) does not prevent a creditor from treating the right to draw on any credit as restricted or deferred and taking such steps as may be necessary to make the restriction or deferment effective.

(5) Regulations may provide that subsection (1) is not to apply to agreements described by the regulations.

(6) Subsection (1) does not apply to a right of enforcement arising by reason of any breach by the debtor or hirer of the regulated agreement.

77   *Duty to give information to debtor under fixed-sum credit agreement.*

(1) The creditor under a regulated agreement for fixed-sum credit, within the prescribed period after receiving a request in writing to that effect from the debtor and payment of a fee of ...£1, shall give the debtor a copy of the executed agreement (if any) and of any other document referred to in it, together with a statement signed by or on behalf of the creditor showing, according to the information to which it is practicable for him to refer—

(a) the total sum paid under the agreement by the debtor;

(b) the total sum which has become payable under the agreement by the debtor but remains unpaid, and the various amounts comprised in that total sum, with the date when each became due; and

(c) the total sum which is to become payable under the agreement by the debtor, and the various amounts comprised in that total sum, with the date, or mode of determining the date, when each becomes due.

(2) If the creditor possesses insufficient information to enable him to ascertain the amounts and dates mentioned in subsection (1)(c), he shall be taken to comply with that paragraph if his statement under subsection (1) gives the basis on which, under the regulated agreement, they would fall to be ascertained.

(3) Subsection (1) does not apply to—

(a) an agreement under which no sum is, or will or may become, payable by the debtor, or

(b) a request made less than one month after a previous request under that subsection relating to the same agreement was complied with.

(4) If the creditor under an agreement fails to comply with subsection (1)—

(a) he is not entitled, while the default continues, to enforce the agreement.

(b) ...

(5) This section does not apply to a non-commercial agreement.

77A   *Statements to be provided in relation to fixed-sum credit agreements*

(1) The creditor under a regulated agreement for fixed-sum credit—

(a)   shall, within the period of one year beginning with the day after the day on which the agreement is made, give the debtor a statement under this section; and

(b)   after the giving of that statement, shall give the debtor further statements under this section at intervals of not more than one year.

(2)   Regulations may make provision about the form and content of statements under this section.

(3)   The debtor shall have no liability to pay any sum in connection with the preparation or the giving to him of a statement under this section.

(4)   The creditor is not required to give the debtor any statement under this section once the following conditions are satisfied—

(a)   that there is no sum payable under the agreement by the debtor; and

(b)   that there is no sum which will or may become so payable.

(5)   Subsection (6) applies if at a time before the conditions mentioned in subsection (4) are satisfied the creditor fails to give the debtor—

(a)   a statement under this section within the period mentioned in subsection (1)(a); or

(b)   such a statement within the period of one year beginning with the day after the day on which such a statement was last given to him.

(6)   Where this subsection applies in relation to a failure to give a statement under this section to the debtor—

(a)   the creditor shall not be entitled to enforce the agreement during the period of non-compliance;

(b)   the debtor shall have no liability to pay any sum of interest to the extent calculated by reference to the period of non-compliance or to any part of it; and

(c)   the debtor shall have no liability to pay any default sum which (apart from this paragraph)—

(i)   would have become payable during the period of non-compliance; or

(ii)   would have become payable after the end of that period in connection with a breach of the agreement which occurs during that period (whether or not the breach continues after the end of that period).

(7)   In this section 'the period of non-compliance' means, in relation to a failure to give a statement under this section to the debtor, the period which—

(a)   begins immediately after the end of the period mentioned in paragraph (a) or (as the case may be) paragraph (b) of subsection (5); and

(b)   ends at the end of the day on which the statement is given to the debtor or on which the conditions mentioned in subsection (4) are satisfied, whichever is earlier.

(8)   This section does not apply in relation to a non-commercial agreement or to a small agreement.

78   *Duty to give information to debtor under running-account credit agreement.*

(1)   The creditor under a regulated agreement for running-account credit, within the prescribed period after receiving a request in writing to that effect from the debtor and payment of a fee of £1, shall give the debtor a copy of the executed agreement (if any) and of

any other document referred to in it, together with a statement signed by or on behalf of the creditor showing, according to the information to which it is practicable for him to refer—

(a) the state of the account, and

(b) the amount, if any currently payable under the agreement by the debtor to the creditor, and

(c) the amounts and due dates of any payments which, if the debtor does not draw further on the account, will later become payable under the agreement by the debtor to the creditor.

(2) If the creditor possesses insufficient information to enable him to ascertain the amounts and dates mentioned in subsection (1)(c), he shall be taken to comply with that paragraph if his statement under subsection (1) gives the basis on which, under the regulated agreement, they would fall to be ascertained.

(3) Subsection (1) does not apply to—

(a) an agreement under which no sum is, or will or may become, payable by the debtor, or

(b) a request made less than one month after a previous request under that subsection relating to the same agreement was complied with.

(4) Where running-account credit is provided under a regulated agreement, the creditor shall give the debtor statements in the prescribed form, and with the prescribed contents—

(a) showing according to the information to which it is practicable for him to refer, the state of the account at regular intervals of not more than twelve months, and

(b) where the agreement provides, in relation to specified periods, for the making of payments by the debtor, or the charging against him of interest or any other sum, showing according to the information to which it is practicable for him to refer the state of the account at the end of each of those periods during which there is any movement in the account.

(4A) Regulations may require a statement under subsection (4) to contain also information in the prescribed terms about the consequences of the debtor—

(a) failing to make payments as required by the agreement; or

(b) only making payments of a prescribed description in prescribed circumstances.

(5) A statement under subsection (4) shall be given within the prescribed period after the end of the period to which the statement relates.

(6) If the creditor under an agreement fails to comply with subsection (1)—

(a) he is not entitled, while the default continues, to enforce the agreement.

(b) ...

(7) This section does not apply to a non-commercial agreement, and subsections (4) to (5) do not apply to a small agreement.

79 *Duty to give hirer information.*

(1) The owner under a regulated consumer hire agreement, within the prescribed period after receiving a request in writing to that effect from the hirer and payment of a fee of £1, shall give to the hirer a copy of the executed agreement and of any other document referred to

in it, together with a statement signed by or on behalf of the owner showing, according to the information to which it is practicable for him to refer, the total sum which has become payable under the agreement by the hirer but remains unpaid and the various amounts comprised in that total sum, with the date when each became due.

(2)   Subsection (1) does not apply to—

(a)   an agreement under which no sum is, or will or may become, payable by the hirer, or

(b)   a request made less than one month after a previous request under that subsection relating to the same agreement was complied with.

(3)   If the owner under an agreement fails to comply with subsection (1)—

(a)   he is not entitled, while the default continues, to enforce the agreement.

(b)   . . .

(4)   This section does not apply to a non-commercial agreement.

80   *Debtor or hirer to give information about goods.*

(1)   Where a regulated agreement, other than a non-commercial agreement, requires the debtor or hirer to keep goods to which the agreement relates in his possession or control, he shall, within seven working days after he has received a request in writing to that effect from the creditor or owner, tell the creditor or owner where the goods are.

(2)   If the debtor or hirer fails to comply with subsection (1), and the default continues for 14 days, he commits an offence.

81   *Appropriation of payments.*

(1)   Where a debtor or hirer is liable to make to the same person payments in respect of two or more regulated agreements, he shall be entitled, on making any payment in respect of the agreements which is not sufficient to discharge the total amount then due under all the agreements, to appropriate the sum so paid by him—

(a)   in or towards the satisfaction of the sum due under any one of the agreements, or

(b)   in or towards the satisfaction of the sums due under any two or more of the agreements in such proportions as he thinks fit.

(2)   If the debtor or hirer fails to make any such appropriation where one or more of the agreements is—

(a)   a hire-purchase agreement or conditional sale agreement, or

(b)   a consumer hire agreement, or

(c)   an agreement in relation to which any security is provided,

the payment shall be appropriated towards the satisfaction of the sums due under the several agreements respectively in the proportions which those sums bear to one another.

82   *Variation of agreements.*

(1)   Where, under a power contained in a regulated agreement, the creditor or owner varies the agreement, the variation shall not take effect before notice of it is given to the debtor or hirer in the prescribed manner.

(2) Where an agreement (a 'modifying agreement') varies or supplements an earlier agreement, the modifying agreement shall for the purposes of this Act be treated as—

(a) revoking the earlier agreement, and

(b) containing provisions reproducing the combined effect of the two agreements,

and obligations outstanding in relation to the earlier agreement shall accordingly be treated as outstanding instead in relation to the modifying agreement.

(2A) Subsection (2) does not apply if the earlier agreement or the modifying agreement is an exempt agreement as a result of section 16(6C).

(3) If the earlier agreement is a regulated agreement but (apart from this subsection) the modifying agreement is not then, unless the modifying agreement is—

(a) for running account credit; or

(b) an exempt agreement as a result of section 16(6C),

it shall be treated as a regulated agreement.

(4) If the earlier agreement is a regulated agreement for running-account credit, and by the modifying agreement the creditor allows the credit limit to be exceeded but intends the excess to be merely temporary, Part V (except section 56) shall not apply to the modifying agreement.

(5) If—

(a) the earlier agreement is a cancellable agreement, and

(b) the modifying agreement is made within the period applicable under section 68 to the earlier agreement,

then, whether or not the modifying agreement would, apart from this subsection, be a cancellable agreement, it shall be treated as a cancellable agreement in respect of which a notice may be served under section 68 not later than the end of the period applicable under that section to the earlier agreement.

(5A) Subsection (5) does not apply where the modifying agreement is an exempt agreement as a result of section 16(6C).

(6) Except under subsection (5), a modifying agreement shall not be treated as a cancellable agreement.

(7) This section does not apply to a non-commercial agreement.

83 *Liability for misuse of credit facilities.*

(1) The debtor under a regulated consumer credit agreement shall not be liable to the creditor for any loss arising from use of the credit facility by another person not acting, or to be treated as acting, as the debtor's agent.

(2) This section does not apply to a non-commercial agreement, or to any loss in so far as it arises from misuse of an instrument to which section 4 of the Cheques Act 1957 applies.

84 *Misuse of credit-tokens.*

(1) Section 83 does not prevent the debtor under a credit-token agreement from being made liable to the extent of £50 (or the credit limit if lower) for loss to the creditor arising from

use of the credit-token by other persons during a period beginning when the credit-token ceases to be in the possession of any authorised person and ending when the credit-token is once more in the possession of an authorised person.

(2)   Section 83 does not prevent the debtor under a credit-token agreement from being made liable to any extent for loss to the creditor from use of the credit-token by a person who acquired possession of it with the debtor's consent.

(3)   Subsections (1) and (2) shall not apply to any use of the credit-token after the creditor has been given oral or written notice that it is lost or stolen, or is for any other reason liable to misuse.

(3A) Subsections (1) and (2) shall not apply to any use, in connection with a distance contract (other than an excepted contract), of a card which is a credit-token.

(3B) In subsection (3A), 'distance contract' and 'excepted contract' have the meanings given in the Consumer Protection (Distance Selling) Regulations 2000.

(3C) Subsections (1) and (2) shall not apply to any use, in connection with a distance contract within the meaning of the Financial Services (Distance Marketing) Regulations 2004, of a card which is a credit-token.

(4)   Subsections (1) and (2) shall not apply unless there are contained in the credit-token agreement in the prescribed manner particulars of the name, address and telephone number of a person stated to be the person to whom notice is to be given under subsection (3).

(5)   Notice under subsection (3) takes effect when received, but where it is given orally, and the agreement so requires, it shall be treated as not taking effect if not confirmed in writing within seven days.

(6)   Any sum paid by the debtor for the issue of the credit-token, to the extent (if any) that it has not been previously offset by use made of the credit-token, shall be treated as paid towards satisfaction of any liability under subsection (1) or (2).

(7)   The debtor, the creditor, and any person authorised by the debtor to use the credit-token, shall be authorised persons for the purposes of subsection (1).

(8)   Where two or more credit-tokens are given under one credit-token agreement, the preceding provisions of this section apply to each credit-token separately.

85   Duty on issue of new credit-tokens.

(1)   Whenever, in connection with a credit-token agreement, a credit-token (other than the first) is given by the creditor to the debtor, the creditor shall give the debtor a copy of the executed agreement (if any) and of any other document referred to in it.

(2)   If the creditor fails to comply with this section—

    (a)   he is not entitled, while the default continues, to enforce the agreement.

    (b)   . . .

(3)   This section does not apply to a small agreement.

86   Death of debtor or hirer.

(1)   The creditor or owner under a regulated agreement is not entitled, by reason of the death of the debtor or hirer, to do an act specified in paragraphs (a) to (e) of section 87(1) if at the death the agreement is fully secured.

(2) If at the death of the debtor or hirer a regulated agreement is only partly secured or is unsecured, the creditor or owner is entitled, by reason of the death of the debtor or hirer, to do an act specified in paragraphs (a) to (e) of section 87(1) on an order of the court only.

(3) This section applies in relation to the termination of an agreement only where—

(a) a period for its duration is specified in the agreement, and

(b) that period has not ended when the creditor or owner purports to terminate the agreement,

but so applies notwithstanding that, under the agreement, any party is entitled to terminate it before the end of the period so specified.

(4) This section does not prevent the creditor from treating the right to draw on any credit as restricted or deferred, and taking such steps as may be necessary to make the restriction or deferment effective.

(5) This section does not affect the operation of any agreement providing for payment of sums—

(a) due under the regulated agreement, or

(b) becoming due under it on the death of the debtor or hirer,

out of the proceeds of a policy of assurance on his life.

(6) For the purposes of this section an act is done by reason of the death of the debtor or hirer if it is done under a power conferred by the agreement which is—

(a) exercisable on his death, or

(b) exercisable at will and exercised at any time after his death.

Information sheets

86A   OFT to prepare information sheets on arrears and default

(1) The OFT shall prepare, and give general notice of, an arrears information sheet and a default information sheet.

(2) The arrears information sheet shall include information to help debtors and hirers who receive notices under section 86B or 86C.

(3) The default information sheet shall include information to help debtors and hirers who receive default notices.

(4) Regulations may make provision about the information to be included in an information sheet.

(5) An information sheet takes effect for the purposes of this Part at the end of the period of three months beginning with the day on which general notice of it is given.

(6) If the OFT revises an information sheet after general notice of it has been given, it shall give general notice of the information sheet as revised.

(7) A revised information sheet takes effect for the purposes of this Part at the end of the period of three months beginning with the day on which general notice of it is given.

Sums in arrears and default sums

86B   Notice of sums in arrears under fixed-sum credit agreements etc

(1)   This section applies where at any time the following conditions are satisfied—

    (a)   that the debtor or hirer under an applicable agreement is required to have made at least two payments under the agreement before that time;

    (b)   that the total sum paid under the agreement by him is less than the total sum which he is required to have paid before that time;

    (c)   that the amount of the shortfall is no less than the sum of the last two payments which he is required to have made before that time;

    (d)   that the creditor or owner is not already under a duty to give him notices under this section in relation to the agreement; and

    (e)   if a judgment has been given in relation to the agreement before that time, that there is no sum still to be paid under the judgment by the debtor or hirer.

(2)   The creditor or owner—

    (a)   shall, within the period of 14 days beginning with the day on which the conditions mentioned in subsection (1) are satisfied, give the debtor or hirer a notice under this section; and

    (b)   after the giving of that notice, shall give him further notices under this section at intervals of not more than six months.

(3)   The duty of the creditor or owner to give the debtor or hirer notices under this section shall cease when either of the conditions mentioned in subsection (4) is satisfied; but if either of those conditions is satisfied before the notice required by subsection (2)(a) is given, the duty shall not cease until that notice is given.

(4)   The conditions referred to in subsection (3) are—

    (a)   that the debtor or hirer ceases to be in arrears;

    (b)   that a judgment is given in relation to the agreement under which a sum is required to be paid by the debtor or hirer.

(5)   For the purposes of subsection (4)(a) the debtor or hirer ceases to be in arrears when—

    (a)   no sum, which he has ever failed to pay under the agreement when required, is still owing;

    (b)   no default sum, which has ever become payable under the agreement in connection with his failure to pay any sum under the agreement when required, is still owing;

    (c)   no sum of interest, which has ever become payable under the agreement in connection with such a default sum, is still owing; and

    (d)   no other sum of interest, which has ever become payable under the agreement in connection with his failure to pay any sum under the agreement when required, is still owing.

(6)   A notice under this section shall include a copy of the current arrears information sheet under section 86A.

(7)   The debtor or hirer shall have no liability to pay any sum in connection with the preparation or the giving to him of a notice under this section.

(8) Regulations may make provision about the form and content of notices under this section.

(9) In the case of an applicable agreement under which the debtor or hirer must make all payments he is required to make at intervals of one week or less, this section shall have effect as if in subsection (1)(a) and (c) for 'two' there were substituted 'four'.

(10) If an agreement mentioned in subsection (9) was made before the beginning of the relevant period, only amounts resulting from failures by the debtor or hirer to make payments he is required to have made during that period shall be taken into account in determining any shortfall for the purposes of subsection (1)(c).

(11) In subsection (10) 'relevant period' means the period of 20 weeks ending with the day on which the debtor or hirer is required to have made the most recent payment under the agreement.

(12) In this section 'applicable agreement' means an agreement which—

    (a) is a regulated agreement for fixed-sum credit or a regulated consumer hire agreement; and

    (b) is neither a non-commercial agreement nor a small agreement.

86C   Notice of sums in arrears under running-account credit agreements

(1) This section applies where at any time the following conditions are satisfied—

    (a) that the debtor under an applicable agreement is required to have made at least two payments under the agreement before that time;

    (b) that the last two payments which he is required to have made before that time have not been made;

    (c) that the creditor has not already been required to give a notice under this section in relation to either of those payments; and

    (d) if a judgment has been given in relation to the agreement before that time, that there is no sum still to be paid under the judgment by the debtor.

(2) The creditor shall, no later than the end of the period within which he is next required to give a statement under section 78(4) in relation to the agreement, give the debtor a notice under this section.

(3) The notice shall include a copy of the current arrears information sheet under section 86A.

(4) The notice may be incorporated in a statement or other notice which the creditor gives the debtor in relation to the agreement by virtue of another provision of this Act.

(5) The debtor shall have no liability to pay any sum in connection with the preparation or the giving to him of the notice.

(6) Regulations may make provision about the form and content of notices under this section.

(7) In this section 'applicable agreement' means an agreement which—

    (a) is a regulated agreement for running-account credit; and

    (b) is neither a non-commercial agreement nor a small agreement.

86D   Failure to give notice of sums in arrear

(1)   This section applies where the creditor or owner under an agreement is under a duty to give the debtor or hirer notices under section 86B but fails to give him such a notice–

    (a)   within the period mentioned in subsection (2)(a) of that section; or

    (b)   within the period of six months beginning with the day after the day on which such a notice was last given to him.

(2)   This section also applies where the creditor under an agreement is under a duty to give the debtor a notice under section 86C but fails to do so before the end of the period mentioned in subsection (2) of that section.

(3)   The creditor or owner shall not be entitled to enforce the agreement during the period of non-compliance.

(4)   The debtor or hirer shall have no liability to pay—

    (a)   any sum of interest to the extent calculated by reference to the period of non-compliance or to any part of it; or

    (b)   any default sum which (apart from this paragraph)—

        (i)   would have become payable during the period of non-compliance; or

        (ii)   would have become payable after the end of that period in connection with a breach of the agreement which occurs during that period (whether or not the breach continues after the end of that period).

(5)   In this section 'the period of non-compliance' means, in relation to a failure to give a notice under section 86B or 86C to the debtor or hirer, the period which—

    (a)   begins immediately after the end of the period mentioned in (as the case may be) subsection (1)(a) or (b) or (2); and

    (b)   ends at the end of the day mentioned in subsection (6).

(6)   That day is—

    (a)   in the case of a failure to give a notice under section 86B as mentioned in subsection (1)(a) of this section, the day on which the notice is given to the debtor or hirer; (b) in the case of a failure to give a notice under that section as mentioned in subsection (1)(b) of this section, the earlier of the following—

        (i)   the day on which the notice is given to the debtor or hirer;

        (ii)   the day on which the condition mentioned in subsection (4)(a) of that section is satisfied;

    (c)   in the case of a failure to give a notice under section 86C, the day on which the notice is given to the debtor.'

86E   Notice of default sums

(1)   This section applies where a default sum becomes payable under a regulated agreement by the debtor or hirer.

(2)   The creditor or owner shall, within the prescribed period after the default sum becomes payable, give the debtor or hirer a notice under this section.

(3)   The notice under this section may be incorporated in a statement or other notice which the creditor or owner gives the debtor or hirer in relation to the agreement by virtue of another provision of this Act.

(4) The debtor or hirer shall have no liability to pay interest in connection with the default sum to the extent that the interest is calculated by reference to a period occurring before the 29th day after the day on which the debtor or hirer is given the notice under this section.

(5) If the creditor or owner fails to give the debtor or hirer the notice under this section within the period mentioned in subsection (2), he shall not be entitled to enforce the agreement until the notice is given to the debtor or hirer.

(6) The debtor or hirer shall have no liability to pay any sum in connection with the preparation or the giving to him of the notice under this section.

(7) Regulations may—

    (a) Provide that this section does not apply in relation to a default sum which is less than a prescribed amount;

    (b) make provision about the form and content of notices under this section.

(8) This section does not apply in relation to a non-commercial agreement or to a small agreement.

86F Interest on default sum

(1) This section applies where a default sum becomes payable under a regulated agreement by the debtor or hirer.

(2) The debtor or hirer shall only be liable to pay interest in connection with the default sum if the interest is simple interest.'

PART VII DEFAULT AND TERMINATION

Default notices

87 Need for default notice.

(1) Service of a notice on the debtor or hirer in accordance with section 88 (a 'default notice') is necessary before the creditor or owner can become entitled, by reason of any breach by the debtor or hirer of a regulated agreement,—

    (a) to terminate the agreement, or

    (b) to demand earlier payment of any sum, or

    (c) to recover possession of any goods or land, or

    (d) to treat any right conferred on the debtor or hirer by the agreement as terminated, restricted or deferred, or

    (e) to enforce any security.

(2) Subsection (1) does not prevent the creditor from treating the right to draw upon any credit as restricted or deferred, and taking such steps as may be necessary to make the restriction or deferment effective.

(3) The doing of an act by which a floating charge becomes fixed is not enforcement of a security.

(4) Regulations may provide that subsection (1) is not to apply to agreements described by the regulations.

88   Contents and effect of default notice.

(1) The default notice must be in the prescribed form and specify—

    (a) the nature of the alleged breach;

    (b) if the breach is capable of remedy, what action is required to remedy it and the date before which that action is to be taken;

    (c) if the breach is not capable of remedy, the sum (if any) required to be paid as compensation for the breach, and the date before which it is to be paid.

(2) A date specified under subsection (1) must not be less than 14 days after the date of service of the default notice, and the creditor or owner shall not take action such as is mentioned in section 87(1) before the date so specified or (if no requirement is made under subsection (1)) before those 14 days have elapsed.

(3) The default notice must not treat as a breach failure to comply with a provision of the agreement which becomes operative only on breach of some other provision, but if the breach of that other provision is not duly remedied or compensation demanded under subsection (1) is not duly paid, or (where no requirement is made under subsection (1)) if the 14 days mentioned in subsection (2) have elapsed, the creditor or owner may treat the failure as a breach and section 87(1) shall not apply to it.

(4) The default notice must contain information in the prescribed terms about the consequences of failure to comply with it and any other prescribed matters relating to the agreement.

(5) A default notice making a requirement under subsection (1) may include a provision for the taking of action such as is mentioned in section 87(1) at any time after the restriction imposed by subsection (2) will cease, together with a statement that the provision will be ineffective if the breach is duly remedied or the compensation duly paid.

89   Compliance with default notice.

If before the date specified for that purpose in the default notice the debtor or hirer takes the action specified under section 88(1)(b) or (c) the breach shall be treated as not having occurred.

Further restriction of remedies for default

90   Retaking of protected hire-purchase etc. goods.

(1) At any time when—

    (a) the debtor is in breach of a regulated hire-purchase or a regulated conditional sale agreement relating to goods, and

    (b) the debtor has paid to the creditor one-third or more of the total price of the goods, and

    (c) the property in the goods remains in the creditor,

the creditor is not entitled to recover possession of the goods from the debtor except on an order of the court.

(2) Where under a hire-purchase or conditional sale agreement the creditor is required to carry out any installation and the agreement specifies, as part of the total price, the amount to be paid in respect of the installation (the 'installation charge') the reference in subsection (1)(b) to one-third of the total price shall be construed as a reference to the aggregate of the installation charge and one-third of the remainder of the total price.

(3) In a case where—

(a) subsection (1)(a) is satisfied, but not subsection (1)(b), and

(b) subsection (1)(b) was satisfied on a previous occasion in relation to an earlier agreement, being a regulated hire-purchase or regulated conditional sale agreement, between the same parties, and relating to any of the goods comprised in the later agreement (whether or not other goods were also included),

Subsection (1) shall apply to the later agreement with the omission of paragraph (b).

(4) If the later agreement is a modifying agreement, subsection (3) shall apply with the substitution, for the second reference to the later agreement, of a reference to the modifying agreement.

(5) Subsection (1) shall not apply, or shall cease to apply, to an agreement if the debtor has terminated, or terminates, the agreement.

(6) Where subsection (1) applies to an agreement at the death of the debtor, it shall continue to apply (in relation to the possessor of the goods) until the grant of probate or administration, or (in Scotland) confirmation (on which the personal representative would fall to be treated as the debtor).

(7) Goods falling within this section are in this Act referred to as 'protected goods'.

91 Consequences of breach of s. 90.

If goods are recovered by the creditor in contravention of section 90—

(a) the regulated agreement, if not previous terminated, shall terminate, and

(b) the debtor shall be released from all liability under the agreement, and shall be entitled to recover from the creditor all sums paid by the debtor under the agreement.

92 Recovery of possession of goods or land.

(1) Except under an order of the court, the creditor or owner shall not be entitled to enter any premises to take possession of goods subject to a regulated hire-purchase agreement, regulated conditional sale agreement or regulated consumer hire agreement.

(2) At any time when the debtor is in breach of a regulated conditional sale agreement relating to land, the creditor is entitled to recover possession of the land from the debtor, or any person claiming under him, on an order of the court only.

(3) An entry in contravention of subsection (1) or (2) is actionable as a breach of statutory duty.

93 Interest not to be increased on default.

The debtor under a regulated consumer credit agreement shall not be obliged to pay interest on sums which, in breach of the agreement, are unpaid by him at a rate—

(a) where the total charge for credit includes an item in respect of interest, exceeding the rate of that interest, or

(b)   in any other case, exceeding what would be the rate of the total charge for credit if any items included in the total charge for credit by virtue of section 20(2) were disregarded.

93A   Summary diligence not competent in Scotland

Summary diligence shall not be competent in Scotland to enforce payment of a debt due under a regulated agreement or under any security related thereto.

Early payment by debtor

94   Right to complete payments ahead of time.

(1)   The debtor under a regulated consumer credit agreement is entitled at any time, by notice to the creditor and the payment to the creditor of all amounts payable by the debtor to him under the agreement (less any rebate allowable under section 95), to discharge the debtor's indebtedness under the agreement.

(2)   A notice under subsection (1) may embody the exercise by the debtor of any option to purchase goods conferred on him by the agreement, and deal with any other matter arising on, or in relation to, the termination of the agreement.

95   Rebate on early settlement.

(1)   Regulations may provide for the allowance of a rebate of charges for credit to the debtor under a regulated consumer credit agreement where, under section 94, on refinancing, on breach of the agreement, or for any other reason, his indebtedness is discharged or becomes payable before the time fixed by the agreement, or any sum becomes payable by him before the time so fixed.

(2)   Regulations under subsection (1) may provide for calculation of the rebate by reference to any sums paid or payable by the debtor or his relative under or in connection with the agreement (whether to the creditor or some other person), including sums under linked transactions and other items in the total charge for credit.

96   Effect on linked transactions.

(1)   Where for any reason the indebtedness of the debtor under a regulated consumer credit agreement is discharged before the time fixed by the agreement, he, and any relative of his, shall at the same time be discharged from any liability under a linked transaction, other than a debt which has already become payable.

(2)   Subsection (1) does not apply to a linked transaction which is itself an agreement providing the debtor or his relative with credit.

(3)   Regulations may exclude linked transactions of the prescribed description from the operation of subsection (1).

97   Duty to give information.

(1)   The creditor under a regulated consumer credit agreement, within the prescribed period after he has received a request in writing to that effect from the debtor, shall give the debtor a statement in the prescribed form indicating, according to the information to which it is practicable for him to refer, the amount of the payment required to discharge

the debtor's indebtedness under the agreement, together with the prescribed particulars showing how the amount is arrived at.

(2) Subsection (1) does not apply to a request made less than one month after a previous request under that subsection relating to the same agreement was complied with.

(3) If the creditor fails to comply with subsection (1)—

(a)   he is not entitled, while the default continues, to enforce the agreement.

(b)   ...

Termination of agreements

98   *Duty to give notice of termination (non-default cases).*

(1)   The creditor or owner is not entitled to terminate a regulated agreement except by or after giving the debtor or hirer not less than seven days' notice of the termination.

(2)   Subsection (1) applies only where—

(a)   a period for the duration of the agreement is specified in the agreement, and

(b)   that period has not ended when the creditor or owner does an act mentioned in subsection (1),

but so applies notwithstanding that, under the agreement, any party is entitled to terminate it before the end of the period so specified.

(3)   A notice under subsection (1) is ineffective if not in the prescribed form.

(4)   Subsection (1) does not prevent a creditor from treating the right to draw on any credit as restricted or deferred and taking such steps as may be necessary to make the restriction or deferment effective.

(5)   Regulations may provide that subsection (1) is not to apply to agreements described by the regulations.

(6)   Subsection (1) does not apply to the termination of a regulated agreement by reason of any breach by the debtor or hirer of the agreement.

99   *Right to terminate hire-purchase etc. agreements.*

(1)   At any time before the final payment by the debtor under a regulated hire-purchase or regulated conditional sale agreement falls due, the debtor shall be entitled to terminate the agreement by giving notice to any person entitled or authorised to receive the sums payable under the agreement.

(2)   Termination of an agreement under subsection (1) does not affect any liability under the agreement which has accrued before the termination.

(3)   Subsection (1) does not apply to a conditional sale agreement relating to land after the title to the land has passed to the debtor.

(4)   In the case of a conditional sale agreement relating to goods, where the property in the goods, having become vested in the debtor, is transferred to a person who does not become the debtor under the agreement, the debtor shall not thereafter be entitled to terminate the agreement under subsection (1).

(5)   Subject to subsection (4), where a debtor under a conditional sale agreement relating to goods terminates the agreement under this section after the property in the goods has become vested in him, the property in the goods shall thereupon vest in the person (the 'previous owner') in whom it was vested immediately before it became vested in the debtor:

Provided that if the previous owner has died, or any other event has occurred whereby that property, if vested in him immediately before that event, would thereupon have vested in some other person, the property shall be treated as having devolved as if it had been vested in the previous owner immediately before his death or immediately before that event, as the case may be.

100   Liability of debtor on termination of hire-purchase etc. agreement.

(1)   Where a regulated hire-purchase or regulated conditional sale agreement is terminated under section 99 the debtor shall be liable, unless the agreement provides for a smaller payment, or does not provide for any payment, to pay to the creditor the amount (if any) by which one-half of the total price exceeds the aggregate of the sums paid and the sums due in respect of the total price immediately before the termination.

(2)   Where under a hire-purchase or conditional sale agreement the creditor is required to carry out any installation and the agreement specifies, as part of the total price, the amount to be paid in respect of the installation (the 'installation charge') the reference in subsection (1) to one-half of the total price shall be construed as a reference to the aggregate of the installation charge and one-half of the remainder of the total price.

(3)   If in any action the court is satisfied that a sum less than the amount specified in subsection (1) would be equal to the loss sustained by the creditor in consequence of the termination of the agreement by the debtor, the court may make an order for the payment of that sum in lieu of the amount specified in subsection (1).

(4)   If the debtor has contravened an obligation to take reasonable care of the goods or land, the amount arrived at under subsection (1) shall be increased by the sum required to recompense the creditor for that contravention, and subsection (2) shall have effect accordingly.

(5)   Where the debtor, on the termination of the agreement, wrongfully retains possession of goods to which the agreement relates, then, in any action brought by the creditor to recover possession of the goods from the debtor, the court, unless it is satisfied that having regard to the circumstances it would not be just to do so, shall order the goods to be delivered to the creditor without giving the debtor an option to pay the value of the goods.

101   Right to terminate hire agreement.

(1)   The hirer under a regulated consumer hire agreement is entitled to terminate the agreement by giving notice to any person entitled or authorised to receive the sums payable under the agreement.

(2)   Termination of an agreement under subsection (1) does not affect any liability under the agreement which has accrued before the termination.

(3)   A notice under subsection (1) shall not expire earlier than eighteen months after the making of the agreement, but apart from that the minimum period of notice to be given under subsection (1), unless the agreement provides for a shorter period, is as follows.

(4)   If the agreement provides for the making of payments by the hirer to the owner at equal intervals, the minimum period of notice is the length of one interval or three months, whichever is less.

(5) If the agreement provides for the making of such payments at differing intervals, the minimum period of notice is the length of the shortest interval or three months, whichever is less.

(6) In any other case, the minimum period of notice is three months.

(7) This section does not apply to—

    (a) any agreement which provides for the making by the hirer of payments which in total (and without breach of the agreement) exceed £1,500 in any year, or

    (b) any agreement where—

        (i) goods are bailed or (in Scotland) hired to the hirer for the purposes of a business carried on by him, or the hirer holds himself out as requiring the goods for those purposes, and

        (ii) the goods are selected by the hirer, and acquired by the owner for the purposes of the agreement at the request of the hirer from any person other than the owner's associate, or

    (c) any agreement where the hirer requires, or holds himself out as requiring, the goods for the purpose of bailing or hiring them to other persons in the course of a business carried on by him.

(8) If, on an application made to the OFT by a person carrying on a consumer hire business, it appears to the OFT that it would be in the interest of hirers to do so, it may by notice to the applicant direct that, subject to such conditions (if any) as it may specify, this section shall not apply to consumer hire agreements made by the applicant; and this Act shall have effect accordingly.

(8A) If it appears to the OFT that it would be in the interests of hirers to do so, it may by general notice direct that, subject to such conditions (if any) as it may specify, this section shall not apply to a consumer hire agreement if the agreement falls within a specified description; and this Act shall have effect accordingly.

(9) In the case of a modifying agreement, subsection (3) shall apply with the substitution, for 'the making of the agreement' of 'the making of the original agreement'.

102 Agency for receiving notice of rescission.

(1) Where the debtor or hirer under a regulated agreement claims to have a right to rescind the agreement, each of the following shall be deemed to be the agent of the creditor or owner for the purpose of receiving any notice rescinding the agreement which is served by the debtor or hirer—

    (a) a credit-broker or supplier who was the negotiator in antecedent negotiations, and

    (b) any person who, in the course of a business carried on by him, acted on behalf of the debtor or hirer in any negotiations for the agreement.

(2) In subsection (1) 'rescind' does not include—

    (a) service of a notice of cancellation, or

    (b) termination of an agreement under section 99 or 101 or by the exercise of a right or power in that behalf expressly conferred by the agreement.

103 Termination statements.

(1) If an individual (the 'customer') serves on any person (the 'trader') a notice—

(a)   stating that—

   (i)   the customer was the debtor or hirer under a regulated agreement described in the notice, and the trader was the creditor or owner under the agreement, and

   (ii)   the customer has discharged his indebtedness to the trader under the agreement, and

   (iii)   the agreement has ceased to have any operation; and

(b)   requiring the trader to give the customer a notice, signed by or on behalf of the trader, confirming that those statements are correct,

the trader shall, within the prescribed period after receiving the notice, either comply with it or serve on the customer a counter-notice stating that, as the case may be, he disputes the correctness of the notice or asserts that the customer is not indebted to him under the agreement.

(2)   Where the trader disputes the correctness of the notice he shall give particulars of the way in which he alleges it to be wrong.

(3)   Subsection (1) does not apply in relation to any agreement if the trader has previously complied with that subsection on the service of a notice under it with respect to that agreement.

(4)   Subsection (1) does not apply to a non-commercial agreement.

(5)   If the trader fails to comply with subsection (1), and the default continues for one month, he commits an offence.

(6)   A breach of the duty imposed by subsection (1) is actionable as a breach of statutory duty.

104   *Goods not to be treated as subject to landlord's hypothec in Scotland.*

Goods comprised in a hire-purchase agreement or goods comprised in a conditional sale agreement which have not become vested in the debtor shall not be treated in Scotland as subject to the landlord's hypothec—

(a)   during the period between the service of a default notice in respect of the goods and the date on which the notice expires or is earlier complied with; or

(b)   if the agreement is enforceable on an order of the court only, during the period between the commencement and termination of an action by the creditor to enforce the agreement.

PART VIII SECURITY

General

105   *Form and content of securities.*

(1)   Any security provided in relation to a regulated agreement shall be expressed in writing.

(2)   Regulations may prescribe the form and content of documents ('security instruments') to be made in compliance with subsection (1).

(3)   Regulations under subsection (2) may in particular—

(a)   require specified information to be included in the prescribed manner in documents, and other specified material to be excluded;

    (b) contain requirements to ensure that specified information is clearly brought to the attention of the surety, and that one part of a document is not given insufficient or excessive prominence compared with another.

(4) A security instrument is not properly executed unless—

    (a) a document in the prescribed form, itself containing all the prescribed terms and conforming to regulations under subsection (2), is signed in the prescribed manner by or on behalf of the surety, and

    (b) the document embodies all the terms of the security, other than implied terms, and

    (c) the document, when presented or sent for the purpose of being signed by or on behalf of the surety, is in such state that its terms are readily legible, and

    (d) when the document is presented or sent for the purpose of being signed by or on behalf of the surety there is also presented or sent a copy of the document.

(5) A security instrument is not properly executed unless—

    (a) where the security is provided after, or at the time when, the regulated agreement is made, a copy of the executed agreement, together with a copy of any other document referred to in it, is given to the surety at the time the security is provided, or

    (b) where the security is provided before the regulated agreement is made, a copy of the executed agreement, together with a copy of any other document referred to in it, is given to the surety within seven days after the regulated agreement is made.

(6) Subsection (1) does not apply to a security provided by the debtor or hirer.

(7) If—

    (a) in contravention of subsection (1) a security is not expressed in writing, or

    (b) a security instrument is improperly executed,

the security, so far as provided in relation to a regulated agreement, is enforceable against the surety on an order of the court only.

(8) If an application for an order under subsection (7) is dismissed (except on technical grounds only) section 106 (ineffective securities) shall apply to the security.

(9) Regulations under section 60(1) shall include provision requiring documents embodying regulated agreements also to embody any security provided in relation to a regulated agreement by the debtor or hirer.

106 Ineffective securities.

Where, under any provision of this Act, this section is applied to any security provided in relation to a regulated agreement, then, subject to section 177 (saving for registered charges)—

    (a) the security, so far as it is so provided, shall be treated as never having effect;

    (b) any property lodged with the creditor or owner solely for the purposes of the security as so provided shall be returned by him forthwith;

    (c) the creditor or owner shall take any necessary action to remove or cancel an entry in any register, so far as the entry relates to the security as so provided; and

    (d) any amount received by the creditor or owner on realisation of the security shall, so far as it is referable to the agreement, be repaid to the surety.

107 Duty to give information to surety under fixed-sum credit agreement.

(1) The creditor under a regulated agreement for fixed-sum credit in relation to which security is provided, within the prescribed period after receiving a request in writing to that effect from the surety and payment of a fee of £1, shall give to the surety (if a different person from the debtor)—

    (a) a copy of the executed agreement (if any) and of any other document referred to in it;

    (b) a copy of the security instrument (if any); and

    (c) a statement signed by or on behalf of the creditor showing, according to the information to which it is practicable for him to refer—

        (i) the total sum paid under the agreement by the debtor,

        (ii) the total sum which has become payable under the agreement by the debtor but remains unpaid, and the various amounts comprised in that total sum, with the date when each became due, and

        (iii) the total sum which is to become payable under the agreement by the debtor, and the various amounts comprised in that total sum, with the date, or mode of determining the date, when each becomes due.

(2) If the creditor possesses insufficient information to enable him to ascertain the amounts and dates mentioned in subsection (1)(c)(iii), he shall be taken to comply with that sub-paragraph if his statement under subsection (1)(c) gives the basis on which, under the regulated agreement, they would fall to be ascertained.

(3) Subsection (1) does not apply to—

    (a) an agreement under which no sum is, or will or may become, payable by the debtor, or

    (b) a request made less than one month after a previous request under that subsection relating to the same agreement was complied with.

(4) If the creditor under an agreement fails to comply with subsection (1)—

    (a) he is not entitled, while the default continues, to enforce the security, so far as provided in relation to the agreement.

    (b) ...

(5) This section does not apply to a non-commercial agreement.

108 Duty to give information to surety under running-account credit agreement.

(1) The creditor under a regulated agreement for running-account credit in relation to which security is provided, within the prescribed period after receiving a request in writing to that effect from the surety and payment of a fee of £1, shall give to the surety (if a different person from the debtor)—

    (a) a copy of the executed agreement (if any) and of any other document referred to in it;

    (b) a copy of the security instrument (if any); and

    (c) a statement signed by or on behalf of the creditor showing, according to the information to which it is practicable for him to refer—

        (i) the state of the account, and

(ii) the amount, if any, currently payable under the agreement by the debtor to the creditor, and

(iii) the amounts and due dates of any payments which, if the debtor does not draw further on the account, will later become payable under the agreement by the debtor to the creditor.

(2) If the creditor possesses insufficient information to enable him to ascertain the amounts and dates mentioned in subsection (1)(c)(iii), he shall be taken to comply with that sub-paragraph if his statement under subsection (1)(c) gives the basis on which, under the regulated agreement, they would fall to be ascertained.

(3) Subsection (1) does not apply to—

(a) an agreement under which no sum is, or will or may become, payable by the debtor, or

(b) a request made less than one month after a previous request under that subsection relating to the same agreement was complied with.

(4) If the creditor under an agreement fails to comply with subsection (1)—

(a) he is not entitled, while the default continues, to enforce the security, so far as provided in relation to the agreement.

(b) . . .

(5) This section does not apply to a non-commercial agreement.

109   Duty to give information to surety under consumer hire agreement.

(1) The owner under a regulated consumer hire agreement in relation to which security is provided, within the prescribed period after receiving a request in writing to that effect from the surety and payment of a fee of £1, shall give to the surety (if a different person from the hirer)—

(a) a copy of the executed agreement and of any other document referred to in it;

(b) a copy of the security instrument (if any); and

(c) a statement signed by or on behalf of the owner showing, according to the information to which it is practicable for him to refer, the total sum which has become payable under the agreement by the hirer but remains unpaid and the various amounts comprised in that total sum, with the date when each became due.

(2) Subsection (1) does not apply to—

(a) an agreement under which no sum is, or will or may become, payable by the hirer, or

(b) a request made less than one month after a previous request under that subsection relating to the same agreement was complied with.

(3) If the owner under an agreement fails to comply with subsection (1)—

(a) he is not entitled, while the default continues, to enforce the security, so far as provided in relation to the agreement.

(b) . . .

(4) This section does not apply to a non-commercial agreement.

110   Duty to give information to debtor or hirer.

(1)   The creditor or owner under a regulated agreement, within the prescribed period after receiving a request in writing to that effect from the debtor or hirer and payment of a fee of £1, shall give the debtor or hirer a copy of any security instrument executed in relation to the agreement after the making of the agreement.

(2)   Subsection (1) does not apply to—

    (a)   a non-commercial agreement, or

    (b)   an agreement under which no sum is, or will or may become, payable by the debtor or hirer, or

    (c)   a request made less than one month after a previous request under subsection (1) relating to the same agreement was complied with.

(3)   If the creditor or owner under an agreement fails to comply with subsection (1)—

    (a)   he is not entitled, while the default continues, to enforce the security (so far as provided in relation to the agreement).

    (b)   ...

111   Duty to give surety copy of default etc. notice.

(1)   When a default notice or a notice under section 76(1) or 98(1) is served on a debtor or hirer, a copy of the notice shall be served by the creditor or owner on any surety (if a different person from the debtor or hirer).

(2)   If the creditor or owner fails to comply with subsection (1) in the case of any surety, the security is enforceable against the surety (in respect of the breach or other matter to which the notice relates) on an order of the court only.

112   Realisation of securities.

Subject to section 121, regulations may provide for any matters relating to the sale or other realisation, by the creditor or owner, of property over which any right has been provided by way of security in relation to an actual or prospective regulated agreement, other than a non-commercial agreement.

113   Act not to be evaded by use of security.

(1)   Where a security is provided in relation to an actual or prospective regulated agreement, the security shall not be enforced so as to benefit the creditor or owner, directly or indirectly, to an extent greater (whether as respects the amount of any payment or the time or manner of its being made) than would be the case if the security were not provided and any obligations of the debtor or hirer, or his relative, under or in relation to the agreement were carried out to the extent (if any) to which they would be enforced under this Act.

(2)   In accordance with subsection (1), where a regulated agreement is enforceable on an order of the court or the OFT only, any security provided in relation to the agreement is enforceable (so far as provided in relation to the agreement) where such an order has been made in relation to the agreement, but not otherwise.

(3)   Where—

    (a)   a regulated agreement is cancelled under section 69(1) or becomes subject to section 69(2), or

(b) a regulated agreement is terminated under section 91, or

(c) in relation to any agreement an application for an order under section 40(2), 65(1), 124(1) or 149(2) is dismissed (except on technical grounds only), or

(d) a declaration is made by the court under section 142(1) (refusal of enforcement order) as respects any regulated agreement,

section 106 shall apply to any security provided in relation to the agreement.

(4) Where subsection (3)(d) applies and the declaration relates to a part only of the regulated agreement, section 106 shall apply to the security only so far as it concerns that part.

(5) In the case of a cancelled agreement, the duty imposed on the debtor or hirer by section 71 or 72 shall not be enforceable before the creditor or owner has discharged any duty imposed on him by section 106 (as applied by subsection (3)(a)).

(6) If the security is provided in relation to a prospective agreement or transaction, the security shall be enforceable in relation to the agreement or transaction only after the time (if any) when the agreement is made; and until that time the person providing the security shall be entitled, by notice to the creditor or owner, to require that section 106 shall thereupon apply to the security.

(7) Where an indemnity or guarantee is given in a case where the debtor or hirer is a minor, or an indemnity is given in a case where he is otherwise not of full capacity, the reference in subsection (1) to the extent to which his obligations would be enforced shall be read in relation to the indemnity or guarantee as a reference to the extent to which those obligations would be enforced if he were of full capacity.

(8) Subsections (1) to (3) also apply where a security is provided in relation to an actual or prospective linked transaction, and in that case—

(a) references to the agreement shall be read as references to the linked transaction, and

(b) references to the creditor or owner shall be read as references to any person (other than the debtor or hirer, or his relative) who is a party, or prospective party, to the linked transaction.

Pledges

114 Pawn-receipts.

(1) At the time he receives the article, a person who takes any article in pawn under a regulated agreement shall give to the person from whom he receives it a receipt in the prescribed form (a 'pawn-receipt').

(2) A person who takes any article in pawn from an individual whom he knows to be, or who appears to be and is, a minor commits an offence.

(3) This section and sections 115 to 122 do not apply to—

(a) a pledge of documents of title or of bearer bonds , or

(b) a non-commercial agreement.

115 Penalty for failure to supply copies of pledge agreement, etc.

If the creditor under a regulated agreement to take any article in pawn fails to observe the requirements of sections 62 to 64 or 114(1) in relation to the agreement he commits an offence.

116   Redemption period.

(1)   A pawn is redeemable at any time within six months after it was taken.

(2)   Subject to subsection (1), the period within which a pawn is redeemable shall be the same as the period fixed by the parties for the duration of the credit secured by the pledge, or such longer period as they may agree.

(3)   If the pawn is not redeemed by the end of the period laid down by subsections (1) and (2) (the 'redemption period'), it nevertheless remains redeemable until it is realised by the pawnee under section 121 except where under section 120(1)(a) the property in it passes to the pawnee.

(4)   No special charge shall be made for redemption of a pawn after the end of the redemption period, and charges in respect of the safe keeping of the pawn shall not be at a higher rate after the end of the redemption period than before.

117   Redemption procedure.

(1)   On surrender of the pawn-receipt, and payment of the amount owing, at any time when the pawn is redeemable, the pawnee shall deliver the pawn to the bearer of the pawn-receipt.

(2)   Subsection (1) does not apply if the pawnee knows or has reasonable cause to suspect that the bearer of the pawn-receipt is neither the owner of the pawn nor authorised by the owner to redeem it.

(3)   The pawnee is not liable to any person in tort or delict for delivering the pawn where subsection (1) applies, or refusing to deliver it where the person demanding delivery does not comply with subsection (1) or, by reason of subsection (2), subsection (1) does not apply.

118   Loss etc of pawn-receipt.

(1)   A person (the 'claimant') who is not in possession of the pawn-receipt but claims to be the owner of the pawn, or to be otherwise entitled or authorised to redeem it, may do so at any time when it is redeemable by tendering to the pawnee in place of the pawn-receipt—

   (a)   a statutory declaration made by the claimant in the prescribed form, and with the prescribed contents, or

   (b)   where the pawn is security for fixed-sum credit not exceeding £75 or running-account credit on which the credit limit does not exceed £75, and the pawnee agrees, a statement in writing in the prescribed form, and with the prescribed contents, signed by the claimant.

(2)   On compliance by the claimant with subsection (1), section 117 shall apply as if the declaration or statement were the pawn-receipt, and the pawn-receipt itself shall become inoperative for the purposes of section 117.

119   Unreasonable refusal to deliver pawn.

(1)   If a person who has taken a pawn under a regulated agreement refuses without reasonable cause to allow the pawn to be redeemed, he commits an offence.

(2)   On the conviction in England or Wales of a pawnee under subsection (1) where the offence does not amount to theft, section 148 of the Powers of Criminal Courts (Sentencing) Act

2000 (restitution orders) shall apply as if the pawnee had been convicted of stealing the pawn.

(3) On the conviction in Northern Ireland of a pawnee under subsection (1) where the offence does not amount to theft, section 27 (orders for restitution) of the Theft Act (Northern Ireland) 1969, and any provision of the Theft Act (Northern Ireland) 1969 relating to that section, shall apply as if the pawnee had been convicted of stealing the pawn.

Amendment as at: May 1, 1998

120   Consequence of failure to redeem.

(1) If at the end of the redemption period the pawn has not been redeemed—

   (a) notwithstanding anything in section 113, the property in the pawn passes to the pawnee where the redemption period is six months and the pawn is security for fixed-sum credit not exceeding £75 or running-account credit on which the credit limit does not exceed £75; or

   (b) in any other case the pawn becomes realisable by the pawnee.

(2) Where the debtor or hirer is entitled to apply to the court for a time order under section 129, subsection (1) shall apply with the substitution, for 'at the end of the redemption period' of 'after the expiry of five days following the end of the redemption period'.

121   Realisation of pawn.

(1) When a pawn has become realisable by him, the pawnee may sell it, after giving to the pawnor (except in such cases as may be prescribed) not less than the prescribed period of notice of the intention to sell, indicating in the notice the asking price and such other particulars as may be prescribed.

(2) Within the prescribed period after the sale takes place, the pawnee shall give the pawnor the prescribed information in writing as to the sale, its proceeds and expenses.

(3) Where the net proceeds of sale are not less than the sum which, if the pawn had been redeemed on the date of the sale, would have been payable for its redemption, the debt secured by the pawn is discharged and any surplus shall be paid by the pawnee to the pawnor.

(4) Where subsection (3) does not apply, the debt shall be treated as from the date of sale as equal to the amount by which the net proceeds of sale fall short of the sum which would have been payable for the redemption of the pawn on that date.

(5) In this section the 'net proceeds of sale' is the amount realised (the 'gross amount') less the expenses (if any) of the sale.

(6) If the pawnor alleges that the gross amount is less than the true market value of the pawn on the date of sale, it is for the pawnee to prove that he and any agents employed by him in the sale used reasonable care to ensure that the true market value was obtained, and if he fails to do so subsections (3) and (4) shall have effect as if the reference in subsection (5) to the gross amount were a reference to the true market value.

(7) If the pawnor alleges that the expenses of the sale were unreasonably high, it is for the pawnee to prove that they were reasonable, and if he fails to do so subsections (3) and (4) shall have effect as if the reference in subsection (5) to expenses were a reference to reasonable expenses.

122   Order in Scotland to deliver pawn.

(1)   As respects Scotland where—

    (a)   a pawn is either—

        (i)   an article which has been stolen, or

        (ii)   an article which has been obtained by fraud, and a person is convicted of any offence in relation to the theft or, as the case may be, the fraud; or

    (b)   a person is convicted of an offence under section 119(1),

the court by which that person is so convicted may order delivery of the pawn to the owner or the person otherwise entitled thereto.

(2)   A court making an order under subsection (1)(a) for delivery of a pawn may make the order subject to such conditions as to payment of the debt secured by the pawn as it thinks fit.

Negotiable instruments

123   Restrictions on taking and negotiating instruments.

(1)   A creditor or owner shall not take a negotiable instrument, other than a bank note or cheque, in discharge of any sum payable—

    (a)   by the debtor or hirer under a regulated agreement, or

    (b)   by any person as surety in relation to the agreement.

(2)   The creditor or owner shall not negotiate a cheque taken by him in discharge of a sum payable as mentioned in subsection (1) except to a banker (within the meaning of the Bills of Exchange Act 1882).

(3)   The creditor or owner shall not take a negotiable instrument as security for the discharge of any sum payable as mentioned in subsection (1).

(4)   A person takes a negotiable instrument as security for the discharge of a sum if the sum is intended to be paid in some other way, and the negotiable instrument is to be presented for payment only if the sum is not paid in that way.

(5)   This section does not apply where the regulated agreement is a non-commercial agreement.

(6)   The Secretary of State may by order provide that this section shall not apply where the regulated agreement has a connection with a country outside the United Kingdom.

124   Consequences of breach of s 123.

(1)   After any contravention of section 123 has occurred in relation to a sum payable as mentioned in section 123(1)(a), the agreement under which the sum is payable is enforceable against the debtor or hirer on an order of the court only.

(2)   After any contravention of section 123 has occurred in relation to a sum payable by any surety, the security is enforceable on an order of the court only.

(3)   Where an application for an order under subsection (2) is dismissed (except on technical grounds only) section 106 shall apply to the security.

125   Holders in due course.

(1)   A person who takes a negotiable instrument in contravention of section 123(1) or (3) is not a holder in due course, and is not entitled to enforce the instrument.

(2)   Where a person negotiates a cheque in contravention of section 123(2), his doing so constitutes a defect in his title within the meaning of the Bills of Exchange Act 1882.

(3)   If a person mentioned in section 123(1)(a) or (b) ('the protected person') becomes liable to a holder in due course of an instrument taken from the protected person in contravention of section 123(1) or (3), or taken from the protected person and negotiated in contravention of section 123(2), the creditor or owner shall indemnify the protected person in respect of that liability.

(4)   Nothing in this Act affects the rights of the holder in due course of any negotiable instrument.

Land mortgages

126   Enforcement of land mortgages.

A land mortgage securing a regulated agreement is enforceable (so far as provided in relation to the agreement) on an order of the court only.

PART IX JUDICIAL CONTROL

Enforcement of certain regulated agreements and securities

127   Enforcement orders in cases of infringement.

(1)   In the case of an application for an enforcement order under—

(a)   section 65(1) (improperly executed agreements), or

(b)   section 105(7)(a) or (b) (improperly executed security instruments), or

(c)   section 111(2) (failure to serve copy of notice on surety), or

(d)   section 124(1) or (2) (taking of negotiable instrument in contravention of section 123),

the court shall dismiss the application if, but only if, it considers it just to do so having regard to—

(i)   Prejudice caused to any person by the contravention in question, and the degree of culpability for it; and

(ii)   the powers conferred on the court by subsection (2) and sections 135 and 136.

(2)   If it appears to the court just to do so, it may in an enforcement order reduce or discharge any sum payable by the debtor or hirer, or any surety, so as to compensate him for prejudice suffered as a result of the contravention in question.

(3)   . . .

(4)   . . .

(5)   . . .

128   Enforcement orders on death of debtor or hirer.

The court shall make an order under section 86(2) if, but only if, the creditor or owner proves that he has been unable to satisfy himself that the present and future obligations of the debtor or hirer under the agreement are likely to be discharged.

Extension of time

129   Time orders.

(1)   Subject to subsection (3) below, if it appears to the court just to do so—

    (a)   on an application for an enforcement order; or

    (b)   on an application made by a debtor or hirer under this paragraph after service on him of—

        (i)   a default notice, or

        (ii)   a notice under section 76(1) or 98(1); or

    (ba)   on an application made by a debtor or hirer under this paragraph after he has been given a notice under section 86B or 86C; or

    (c)   in an action brought by a creditor or owner to enforce a regulated agreement or any security, or recover possession of any goods or land to which a regulated agreement relates,

the court may make an order under this section (a 'time order').

(2)   A time order shall provide for one or both of the following, as the court considers just—

    (a)   the payment by the debtor or hirer or any surety of any sum owed under a regulated agreement or a security by such instalments, payable at such times, as the court, having regard to the means of the debtor or hirer and any surety, considers reasonable;

    (b)   the remedying by the debtor or hirer of any breach of a regulated agreement (other than non-payment of money) within such period as the court may specify.

(3)   Where in Scotland a time to pay direction or a time to pay order has been made in relation to a debt, it shall not thereafter be competent to make a time order in relation to the same debt.

129A   Debtor or hirer to give notice of intent etc. to creditor or owner

(1)   A debtor or hirer may make an application under section 129(1)(ba) in relation to a regulated agreement only if–

    (a)   following his being given the notice under section 86B or 86C, he gave a notice within subsection (2) to the creditor or owner; and

    (b)   a period of at least 14 days has elapsed after the day on which he gave that notice to the creditor or owner.

(2)   A notice is within this subsection if it–

    (a)   indicates that the debtor or hirer intends to make the application;

    (b)   indicates that he wants to make a proposal to the creditor or owner in relation to his making of payments under the agreement; and

    (c)   gives details of that proposal.

130   Supplemental provisions about time orders.

(1)   Where in accordance with rules of court an offer to pay any sum by instalments is made by the debtor or hirer and accepted by the creditor or owner, the court may in accordance with rules of court make a time order under section 129(2)(a) giving effect to the offer without hearing evidence of means.

(2)   In the case of a hire-purchase or conditional sale agreement only, a time order under section 129(2)(a) may deal with sums which, although not payable by the debtor at the time the order is made, would if the agreement continued in force become payable under it subsequently.

(3)   A time order under section 129(2)(a) shall not be made where the regulated agreement is secured by a pledge if, by virtue of regulations made under section 76(5), 87(4) or 98(5), service of a notice is not necessary for enforcement of the pledge.

(4)   Where, following the making of a time order in relation to a regulated hire-purchase or conditional sale agreement or a regulated consumer hire agreement, the debtor or hirer is in possession of the goods, he shall be treated (except in the case of a debtor to whom the creditor's title has passed) as a bailee or (in Scotland) a custodier of the goods under the terms of the agreement, notwithstanding that the agreement has been terminated.

(5)   Without prejudice to anything done by the creditor or owner before the commencement of the period specified in a time order made under section 129(2)(b) ('the relevant period')—

(a)   he shall not while the relevant period subsists take in relation to the agreement any action such as is mentioned in section 87(1);

(b)   where—

(i)   a provision of the agreement ('the secondary provision') becomes operative only on breach of another provision of the agreement ('the primary provision'), and

(ii)   the time order provides for the remedying of such a breach of the primary provision within the relevant period,

he shall not treat the secondary provision as operative before the end of that period;

(c)   if while the relevant period subsists the breach to which the order relates is remedied it shall be treated as not having occurred.

(6)   On the application of any person affected by a time order, the court may vary or revoke the order.

Interest

130A   Interest payable on judgment debts etc.

(1)   If the creditor or owner under a regulated agreement wants to be able to recover from the debtor or hirer post-judgment interest in connection with a sum that is required to be paid under a judgment given in relation to the agreement (the 'judgment sum'), he—

(a)   after the giving of that judgment, shall give the debtor or hirer a notice under this section (the 'first required notice'); and

(b)   after the giving of the first required notice, shall give the debtor or hirer further notices under this section at intervals of not more than six months.

(2)   The debtor or hirer shall have no liability to pay post-judgment interest in connection with the judgment sum to the extent that the interest is calculated by reference to a period occurring before the day on which he is given the first required notice.

(3)   If the creditor or owner fails to give the debtor or hirer a notice under this section within the period of six months beginning with the day after the day on which such a notice was last given to the debtor or hirer, the debtor or hirer shall have no liability to pay post-judgment interest in connection with the judgment sum to the extent that the interest is calculated by reference to the whole or to a part of the period which—

(a)   begins immediately after the end of that period of six months; and

(b)   ends at the end of the day on which the notice is given to the debtor or hirer.

(4)   The debtor or hirer shall have no liability to pay any sum in connection with the preparation or the giving to him of a notice under this section.

(5)   A notice under this section may be incorporated in a statement or other notice which the creditor or owner gives the debtor or hirer in relation to the agreement by virtue of another provision of this Act.

(6)   Regulations may make provision about the form and content of notices under this section.

(7)   This section does not apply in relation to post-judgment interest which is required to be paid by virtue of any of the following—

(a)   section 4 of the Administration of Justice (Scotland) Act 1972;

(b)   Article 127 of the Judgments Enforcement (Northern Ireland) Order 1981;

(c)   section 74 of the County Courts Act 1984.

(8)   This section does not apply in relation to a non-commercial agreement or to a small agreement.

(9)   In this section 'post-judgment interest' means interest to the extent calculated by reference to a period occurring after the giving of the judgment under which the judgment sum is required to be paid.

Protection of property pending proceedings

131   *Protection orders.*

The court, on the application of the creditor or owner under a regulated agreement, may make such orders as it thinks just for protecting any property of the creditor or owner, or property subject to any security, from damage or depreciation pending the determination of any proceedings under this Act, including orders restricting or prohibiting use of the property or giving directions as to its custody.

Hire and hire-purchase etc agreements

132   *Financial relief for hirer.*

(1)   Where the owner under a regulated consumer hire agreement recovers possession of goods to which the agreement relates otherwise than by action, the hirer may apply to the court for an order that—

(a) the whole or part of any sum paid by the hirer to the owner in respect of the goods shall be repaid, and

(b) the obligation to pay the whole or part of any sum owed by the hirer to the owner in respect of the goods shall cease,

and if it appears to the court just to do so, having regard to the extent of the enjoyment of the goods by the hirer, the court shall grant the application in full or in part.

(2) Where in proceedings relating to a regulated consumer hire agreement the court makes an order for the delivery to the owner of goods to which the agreement relates the court may include in the order the like provision as may be made in an order under subsection (1).

133   Hire-purchase etc agreements: special powers of court.

(1) If, in relation to a regulated hire-purchase or conditional sale agreement, it appears to the court just to do so—

(a) on an application for an enforcement order or time order; or

(b) in an action brought by the creditor to recover possession of goods to which the agreement relates,

the court may—

(i) make an order (a 'return order') for the return to the creditor of goods to which the agreement relates;

(ii) make an order (a 'transfer order') for the transfer to the debtor of the creditor's title to certain goods to which the agreement relates ('the transferred goods'), and the return to the creditor of the remainder of the goods.

(2) In determining for the purposes of this section how much of the total price has been paid ('the paid-up sum'), the court may—

(a) treat any sum paid by the debtor, or owed by the creditor, in relation to the goods as part of the paid-up sum;

(b) deduct any sum owed by the debtor in relation to the goods (otherwise than as part of the total price) from the paid-up sum,

and make corresponding reductions in amounts so owed.

(3) Where a transfer order is made, the transferred goods shall be such of the goods to which the agreement relates as the court thinks just; but a transfer order shall be made only where the paid-up sum exceeds the part of the total price referable to the transferred goods by an amount equal to at least one-third of the unpaid balance of the total price.

(4) Notwithstanding the making of a return order or transfer order, the debtor may at any time before the goods enter the possession of the creditor, on payment of the balance of the total price and the fulfilment of any other necessary conditions, claim the goods ordered to be returned to the creditor.

(5) When, in pursuance of a time order or under this section, the total price of goods under a regulated hire-purchase agreement or regulated conditional sale agreement is paid and any other necessary conditions are fulfilled, the creditor's title to the goods vests in the debtor.

(6) If, in contravention of a return order or transfer order, any goods to which the order relates are not returned to the creditor, the court, on the application of the creditor, may—

(a) revoke so much of the order as relates to those goods, and

(b) order the debtor to pay the creditor the unpaid portion of so much of the total price as is referable to those goods.

(7) For the purposes of this section, the part of the total price referable to any goods is the part assigned to those goods by the agreement or (if no such assignment is made) the part determined by the court to be reasonable.

134 *Evidence of adverse detention in hire-purchase etc. cases.*

(1) Where goods are comprised in a regulated hire-purchase agreement, regulated conditional sale agreement or regulated consumer hire agreement, and the creditor or owner—

(a) brings an action or makes an application to enforce a right to recover possession of the goods from the debtor or hirer, and

(b) proves that a demand for the delivery of the goods was included in the default notice under section 88(5), or that, after the right to recover possession of the goods accrued but before the action was begun or the application was made, he made a request in writing to the debtor or hirer to surrender the goods,

then, for the purposes of the claim of the creditor or owner to recover possession of the goods, the possession of them by the debtor or hirer shall be deemed to be adverse to the creditor or owner.

(2) In subsection (1) 'the debtor or hirer' includes a person in possession of the goods at any time between the debtor's or hirer's death and the grant of probate or administration, or (in Scotland) confirmation.

(3) Nothing in this section affects a claim for damages for conversion or (in Scotland) for delict.

Supplemental provisions as to orders

135 *Power to impose conditions, or suspend operation of order.*

(1) If it considers it just to do so, the court may in an order made by it in relation to a regulated agreement include provisions—

(a) making the operation of any term of the order conditional on the doing of specified acts by any party to the proceedings;

(b) suspending the operation of any term of the order either—

(i) until such time as the court subsequently directs, or

(ii) until the occurrence of a specified act or omission.

(2) The court shall not suspend the operation of a term requiring the delivery up of goods by any person unless satisfied that the goods are in his possession or control.

(3) In the case of a consumer hire agreement, the court shall not so use its powers under subsection (1)(b) as to extend the period for which, under the terms of the agreement, the hirer is entitled to possession of the goods to which the agreement relates.

(4) On the application of any person affected by a provision included under subsection (1), the court may vary the provision.

136 *Power to vary agreements and securities.*

The court may in an order made by it under this Act include such provision as it considers just for amending any agreement or security in consequence of a term of the order.

Extortionate credit bargains

137

...

138

...

139

...

140

...

Unfair relationships

140A Unfair relationships between creditors and debtors

(1) The court may make an order under section 140B in connection with a credit agreement if it determines that the relationship between the creditor and the debtor arising out of the agreement (or the agreement taken with any related agreement) is unfair to the debtor because of one or more of the following—

    (a) any of the terms of the agreement or of any related agreement;

    (b) the way in which the creditor has exercised or enforced any of his rights under the agreement or any related agreement;

    (c) any other thing done (or not done) by, or on behalf of, the creditor (either before or after the making of the agreement or any related agreement).

(2) In deciding whether to make a determination under this section the court shall have regard to all matters it thinks relevant (including matters relating to the creditor and matters relating to the debtor).

(3) For the purposes of this section the court shall (except to the extent that it is not appropriate to do so) treat anything done (or not done) by, or on behalf of, or in relation to, an associate or a former associate of the creditor as if done (or not done) by, or on behalf of, or in relation to, the creditor.

(4) A determination may be made under this section in relation to a relationship notwithstanding that the relationship may have ended.

(5) An order under section 140B shall not be made in connection with a credit agreement which is an exempt agreement by virtue of section 16(6C).

140B Powers of court in relation to unfair relationships

(1) An order under this section in connection with a credit agreement may do one or more of the following—

    (a) require the creditor, or any associate or former associate of his, to repay (in whole or in part) any sum paid by the debtor or by a surety by virtue of the agreement or any related agreement (whether paid to the creditor, the associate or the former associate or to any other person);

(b) require the creditor, or any associate or former associate of his, to do or not to do (or to cease doing) anything specified in the order in connection with the agreement or any related agreement;

(c) reduce or discharge any sum payable by the debtor or by a surety by virtue of the agreement or any related agreement;

(d) direct the return to a surety of any property provided by him for the purposes of a security;

(e) otherwise set aside (in whole or in part) any duty imposed on the debtor or on a surety by virtue of the agreement or any related agreement;

(f) alter the terms of the agreement or of any related agreement;

(g) direct accounts to be taken, or (in Scotland) an accounting to be made, between any persons.

(2) An order under this section may be made in connection with a credit agreement only—

(a) on an application made by the debtor or by a surety;

(b) at the instance of the debtor or a surety in any proceedings in any court to which the debtor and the creditor are parties, being proceedings to enforce the agreement or any related agreement; or

(c) at the instance of the debtor or a surety in any other proceedings in any court where the amount paid or payable under the agreement or any related agreement is relevant.

(3) An order under this section may be made notwithstanding that its effect is to place on the creditor, or any associate or former associate of his, a burden in respect of an advantage enjoyed by another person.

(4) An application under subsection (2)(a) may only be made—

(a) in England and Wales, to the county court;

(b) in Scotland, to the sheriff court;

(c) in Northern Ireland, to the High Court (subject to subsection (6)).

(5) In Scotland such an application may be made in the sheriff court for the district in which the debtor or surety resides or carries on business.

(6) In Northern Ireland such an application may be made to the county court if the credit agreement is an agreement under which the creditor provides the debtor with—

(a) fixed-sum credit not exceeding £15,000; or

(b) running-account credit on which the credit limit does not exceed £15,000.

(7) Without prejudice to any provision which may be made by rules of court made in relation to county courts in Northern Ireland, such rules may provide that an application made by virtue of subsection (6) may be made in the county court for the division in which the debtor or surety resides or carries on business.

(8) A party to any proceedings mentioned in subsection (2) shall be entitled, in accordance with rules of court, to have any person who might be the subject of an order under this section made a party to the proceedings.

(9) If, in any such proceedings, the debtor or a surety alleges that the relationship between the creditor and the debtor is unfair to the debtor, it is for the creditor to prove to the contrary.

140C   Interpretation of ss 140A and 140B

(1)   In this section and in sections 140A and 140B 'credit agreement' means any agreement between an individual (the 'debtor') and any other person (the 'creditor') by which the creditor provides the debtor with credit of any amount.

(2)   References in this section and in sections 140A and 140B to the creditor or to the debtor under a credit agreement include—

   (a)   references to the person to whom his rights and duties under the agreement have passed by assignment or operation of law;

   (b)   where two or more persons are the creditor or the debtor, references to any one or more of those persons.

(3)   The definition of 'court' in section 189(1) does not apply for the purposes of sections 140A and 140B.

(4)   References in sections 140A and 140B to an agreement related to a credit agreement (the 'main agreement') are references to—

   (a)   a credit agreement consolidated by the main agreement;

   (b)   a linked transaction in relation to the main agreement or to a credit agreement within paragraph (a);

   (c)   a security provided in relation to the main agreement, to a credit agreement within paragraph (a) or to a linked transaction within paragraph (b).

(5)   In the case of a credit agreement which is not a regulated consumer credit agreement, for the purposes of subsection (4) a transaction shall be treated as being a linked transaction in relation to that agreement if it would have been such a transaction had that agreement been a regulated consumer credit agreement.

(6)   For the purposes of this section and section 140B the definitions of 'security' and 'surety' in section 189(1) apply (with any appropriate changes) in relation to—

   (a)   a credit agreement which is not a consumer credit agreement as if it were a consumer credit agreement; and

   (b)   a transaction which is a linked transaction by virtue of subsection (5).

(7)   For the purposes of this section a credit agreement (the 'earlier agreement') is consolidated by another credit agreement (the 'later agreement') if—

   (a)   the later agreement is entered into by the debtor (in whole or in part) for purposes connected with debts owed by virtue of the earlier agreement; and

   (b)   at any time prior to the later agreement being entered into the parties to the earlier agreement included—

      (i)   the debtor under the later agreement; and

      (ii)   the creditor under the later agreement or an associate or a former associate of his.

(8)   Further, if the later agreement is itself consolidated by another credit agreement (whether by virtue of this subsection or subsection (7)), then the earlier agreement is consolidated by that other agreement as well.

140D   Advice and information

The advice and information published by the OFT under section 229 of the Enterprise Act 2002 shall indicate how the OFT expects sections 140A to 140C of this Act to interact with Part 8 of that Act.

Miscellaneous

141   Jurisdiction and parties.

(1)   In England and Wales the county court shall have jurisdiction to hear and determine—

    (a)   any action by the creditor or owner to enforce a regulated agreement or any security relating to it;

    (b)   any action to enforce any linked transaction against the debtor or hirer or his relative,

and such an action shall not be brought in any other court.

(2)   Where an action or application is brought in the High Court which, by virtue of this Act, ought to have been brought in the county court it shall not be treated as improperly brought, but shall be transferred to the county court.

(3)   In Scotland the sheriff court shall have jurisdiction to hear and determine any action referred to in subsection (1) and such an action shall not be brought in any other court.

(3A) Subject to subsection (3B) an action which is brought in the sheriff court by virtue of subsection (3) shall be brought only in one of the following courts, namely—

    (a)   the court for the place where the debtor or hirer is domiciled (within the meaning of section 41 or 42 of the Civil Jurisdiction and Judgments Act 1982);

    (b)   the court for the place where the debtor or hirer carries on business; and

    (c)   where the purpose of the action is to assert, declare or determine proprietary or possessory rights, or rights of security, in or over moveable property, or to obtain authority to dispose of moveable property, the court for the place where the property is situated.

(3B) Subsection (3A) shall not apply—

    (a)   where Rule 3 of Schedule 8 to the said Act of 1982 applies; or

    (b)   where the jurisdiction of another court has been prorogated by an agreement entered into after the dispute has arisen.

(4)   In Northern Ireland the county court shall have jurisdiction to hear and determine any action or application falling within subsection (1).

(5)   Except as may be provided by rules of court, all the parties to a regulated agreement, and any surety, shall be made parties to any proceedings relating to the agreement.

142   Power to declare rights of parties.

(1)   Where under any provision of this Act a thing can be done by a creditor or owner on an enforcement order only, and either—

    (a)   the court dismisses (except on technical grounds only) an application for an enforcement order, or

    (b)   where no such application has been made or such an application has been dismissed on technical grounds only, an interested party applies to the court for a declaration under this subsection,

the court may if it thinks just make a declaration that the creditor or owner is not entitled to do that thing, and thereafter no application for an enforcement order in respect of it shall be entertained.

(2) Where—

    (a) a regulated agreement or linked transaction is cancelled under section 69(1), or becomes subject to section 69(2), or

    (b) a regulated agreement is terminated under section 91,

and an interested party applies to the court for a declaration under this subsection, the court may make a declaration to that effect.

Northern Ireland

143 Jurisdiction of county court in Northern Ireland.

Without prejudice to any provision which may be made by rules of court made in relation to county courts in Northern Ireland such rules may provide—

    (a) that any action or application such as is mentioned in section 141(4) which is brought against the debtor or hirer in the county court may be brought in the county court for the division in which the debtor or hirer resided or carried on business at the date on which he last made a payment under the regulated agreement;

    (b) that an application by a debtor or hirer or any surety under section129(1)(b), 132(1) or 142(1)(b) which is brought in the county court may be brought in the county court for the division in which the debtor, or, as the case may be, the hirer or surety resides or carries on business;

    (c) for service of process on persons outside Northern Ireland.

144 Appeal from county court in Northern Ireland.

Any person dissatisfied—

    (a) with an order, whether adverse to him or in his favour, made by a county court in Northern Ireland in the exercise of any jurisdiction conferred by this Act, or

    (b) with the dismissal or refusal by such a county court of any action or application instituted by him under the provisions of this Act,

shall be entitled to appeal from the order or from the dismissal or refusal as if the order, dismissal or refusal had been made in exercise of the jurisdiction conferred by Part III of the County Courts Act (Northern Ireland) 1959 and the appeal brought under the County Court Appeals Act (Northern Ireland) 1964 and sections 2 (cases stated by county court judge) and 3 (cases stated by assize judge or High Court on appeal from county court) of the last-mentioned Act shall apply accordingly.

PART X ANCILLARY CREDIT BUSINESSES

Definitions

145 Types of ancillary credit business.

(1) An ancillary credit business is any business so far as it comprises or relates to—

    (a) credit brokerage,

    (b) debt-adjusting,

    (c) debt-counselling,

   (d)   debt-collecting,

   (da) debt administration, or

   (e)   the operation of a credit reference agency.

(2) Subject to section 146(5) and (5A), credit brokerage is the effecting of introductions—

   (a)   of individuals desiring to obtain credit—

      (i)   to persons carrying on businesses to which this sub-paragraph applies, or

      (ii) in the case of an individual desiring to obtain credit to finance the acquisition or provision of a dwelling occupied or to be occupied by himself or his relative, to any person carrying on a business in the course of which he provides credit secured on land, or

   (b)   of individuals desiring to obtain goods on hire to persons carrying on businesses to which this paragraph applies, or

   (c)   of individuals desiring to obtain credit, or to obtain goods on hire, to other credit-brokers.

(3) Subsection (2)(a)(i) applies to—

   (a)   a consumer credit business;

   (b)   a business which comprises or relates to consumer credit agreements being, otherwise than by virtue of section 16(5)(a), exempt agreements;

   (c)   a business which comprises or relates to unregulated agreements where—

      (i)   the law applicable to the agreement is the law of a country outside the United Kingdom, and

      (ii) if the law applicable to the agreement were the law of a part of the United Kingdom it would be a regulated consumer credit agreement.

(4) Subsection (2)(b) applies to—

   (a)   a consumer hire business;

   (aa) a business which comprises or relates to consumer hire agreements being, otherwise than by virtue of section 16(6), exempt agreements;

   (b)   a business which comprises or relates to unregulated agreements where—

      (i)   the law applicable to the agreement is the law of a country outside the United Kingdom, and

      (ii) if the law applicable to the agreement were the law of a part of the United Kingdom it would be a regulated consumer hire agreement.

(5) Subject to section 146(5B) and (6), debt-adjusting is, in relation to debts due under consumer credit agreements or consumer hire agreements,—

   (a)   negotiating with the creditor or owner, on behalf of the debtor or hirer, terms for the discharge of a debt, or

   (b)   taking over, in return for payments by the debtor or hirer, his obligation to discharge a debt, or

   (c)   any similar activity concerned with the liquidation of a debt.

(6) Subject to section 146(5C) and (6), debt-counselling is the giving of advice to debtors or hirers about the liquidation of debts due under consumer credit agreements or consumer hire agreements.

(7)   Subject to section 146(6), debt-collecting is the taking of steps to procure payment of debts due under consumer credit agreements or consumer hire agreements.

(7A) Subject to section 146(7), debt administration is the taking of steps—

   (a)   to perform duties under a consumer credit agreement or a consumer hire agreement on behalf of the creditor or owner, or

   (b)   to exercise or to enforce rights under such an agreement on behalf of the creditor or owner,

   so far as the taking of such steps is not debt-collecting.

(7B) A person provides credit information services if—

   (a)   he takes any steps mentioned in subsection (7C) on behalf of an individual; or

   (b)   he gives advice to an individual in relation to the taking of any such steps.

(7C) Those steps are steps taken with a view—

   (a)   to ascertaining whether a credit information agency (other than that person himself if he is one) holds information relevant to the financial standing of an individual;

   (b)   to ascertaining the contents of such information held by such an agency;

   (c)   to securing the correction of, the omission of anything from, or the making of any other kind of modification of, such information so held; or

   (d)   to securing that such an agency which holds such information—

      (i)   stops holding it; or

      (ii)   does not provide it to another person.

(7D) In subsection (7C) 'credit information agency' means—

   (a)   a person carrying on a consumer credit business or a consumer hire business;

   (b)   a person carrying on a business so far as it comprises or relates to credit brokerage, debt-adjusting, debt-counselling, debt collecting, debt administration or the operation of a credit reference agency;

   (c)   a person carrying on a business which would be a consumer credit business except that it comprises or relates to consumer credit agreements being, otherwise than by virtue of section 16(5)(a), exempt agreements; or

   (d)   a person carrying on a business which would be a consumer hire business except that it comprises or relates to consumer hire agreements being, otherwise than by virtue of section 16(6), exempt agreements.

(8)   A credit reference agency is a person carrying on a business comprising the furnishing of persons with information relevant to the financial standing of individuals, being information collected by the agency for that purpose.

146   Exceptions from section 145.

(1)   A barrister or advocate acting in that capacity is not to be treated as doing so in the course of any ancillary credit business.

(2)   A solicitor engaging in contentious business (as defined in section 87(1) of the Solicitors Act 1974) is not to be treated as doing so in the course of any ancillary credit business.

(3) A solicitor within the meaning of the Solicitors (Scotland) Act 1933 engaging in business done in or for the purposes of proceedings before a court or before an arbiter is not to be treated as doing so in the course of any ancillary credit business.

(4) A solicitor in Northern Ireland engaging in contentious business (as defined in Article 3(2) of the Solicitors (Northern Ireland) Order 1976 , is not to be treated as doing so in the course of any ancillary credit business.

(5) For the purposes of section 145(2), introductions effected by an individual by canvassing off trade premises either debtor-creditor-supplier agreements falling within section 12(a) or regulated consumer hire agreements shall be disregarded if—

(a)   the introductions are not effected by him in the capacity of an employee, and

(b)   he does not by any other method effect introductions falling within section 145(2).

(5A) It is not credit brokerage for a person to effect the introduction of an individual desiring to obtain credit if the introduction is made—

(a)   to an authorised person, within the meaning of the 2000 Act, who has permission under that Act to enter into a relevant agreement as lender or home purchase provider (as the case may be); or

(b)   to a qualifying broker,

with a view to that individual obtaining credit under the relevant agreement.

(5B) It is not debt-adjusting for a person to carry on an activity mentioned in paragraph (a),(b) or (c) of section 145(5) if—

(a)   the debt in question is due under a relevant agreement; and

(b)   that activity is a regulated activity for the purposes of the 2000 Act.

(5C) It is not debt-counselling for a person to give advice to debtors about the liquidation of debts if—

(a)   the debt in question is due under a relevant agreement; and

(b)   giving that advice is a regulated activity for the purposes of the 2000 Act.

(5D) In this section—
'the 2000 Act' means the Financial Services and Markets Act 2000;
'relevant agreement' means an agreement which—

(a)   is secured by a land mortgage, or

(b)   is or forms part of a regulated home purchase plan,

but only if entering into the agreement as lender or home purchase provider (as the case may be) is a regulated activity for the purposes of the 2000 Act;
'qualifying broker' means a person who may effect introductions of the kind mentioned in subsection (5A) without contravening the general prohibition, within the meaning of section 19 of the 2000 Act,
and references to 'regulated activities', 'regulated home purchase plan' and 'home purchase provider' and the definition of 'qualifying broker' must be read with—

(a)   section 22 of the 2000 Act (regulated activities: power to specify classes of activity and categories of investment);

(b)   any order for the time being in force under that section; and

(c)   Schedule 2 to that Act.

(6) It is not debt-adjusting, debt-counselling or debt-collecting for a person to do anything in relation to a debt arising under an agreement if—

    (a) he is the creditor or owner under the agreement, otherwise than by virtue of an assignment, or

    (b) he is the creditor or owner under the agreement by virtue of an assignment made in connection with the transfer to the assignee of any business other than a debt-collecting business, or

    (c) he is the supplier in relation to the agreement, or

    (d) he is a credit-broker who has acquired the business of the person who was the supplier in relation to the agreement, or

    (e) he is a person prevented by subsection (5) from being treated as a credit-broker, and the agreement was made in consequence of an introduction (whether made by him or another person) which, under subsection (5), is to be disregarded.

(7) It is not debt administration for a person to take steps to perform duties, or to exercise or enforce rights, under an agreement on behalf of the creditor or owner if any of the conditions mentioned in subsection (6)(aa) to(e) is satisfied in relation to that person.

Definition substituted by SI 2006/2383 (Financial Services and Markets Act 2000 (Regulated Activities) (Amendment) (No.2) Order), Pt 3 Art 25(4)(b) (i)

Licensing

147   Application of Part III.

(1)   ...

(2) Without prejudice to the generality of section 26, regulations under that section may include provisions regulating the collection and dissemination of information by credit reference agencies.

148   Agreement for services of unlicensed trader.

(1) An agreement for the services of a person carrying on an ancillary credit business (the 'trader'), if made when the trader was unlicensed, is enforceable against the other party (the 'customer') only where the OFT has made an order under subsection (2) which applies to the agreement.

(2) The trader or his successor in title may apply to the OFT for an order that agreements within subsection (1) are to be treated as if made when the trader was licensed.

(3) Unless the OFT determines to make an order under subsection (2) in accordance with the application, it shall, before determining the application, by notice—

    (a) inform the trader, giving its reasons, that, as the case may be, it is minded to refuse the application, or to grant it in terms different from those applied for, describing them, and

    (b) invite the trader to submit to the OFT representations in support of his application in accordance with section 34.

(4) In determining whether or not to make an order under subsection (2) in respect of any period the OFT shall consider, in addition to any other relevant factors—

- (a) how far, if at all, customers, under agreements made by the trader during that period were prejudiced by the trader's conduct,

- (b) whether or not the OFT would have been likely to grant a licence covering that period on an application by the trader, and

- (c) the degree of culpability for the failure to obtain a licence.

(5) If the OFT thinks fit, it may in an order under subsection (2)—

- (a) limit the order to specified agreements, or agreements of a specified description or made at a specified time;

- (b) make the order conditional on the doing of specified acts by the trader.

(6) This section does not apply to an agreement made by a consumer credit EEA firm unless at the time it was made that firm was precluded from entering into it as a result of—

- (a) a consumer credit prohibition imposed under section 203 of the Financial Services and Markets Act 2000; or

- (b) a restriction imposed on the firm under section 204 of that Act.

149 *Regulated agreements made on introductions by unlicensed credit-broker.*

(1) A regulated agreement made by a debtor or hirer who, for the purpose of making that agreement, was introduced to the creditor or owner by an unlicensed credit-broker is enforceable against the debtor or hirer only where—

- (a) on the application of the credit-broker, the OFT has made an order under section 148(2) in respect of a period including the time when the introduction was made, and the order does not (whether in general terms or specifically) exclude the application of this paragraph to the regulated agreement, or

- (b) the OFT has made an order under subsection (2) which applies to the agreement.

(2) Where during any period individuals were introduced to a person carrying on a consumer credit business or consumer hire business by an unlicensed credit-broker for the purpose of making regulated agreements with the person carrying on that business, that person or his successor in title may apply to the OFT for an order that regulated agreements so made are to be treated as if the credit-broker had been licensed at the time of the introduction.

(3) Unless the OFT determines to make an order under subsection (2) in accordance with the application, it shall, before determining the application, by notice—

- (a) inform the applicant, giving its reasons, that, as the case may be, it is minded to refuse the application, or to grant it in terms different from those applied for, describing them, and

- (b) invite the applicant to submit to the OFT representations in support of his application in accordance with section 34.

(4) In determining whether or not to make an order under subsection (2) the OFT shall consider, in addition to any other relevant factors—

- (a) how far, if at all, debtors or hirers under regulated agreements to which the application relates were prejudiced by the credit-broker's conduct, and

- (b) the degree of culpability of the applicant in facilitating the carrying on by the credit-broker of his business when unlicensed.

(5) If the OFT thinks fit, it may in an order under subsection (2)—

(a) limit the order to specified agreements, or agreements of a specified description or made at a specified time;

(b) make the order conditional on the doing of specified acts by the applicant.

(6) For the purposes of this section, 'unlicensed credit-broker' does not include a consumer credit EEA firm unless at the time the introduction was made that firm was precluded from making it as a result of—

(a) a consumer credit prohibition imposed under section 203 of the Financial Services and Markets Act 2000; or

(b) a restriction imposed on the firm under section 204 of that Act.

150

...

Seeking business

151   Advertisements.

(1) Sections 44 to 47 apply to an advertisement published for the purposes of a business of credit brokerage carried on by any person, whether it advertises the services of that person or the services of persons to whom he effects introductions, as they apply to an advertisement to which Part IV applies.

(2) Sections 44 and 47 apply to an advertisement, published for the purposes of a business carried on by the advertiser, indicating that he is willing to advise on debts, or engage in transactions concerned with the liquidation of debts or to provide credit information services, as they apply to an advertisement to which Part IV applies.

(2A) An advertisement does not fall within subsection (1) or (2) in so far as it is a communication of an invitation or inducement to engage in investment activity within the meaning of section 21 of the Financial Services and Markets Act 2000, other than an exempt generic communication (as defined in section 43(3B)).

(3) The Secretary of State may by order provide that an advertisement published for the purposes of a business of credit brokerage, debt adjusting debt counselling or the provision of credit information services shall not fall within subsection (1) or (2) if it is of a description specified in the order.

(4) An advertisement (other than one for credit information services) does not fall within subsection (2) if it indicates that the advertiser is not willing to act in relation to consumer credit agreements and consumer hire agreements.

(5) In subsections (1) and (3) 'credit brokerage' includes the effecting of introductions of individuals desiring to obtain credit to any person carrying on a business in the course of which he provides credit secured on land.

152   Application of section 52 to 54 to credit brokerage etc.

(1) Sections 52 to 54 apply to a business of credit brokerage, debt-adjusting debt counselling or the provision of credit information services as they apply to a consumer credit business.

(2) In their application to a business of credit brokerage, sections 52 and 53 shall apply to the giving of quotations and information about the business of any person to whom the credit-broker effects introductions as well as to the giving of quotations and information about his own business.

153 *Definition of canvassing off trade premises (agreements for ancillary credit services).*

(1) An individual (the 'canvasser') canvasses off trade premises the services of a person carrying on an ancillary credit business if he solicits the entry of another individual (the 'consumer') into an agreement for the provision to the consumer of those services by making oral representations to the consumer, or any other individual, during a visit by the canvasser to any place (not excluded by subsection (2)) where the consumer, or that other individual as the case may be, is, being a visit—

  (a) carried out for the purpose of making such oral representations to individuals who are at that place, but

  (b) not carried out in response to a request made on a previous occasion.

(2) A place is excluded from subsection (1) if it is a place where (whether on a permanent or temporary basis)—

  (a) the ancillary credit business is carried on, or

  (b) any business is carried on by the canvasser or the person whose employee or agent the canvasser is, or by the consumer.

154 *Prohibition of canvassing certain ancillary credit services off trade premises.*

It is an offence to canvass off trade premises the services of a person carrying on a business of credit-brokerage, debt-adjusting, debt counselling or the provision of credit information services.

155 *Right to recover brokerage fees.*

(1) Subject to subsection (2A), the excess over £5 of a fee or commission for his services charged by a credit-broker to an individual to whom this subsection applies shall cease to be payable or, as the case may be, shall be recoverable by the individual if the introduction does not result in his entering into a relevant agreement within the six months following the introduction (disregarding any agreement which is cancelled under section 69(1) or becomes subject to section 69(2)).

(2) Subsection (1) applies to an individual who sought an introduction for a purpose which would have been fulfilled by his entry into—

  (a) a regulated agreement, or

  (b) in the case of an individual such as is referred to in section 145(2)(a)(ii), an agreement for credit secured on land, or

  (c) an agreement such as is referred to in section 145(3)(b) or (c) or (4)(b).

(2A) But subsection (1) does not apply where—

  (a) the fee or commission relates to the effecting of an introduction of a kind mentioned in section 146(5A); and

  (b) the person charging that fee or commission is an authorised person or an appointed representative, within the meaning of the Financial Services and Markets Act 2000.

(3) An agreement is a relevant agreement for the purposes of subsection (1) in relation to an individual if it is an agreement such as is referred to in subsection (2) in relation to that individual.

(4) In the case of an individual desiring to obtain credit under a consumer credit agreement, any sum payable or paid by him to a credit-broker otherwise than as a fee or commission for the credit-broker's services shall for the purposes of subsection (1) be treated as such a fee or commission if it enters, or would enter, into the total charge for credit.

Entry into agreements

156   Entry into agreements.

Regulations may make provision, in relation to agreements entered into in the course of a business of credit brokerage, debt-adjusting, debt counselling or the provision of credit information services, corresponding, with such modifications as the Secretary of State thinks fit, to the provision which is or may be made by or under sections 55, 60, 61, 62, 63, 65, 127, 179 or 180 in relation to agreements to which those sections apply.

157   Duty to disclose name etc of agency.

(1) A creditor, owner or negotiator, within the prescribed period after receiving a request in writing to that effect from the debtor or hirer, shall give him notice of the name and address of any credit reference agency from which the creditor, owner or negotiator has, during the antecedent negotiations, applied for information about his financial standing.

(2) Subsection (1) does not apply to a request received more than 28 days after the termination of the antecedent negotiations, whether on the making of the regulated agreement or otherwise.

(3) If the creditor, owner or negotiator fails to comply with subsection (1) he commits an offence.

158   Duty of agency to disclose filed information.

(1) A credit reference agency, within the prescribed period after receiving,—

   (a)   a request in writing to that effect from a consumer,

   (b)   such particulars as the agency may reasonably require to enable them to identify the file, and

   (c)   a fee of £2,

shall give the consumer a copy of the file relating to it kept by the agency.

(2) When giving a copy of the file under subsection (1), the agency shall also give the consumer a statement in the prescribed form of the consumer's rights under section 159.

(3) If the agency does not keep a file relating to the consumer it shall give the consumer notice of that fact, but need not return any money paid.

(4) If the agency contravenes any provision of this section it commits an offence.

(4A) In this section 'consumer' means—

   (a)   a partnership consisting of two or three persons not all of whom are bodies corporate; or

    (b)   an unincorporated body of persons which does not consist entirely of bodies corporate and is not a partnership.

(5)   In this Act 'file', in relation to an individual, means all the information about him kept by a credit reference agency, regardless of how the information is stored, and 'copy of the file', as respects information not in plain English, means a transcript reduced into plain English.

159   *Correction of wrong information.*

(1)   Any individual (the 'objector') given—

    (a)   information under section 7 of the Data Protection Act 1998 by a credit reference agency, or

    (b)   information under section 158,

who considers that an entry in his file is incorrect, and that if it is not corrected he is likely to be prejudiced, may give notice to the agency requiring it either to remove the entry from the file or amend it.

(2)   Within 28 days after receiving a notice under subsection (1), the agency shall by notice inform the objector that it has—

    (a)   removed the entry from the file, or

    (b)   amended the entry, or

    (c)   taken no action,

and if the notice states that the agency has amended the entry it shall include a copy of the file so far as it comprises the amended entry.

(3)   Within 28 days after receiving a notice under subsection (2), or where no such notice was given, within 28 days after the expiry of the period mentioned in subsection (2), the objector may, unless he has been informed by the agency that it has removed the entry from his file, serve a further notice on the agency requiring it to add to the file an accompanying notice of correction (not exceeding 200 words) drawn up by the objector, and include a copy of it when furnishing information included in or based on that entry.

(4)   Within 28 days after receiving a notice under subsection (3), the agency, unless it intends to apply to the relevant authority under subsection (5), shall by notice inform the objector that it has received the notice under subsection (3) and intends to comply with it.

(5)   If—

    (a)   the objector has not received a notice under subsection (4) within the time required, or

    (b)   it appears to the agency that it would be improper for it to publish a notice of correction because it is incorrect, or unjustly defames any person, or is frivolous or scandalous, or is for any other reason unsuitable,

the objector or, as the case may be, the agency may, in the prescribed manner and on payment of the specified fee, apply to the relevant authority, who may make such order on the application as he thinks fit.

(6)   If a person to whom an order under this section is directed fails to comply with it within the period specified in the order he commits an offence.

(7)   The Information Commissioner may vary or revoke any order made by him under this section.

(8)   In this section 'the relevant authority' means—

(a)   where the objector is a partnership or other unincorporated body of persons, the OFT, and

(b)   in any other case, the Information Commissioner.

160   Alternative procedure for business consumers.

(1)   The OFT, on an application made by a credit reference agency, may direct that this section shall apply to the agency if it is satisfied—

(a)   that compliance with section 158 in the case of consumers who carry on a business would adversely affect the service provided to its customers by the agency, and

(b)   that, having regard to the methods employed by the agency and to any other relevant factors, it is probable that consumers carrying on a business would not be prejudiced by the making of the direction.

(2)   Where an agency to which this section applies receives a request, particulars and a fee under section 158(1) from a consumer who carries on a business, and section 158(3) does not apply, the agency, instead of complying with section 158, may elect to deal with the matter under the following subsections.

(3)   Instead of giving the consumer a copy of the file, the agency shall within the prescribed period give notice to the consumer that it is proceeding under this section, and by notice give the consumer such information included in or based on entries in the file as the OFT may direct, together with a statement in the prescribed form of the consumer's rights under subsections (4) and (5).

(4)   If within 28 days after receiving the information given to the consumer under subsection (3), or such longer period as the OFT may allow, the consumer—

(a)   gives notice to the OFT that the consumer is dissatisfied with the information, and

(b)   satisfies the OFT that the consumer has taken such steps in relation to the agency as may be reasonable with a view to removing the cause of the consumer's dissatisfaction, and

(c)   Pays the OFT the specified fee,

the OFT may direct the agency to give the OFT a copy of the file, and the OFT may disclose to the consumer such of the information on the file as the OFT thinks fit.

(5)   Section 159 applies with any necessary modifications to information given to the consumer under this section as it applies to information given under section 158.

(6)   If an agency making an election under subsection (2) fails to comply with subsection (3) or (4) it commits an offence.

(7)   In this section 'consumer' has the same meaning as in section 158.

PART XI ENFORCEMENT OF ACT

161   Enforcement authorities.

(1)   The following authorities ('enforcement authorities') have a duty to enforce this Act and regulations made under it—

    (a)   the OFT,

    (b)   in Great Britain, the local weights and measures authority,

    (c)   in Northern Ireland, the Department of Commerce for Northern Ireland.

(3)   Every local weights and measures authority shall, whenever the OFT requires, report to it in such form and with such particulars as it requires on the exercise of their functions under this Act.

Amendment as at: April 6, 2008

162   Powers of entry and inspection.

(1)   A duly authorised officer of an enforcement authority, at all reasonable hours and on production, if required, of his credentials, may—

    (a)   in order to ascertain whether a breach of any provision of or under this Act has been committed, inspect any goods and enter any premises (other than premises used only as a dwelling);

    (b)   if he has reasonable cause to suspect that a breach of any provision of or under this Act has been committed, in order to ascertain whether it has been committed, require any person—

        (i)   carrying on, or employed in connection with, a business to produce any documents relating to it; or

        (ii)   having control of any information relating to a business to provide him with that information,

    (c)   if he has reasonable cause to believe that a breach of any provision of or under this Act has been committed, seize and detain any goods in order to ascertain (by testing or otherwise) whether such a breach has been committed;

    (d)   seize and detain any goods, documents which he has reason to believe may be required as evidence in proceedings for an offence under this Act;

    (e)   for the purpose of exercising his powers under this subsection to seize goods, documents, but only if and to the extent that it is reasonably necessary for securing that the provisions of this Act and of any regulations made under it are duly observed, require any person having authority to do so to break open any container and, if that person does not comply, break it open himself.

(2)   An officer seizing goods, documents in exercise of his powers under this section shall not do so without informing the person he seizes them from.

(3)   If a justice of the peace, on sworn information in writing, or, in Scotland, a sheriff or a magistrate or justice of the peace, on evidence on oath,—

    (a)   is satisfied that there is reasonable ground to believe either—

        (i)   that any goods, documents which a duly authorised officer has power to inspect under this section are on any premises and their inspection is likely to disclose evidence of a breach of any provision of or under this Act; or

        (ii)   that a breach of any provision of or under this Act has been, is being or is about to be committed on any premises; and

    (b)   is also satisfied either—

        (i)   that admission to the premises has been or is likely to be refused and that notice of intention to apply for a warrant under this subsection has been given to the occupier; or

(ii) that an application for admission, or the giving of such a notice, would defeat the object of the entry or that the premises are unoccupied or that the occupier is temporarily absent and it might defeat the object of the entry to wait for his return,

the justice or, as the case may be, the sheriff or magistrate may by warrant under his hand, which shall continue in force for a period of one month, authorise an officer of an enforcement authority to enter the premises (by force if need be).

(4) An officer entering premises by virtue of this section may take such other persons and equipment with him as he thinks necessary; and on leaving premises entered by virtue of a warrant under subsection (3) shall, if they are unoccupied or the occupier is temporarily absent, leave them as effectively secured against trespassers as he found them.

(5) Regulations may provide that, in cases described by the regulations, an officer of a local weights and measures authority is not to be taken to be duly authorised for the purposes of this section unless he is authorised by the OFT.

(6) A person who is not a duly authorised officer of an enforcement authority, but purports to act as such under this section, commits an offence.

(7) ...

(8) References in this section to a breach of any provision of or under this Act do not include references to—

(a) a failure to comply with a requirement imposed under section 33A or 33B;

(b) a failure to comply with section 36A; or

(c) a failure in relation to which the OFT can apply for an order under section 36E.

163 Compensation for loss.

(1) Where, in exercising his powers under section 162, an officer of an enforcement authority seizes and detains goods and their owner suffers loss by reason of—

(a) that seizure, or

(b) the loss, damage or deterioration of the goods during detention,

then, unless the owner is convicted of an offence under this Act committed in relation to the goods, the authority shall compensate him for the loss so suffered.

(2) Any dispute as to the right to or amount of any compensation under subsection (1) shall be determined by arbitration.

164 Power to make test purchases etc.

(1) An enforcement authority may—

(a) make, or authorise any of their officers to make on their behalf, such purchases of goods; and

(b) authorise any of their officers to procure the provision of such services or facilities or to enter into such agreements or other transactions,

as may appear to them expedient for determining whether any provisions made by or under this Act are being complied with.

(2) Any act done by an officer authorised to do it under subsection (1) shall be treated for the purposes of this Act as done by him as an individual on his own behalf.

(3)   Any goods seized by an officer under this Act may be tested, and in the event of such a test he shall inform the person mentioned in section 162(2) of the test results.

(4)   Where any test leads to proceedings under this Act, the enforcement authority shall—

(a)   if the goods were purchased, inform the person they were purchased from of the test results, and

(b)   allow any person against whom the proceedings are taken to have the goods tested on his behalf if it is reasonably practicable to do so.

165   Obstruction of authorised officers.

(1)   Any person who—

(a)   wilfully obstructs an officer of an enforcement authority acting in pursuance of this Act; or

(b)   wilfully fails to comply with any requirement properly made to him by such an officer under section 162; or

(c)   without reasonable cause fails to give such an officer (so acting) other assistance or information he may reasonably require in performing his functions under this Act,

commits an offence.

(1A)A failure to give assistance or information shall not constitute an offence under subsection (1)(c) if it is also—

(a)   a failure to comply with a requirement imposed under section 33A or 33B;

(b)   a failure to comply with section 36A; or

(c)   a failure in relation to which the OFT can apply for an order under section 36E.

(2)   If any person, in giving such information as is mentioned in subsection (1)(c), makes any statement which he knows to be false, he commits an offence.

(3)   Nothing in this section requires a person to answer any question or give any information if to do so might incriminate that person or (where that person is married or a civil partner) the spouse or civil partner of that person.

166   Notification of convictions and judgments to OFT.

Where a person is convicted of an offence or has a judgment given against him by or before any court in the United Kingdom and it appears to the court—

(a)   having regard to the functions of the OFT under this Act, that the conviction or judgment should be brought to the OFT's attention, and

(b)   that it may not be brought to its attention unless arrangements for that purpose are made by the court,

the court may make such arrangements notwithstanding that the proceedings have been finally disposed of.

167   Penalties.

(1)   An offence under a provision of this Act specified in column 1 of Schedule 1 is triable in the mode or modes indicated in column 3, and on conviction is punishable as indicated in column 4 (where a period of time indicates the maximum term of imprisonment, and a monetary amount indicates the maximum fine, for the offence in question).

(2) A person who contravenes any regulations made under section 44, 52, 53 or 112, or made under section 26 by virtue of section 54, commits an offence.

168 Defences.

(1) In any proceedings for an offence under this Act it is a defence for the person charged to prove—

  (a) that his act or omission was due to a mistake, or to reliance on information supplied to him, or to an act or omission by another person, or to an accident or some other cause beyond his control, and

  (b) that he took all reasonable precautions and exercised all due diligence to avoid such an act or omission by himself or any person under his control.

(2) If in any case the defence provided by subsection (1) involves the allegation that the act or omission was due to an act or omission by another person or to reliance on information supplied by another person, the person charged shall not, without leave of the court, be entitled to rely on that defence unless, within a period ending seven clear days before the hearing, he has served on the prosecutor a notice giving such information identifying or assisting in the identification of that other person as was then in his possession.

169 Offences by bodies corporate.

Where at any time a body corporate commits an offence under this Act with the consent or connivance of, or because of neglect by, any individual, the individual commits the like offence if at that time—

  (a) he is a director, manager, secretary or similar officer of the body corporate, or

  (b) he is purporting to act as such an officer, or

  (c) the body corporate is managed by its members of whom he is one.

170 No further sanctions for breach of Act.

(1) A breach of any requirement made (otherwise than by any court) by or under this Act shall incur no civil or criminal sanction as being such a breach, except to the extent (if any) expressly provided by or under this Act.

(2) In exercising its functions under this Act the OFT may take account of any matter appearing to it to constitute a breach of a requirement made by or under this Act, whether or not any sanction for that breach is provided by or under this Act and, if it is so provided, whether or not proceedings have been brought in respect of the breach.

(3) Subsection (1) does not prevent the grant of an injunction, or the making of an order of certiorari, mandamus or prohibition or as respects Scotland the grant of an interdict or of an order under section 91 of the Court of Session Act 1868 (order for specific performance of statutory duty).

171 Onus of proof in various proceedings.

(1) If an agreement contains a term signifying that in the opinion of the parties section 10(3)(b)(iii) does not apply to the agreement, it shall be taken not to apply unless the contrary is proved.

(2) It shall be assumed in any proceedings, unless the contrary is proved, that when a person initiated a transaction as mentioned in section 19(1)(c) he knew the principal agreement had been made, or contemplated that it might be made.

(3)   Regulations under section 44 or 52 may make provision as to the onus of proof in any proceedings to enforce the regulations.

(4)   In proceedings brought by the creditor under a credit-token agreement—

    (a)   it is for the creditor to prove that the credit-token was lawfully supplied to the debtor, and was accepted by him, and

    (b)   if the debtor alleges that any use made of the credit-token was not authorised by him, it is for the creditor to prove either—

        (i)   that the use was so authorised, or

        (ii)   that the use occurred before the creditor had been given notice under section 84(3).

(5)   In proceedings under section 50(1) in respect of a document received by a minor at any school or other educational establishment for minors, it is for the person sending it to him at that establishment to prove that he did not know or suspect it to be such an establishment.

(6)   In proceedings under section 119(1) it is for the pawnee to prove that he had reasonable cause to refuse to allow the pawn to be redeemed.

(7)   ...

172   *Statements by creditor or owner to be binding.*

(1)   A statement by a creditor or owner is binding on him if given under—

section 77(1),

section 78(1),

section 79(1),

section 97(1),

section 107(1)(c),

section 108(1)(c), or

section 109(1)(c),

(2)   Where a trader—

    (a)   gives a customer a notice in compliance with section 103(1)(b), or

    (b)   gives a customer a notice under section 103(1) asserting that the customer is not indebted to him under an agreement,

the notice is binding on the trader.

(3)   Where in proceedings before any court—

    (a)   it is sought to reply on a statement or notice given as mentioned in subsection (1) or (2), and

    (b)   the statement or notice is shown to be incorrect,

the court may direct such relief (if any) to be given to the creditor or owner from the operation of subsection (1) or (2) as appears to the court to be just.

173   *Contracting-out forbidden.*

(1)   A term contained in a regulated agreement or linked transaction, or in any other agreement relating to an actual or prospective regulated agreement or linked transaction, is

void if, and to the extent that, it is inconsistent with a provision for the protection of the debtor or hirer or his relative or any surety contained in this Act or in any regulation made under this Act.

(2) Where a provision specifies the duty or liability of the debtor or hirer or his relative or any surety in certain circumstances, a term is inconsistent with that provision if it purports to impose, directly or indirectly, an additional duty or liability on him in those circumstances.

(3) Notwithstanding subsection (1), a provision of this Act under which a thing may be done in relation to any person on an order of the court or the OFT only shall not be taken to prevent its being done at any time with that person's consent given at that time, but the refusal of such consent shall not give rise to any liability.

PART XII SUPPLEMENTAL

174

...

174A Powers to require provision of information or documents etc

(1) Every power conferred on a relevant authority by or under this Act (however expressed) to require the provision or production of information or documents includes the power—

    (a) to require information to be provided or produced in such form as the authority may specify, including, in relation to information recorded otherwise than in a legible form, in a legible form;

    (b) to take copies of, or extracts from, any documents provided or produced by virtue of the exercise of the power;

    (c) to require the person who is required to provide or produce any information or document by virtue of the exercise of the power—

        (i) to state, to the best of his knowledge and belief, where the information or document is;

        (ii) to give an explanation of the information or document;

        (iii) to secure that any information provided or produced, whether in a document or otherwise, is verified in such manner as may be specified by the authority;

        (iv) to secure that any document provided or produced is authenticated in such manner as may be so specified;

    (d) to specify a time at or by which a requirement imposed by virtue of paragraph (c) must be complied with.

(2) Every power conferred on a relevant authority by or under this Act (however expressed) to inspect or to seize documents at any premises includes the power to take copies of, or extracts from, any documents inspected or seized by virtue of the exercise of the power.

(3) But a relevant authority has no power under this Act—

    (a) to require another person to provide or to produce,

    (b) to seize from another person, or

    (c) to require another person to give access to premises for the purposes of the inspection of, any information or document which the other person would be entitled to refuse to provide or produce in proceedings in the High Court on the grounds of legal professional privilege or (in Scotland) in proceedings in the Court of Session on the grounds of confidentiality of communications.

(4)   In subsection (3) 'communications' means—

   (a)   communications between a professional legal adviser and his client;

   (b)   communications made in connection with or in contemplation of legal proceedings and for the purposes of those proceedings.

(5)   In this section 'relevant authority' means—

   (a)   the OFT or an enforcement authority (other than the OFT);

   (b)   an officer of the OFT or of an enforcement authority (other than the OFT).

175   *Duty of persons deemed to be agents.*

Where under this Act a person is deemed to receive a notice or payment as agent of the creditor or owner under a regulated agreement, he shall be deemed to be under a contractual duty to the creditor or owner to transmit the notice, or remit the payment, to him forthwith.

176   *Service of documents.*

(1)   A document to be served under this Act by one person ('the server') on another person ('the subject') is to be treated as properly served on the subject if dealt with as mentioned in the following subsections.

(2)   The document may be delivered or sent by an appropriate method to the subject, or addressed to him by name and left at his proper address.

(3)   For the purposes of this Act, a document sent by post to, or left at, the address last known to the server as the address of a person shall be treated as sent by post to, or left at, his proper address.

(4)   Where the document is to be served on the subject as being the person having any interest in land, and it is not practicable after reasonable inquiry to ascertain the subject's name or address, the document may be served by—

   (a)   addressing it to the subject by the description of the person having that interest in the land (naming it), and

   (b)   delivering the document to some responsible person on the land or affixing it, or a copy of it, in a conspicuous position on the land.

(5)   Where a document to be served on the subject as being a debtor, hirer or surety, or as having any other capacity relevant for the purposes of this Act, is served at any time on another person who—

   (a)   is the person last known to the server as having that capacity, but

   (b)   before that time had ceased to have it,

the document shall be treated as having been served at that time on the subject.

(6)   Anything done to a document in relation to a person who (whether to the knowledge of the server or not) has died shall be treated for the purposes of subsection (5) as service of the document on that person if it would have been so treated had he not died.

(7) The following enactments shall not be construed as authorising service on the Public Trustee (in England and Wales) or the Probate Judge (in Northern Ireland) of any document which is to be served under this Act—

section 9 of the Administration of Estates Act 1925;

section 3 of the Administration of Estates Act (Northern Ireland) 1955.

(8) References in the preceding subsections to the serving of a document on a person include the giving of the document to that person.

176A Electronic transmission of documents

(1) A document is transmitted in accordance with this subsection if—

(a) the person to whom it is transmitted agrees that it may be delivered to him by being transmitted to a particular electronic address in a particular electronic form,

(b) it is transmitted to that address in that form, and

(c) the form in which the document is transmitted is such that any information in the document which is addressed to the person to whom the document is transmitted is capable of being stored for future reference for an appropriate period in a way which allows the information to be reproduced without change.

(2) A document transmitted in accordance with subsection (1) shall, unless the contrary is proved, be treated for the purposes of this Act, except section 69, as having been delivered on the working day immediately following the day on which it is transmitted.

(3) In this section, 'electronic address' includes any number or address used for the purposes of receiving electronic communications.

177 Saving for registered charges.

(1) Nothing in this Act affects the rights of a proprietor of a registered charge (within the meaning of the Land Registration Act 2002), who—

(a) became the proprietor under a transfer for valuable consideration without notice of any defect in the title arising (apart from this section) by virtue of this Act, or

(b) derives title from such a proprietor.

(2) Nothing in this Act affects the operation of section 104 of the Law of Property Act 1925 (protection of purchaser where mortgagee exercises power of sale).

(3) Subsection (1) does not apply to a proprietor carrying on a business of debt-collecting.

(4) Where, by virtue of subsection (1), a land mortgage is enforced which apart from this section would be treated as never having effect, the original creditor or owner shall be liable to indemnify the debtor or hirer against any loss thereby suffered by him.

(5) In the application of this section to Scotland for subsections (1) to (3) there shall be substituted the following subsections—

'(1) Nothing in this Act affects the rights of a creditor in a heritable security who—

(a) became the creditor under a transfer for value without notice of any defect in the title arising (apart from this section) by virtue of this Act; or

(b) derives title from such a creditor.

(2)   Nothing in this Act affects the operation of section 41 of the Conveyancing (Scotland) Act 1924 (protection of purchasers), or of that section as applied to standard securities by section 32 of the Conveyancing and Feudal Reform (Scotland) Act 1970.

(3)   Subsection (1) does not apply to a creditor carrying on a business of debt-collecting.'.

(6)   In the application of this section to Northern Ireland—

(a)   any reference to the proprietor of a registered charge (within the meaning of the Land Registration Act 2002) shall be construed as a reference to the registered owner of a charge under the Local Registration of Title (Ireland) Act 1891 or Part IV of the Land Registration Act (Northern Ireland) 1970, and

(b)   for the reference to section 104 of the Law of Property Act 1925 there shall be substituted a reference to section 21 of the Conveyancing and Law of Property Act 1881 and section 5 of the Conveyancing Act 1911.

178   Local Acts.

The Secretary of State or the Department of Commerce for Northern Ireland may by order make such amendments or repeals of any provision of any local Act as appears to the Secretary of State or, as the case may be, the Department, necessary or expedient in consequence of the replacement by this Act of the enactments relating to pawnbrokers and moneylenders.

Regulations, orders etc

179   Power to prescribe form etc of secondary documents.

(1)   Regulations may be made as to the form and content of credit-cards, trading-checks, receipts, vouchers and other documents or things issued by creditors, owners or suppliers under or in connection with regulated agreements or by other persons in connection with linked transactions, and may in particular—

(a)   require specified information to be included in the prescribed manner in documents, and other specified material to be excluded;

(b)   contain requirements to ensure that specified information is clearly brought to the attention of the debtor or hirer, or his relative, and that one part of a document is not given insufficient or excessive prominence compared with another.

(2)   If a person issues any document or thing in contravention of regulations under subsection (1) then, as from the time of the contravention but without prejudice to anything done before it, this Act shall apply as if the regulated agreement had been improperly executed by reason of a contravention of regulations under section 60(1).

180   Power to prescribe form etc. of copies.

(1)   Regulations may be made as to the form and content of documents to be issued as copies of any executed agreement, security instrument or other document referred to in this Act, and may in particular—

(a)   require specified information to be included in the prescribed manner in any copy, and contain requirements to ensure that such information is clearly brought to the attention of a reader of the copy;

(b)   authorise the omission from a copy of certain material contained in the original, or the inclusion of such material in condensed form.

(2) A duty imposed by any provision of this Act (except section 35) to supply a copy of any document—

(a) is not satisfied unless the copy supplied is in the prescribed form and conforms to the prescribed requirements;

(b) is not infringed by the omission of any material, or its inclusion in condensed form, if that is authorised by regulations;

and references in this Act to copies shall be construed accordingly.

(3) Regulations may provide that a duty imposed by this Act to supply a copy of a document referred to in an unexecuted agreement or an executed agreement shall not apply to documents of a kind specified in the regulations.

181 Power to alter monetary limits etc.

(1) The Secretary of State may by order made by statutory instrument amend, or further amend, any of the following provisions of this Act so as to reduce or increase a sum mentioned in that provision, namely, sections 16B(1), 17(1), 39A(3), 70(6), 75(3)(b), 77(1), 78(1), 79(1), 84(1), 101(7)(a), 107(1), 108(1), 109(1), 110(1), 118(1)(b), 120(1)(a), 140B(6), 155(1) and 158(1).

(2) An order under subsection (1) amending section 16B(1), 17(1), 39A(3), 75(3)(b)or 140B(6) shall be of no effect unless a draft of the order has been laid before and approved by each House of Parliament.

182 Regulations and orders.

(1) Any power of the Secretary of State to make regulations or orders under this Act, except the power conferred by sections 2(1)(a), 181 and 192 shall be exercisable by statutory instrument subject to annulment in pursuance of a resolution of either House of Parliament.

(1A) The power of the Lord Chancellor to make rules under section 40A(3) shall be exercisable by statutory instrument subject to annulment in pursuance of a resolution of either House of Parliament.

(2) Where a power to make regulations or orders or rules is exercisable by the Secretary of State or by the Lord Chancellor by virtue of this Act, regulations or orders or rules made in the exercise of that power may—

(a) make different provision in relation to different cases or classes of case, and

(b) exclude certain cases or classes of case, and

(c) contain such transitional provisions as the person making them thinks fit.

(3) Regulations may provide that specified expressions, when used as described by the regulations, are to be given the prescribed meaning, notwithstanding that another meaning is intended by the person using them.

(4) Any power conferred on the Secretary of State by this Act to make orders includes power to vary or revoke an order so made.

183 Determinations etc. by OFT.

(1) The OFT may vary or revoke any determination made, or direction given, by it under this Act.

(2) Subsection (1) does not apply to—

    (a) a determination to issue, renew or vary a licence;

    (b) a determination to extend a period under section 28B or to refuse to extend a period under that section;

    (c) a determination to end a suspension under section 33;

    (d) a determination to make an order under section 40(2), 148(2) or 149(2);

    (e) a determination mentioned in column 1 of the Table in section 41.

Interpretation

184 Associates.

(1) A person is an associate of an individual if that person is—

    (a) the individual's husband or wife or civil partner,

    (b) a relative of—

        (i) the individual, or

        (ii) the individual's husband or wife or civil partner, or

    (c) the husband or wife or civil partner of a relative of—

        (i) the individual, or

        (ii) the individual's husband or wife or civil partner.

(2) A person is an associate of any person with whom he is in partnership, and of the husband or wife or civil partner or a relative of any individual with whom he is in partnership.

(3) A body corporate is an associate of another body corporate—

    (a) if the same person is a controller of both, or a person is a controller of one and persons who are his associates, or he and persons who are his associates, are controllers of the other; or

    (b) if a group of two or more persons is a controller of each company, and the groups either consist of the same persons or could be regarded as consisting of the same persons by treating (in one or more cases) a member of either group as replaced by a person of whom he is an associate.

(4) A body corporate is an associate of another person if that person is a controller of it or if that person and persons who are his associates together are controllers of it.

(5) In this section 'relative' means brother, sister, uncle, aunt, nephew, niece, lineal ancestor or lineal descendant, references to a husband or wife include a former husband or wife and a reputed husband or wife, references to a civil partner include a former civil partner and a reputed civil partner; and for the purposes of this subsection a relationship shall be established as if any illegitimate child, step-child or adopted child of a person were the legitimate child of the relationship in question.

185 Agreement with more than one debtor or hirer.

(1) Where an actual or prospective regulated agreement has two or more debtors or hirers (not being a partnership or an unincorporated body of persons)—

    (a) anything required by or under this Act to be done to or in relation to the debtor or hirer shall be done to or in relation to each of them; and

   (b)   anything done under this Act by or on behalf of one of them shall have effect as if done by or on behalf of all of them.

(2)   Notwithstanding subsection (1)(a), where credit is provided under an agreement to two or more debtors jointly, in performing his duties—

   (a)   in the case of fixed-sum credit, under section 77A, or

   (b)   in the case of running-account credit, under section 78(4),

the creditor need not give statements to any debtor who has signed and given to him a notice (a ' dispensing notice') authorising him not to comply in the debtor's case with section 77A or (as the case may be) 78(4).

(2A) A dispensing notice given by a debtor is operative from when it is given to the creditor until it is revoked by a further notice given to the creditor by the debtor.

(2B) But subsection (2) does not apply if (apart from this subsection) dispensing notices would be operative in relation to all of the debtors to whom the credit is provided.

(2C) Any dispensing notices operative in relation to an agreement shall cease to have effect if any of the debtors dies.

(2D) A dispensing notice which is operative in relation to an agreement shall be operative also in relation to any subsequent agreement which, in relation to the earlier agreement, is a modifying agreement.'

(3)   Subsection (1)(b) does not apply for the purposes of section 61(1)(a).

(4)   Where a regulated agreement has two or more debtors or hirers (not being a partnership or an unincorporated body of persons), section 86 applies to the death of any of them.

(5)   An agreement for the provision of credit, or the bailment or (in Scotland) the hiring of goods, to two or more persons jointly where—

   (a)   one or more of those persons is an individual, and

   (b)   one or more of them is not an individual,

is a consumer credit agreement or consumer hire agreement if it would have been one had they all been individuals; and each person within paragraph (b) shall accordingly be included among the debtors or hirers under the agreement.

(6)   Where subsection (5) applies, references in this Act to the signing of any document by the debtor or hirer shall be construed in relation to a body corporate within paragraph (b) of that subsection as referring to a signing on behalf of the body corporate.

186   Agreement with more than one creditor or owner.

Where an actual or prospective regulated agreement has two or more creditors or owners, anything required by or under this Act to be done to, or in relation to, or by, the creditor or owner shall be effective if done to, or in relation to, or by, any one of them.

187   Arrangements between creditor and supplier.

(1)   A consumer credit agreement shall be treated as entered into under pre-existing arrangements between a creditor and a supplier if it is entered into in accordance with, or in furtherance of, arrangements previously made between persons mentioned in subsection (4)(a), (b) or (c).

(2) A consumer credit agreement shall be treated as entered into in contemplation of future arrangements between a creditor and a supplier if it is entered into in the expectation that arrangements will subsequently be made between persons mentioned in subsection (4)(a), (b) or (c) for the supply of cash, goods and services (or any of them) to be financed by the consumer credit agreement.

(3) Arrangements shall be disregarded for the purposes of subsection (1) or (2) if—

(a)   they are arrangements for the making, in specified circumstances, of payments to the supplier by the creditor, and

(b)   the creditor holds himself out as willing to make, in such circumstances, payments of the kind to suppliers generally.

(3A) Arrangements shall also be disregarded for the purposes of subsections (1) and (2) if they are arrangements for the electronic transfer of funds from a current account at a bank within the meaning of the Bankers' Books Evidence Act 1879.

(4) The persons referred to in subsections (1) and (2) are—

(a)   the creditor and the supplier;

(b)   one of them and an associate of the other's;

(c)   an associate of one and an associate of the other's.

(5) Where the creditor is an associate of the supplier's, the consumer credit agreement shall be treated, unless the contrary is proved, as entered into under pre-existing arrangements between the creditor and the supplier.

187A   Definition of 'default sum'

(1) In this Act 'default sum' means, in relation to the debtor or hirer under a regulated agreement, a sum (other than a sum of interest) which is payable by him under the agreement in connection with a breach of the agreement by him.

(2) But a sum is not a default sum in relation to the debtor or hirer simply because, as a consequence of his breach of the agreement, he is required to pay it earlier than he would otherwise have had to.

188   Examples of use of new terminology.

(1) Schedule 2 shall have effect for illustrating the use of terminology employed in this Act.

(2) The examples given in Schedule 2 are not exhaustive.

(3) In the case of conflict between Schedule 2 and any other provision of this Act, that other provision shall prevail.

(4) The Secretary of State may by order amend Schedule 2 by adding further examples or in any other way.

189   Definitions.

(1) In this Act, unless the context otherwise requires—

'advertisement' includes every form of advertising, whether in a publication, by television or radio, by display of notices, signs, labels, showcards or goods, by distribution of samples, circulars, catalogues, price lists or other material, by exhibition of pictures, models or films, or in any other way, and references to the publishing of advertisements shall be construed accordingly;

'advertiser' in relation to an advertisement, means any person indicated by the advertisement as willing to enter into transactions to which the advertisement relates;

'ancillary credit business' has the meaning given by section 145(1);

'antecedent negotiations' has the meaning given by section 56;

'appeal period' means the period beginning on the first day on which an appeal to the Tribunal may be brought and ending on the last day on which it may be brought or, if it is brought, ending on its final determination, or abandonment;

'appropriate method' means—

    (a)   Post, or

    (b)   transmission in the form of an electronic communication in accordance with section 176A(1);

'assignment', in relation to Scotland, means assignation;

'associate' shall be construed in accordance with section 184;

'bill of sale' has the meaning given by section 4 of the Bills of Sale Act 1878 or, for Northern Ireland, by section 4 of the Bills of Sale (Ireland) Act 1879;

'building society' means a building society within the meaning of the Building Societies Act 1986;

'business' includes profession or trade, and references to a business apply subject to subsection (2);

'cancellable agreement' means a regulated agreement which, by virtue of section 67, may be cancelled by the debtor or hirer;

'canvass' shall be construed in accordance with sections 48 and 153;

'cash' includes money in any form;

'charity' means as respects England and Wales a charity registered under the Charities Act 1993 or an exempt charity (within the meaning of that Act), as respects Northern Ireland an institution or other organisation established for charitable purposes only ('organisation' including any persons administering a trust and 'charitable' being construed in the same way as if it were contained in the Income Tax Acts) and as respects Scotland a body entered in the Scottish Charity Register;

'conditional sale agreement' means an agreement for the sale of goods or land under which the purchase price or part of it is payable by instalments, and the property in the goods or land is to remain in the seller (notwithstanding that the buyer is to be in possession of the goods or land) until such conditions as to the payment of instalments or otherwise as may be specified in the agreement are fulfilled;

'consumer credit agreement' has the meaning given by section 8, and includes a consumer credit agreement which is cancelled under section 69(1), or becomes subject to section 69(2), so far as the agreement remains in force;

'consumer credit business' means any business being carried on by a person so far as it comprises or relates to—

    (a)   the provision of credit by him, or

    (b)   otherwise his being a creditor,

under regulated consumer credit agreements;

'consumer hire agreement' has the meaning given by section 15;

'consumer hire business' means any business being carried on by a person so far as it comprises or relates to—

(a) the bailment or (in Scotland) the hiring of goods by him, or

(b) otherwise his being an owner,

under regulated consumer hire agreements;

'controller', in relation to a body corporate, means a person—

(a) in accordance with whose directions or instructions the directors of the body corporate or of another body corporate which is its controller (or any of them) are accustomed to act, or

(b) who, either alone or with any associate or associates, is entitled to exercise, or control the exercise of, one third or more of the voting power at any general meeting of the body corporate or of another body corporate which is its controller;

'copy' shall be construed in accordance with section 180;

'court' means in relation to England and Wales the county court, in relation to Scotland the sheriff court and in relation to Northern Ireland the High Court or the county court;

'credit' shall be construed in accordance with section 9;

'credit-broker' means a person carrying on a business of credit brokerage;

'credit brokerage' has the meaning given by section 145(2);

'credit information services' has the meaning given by section 145(7B).

'credit limit' has the meaning given by section 10(2);

'creditor' means the person providing credit under a consumer credit agreement or the person to whom his rights and duties under the agreement have passed by assignment or operation of law, and in relation to a prospective consumer credit agreement, includes the prospective creditor;

'credit reference agency' has the meaning given by section 145(8);

'credit-sale agreement' means an agreement for the sale of goods, under which the purchase price or part of it is payable by instalments, but which is not a conditional sale agreement;

'credit-token' has the meaning given by section 14(1);

'credit-token agreement' means a regulated agreement for the provision of credit in connection with the use of a credit-token;

'debt-adjusting' has the meaning given by section 145(5);

'debt administration' has the meaning given by section 145(7A);

'debt-collecting' has the meaning given by section 145(7);

'debt-counselling' has the meaning given by section 145(6);

'debtor' means the individual receiving credit under a consumer credit agreement or the person to whom his rights and duties under the agreement have passed by assignment or operation of law, and in relation to a prospective consumer credit agreement includes the prospective debtor;

'debtor-creditor agreement' has the meaning given by section 13;

'debtor-creditor-supplier agreement' has the meaning given by section 12;

'default notice' has the meaning given by section 87(1);

'default sum' has the meaning given by section 187A;

'deposit' means (except in section 16(10) and 25(1B)) any sum payable by a debtor or hirer by way of deposit or down-payment, or credited or to be credited to him on account of any deposit or down-payment, whether the sum is to be or has been paid to the creditor or owner or any other person, or is to be or has been discharged by a payment of money or a transfer or delivery of goods or by any other means;

'documents' includes information recorded in any form;

'electric line' has the meaning given by the Electricity Act 1989 or, for Northern Ireland, the Electricity Supply (Northern Ireland) Order 1972;

'electronic communication' means an electronic communication within the meaning of the Electronic Communications Act 2000 (c.7);

'embodies' and related words shall be construed in accordance with subsection (4);

'enforcement authority' has the meaning given by section 161(1);

'enforcement order' means an order under section 65(1), 105(7)(a) or (b), 111(2) or 124(1) or (2);

'executed agreement' means a document, signed by or on behalf of the parties, embodying the terms of a regulated agreement, or such of them as have been reduced to writing;

'exempt agreement' means an agreement specified in or under section 16, 16A or 16B;

'finance' means to finance wholly or partly, and 'financed' and 'refinanced' shall be construed accordingly

'file' and 'copy of the file' have the meanings given by section 158(5);

'fixed-sum credit' has the meaning given by section 10(1)(b);

'friendly society' means a society registered or treated as registered under the Friendly Societies Act 1974 or the Friendly Societies Act 1992;

'future arrangements' shall be construed in accordance with section 187;

'general notice' means a notice published by the OFT at a time and in a manner appearing to it suitable for securing that the notice is seen within a reasonable time by persons likely to be affected by it;

'give' means deliver or send by an appropriate method to;

'goods' has the meaning given by section 61(1) of the Sale of Goods Act 1979;

'group licence' has the meaning given by section 22(1)(b);

'High Court' means Her Majesty's High Court of Justice, or the Court of Session in Scotland or the High Court of Justice in Northern Ireland;

'hire-purchase agreement' means an agreement, other than a conditional sale agreement, under which—

(a) goods are bailed or (in Scotland) hired in return for periodical payments by the person to whom they are bailed or hired, and

(b) the property in the goods will pass to that person if the terms of the agreement are complied with and one or more of the following occurs—

(i) the exercise of an option to purchase by that person,

(ii) the doing of any other specified act by any party to the agreement,

(iii) the happening of any other specified event;

'hirer' means the individual to whom goods are bailed or (in Scotland) hired under a consumer hire agreement, or the person to whom his rights and duties under the agreement have passed by assignment or operation of law, and in relation to a prospective consumer hire agreement includes the prospective hirer;

'individual' includes—

    (a)   a partnership consisting of two or three persons not all of whom are bodies corporate; and

    (b)   an unincorporated body of persons which does not consist entirely of bodies corporate and is not a partnership;

'installation' means —

    (a)   the installing of any electric line or any gas or water pipe,

    (b)   the fixing of goods to the premises where they are to be used, and the alteration of premises to enable goods to be used on them,

    (c)   where it is reasonably necessary that goods should be constructed or erected on the premises where they are to be used, any work carried out for the purpose of constructing or erecting them on those premises;

'judgment' includes an order or decree made by any court;

'land' , includes an interest in land, and in relation to Scotland includes heritable subjects of whatever description;

'land improvement company' means an improvement company as defined by section 7 of the Improvement of Land Act 1899;

'land mortgage' includes any security charged on land;

'licence' means a licence under Part III ;

'licensed', in relation to any act, means authorised by a licence to do the act or cause or permit another person to do it;

'licensee', in the case of a group licence, includes any person covered by the licence;

'linked transaction' has the meaning given by section 19(1);

'local authority', in relation to England, means a county council, a London borough council, a district council, the Common Council of the City of London, or the Council of the Isles of Scilly, in relation to Wales means a county council or a county borough council, and in relation to Scotland, means a council constituted under section 2 of the Local Government etc. (Scotland) Act 1994, and, in relation to Northern Ireland, means a district council;

'modifying agreement' has the meaning given by section 82(2);

'mortgage', in relation to Scotland, includes any heritable security;

'multiple agreement' has the meaning given by section 18(1);

'negotiator' has the meaning given by section 56(1);

'non-commercial agreement' means a consumer credit agreement or a consumer hire agreement not made by the creditor or owner in the course of a business carried on by him;

'notice' means notice in writing;

'notice of cancellation' has the meaning given by section 69(1);

'OFT' means the Office of Fair Trading;

'owner' means a person who bails or (in Scotland) hires out goods under a consumer hire agreement or the person to whom his rights and duties under the agreement have passed by assignment or operation of law, and in relation to a prospective consumer hire agreement, includes the prospective bailor or person from whom the goods are to be hired;

'pawn' means any article subject to a pledge;

'pawn-receipt' has the meaning given by section 114;

'pawnee' and 'pawnor' include any person to whom the rights and duties of the original pawnee or the original pawnor, as the case may be, have passed by assignment or operation of law;

'payment' includes tender;

'pledge' means the pawnee's rights over an article taken in pawn;

'prescribed' means prescribed by regulations made by the Secretary of State;

'pre-existing arrangements' shall be construed in accordance with section 187;

'principal agreement' has the meaning given by section 19(1);

'protected goods' has the meaning given by section 90(7);

'quotation' has the meaning given by section 52(1)(a);

'redemption period' has the meaning given by section 116(3);

'register' means the register kept by the OFT under section 35;

'regulated agreement' means a consumer credit agreement, or consumer hire agreement, other than an exempt agreement, and 'regulated' and 'unregulated' shall be construed accordingly;

'regulations' means regulations made by the Secretary of State;

'relative', except in section 184, means a person who is an associate by virtue of section 184(1);

'representation' includes any condition or warranty, and any other statement or undertaking, whether oral or in writing;

'restricted-use credit agreement' and 'restricted-use credit' have the meanings given by section 11(1);

'rules of court', in relation to Northern Ireland means , in relation to the High Court, rules made under section 7 of the Northern Ireland Act 1962, and, in relation to any other court, rules made by the authority having for the time being power to make rules regulating the practice and procedure in that court;

'running-account credit' shall be construed in accordance with section 10;

'security', in relation to an actual or prospective consumer credit agreement or consumer hire agreement, or any linked transaction, means a mortgage, charge, pledge, bond, debenture, indemnity, guarantee, bill, note or other right provided by the debtor or hirer, or at his request (express or implied), to secure the carrying out of the obligations of the debtor or hirer under the agreement;

'security instrument' has the meaning given by section 105(2);

'serve on' means deliver or send by an appropriate method to;

'signed' shall be construed in accordance with subsection (3);

'small agreement' has the meaning given by section 17(1), and 'small' in relation to an agreement within any category shall be construed accordingly;

'specified fee' shall be construed in accordance with section 2(4) and (5);

'standard licence' has the meaning given by section 22(1)(a);

'supplier' has the meaning given by section 11(1)(b) or 12(c) or 13(c) or, in relation to an agreement falling within section 11(1)(a), means the creditor, and includes a person to whom the rights and duties of a supplier (as so defined) have passed by assignment or operation of law, or (in relation to a prospective agreement) the prospective supplier;

'surety' means the person by whom any security is provided, or the person to whom his rights and duties in relation to the security have passed by assignment or operation of law;

'technical grounds' shall be construed in accordance with subsection (5);

'time order' has the meaning given by section 129(1);

'total charge for credit' means a sum calculated in accordance with regulations under section 20(1);

'total price' means the total sum payable by the debtor under a hire-purchase agreement or a conditional sale agreement, including any sum payable on the exercise of an option to purchase, but excluding any sum payable as a penalty or as compensation or damages for a breach of the agreement;

'the Tribunal' means the Consumer Credit Appeals Tribunal;

'unexecuted agreement' means a document embodying the terms of a prospective regulated agreement, or such of them as it is intended to reduce to writing;

'unlicensed' means without a licence, but applies only in relation to acts for which a licence is required;

'unrestricted-use credit agreement' and 'unrestricted-use credit' have the meanings given by section 11(2);

'working day' means any day other than—

(a)   Saturday or Sunday,

(b)   Christmas Day or Good Friday,

(c)   a bank holiday within the meaning given by section 1 of the Banking and Financial Dealings Act 1971.

(1A) In sections 36E(3), 70(4), 73(4) and 75(2) and paragraphs 14 and 15 of Schedule A1 'costs', in relation to proceedings in Scotland, means expenses.

(2)   A person is not to be treated as carrying on a particular type of business merely because occasionally he enters into transactions belonging to a business of that type.

(3)   Any provision of this Act requiring a document to be signed is complied with by a body corporate if the document is sealed by that body.

This subsection does not apply to Scotland.

(4)   A document embodies a provision if the provision is set out either in the document itself or in another document referred to in it.

(5)   An application dismissed by the court or the OFT shall, if the court or the OFT (as the case may be) so certifies, be taken to be dismissed on technical grounds only.

(6)   Except in so far as the context otherwise requires, any reference in this Act to an enactment shall be construed as a reference to that enactment as amended by or under any other enactment, including this Act.

(7)   In this Act, except where otherwise indicated—

(a)   a reference to a numbered Part, section or Schedule is a reference to the Part or section of, or the Schedule to, this Act so numbered, and

(b)   a reference in a section to a numbered subsection is a reference to the subsection of that section so numbered, and

(c)   a reference in a section, subsection or Schedule to a numbered paragraph is a reference to the paragraph of that section, subsection or Schedule so numbered.

189A   Meaning of 'consumer credit EEA firm'

In this Act 'consumer credit EEA firm' means an EEA firm falling within sub-paragraph (a),(b) or (c) of paragraph 5 of Schedule 3 to the Financial Services and Markets Act 2000 carrying on, or seeking to carry on, consumer credit business, consumer hire business or ancillary credit business for which a licence would be required under this Act but for paragraph 15(3) of Schedule 3 to the Financial Services and Markets Act 2000.

190   Financial provisions.

(1)   There shall be defrayed out of money provided by Parliament—

   (a)   all expenses incurred by the Secretary of State in consequence of the provisions of this Act;

   (b)   any expenses incurred in consequence of those provisions by any other Minister of the Crown or Government department;

   (c)   any increase attributable to this Act in the sums payable out of money so provided under the Superannuation Act 1972 or the Fair Trading Act 1973.

(2)   Any fees, charges, penalties or other sums received by the Director under this Act shall be paid into the Consolidated Fund.

191   Special provisions as to Northern Ireland.

(1)   The OFT may make arrangements with the Department of Commerce for Northern Ireland for the Department, on the OFT's behalf—

   (a)   to receive applications, notices, charges and fees;

   (b)   to maintain, and make available for inspection and copying, copies of entries in the register; and

   (c)   to provide certified copies of entries in the register,

   to the extent that seems to the OFT desirable for the convenience of persons in Northern Ireland.

(2)   The OFT shall give general notice of any arrangements made under subsection (1).

(3)   Nothing in this Act shall authorise any Northern Ireland department to incur any expenses attributable to the provisions of this Act until provision has been made for those expenses to be defrayed out of money appropriated for the purpose.

(4)   The power of the Department of Commerce for Northern Ireland to make an order under section 178 shall be exercisable by statutory rule for the purposes of the Statutory Rules (Northern Ireland) Order 1979, and any such order shall be subject to negative resolution within the meaning of the Interpretation Act (Northern Ireland) 1954 as if it were a statutory instrument within the meaning of that Act.

(5)   In this Act 'enactment' includes an enactment of the Parliament of Northern Ireland or the Northern Ireland Assembly, and 'Act' shall be construed in a corresponding manner; and (without prejudice to section 189(6)) any reference in this Act to such an enactment shall include a reference to any enactment re-enacting it with or without modifications.

(6)   Section 38 of the Interpretation Act 1889 (effect of repeals) shall have the same operation in relation to any repeal by this Act of an enactment of the Parliament of Northern Ireland as it has in relation to the repeal of an Act of the Parliament of the United Kingdom, references in that section of the Act of 1889 to Acts and enactments being construed accordingly.

192   Transitional and commencement provisions, amendments and repeals.

(1)   The provisions of Schedule 3 shall have effect for the purposes of this Act.

(2)   The appointment of a day for the purposes of any provision of Schedule 3 shall be effected by an order of the Secretary of State made by statutory instrument; and any such order shall include a provision amending Schedule 3 so as to insert an express reference to the day appointed.

(3)

   (a)   . . .

   (b)   . . .

(4)   The Secretary of State shall by order made by statutory instrument provide for the coming into operation of the amendments contained in Schedule 4 and the repeals contained in Schedule 5, and those amendments and repeals shall have effect only as provided by an order so made.

193   Short title and extent.

(1)   This Act may be cited as the Consumer Credit Act 1974.

(2)   This Act extends to Northern Ireland.

SCHEDULE A1 THE CONSUMER CREDIT APPEALS TRIBUNAL

Part 1 Interpretation

1

In this Schedule—

'the Deputy President' means the Deputy President of the Consumer Credit Appeals Tribunal;

'lay panel' means the panel established under paragraph 3(3);

'panel of chairmen' means the panel established under paragraph 3(1);

'party' means, in relation to an appeal, the appellant or the OFT;

'the President' means the President of the Consumer Credit Appeals Tribunal;

'rules' means rules under section 40A(3) of this Act;

'specified' means specified by rules.

Part 2 The Tribunal

2   The President and the Deputy President.

(1)   The Lord Chancellor shall appoint one of the members of the panel of chairmen to preside over the discharge of the Tribunal's functions.

(2)   The person so appointed shall be known as the President of the Consumer Credit Appeals Tribunal.

(3) The Lord Chancellor may appoint one of the members of the panel of chairmen to be the Deputy President of the Consumer Credit Appeals Tribunal.

(4) The Deputy President shall have such functions in relation to the Tribunal as the President may assign to him.

(5) If the President or the Deputy President ceases to be a member of the panel of chairmen, he shall also cease to be the President or (as the case may be) the Deputy President.

(6) The functions of the President may, if he is absent or is otherwise unable to act, be discharged—

   (a) by the Deputy President; or

   (b) if there is no Deputy President or he too is absent or otherwise unable to act, by a person appointed for that purpose from the panel of chairmen by the Lord Chancellor.

3   Panels.

(1) The Lord Chancellor shall appoint a panel of persons for the purpose of serving as chairmen of the Tribunal.

(2) A person shall not be appointed to the panel of chairmen unless he—

   (a) has a seven year general qualification within the meaning of section 71 of the Courts and Legal Services Act 1990;

   (b) is an advocate or solicitor in Scotland of at least seven years' standing; or

   (c) is a member of the Bar of Northern Ireland, or a solicitor of the Supreme Court of Northern Ireland, of at least seven years' standing.

(3) The Lord Chancellor shall also appoint a panel of persons who appear to him to be qualified by experience or otherwise to deal with appeals of the kind that may be made to the Tribunal.

4   Terms of office etc.

(1) Each member of the panel of chairmen or the lay panel shall hold and vacate office in accordance with the terms of his appointment.

(2) The Lord Chancellor may remove a member of either panel from office on the ground of incapacity or misbehaviour.

(3) A member of either panel—

   (a) may at any time resign office by notice in writing to the Lord Chancellor;

   (b) is eligible for re-appointment if he ceases to hold office.

5   Remuneration and allowances.

The Lord Chancellor may pay to a person in respect of his service—

   (a) as the President or the Deputy President,

   (b) as a member of the Tribunal, or

   (c) as a person appointed under paragraph 7(4),

such remuneration and allowances as the Lord Chancellor may determine.

6   *Staff and costs.*

(1)   The Lord Chancellor may appoint such staff for the Tribunal as he may determine.

(2)   The Lord Chancellor shall defray—

    (a)   the remuneration of the Tribunal's staff; and

    (b)   such other costs of the Tribunal as he may determine.

Part 3 Constitution of the tribunal

7

(1)   On an appeal to the Tribunal, the persons to act as members of the Tribunal for the purposes of the appeal shall be selected from the panel of chairmen or the lay panel.

(2)   The selection shall be in accordance with arrangements made by the President for the purposes of this paragraph.

(3)   Those arrangements shall provide for at least one member to be a person selected from the panel of chairmen.

(4)   If it appears to the Tribunal that a matter before it involves a question of fact of special difficulty, it may appoint one or more experts to provide assistance.

Part 4 Tribunal powers and procedure sittings

8

The Tribunal shall sit at such times and in such places as the Lord Chancellor may direct.

9

(1)   Subject to sub-paragraph (2), the Tribunal may, on an appeal, consider any evidence that it thinks relevant, whether or not it was available to the OFT at the time it made the determination appealed against.

(2)   Rules may make provision restricting the evidence that the Tribunal may consider on an appeal in specified circumstances.

10

Rules may include, amongst other things, provision—

    (a)   about the withdrawal of appeals;

    (b)   about persons who may appear on behalf of a party to an appeal;

    (c)   about how an appeal is to be dealt with if a person acting as member of the Tribunal in respect of the appeal becomes unable to act;

    (d)   setting time limits in relation to anything that is to be done for the purposes of an appeal or for such limits to be set by the Tribunal or a member of the panel of chairmen;

    (e)   for time limits (including the period specified for the purposes of section 41(1) of this Act) to be extended by the Tribunal or a member of the panel of chairmen;

(f)   conferring powers on the Tribunal or a member of the panel of chairmen to give such directions to the parties to an appeal as it or he thinks fit for purposes connected with the conduct and disposal of the appeal;

(g)   about the holding of hearings by the Tribunal or a member of the panel of chairmen (including for such hearings to be held in private);

(h)   Placing restrictions on the disclosure of information and documents or for such restrictions to be imposed by the Tribunal or a member of the panel of chairmen;

(i)   about the consequences of a failure to comply with a requirement imposed by or under any rule (including for the immediate dismissal or allowing of an appeal if the Tribunal or a member of the panel of chairmen thinks fit);

(j)   for proceedings on different appeals (including appeals with different appellants) to take place concurrently;

(k)   for the suspension of determinations of the OFT;

(l)   for the suspension of decisions of the Tribunal;

(m)   for the Tribunal to reconsider its decision disposing of an appeal where it has reason to believe that the decision was wrongly made because of an administrative error made by a member of its staff.

II

A member of the Council on Tribunals or of its Scottish Committee shall be entitled—

(a)   to attend any hearing held by the Tribunal or a member of the panel of chairmen whether or not it is held in public; and

(b)   to attend any deliberations of the Tribunal in relation to an appeal.

I2

(1)   The Tribunal shall decide an appeal by reference to the grounds of appeal set out in the notice of appeal.

(2)   In disposing of an appeal the Tribunal may do one or more of the following—

(a)   confirm the determination appealed against;

(b)   quash that determination;

(c)   vary that determination;

(d)   remit the matter to the OFT for reconsideration and determination in accordance with the directions (if any) given to it by the Tribunal;

(e)   give the OFT directions for the purpose of giving effect to its decision.

(3)   In the case of an appeal against a determination to impose a penalty, the Tribunal—

(a)   has no power by virtue of sub-paragraph (2)(c) to increase the penalty;

(b)   may extend the period within which the penalty is to be paid (including in cases where that period has already ended).

(4)   Sub-paragraph (3) does not affect—

(a)   the Tribunal's power to give directions to the OFT under sub-paragraph (2)(d); or

(b)   what the OFT can do where a matter is remitted to it under sub-paragraph (2)(d).

(5)   Where the Tribunal remits a matter to the OFT, it may direct that the requirements of section 34 of this Act are not to apply, or are only to apply to a specified extent, in relation to the OFT's reconsideration of the matter.

(6) Subject to sub-paragraphs (7) and (8), where the Tribunal remits an application to the OFT, section 6(1) and (3) to (9) of this Act shall apply as if the application had not been previously determined by the OFT.

(7) In the case of a general notice which came into effect after the determination appealed against was made but before the application was remitted, the applicant shall provide any information or document which he is required to provide under section 6(6) within—

    (a) the period of 28 days beginning with the day on which the application was remitted; or

    (b) such longer period as the OFT may allow.

(8) In the case of—

    (a) any information or document which was superseded,

    (b) any change in circumstances which occurred, or

    (c) any error or omission of which the applicant became aware,

after the determination appealed against was made but before the application was remitted, any notification that is required to be given by the applicant under section 6(7) shall be given within the period of 28 days beginning with the day on which the application was remitted.

13

(1) A decision of the Tribunal may be taken by majority.

(2) A decision of the Tribunal disposing of an appeal shall—

    (a) state whether it was unanimous or taken by majority; and

    (b) be recorded in a document which—

        (i) contains a statement of the reasons for the decision and any other specified information; and

        (ii) is signed and dated by a member of the panel of chairmen.

(3) Where the Tribunal disposes of an appeal it shall—

    (a) send to each party to the appeal a copy of the document mentioned in sub-paragraph (2)(b); and

    (b) Publish that document in such manner as it thinks fit.

(4) The Tribunal may exclude from what it publishes under sub-paragraph (3)(b) information of a specified description.

14

(1) Where the Tribunal disposes of an appeal and—

    (a) it decides that the OFT was wrong to make the determination appealed against, or

    (b) during the course of the appeal the OFT accepted that it was wrong to make that determination,

it may order the OFT to pay to the appellant the whole or a part of the costs incurred by the appellant in relation to the appeal.

(2) In determining whether to make such an order, and the terms of such an order, the Tribunal shall have regard to whether it was unreasonable for the OFT to make the determination appealed against.

15

Where—

(a) the Tribunal disposes of an appeal or an appeal is withdrawn before the Tribunal disposes of it, and

(b) the Tribunal thinks that a party to the appeal acted vexatiously, frivolously or unreasonably in bringing the appeal or otherwise in relation to the appeal,

it may order that party to pay to the other party the whole or a part of the costs incurred by the other party in relation to the appeal.

16

An order of the Tribunal under paragraph 14 or 15 may be enforced—

(a) as if it were an order of the county court; or

(b) in Scotland, as if it were an interlocutor of the Court of Session.

SCHEDULE 1 PROSECUTION AND PUNISHMENT OF OFFENCES

1 Section	2 Offence	3 Mode of prosecution	4 Imprisonment or fine
7	Knowingly or recklessly giving false information to OFT.	(a) Summarily. (b) On indictment.	The prescribed sum. 2 years or a fine or both.
39(1)	Engaging in activities requiring a licence when not a licensee.	(a) Summarily. (b) On indictment.	The prescribed sum. 2 years or a fine or both.
39(2)	Carrying on business under a name not specified in licence.	(a) Summarily. (b) On indictment.	The prescribed sum. 2 years or a fine or both.
39(3)	Failure to notify changes in registered particulars.	(a) Summarily. (b) On indictment.	The prescribed sum. 2 years or a fine or both.
45	Advertising credit where goods etc not available for cash.	(a) Summarily. (b) On indictment.	The prescribed sum. 2 years or a fine or both.
. . .	. . .	. . .	. . .
47(1)	Advertising infringements.	(a) Summarily. (b) On indictment.	The prescribed sum. 2 years or a fine or both.
49(1)	Canvassing debtor-creditor agreements off trade premises.	(a) Summarily. (b) On indictment.	The prescribed sum. 1 year or a fine or both.
49(2)	Soliciting debtor-creditor agreements during visits made in response to previous oral requests.	(a) Summarily. (b) On indictment.	The prescribed sum. 1 year or a fine or both.

1 Section	2 Offence	3 Mode of prosecution	4 Imprisonment or fine
50(1)	Sending circulars to minors.	(a) Summarily. (b) On indictment.	The prescribed sum. 1 year or a fine or both.
51(1)	Supplying unsolicited credit-tokens.	(a) Summarily. (b) On indictment.	The prescribed sum. 2 years or a fine or both.
...	...	...	...
79(3)	Failure of owner under consumer hire agreement to supply copies of documents etc.	Summarily.	Level 4 on the standard scale.
80(2)	Failure to tell creditor or owner whereabouts of goods.	Summarily.	Level 3 on the standard scale.
...	...	...	...
114(2)	Taking pledges from minors.	(a) Summarily. (b) On indictment.	The prescribed sum. 1 year or a fine or both.
115	Failure to supply copies of a pledge agreement or pawn-receipt.	Summarily.	Level 4 on the standard scale.
119(1)	Unreasonable refusal to allow pawn to be redeemed.	Summarily.	Level 4 on the standard scale.
154	Canvassing ancillary credit services off trade premises.	(a) Summarily. (b) On indictment.	The prescribed sum. 1 year or a fine or both.
157(3)	Refusal to give name etc of credit reference agency.	Summarily.	Level 4 on the standard scale.
158(4)	Failure of credit reference agency to disclose filed information.	Summarily. standard scale.	Level 4 on the
159(6)	Failure of credit reference agency to correct information.	Summarily.	Level 4 on the standard scale.
160(6)	Failure of credit reference agency to comply with section 160(3) or (4).	Summarily.	Level 4 on the standard scale.
162(6)	Impersonation of enforcement authority officers.	(a) Summarily. (b) On indictment.	The prescribed sum. 2 years or a fine or both.
165(1)	Obstruction of enforcement authority officers.	Summarily.	Level 4 on the standard scale.
165(2)	Giving false information to enforcement authority officers.	(a) Summarily. (b) On indictment.	The prescribed sum. 2 years or a fine or both.
167(2)	Contravention of regulations under section 44, 52, 53, 54 or 112.	(a) Summarily. (b) On indictment.	The prescribed sum. 2 years or a fine or both.
174(5)	Wrongful disclosure of information.	(a) Summarily. (b) On indictment.	The prescribed sum. 2 years or a fine or both.

SCHEDULE 2 EXAMPLES OF USE OF NEW TERMINOLOGY

Part I Lists of terms

Term	Defined in section	Illustrated by example(s)
Advertisement	189(1)	2
Advertiser	189(1)	2
Antecedent negotiations	56	1, 2, 3, 4
Cancellable agreement	67	4
Consumer credit agreement	8	5, 6, 7, 15, 19, 21
Consumer hire agreement	15	20, 24
Credit	9	16, 19, 21
Credit-broker	189(1)	2
Credit limit	10(2)	6, 7, 19, 22, 23
Creditor	189(1)	1, 2, 3, 4
Credit-sale agreement	189(1)	5
Credit-token	14	3, 14, 16
Credit-token agreement	14	3, 14, 16, 22
Debtor-creditor agreement	13	8, 16, 17, 18
Debtor-creditor-supplier agreement	12	8, 16
Fixed-sum credit	10	9, 10, 17, 23
Hire-purchase agreement	189(1)	10
Individual	189(1)	19, 24
Linked transaction	19	11
Term	Defined in section	Illustrated by example(s)
Modifying agreement	82(2)	24
Multiple agreement	18	16, 18
Negotiator	56(1)	1, 2, 3, 4
...	...	...
Pre-existing arrangements	187	8, 21
Restricted-use credit	11	10, 12, 13, 14, 16
Running-account credit	10	15, 16, 18, 23
Small agreement	17	16, 17, 22
Supplier	189(1)	3, 14
Total charge for credit	20	5, 10
Total price	189(1)	10
Unrestricted-use credit	11	8, 12, 16, 17, 18

Part II Examples

EXAMPLE 1

Facts. Correspondence passes between an employee of a moneylending company (writing on behalf of the company) and an individual about the terms on which the company would grant him a loan under a regulated agreement.

Analysis. The correspondence constitutes antecedent negotiations falling within section 56(1)(a), the moneylending company being both creditor and negotiator.

EXAMPLE 2

Facts. Representations are made about goods in a poster displayed by a shopkeeper near the goods, the goods being selected by a customer who has read the poster and then sold by the shopkeeper to a finance company introduced by him (with whom he has a business relation-ship). The goods are disposed of by the finance company to the customer under a regulated hire-purchase agreement.

Analysis. The representations in the poster constitute antecedent negotiations falling within section 56(1)(b), the shopkeeper being the credit-broker and negotiator and the finance company being the creditor. The poster is an advertisement and the shopkeeper is the advertiser.

EXAMPLE 3

Facts. Discussions take place between a shopkeeper and a customer about goods the customer wishes to buy using a credit-card issued by the D Bank under a regulated agreement.

Analysis. The discussions constitute antecedent negotiations falling within section 56(1)(c), the shopkeeper being the supplier and negotiator and the D Bank the creditor. The credit-card is a credit-token as defined in section 14(1), and the regulated agreement under which it was issued is a credit-token agreement as defined in section 14(2).

EXAMPLE 4

Facts. Discussions take place and correspondence passes between a secondhand car dealer and a customer about a car, which is then sold by the dealer to the customer under a regulated conditional sale agreement. Subsequently, on a revocation of that agreement by consent, the car is resold by the dealer to a finance company introduced by him (with whom he has a business relationship), who in turn dispose of it to the same customer under a regulated hire-purchase agreement.

Analysis. The discussions and correspondence constitute antecedent negotiations in relation both to the conditional sale agreement and the hire-purchase agreement. They fall under section 56(1)(a) in relation to the conditional sale agreement, the dealer being the creditor and the negotiator. In relation to the hire-purchase agreement they fall within section 56(1)(b), the dealer continuing to be treated as the negotiator but the finance company now being the creditor. Both agreements are cancellable if the discussions took place when the individual conducting the negotiations (whether the 'negotiator' or his employee or agent) was in the presence of the debtor, unless the unexecuted agreement was signed by the debtor at trade premises (as defined in section 67(b)). If the discussions all took place by telephone however, or the unexecuted agreement was signed by the debtor on trade premises (as so defined) the agreements are not cancellable.

EXAMPLE 5

Facts. E agrees to sell to F (an individual) an item of furniture in return for 24 monthly instalments of £10 payable in arrear. The property in the goods passes to F immediately.

Analysis. This is a credit-sale agreement (see definition of 'credit-sale agreement' in section 189(1)). The credit provided amounts to £240 less the amount which, according to regulations made under section 20(1), constitutes the total charge for credit. (This amount is required to be deducted by section 9(4)). Accordingly the agreement falls within section 8(2) and is a consumer credit agreement.

EXAMPLE 6

Facts. The G Bank grants H (an individual) an unlimited overdraft, with an increased rate of interest on so much of any debit balance as exceeds £2,000.

Analysis. Although the overdraft purports to be unlimited, the stipulation for increased interest above £2,000 brings the agreement within section 10(3)(b)(ii) and it is a consumer credit agreement.

EXAMPLE 7

Facts. J is an individual who owns a small shop which usually carries a stock worth about £1,000. K makes a stocking agreement under which he undertakes to provide on short-term credit the stock needed from time to time by J without any specified limit.

Analysis. Although the agreement appears to provide unlimited credit, it is probable, having regard to the stock usually carried by J, that his indebtedness to K will not at any time rise above £5,000. Accordingly the agreement falls within section 10(3)(b)(iii) and is a consumer credit agreement.

EXAMPLE 8

Facts. U, a moneylender, lends £500 to V (an individual) knowing he intends to use it to buy office equipment from W. W introduced V to U, it being his practice to introduce customers needing finance to him. Sometimes U gives W a commission for this and sometimes not. U pays the £500 direct to V.

Analysis. Although this appears to fall under section 11(1)(b), it is excluded by section 11(3) and is therefore (by section 11(2)) an unrestricted-use credit agreement. Whether it is a debtor-creditor agreement (by section 13(c)) or a debtor-creditor-supplier agreement (by section 12(c)) depends on whether the previous dealings between U and W amount to 'pre-existing arrangements', that is whether the agreement can be taken to have been entered into 'in accordance with, or in furtherance of' arrangements previously made between U and W, as laid down in section 187(1).

EXAMPLE 9

Facts. A agrees to lend B (an individual) £4,500 in nine monthly instalments of £500.

Analysis. This is a cash loan and is a form of credit (see section 9 and definition of 'cash' in section 189(1)). Accordingly it falls within section 10(1)(b) and is fixed-sum credit amounting to £4,500.

EXAMPLE 10

Facts. C (in England) agrees to bail goods to D (an individual) in return for periodical payments. The agreement provides for the property in the goods to pass to D on payment of a total of £7,500 and the exercise by D of an option to purchase. The sum of £7,500 includes a down-payment of £1,000. It also includes an amount which, according to regulations made under section 20(1), constitutes a total charge for credit of £1,500.

Analysis. This is a hire-purchase agreement with a deposit of £1,000 and a total price of £7,500 (see definitions of 'hire-purchase agreement', 'deposit' and 'total price' in section 189(1)). By section 9(3), it is taken to provide credit amounting to £7,500 – (£1,500 + £1,000), which equals £5,000. Under section 8(2), the agreement is therefore a consumer credit agreement, and under sections 9(3) and 11(1) it is a restricted-use credit agreement for fixed-sum credit. A similar result would follow if the agreement by C had been a hiring agreement in Scotland.

EXAMPLE 11

Facts. X (an individual) borrows £500 from Y (Finance). As a condition of the granting of the loan X is required—

(a) to execute a second mortgage on his house in favour of Y (Finance), and

(b) to take out a policy of insurance on his life with Y (Insurances).

In accordance with the loan agreement, the policy is charged to Y (Finance) as collateral security for the loan. The two companies are associates within the meaning of section 184(3).

Analysis. The second mortgage is a transaction for the provision of security and accordingly does not fall within section 19(1), but the taking out of the insurance policy is a linked transaction falling within section 19(1)(a). The charging of the policy is a separate transaction (made between different parties) for the provision of security and again is excluded from section 19(1). The only linked transaction is therefore the taking out of the insurance policy. If X had not been required by the loan agreement to take out the policy, but it had been done at the suggestion of Y (Finance) to induce them to enter into the loan agreement, it would have been a linked transaction under section 19(1)(c)(i) by virtue of section 19(2)(a).

EXAMPLE 12

Facts. The N Bank agrees to lend O (an individual) £2,000 to buy a car from P. To make sure the loan is used as intended, the N Bank stipulates that the money must be paid by it direct to P.

Analysis. The agreement is a consumer credit agreement by virtue of section 8(2). Since it falls within section 11(1)(b), it is a restricted-use credit agreement, P being the supplier. If the N Bank had not stipulated for direct payment to the supplier, section 11(3) would have operated and made the agreement into one for unrestricted-use credit.

EXAMPLE 13

Facts. Q, a debt-adjuster, agrees to pay off debts owed by R (an individual) to various money-lenders. For this purpose the agreement provides for the making of a loan by Q to R in return for R's agreeing to repay the loan by instalments with interest. The loan money is not paid over to R but retained by Q and used to pay off the moneylenders.

Analysis. This is an agreement to refinance existing indebtedness of the debtor's, and if the loan by Q does not exceed £5,000 is a restricted-use credit agreement falling within section 11(1)(c).

EXAMPLE 14

Facts. On payment of £1, S issues to T (an individual) a trading check under which T can spend up to £20 at any shop which has agreed, or in future agrees, to accept S's trading checks.

Analysis The trading check is a credit-token falling within section 14(1)(b). The credit-token agreements a restricted-use credit agreement within section 11(1)(b), any shop in which the credit-token is used being the 'supplier'. The fact that further shops may be added after the issue of the credit-token is irrelevant in view of section 11(4).

EXAMPLE 15

Facts. A retailer L agrees with M (an individual) to open an account in M's name and, in return for M's promise to pay a specified minimum sum into the account each month and to pay a monthly charge for credit, agrees to allow to be debited to the account, in respect of purchases made by M from L, such sums as will not increase the debit balance at any time beyond the credit limit, defined in the agreement as a given multiple of the specified minimum sum.

Analysis. This agreement provides credit falling within the definition of running-account credit in section 10(1)(a).

Provided the credit limit is not over £5,000, the agreement falls within section 8(2) and is a consumer credit agreement for running-account credit.

EXAMPLE 16

Facts. Under an unsecured agreement, A (Credit), an associate of the A Bank, issues to B (an individual) a credit-card for use in obtaining cash on credit from A (Credit), to be paid by branches of the A Bank (acting as agent of A (Credit)), or goods or cash from suppliers or banks who have agreed to honour credit-cards issued by A (Credit). The credit limit is £30.

Analysis. This is a credit-token agreement falling within section 14(1)(a) and (b). It is a regulated consumer credit agreement for running-account credit. Since the credit limit does not exceed £30, the agreement is a small agreement. So far as the agreement relates to goods it is a debtor-creditor-supplier agreement within section 12(b), since it provides restricted-use credit under section 11(1)(b). So far as it relates to cash it is a debtor-creditor agreement within section 13(c) and the credit it provides is unrestricted-use credit. This is therefore a multiple agreement. In that the whole agreement falls within several of the categories of agreement mentioned in this Act, it is, by section 18(3), to be treated as an agreement in each of those categories. So far as it is a debtor-creditor-supplier agreement providing restricted-use credit it is, by section 18(2), to be treated as a separate agreement; and similarly so far as it is a debtor-creditor agreement providing unrestricted-use credit. (See also Example 22.)

EXAMPLE 17

Facts. The manager of the C Bank agrees orally with D (an individual) to open a current account in D's name. Nothing is said about overdraft facilities. After maintaining the account in credit for some weeks, D draws a cheque in favour of E for an amount exceeding D's credit balance by £20. E presents the cheque and the Bank pay it.

Analysis. In drawing the cheque D, by implication, requests the Bank to grant him an overdraft of £20 on its usual terms as to interest and other charges. In deciding to honour the cheque, the Bank by implication accept the offer. This constitutes a regulated small consumer credit agreement for unrestricted-use, fixed-sum credit. It is a debtor-creditor agreement, and falls within section 74(1)(b) if covered by a determination under section 74(3). (Compare Example 18.)

EXAMPLE 18

Facts. F (an individual) has had a current account with the G Bank for many years. Although usually in credit, the account has been allowed by the Bank to become overdrawn from time to time. The maximum such overdraft has been is about £1,000. No explicit agreement has ever been made about overdraft facilities. Now, with a credit balance of £500, F draws a cheque for £1,300.

Analysis. It might well be held that the agreement with F (express or implied) under which the Bank operate his account includes an implied term giving him the right to overdraft facilities up to say £1,000. If so, the agreement is a regulated consumer credit agreement for unrestricted-use, running-account credit. It is a debtor-creditor agreement, and falls within section 74(1)(b) if covered by a direction under section 74(3). It is also a multiple agreement, part of which (i.e. the part not dealing with the overdraft), as referred to in section 18(1)(a), falls within a category of agreement not mentioned in this Act. (Compare Example 17.)

EXAMPLE 19

Facts. H (a finance house) agrees with J (a partnership of individuals) to open an unsecured loan account in J's name on which the debit balance is not to exceed £7,000 (having regard to payments into the account made from time to time by J). Interest is to be payable in advance on this sum, with provision for yearly adjustments. H is entitled to debit the account with interest, a 'setting-up' charge, and other charges. Before J has an opportunity to draw on the account it is initially debited with £2,250 for advance interest and other charges.

Analysis. This is a personal running-account credit agreement (see sections 8(1) and 10(1)(a), and definition of 'individual' in section 189(1)). By section 10(2) the credit limit is £7,000. By section 9(4) however the initial debit of £2,250, and any other charges later debited to the account by H, are not to be treated as credit even though time is allowed for their payment. Effects is given to this by section 10(3). Although the credit limit of £7,000 exceeds the amount (£5,000) specified in section 8(2) as the maximum for a consumer credit agreement, so that the agreement is not within section 10(3)(a), it is caught by section 10(3)(b)(i). At the beginning J can effectively draw (as credit) no more than £4,750, so the agreement is a consumer credit agreement.

EXAMPLE 20

Facts. K (in England) agrees with L (an individual) to bail goods to L for a period of three years certain at £2,000 a year, payable quarterly. The agreement contains no provision for the passing of the property in the goods to L.

Analysis. This is not a hire-purchase agreement (see paragraph (b) of the definition of that term in section 189(1)), and is capable of subsisting for more than three months. Paragraphs

(a) and (b) of section 15(1) are therefore satisfied, but paragraph (c) is not. The payments by L must exceed £5,000 if he conforms to the agreement. It is true that under section 101 L has a right to terminate the agreement on giving K three months' notice expiring not earlier than eighteen months after the making of the agreement, but that section applies only where the agreement is a regulated consumer hire agreement apart from the section (see subsection (1)). So the agreement is not a consumer hire agreement, though it would be if the hire charge were say £1,500 a year, or there were a 'break' clause in it operable by either party before the hire charges exceeded £5,000. A similar result would follow if the agreement by K had been a hiring agreement in Scotland.

EXAMPLE 21

Facts. The P Bank decides to issue cheque cards to its customers under a scheme whereby the bank undertakes to honour cheques of up to £30 in every case where the payee has taken the cheque in reliance on the cheque card, whether the customer has funds in his account or not. The P Bank writes to the major retailers advising them of this scheme and also publicises it by advertising. The Bank issues a cheque card to Q (an individual), who uses it to pay by cheque for goods costing £20 bought by Q from R, a major retailer. At the time, Q has £500 in his account at the P Bank.

Analysis. The agreement under which the cheque card is issued to Q is a consumer credit agreement even though at all relevant times Q has more than £30 in his account. This is because Q is free to draw out his whole balance and then use the cheque card, in which case the Bank has bound itself to honour the cheque. In other words the cheque card agreement provides Q with credit, whether he avails himself of it or not. Since the amount of the credit is not subject to any express limit, the cheque card can be used any number of times. It may be presumed however that section 10(3)(b)(iii) will apply. The agreement is an unrestricted-use debtor-creditor agreement (by section 13(c)). Although the P Bank wrote to R informing R of the P Bank's willingness to honour any cheque taken by R in reliance on a cheque card, this does not constitute pre-existing arrangements as mentioned in section 13(c) because section 187(3) operates to prevent it. The agreement is not a credit-token agreement within section 14(1)(b) because payment by the P Bank to R, would be a payment of the cheque and not a payment for the goods.

EXAMPLE 22

Facts. The facts are as in Example 16. On one occasion B uses the credit-card in a way which increases his debit balance with A (Credit) to £40. A (Credit) writers to B agreeing to allow the excess on that occasion only, but stating that it must be paid off within one month.

Analysis. In exceeding his credit limit B, by implication, requests A (Credit) to allow him a temporary excess (compare Example 17). A (Credit) is thus faced by B's action with the choice of treating it as a breach of contract or granting his implied request. He does the latter. If he had done the former, B would be treated as taking credit to which he was not entitled (see section 14(3)) and, subject to the terms of his contract with A (Credit), would be liable to damages for breach of contract. As it is, the agreement to allow the excess varies the original credit-token agreement by adding a new term. Under section 10(2), the new term is to be disregarded in arriving at the credit limit, so that the credit-token agreement at no time ceases to be a small agreement. By section 82(2) the later agreement is deemed to revoke the original agreement and contain provisions reproducing the combined effect of the two agreements. By section 82(4), this later agreement is exempted from Part V (except section 56).

EXAMPLE 23

Facts. Under an oral agreement made on 10th January, X (an individual) has an overdraft on his current account at the Y bank with a credit limit of £100. On 15th February, when his overdraft stands at £90, X draws a cheque for £25. It is the first time that X has exceeded his credit limit, and on 16th February the bank honours the cheque.

Analysis. The agreement of 10th January is a consumer credit agreement for running-account credit. The agreement of 15th–16th February varies the earlier agreement by adding a term allowing the credit limit to be exceeded merely temporarily. By section 82(2) the later agreement is deemed to revoke the earlier agreement and reproduce the combined effect of the two agreements. By section 82(4), Part V of this Act (except section 56) does not apply to the later agreement. By section 18(5), a term allowing a merely temporary excess over the credit limit is not to be treated as a separate agreement, or as providing fixed-sum credit. The whole of the £115 owed to the bank by X on 16th February is therefore running-account credit.

EXAMPLE 24

Facts. On 1st March 1975 Z (in England) enters into an agreement with A (an unincorporated body of persons) to bail to A equipment consisting of two components (component P and component Q). The agreement is not a hire-purchase agreement and is for a fixed term of 3 years, so paragraphs (a) and (b) of section 15(1) are both satisfied. The rental is payable monthly at a rate of £2,400 a year, but the agreement provides that this is to be reduced to £1,200 a year for the remainder of the agreement if at any time during its currency A returns component Q to the owner Z. On 5th May 1976 A is incorporated as A Ltd., taking over A's assets and liabilities. On 1st March 1977, A Ltd. returns component Q. On 1st January 1978, Z and A Ltd. agree to extend the earlier agreement by one year, increasing the rental for the final year by £250 to £1,450.

Analysis. When entered into on 1st March 1975, the agreement is a consumer hire agreement. A falls within the definition of 'individual' in section 189(1) and if A returns component Q before 1st May 1976 the total rental will not exceed £5,000 (see section 15(1)(c)). When this date is passed without component Q having been returned it is obvious that the total rental must now exceed £5,000. Does this mean that the agreement then ceases to be a consumer hire agreement? The answer is no, because there has been no change in the terms of the agreement, and without such a change the agreement cannot move from one category to the other. Similarly, the fact that A's rights and duties under the agreement pass to a body corporate on 5th May 1976 does not cause the agreement to cease to be a consumer hire agreement (see the definition of 'hirer' in section 189(1)).

The effect of the modifying agreement of 1st January 1978 is governed by section 82(2), which requires it to be treated as containing provisions reproducing the combined effect of the two actual agreements, that is to say as providing that—

(a) obligations outstanding on 1st January 1978 are to be treated as outstanding under the modifying agreement;

(b) the modifying agreement applies at the old rate of hire for the months of January and February 1978, and

(c) for the year beginning 1st March 1978 A Ltd. will be the bailee of component P at a rental of £1,450.

The total rental under the modifying agreement is £1,850. Accordingly the modifying agreement is a regulated agreement. Even if the total rental under the modifying agreement exceeded £5,000 it would still be regulated because of the provisions of section 82(3).

Index

[all references are to paragraph number]